The International Yearbook of Environmental and Resource Economics 2002/2003

NEW HORIZONS IN ENVIRONMENTAL ECONOMICS

Series Editors: Wallace E. Oates, *Professor of Economics, University of Maryland, USA* and Henk Folmer, *Professor of General Economics, Wageningen University, The Netherlands and Professor of Environmental Economics, Tilburg University, The Netherlands*

This important series is designed to make a significant contribution to the development of the principles and practices of environmental economics. It includes both theoretical and empirical work. International in scope, it addresses issues of current and future concern in both East and West and in developed and developing countries.

The main purpose of the series is to create a forum for the publication of high-quality work and to show how economic analysis can make a contribution to understanding and resolving the environmental problems confronting the world in the twenty-first century.

Recent titles in the series include:

The International Yearbook of Environmental and Resource Economics 2002/2003

A Survey of Current Issues

Edited by
Tom Tietenberg

Mitchell Family Professor of Economics, Colby College, USA

Henk Folmer

*Professor of General Economics, Wageningen University,
The Netherlands and Professor of Environmental Economics,
Tilburg University, The Netherlands*

NEW HORIZONS IN ENVIRONMENTAL ECONOMICS

Edward Elgar

Cheltenham, UK • Northampton, MA, USA

Published by
Edward Elgar Publishing Limited
Glensanda House
Montpellier Parade
Cheltenham
Glos GL50 1UA
UK

Edward Elgar Publishing, Inc.
136 West Street
Suite 202
Northampton
Massachusetts 01060
USA

A catalogue record for this book is available from the British Library

ISSN 1460 7352

ISBN 1 84064 949 6 (cased)
Printed and bound in Great Britain by MPG Books Ltd, Bodmin, Cornwall

Contents

List of figures

List of panels

List of tables

Contributors

Anna Alberini, Assistant Professor of Agricultural and Resource Economics, University of Maryland, USA

John M. Antle, Professor of Agricultural Economics & Economics, Montana State University, USA

Carlo Carraro, Professor of Econometrics and Environmental Economics, University of Venice and FEEM, Italy

Klaus Conrad, Professor Doctor, Mannheim University, Germany

David Harrison, Jr, Senior Vice President, National Economic Research Associates, Inc., USA

Alan Krupnick, Director, Quality of the Environment Division, Resources for the Future, Washington, DC, USA

Bruce A. McCarl, Professor of Agricultural Economics, Texas A&M University, USA

Ben A. Minteer, Visiting Assistant Professor, School of Public Policy, Georgia Institute of Technology, USA

Bryan Norton, Professor, School of Public Policy, Georgia Institute of Technology, USA

Raymond B. Palmquist, Professor of Economics, North Carolina State University, USA

John C.V. Pezzey, Fellow, Centre for Resource and Environmental Studies, Australian National University, Australia, and Visiting Fellow, Department of Economics, University of Bath, UK

V. Kerry Smith, University Distingushed Professor, Agricultural and Resource Economics, North Carolina State University, USA

Michael A. Toman, Senior Fellow, Energy and Natural Resources Division, Resources for the Future, Washington, DC, USA

Preface

As a discipline Environmental and Resource Economics has undergone a rapid evolution over the past three decades. Originally the literature focused on valuing environmental resources and on the design of policy instruments to correct externalities and to provide for the optimal exploitation of resources. The relatively narrow focus of the field and the limited number of contributors made the task of keeping up with the literature relatively simple.

More recently, Environmental and Resource Economics has broadened its focus by making connections with many other subdisciplines in economics as well as the natural and physical sciences. It has also attracted a much larger group of contributors. Thus the literature is exploding in terms of the number of topics addressed, the number of methodological approaches being applied and the sheer number of articles being written. Coupled with the high degree of specialization that characterizes modern academic life, this proliferation of topics and methodologies makes it impossible for anyone, even those who specialize in Environmental and Resource Economics, to keep up with the developments in the field.

The International Yearbook of Environmental and Resource Economics: A Survey of Current Issues was designed to fill this niche. The *Yearbook* publishes state-of-the-art papers by top specialists in their fields who have made substantial contributions to the area that they are surveying. Authors are invited by the editors, in consultation with members of the editorial board. Each paper is critically reviewed by the editors and by several members of the editorial board.

The editors would like to thank Wallace Oates for his help in getting the project started. We also very much appreciate the assistance of Jim Shortle, Hans Andersson, Bryon Swift, Gert Tinggaard Svendson, Bengt Kriström, Shelby Gerking, Larry Goulder, Richard Howarth, Douglas Shaw, Stale Navrud, G. CornelisVan Kooten, Clive Spash, Peter Bohm and Scott Barrett in shaping this collection of papers. Special thanks to Sjak Smulders for reviewing and commenting on two articles.

Tom Tietenberg

Henk Folmer

Editorial board

EDITORS

Tom Tietenberg, Colby College, USA
Henk Folmer, Wageningen University and Tilburg University, The Netherlands

EDITORIAL BOARD

1. Climate change policy: models, controversies and strategies

Carlo Carraro*

1. INTRODUCTION

The political agenda on climate change is dominated by the 1992 UN Framework Convention on Climate Change (UNFCCC), its 1997 Kyoto Protocol, and the diverse ways of interpreting, refining and implementing the commitments under the two treaties. While many scientists and policy-makers welcome the UNFCCC and the Kyoto Protocol for the signals they send to society and industry, they are afraid that lack of political will and the loopholes in the treaties may minimize their impacts. In addition, some environmentalists, academicians and business NGOs (non-governmental organizations) think that the design of the Kyoto Protocol is inadequate in its choice of instruments – but they disagree on the definition of the appropriate instruments – while its targets are considered either too weak or too ambitious. The diverging views on the science of climate change and the associated risks, and the need for fair and politically feasible mechanisms for implementing the international agreements have been lurking under the surface of the negotiations, becoming more explicit during the ratification process. For a while, the European Union countries have been waiting for other developed countries to take action at the same time (see, for example, the EU Council Conclusions of 1997). In 1999, the US Senate linked the ratification of the Kyoto Protocol with the 'meaningful participation' of key developing countries. In addition, developed countries have been unable to reach agreement on some aspects of the treaty – specifically the balance between domestic actions and Kyoto mechanisms, the role of sinks, the implementation of sanctions, and so on. All this led to a negotiation deadlock, as shown by the failure of the Sixth Conference of the Parties (COP6) in The Hague in 2001 and its follow-up in Bonn a few months later. The European Union is currently leading a group of countries which plan to ratify the Kyoto Protocol even without US participation in the agreement. However, there are doubts about the environmental effectiveness of this policy option.

Independently of the future outcomes of climate negotiations, the above short summary raises some important questions. Why is it so difficult to reach agreement on strategies to control climate changes? What is peculiar to this environmental problem that prevents other environmental agreements from being adapted to climate changes? At least seven peculiar features characterize the issue of climate change. Even though other environmental problems also possess some of these features, the climate problem stands out in relation to both their intensity and their strong interdependencies.

1. The problem is global. This implies that climate change control is a public good, that is, the climate that we all enjoy is the product of everyone's behaviour. This provides an important motivation for collective, global action, but also strong incentives to free-riding. Moreover, emissions and their consequences are heterogeneous around the world. This exacerbates the basic public-good nature of the problem. Countries are distributed across a spectrum of high emitters–low emitters and high impact–low impact. Nations with high emissions and low expected impacts have a high potential to control concentrations, but little incentive. On the other hand, nations with low emissions and high impacts have great incentive to control emissions, but little capability. While side payments could in principle resolve this dilemma, transaction costs may be significant and present income distributions may lead to unacceptable outcomes.

2. The problem is long term. Hence, it is concentrations not emissions that matter. Climate change is related to the concentration of greenhouse gases (GHGs) and not to any individual year's emissions. Carbon dioxide (CO_2) concentrations are closely related to the net accumulation of emissions over long periods of time. Therefore, strategies to control net emissions must take long periods of time into account in a meaningful way. Moreover, intergeneration transfers are inevitable because the consequences of climate change will affect primarily those who will be alive in the future. The fact that most of the affected parties are not present to participate in the decision-making process raises complicated ethical questions. Indeed, the implications of their absence are not immediately obvious. Because climate change is anticipated to be greater in the future than it is at present, those who live in the future will reap most of the benefits that accrue to near-term actions to limit emissions. Intergenerational asymmetry can lead to a form of public-good problem in which the willingness to undertake emissions mitigation in the near term may be less than would have been the case if decision-makers were infinitely lived.

3. Narrowly defined technological solutions are unavailable. Emissions of greenhouse gases are associated with an extraordinary array of human activities. CO_2 emissions alone are associated with the combustion of fossil fuels and changes in land use, thus affecting activities ranging from agriculture to manufacture. As a consequence, GHGs emissions are greatly affected by other, exogenous and non-climate-policy factors. Narrowly defined technological solutions, such as those which were available to address the problem of stratospheric ozone depletion, are not yet available to reduce GHG emissions. Hence, a mix of internationally agreed policies is likely to be necessary to control climate changes, thus raising issues of appropriate negotiation processes, well-designed international regimes, adequate incentives to participation, and so on.

4. Policy interactions are strong. Future emissions depend to a large degree on the rate and direction of technological developments in a broad array of human endeavours. For example, China's policies to stabilize its population's size, made for reasons unrelated to climate change, will have a profound effect on Chinese emissions of greenhouse gases to the atmosphere. Policies to control non-greenhouse air pollutants can greatly affect greenhouse gas emissions. For example, measures to substitute natural gas and non-carbon-emitting energy forms, such as solar and nuclear power, for coal in electric power generation to control local and regional air pollution can affect greenhouse gas emissions as well. On the other hand, some policies that reduce local air pollution, such as scrubbing power plants for sulphur, can reduce power plant efficiency and increase greenhouse gas emissions. This raises several forms of interaction between domestic and international policies and makes it difficult to define baselines for negotiations and net costs and benefits from climate policies. It also raises domestic economic conflicts between different economic interests in addition to the international ones.

5. Uncertainty is pervasive. Uncertainty surrounds the climate change problem at every point. Researchers disagree as to the rate and extent of emissions to the atmosphere in the absence of climate change. Researchers disagree as to the change in concentration of greenhouse gases which would result from a given emission rate. Researchers disagree as to the timing, extent and distribution of climate change and sea level rise for a given concentration of greenhouse gases. Researchers disagree as to whether some climate change is an aggregate net benefit or net cost to ecosystems and humanity. The potential for an unspecified, low-probability, but catastrophic turn of events haunts the problem. While uncertainties are great, they are not distributed evenly throughout the problem. The implications of emissions mitigation are better known than the more long-term potential benefits from mitigation. Uncertainty and the uneven distribution of uncertainty is another factor that explains the difficulty of agreeing on an effective international regime to control climate changes.

6. The consequences are potentially irreversible. Many global bio-geochemical processes have long characteristic time scales. Sea level changes as a consequence of changes in mean global temperature can take more than 1000 years to play out. Similarly, changes in the concentration of greenhouse gases can rise rapidly, but decline slowly. And, even if concentrations can be reduced, the nature of the climate system is such that it might not return to the same climatic state associated with an earlier concentration.

7. The global institutions needed to address the issue are only partially formed. The UNFCCC has been ratified by more than 170 parties and entered into force in 1994. It provides the institutional foundations upon which international climate change negotiations occur. It sets, as its ultimate objective, the stabilization of the concentration of greenhouse gases in the atmosphere at levels that would prevent dangerous anthropogenic interferences with the climate. But the UNFCCC establishes a process rather than creating the institutions for implementing the objective. The objective has not been quantified. The term 'dangerous' has been left open to interpretation by the parties. The Kyoto Protocol of December 1997 represents a further important step in international regime formation under the UNFCCC. It has introduced a number of new elements and broadened the context of the decision-making process regarding the implementation of climate change policy.[1] However, several issues need to be clarified for the Kyoto Protocol to be implemented. In particular, countries do not completely agree on the meaning of the supplementarity condition, the role of sinks, the liability rules, the enforcement process, the extension of the emission trading market, and so on. More generally, there is no supranational institution with the power to enforce and monitor the objectives agreed upon in Kyoto which will therefore be implemented on a voluntary basis. Hence, again, a problem of incentives to free-riding and the difficulty of establishing a stable and effective international regime to control climate changes.

Given the above peculiar features of the climate policy problem, it obviously raises a few fundamental questions. What is the future of the UNFCCC and of the Kyoto Protocol? Are there any chances for the Kyoto Protocol to be ratified and implemented by a sufficiently large number of countries within a time limit which actually enables these countries to fulfil their commitments? Is there any strategy that could enhance the chances of implementation of the Kyoto Protocol? Or should countries move to a different type of agreement? Is it reasonable to pursue an 'evolutionary approach' in which the UNFCCC and the Kyoto Protocol are updated to achieve the consensus of all industrialized countries and the most important developing countries? Or is it more reasonable to follow a 'revolutionary approach' in which the Kyoto Protocol is abandoned and climate policy is structured according to very different principles and measures?

In order to answer these questions, it is important to assess the costs and benefits of GHG emission reductions in the presence of the above features of the climate change policy problem and under alternative international regimes, namely different structures of the agreements (number and identity of signatories), different policy mixes to achieve emission control, different cooperation policies with developing countries, and so on. This will enable us to identify the incentives, if any, that different countries have in ratifying the Kyoto Protocol or any other climate agreements. Given these incentives, it will be possible to construct a scenario on the likely evolutions of climate negotiations.

In particular, we would like to identify which policies can be designed to lower the costs and increase the incentives to ratify a given international agreement on climate. There are studies (see the collection of papers in Carraro, 1999a, 1999b, 2000; Carraro and Hourcade, 1999; Weyant, 1999) that analyse the costs of implementing the Kyoto Protocol either through a set of domestic policies and measures or through a system of international tradable permits, keeping as given the number of participating countries. But the adoption of either policy crucially affects the number of participating countries, which can be larger or smaller under policies and measures than under tradable permits. And the number (and identity) of the participating countries crucially affects the costs and benefits of different policy strategies. Therefore, this paper has two objectives:

1. to provide an analysis of the environmental and cost-effectiveness of different climate policies;
2. to emphasize the bi-directional link between policy options and structure of the agreement, that is, the number of countries which sign and ratify the agreement.

The equity issue is also very important in understanding which countries are going to reduce/control their emissions. As a consequence, given that the number and identity of participating countries affect the costs of emission reductions, equity is crucial in adequately assessing the costs of emission reductions at the global and country level. Accordingly, recent studies address the problem of optimal burden-sharing (the distribution of costs) of climate change control. For example, it has been argued that some countries are allowed to reduce emissions less than other countries, both within (Kram, 1998) and outside the EU bubble (Metz, 2000; Bosello and Roson, 2000; Rose and Stevens, 2000). And that even when applying flexibility mechanisms, some countries will benefit from the agreements more than others (Nordhaus and Boyer, 1999). These studies analyse the burden-sharing issue without relating it to the incentives to implement measures to achieve emission control. However, burden-sharing and participation in an international agreement to control GHG emissions are closely interrelated. On the one hand, an increasing number of participating countries reduces the burden for each signatory; on the other hand, an agreement in which the burden is shared equitably is more likely to be signed by a large number of countries (Convery, 2000). Therefore, equity and the structure of the international agreement (number and identity of signatories) are intimately linked. But the number of signatories affects and is affected by costs. Hence, equity and efficiency cannot be separated.

This leads to a further set of issues. If a larger number of participating countries reduces the implementation costs, thus opening the way for further extensions of a climate agreement, what are the negotiating strategies that could help increase the number of countries which sign and ratify the agreement? Are there negotiating and institutional rules which favour countries' participation? Are there policy strategies that could provide the right incentives for countries to participate in a climate agreement?

Therefore, this paper will also analyse which policy strategies and negotiation rules can provide the right incentives for a sufficiently large number of countries – and the big countries in particular – to sign and ratify the Kyoto Protocol or any other climate agreements. This analysis will enable us to identify a set of policy guidelines that could help the future evolution of climate agreements.

The structure of this chapter is as follows. Section 2 reviews the main features and the effects of different climate policy instruments, whereas section 3 describes the properties of the most popular economic climate models. Given these tools, section 4 analyses some controversial issues in climate change policy. Section 5 explores the incentives to ratify a climate agreement and discusses strategies designed to improve the prospects of the Kyoto Protocol or of other climate agreements that could be proposed in the future. Finally a concluding section will summarize the main results and identify topics where further research is needed.

2.   CLIMATE POLICY INSTRUMENTS

Climate policy instruments are usually grouped into either command-and-control or market-based approaches. Market-based instruments (MBIs) are mechanisms that encourage behaviour through market signals rather than through explicit directives regarding pollution control levels or methods. These policy instruments, such as pollution charges, subsidies, tradable permits, and some types of information programmes, have been described as 'harnessing market forces'.[2] This is because, if they are well designed and implemented, they encourage firms (and/or individuals) to undertake pollution control efforts that are in their own interests and that collectively meet policy goals.

Conventional approaches to regulating the environment are often referred to as command-and-control (CAC) regulations since they allow relatively little flexibility in the means of achieving goals. Such regulations tend to force firms to take on similar shares of the pollution control burden, regardless of the cost.

Command-and-control regulations do this by setting uniform standards for firms, the most prevalent of which are technology and performance-based standards. Technology-based standards specify the method, and sometimes the actual equipment, which firms must use to comply with a particular regulation. A performance-based standard sets a uniform control target for firms, while allowing some latitude in how this target is met.

Holding all firms to the same target can be expensive and, in some circumstances, counterproductive. While standards may effectively limit emissions of pollutants, they typically imply relatively high costs in the process, by forcing some firms to resort to unduly expensive means of controlling pollution. Because the costs of controlling emissions may vary greatly among firms, and even among sources within the same firm, the appropriate technology in one situation may not be appropriate (that is, cost effective) in another.

To the above list of instruments we should add negotiated environmental agreements (NEAs) [3] and project-based instruments (PBIs), such as joint implementation and CDM (clean development mechanism).

NEAs are not easily classified: including reduction obligations makes an NEA like a regulatory measure; receipt by participating firms of financial incentives for complying with certain environmental goals makes NEAs fall in the economic tools category. Loosely speaking, PBIs consist of new investment in technical projects that are beneficial for the environment.

While on theoretical grounds MBIs are generally preferred because they are more cost-effective, in practice CAC policies have been predominant. In recent years, however, economic instruments have played an ever-increasing role, reflecting their perceived superiority. This process has culminated in the official recognition of these policy tools in the Kyoto Protocol. Indeed, much of the debate surrounding the Protocol has centred on the use of MBIs, and on emission trading in particular, precisely because of the large potential cost savings that economic tools offer relative to CAC measures.

Policy-makers became sympathetic to the application of MBIs due to a mixture of push and pull factors. The push factor was that regulation had not always been effective. It proved expensive and lengthy to bring offenders to court, thereby reducing the possibility of enforcing effective compliance. The level of sanctions was not sufficient to ensure compliance. Procedures for permits and licensing have become increasingly cumbersome, pushing up administrative costs. Pull factors included the prospect for less bureaucracy and better environmental performance due to more effective implementation (Pelkmans and Egenhofer, 1993; Delbeke, 1996) and the revenue-raising function – in the cases of taxation and tradable permits, if allowances are auctioned – which has still remained the prevailing function (EEA, 1996; Potier, 1996).

Another strong argument in favour of incentive-based instruments is their dynamic efficiency, that is, their incentives to innovate and improve environ-

Table 1.1   Incentives for innovation created by environmental policies

Policy	Direct gains to innovating firm	Potential rents from adoption
Command-and-control	None	None
Best available technology	Negative. New standard raises overall compliance costs	Very high. Tighter standard raises incentives to adopt
Performance standards	Positive. Limited to existing abatement costs	Positive. Limited to existing abatement costs
Emission tax	High. Lowers abatement costs and taxed emissions	High. Lowers abatement costs and taxed emissions
Auctioned emission permits	High. Lowers abatement costs and costs of all permits purchased	Small. Buying permits becomes cheaper alternative
Grandfathered emission permits	Small. Lowers abatement costs	Small. Buying permits becomes cheaper alternative

Source: Fischer (2000).

mental performance. While standards – if adhered to and properly implemented – effectively limit pollution, they tend to increase costs by forcing some firms to apply expensive technologies to comply with a given standard. In addition to typically incurring high costs, technical standards tend to freeze the development of technologies in the absence of financial incentives to exceed a control target. Technical standards do not reward companies to go beyond the mandated standards (see Clinch, 2000; Stavins, 2001). By contrast, market-based instruments foster the adoption of new technologies with relevant impacts on emission reductions both in the short and in the long term (see Table 1.1 for an overview of the effects of different policy instruments on technological innovation).

Empirical evidence suggests that society's economic benefits from the application of incentive-based instruments are considerable. One survey of ten empirical studies of air pollution control in the USA found that the ratio of actual aggregate costs of command-and-control regulations to the aggregate costs of least-cost benchmarks ranged from 1.07 for sulphate emissions in Los Angeles to 22.0 for hydrocarbons emissions at all domestic DuPont plants (see Table 1.2).

Even though these figures cannot easily be extended to a global scale, they actually suggest that large cost reductions can be achieved by adopting MBIs to deal with GHG emission control. Indeed, the focus on market-based policy instruments was further increased by the adoption of the Kyoto Protocol in 1997. The Kyoto Protocol foresees a number of flexibility provisions permitting the transfer or exchange of emission reduction obligations between the contracting governments. These flexibility provisions include the well-known Kyoto mechanisms (JI, CDM and emissions trading) as well as the (EU) bubble provision and banking. All these provisions aim at increasing flexibility either to reduce compliance costs or to address equity (geographical or between generations) or both, driven by the desire to provide sufficient incentives to governments, industry and other stakeholders to adhere to the Kyoto Protocol.

The clean development mechanism (CDM)[4] addresses both equity and efficiency concerns. The main objective of the CDM is to enhance developing-country investment and technology transfer by the industrialized countries and thereby address equity issues between industrialized and developing countries. At the same time, the CDM, like the other flexible mechanisms, aims to increase the efficiency of abatement by least-cost emission reductions.[5] The tensions between equity and efficiency concerns can be found in the COP6 discussions on share of proceeds of CDM projects and sinks, both of which constitute an additional transfer to developing countries. However, the CDM also raised equity issues among developing countries. For example, African countries, which fear that most CDM investments will bypass them, have insisted on regional CDM quotas. Both quotas and share of proceeds, in effect a tax on CDM projects recycled to developing countries, reduce the efficiency and risk

Table 1.2 The gains from least-cost air pollution control

Study	Pollutants covered	Area of the USA	Command-and-control policy benchmark	Ratio of CAC cost to least-cost policy
Atkinson and Lewis (1974)	Particulates	St Louis	State Implementation Plan (SIP) regulations	6.00
Roach et al. (1981)	Sulphur dioxide	Four Corners: Utah, Col., Arizona, New Mexico	State Implementation Plan (SIP) regulations	4.25
Hahn and Noll (1982)	Sulphates standards	Los Angeles	California emission standards	1.07
Krupnick (1986)	Nitrogen dioxide regulations	Baltimore	Proposed RACT (technology requirements)	5.96
Seskin et al. (1983)	Nitrogen dioxide regulations	Chicago	Proposed RACT (technology requirements)	14.40
McGartland (1984)	Particulates	Baltimore	State Implementation Plan (SIP) regulations	4.18
Spofford (1984)	Sulphur dioxide	Lower Delaware Valley	Uniform percentage reductions	1.78
	Particulates			22.00
Harrison (1983)	Airport noise	USA	Mandatory Refit	1.72
Maloney and Yandle (1984)	Hydrocarbons	US DuPont plants	Uniform percentage reductions	4.15
Palmer et al. (1980)	CFC emissions ex. aerosols	USA	Proposed emissions standards	1.96

Source: Clinch (2000).

to undermine the incentives to undertake such projects. The incentive structure will also depend on the eligibility of CDM projects. Since it is generally assumed that CDM projects will have considerable transaction costs, the reward in terms of credits must match the risk of an investor in countries with occasionally unstable economic climates.

Joint implementation (JI),[6] similarly to the CDM, aims at efficiency improvements via international trading. But it attempts to address equity concerns through investment promotion and technology transfer within industrialized countries, contrary to CDM. Operating within Annex B countries, JI puts more emphasis on environmental effectiveness. Permits can only be traded if they reflect emissions reductions achieved via new investment, which would not have been achieved without JI provisions. As in the case of CDM, shares or proceeds, eligibility criteria and transaction costs will be crucial in deciding the exact scope of JI projects.

International emissions trading (ET)[7] is mainly driven by efficiency and effectiveness concerns aimed at providing incentives to Annex B counties and industry to implement the Kyoto Protocol. Emissions trading produces least-cost emissions reductions by placing the same price on emissions. A precondition of being an effective instrument was that those counties potentially participating in trading (that is, Annex B) accept a cap on overall emissions (that is, assigned amounts). Emissions trading however has indirect features of transfers in the form of hot air.[8] While hot air will reduce compliance costs for importing countries, it will constitute a transfer for exporting countries. The Kyoto Protocol's supplementarity clause whereby the use of the flexible mechanisms need to be supplemental to domestic action is consequently driven by equity concerns. The supplementarity clause is a further attempt to apply in a narrow sense – at least to some extent – the polluter pays principle.[9] Those countries that historically have been responsible for GHG concentrations should undertake most of the abatement effort. The tension with efficiency is evident. Further tensions between efficiency and effectiveness are inherent when deciding on the rules and procedures by which ET should be governed. This is especially true for the liability regime that will be applied. The ill-fated attempt by the EU environment ministers at COP6 to combine seller liability with buyer liability is an attempt to value environmental effectiveness higher than economic efficiency.

In addition, the Kyoto Protocol foresees a banking provision in Art. 3(13) addressing intergenerational equity concerns. Borrowing is not permitted. Finally, the Kyoto Protocol foresees, under joint commitments in Article 4, that Annex B countries are allowed to fulfil their obligations jointly. This is usually referred to as the EU bubble since the provision is presently only used by the EU.[10] The EU bubble can be interpreted as an incentive to address geographical equity as well as to equalize marginal cost differences through an internal EU emissions trading scheme that this provision allows.

As a consequence of the increased focus of climate policy on MBIs, even economic research moved from the comparison of command-and-control regulation with incentive-based policy measures to the comparison of different types of MBIs. For example, several studies have considered the relative merits of emission taxes and tradable pollution permits by comparing them in both first-best and second-best worlds (see Norregaard and Reppelin-Hill, 2000, for a survey). A summary is reported in Table 1.3.

One interesting aspect of the comparison is the revenue-raising potential. Both an emission tax and a system of auctioned pollution permits (as opposed to freely allocated, or grandfathered, permits) generate government revenues which may be used for pursuing some policy goal. The possibility of improving the environment and, at the same time, increasing overall welfare has been termed the 'double dividend' and its emergence under alternative forms of revenue recycling has been much studied in recent years (for a comprehensive review see Bosello, Carraro and Galeotti, 2000).

NEAs have been typically used to solve environmental problems other than climate change mitigation. Because they do not encounter the resistance of CAC and other policies, they have also come to be considered as means for industry to contribute to reducing GHG emissions. In the early 1990s, many countries adopted NEAs as part of their national policy for CO_2 reduction and/or for improving energy efficiency. Since the UNFCCC was agreed in Rio, the use of NEAs for energy efficiency has increased (Chidiak, 1998; Storey, 1997). However, none of these NEAs were designed with a view to binding targets. Examples of these pre-Kyoto voluntary agreements include the 'Long Term Energy Efficiency Agreements' (1992) in the Netherlands (see Dutch Ministry of Economic Affairs, 1998), the 'Declaration by German Industry on Global Warming' established in 1995, then amended in 1996 (and 2000) in Germany (see BDI, 1995, 1996a, 1996b, 1999) and the Danish Agreements on CO_2 Emission Abatement (1996–97) in Denmark (see Millock, 1999).

In contrast, since the Kyoto Protocol, agreements are being defined with consideration for a priori targets. Among these new initiatives are Switzerland's 'Action Program Energy 2000', Italy's 'Climate Pact' between government, industry and NGOs (November 1998), which specifies that NEAs are to be the favoured policy tool to address climate change, and the UK's Climate Change Levy (CCL) which defines a group of NEAs as complementary measures. The group of NEAs signed in 1999 have been designed as a complement to the recently established CCL which is to be used in conjunction with the domestic tradable permit system. This policy mix represents the main tool that will be used in the UK to meet the Kyoto commitment.

Table 1.3 Summary of the basic criteria for the choice of taxes vs tradable permits

Criteria	Tax versus tradable permits
Information intensity	*First-best scenario* • Emissions taxes and tradable permits are equally preferred under a first-best scenario (when knowledge on marginal damages (MD) and marginal abatement costs (MAC) is available) • Under uncertainty about MD, both are equally inefficient • Under uncertainty about MACs, efficiency losses are minimized with an emissions tax if the MD curve is relatively flatter than the MAC curve and vice versa *Second-best scenario* • Tradable permits are preferred if the regulator wants to achieve an absolute target
Efficiency in non-competitive market	• When the output market is non-competitive, neither instrument is efficient but efficiency losses are smaller under a permit scheme with heterogeneous firms (with different abatement technologies). • When the permit market is non-competitive, the permit programme is inefficient
Monitoring/enforcement	• Tax is preferable since requiring monitoring of emissions only, while a permit system also requires the monitoring of trades.
Flexibility in the face of change	• Permits are preferred since, once established, such systems maintain the desired level of emissions. A tax needs to be adjusted in the face of change of the ambient air quality.
Dynamic incentives	• Both are equivalent in terms of encouraging new *technologies*, except if permit market does not function • In terms of *industry*, grandfathering may create a barrier to entry
Revenue-raising	• If permits are auctioned, both systems are equivalent. If permits are grandfathered, tax has higher potential
Distribution	• If permits are auctioned, both systems have the same effect • If permits are grandfathered, new entrants are discriminated against
Competitiveness	• Tradable permits are preferred since they make the cost of environmental protection less visible.

Source: Norregaard and Reppelin-Hill (2000); Stavins (2001).

In addition to these agreements, a number of companies have also launched purely self-commitments (no negotiations and no discussions), two key examples being Shell and BP. Shell promised to cut greenhouse gases (GHGs) by at least 10 per cent from 1990 levels by 2002. In addition, these two companies have launched voluntary emissions trading initiatives to understand the likely effects of this particular Kyoto mechanism.

To date no systematic analysis on the link between the Kyoto Protocol approach to climate change, the role of the Kyoto mechanisms and NEAs exists. This neglect is surprising given that specific targets of NEAs appear to be incompatible both with absolute national targets and allowance-based emissions trading (CCAP, 1999; Zapfel, 1999; FIELD, 2000) that have been proposed by the European Commission (CEC, 2000).

Most of the focus of economic analysis has instead concentrated on emissions trading at different geographical scales and/or in association with other policy instruments. Table 1.4 reorganizes the existing literature on climate policies in a way that enables us to identify the costs and benefits of different combinations of policy mixes and participatory regimes. The papers mentioned in Table 1.4 are only a subset of the available papers (see Carraro, 1998, 1999b, 2000; OECD, 1998. See also Burniaux, 1998; Capros, 1998, Ellerman et al. 1998; Grubb and Vrolijk, 1998; Holtzmark, 1998, Manne and Richels, 1998; Mensbrugghe, 1998; Nordhaus and Boyer, 1999; and the surveys by Metz, 2000 and Convery, 2000, among others). For a more complete survey, see chapter 8 of the IPCC Third Assessment Report.

A careful analysis of the papers listed in Table 1.4 leads to three conclusions which find consensus among most researchers in climate policy:

1. An increased number of countries ratifying the Protocol reduces the implementation costs in all participating countries and increases the abated emissions. Hence, strategies that increase the size and the number of ratifying countries also increase the environmental and cost-effectiveness of the Protocol[11] and more generally of any climate agreements.
2. A reduced cost of implementing the Protocol increases the incentives for countries to ratify it. Hence, strategies designed to reduce implementation costs also increase the number of participating countries, thus further reducing the cost of achieving the Kyoto commitments.
3. Climate policy has clear objectives both in terms of cost-efficiency and in terms of equity. Hence, a policy mix in which different policy instruments are optimally designed is likely to be the preferred policy option. This issue will be further explored in section 4.

We shall use these conclusions in section 5 to identify a set of policy strategies that will help in the negotiation process which could lead to an

Table 1.4 Coalition structures and policy options

Policy options / Coalitions	Domestic measures only	Coordinated carbon tax	Flexibility mechanisms with ceilings	Free flexibility mechanisms	Flexibility mechanisms with banking	Flexibility mechanisms with R&D	Flexibility mechanisms with mkt imperfections
No participation Unilateral participation	IPCC (1995) Jorgenson and Wilcoxen (1993) Barrett (1992)						
EU only	Carraro and Siniscalco (1992)	Bosello and Carraro (1999a, 1999b) Barker (1998)	Schmidt and Koschel (1998)				
OECD only	Burniaux et al. (1992) McKibbin et al. (1998)	Capros (1998) Mensbrugghe (1998)		Harrison and Rutherford (1999) Holtzmark (1998) Capros (1998)			
Annex B countries			Ellerman et al. (1998, 1999) Buonanno et al. (1999) Manne and Richels (1998)	Ellerman et al. (1998) Grubb and Vrolijk (1998) Holtzmark (1998) McKibbin et al. (1998) Manne and Richels (1999, 2000) Mensbrugghe (1998) Nordhaus and Boyer (1999) Schackleton (1998)	Bosello and Roson (2000) Westkog (1999)	Nordhaus (1997) Buonanno et al. (1999)	Burniaux (1998) Ellerman et al. (1998)
Double umbrella				McKibbin et al. (1998) Schackleton (1998)			Ellerman et al. (1998)
All countries	Nordhaus and Yang (1996)		Ellerman et al. (1998) Buonanno et al. (1999)	Bohm (1999) Ellerman et al. (1998) Manne and Richels (1998,1999,2000) Nordhaus and Boyer (1999) Schackleton (1998)	Bosello and Roson (2000) Westkog (1999)	Nordhaus (1997) Buonanno et al. (1999)	

Source: Carraro (2001)

15

effective and efficient climate policy. Here, we want to stress the increasing role of policy mixes in climate policy. For example, ET and NEAs can have important synergies, as ten Brink and Morère (2000) argue. NEAS can function as a starting-point and learning process in the design and implementation of the project mechanisms. They can bridge the transition period to the first commitment period, and can be a means of early action, preparing industry for the kind of carbon constraints they face in the first and following commitment periods. NEAs are also a means to provide regulators with information regarding future allowance allocations (FIELD, 2000). The Center for Clean Air Policy (CCAP, 1999) maintains that NEAs are unlikely to survive the introduction of an ET system since double regulation would increase costs. Companies have accepted NEAs to avoid additional regulation. Torvanger and Skodvin (2001) argue that NEAs can play a role as a 'soft' transition stage from traditional regulation to domestic emissions trading.

More recently the idea of combining taxes and permits has been proposed. A hybrid system of permits and taxes is seen as a safety valve in light of the high uncertainty – as in the case of climate change – in relation to the risk of ever-rising permit prices (Kolstad and Toman, 2000). This policy mix would set the target via an initial distribution of allowances, but allow additional permits to be purchased at a fixed price (McKibbin and Wilcoxen, 1997) or set floor and ceiling prices for permits to reduce the impact of hot air, respectively to avoid excessive costs (Hourcade and Fortin, 2000). In the case of ceiling prices, the system works like a permit system by fixing the level of emissions as long as the marginal cost – reflected in the permit price – lies below the fixed price ceiling. They work like tax schemes by fixing marginal costs through the fixed price ceiling when the marginal costs hit that ceiling. In the case of floor prices, designed to avoid possible negative effects of hot air, the system works like a permit system unless the permit price becomes lower than a given level, in which case the tax system applies. In light of the fact that the hybrid policies have not yet been implemented, 'real-world' experience is still missing. Pizer (1997) maintains, on the basis of a modelling exercise, that sub-optimal hybrid policies, based both on targets and on emission prices, can generate better welfare than straight permit systems and thereby provide an alternative to either straight tax or permit policy.

3.   CLIMATE MODELS

Climate models played an important role in the policy debate and negotiation process that preceded and followed the Kyoto agreement. Climate changes are indeed the outcome of complex human, social, economic, biological and physical phenomena. The interactions between and the effects of these phenomena can hardly be assessed altogether, and only huge modelling efforts can achieve approximate representations of the causes and impacts of climate changes. Needless to say, policy analyses are highly dependent on these imperfect representations of climate dynamics and its relationships with human activities.

At the beginning of the 1970s, the first environmental models attempting to assess environmental impacts were developed, mainly focusing on greenhouse gas (GHG) emissions. These models, usually constructed by natural scientists, were generally technical–climatic models rather than economic models, and were based on a small number of parameters and on qualitative/quantitative expert opinions.

Economists began to get involved in GHGs and environmental modelling in general at the end of the 1970s. This type of research was stimulated by the Toronto Climate Conference in 1988, which stressed the need to reduce CO_2 emissions to 20 per cent below 1988 levels. As a consequence, climate modelling boomed and a large amount of regional and global work on the costs and benefits of CO_2 abatement appeared in journals and books.

In recent years, modelling techniques have changed. First, input–output and 'macro-Keynesian' models were replaced by applied general equilibrium models, in part reflecting improvements in computer technology and algorithm solver methods. Subsequently, these model approaches were replaced by 'eclectic' models with both 'bottom-up' and 'top-down' characteristics, which could also account for the possibility of temporary disequilibria in factor markets. Currently, with the so-called Integrated Assessment Models (IAMs), environmental modelling aims to amalgamate the knowledge from different scientific fields – economics, bio-geophysics, engineering, demography, and so on – in order to tackle environmental issues in the most comprehensive way possible.

The so-called bottom-up/top-down controversy dominated the late 1980s and the early 1990s. Bottom up models aim at identifying alternative ways to provide energy services. The objective is pursued through a high level of dis-aggregation of the energy system, both on the supply and on the demand side, and through a detailed micro-description of available technologies. The main limit of this approach is that bottom-up models generally neglect feedbacks to the economy and rebound effects through international energy markets. Moreover, they do not take into account the uncertainty concerning many environmental phenomena, the actual diffusion process of new technologies, and the effects of environmental policies.

In top-down models, energy–economy interactions are modelled at the macro level, for a single country, for a group of nations or for the world as a whole. They allow for varying degrees of disaggregation, particularly of the energy sector, yet top-down models contain a fairly aggregate representation of production systems and technologies. Many types of models follow this approach. In particular, we can distinguish three major ones: the traditional macroeconomic models, the technical–economic sectoral models, and the computable general equilibrium models.

The traditional macroeconometric models (for example Capros and Karadeloglou, 1992) follow a neo-Keynesian theoretical approach: the assumed structure is 'demand driven' and under-utilization of productive capacity is possible in the short and medium term. Hence, they are not suitable for very long-run analyses which are necessary when estimating the dynamics of policy changes aimed at reducing GHGs. Moreover, they have not yet convincingly considered the role of uncertainty, nor that of technical change which is generally represented by an exogenous time trend.

A second type of top-down modelling approach is the technical–economic models which generally combine a simplified description of the economic relationships with a detailed representation of the energy sector. The most important global models in this group are the Edmonds–Reilly–Barns model and the Global 2100 model of Manne and Richels (see Table 1.5). They present different levels of detail of energy-supply technologies and contain a simplified representation of macroeconomic and trade linkages. They extend the analysis over a very long time horizon. Technical progress is represented by an exogenous index measuring the autonomous energy efficiency improvement (AEEI). Therefore, both the international dimensions and technical progress are unsatisfactorily dealt with in these models. Uncertainty is examined only in the work by Manne and Richels (1992).

The third type of top-down models, the computable general equilibrium class, has been developed in more recent years. These models have the theoretical assumption of a Walrasian representation of the economy in common, but they differ in many other respects: the behaviour of economic agents; the calibration or the estimation of the model parameters; the time horizon; the geographic extension; and the representation of technology options. Among the global models (see Table 1.5), the Whalley and Wigle and the OECD's GREEN are the best known. In Europe, GEM-E3 and WARM were developed under the auspices of the European Commission. These models suffer from limitations similar to those of the previous approaches. In particular, they do not provide an endogenous representation of technological change,[12] which is described through the AEEI, and the elasticity of substitution (ESUB) parameters, which are generally guess-estimated: the independence of such parameters from any other model variable, and their constancy, jeopardize the possibility of measuring the role of non-price policies in affecting energy efficiency. Moreover, uncertainty and environmental impacts and feedback are also largely neglected.

Table 1.5   *Climate models: a taxonomy*

Models	National	EU	Global	Global/regionalized
Input–output	MIS MEPA			
LP/NLP	MARKAL ETSAP MESSAGE III	HERMES–MIDAS MARKAL		IEA (10 world regions) MARKAL
IA		ESCAPE	DICE, R&DICE, PRICE SLICE CETA Yohe Gjerde et al.	IMAGE 2.0 (13 world regions) RICE (6 world regions) FUND (9 world regions) PAGE (4 world regions) MERGE (5 world regions) IIAM (26 world regions) ICAM (7 world regions) MINICAM (9 world regions)
CGE/AGE	Konrad (D) Bovenberg–Goulder (USA) Jorgenson–Wilcoxen (USA)	GEM-E3 Boehringer et al. LEAN		ERM (9 world regions) EPPA (12 world regions) SGM (20 world regions) GREEN (12 world regions) G-Cubed (8 world regions) Whalley–Wigle (6 world regions)
Econometric	MDM (UK)	QUEST WARM E3ME		WORLDSCAN POLES

Note: For a description of the models see Manne and Richels (1992); MERGE, Nordhaus (1993); DICE; Peck and Teisberg (1992): CETA; Barns et al. (1992): ERM; CEC (1991): QUEST; Nordhaus and Yang (1996): RICE; Barker (1994): MDM; Barker and Zagame (1995) E3ME; Rotmans et al. (1994): ESCAPE; Rotmans (1990): IMAGE; Alcamo (1994): IMAGE 2.0; Capros and Karadeloglou (1992): HERMES–MIDAS; Tol (1997) FUND; Bernstein et al. (1997): IIAM; Dowlatabadi and Kandlikar (1995) ICAM; Hope et al. (1993): PAGE; Rowe and Hill (1989): IEA; Gjerde et al. (1998); McKibbin and Wilcoxen (1995): G-Cubed; Fisher–Vaden et al. (1993): SGM; Yang et al. (1996): EPPA; Kolstad (1994): SLICE.

Source: Bosello et al. (1999).

19

Both bottom-up and top-down models have been used to answer the question of how much it would cost to limit GHG emissions. Each yields very different results. Bottom-up models indicate that much can be done significantly to reduce GHG emissions due to the existence of a wide range of technological opportunities and the assumption that the economy will be able to exploit them immediately and at low costs. Top-down models represent a world in which there is limited scope for technological improvements and cost-effective opportunities. Hence, substantive action to curb GHGs is only achievable through costly changes.

This debate on the costs of reducing GHG emissions, and the results provided by models available at the beginning of the 1990s, substantially affected policy analyses and decisions, despite the models' intrinsic limitations, such as short time horizons, lack of treatment of uncertainty and a rather conventional representation of technical change.[13]

These limitations appeared clearly when the Conference of Parties decided (in Berlin, 1994) to put the adoption of legally binding emission reductions in the Kyoto agenda in order to meet the objective of the Framework Convention on Climate Change (FCCC), namely the stabilization of GHG concentrations in the atmosphere. This stabilization goal is associated with three politically intertwined but analytically separable issues: the determination of the desired level of concentrations; the definition of the most cost-effective abatement profile towards such a level; and the efficient and equitable distribution of efforts among countries. Most top-down and bottom-up models could not provide an adequate analysis of these three issues. This is why, following the pioneering work of Nordhaus (1993), a wave of integrated assessment models was developed, in which the time and geographic dimension, the role of uncertainty, and the effects of technical change were increasingly taken into account. These new models focused on the determination of optimal climate policies in order to scrutinize the consistency between short-term decisions and long-term objectives, as implied by the Berlin Mandate.

It should be clear why technical change cannot be modelled as an *ad hoc* and exogenous process in climate models. The time profile of abatement strategies can be carefully designed only if the dynamics of technical progress are endogenized and linked to the other economic dimensions represented by the model. Any policy strategy which increases the costs of emissions can indeed induce energy-saving innovation and technological adoption, thus reducing the need for emission abatement in the future. At the same time, the high degree of uncertainty over the magnitude of climate changes and, above all, of their economic impacts also affect both innovation and investment plans and optimal policy strategies, which can feed back to innovation.

Various types of model represent in different ways the relationship between economic stimuli such as research and development (R&D) expenditures, energy prices, taxes and subsidies, and the direction and rate of technological change, as well as the subsequent effect on societal cost. In bottom-up models, the rate of technological change depends on how different the alternatives are to the present technology, as well as how quickly they substitute for one another. In top-down models employing endogenous technological change, technological change is often represented as a function of past production (learning by doing), the amount of past R&D (stock of knowledge), or the extent of energy price changes. Thus, even these endogenous models operate on the basis of an assumption about what determines technological effort and how that effort translates into progress. Thus, regardless of their different structures, all models of technological progress rely on some fundamental assumption about future technology, an assumption that plays a central role in determining model results.

In the model of knowledge accumulation of Goulder and Mathai (2000), a central planner chooses time paths of abatement and R&D efforts in order to minimize the present value of the costs of abating emissions and of R&D expenditures subject to an emission target. The abatement cost function depends both on abatement and on the stock of knowledge, which increases over time via R&D investment. By assuming a central planner, this model sidesteps the problem of explicitly modelling innovation incentives and appropriability. A second model studied by Goulder and Mathai (2000) assumes that the rate of change of the knowledge stock is governed by abatement efforts themselves. This form of technological change is termed 'learning by doing'. In this respect, another recent development of the literature is constituted by models based on the concept of learning curves (see Grubler and Messner, 1998) describing future costs and performance improvements of new technologies as a function of accumulated R&D, and learning and experience gained in diffusion of new technologies. Thus, technological learning depends on previous, accumulated investments in R&D, demonstration plants and gradually expanding niche markets.[14]

Other top-down models containing a direct modelling of investment in knowledge/innovation are applied general equilibrium (AGE) models and neoclassical growth models. One example of AGE models is the OECD's GREEN model, which allows for three back-stop options: a carbon-based synthetic fuel and two carbon-free possibilities. The main hypotheses concern prices and timing of diffusion: the prices are exogenous and the back-stop technologies, once they come on stream, are available in all regions in unlimited quantities at constant marginal costs. The only key variable of this approach is the relative price of the technological substitution options, which is exogenously imposed at current levels; on the contrary, the technological innovation possibilities are assumed to be fixed at the present level of knowledge for the entire simulation path.

As previously said, new technologies are typically developed by the most innovative firms and are not immediately available to all. Factors that influence the rate and timing of diffusion are of fundamental importance in assessing the ultimate effectiveness of the innovation. Modelling this factor is obstructed by certain characteristics of empirical environmental models. Usually, top-down models do not provide the degree of sector disaggregation that would be required for analysis at the level of the firm, while bottom-up studies do not consider strategic market behaviour that may delay the diffusion of innovation. There are, however, some attempts to model spillovers and diffusion.

One significant example is the AGE model by Goulder and Schneider (1999). The model quantifies the costs of carbon taxes in the presence of induced technical change and crowding out. If there are no prior inefficiencies in R&D markets, policies that stimulate environmental R&D crowd out other forms of R&D, which implies that the gross costs (before accounting for environment-related benefits) of carbon taxes are higher than they would be if there were no induced technical change. The result may be reversed in the presence of inefficiencies in R&D markets. More importantly, the environmental benefits are likely to be larger when induced technical change is taken into account (because there is more abatement) and the benefits from the additional abatement more than compensate for the higher gross costs (whenever this is actually the case).

Recently, so-called 'integrated assessment models' (IAMs) have been used to describe intertemporal optimization decisions, combining the economic macro-framework, and sometimes a detailed modelling of the energy sector, with environmental or climate change sub-models. IAMs, often applied in global economic and environmental optimization exercises, can incorporate uncertainties and risk analysis, calculating costs and benefits of environmental policy. IAMs generally contain a production function approach comprised of capital, labour and energy and a so-called 'Hicks-neutral' technical progress factor (AEEI). Until today, the majority of IAMs have not taken account of endogenous technical changes. Following their theoretical approach, IAMs maximize discounted intertemporal utility of a representative agent subject to the budget constraint.

Three categories of IAMs can be identified: models which state the effect of anthropogenic activities on the environment; models which state the effect of anthropogenic activities on the environment and the related feedback in terms of human health; and models which attempt to assess the anthropogenic effects of human activities on the environment and the related feedback in terms of market and non-market costs and benefits. In the first two cases, the models are strongly 'environment-oriented', whereas in the latter, the environmental and the economic components are considered to be of equal importance. In fact, cost–benefit analysis requires an accurate definition of the environmental system coupled with a detailed description of the functioning of the economic system and of the linkages between the two.

These last 'economic' IAMs are and have been used both for simulation and for optimization. Nevertheless, they maintain an 'optimizing perspective' (they answer the question of how to obtain a desired result in the most efficient way) from which 'pure' optimization models and evaluation models have developed.

The purpose of an optimization model is the definition of the optimal level of environmental externality that is sustainable by the economic–environmental system, for example defining the amount of pollution that can be emitted to the atmosphere or the amount of acid rain that can be tolerated. Indeed, the 'philosophy' of evaluation models is to assess the optimal path to accomplishing a given environmental target.

In dealing with IAMs the following should be taken into account:

- Uncertainty plays an important role. The direct consequence is that it is difficult to choose one policy in preference to others based on current knowledge about the climate system and human interactions with it. Thus research aimed at stating the various 'uncertainty effects' (effects on natural variables forecasts, effects of the propagation of uncertainty among natural and economical variables, effects on policy options) are crucial to improving integrated assessment (IA).
- The issue of endogenous technical progress is still largely unexplored.
- Most current models do not match the social and economic organization of developing economies well. This can lead to biases in global assessments when impacts in developing countries are evaluated as if their economies operated like those of developed countries.

The RICE model proposed by Nordhaus and Yang (1996) is one of the most popular integrated assessment tools for the study of climate change. It is basically a single-sector optimal growth model suitably extended to incorporate the interactions between economic activities and climate. There is one such model for each macro-region into which the world is divided (the USA, Japan, Europe, China, the Former Soviet Union, the Rest of the World). Within each region a central planner chooses the optimal paths of fixed investment and emission abatement that maximize the present value of per capita consumption. Technology levels affect output production (non-environmental technical change) and the ratio between emissions and output (environmental technical change), but grow over time in an exogenous fashion. Nordhaus (1997) starts from this aspect and sets out a model of induced innovation brought about by R&D efforts. In particular, technological change displays its effects through changes in the emissions–output ratio. This aspect is then embedded in the non-regional version of the author's RICE model for climate change policy analysis, called DICE (Nordhaus, 1993).

Buonanno et al. (2000) extend the RICE model by endogenizing both environmental and non-environmental technical change and by allowing for technological spillovers. In the model, each country plays a non-cooperative Nash game in a dynamic setting, which yields an open-loop Nash equilibrium. It is assumed that innovation is brought about by R&D spending, which contributes to the accumulation of knowledge. The stock of existing knowledge is a factor of production, which therefore enhances the rate of productivity. This is a form of endogenous technical change. Besides this channel, however, knowledge also serves the purpose of reducing, *ceteris paribus*, the level of carbon emissions per unit of output. This is referred to in the literature as induced technical change. Finally, the knowledge accumulated in one country positively affects production and environmental efficiency in the other countries, thus inducing technological spillovers. Therefore, using this model, it is possible to assess the incremental effects of different forms of technological innovation and diffusion.

Dowlatabady and Orawitz (1997) have estimated the relationship between the observed AEEI and energy prices and have then integrated this relationship in their ICAM 3 model so that each variation in price is directly reflected by a variation in AEEI. In DICE, Nordhaus (1997) tries to define how technological innovation reacts endogenously to price variations. This is accomplished by adding an energy/carbon input, dependent on energy prices, to the DICE Cobb–Douglas production function. Then he performs simulations, including carbon taxes, which increase energy prices. Thus the model determines, along with the 'optimal' level of carbon taxes, the level of R&D in the energy/carbon sector that optimizes world income. The carbon tax is the policy variable and R&D reacts to maximize private profits. A major limitation of all these approaches is that they fail to consider innovation which is not induced by prices.

In addition to these advances in the modelling of technical change, IAMs have tackled the problem of their geographical disaggregation. This is a difficult problem, both from a scientific and economic viewpoint. Scientists have difficulties in assessing the regional impacts of climate changes. Economists have problems in integrating the environmental and economic heterogeneity of climate change impacts and their related effects and feedbacks. These issues are specifically investigated by those IAMs which split the world into macro-regions. With regard to the heterogeneous impacts on welfare of climate change, IAMs incorporate a functional relationship in the region-specific welfare functions which accounts for the negative effect of environmental damage and the costs of environmental protection on agents' utility, usually represented by per capita consumption. IAMs are able to find the 'optimal' balance between the two types of cost. Environmental feedbacks on utility are calculated by a damage–benefit function which expresses world temperature changes (which depend on overall emissions) in terms of GDP losses. Country specificities are thus accounted for through two channels: the key parameters of the production functions (which in turn define consumption) are differentiated among regions; moreover, the utility functions of different countries are weighted with country- (and time-)specific weights, which are intended to assess the different 'perception' of utility changes. This is the approach adopted for models such as RICE, MERGE, FUND and IIAM.

As for the different physical impacts, some IAMs incorporate a 'distributive' element in their environmental module which takes into account the fact that the increase in world temperature (and therefore in damages) is highly non-homogeneous at different latitudes. PAGE95, for example, includes in its analysis the changes in regional temperature which result from the effect of sulphate aerosol on radiative forcing, which has a 'typical' regional relevance. The ESCAPE model includes a specific module – CLIMAPS – which uses the global mean temperature projections from other sub-models to construct regional climate scenarios.

Given these 'regionalized' characteristics, IAMs are particularly suited to evaluate the possible outcomes of different options of internationally coordinated actions to cope with environmental issues. First, they measure how pollution control (generally represented by different emission stabilization targets) in a country or group of countries would be translated into an increase in pollution outside the given area, and second, how its costs and benefits would be distributed among different regions. This provides a useful framework for deciding where and when to act and how to design proper compensations in order to find a 'fair balance' between efficiency and equity.

What can be said about the results achieved by the different modelling approaches described above? A brief summary of the main conclusions, which obviously neglects some of the specific outputs of existing models, is as follows:

- The cost of controlling emissions, for example of complying with the Kyoto Protocol, is generally higher in top-down models than in bottom-up models. In these latter models, some emission reductions can be achieved at no cost or at a negative cost (the marginal abatement cost curve is initially negative). Of course this raises the question of why these emission reductions are not undertaken anyway, independently of any climate policies. Where does technological inertia come from? What are the costs of moving away from the technologies into which present economic systems are locked? In other words, what are the costs of diffusing the technological potential identified in bottom-up models?[15]
- The endogenization of technical change reduces the costs of controlling GHG emissions. Therefore, if technical change responds to incentives

(through price changes and/or policy changes) and externalities, then long-run abatement costs are generally lower despite possible crowding-out effects (more climate-related technical change may replace other forms of technical change and the use of permits). However, how relevant is this effect? How much technical change can actually be induced by climate policy instruments?

- All models agree that, consistent with economic theory, the introduction of emissions trading and other market-based mechanisms reduces the costs of controlling GHG emissions, both in the short and in the long run (even though global trading may reduce the incentives to innovate; see Buonanno et al., 1999).

- Most models also find, again consistent with economic theory, that more flexibility reduces the economic costs of controlling emissions. Therefore, no ceilings on trading, the use of carbon sinks, the possibility of setting emission targets over the six GHGs and the use of multiple policy instruments all contribute to reducing abatement costs. However, these results are mostly achieved using a perfectly competitive representation of world markets and economic systems. This is particularly inadequate when dealing with developing and transition economies. Moreover, the representation of technical change in climate models is often deficient.

It is important to stress the crucial role of technical change in all the above results. Indeed, the representation of technical change is probably the crucial factor in explaining the different results achieved by different models. Therefore, the next section will further explore the relationship between climate policy and climate-related technological innovation and diffusion.

4.   HOT POLICY ISSUES AND CONTROVERSIES

In this section, we deal with some policy issues and controversies that characterize the recent debate on climate policy. The focus will be on issues that have been dealt with using either theoretical or empirical models. The previous two sections have identified those policy instruments and modelling tools that are crucial is assessing the policy issues that will be examined below. Of course, the current list of issues and controversies in climate policy is wider than the one presented in this section. We do not discuss topics such as sinks, liability and sanctions that have been largely debated in recent Conferences of Parties and international meetings. We concentrate on those issues where economic theory has produced sound analyses and results that can be used to assess different opinions and viewpoints.

4.1 Do Ceilings Enhance Equity and Dynamic Efficiency?

Article 17 of the Kyoto Protocol calls for emissions trading to be only 'supplemental to domestic actions for the purpose of meeting quantified emissions limitation and reduction commitments under Article 3'. To make it operational, it has been suggested that quantitative constraints on imports of emissions reduction be introduced. In the recent debate on the costs and benefits of different climate policies (OECD, 1998; Carraro, 1999a, 1999b, 2000) the role of restrictions in the market for GHG emission permits is an issue that has been increasingly discussed. These restrictions are often advocated for equity reasons: in particular, developed countries should not be allowed to trade freely in the permit market in order to be induced to abate their own emissions through domestic policy and measures, rather than by 'exploiting' the lower abatement costs of developing countries. But restrictions on emissions trading are also advocated for efficiency reasons, since they would stimulate environmental innovation and the adoption of environmentally friendly technologies, thus reducing abatement costs, at least in the long run (see, for instance, Grubb et al., 1999; Schleicher et al., 2000; Zhang, 2000a, 2000b; Rose and Stevens, 2000). On practical grounds, as the Kyoto Protocol stops short of defining the precise meaning of 'supplementarity', some current and prospective EU member states proposed a set of guidelines for trade in emission reductions in June 1999 (CEC, 2000). In particular, the proposal defines a set of concrete ceilings for selling and buying emission reductions for all Annex 1 countries (see 2000).

The efficiency argument seems to be in contrast with the basic economic result which says that the equalization of marginal abatement costs across countries (achieved through free trading) minimizes overall abatement costs. Indeed, Chander et al. (1999) show that the application of simple economic principles is sufficient to prove that: (i) flexibility mechanisms reduce total compliance costs; (ii) the largest cost reduction is achieved when no constraint is imposed on the trading system (that is, no ceilings); and (iii) there exists a system of transfers such that this cost reduction benefits all countries.

However, the theoretical conclusions by Chander et al. (1999) are achieved within the framework of a static model, and it is not a priori clear whether they can be generalized to the case in which investment, stock pollution, R&D and technical change are accounted for. This is why several empirical models have been used to assess the role of ceilings within a dynamic framework where the most relevant variables are taken into account. For example, on the basis of model simulations, Manne and Richels (2000) state that 'losses in 2010 are two and one-half times higher with the constraint on the purchase of carbon emission rights; international co-operation through trade is essential if we are to reduce mitigation costs'.[16]

Still, most of these models do not satisfactorily specify the role of technical progress and, above all, are unable to take into account the link between the presence of ceilings and the path of environmental innovation and diffusion. Indeed, the issue of technical change is very controversial and not yet sufficiently studied in that context. As said above, arguments offered in support of the introduction of ceilings on emissions trading are based on the view that the widespread adoption of flexibility mechanisms reduces the incentives to carry out environmental R&D, thereby reducing the effectiveness and increasing the costs of abatement options in the long run. Moreover, the incentives to R&D induced by the presence of ceilings on the use of flexibility mechanisms may spill over on to other sectors, thus speeding up the 'engine of growth', and reducing the impact of climate change control on long-run per capita income and welfare.

This is why it is important to study the problem of ceilings with a model which, on the one hand, endogenizes the process of adoption and diffusion of environmental technical change, and on the other hand captures the link between this process and the introduction of ceilings on emissions trading. This is done in Buonanno et al. (2000), where the well-known RICE model of integrated assessment (Nordhaus and Yang, 1996) is modified to incorporate a version of the endogenous environmental technical change (ETC) model proposed by Goulder and Mathai (2000) (see also Nordhaus, 1999).[17] In this model, agents choose the optimal R&D effort which increases the stock of technological knowledge. This stock in turn enters the production function as one of the production factors and, at the same time, affects the emission–output ratio. R&D is thus a strategic variable, the idea being that more knowledge helps increase a firm's productivity and reduces the negative impact on the environment. The model so obtained is also extended to include a market for pollution permits.

The analysis of Buonanno et al. (2000) provides little support for quantitative restrictions on emissions trading. Even if the introduction of ceilings increases the R&D efforts of buyer countries and fosters technological innovation, the overall effect on abatement costs and economic growth is negative. The reason is that the benefits from technological innovation are lower, even in the long run, than the costs of adopting a more costly approach to climate change control. In other words, firms benefit more from climate policies with a low impact on their costs than from the stimulus to innovation that these policies induce.

Even equity is not positively affected by ceilings. Buonanno et al. (2000) find that flexibility mechanisms in the presence of endogenous technical change increase equity and that the highest equity levels are achieved without ceilings, both in the short and in the long run. The main reason is that developing countries receive important transfers from developed countries through the trading of permits, and this tends to reduce income inequalities (see also Nordhaus and Boyer, 1999). Moreover, the introduction of R&D and technical change gives developing countries the possibility to use R&D strategically to increase their sale of permits.

These conclusions are confirmed by Convery (2000), who states that

> to the extent that constraints are placed on carbon trade, the costs of compliance will be increased ... the negative effects would spill over also to the countries likely to export carbon credits, since the volume of their sales and the price they get will be lower because of lower demand induced by higher costs of mitigation measures taken at home by the EU and the USA. All countries lose, and emissions reduction commitments in subsequent periods will be made more expensive and therefore less likely to be significant. Since the gains from trade experienced by Russia and Ukraine will be reduced, it will also reduce the prospects for trade gains from potential entrants from the developing countries in the future.

Similarly, Bohm (1999) asserts that ceilings 'can be expected to increase marginal costs or shadow prices of emissions reductions in the importing countries', and

> forcing countries to produce more of the emissions reduction quantity commodity at home than it wants to is like forcing cold Nordic countries to grow some minimum share of bananas before it is allowed to import bananas from countries that have a comparative advantage in banana production. ... Supplementarity will not only make present Annex B countries less likely to accept more stringent future commitments, it will also make it harder to get new countries to join the set of Annex B countries. Finally, in the more immediate time frame, the success of the Kyoto Protocol stands and falls with the US ratifying it,

which will require maximum flexibility.

4.2 Does Technical Change Provide Low-cost, Short-term Options to Reduce GHG Emissions?

This is another issue at the heart of several discussions and with important implications for climate policy. Indeed, as also stressed in the recent IPCC Report (2001), it seems that technical change can provide opportunities to reduce GHG emissions at very low, or even negative, costs, both in the short and in the long run. Where this is true, the climate policy problem could be easily solved and it would be difficult to understand why many countries were so reluctant to adopt effective climate policies. However, as Shogren (2000) notes, 'engineers argue that the origins of technological advance are firmly rooted in non-price responses; but for economists it is the search for profits that can create R&D breakthroughs that reduce the costs of backstop technologies'.

Hence it is not at all clear whether these low-cost technological opportunities, whenever they exist, are actually adopted by economic agents.

A comprehensive evaluation of the role of technology requires separate consideration of the different phases in which the process of technological innovation can be divided. This takes us back to the controversy between bottom-up and top-down models (see section 3) because the often sharp differences between the role and costs of technical change crucially depend on how these two modelling approaches represent technical change. For example, bottom-up studies focus on the potential achievement of replacing the existing capital stock with more energy-efficient technologies. Most of them consider already available technologies only, omitting reference to those that might be developed in the future.[18] Top-down models introduce the concept of backstop technologies, which includes those not yet adopted in the market. Costs are the driving factor for choosing among alternative technologies. Policy instruments, that is, taxes or permits, which raise the price of existing production techniques, make it profitable to switch to less polluting options. Backstop technologies not yet available will be more costly because they include costs of engaging in R&D.

Both types of model are weak in taking into account factors that influence the rate and timing of technological diffusion, which are of fundamental importance in assessing the final effectiveness of the innovation. Usually, top-down models do not provide the degree of sector disaggregation that would be required for analysis at the firm level, while bottom-up studies do not consider strategic market behaviour that may delay the diffusion of innovation.

In addition, the engineering approach considers the possibility of substitution among different techniques through absolute shifts. Therefore, it risks underestimating transaction costs and being too optimistic about the potential for market penetration. At the firm level, elements that deserve more consideration are all those factors which impose a degree of inertia on the energy system, thereby reducing the scope for immediate adoption of available technologies. At the consumer level, market failures such as information costs and high discount rates can result in a limited exploitation of available options. In top-down studies the possibility of substituting the existing technologies is no longer absolute, as in the previous case, but relative to variation in the prices of the techniques, that is, costs are typically expressed through the concept of elasticity. Most models assign constant values to the parameters representing the elasticities. Price substitution along a given production isoquant is likely to underestimate the real impact of technology on the emission–output ratio; in particular, it does not account for changes in factor demand (that is, energy) which take place through shifts of the production isoquant. The possibility of non-price-induced energy intensity reduction is assumed to be extremely limited in the majority of cases.

Finally, advanced technologies are likely to be developed by industrialized countries. However, they will achieve their full potential in counteracting global warming only if applied by developing countries as well. Barriers to and opportunities for applying the technology to developing countries are being examined in the literature.[19] They are not yet specifically addressed in the models. Bottom-up models analyse options at the national level. Difficulty in accounting for the interdependence of countries' markets at the international level prevents a wider scope for these models. Moreover, wide variation of data used in the analysis does not allow results obtained for one place to be extended to others. By contrast, multi-country top-down models account for international trade flows; therefore, it is possible to assess the effects of policies aimed at increasing the geographical diffusion of the new technologies.

Summing up, it is important to acknowledge the great potential of technological options revealed by bottom-up studies. However, at the same time, barriers can arise at different stages, limiting the effectiveness of technological development. Some of these barriers raise issues that would be difficult to deal with in the context of existing models. This appears to be the case in particular with the problems of innovation, technologies not already available, diffusion of technologies among firms and on a global scale.

A recent model which tries to address these issues, even though using a top-down approach, is the one developed by Buonanno et al. (2001), where R&D, innovation and its diffusion are explicitly modelled within a world optimization model. Hence, both domestic and international spillovers are taken into account.

Buonanno et al. (2001) use three main differing specifications of technical change. In the first, technical change is endogenous and enters the production function through the domestic stock of knowledge, thus inducing endogenous growth. In the second, there is an additional effect of the domestic stock of knowledge on the emission–output ratio. This yields a model with induced technical change, that is, environmental policies directly affect the incentives to carry out R&D. In the third formulation, the outcomes of domestic R&D spill over to the other regions' productivity and emission–output ratio.

This type of model can be used to assess the impacts of different ways of modelling technical change. For example, Nordhaus (1999) argues that the endogenization of technical change is likely to have small effects on the main climate-related economic and environmental variables, and in particular on the costs of complying with the Kyoto Protocol. By contrast, Buonanno et al. (2001), using the same RICE model used by Nordhaus (1999), and a specification of technical change taken from Goulder and Mathai (2000), reach different conclusions. The overall costs of complying with the Kyoto Protocol under different policy options and for different specifications of technical change are presented in Table 1.6. The notion of costs considered here is the sum of abatement costs, R&D spending and, whenever applicable, outlays/receipts due to purchasing/selling pollution permits. For ease of presentation, average figures over the simulation period 2010–2100 are displayed.

Table 1.6   Total compliance costs under alternative specifications of technical change and for alternative policy options

Specification of technical change	Policy option	USA	Japan	Europe	FSU	China	ROW
ETC	Kyoto	0.480	0.308	0.512	0.080	0.044	0.356
	ET-A1	0.478	0.293	0.500	0.056	0.044	0.356
	ET-All	0.412	0.242	0.387	0.050	0.033	0.335
ETC+ITC	Kyoto	0.550	0.321	0.549	0.066	0.045	0.360
	ET-A1	0.546	0.292	0.513	0.002	0.045	0.360
	ET-All	0.409	0.239	0.380	0.050	0.050	0.379
ETC+ITC with spillovers	Kyoto	0.575	0.296	0.583	0.091	0.058	0.412
	ET-A1	0.591	0.279	0.558	0.047	0.058	0.412
	ET-All	0.446	0.224	0.408	0.067	0.046	0.393

Note: The figures reported are expressed in 1990 trillion USD and are averages over the period 2010–2100. ETC refers to the model with only environmental technical change; ETC+ITC also incorporates induced technical change; ETC+ITC with spillovers includes international knowledge and technological spillovers.

The general picture that emerges from the table is consistent across model specifications. First, the Kyoto scenario entails the highest overall costs as no emission reduction can be traded away and emission limits cannot be overcome. The possibility of emissions trading leads to a reduction in compliance costs for all Annex 1 countries when trade takes place only among these countries (ET-A1 scenario), and for all countries under global trade (ET-All scenario). There are a couple of exceptions to this rule. The first is the case of the Former Soviet Union (FSU) in the two versions of the model with induced technical change (ITC). Notice that FSU total costs increase in the global trade scenario with respect to the ET-A1 scenario. This situation can be explained by the fact that, under ET-A1 trading, the FSU sells permits, thus receiving a relevant financial transfer. Under global trading, China and the rest of the world (ROW) become the main sellers of permits. Moreover, supply increases and the price of permits becomes lower. Hence, financial transfers to the FSU are much smaller under global trading and the total costs increase.

A second case concerns China and ROW and depends on the strategic use of R&D. As shown below, sellers of permits have an incentive to invest in R&D

to increase their supply of permits and the related revenue. This incentive, and the non-cooperative framework through which decisions are taken, may lead some countries – notably sellers of permits – to over-invest in R&D. This may induce an excess supply of permits and a too low price in the market for permits. The consequence is that total costs for seller countries under global trading – total costs include the cost of R&D investments – may increase as shown in Table 1.6 for China and ROW in the ETC+ITC case, where both endogenous and induced technical change are considered. Notice that the incentive to over-invest in R&D is lower in the presence of spillovers, because of the well-known free-riding incentive. As a consequence, the effect described above is smaller and global trading induces a reduction of total costs even for China and ROW in the model versions with spillovers.

We can also consider the results of Table 1.6 from the viewpoint of alternative models of technical change. When induced technical change is allowed for, R&D is used also to lower the emission–output ratio. In this case, spending on domestic abatement can be replaced by investments in R&D activities. The net impact on total compliance costs of this substitution effect of induced technical change cannot be predicted a priori. Costs turn out to be higher for all countries under Kyoto and ET-A1 regimes, the only exception being the FSU. Costs are instead lower under global trading, but only for the three industrialized regions. Considering the role of knowledge spillovers, our assumption is that free-riding induces countries to undertake less R&D relative to the absence of this type of global externality. This entails more domestic abatement activities and therefore costs. Again, however, the net effect on compliance costs is not defined a priori and the results show that for all countries, with the single exception of Japan, costs go up when spillovers are part of the picture.

The conclusion of this chapter is that different ways of modelling technical change affect the costs of climate policy, even though these effects are not very large. None the less the uncertainty surrounding an appropriate modelling of technical change makes all estimates of the costs of reducing GHGs emissions quite unreliable, particularly in the long term. Therefore, it is important (i) to be cautious when assessing the costs of reducing GHGs emissions and (ii) to increase efforts to produce better models of technical change which embody both bottom-up and top-down features.

There are, however, two results that seem quite robust and consistent with theoretic predictions:

1. the presence of induced technical change largely reduces the costs of complying with Kyoto, both by increasing R&D efforts – because R&D is used strategically both to reduce emissions and to increase the supply of permits – and by reducing the price of permits;

2. the presence of spillovers becomes relevant in the presence of induced technical change. In this latter case, spillovers reduce the incentive to carry out R&D, thus increasing the price of permits. Overall abatement costs do not increase because of the positive effect of a globally diffused R&D on the emission level.

4.3   Should Climate Policy Focus on Adaptation as Much as on Mitigation?

The principal objective of mitigation activities is to reduce the amount of anthropogenic CO_2 and other GHG emissions in order to slow down and thus delay climate change. In contrast, climate change adaptation aims to reduce adverse consequences of climate change and to enhance positive impacts, through private action and/or public measures. Adaptation activities include a wide array of potential strategies, such as coastal protection, establishing corridors for migrating species, searching for drought-resistant crops, altering planting patterns, forest management, as well as personal savings or insurance that may cover the damage expected by individuals (Toman and Bierbaum, 1996).

Whereas mitigation deals with the causes of climate change, adaptation tackles the consequences. As a result, the distribution of benefits from mitigation and adaptation policies is fundamentally different in terms of damage avoided. Mitigation will have only a long-term global impact on climate change damage, while adaptation options usually generate a positive effect in the shorter term. Adaptation activities mainly benefit those who implement them, while gains from mitigation activities also accrue to those who have not invested in the abatement policies. Mitigation is plagued by the free-rider problem and might create severe problems for decision-making (see section 5) as opposed to adaptation, in which free-riding is much more limited. Hence the output of mitigation activities can be viewed as a global public good, while the output of adaptation measures is either a private good in the case of autonomous adaptation or a regional or national public good in the case of public strategies. Mitigation policies on a global scale are efficient only if all major emitters implement their accepted reduction commitments. In contrast, most adaptation policies are carried out by those for whom averted damage exceeds the respective costs (Jepma and Munasinghe, 1998).

What adaptation and mitigation actions have in common is that they both avoid climate change damages. So far the debate about climate change policy has been dominated by emission reduction activities. The strong bias towards mitigation schemes has resulted in a relatively poor incorporation of adaptive response strategies into climate change analysis, although methods for evaluating and assessing adaptive response strategies have already been elaborated (Parry and Carter, 1998). The reasons for this are diverse. Adaptation has been associated with an attitude of fatalism and acceptance. Putting too much emphasis on adaptation strategies might raise the notions that mitigation efforts have little effect, that climate change is inevitable, and/or that mitigation measures are unnecessary. Approaching the climate issue from the adaptive side might inhibit concerted rational action by governments, as adaptation measures are conducted and rewarded locally. Consequently, there is no incentive to participate in international negotiations if a country considers itself to be able to adapt fully to climate change (Pielke, 1998).

Emission reduction is recognized as attacking the immediate cause. However, past emissions of GHGs together with their long atmospheric lifetime leave the earth with unavoidable adverse climate change impacts, irrespective of current mitigation actions (see Smith, 1997; Jepma and Munasinghe, 1998; Rayner and Malone, 1998a, 1998b). Hence, independently of the important decisions on mitigation that need to be taken, it is crucial to start planning effective and large-scale adaptation policies.

The challenge is to find the right balance of adaptation and mitigation measures that represents an effective and complementary response strategy to climate change. For this purpose it is important to recognize the potential economic trade-off between mitigation and adaptation strategies. This trade-off entails the use of scarce resources in mitigation activities, like restructuring a nation's energy system, versus adaptation strategies, like protection against changing flood and/or drought patterns or sea-level increase.

From an economic point of view, the task is to compare the marginal costs and benefits of both strategies, and – in an optimization framework – to minimize the overall welfare loss or macroeconomic costs. In this context, the quantity of adaptation depends on the level of mitigation, but the perceived level and costs of adaptation influence the level of mitigation. The task is then to set the share of mitigation and adaptation costs within the overall costs, which include the residual damage costs (Jepma and Munasinghe, 1998). In the IAMs, which use a cost–benefit framework, the optimal mitigation and adaptation levels are theoretically resolved by comparing the marginal costs of further action with the marginal benefits of avoided damage. However, many uncertainties characterize this framework, such as sector- and country-specific damage functions, and adaptation options and their costs are largely unknown, especially in developing countries. Assumptions and data behind the mitigation cost functions differ widely as well.

Integrated studies do not yet explicitly report adaptation costs and possible secondary benefits of adaptation strategies. In fact, they take into account individual market adjustments driven by changes in relative prices and changing consumption, investment and production decisions to balance the private marginal benefits and costs. However, most IAMs do not balance the marginal costs of controlling GHG emissions against those of adapting explicitly to any level of climate change. Tol and Fankhauser (1998) give an overview of IAMs and their treatment of adaptation strategies. Tol et al. (1998) approximate that about 7–25 per cent of the estimated global damage costs may be attributed to adaptation activities.

Giving policy advice on the basis of the efficiency concept within the IAM framework is often difficult, partly because IAMs capture only some elements of the potential coping strategies and are thus biased towards mitigation activities, and partly because damage estimates still have a rather low confidence (Tol, 1999, 2000). Nevertheless, IAMs are a useful tool in exploring the implications of new types of policies. They help to manage scientific knowledge and give insights into the major driving forces for present and future development with respect to social, economic and ecological structures (Rotmans and Dowlatabadi, 1998).

4.4   Can More Equity Provide Additional Incentives to Ratify the Kyoto Protocol?

As argued in the Introduction, equity is certainly an important dimension of current climate negotiations. On the one hand, developing countries' request for an equitable division of the abatement effort is based on principles of justice and fairness, which play a major role in practically all modern international agreements. On the other hand, some developed countries, and in particular NGOs, believe that an increased focus on equity can help induce a larger number of countries to sign and/or ratify a climate agreement.

The background of the equity debate in mitigating the risks of global climate change can be found in the 1992 UN Framework Convention on Climate Change. Article 3 states that the Parties have to engage in the protection of the climate system with 'common but differentiated responsibilities'. This phrase characterizes the real beginning of the search for equity proposals, both in the international and intergenerational sphere. Since the debate about the adequacy of scope and timing of emission reduction commitments is still ongoing, it becomes more and more obvious that the definition of 'fairness' or 'equity' in the context of climate change control is not a straightforward task. Different preconditions and characteristics of the countries, such as strong and diverse self-interests, and incentives to free-ride, as well as the special features of climate change, render the approval and acceptance of equity criteria difficult.

There are a number of proposals regarding what could constitute equity in GHG mitigation. Corresponding to the wide variety of equity principles, a range of possible burden-sharing rules has emerged[20]. Equity proposals can usually be classified by distinguishing whether the applied equity criterion has been chosen according to the initial allocation of emissions ('allocation-based equity criteria'), according to the final outcome of the implementation of the policy instruments ('outcome-based equity criteria') or according to the process by which the criterion has been chosen ('process-based equity criteria').[21]

Tables 1.7–1.9 summarize the main features of these three different groups of equity proposals and describe the way in which they are usually implemented. Notice that 'allocation-based equity criteria' are implemented with reference to the abatement cost function. They are the dominating concepts used and examined in the literature, because they can be easily applied without specifying the welfare function for each country. Nevertheless, a number of other possible equity formulations have recently emerged, mainly related to a redistribution of total welfare.

With a few exceptions, most empirical studies of equity rules focus on 'allocation-based equity criteria' (for example, Eyckmans and Cornillie, 2000; Schmidt and Koschel, 1998). A notable exception is Tol (1999, 2000), where three equity concepts based on welfare distribution are analysed. The first relates to Kant with a 'Rawlsian touch' ('Do not do to others what you do not want to be done to you', whereby the 'others' are the least well-off regions, thus 'act as if the impact on the worst-off country is your own'). The second can be seen as a principle based on Varian's no-envy criterion (for all regions, at all times, the sum of costs of emissions reductions and the costs of climate change should be equal; income distribution should be at the same level where it would have been without climate policy). The third maximizes a global welfare function which explicitly includes an inequality aversion.

The reasons why most empirical studies focus on cost-related equity concepts are their simple implementation and the possibility of comparing the results across studies. Indeed, criteria based on welfare distribution depend on the specification of the welfare function. Existing specifications largely differ across models. In some models, the welfare function is not even defined. By contrast, the specification of abatement costs, and in particular of marginal abatement costs, is subject to much lower variability across models.

However, most studies of the relationship between climate change and equity analyse the *ex-post* implications on abatement efforts and costs of applying different equity principles to the *ex-ante* allocation of emission rights (see Rose, 1999; Rose et al., 1998; Rose and Stevens, 1993, 2000; Tol, 1999, 2000). It would be important, rather, to assess the implications on the decision to participate in a climate agreement of the *ex-post* implementation of different equity principles. This is done in Bosello et al. (2001), where the following three outcome-based equity criteria are analysed: (i) equal average abatement costs; (ii) equal per capita abatement costs; and (iii) equal abatement costs per unit of GDP.

Their results can be summarized as follows. The conjecture that a more equitable *ex-post* distribution of the burden of reducing emissions could provide the right incentives for more countries – particularly big emitters – to accept an

Table 1.7   Allocation-based equity criteria

Equity principle	Definition	Implied burden-sharing rule
Egalitarian	All people have an equal right to pollute and to be protected from pollution.	Equal emissions reductions (abatement costs) per capita (in proportion to population or historic responsibilities). Implementation criterion: **equal per capita abatement costs**
Ability to pay	Abatement costs should vary directly with economic circumstances and national well-being.	Equal emissions reductions (abatement costs) per unit of GDP Implementation criterion: **equal abatement costs per unit of GDP**
Sovereignty	All nations have an equal right to pollute and to be protected from pollution.	Grandfathering (equal emissions reductions or abatement costs in proportion to emissions). Implementation criterion: **equal average abatement costs**

Sources: Adapted from Cazorla and Toman (2000), Tol (1999, 2000), Rose and Stevens (1993, 2000), Rose et al. (1998) and Schmidt and Koschel (1998).

Table 1.8   Outcome-based equity criteria

Equity principle	Definition	Implied burden-sharing rule
Horizontal	All nations have the right to be treated equally both concerning emission rights and burden-sharing responsibilities.	Welfare changes across nations such that welfare costs or net abatement costs as a proportion of GDP or of population are the same in each country. Implementation criterion: **equal welfare costs per unit of GDP or per capita**
Vertical	Welfare gains should vary inversely with national economic well-being; welfare losses should vary directly with GDP. The greater the ability to pay, the greater the economic burden.	Emissions reductions such that net abatement costs grow with GDP. Implementation criterion: **equal abatement costs per unit of GDP**
Compensation (Pareto rule)	'Winners' should compensate 'losers' so that both are better off after mitigation.	Distribute abatement costs so that no nation suffers a net loss of welfare. Implementation criterion: **strong profitability**

Sources: As for Table 1.7.

Table 1.9   Process-based equity criteria

Equity principle	Definition	Implied burden-sharing rule
Rawls's max–min	The welfare of the worst-off nation should be maximized, thus maximize the net benefit to the poorest nations.	Distribute largest proportion of net welfare change to poorest nations; majority of emissions reductions (abatement costs) imposed on wealthier nations.
Market justice	The market is 'fair', thus make greater use of markets.	Distribute emissions reductions to highest bidder; lowest net abatement costs by using flexible mechanisms (ET).
Consensus	The international negotiation process is fair; thus seek a political solution promoting stability.	Distribute abatement costs (power weighted) so the majority of nations are satisfied.
Sovereign bargaining	Principles of fairness emerge endogenously as a result of multi-stage negotiations.	Distribute abatement costs according to equity principles that result from international bargaining and negotiation over time.
Kantian allocation rule*	Each country chooses an abatement level at least as large as the uniform abatement level it would like all countries to undertake.	Differentiate emissions reductions by country's preferred world abatement, possibly in tiers or groups.

Note: * According to Rose et al. (1998), this rule can be considered roughly equal to the principle of sovereignty plus elements of the principle of consensus.

Sources: As for Table 1.7.

emissions reduction scheme defined within an international climate agreement is not supported by the empirical analysis carried out in Bosello et al. (2001). Even though more equitable burden-sharing rules provide better incentives to sign and ratify a climate agreement than the burden-sharing rule implicit in the Kyoto Protocol, a stable agreement cannot generally be achieved; that is, equity seems to enhance the profitability of climate agreements but it does not offset the incentives to free-ride.

This is consistent with the findings in Victor (1999) who examines the relationship between fairness and compliance with international environmental agreements through the lessons learned about implementation and effectiveness of numerous earlier treaties. His conclusion is that equity concerns matter little in the success of negotiating and implementing such agreements. Even for cases in which fairness seems to play some role, willingness to pay had a stronger role.

Bosello et al. (2001) also verify whether there is a transfer mechanism that could help to broaden an initially stable, but partial, coalition achieved by agreeing on an equitable burden-sharing scheme (see the next section for a discussion of the role of transfers in climate policy). Their results suggest that transfers can indeed help to broaden a given coalition. However, at least with the three outcome-based equity rules described above, the grand coalition cannot be achieved. The only strategy shown to achieve a global agreement without free-riding incentives is a policy mix in which global emissions trading is coupled with a transfer mechanism designed to offset *ex-post* incentives to free-ride. This policy mix can achieve a stable global agreement whatever the initially stable coalition and whatever the *ex-ante* burden-sharing rule.

As a consequence, these results seem to suggest that an excessive focus on equity rules is not fruitful. It is more effective to minimize overall abatement costs via emissions trading and then use the resulting surplus to provide incentives for free-riding countries to join the initial coalition.

Albeit preliminary, these results support the conclusion that a global and unrestricted emissions trading scheme coupled with additional transfers, whenever necessary to induce some countries to enter the scheme, is the best option to achieve both equity and efficiency goals. The next section will further explore this issue from a different perspective, shedding more light on the link between equity, efficiency and the size of climate coalitions.

5. THE FUTURE OF CLIMATE NEGOTIATIONS

The actual difficulties underlying negotiations on climate change have been described in the Introduction and stressed again in the previous section. Even recent game-theoretic analyses confirm that the emergence of a global agreement on climate change is quite unlikely (see Barrett, 1994, 1997a, 1997b; Bloch, 1997; Carraro and Moriconi, 1998; Carraro and Siniscalco, 1993, Hart and Kurz, 1983; Hoel, 1992, 1994; Ray and Vohra, 1997; Yi, 1997).[22] This depends upon four main factors:

(i) The heterogeneity of countries with respect to the causes of climate change, the impacts, and the mitigation and adaptation costs. This factor mainly influences the profitability of the decision to sign a climate agreement. Some countries may lose when signing the agreement, even when environmental benefits are fully accounted for. As shown by Chander and Tulkens (1995, 1997), there is always a system of transfers that may make all countries gain. But this again opens the door to the equity problem and the related burden-sharing issue. Equity may have a large impact on the existence and size of a climate coalition. As shown in Botteon and Carraro (1998, 1999), and as argued by many policy-makers and scientists, the way in which the burden of controlling emissions is shared across countries crucially affects a country's decision to join a coalition. On the one hand, if the burden is not equitably shared, some countries may not find it profitable to sign the agreement. Profitability depends indeed on two main factors: (i) the distribution of costs within the coalition; and (ii) the size of the coalition. It is indeed possible that there exists a minimum size of the coalition above which the coalition becomes profitable. And these two factors are strictly interdependent. On the other hand, equity also affects free-riding incentives. As discussed below, in some cases it may be reasonable for some countries to transfer resources to other countries to induce them to join the coalition on which they would otherwise free-ride. In this case, the final outcome is not equitable – free-riders would gain more than countries in the starting coalition – but it may be environmentally and economically efficient.

(ii) The strong incentives to free-ride on the global agreement and the lack of related sanctions. When a large number of countries accept to control emissions, a defecting country achieves the whole benefit, because its effect on global emission is marginal (with a few exceptions) and pays no cost. Hence a defection with respect to a large coalition is the optimal strategy if there are no sanctions. However, credible sanctions are difficult to design (Barrett, 1994). Emissions themselves are hardly a credible sanction, because countries are unlikely to sustain self-damaging policies. Moreover, in this case, asymmetries play a double role. On the one hand, some countries may not gain from signing the environmental agreement; on the other hand, some countries, even when gaining from environmental cooperation, may lose from carrying out the economic sanctions (Barrett, 1997a, 1997b; Schmidt, 1997).

(iii) The absence of environmental leadership. It has been shown that the process of achieving a global agreement can be a sequential one (Carraro and Siniscalco, 1993). In this case a group of countries takes the leadership, starts reducing/controlling emissions and implement strategies so as to induce other countries to follow.[23] The presence of low-cost climate policies and equitable burden-sharing are again important elements for the formation of an initial profitable coalition. As stated, our definition of profitability accounts for the environmental benefits of emission control. Hence, on the one hand, benefits should be increased by increasing the number of countries that control emissions. On the other hand, abatement costs should be minimized by exploiting all possible opportunities (including emissions trading). This is a prerequisite to achieving a strong leader coalition that can then exert its leadership through the design of better *negotiation rules*, the implementation of *transfer mechanisms*, and the credibility of *international issue linkages* (see below). A preliminary modelling of the effects of leadership is in Jacoby et al. (1998), which shows how and when developing countries may join a leader coalition formed by Annex B countries.

(iv) The focus on a single international climate agreement. If countries can join different coalitions, which means that several agreements can be signed by groups of countries in the same way as countries form trade blocs, then the likelihood that all or almost all countries set emission reduction targets increases (Bloch, 1997; Carraro, 1997, 1998; Yi, 1997; Yi and Shin, 1994). The outcome of negotiations in which more agreements can be signed is usually a situation with several small environmental blocs (Carraro and Moriconi, 1998; Yi, 1997), but this can be considered another step in the right direction. If all or almost all countries set emission reduction targets within their own bloc (that is, regional environmental agreements are signed), then, in a subsequent phase, negotiations among blocs may lead to more ambitious emission reductions.

Despite the warning that global agreements may be difficult to reach, many articles analyse the costs of agreements in which all countries participate, in one form or another (see, for example, Bosello and Roson, 2000; Capros, 1998; Ellerman et al., 1998; Manne and Richels, 1998, Nordhaus and Boyer, 1999; Schackleton, 1998). The weakest form is the one in which a few countries commit to emission reductions, but all accept to trade emissions in a single global market. The strongest form is the one in which a central planner is assumed to set optimal emission levels for all countries. This optimal solution is often proposed as a benchmark for actual negotiations and was often analysed before Kyoto (see the collection of papers in Carraro, 1999a, 1999b).

Other studies deal with the costs and benefits of the Kyoto agreement as a partial agreement among Annex 1 countries (see Table 1.4) and with the possible strategies to increase the number of countries which commit themselves to emission control targets (see the papers gathered in OECD, 1998 and in Carraro, 1999a, 1999b, 2000; see also Burniaux, 1998; Capros, 1998; Ellerman et al., 1998; Grubb and Vrolijk, 1998; Holtzmark, 1998; Manne and Richels, 1998; Mensbrugghe, 1998; Nordhaus and Boyer, 1999; and the surveys by Metz, 2000; Convery, 2000).

Usually the conclusion that can be derived from these papers is that Kyoto is neither economically nor environmentally optimal. However, the notion of optimality is not very useful when analysing coalition formation. Indeed, what matters is the notion of stability of a coalition, which identifies which countries have an incentive to join the coalition (sign the agreement) for different membership rules (Carraro and Moriconi, 1998; Botteon and Carraro, 1998, 1999), business-as-usual scenarios, abatement costs (and therefore climate policies, including the degree of adoption of flexibility mechanisms), environmental benefits (and therefore impacts, adaptation costs, and so on).

More interesting is the attempt made by Peck and Teisberg (1999) to model the negotiations between developed and developing countries to achieve a global agreement. This paper shows the potential for cooperation to be achieved – the Pareto frontier is small, but not empty – but does not analyse the incentives to actually sign the agreement. However, the paper suggests a research direction which at least helps in identifying the optimal emission reductions which are profitable for all negotiating countries. In particular, the paper shows that the Pareto frontier increases with damages from climate change, and that the optimal amount of emissions is virtually unaffected by the allocation of emission permits between regions, which tends to simplify the negotiation process somewhat.

What are the implications of the existing literature for the costs of Kyoto? There are many studies that try to assess the cost for Annex 1 countries of achieving given emission targets under alternative policy options (see Table 1.4). These policy options include the timing of the mitigation responses (see the special issue of *Energy Economics* edited by Carraro and Hourcade, 1999), the degree of adoption of the Kyoto flexibility mechanisms and their features (that is, the role of ceilings; see the papers in OECD, 1998; Carraro, 1999a, 1999b), the role of complementary industrial policies, mainly designed to foster innovation (see Nordhaus, 1997; Goulder and Schneider, 1998; Kopp et al., 1998; Buonanno et al., 1999), the effects of uncertainty about climate impacts or abatement costs (Carraro and Hourcade, 1999), and others.

The main result can be summarized as follows. Despite their high variability, all studies show that the Kyoto flexibility mechanisms sensibly reduce the costs of compliance, whatever the coalition structure. Shogren (2000) notes that 'it is estimated that any agreement without the cost flexibility provided by trading will at least double the USA costs, ... the key is to distribute emissions internationally so as to minimise the costs of climate policy'. Manne and Richels (1999) state that 'losses in 2010 are two and one-half times higher with the constraint on the purchase of carbon emission rights; international co-operation through trade is essential if we are to reduce mitigation costs'. Hence emissions trading, and more generally the application of the flexibility mechanisms, can reduce overall mitigation costs without reducing the effectiveness of the climate policy (see also Burniaux, 1998; Capros, 1998; Ellerman et al., 1998; Glomstrød et al., 1992; Mensbrugghe, 1998; Nordhaus, 1999; Rose and Stevens, 2000; Hourcade et al., 1999; Tol, 1999, 2000).

If flexibility mechanisms can fully exploit both their intertemporal (banking or banking and borrowing) and geographical dimensions (global emissions trading), then compliance costs are further lowered. This result is shown in Bosello and Roson (2000) for banking, Westkog (1999) for banking and borrowing, Manne and Richels (1999, 2000), McKibbin et al. (1998) and many others for global emissions trading. If in addition the incentives to innovation provided by flexibility mechanisms are taken into account, then compliance costs are even lower (Buonanno et al., 1999).

Hence a well-designed climate policy may have low costs, at least in the short run. Moreover, all the above papers also show that the size of the coalition crucially affects the size of the benefits deriving from the adoption of flexibility mechanisms. The larger the number of participating countries, and the higher the variability of marginal abatement costs across them, the larger the benefits from emissions trading, JI and CDM. Hence, in order to reduce abatement costs and increase environmental benefits, policies, rules and institutions should be designed to achieve the largest possible coalition.

One option is to design policies that induce countries which are not committed to emission control to accept this commitment. This can be done through appropriate policies that, on the one hand, reduce the cost of the commitment (that is, competitive emissions trading again) and, on the other hand, increase the benefit of the commitment by means of transfers or by linking the climate agreement to other economic agreements (that is, on technological cooperation). A second option is to recognize that countries' main incentive is to form several coalitions which may adopt different policy measures. A third option is to focus on treaty design and check whether there are negotiation and accession rules that could increase the incentives to sign and ratify a climate agreement. Let us analyse these options.

5.1 Transfers

We first consider transfers. It is quite natural to propose transfers to compensate those countries which may lose by signing the environmental agreement. In other words, a redistribution mechanism among signatories, from gainers to losers, may provide the basic requirement for a self-enforcing agreement to exist, that is, the profitability of the agreement for all signatories. Therefore, if well designed, transfers can guarantee that no country refuses to sign the agreement because it is not profitable. Moreover, Chander and Tulkens (1995, 1997) and Chander et al. (1999) show that there exist transfers such that not only is each country better off with global cooperation than it is with no cooperation at all (the no-participation case), but it is also better off with global cooperation than it is in any sub-coalition, provided the remaining countries behave non-cooperatively (see also Germain et al., 1997; Markusen, 1975). This result is important because it implies that no country or group of countries has an incentive to exclude other countries from the environmental coalition; that is, the grand coalition is optimal (but it may not be stable).

Transfers play a major role also with respect to the stability issue (Carraro and Siniscalco, 1993; Petrakis and Xepapadeas, 1996; Schmidt, 1997). Indeed, it is not sufficient to guarantee the profitability of the environmental agreement. Incentives to free-ride must also be offset. The possibility of using self-financed transfers to stabilize environmental agreements is analysed in Carraro and Siniscalco (1993) and Hoel (1994), which show that transfers may be successful only if associated with a certain degree of commitment. For example, when countries are fairly symmetric, only if a group of countries is committed to cooperation can another group of uncommitted countries be induced to sign the agreement by a system of transfers (Carraro and Siniscalco, 1993).[24] This gives developed countries the responsibility to lead the expansion of the coalition. However, the amount of resources that would be necessary to induce large developing countries to join the agreement may be such that some developed countries perceive the economic costs of a climate agreement larger than its environmental benefit. In this case, the transfer mechanism would undermine the existence of the leader coalition and would therefore be ineffective. This is why countries in the leader coalition must be strongly committed to cooperation on emission control.

Three types of partial commitment that could serve as possible blue-prints for environmental cooperation can be proposed (of course, other types of institutional mechanisms could be proposed as well): stable coalition commitment when only the j countries belonging to the stable coalition commit to cooperation; sequential commitment when the j countries are committed to cooperation and any new signatory, as soon as it enters the expanded coalition, must commit to cooperation as well; external commitment when a subset of non-cooperating countries commits to transfer welfare in order to induce the remaining non-signatories to cooperate, and to guarantee the stability of the resulting coalition. Assuming these alternative commitment schemes, Carraro and Siniscalco (1993) analyse the formal conditions to expand coalitions.[25]

Another general conclusion emerges from the analysis carried out in Carraro and Siniscalco (1993): both the existence of stable coalitions, and the possibilities of expanding them, depend on the pattern of interdependence among countries. If there is leakage, that is, a non-cooperating country expands its emissions when the coalition restricts them, thus offsetting the effort of the cooperating countries, then environmental benefits from cooperation are low, the incentive to free-ride is high, and conditions for transfers to be effective are unlikely to be met. If, on the contrary, there is no leakage, that is, the free-riders simply enjoy the cleaner environment without paying for it, but do not offset the emission reduction by the cooperating countries, then environmental benefits are larger, free-riding is less profitable and transfers may achieve their goal of expanding the coalition.

The stability issue has been often analysed within a theoretical framework in which all countries are identical (symmetric). However, there are a few attempts to analyse the existence of self-enforcing agreements and the role of transfers in the case of asymmetric or heterogeneous countries. This is done both in Barrett (1997a) and in Botteon and Carraro (1998, 1999). These papers show that asymmetries can increase the effectiveness of transfers rather than reduce it. For example, a commitment may not be necessary (in this case an agreement with transfers would also be self-enforcing). Moreover, they address the issue of burden-sharing by showing that the way in which gains are redistributed affects both profitability, as previously stressed, and the stability of the agreement, thus modifying the effectiveness of transfers and the role of commitment. In other words, there are two types of transfers: those which make the agreement profitable to all countries; and those which make it stable. There are therefore two objectives (profitability and stability) with a single instrument (transfers), a situation that economists immediately recognize as inefficient.

5.2   Issue Linkage

This is why a second approach to address the profitability and stability problems has been proposed. The basic idea is to design a negotiation mechanism in which countries do not negotiate only on the environmental issue, but also on another interrelated (economic) issue. For example, Barrett (1995, 1997a, 1997b) proposes to link climate negotiations to negotiations on trade liberalization; Carraro and Siniscalco (1995, 1997) and Katsoulacos (1997) propose to link them to negotiations on R&D cooperation; and Mohr (1995) proposes to link them to international debt.

Again we must distinguish the profitability from the stability problem. The idea of 'issue linkage' was originally proposed by Folmer et al. (1993) and Cesar and De Zeeuw (1996) to solve the problem of asymmetries among countries. The intuition is that some countries gain on a given issue, whereas other countries gain on a second one. By 'linking' the two issues it may be possible that the agreement, in which the countries decide to cooperate on both issues, is profitable to all of them.

The idea of 'issue linkage' can also be used to achieve the stability goal. Suppose there is no profitability concern (either because countries are symmetric or because a transfer scheme is implemented to make the agreement profitable to all countries). Consider the case in which it is Pareto optimal to link the environment to another economic issue (see Carraro and Siniscalco, 1995 for a formal definition). Then, if stable, the linked agreement is also self-enforcing (no commitment is necessary).

Let us consider the stability of the linked agreement. Suppose the environmental negotiation is linked to the negotiation on R&D cooperation,[26] which involves an excludable positive externality and increases the joint coalition welfare. In this way, the incentive to free-ride on the benefit of a cleaner environment (which is a public good fully appropriable by all countries) is offset by the incentive to appropriate the benefit stemming from the positive R&D externality (which is a club good fully appropriable only by the parties). The latter incentive can stabilize the joint agreement, thus increasing its profitability because countries can reap both the R&D cooperation and the environmental benefit (this second benefit would be lost without the linkage).

This idea is also exploited in Katsoulacos (1997). This paper, which accounts for information asymmetries, provides additional support to the conclusion that 'issue linkage' can be very effective in guaranteeing the stability of an environmental agreement.[27] However, the benefit function which relates gains from cooperation on the issue characterized by excludable benefit with the number of cooperating countries is generally humped-shaped. In other words, the grand coalition is not optimal when the negotiation takes place on this issue. By contrast, negotiations on the environmental issue lead to a monotonically increasing function (this is an implication of Chander and Tulkens, 1997). The behaviour of the benefit function for the joint coalition depends on the relative weight of the two issues. There are cases in which the optimal number of countries in the joint coalition is lower than the number of countries belonging to the stable group of signatories of the joint agreement. Hence three groups of countries may emerge (three roles): those which cooperate; those which would like to cooperate but are excluded from the agreement (and are therefore forced to non-cooperation); and those which prefer not to cooperate. This conclusion holds both when countries are symmetric (Carraro and Siniscalco, 1997) and when they are asymmetric (Botteon and Carraro, 1998). In the asymmetric case a further result arises. A given country i may prefer some countries, say j and h, as partners in the cooperating group, but these countries may want to sign the agreement with country k, rather than with i. And k may prefer i and h rather than j. In this case, an equilibrium may not exist; that is, a stable international environmental agreement may not be signed (Carraro and Siniscalco, 1998).

These latter insights lead to the conclusion that issue linkage may damage environmental protection rather than benefit it. This is the case whenever the incentives to exclude some countries from the linked agreement, or the possible political economy problem that undermines the emergence of an equilibrium, dominate the benefits of linking two synergetic (in terms of profitability and stability) issues.

Despite these possible emerging conflicts, issue linkage may be a powerful tool to address the enlargement issue. If developed countries on the one hand increase their financial and technological support to developing countries, and on the other hand make this support conditional on the achievement of given environmental targets, then a number of countries are likely to be induced to join the environmental coalition, that is, to sign a treaty in which they commit themselves to adequate reductions in their emissions growth.

Notice again the importance of technological development and diffusion, which is crucial in creating the incentives for issue linkage to be effective. Hence climate-related technical change accomplishes a twofold task. On the one hand, it reduces abatement costs; on the other hand, it supports the emergence of a larger, stable coalition, that is, a greater number of countries participate in the cooperative GHG emission reduction.

5.3   Minimum Participation Rules

The economic mechanisms described above are not the only possible way by which the EU or other leader coalitions can exert their leadership in climate negotiations in order to achieve an enlargement of the climate coalition. There are other interesting ways, closely related to the institutional design of the negotiation, that is, the rules which govern the negotiation process. Here we would like to address two of them:

1. The possibility of setting a minimum participation rule, that is, a minimum number of signatories below which the treaty is not operational. This provision is already included in the Kyoto Protocol (at least 55 countries whose emissions amount to at least 55 per cent of total emissions from Annex 1 countries), but we wonder whether this type of rule could be modified to increase its effectiveness.
2. The possibility of giving countries the freedom to negotiate on more than one agreement in the same way in which regional agreements can be established on trade issues. We would therefore have the emergence of climate blocs similar to the trade blocs already at work.

Let us focus on the minimum participation rule first. The main result, derived in Carraro et al. (1999), is that all players agree on a rule that leads to the formation of a coalition whose size is larger than the one that would form without any minimum participation rule. The basic intuition behind this result is that all players have an incentive to reduce their freedom to free-ride in order to achieve a larger payoff. However, this does not necessarily lead to the grand coalition because all players also have an incentive to undercut on this limitation to their freedom. The balance of these two incentives leads to the formation of a coalition which is larger than the one that forms when no minimum participation rule is introduced, but generally smaller than the grand coalition.

This result is only partly positive. Indeed, the coalition that forms under the minimum participation rule is larger but may not be sufficiently large to be environmentally effective. And, given the results shown above, one may wonder why at Kyoto a more stringent minimum participation rule was not approved. The answer is that, despite a minimum participation rule which guarantees a larger coalition, free-riders have no incentive to agree on a stringent rule. This is why in the Kyoto Protocol the rule is that the treaty is effective if at least 55 countries producing at least 55 per cent of total emissions commit to emission reductions. A more stringent rule would have forced more countries to commit to emission reductions, but there were not the incentives, because of free-riding, to sign a more stringent rule.

Given the above results, how can a coalition be expanded? One possible answer is that economic mechanisms like transfers and issue linkage should be designed to achieve two goals:

1. to make the climate agreement profitable for the largest number of countries;
2. to induce countries to accept a more stringent minimum participation rule.

In this way, the free-riding incentives would be partly, and if possible almost completely, offset, thus leading to the formation of a very large climate coalition.

5.4   Regional Agreements

Another important change of the negotiation rules concerns the possibility that more than one treaty to control GHG emissions is signed by the negotiating countries, that can thus form two or more 'climate blocs'. Indeed, the results proposed above crucially depend on the assumption that countries can negotiate on a single agreement. If instead countries can choose whether to sign a single global agreement or a region-specific agreement, results may change drastically.

Within this new theoretical framework, the main problem is to determine which equilibrium structure is most likely: whether one in which one coalition is formed, or one in which $k>1$ coalitions, which interact among each other, characterize the equilibrium of the coalition game. The implications for environmental negotiations are clear. In the latter case, there would not be one environmental agreement, but k agreements signed by k groups of countries.

The multiplicity of coalitions may allow for region-specific agreements in which the characteristics of countries in the region are better reflected by the contents of the agreement.

The free-riding incentive, which naturally arises in a game with positive externalities, can be described as follows in a multi-coalition game. In any coalition structure, members of small coalitions have higher payoffs than members of big coalitions, because members of small coalitions receive positive environmental spillovers from big coalitions and pay lower abatement costs. The limit case is that of singletons (that is, coalitions formed by one player only), which receive the greatest net benefit from the other coalitions' abatement.

The equilibrium of the game is still defined by the stability and the profitability conditions. A coalition structure π is profitable if any coalition s in π is profitable. A coalition $s \in \pi$ is profitable if each cooperating player belonging to s gets a payoff larger than the one he would get in the singleton structure. A coalition structure π is stable if any coalition s in π is stable. A coalition $s \in \pi$ is stable if no players in s have an incentive to leave the coalition either to behave as a singleton or to join another coalition (intracoalitional stability). At the same time no singletons and no players belonging to other coalitions have an incentive to join the coalition s.

The specific results on the size of the equilibrium coalitions depend on the model structure and in particular on the slope of countries' reaction functions; that is, on the presence of carbon leakage. If there is no leakage and countries are symmetric, then the equilibrium of the multi-coalition game is characterized by many small coalitions, each one satisfying the properties of internal and external stability (this result is shown in Carraro and Moriconi, 1998). The intuition is as follows. When one coalition forms, the other players receive positive spillovers from the existing coalition but can still choose whether to form a second coalition or to behave as singletons. Since in a Nash game the decision of the other players is taken as given, players outside the initial coalition have the same incentive to form a coalition as those in the first one. Hence a second coalition forms and so on. The equilibrium coalition structure is formed by several (almost identical) coalitions. By refining the equilibrium concept, for example by using the coalition proof equilibrium concept, the number of equilibrium coalitions can be reduced, but still more than one coalition forms at the equilibrium. In addition, they have similar sizes.

From a normative viewpoint, some preliminary analyses of specific examples (see Carraro, 1998) show that social welfare when more than one agreement is signed is larger than social welfare when countries are constrained to sign a single agreement. In other words, even if a single agreement is signed by more countries than each of the many agreements, and even if each country's abatement is larger when a single agreement is signed, total abatement is larger when many regional agreements are signed, and these are therefore to be preferred from both an economic and an environmental viewpoint.

Is this conclusion general enough to provide sound support for policy recommendations? The answer is no, because there may be other examples in which a single agreement is preferred, at least from an environmental viewpoint, to many small regional agreements. Moreover, the conclusion crucially depends on the choice of the equilibrium concept and on the absence of leakage. However, it provides important insights into the feasible outcomes of environmental negotiation processes. The problem still to be solved can be phrased as follows. If countries are free to choose the number and features of agreements, then the negotiation process is likely to lead to several agreements. As a consequence, if the negotiating agenda focuses on a single agreement, will it reduce the probability of stabilizing climate change? Should countries and international institutions recognize that climate change control can be easier to achieve if many regional agreements, which account for the specific characteristics of countries in the region, are proposed?

Notice also that these questions and doubts implicitly contain an extension of previous theoretical results – derived for the case of symmetric countries – to the case of asymmetric countries. Unfortunately, there are no theoretical analyses that support this type of extension, which can therefore be accepted only as very preliminary. However, results contained in Barrett (1997a) and Botteon and Carraro (1998, 1999) for the case in which a single coalition is assumed at the equilibrium suggest that theoretical results derived for the case of symmetric countries are largely confirmed when countries' asymmetries are introduced into the model. A few preliminary results are in Bosello et al. (2001), which, however, suggest that the possibility of forming multiple coalitions does not increase the probability of observing a non-trivial equilibrium coalition structure (that is, an equilibrium in which coalitions with at least two members form). Therefore, more work on this issue will be very important.

The consequence of the results proposed in this section, albeit preliminary and restricted to the case of symmetric countries, is that the structure of the international climate agreement is a crucial dimension of the negotiating process. If all countries negotiate on a single agreement, the incentives to sign are lower than those that characterize a multiple agreement negotiating process. At the equilibrium, the environmental benefit (quality) would also be lower. Should a change of strategy be proposed at the institutional level or will it emerge endogenously? This question should receive the same attention as similar questions have received in the case of trade policies.

Notice that in practice the recent evolution of climate negotiations seems to show an increasing tendency towards the formation of groups (coalitions) which negotiate with each other (for example the EU, the Umbrella group, the Group of 77, AOSIS, and so on). The Kyoto Protocol itself incorporates special provisions for several different groups of countries. The Non-Annex 1 countries have no commitments and can benefit from emission reduction investments through the CDM. The most vulnerable Non-Annex I countries can also receive financial assistance for adaptation from the levy imposed on the CDM (and possibly on the other mechanisms). The economies in transition have generally less ambitious commitments and have the flexibility to choose their base year. The European Union has the ability under Article 4 to redistribute the emissions reduction burden.

Therefore, there seems to be a trend towards a multiple coalition structure. It is likely that this tendency will further increase in the future and will give rise to a sequential multicoalitional formation of climate agreements. Some countries, possibly developed ones, will initially form a coalition, whereas other regions of the world will take measures to control GHG emissions according to different rules and principles. These other regions will then form coalitions which, in a subsequent stage, will negotiate among themselves to form a bigger one, eventually achieving a global coalition.

6.   CONCLUSIONS

The goal of this paper was twofold: on the one hand, to review the theoretical and modelling tools which are used by economists when dealing with climate change issues; and on the other, to use these tools to assess the prospects of a global agreement to control GHG emissions.

From a methodological viewpoint, the results described in previous sections emphasize a dichotomy between theoretical and empirical analysis. Climate models do not deal with the strategic aspects of policy-making described in section 5, but the structure of theoretical models is much simpler than that of the empirical models described in Section 3. Therefore, theoretical models can only provide intuitions that need to be verified by using empirical models more appropriately.

There are a few issues on which theories and empirical models provide convergent conclusions. For example, in the case of ceilings, the idea that an unconstrained trading scheme achieves both static and dynamic efficiency seems widely accepted (see section 4). On other issues, the controversy is still open and better models and further cooperation among scientists are probably necessary to achieve robust policy conclusions (for example, on the right balance between adaptation and mitigation policies).

One theme has been stressed throughout all sections of this chapter and is very important for the future of climate policy: technical change. Unfortunately, most empirical models, in particular CGE models, are unable to provide an adequate representation of technical change. Theoretical models that are used to assess the strategic aspects of climate policy do not deal with technical change at all. Techno-economic and bottom-up models provide an unsatisfactory representation of economic dynamics. Therefore, further work is necessary to produce analyses of climate policy in which strategic incentives and technical change are jointly taken into account within a comprehensive and convincing modelling framework.[28]

Further research is also necessary to reduce uncertainty concerning climate phenomena, their origins, their impacts (in particular the distribution of these impacts) and consequently the most suitable policy mixes. More work is also necessary to model the economies of developing and less developed countries. In many cases, either these big regions of the world are neglected or their economies are represented using the same (perfectly competitive) framework that is used for developed countries.

As for the second goal of this chapter, assessing the prospects of a global climate agreement, the difficulty of achieving such an agreement has been emphasized and the importance of designing policies that are not only cost-effective in reducing emissions, but also effective in providing the right incentives for a large number of countries to participate in the climate agreement, has been stressed. These policies should be able to offset the negative incentives that characterize climate negotiations and that arise because of the peculiar features of the climate problem described in the Introduction (countries' heterogeneity, free-riding, uncertainties, irreversibilities, technical change, lack of global institutions, and so on).

Some examples of these policies have been provided. The role of transfers, issue linkage, negotiation rules, regional agreements and of an equitable sharing of abatement costs has been assessed. However, these suggestions and proposals need a more extensive empirical verification and support. Moreover, it is likely that only a combination of these policies can actually provide the right incentives for a large group of countries, in particular the big emitters, to sign an effective climate agreement.

This conclusion is not only based on the theoretical analysis proposed in section 5, but also on a few results provided by the empirical models which are used to assess the effectiveness and equity of different policy tools (see Table 1.4). None the less, these conclusions remain very general. Additional, reliable and uncontroversial policy guidelines would benefit from an improvement of the modelling framework which is actually used to undertake economic analyses of climate-related policy strategies (see section 3).

Finally, more attention should be devoted to institutional issues. Climate change control is one of the problems whose solution requires new forms of global governance, but it is not the only one. Hence environmental research should interact more closely with the research efforts which other fields (for example industrial organization, political science, macroeconomics, trade theory, and so on) are undertaking on global governance. In particular, the issues of negotiation rules, treaty design, equitable procedures and outcomes should be further studied both in empirical and in theoretical models.

NOTES

* The author is grateful to Marzio Galeotti, Alessandra Goria, Josef Janssen, Claudia Kemfert, Francesco Bosello, Barbara Buchner and all other members of the FEEM Climate Modeling and Policy Research Unit for helpful discussions and research support. The author is also grateful to Christian Egenhofer, Patrick ten Brink, Marina Morere and Jane Wallace Jones whose cooperation on a CEPS Report on Climate Change helped in developing part of the contents of this paper. Many helpful suggestions and comments were provided by Henk Folmer, Tom Tietenberg and two anonymous referees. The usual disclaimer applies.

1. The concrete results of Kyoto include the setting of legally binding emission limitations or reduction targets, the expansion of the number of controlled gases from three to six, and the adoption of flexible mechanisms, such as the clean development mechanisms (CDM), joint implementation (JI) and emissions trading (ET) to increase the cost-effectiveness of GHG emission abatement.
2. The OECD has identified five categories: (i) charges and taxes; (ii) deposit refund systems; (iii) tradable permits; (iv) financial enforcement incentives; and (v) subsidies (OECD, 1994). Others also include subsidy reform, voluntary agreements, liability regimes and information and labelling programmes (see Clinch, 2000; Stavins, 2001).
3. Under the label negotiated environmental agreements (NEAs) we also include those self-commitments and public voluntary programmes that contain similar elements, that is, stakeholder involvement and objective setting. This therefore includes the last four of the recent OECD classifications (OECD, 1999), which distinguishes between instruments according to the parties involved: (i) unilateral commitments made by polluters; (ii) agreements achieved through direct bargaining between polluters and pollutees; (iii) environmental agreements (NEAs) negotiated between industry and public authorities; and (iv) voluntary programmes developed by public authorities (that is, environmental agencies) in which individual firms are invited to participate.
4. Under Art. 12 of the Protocol, Annex B countries – parties that have accepted a target, mainly industrialized countries – can obtain 'credit' for actions undertaken between the entrance into operation and the first budget period (2008–12). These certified emissions reductions (CERs) will be additional to total Annex B assigned amounts. Activities under this article have to be 'supplemental' to domestic action. Private sector entities are specifically allowed to be involved.
5. As noted by one of the referees, the efficiency of CDM can be undermined by significant baseline uncertainties and by the presence of incentive problems.
6. Under Art. 6, Annex B parties may transfer or acquire from each other emissions reduction units (ERUs) on a project basis. Private sector entities are specifically allowed to be involved. Activities under this article have to be 'supplemental' to domestic action.
7. Trading of assigned amounts between Annex B countries is permitted under Article 17 Kyoto Protocol. Similar to JI, ET 'shall be supplemental to domestic action'. The Kyoto Protocol refers only to parties as being allowed to trade.
8. Hot air is the name given to the difference between 1990 emission levels in Russia and Ukraine and their present emission levels. As the latter are lower, Russia and Ukraine can sell this difference in the trading market, thus receiving relevant financial transfers.
9. Of course, the polluter pays principle is applied *in primis* through the allocation of binding commitments to the developed countries.
10. The EU has met its obligation by agreeing on the so-called burden-sharing scheme in the Environment Council on 16 June 1998, where the commitments of all member states were

decided. The burden-sharing scheme foresees different targets among the 15 EU member states ranging from –21 per cent for Germany to +27 per cent for Portugal, taking into account historical emissions. (See Conclusions of the EU Council of Ministers, Environment Council from 16 June 1998.) The burden-sharing scheme will become legally binding with ratification of the Kyoto Protocol by the EU and its 15 member states.

11. A referee pointed out that abated emissions may not increase when the number of countries which ratify the Protocol increases. The reason is the presence of hot air. If, for example, the additional country which ratifies the Protocol is Russia, abatement costs will fall, but abated emissions will fall, too. However, as argued above, the presence of hot hair is crucial to induce some countries, including Russia, to participate in the agreement.

12. A notable exception is WARM. See Carraro and Galeotti (1996).

13. There are many good reasons for the poor representation of technical change in climate (and economic) models, most notably the difficulty in model identification and estimation from empirical evidence.

14. A very recent model which stands halfway between bottom-up and top-down approaches is due to Van der Zwaan et al. (1999). A macroeconomic (top-down) model is expanded with learning curves previously used in energy systems (bottom-up) models. Technological change is represented through a learning curve describing decreasing non-carbon energy prices as a function of cumulative installed capacity.

15. On these matters, see the report prepared by ETAN (1999), the special issue of *Energy Journal, International Association for Energy Economics* edited by Weyant (1999) and the one of *Energy Economics* edited by Carraro and Hourcade (1999).

16. Similar conclusions are achieved by Shogren (2000), Rose and Stevens (2000), Bosello and Roson (2000), Tol (2000), and several others.

17. For a more complete treatment of the endogenous technical change issue in the environmental policy analysis, see Goulder and Schneider (1999). A valuable and exhaustive survey on the topic is Jaffee et al. (2000).

18. Wilson and Swisher (1993) argue that the reason could be the greater difficulties of making assumptions about costs of technologies not marketed today. For an example of the implications of including ongoing R&D in a bottom-up model, see Johansson and Swisher (1993).

19. For a comprehensive survey see Munasinghe and Munasinghe (1993).

20. For further details see for example Cazorla and Toman (2000), Tol (1999, 2000), Rose and Stevens (1993, 2000), Rose et al. (1998) and Schmidt and Koschel (1998).

21. For further explanations regarding this distinction see, among others, Rose et al. (1998) and Schmidt and Koschel (1998).

22. Most papers in the game-theoretic literature on coalition formation applied to environmental agreements propose the following conclusions: (i) when self-enforcing international environmental agreements exist, they are signed by a limited number of countries (Hoel, 1991, 1994; Carraro and Siniscalco, 1992; Barrett, 1994); (ii) when the number of signatories is large, the difference between the cooperative behaviour adopted by the coalition and the non-cooperative behaviour is very small (Barrett, 1997b).

23. See Carraro (1999b) and Grubb et al. (1999) for a more detailed analysis.

24. This condition is less stringent when countries are asymmetric. See Botteon and Carraro (1998).

25. However, recall that the idea of commitment, albeit partial, that is, confined to a group of countries, cannot be entirely consistent with the concept of self-enforcing agreement stressed in the previous sections.

26. See Carraro and Siniscalco (1997) for a full presentation of the model.

27. Information asymmetries are also dealt with in Petrakis and Xepapadeas (1996). This paper designs implementation mechanisms which can induce countries to sign an environmental agreement even when emission levels are not observable.

28. Some preliminary results have been obtained within the CLIMNEG project. See Hourcade et al. (2001), Bosello et al. (2001).

REFERENCES

Alcamo, J. (1994), *IMAGE 2.0: Integrated Modeling of Global Climate Change*, Dordrecht, Boston, London: Kluwer Academic Publishers.

Barker, T. (1994), 'Taxing pollution instead of taxing jobs: toward more employment without more inflation through fiscal reform in the U.K.', Cambridge University.

Barker, T. (1998), 'Achieving a 10% cut in Europe's CO_2 emissions using additional excise duties: multilateral versus unilateral action using E3ME', E3ME Working Paper No. 29, presented at the European–US Conference on Post-Kyoto Strategies, Vienna, 6–8 September.

Barker, T. and P. Zagame (1995), 'E3ME: An Energy–Environment–Economy Model For Europe', Brussels: European Commission.

Barns, D., J. Edmonds and J. Reilly (1992),' The use of the Edmonds–Reilly model to model energy-related greenhouse gas emissions', Paris: OECD.

Barrett, S. (1992), 'Reaching a CO_2-emission limitation agreement for the Community: implications for equity and cost-effectiveness', *European Economy*, Special Edition No. 1, pp. 3–23.

Barrett, S. (1994), 'Self-Enforcing International Environmental Agreements', *Oxford Economic Papers*, **46**, 878–94.

Barrett, S. (1997a), 'Heterogeneous International Environmental Agreements', in C. Carraro, ed., *International Environmental Agreements: Strategic Policy Issues*, Cheltenham, UK and Lyme, USA: Edward Elgar.

Barrett, S. (1997b), 'Towards a Theory of International Co-operation' in C. Carraro and D. Siniscalco (eds), *New Directions in the Economic Theory of the Environment*, Cambridge: Cambridge University Press.

BDI (Bund Deutscher Industrie) (1995), 'Declaration by German Industry and Trade on Global Warming Prevention', March. Cologne, Germany: BDI.

BDI (1996a), 'Updated and Extended Declaration by German Industry and Trade on Global Warming Prevention', 27 March. Cologne, Germany: BDI.

BDI (1996b), 'CO_2 monitoring. Concept for Regular Reporting to provide Transparent and Intelligible Verification of the Declaration by German Industry and Trade on Global Warming Prevention', 26 February. Cologne, Germany: BDI.

BDI (1999), 'Voluntary Agreement and Self-commitments by Industry in the Field of Environmental Protection. Situation Analysis',Cologne, Germany: BDI.

Bernstein, P.M., W.D. Montgomery and T.F. Rutherford (1997), 'World economic impacts of US commitments to medium term carbon emissions limits', *Final Report to the American Petroleum Institute*, Charles River Associates, Report No. 837–06.

Bloch, F. (1997), 'Non-co-operative Models of Coalition Formation in Games with Spillovers', in C. Carraro and D. Siniscalco (eds), *New Directions in the Economic Theory of the Environment*, Cambridge: Cambridge University Press.

Bohm, P. (1999), 'International Greenhouse Gas Emission Trading', Nordic Council of Ministers, TemaNord 1999: 506.

Bosello, F. and C. Carraro (1999), 'Recycling Energy Taxes. Impacts on Disaggregated Labour Market', FEEM Nota di Lavoro No. 79.99. Forthcoming in *Energy Economics* **23**, 569–94.

Bosello, F. and R. Roson (2000), 'Carbon Emissions Trading and Equity in International Agreements', in C. Carraro (ed.), *Efficiency and Equity of Climate Change Policy*, Dordrecht: Kluwer Academic Publishers.

Bosello, F., C. Carraro and C. Kemfert (1999), 'Advances of Climate Modelling for Policy Analysis', in *Proceedings of the ENEA Symposium on Energy and the Environment*, ENEA, Rome.

Bosello, F., C. Carraro and M. Galeotti (2000), 'The Double Dividend Issue: Modeling Strategies and Empirical Findings', *Environment and Development Economics*, **6**, 9–45.

Bosello, F., B. Buchner, C. Carraro and D. Raggi (2001), 'Can Equity Enhance Efficiency? Lessons from the Kyoto Protocol', FEEM Nota di Lavoro 49.2001, Milan.

Botteon, M. and C. Carraro (1998), 'Burden-Sharing and Coalition Stability in Environmental Negotiations with Asymmetric Countries', in C. Carraro (ed.), *International Environmental Agreements: Strategic Policy Issues*, Cheltenham, UK and Northampton, USA: Edward Elgar.

Botteon, M. and C. Carraro (1999), ' Strategies for Environmental Negotiations: Issue Linkage with Heterogeneous Countries', in H. Folmer and N. Hanley (eds), *Game Theory and the Global Environment*, Cheltenham, UK and Northampton, USA: Edward Elgar..

Brink, P. ten and M. Morère (2000), 'Voluntary Initiatives to Address Climate Change in the EU', *European Environment*, **10**, 178–92.

Buonanno, P., C. Carraro, E. Castelnuovo and M. Galeotti (1999), 'Efficiency and Equity of Emission Trading with Endogenous Environmental Technical Change', in C. Carraro (ed.), *Efficiency and Equity of Climate Change Policy*, Dordrecht: Kluwer Academic Publishers.

Buonanno, P., C. Carraro, E. Castelnuovo and M. Galeotti (2000), 'Emission Trading Restrictions with Endogenous Technological Change', FEEM Nota di Lavoro No. 43.00, Milan; forthcoming in *International Environmental Agreements*.

Buonanno, P., C. Carraro and M. Galeotti (2001), 'Endogenous Induced Technical Change and the Costs of Kyoto', FEEM Nota di Lavoro, 80.2000, Milan.

Burniaux, J.M. (1998), 'How Important is Market Power in Achieving Kyoto?: An Assessment Based on the GREEN Model', paper presented at the OECD Experts Workshop on Climate Change and Economic Modeling: Background Analysis for the Kyoto Protocol, Paris, 17–18 September.

Burniaux, J.-M., J-P., Martin, G. Nicoletti and J.O. Martins (1992), 'The Cost of International Agreements to Reduce CO_2 Emissions', *European Economy*, special edition, No. 1, 271–98.

Capros, P. (1998), 'Economic and Energy System Implications of European CO_2 Mitigation Strategy: Synthesis of Results from Model Based Analysis', paper presented at the OECD Experts Workshop on Climate Change and Economic Modeling: Background Analysis for the Kyoto Protocol, Paris, 17–18 September.

Capros, P. and P. Karadeloglou (1992), 'Energy and carbon tax a quantitative analysis using the HERMES MIDAS model', in *An Energy Tax in Europe*, proceedings of the SEO conference, Amsterdam 13 December 1991.

Carraro, C. (1997) (ed.), *International Environmental Agreements: Strategic Policy Issues*, Cheltenham, UK and Northampton, USA: Edward Elgar.

Carraro C. (1998), 'Beyond Kyoto: A Game-Theoretic Perspective', paper presented at the 'OECD Experts Workshop on Climate Change and Economic Modeling: Background Analysis for the Kyoto Protocol', Paris, 17–18 September.

Carraro, C. (1999a), 'The Economics of International Coalition Formation and EU Leadership', in M. Grubb and J. Gupta (eds), *European Leadership of Climate Change Regimes*, Dordrecht: Kluwer Academic Publishers.

Carraro, C. (1999b) (ed.), *International Environmental Agreements on Climate Change*, Dordrecht: Kluwer Academic Publishers.

Carraro, C. (2000), *Efficiency and Equity of Climate Change Policy*, Dordrecht: Kluwer Academic Publishers.

Carraro, C. (2001), 'GSTs, Structure and Equity of International Regimes for Climate Change Mitigation', FEEM Nota di Lavoro No. 61.2000, Milan.

Carraro, C. and M. Galeotti (1996), 'WARM: A European Model for Energy and Environmental Analysis', *Environmental Modeling and Assessment*, **1**.

Carraro, C. and J.C. Hourcade (1999) (eds), *Optimal Timing of Climate Change Policies*, special issue of *Energy Economics*, Amsterdam: Elsevier.

Carraro, C. and F. Moriconi (1998), 'Endogenous Formation of Environmental Coalitions', presented at the Coalition Theory Network Workshop on Coalition Formation: Applications to Economic Issues, Venice, 8–10 January.

Carraro, C. and D. Siniscalco (1992), 'The International Protection of the Environment: Voluntary Agreements among Sovereign Countries', in P. Dasgupta, K.G. Maler and A. Vercelli (eds), *The Economics of Transnational Commons*, Oxford: Clarendon Press.

Carraro, C. and D. Siniscalco (1993), 'Strategies for the International Protection of the Environment', *Journal of Public Economics*, **52**, 309–28.

Carraro, C. and D. Siniscalco (1995), 'Policy Coordination for Sustainability: Commitments, Transfers, and Linked Negotiations', in I. Goldin and A. Winters (eds), *The Economics of Sustainable Development*, Cambridge: Cambridge University Press.

Carraro, C. and D. Siniscalco (1997), 'R&D Cooperation and the Stability of International Environmental Agreements', in C. Carraro (ed.), *International Environmental Agreements: Strategic Policy Issues*, Cheltenham, UK and Lyme, USA: Edward Elgar.

Carraro, C. and D. Siniscalco (1998), 'International Environmental Agreements: Incentives and Political Economy', *European Economic Review*, **42**, 561–72.

Carraro, C., F. Moriconi and S. Oreffice (1999), 'α-Rules and Equilibrium Endogenous Coalitions', presented at the 4th CTN Workshop on Coalition Formation, Aix en Provence, 8–10 January.

Cazorla, M. and M. Toman (2000), 'International Equity and Climate Change Policy', *RFF Climate Issue Brief*, No. 27, Washington.

CCAP (1999), 'Design of a Practical Approach to Greenhouse Gas Emissions Trading Combined with Policies and Measures in the EC', Center for Clean Air Policy, Washington DC. Study prepared for the European Commission, November.

CEC (1991), 'QUEST: A Macroeconometric Model for EUC Countries, in a World Context', *European Economy*, No. 47, part C.

CEC (2000), 'Green Paper on Greenhouse Gas Emissions Trading within the EU', COM (2000) 87 final of 8 March.

Cesar, H. and A. De Zeeuw (1996), 'Issue Linkage in Global Environmental Problems', in A. Xepapadeas (ed.), *Economic Policy for the Environment and Natural Resources*, Cheltenham, UK and Lyme, USA: Edward Elgar.

Chander, P. and H. Tulkens (1995), 'A Core-Theoretical Solution for the Design of Cooperative Agreements on Trans-Frontier Pollution', *International Tax and Public Finance*, **2**, 279–94.

Chander, P. and H. Tulkens (1997), 'The Core of an Economy with Multilateral Environmental Externalities', *International Journal of Game Theory*, **26**, 379–401.

Chander, P., H. Tulkens, J.P. Van Ypersele and S. Willems (1999), 'The Kyoto Protocol: an Economic and Game Theoretic Interpretation', CLIMNEG Working Paper No. 12, CORE, UCL, Louvain.

Chidiak, M. (1998), 'Same Name, but Different Policy Instruments. Voluntary Agreements for Energy Efficiency in five EU Countries', paper presented at CAVA Workshop The Worldwide Use of Voluntary Approaches: State of the Art and National Patterns, Ghent, Belgium, 26–27 November.

Clinch, P. (2000), 'Environmental Policy Reform in the EU', in J. Pelkmans and G. Galli, *Regulatory Reform and Competitiveness in Europe*, Volume 2, Cheltenham, UK and Northampton, USA: Edward Elgar.

Convery, F.J. (2000), 'Blueprints for a Climate Policy: Based on Selected Scientific Contributions', in C. Carraro (ed.), *Integrating Climate Policies in a European Environment*, special issue of *Integrated Assessment*, Baltzer.

Delbeke, J. (1996), 'The Future Use of Economic Instruments in the European Union', in CEPS, *The Rise of Economic Instruments in EU Environmental Policy: Why and How Fast?* CEPS Business Policy Report No. 1.

Dowlatabadi, H., and M. Kandlikar (1995), 'Key Uncertainties in Climate Change Policy: Results from ICAM-2', in Proceedings of The 6th Global Warming Conference, San Francisco, CA.

Dowlatabadi, H. and M. Orawitz (1997), 'U.S. long-term energy intensity: backcast and projection', Carnegie Mellon University.

Dutch Ministry of Economic Affairs (1998), *Long Term Agreement on Energy Efficiency: Progress in 1996*, The Netherlands.

EEA (1996), *Environmental Taxes*, Environmental Issues Series No. 1–Vol. 1, Copenhagen.

Ellerman, A.D., H.D. Jacoby and A. Decaux (1998), 'Analysis of Post-Kyoto Emissions Trading Using Marginal Abatement Curves', paper released under the Joint Program on the Science and Policy of Global Change, MIT.

Ellerman, A.D., H.D. Jacoby and A. Decaux (1999), 'The Effects on Developing Countries of the Kyoto Protocol, and CO_2 Emissions Trading', paper released under the Joint Program on the Science and Policy of Global Change, MIT.

ETAN (1999), 'Climate Change and the Challenge for Research and Technological Development (RTD) Policy', European Commission Directorate General XII, Environment and Climate RTD Programme, Targeted Socio-Economic Research Programme.

Eyckmans, J. and J. Cornillie (2000), 'Efficiency and equity in the EU Bubble', paper presented at the Conference on Instruments for Climate Policy: Limited versus Unlimited Flexibility, University of Ghent, Belgium, 19–20 October.

FIELD (2000), 'Designing Options for Implementing an Emissions Trading Regime for Greenhouse Gases in the EC', London: Foundation for International Environmental Law and Development.

Fischer, C. (2000), 'Climate Change Policy Choices and Technical Innovation', Resources for the Future, Climate Issue Brief No. 20.

Fisher-Vaden, K.E.J., H. Pitcher, D. Barns, R. Baron, S. Kim, C. MacKracken, E.L. Malone, R.D. Sands and M. Wise (1993), 'The second generation model of energy use, the economy and greenhouse gas emissions', presented to the 6th Annual Federal Forecaster Conference, Crystal City.

Folmer, H., P. Van Mouche and S.E. Ragland (1993), 'Interconnected Games and International Environmental Problems', *Environment and Resources Economics*, 3(4), 313–35.

Germain, M., P. Toint and H. Tulkens (1997), 'Financial transfers to Ensure Co-operation International Optimality in Stock-Pollutant Abatement', *CORE Discussion Paper No. 9701*, Center for Operations Research and Econometrics, Université de Louvain, Belgium.

Gjerde, J., S. Grepperud and S. Kverndokk (1998), 'Optimal climate policy in the possibility of a catastrophe', FEEM, Nota di Lavoro No. 11.98.

Glomstrød, S., H. Vennemo and T. Johnsen (1992), 'Stabilisation of Emissions of CO_2: A Computable General Equilibrium Assessment', *The Scandinavian Journal of Economics*, **94**(1).

Goulder, L.H. and K. Mathai (2000), 'Optimal CO_2 Abatement in the Presence of Induced Technological Change', *Journal of Environmental Economics and Management*, **39**, 1–38.

Goulder, L.H. and S.H. Schneider (1997), 'Achieving Carbon Dioxide Concentration Targets: What Need To Be Done Now?', *Nature*, **389**, 13–14.

Goulder, L.H. and S. H. Schneider (1999), 'Induced Technological Change and the Attractiveness of CO_2 Abatement Policies', *Resource and Energy Economics*, **21**, 211–53.

Grubb, M. and C. Vrolijk (1998), 'The Kyoto Protocol: Specific Commitments and Flexibility Mechanisms', RIIA, EEP Climate Change Briefing, No. 11.

Grubb, M., D. Brack and C. Vrolijk (1999), *The Kyoto Protocol: A Guide and Assessment*, London: Royal Institute of International Affairs.

Grubler, A. and S. Messner (1998), 'Technological Change and the Timing of Abatement Measures', *Energy Economics*, **20**, 495–512.

Harrison, G.W. and T.F. Rutherford (1999), 'Burden Sharing, Joint Implementation, and Carbon Coalition', in C. Carraro (ed.), *International Environmental Agreements on Climate Change*, Dordrecht: Kluwer Academic Publishers, pp. 77–108.

Hart, S. and M. Kurz (1983), 'Endogenous Formation of Coalitions', *Econometrica*, **51**, 1047–64.

Hoel, M. (1992), 'International Environmental Conventions: the Case of Uniform Reductions of Emissions', *Environmental and Resource Economics*, **2**, 141–59.

Hoel, M. (1994), 'Efficient Climate Policy in the Presence of Free-Riders', *Journal of Environmental Economics and Management*, **27**, 259–74.

Holtzmark, B.J. (1998), 'From the Kyoto Protocol to the Fossil Fuel Markets', paper presented at the OECD Experts Workshop on Climate Change and Economic Modeling: Background Analysis for the Kyoto Protocol, Paris, 17–18 September.

Hope, C.W., J. Anderson and P. Wenman (1993), 'Policy Analysis of Greenhouse Effect: an Application of the PAGE Model', *Energy Policy*, **21**(3), 327–38.

Hourcade, J.C. and E. Fortin (2000), 'Impact économique des politiques climatiques: des controverses aux enjeux de coordination', *Economie Internationale*, **82**(2), 45–73.

Hourcade, J.C., M. Minh Ha-Duong and F. Lecoq (1999), 'Dynamic Consistency Problems behind the Kyoto Protocol', report prepared for the EU Commission, CIRED, Paris.

Hourcade, J.C. (2001), 'Preliminary results from the CLIMNEG Project', mimeo, Paris: CIRED.

IPCC (1995), *Second Assessment Report and Summary for Policymakers*, Cambridge: Cambridge University Press.

IPCC (2001), *Third Assessment Report and Summary for Policymakers*, Cambridge: Cambridge University Press.

Jacoby, H.D., R. Prinn and R. Schmalensee (1998), 'Kyoto's Unfinished Business', *Foreign Affairs*, **77**, 54–66.

Jaffee, A.B., R.G. Newell and R.N. Stavins (2000), 'Technological Change and the Environment', Resources for the Future Discussion Paper No. 00–47.

Jepma, C.J. and M. Munasinghe (1998), *Climate Change Policy: Facts, Issues, and Analysis*, Cambridge: Cambridge University Press.

Johansson, T.B. and J.N. Swisher (1993), 'Perspectives on bottom-up analysis of costs of carbon dioxide emissions reductions', OECD/IAE Conference on the Economics of Climate Change, Paris, June.

Jorgenson, D.W. and P.J. Wilcoxen (1993), 'Energy, the environment and economic growth', *Handbook of Natural Resources and Energy Economics*, **3**.

Katsoulacos, Y. (1997), 'R&D Spillovers, R&D Co-operation, Innovation and International Environmental Agreements', in C. Carraro (ed.), *International Environmental Agreements: Strategic Policy Issues*, Cheltenham, UK and Lyme, USA: Edward Elgar.

Kolstad, C.D. (1994), 'George Bush versus Al Gore – Irreversibilities in greenhouse gas accumulation and emission control investment', *Energy Policy*, **22**(9), 772–8.

Kolstad, C. and M. Toman (2000), 'The Economics of Climate Change Policy', Discussion Paper 00–40. Washington, DC: Resources for the Future.

Kopp, R.J., W. Harrington, R.D. Morgenstern, W.A. Pizer and J.S. Shih (1998), 'Diffusion of New Technologies: A Microeconomic Analysis of Firm Decision Making at the Plant Level', Washington, DC: Resources for the Future.

Kram, T. (1998), 'The Energy Technology Systems Analysis Program: History, the ETSAP Kyoto Statement and Post-Kyoto Analysis', paper presented at the OECD Experts Workshop on Climate Change and Economic Modeling: Background Analysis for the Kyoto Protocol, Paris, 17–18 September.

Manne, A. and R. Richels (1992), *Buying Greenhouse Insurance – the Economic Costs of CO_2 Emission Limits*, Cambridge, MA: MIT Press.

Manne, A. and R. Richels (1998), 'Preliminary Analysis of the Costs of the Kyoto Protocol', paper presented at the Conference on Global Carbon Dioxide Abatement, Geneva, 11 June.

Manne, A. and R. Richels (1999), 'On Stabilizing CO_2 Concentrations – Cost-Effective Emission Reduction Strategies', in C. Carraro (ed.), *International Environmental Agreements on Climate Change*, Dordrecht: Kluwer Academic Publishers.

Manne, A. and R. Richels (2000), 'The Kyoto Protocol: A Cost-effective Strategy for Meeting Environmental Objectives?', in C. Carraro (ed.), *Efficiency and Equity of Climate Change Policy*, Dordrecht: Kluwer Academic Publishers.

Markusen, G.R. (1975), 'Co-operation Control of International Pollution and Common Property Resources', *Quarterly Journal of Economics*, **89**, 618–32.

McKibbin, J.W. and P.J. Wilcoxen (1995), 'The theoretical and empirical structure of G-Cubed', working paper, The Australian National University, The University of Texas at Austin, and the Brookings Institution.

McKibbin, J.W. and P.J. Wilcoxen (1997), 'A Better Way to Slow Climate Change', Brookings Policy Briefs No. 17. Washington, DC: Brookings Institution.

McKibbin, J.W., S.E. Schackleton and P.G.J. Wilcoxen (1998), 'What to Expect from an International System of Tradable Permits for Carbon Emissions?', *Brookings Discussion Papers in International Economics*, No. 143.

Mensbrugghe, D. van der (1998), 'A Preliminary Analysis of the Kyoto Protocol Using the OECD GREEN Model', paper presented at the OECD Experts Workshop on Climate Change and Economic Modeling: Background Analysis for the Kyoto Protocol, Paris, 17–18 September.

Metz, B. (2000), 'International Equity in Climate Change Policy', in C. Carraro (ed.), *Integrating Climate Policies in a European Environment*, special issue of *Integrated Assessment*, Baltzer.

Millock, K. (1999), 'The Combined Use of Carbon Taxation and Voluntary Agreements for Energy Policy – a Model Based on Danish Policy', paper presented at CAVA Workshop: The efficiency of Voluntary Approaches in environmental policy – what can be derived from theory?', Copenhagen, Denmark, 25–26 May.

Mohr, E. (1995), 'International Environmental Permits Trade and Debt: The Consequences of Country Sovereignty and Cross Default Policies', *Review of International Economics*, (1), 1–19.

Munasinghe, M. and S. Munasinghe (1993) 'Barriers to and opportunities for technological change in developing countries to reduce global warning', report presented at the IPCC WGIII First Session, Montreal, 3–7 May.

Nordhaus, W.D. (1993), 'Rolling the "DICE": An Optimal Transition Path for Controlling Greenhouse Gases', *Resource and Energy Economics*, **15**, 27–50.

Nordhaus, W.D. (1997), 'Modeling Induced Innovation in Climate-Change Policy: Theory and Estimates in the R&DICE model', paper prepared for the Workshop on Induced Technological Change, IIASA, June.

Nordhaus, W.D. (1999), 'Modeling the Impact of Climate Change', paper presented and the 1999 FEEM–IDEI–INRA Conference, Toulouse, 14–16 June.

Nordhaus, W.D. and J.C. Boyer (1999), ' Requiem for Kyoto: An Economic Analysis of the Protocol', Yale University, draft.

Nordhaus W.D. and Z. Yang (1996), 'RICE: A Regional Dynamic General Equilibrium model of Alternative Climate Change Strategies', *The American Economic Review*, **86**(4), 726–41.

Norregaard, J. and V. Reppelin-Hill (2000), 'Taxes and Tradable Permits as Instruments for Controlling Pollution: Theory and Practice', International Monetary Fund Working Paper No. WP/00/13.

OECD (1994), *Managing the Environment – The Role of Economic Instruments*, Paris: OECD.

OECD (1998), *Proceedings* of the OECD Workshop on Climate Change and Economic Modeling. Background Analysis for the Kyoto Protocol, Paris, 17–18 September.

OECD (1999), *Voluntary Approaches for Environmental Policy: an assessment*, Paris: OECD.

Parry, M., and J. Carter (1998), *Climate Impact and Adaptation Assessment*, London: Earthscan Publications.

Peck, S. and T. Teisberg (1992), 'CETA: A Model for Carbon Emission Trajectory Assessment', *Energy Journal*, **13**(1), 55–77.

Peck, S. and T.J. Teisberg (1999), 'CO$_2$ Concentrations Limits, the Costs and Benefits of Control and the Potential for International Agreements', in C. Carraro (ed.), *International Environmental Agreements on Climate Change*, Dordrecht: Kluwer Academic Publishers.

Pelkmans, J and C. Egenhofer (1993), 'Defizite in Politkfeldern der EG-Integration', in Pelkmans, J. (1997), *European Integration*, Harlow, UK: Longman.

Petrakis, E.A. and A. Xepapadeas (1996), 'Environmental Consciousness and Moral Hazard in International Agreements to Protect the Environment', *Journal of Public Economics*, **60**(1), 95–110.

Pielke, R.A.J. (1998), 'Rethinking the Role of Adaptation in Climate Policy', *Global Environmental Change*, **8**(2), 159–70.

Pizer, W. (1997), 'Prices vs. Quantities Revisited: The case of Climate Change', Discussion Paper 98–00. Washington, DC: Resources for the Future.

Potier, M. (1996), 'The Experience of OECD Countries in Their Domestic Use of Economic Instruments for Environmental Management, in CEPS, *The Rise of Economic Instruments in EU Environmental Policy: Why and How Fast?* CEPS Business Policy Report No. 1.

Ray, D. and R. Vohra (1997), 'Equilibrium Binding Agreements', *Journal of Economic Theory*, **73**, 30–78.

Rayner, S. and E.L. Malone (1998a), 'The challenge of climate change to the social sciences', in *Human Choice & Climate Change: What Have We Learned?*, Vol. 4, Columbus, OH: Battelle Press.

Rayner, S. and E.L. Malone (1998b), *Human Choice & Climate Change. Ten Suggestions For Policymakers: Guidelines from an International Social Science Assessment*, Columbus, OH: Battelle Press.

Rose, A. (1999), 'Burden-sharing and Climate Change Policy Beyond Kyoto: Implications for Developing Countries', *Environment and Development Economics*, 3, 392–8.

Rose, A. and B. Stevens (1993), 'The Efficiency and Equity of Marketable Permits for CO_2 Emissions', *Resource and Energy Economics*, 15(1), 117–46.

Rose, A. and B. Stevens (2000), 'A Dynamic Analysis of Fairness in Global Warming Policy: Kyoto, Buenos Aires and Beyond', in C. Carraro (ed.), *Efficiency and Equity of Climate Change Policy*, Dordrecht: Kluwer Academic Publishers.

Rose, A., B. Stevens, J. Edmonds and M. Wise (1998), 'International Equity and Differentiation in Global Warming Policy: An Application to Tradable Emission Permits', *Environmental and Resource Economics*, 12(1), 25–51.

Rotmans, J. (1990), 'IMAGE: an Integrated Model to Assess the Greenhouse Effect', Dordrecht, Boston, London: Kluwer Academic Publishers.

Rotmans, J. and H. Dowlatabadi (1998), 'Integrated Assessment Modeling', in S. Rayner and E. Malone (eds), *Human Choice and Climate Change Tools for Policy Analysis*, Columbus, OH: Battelle Press, pp. 291–377.

Rotmans, J., M. Hulme and T. Downing (1994), 'Climate change implication for Europe: an application of the ESCAPE model', *Global Environment Change*, June.

Rowe, M.D. and D. Hill (1989), 'Estimating National Costs of Controlling Emissions from the Energy System – A Report of the Energy Technology Systems Analysis Project' IEA, Brookhaven National Lab., New York.

Schackleton, T. (1998), 'HANDOUT: The Potential Effects of International Carbon Emissions Mitigation Under the Kyoto Protocol: What we have learned from the G-Cubed Model', in *Proceedings* of the OECD Workshop on Climate Change and Economic Modeling. Background Analysis for the Kyoto Protocol, Paris, 17–18 September.

Schleicher, S.P., B. Buchner and K. Kratena (2000), 'Why Cost Minimisation Strategies for the Kyoto Mechanisms May Cause Market Failures', University of Graz, mimeo.

Schmidt, C. (1997), 'Enforcement and Cost-effectiveness of International Agreements: The Role of Side Payments', *Discussionbeträge des Sonderforschungbereich 178*, Serie II, NR 350, Universität Konstanz.

Schmidt, T.F.N. and H. Koschel (1998), 'Climate Change Policy and Burden-Sharing Policy in the European Union', *ZEW Discussion Paper Series*, No. 98–12.

Shogren J. (2000), 'Benefits and Costs of Kyoto', in C. Carraro (ed.), *Efficiency and Equity of Climate Change Policy*, Dordrecht: Kluwer Academic Publishers.

Smith, J.B. (1997), 'Setting Priorities for Adapting to Climate Change', *Global Environmental Change*, 7(3), 251–64.

Stavins, R. (2001), 'Experience with Market-based Environmental Policy Instruments'. Draft of Chapter 21 in K.G. Mäler and J. Vincent (eds), *The Handbook of Environmental Economics*, Amsterdam: North-Holland/Elsevier Science.

Storey, M. (1997), 'Demand Side Efficiency: Voluntary Agreements with Industry', Policies and Measures for Common Action working papers, No. 8, OECD, Paris.

Tol, R.S.J. (1997), 'On the Optimal Control of Carbon Dioxide Emissions: an Application of Fund', *Environmental Modeling and Assessment*, 2, 151–63.

Tol, R.S.J. (1999), 'The Optimal Timing of Greenhouse Gas Emission Abatement, Individual Rationality and Intergenerational Equity', in C. Carraro (ed.), *Interna-*

tional Environmental Agreements on Climate Change, Dordrecht: Kluwer Academic Publishers.

Tol, R.S.J. (2000), 'Equitable Cost–Benefit Analysis of Climate Change', in C. Carraro (ed.), *Efficiency and Equity of Climate Change Policy*, Dordrecht: Kluwer Academic Publishers.

Tol, R.S.J. and S. Fankhauser (1998), 'On the Representation of Impacts in Integrated Assessment Models of Climate Change', *Environmental Modeling and Assessment*, **3**, 63–74.

Tol, R.S.J., S. Fankhauser and J.B. Smith (1998), 'The scope for adaptation to climate change: what can we learn from the impact literature?', *Global Environmental Change*, **8**(2), 109–23.

Toman, M. and R. Bierbaum (1996), 'An Overview of Adaptation to Climate Change', in J.B. Smith, N. Bhatti, G.V. Menzhulin, R. Benioff, M. Campos, B. Jallow, F. Rijsberman, M.I. Budyko and R.K. Dixon (eds), *Adapting to Climate Change: An International Perspective*, New York: Springer Verlag, pp. 5–26.

Torvanger, A. and T. Skodvin (2001), 'Environmental Agreements in Climate Politics', in P. ten Brink (ed.), *Voluntary Environmental Agreements: Process, Practice and Future Use*, Greenleaf Publishing.

Van der Zwaan, B.C.C., R. Gerlagh, G. Klaassen and L. Schrattenholzer (1999), 'Endogenous Technological Change in Climate Change Modelling', Report D-99/15, IVM Institute for Environmental Studies, Amsterdam, forthcoming in *Energy Economics*.

Victor, D.G. (1999), 'The Regulation of Greenhouse Gases: Does Fairness Matter?', in F.L. Tóth (ed.), *Fair weather? Equity concerns in climate change*, London: Earthscan Publications, pp. 193–207.

Westkog, H. (1999), paper presented at the EEA Annual Conference, Santiago de Compostela, 26–28 August.

Weyant, J.P. (1999), 'The Costs of the Kyoto Protocol: a Multi-Model Evaluation', special issue of the *Energy Journal*, International Association for Energy Economics.

Wilson, D. and J. Swisher (1993), 'Exploring the Gap: Top-down Versus Bottom-up Analyses of the Cost of Mitigating Global Warming', *Energy policy*, March, 249–63.

Yang, Z., R.S. Eckhaus, A.D. Ellerman and H.D. Jacoby (1996), 'The MIT emissions prediction and policy analysis (EPPA) model' in The MIT Joint Program on the Science and Policy of Global Change, Report No. 6.

Yi, S. (1997), 'Stable Coalition Structures with Externalities', *Games and Economic Behaviour*, **20**, 201–23.

Yi, S. and H. Shin (1994), 'Endogenous Formation of Coalition in Oligopoly: I. Theory', mimeo, Dartmouth College.

Zapfel, P. (1999), 'Negotiated Agreements and "Flexible Mechanisms": Building Blocks for Efficient Kyoto Implementation Strategies in the European Union?', in ZEW, *Flexible Mechanisms for an Efficient Climate Policy*', ZEW (Zentrum für Europäische Wirtschaftsforschung – Centre for European Economic Research).

Zhang, Z. (2000a), 'Estimating the Size of the Potential Market for the Kyoto Mechanisms', *Review of World Economics*, **136**, 491–520.

Zhang, Z. (2000b), 'An Assessment of the EU Proposal for Ceilings on the Use of Kyoto Flexibility Mechanisms', FEEM Nota di Lavoro, 99.00, Milan.

2. Computable general equilibrium models in environmental and resource economics

Klaus Conrad[1]

1. INTRODUCTION

The focus of this survey chapter is on the importance of general equilibrium interactions in assessing efficiency costs of environmental policies. Those inter-actions are relevant to the impacts of a wide range of government policies to control air pollution, deforestation or water quality. These policies raise the costs of output and the distortions in factor markets from pre-existing market imperfections and imply higher social costs than would be indicated by partial equilibrium models. Although computable general equilibrium (CGE) models cannot be used to forecast business cycles, they can indicate likely magnitudes of policy-induced changes from future baselines, and they are indispensable for ranking alternative policy measures. Since these numerical models are based on assumptions concerning the economic development (elasticities of substi-tution, technical change, or the magnitude of exogenous variables), it would be misleading to base policy decisions on a specific numerical result. Rather, CGE models should be used to understand the reasons for particular results, to better frame the policy decisions, and to support the appropriate policy judgments. Using general equilibrium theory, economists can frequently get a good idea of the welfare effect and of the qualitative results from a change in a given policy instrument. However, using theory alone, it is very often not possible to determine the signs of the net effects in general equilibrium inter-actions, to evaluate alternative environmental policy approaches with respect to their different impacts on the economy, and then to rank them according to their welfare effects. Theoretical models can account for general equilibrium issues but, to be analytically tractable, simplicity is required whereas the numer-ically solved CGE models allow for greater complexity.

This chapter provides an overview of the use of CGE models in environ-mental economics. This overview is not meant to be exhaustive; rather we hope to illustrate the types of approaches we know of to give an impression of the scope of applying CGE models. We begin in section 2 by emphasizing the importance of general versus partial equilibrium models and the advantage of CGE models compared to other macroeconomic models. The extension of a standard input–output model with fixed input–output coefficients to a CGE model with price-dependent coefficients is discussed in section 3. In section 4 we describe the development of investment decisions in the model of producer behavior, starting from recursive accumulation of capital under static expectation to the new generation of dynamic models where the manager of a firm accumulates capital over time in order to maximize the value of the firm. A similar approach can be chosen for a consumer who accumulates investment in consumer durables over time. This aspect is part of an intertemporal model of consumer behavior with several stages of budget allocation which we present in section 5. Since environmental regulation may affect international competitiveness, we show in section 6 how in CGE models the trade pattern allows us to adjust to environmental policy measures. Given the variety of modeling of the labor market, we say only a few words on this topic in section 7. Another complex but very important topic is the modeling of technical change. The long-term outcome from an environmental policy measure is particularly sensitive with respect to the assumption on the efficiency improvement in energy use, pollution abatement or waste disposal. Thus, in section 8 we examine some approaches to incorporate technical change in CGE models. Abatement technologies are also an important aspect in environmentally oriented CGE models and we present some approaches to take this aspect into account in section 9. Data required for doing CGE modeling are mentioned in section 10. In section 11 we present several simulation studies in environmental economics based on the use of CGE models. First, we take the double dividend debate as an example for a CGE analysis. We present results from a CO_2 reduction policy for 12 EU member countries whose CGE models are linked by foreign trade (section 11.1). In sections 11.2–11.9 we review environmentally related CGE analyses on topics such as global warming, the costs of environmental regulation under different instruments, and joint implementation. Finally, we describe some models which look at a two-way link between the environment and economic performance (section 12). In those models economic variables generate environmental externalities, but the latter ones also affect the quality of the former ones. Concluding remarks are made in the final section.

2. PARTIAL EQUILIBRIUM MODELS, CGE MODELS AND MACROECONOMIC MODELS

Policies aimed at significantly reducing environmental problems such as global warming, acid rain, deforestation, waste disposal or any other degradation of the quality of air, water, soil or land imply costs in terms of lower growth of GDP, a reduction in international competitiveness or in employment. The implied change in relative prices will induce general equilibrium effects throughout the whole economy. For this reason it is often useful to evaluate the effects of environmental policy measures within the framework of a computable general equilibrium (CGE) model. Although partial equilibrium models make it possible to estimate the costs of environmental policy measures, taking substitution processes in production and consumption as well as market-clearing conditions into account, CGE models additionally allow for adjustments in all sectors, enable us to consider the interactions between the intermediate input market and markets for other commodities or intermediate inputs, and complete the link between factor incomes and consumer expenditures. The link between environmental policy and the economy can rely on partial equilibrium models if feedback effects are not important or if a certain impact is to be demonstrated. However, one has to keep in mind that CGE analysis can yield very different results from what one would obtain from partial equilibrium. Policies that appear to improve efficiency in a partial equilibrium analysis emerge as reducing efficiency when model builders account for general equilibrium effects.[2] Researchers sometimes expect the net effect of the multitude of interdependencies and interactions within the economy to be zero when using a partial equilibrium model. However, if environmental policies raise the costs of output and thereby reduce real factor returns, they enforce the distortions in factor markets from pre-existing taxes and imply higher social costs than would be indicated by partial equilibrium analyses. A good example for illustrating the importance of general versus partial equilibrium models is the highly debated double dividend issue when a revenue-neutral carbon or energy tax is introduced. The open question is whether the positive substitution effect towards labor input will be outweighed by the negative output effect and by the adverse impact from new distortions on the factor market. Another example is to measure the effect of an emission tax on the performance of the economy. This policy raises marginal cost of production due to abatement expenditure and tax payments. Hence the firm will reduce its output under the present price level. If all firms in that industry react in the same way, the market supply function will shift to the left and the market price will rise. Now the firms will revise their output decisions. The higher domestic price will attract imports and will lower exports. The higher price in the environment-intensive industry will induce spillovers to other markets and industries which produce substitutes or complements. On the input side our firm will substitute labor, material and capital for the taxed energy input for keeping costs low. This affects the factor markets and factor prices. This line of reasoning shows the substantial difference between a partial equilibrium analysis and a CGE analysis.

The impact of an environmental policy could also be analyzed with macro-economic models based on Keynesian theory, on monetaristic approaches, on supply-side models, on models with an optimization framework (optimal control, non-linear dynamic optimization) or on dynamic input–output models.[3] These models focus on the impact of environmental policy on unemployment, on inflation, on disequilibrium in some markets, on cyclical developments, on convergence and stability, on long-run growth, and on forecasting. A disadvantage of macroeconomic models is their heterogeneous theoretical underpinning. Since in recent years macroeconomic models have tended to incorporate microeconomic elements, the difference between CGE models and macroeconomic models has become less clear. In principle, a CGE model is a member of the class of macroeconomic models which has as its theoretical underpinning the application of an Arrow–Debreu general equilibrium framework. The commonly made assumption of an underlying optimizing behavior of all agents explains why microeconomic theory and general equilibrium theory have strongly increased their relevance for policy analysis. The outcome of a policy simulation is not generated from a black box but can be traced back to rational behavior. CGE models can provide answers on economic effects of changes in tax rates or of the introduction of new taxes or subsidies in a coherent and consistent way. They are superior to traditional macroeconomic models when the source and the effects of market inefficiencies are to be investigated or when excess burdens caused by price-distorting measures are to be demonstrated. They are the appropriate tool to answer important policy questions such as structural adjustments, tax reforms or trade liberalization. CGE models are therefore primarily focused on long-run impacts whereas macroeconomic models are more appropriate to shed light on the transition from the old equilibrium to the new one.

3.   FROM INPUT–OUTPUT MODELS TO CGE MODELS

Leontief's input–output analysis is based on an input–output table and on inter-industry input–output production relations to model the exchange of commodities by agents. A static input–output model describes the relationship between supply X_i of an industry i and intermediate demands of all industries j ($j = 1, ..., n$) for goods from industry i, X_{ij}, and final demand FD_i:

$$X_i = \sum_{j=1}^{n} X_{ij} + FD_i, \quad i = 1, ..., n. \tag{2.1}$$

For primary factors labor L and capital K, supply $\bar{L}$ ($\bar{K}$) should be equal to the sum of the demand L_j (K_j) by all industries:

$$\bar{L} = \sum_{j=1}^{n} L_j \quad \bar{K} = \sum_{j=1}^{n} K_j. \tag{2.2}$$

Under the assumption of fixed Walras–Leontief input coefficients,

$$X_{ij} = \alpha_{ij} X_j, \quad i,j = 1, ..., n \tag{2.3}$$

$$L_j = \alpha_{Lj} X_j, \quad K_j = \alpha_{Kj} X_j, \qquad j = 1, ..., n$$

(2.1) and (2.2) can be written as

$$X_i = \sum_{j=1}^{n} \alpha_{ij} \cdot X_j + FD_i \tag{2.5}$$

$$\bar{L} = \sum_j \alpha_{Lj} \cdot X_j, \quad \bar{K} = \sum_j \alpha_{Kj} \cdot X_j. \tag{2.6}$$

Given final demand, (2.5) can be solved for the output levels X_i and (2.6) then gives the demand for the primary inputs. Prices PX_i can be determined by using the identity

$$PX_j \cdot X_j = \sum_{i=1}^{n} PX_i \cdot X_{ij} + PL \cdot L_j + PK \cdot K_j$$

and then (2.3) and (2.4):

$$PX_j = \sum_{i=1}^{n} PX_i \cdot \alpha_{ij} + PL \cdot \alpha_{Lj} + PK \cdot \alpha_{Kj} \tag{2.7}$$

where prices for labor and capital are exogenous. The critical features of this model are that input coefficients do not depend on prices and that prices, calculated as an arithmetic mean with input coefficients as weights, have no impact on the economy.

The idea of deriving price-dependent input coefficients as factor demand functions of the neoclassical production theory goes back to Samuelson's (1951) 'non-substitution theorem'. In a path-breaking paper Samuelson (1953) studies the causal relationship between prices and quantities and proves the duality of cost and production functions. The dual characterization of a technology, also shown by Shephard (1953), permits as Shephard's lemma to derive cost-minimizing input coefficients as partial derivative of a unit cost function of the output of an industry. First-order conditions of producer behavior did not have to be solved explicitly for the quantities as function of prices (if this was possible at all) and, in addition, those unit cost functions as a dual characterization of the technology proved to be useful in determining prices. Unlike inter-industry input–output models and other earlier economy-wide planning models, household factor income and expenditures are linked in a theoretically appropriate manner. As will be seen next, the input–output technology is typically embedded in CGE models to characterize inter-industry transfers.

In a dual CGE approach the technology of a cost-minimizing industry is characterized by a cost function C,

$$C_j = C_j(X_j, w, PL, PK) \quad j = 1, ..., n \tag{2.8}$$

where w is the price vector of intermediate inputs. The observed costs are

$$C_j = \sum_{i=1}^{n} w_i \cdot X_{ij} + PL \cdot L_j + PK \cdot K_j.$$

Under the assumption of constant returns to scale, $c_j = C_j(1, w, PL, PK)$ is the unit cost function and $C_j = X_j \cdot c_j(w, PL, PK)$.

From Shephard's lemma we derive demand functions as input coefficients:

$$\frac{X_{ij}}{X_j} = \frac{\partial c_j(\cdot)}{\partial w_i}, \quad i = 1, ..., n, \quad \frac{L_j}{X_j} = \frac{\partial c_j}{\partial PL}, \quad \frac{K_j}{X_j} = \frac{\partial c_j}{\partial PK}. \tag{2.9}$$

Assuming profit maximization under perfect competition ($PX = MC$):

$$PX_j = c_j(w, PL, PK). \tag{2.10}$$

This price-equal average cost condition can be employed to determine the system of n output prices. Since the price vector w of intermediate inputs is exactly the price vector $(PX_1, ..., PX_n)$ of output prices, equation (2.10) for industry j is:

$$PX_j = c_j(PX_1, ..., PX_n, PL, PK), \quad j = 1, ..., n. \tag{2.11}$$

This system of n prices can be solved, given the prices of labor and capital. In order to determine the output levels X_j which are influenced by the price system, we substitute

$$X_{ij} = X_j \frac{\partial c_j(\cdot)}{\partial PX_i}$$

from (2.9) for X_{ij} in (2.1) and obtain

$$X_i = \sum_i X_j \frac{\partial c_j(\cdot)}{\partial PX_i} + FD_i, \quad i = 1, ..., n. \tag{2.12}$$

This system of n equations in the n unknown Xs can be solved, given final demand. A CGE model is therefore a system of linear and nonlinear equations that is solved to simulate market equilibrium. It includes equations describing consumers' and producers' supply and demand behavior that are derived explicitly from conditions for profit or utility maximization (see section 4), and market-clearing conditions in product and input markets (see section 6). In this dual or cost-driven form, pioneered by Johansen and Jorgenson,[4] Leontief's input output model is a special case if consumer behavior and factor market are ignored. If the unit cost function in (2.11) is an arithmetic mean of input prices, as given in (2.7), then (2.12) is identical with (2.5), the basic Leontief model.

CGE models based on the primal approach to production have been used by Shoven and Whalley (1973, 1984). In the primal problem formulation, the agent determines supply quantities as a function of the market prices of commodities, while in the dual problem the supplier is setting the market price of the commodity he is supplying by using the inverse supply function, that is, price equal to marginal cost. In the primal problem form, demand as well as supply depend explicitly on prices which are determined by equating demand and supply. In the dual problem form, the supplier receives the market price of the commodity from average cost pricing. Demand depends explicitly on prices and determines the quantity to be supplied. Supply enters marginal cost, which influences the price. In principle, however, it doesn't matter which approach is used if the equilibrium is unique and the forms of the cost and production functions used are self-dual (Cobb–Douglas or constant elasticity of substitution (CES) specifications).[5] The Shoven–Whalley type of models have their roots in applied welfare economics while the Johansen–Jorgenson type of models originate from input–output analysis (see Johansen, 1979; Hudson and Jorgenson, 1974).

The choice of specifying functional forms for production or cost functions depends on adopting the econometric approach or the calibration approach to CGE modeling. The econometric approach requires time-series or cross-sectional data for estimating the unknown parameters statistically. Calibration may make use of a mix of econometric results and other data taken from the literature. When choosing the econometric approach, flexible functional forms like the translog specification (Jorgenson and Wilcoxen, 1990a, 1990b; Hazilla and Kopp, 1990) or the generalized Leontief specification of cost functions (Glomsrød et al., 1992) can be used. The estimation procedure of the unknown parameters is based on a multi-level nest of input compositions. At the 'top' level, there are two inputs, for instance energy and non-energy, or four inputs, say labor, capital, material and energy. Depending on the focus of the study, land instead of energy can be included in this nesting, or commodities from agriculture or forestry, respectively. At the 'bottom' level, demand for aggregated energy, or material for transportation is further divided into its components using nested flexible sub-functions. Agriculture, for example, can be decomposed into program crops, livestock and dairy, and all other agricultural production if the user of a CGE model wishes to illustrate some of the difficulties of coordinating agricultural and environmental policies (Hrubovcak et al., 1990). The common approach to CGE modeling is to calibrate the parameters of the model so that one-year observations are sufficient. The preferred specification is a series of nested CES functions but with fixed input coefficients for some input components (for example Bergman, 1990b; Capros et al., 1996 or the GREEN model (Burniaux et al. 1992, b)). In the CES approach, the elasticity of substitution will be guessed, and the distribution parameters depend on the particular year chosen for calibration. The elasticities of price-induced substitution are key parameters and will affect the economic costs and environmental benefits from stricter policies towards sustainable development. In general, input categories and nests in a nested production structure should be selected according to the focus of the model. Those nests one would use for an energy-oriented model may not be the same as for a trade and environmental analysis in a developing country that depends on agriculture, fishery and forestry.

To demonstrate the production/cost nesting, let us assume that the first m prices in (2.11) are prices of fossil fuels (gas, oil, coal). Then the unit cost function PE_j of industry j for fossil energy is ($j \in \{1, ..., m\}$):

$$PE_j = CES_j(PX_1, ..., PX_m) = \left[\sum d_i^{\sigma} \cdot PX_i^{1-\sigma} \right]^{\frac{1}{1-\sigma}} \qquad (2.13)$$

where σ is the elasticity of substitution and the d_is are distributional weights which indicate the relative significance of the inputs (we omit an index j on d_i and σ to simplify the notation). This cost function is dual to a CES sub-production function

$$E_j = \left(\sum d_i X_{ij}^{-\rho} \right)^{-\frac{1}{\rho}}$$

where ρ is the substitution parameter$(\sigma = 1/(1 + \rho))$. Using Shephard's lemma, input coefficients for fossil fuels are

$$\frac{X_{ij}}{E_j} = \frac{\partial CES_j(\cdot)}{\partial PX_i} = d_i^{\sigma} \left(\frac{PE_j}{PX_i} \right)^{\sigma}, \quad i = 1, \dots, m. \qquad (2.14)$$

From (2.9) we get, using Shephard's lemma with respect to the price *PE*,

$$\frac{E_j}{X_j} = \frac{\partial c_j \left(PE, PX_{m+1, \dots} \right)}{\partial PE} \qquad (2.15)$$

If we multiply (2.14) by (2.15), we obtain price-dependent energy input coefficients as a subset of the coefficients derived in (2.9).

4.   PRODUCER BEHAVIOR

Given the basic neoclassical approach to model producer behavior in an inter-industry framework, CGE models differ from one another in dealing with the following issues: expectations and planning horizon; the optimal choice of investment with or without adjustment costs; the treatment of technical change, and the incorporation of abatement activities. In this section we deal with producer behavior with respect to investment decision and in separate sections with respect to technical change and abatement technologies.

   In the first generation of CGE models producers were regarded as having static expectations and the dynamics are modeled as a recursive accumulative procedure. The capital stock is fixed in the short run and variable in the long run. Investment is neither determined by savings behavior of private households nor by the behavior of a manager who maximizes the value of the firm (the Tobin, 1969, q-theory of investment). Especially in large-scale CGE models investment of the firm is determined by optimal capital costs in the long run, expectations about future growth of demand for a firm's product and static expectation about its future prices. An adjustment factor determines the percentage a firm wishes to invest in order to narrow the gap between the size of its 'desired' capital stock and its current level. If, however, agents have myopic expectations, they expect future prices to be the same as current ones. Decisions in each period of the transition phase to a new long-run equilibrium will then deviate from optimal decisions if a policy change has affected prices. In such models the requirements for actions in a future period (for example global warming) will not alter the nature of environmental decisions before the requirements come into effect. In the new generation of fully dynamic CGE models investment decisions are based on forward-looking expectations (rational or perfect foresight) and on intertemporal optimization behavior. In addition, adjustment cost functions express the notion that installing new capital necessitates a loss of current output. The coordination of intertemporal savings behavior and investment decisions occurs on perfect capital markets. In models with perfect foresight, the cost estimates of an environmental policy can be lower than for the same model with no foresight because there will be no early, and hence costly, retirement of the capital stock.

An important advantage of an explicit intertemporal optimization framework is that the necessary *ex-post* equality between investment and savings can be warranted, which is not the case in a backward-looking capital accumulation approach (see Dewatripont and Michel, 1987). Therefore, no closure rule has to be chosen, that is, none of the constraints of the model must be relaxed to find a solution when all markets are in equilibrium. In most static CGE models the identity of private gross domestic production from the flow of cost approach with the flow of product approach has been used to choose a residual variable for closing the model. Such a variable could be investment, the public budget or the balance of trade.[6] The *ex-post* identity of gross investment to net savings (household savings, government budget deficit and current account balance) serves as a closure rule, for example in Hudson and Jorgenson (1974), GREEN or in some versions of GEM-E3.

In the new generation of dynamic models the focus is on how a manager should accumulate capital over time in order to maximize the value of the firm.[7] Let π be the firm's profit (or a restricted profit function), then the following cash-flow identity links the firm's sources (left-hand side) and uses of revenues (right-hand side):

$$\pi + BN + VN = DIV + PI\cdot I$$

where BN is new dept issue, VN new share issue, $PI\cdot I$ are investment expenditure and DIV are dividend payments. New share issues are residual because dividend payments are assumed to be a constant fraction, a, of profit net of economic depreciation, and new debt issue to be a constant fraction, b, of the value of net investment:

$$DIV = a\cdot(\pi + (PI - PI_{-1}))\cdot K - \delta\cdot PI\cdot K$$
$$BN = b\cdot(PI\cdot K_{+1} - PI_{-1}\cdot K)$$

where δ is the rate of economic depreciation.[8] Arbitrage possibilities compel the firm to offer its stockholders a rate of return comparable to the interest rate i on alternative assets:[9]

$$DIV + (V_{+1} - V - VN) = i\cdot V. \tag{2.16}$$

The return before tax to stockholders consists of the current dividend plus capital gain on the equity value (V) of the firm net of the value of new share issues. This return must be comparable to the return from an investment of the same value at the market rate of interest, i. Forward substitution of the basic arbitrage condition yields the following expression for the firm's equity value as the discounted value of dividends less share issues:

$$V_t = \sum_{s=t}^{\infty}[DIV_s - VN_s]\cdot \prod_{u=t+1}^{s}(1+i_u)^{-1}$$

The manager maximizes V subject to the capital accumulation condition by choosing optimally in each period the levels of labor, intermediate inputs and investment.

There are theoretical difficulties in extending CGE models but the effort seems to be worthwhile to end up with useful policy models. However, it is important to proceed with caution, adding at each step only as much complication as is needed, and retaining a clear view of the causal mechanisms at work.[10]

5.   CONSUMER BEHAVIOR

In most CGE models the focus of the analysis is on efficiency issues, and all consumers are then aggregated into a single representative consumer. This infinitely lived consumer with perfect foresight maximizes in year t the discounted sum of intra-period utility from 'full consumption' FC consisting of consumption goods and leisure:[11]

$$U_t = \sum_{\tau=t}^{\infty} (1+s)^{t-\tau} \frac{\sigma}{\sigma-1} FC_s^{\frac{\sigma-1}{\sigma}}$$

The parameter σ is the intertemporal elasticity of substitution in full consumption and s is the rate of time preference. Full consumption is a quantity index in the form of an intraperiod aggregate of consumption of goods (C_t) and leisure (LJ_t):

$$FC_t = FC(C_t, LJ_t)$$

The maximization of the weak separable intertemporal utility function is subject to a budget constraint that restricts the present value of expenditures not to exceed the present value of lifetime wealth endowment. This endowment consists of the present value of wages, the imputed value of leisure time, of net transfer, and of the value of current non-human wealth. The determination of full consumption can be seen as the first stage in the allocation procedure of a consumer. At the second stage the consumer maximizes an intraperiod utility function given the full income the consumer has decided to spend in each period. The allocation is usually based on a within-period expenditure function with full consumption as an indicator of within-period utility. At this stage the consumer decides how to allocate full consumption between consumption of goods C_t and of leisure time. The difference between the quantity of leisure consumed and the household's total time endowment determines the quantity of labor supplied. Saving is also determined at this stage and is the difference between current income from the supply of capital and labor services and personal consumption expenditures. At the final stage of the budgeting process, consumption is allocated into several consumption categories. The allocation is normally between a composite of non-energy goods and a composite of energy goods. Then different non-energy goods have to be chosen as well as different energy goods. The several consumption categories are then transferred into consumption by product according to the industry classification used.

Since environmental regulation affects the use and purchase of consumer durables such as cars, electric appliances and heating, a model of consumer behavior should integrate demand for durables and for non-durables. Demand for non-durables and for services from durables has to be reconciled with investment demand for durables to modify the stock of durables towards their optimal levels. Such an approach permits us to model the impact of an energy or gasoline tax on growth and on the age of the stock of durables.[12] Since non-durable goods like gasoline or electricity are linked to durable goods such as cars or electric appliances, prices of durables are stated in terms of user costs which include all costs of using durables.[13] The approach is based on the notion of a variable expenditure function $e(u, p, z)$ which gives minimal expenditure for non-durable goods given the utility level u, the price vector p of the non-durable goods and the vector z of the quasi-fixed stock of durables.

The optimal stock of the durables can be derived from an intertemporal minimization of expenditures. These expenditures consist of expenditures for non-durables, of purchases of new durables as net investment, of purchases for replacement, and of taxes on durables like a motor vehicle tax. If we include the aspect of adjustment costs, the long-run problem facing the consumer is to minimize the present value of the expected sum of variable expenditures, the purchase costs of quasi-fixed assets, and adjustment costs. The analytical solution is similar to the firm's decision on investment facing a variable cost function with quasi-fixed capital.

If consumer behavior is based on a representative consumer, then one of the restrictions of such an approach is that preferences are identical for all consumers. However, expenditure patterns differ with demographic characteristics of individual consumers and therefore environmental policies have different impacts on different households, depending on the size of their stock of consumer durables. In assessing the distributional impacts of policies to restrict air pollution, a disaggregation into several types of households is potentially useful. To capture differences among social groups of households, Jorgenson and Wilcoxen (1993) have subdivided the household sector into demographic groups that differ by characteristics such as family size, age of head, region of residence and urban versus rural location.

Especially in large-scale models consumers have myopic expectations and no perfect foresight. They expect future prices to be the same as current ones. However, as a policy change will induce prices to change, the consumer makes a mistake in each period in the transition phase to a new long-run equilibrium. While with rational expectations, consumers readily adjust their behavior to the announced policy change, consumers with myopic expectations only adjust their behavior when the policy is enacted. In modeling perfect foresight three options can be considered. Besides the Ramsey-type model, which assumes an infinitely living representative consumer, there is the Blanchard-type approach where different generations are alive each period. Each generation has the same constant death probability independent of age. The third type is a model of the Auerbach and Kotlikoff (1987) type where different generations are alive in each period and the individuals face different death probabilities dependent on their age. To my knowledge no CGE model exists with an Auerbach–Kotlikoff type of modeling the household sector whereas a Blanchard-type model has been used (for example Keuschnigg and Kohler, 1994).

Common specifications for the intratemporal allocation of consumption into categories are the linear expenditure system, nested CES or translog demand functions. A linear expenditure system based on a restricted expenditure function with consumer durables as quasi-fixed stocks can be found in Conrad and Schröder (1991b). Calibration of a linear expenditure system requires information on all income elasticities to calculate the parameters of the budget shares as well as information on all own-price elasticities to calculate the minimum required quantity of the good.

6.   FOREIGN TRADE, DOMESTIC SUPPLY AND DEMAND

If all countries implement a more stringent environmental policy, the impact on their GDP and relative prices of goods will be different in each country. As a result trade patterns and domestic production will change. These effects will be more significant if a unilateral action is taken by one of the countries which adversely affects international competitiveness. Since the costs of environmental policies will decline as the number of countries implementing them increases, it is important to model the impact on international competitiveness by endogenizing foreign trade. Most CGE models allow the trade pattern to adjust to environmental policy measures. Since perfect specialization is rarely observed in reality and since two-way trade prevails, the Armington (1969) assumption is widely adopted to model intra-industry trade. Under this assumption, domestically produced goods and imported goods are not perfect substitutes. We next describe a CGE approach to model trade, domestic supply and total demand by adopting the small open-economy framework; that is, the domestic economy is considered as sufficiently small. This assumption implies that the domestic economy does not affect international prices.[14]

Firms substitute between domestic, X, and foreign goods, IM, to minimize the cost of obtaining a given Armington composite good, Y. The dual approach is based on a unit cost function

$$PY = CES(PX,PIM),\qquad(2.17)$$

where PY is the price of the aggregate composite, and $PX(PIM)$ is the price of obtaining the domestic (foreign) good. From this cost function the share for the domestic good in the composite good is derived by Shephard's lemma:

$$\frac{X}{Y} = cx \cdot \left(\frac{PY}{PX}\right)^{\sigma}\qquad(2.18)$$

as well as the aggregate import in the composite good[15]

$$\frac{IM}{Y} = (1 - cx)\left(\frac{PY}{PIM}\right)^{\sigma} \tag{2.19}$$

Y is determined from the input output part of the CGE model, that is, from

$$Y_i = \sum a_{ij}X_j + FD_i = \sum a_{ij} \cdot \left(\frac{X_j}{Y_j}\right)Y_j + FD_i \tag{2.20}$$

with the price-dependent share X_j/Y_j from (2.18). Equations (2.18) and (2.19) therefore allocate Y to X and IM, and (2.17) determines PY. If CGE models are linked by trade flow matrices, then PIM has to be specified as a unit cost function in import prices (equal to export prices) of the trading partners as in the GEM-E3 project. Here,[16] $PIM = PEX_{ROW}/ex$ where PEX is the export price of the rest of the world (ROW) (exogenous) and the exchange rate ex is in dollars per euro (exogenous). This assumption implies that the foreign import supply function is horizontal at PEX_{ROW}.

To determine domestic export supply, firms maximize revenue $PX \cdot X + PEX \cdot EX$ from domestic, X, and foreign supply EX subject to a constant return to scale *CET* (constant elasticity of transformation) function for the composite good Y (determined by (2.20)) as a function of X and EX. Using again the dual approach of a *CET* unit revenue function,

$$PY = CET(PX, PEX), \tag{2.21}$$

we obtain supply functions using Hotelling's lemma, that is, differentiating (2.21) with respect to the product prices:

$$X = Y \cdot \gamma_x \cdot \left(\frac{PY}{PX}\right)^{\sigma_\tau} \tag{2.22}$$

$$EX = Y \cdot \gamma_{EX} \cdot \left(\frac{PY}{PEX}\right)^{\sigma_\tau} \tag{2.23}$$

where $\sigma_T < 0$ is the elasticity of transformation and the γs indicate the significance of the outputs. Equating the export equation (2.23) with import demand of the *ROW* (see IM_{ROW} in (2.24) below) gives the price PEX. Since PY has been determined by (2.17), (2.21) can be solved for *PX*. Then *X* in (2.22) can be calculated. In order to model import demand by the *ROW*, we proceed as in (2.17)–(2.19) by adding an index row to all variables. Dividing the symmetric equation of (2.19) by (2.18) yields import demand of the *ROW*

$$IM_{ROW} = Y_{ROW} \cdot \gamma_{ROW} \left(\frac{PY_{ROW}}{PIM_{ROW}} \right)^{\sigma} \tag{2.24}$$

where $PIM_{ROW} = PEX/ex =$ and *PEX* is determined as mentioned above. World market prices PY_{ROW} and sectoral output levels Y_{ROW} of the *ROW* are exogenous. One of these prices serves as numeraire. Note that the foreign export demand function is not horizontal but is declining in *PEX*.

Finally we can calculate the trade surplus/deficit *TS* by commodity

$$TS = PEX \cdot EX - PIM \cdot IM. \tag{2.25}$$

By summing up over all commodities, the total trade surplus/deficit can be calculated. If the exchange rate is assumed to be exogenous (as in GEM-M3), the current account is not balanced and will change with the policy simulation. Instead of a residual as a world closure, an alternative is to fix *TS* and make the exchange rate endogenous. The models are closed by budget constraints, market-clearing conditions and macroeconomic balances based on the Social Accounting Matrix. These equations include all kinds of taxes, subsidies and transfer payments. They summarize incomes and expenditures of private households, of the government and of the rest of the world. For the government the deficit/surplus could be held fixed and one of the taxes allowed to adjust, or it could be determined endogenously as a residual. Finally, some variables have to be set at an exogenous level because we do not know how the world oil market functions (price of crude oil is exogenous) or because the impact of technical change is uncertain.

7.   LABOR MARKETS

The specification of the labor market could be crucial to the discussion on the effect of environmental policy on employment. A labor market policy of recycling tax revenues from an environmental tax to lower employers' non-wage labor cost depends on how the labor market is modeled. Non-competitive labor markets could provide another potential channel for the so-called 'double dividend' (see section 11.1). In most CGE models the labor market is perfectly competitive and the wage rate adjusts so that supply equals demand. Proost and van Regemorter (1995) consider several income groups and different regimes for the labor market to test the double dividend hypotheses empirically, including equity aspects. Labor supply is fixed and they consider a case with flexible wages and one with fixed real wages. The efficiency gain that can be made by using the tax revenue from an environmental tax to reduce existing distortions from high taxes on labor depends crucially on how flexible labor supply is. In most static models a simple labor supply curve for a skill category is implemented where labor supply is a function of the real wage rate:

$$L^S = \overline{L} \cdot \left(\frac{PL}{PY} \right)^{\eta}.$$

If the supply elasticity η is zero, labor supply is fixed ($\overline{L}$) and if it is infinite, the real wage rate is fixed. In this case, the labor supply equation is dropped from the system and the labor market equilibrium equation states that labor demand is always met by supply. Suppliers will freely supply all labor demanded at the fixed wage and a labor supply function can be used as a side equation to compute involuntary unemployment. If the labor supply curve is not flat, the condition $\Sigma_j L^d_{j,l} = L^s_l$ determines the equilibrium wage rate for a skill category l.

In intertemporal models the representative agent allocates full consumption between goods and leisure, determining personal consumption expenditure, labor supply and savings. The price of labor is determined (for example in McKibbin and Wilcoxen, 1992) by assuming that it adjusts according to an overlapping contracts model where nominal wages are set based on current and expected inflation and on labor demand relative to labor supply. In the long run labor supply is given by the exogenous rate of population growth, but in the short run the hours worked can fluctuate depending on the demand for labor. Then for a given nominal wage, the demand for labor will determine short-run unemployment.

Some model builders do sensitivity analyses to test whether the computed results depend on the labor market specification. Boehringer et al. (2000) incorporate some features of wage bargaining in the presence of initial unemployment in order to represent labor market imperfections. A Phillips curve concept is used to model the empirical evidence that high unemployment rates weaken the level of bargaining power by unions, which in turn implies lower real wages (see also GEM-E3 or Carraro and Galeotti, 1994).

8.   TECHNICAL CHANGE

It is well known that the outcome of an environmental policy measure to mitigate global climate change is very sensitive to the assumption made on the rate of energy efficiency improvement. However, technical progress is in general considered to be a non-economic, exogenous variable in economic policy models. This is not very satisfactory because the neglect of induced technological progress may lead to an overestimation of the costs of greenhouse gas reduction or of the contribution of traffic to air pollution. An inadequate representation of policy-driven technical change in the models will also result in an understatement of the advantages of market-based instruments. In the field of industrial organization partial models have been developed to endogenize the process from R&D expenditure to invention and innovation, and then to diffusion of a new process or product. These models seem, however, not appropriate for implementation and calibration.

The technological change process is usually initiated by public or private R&D and diffuses by 'learning by using', 'learning by doing' and by networking. These processes are not easy to capture in a neoclassical framework because they have evolutionary elements. In most models technological parameters, representing for example efficiency or emission reduction potentials, are treated as inputs and not as results of the technological change process. The impact of technological change on processes, products and on emissions cannot be modeled with only a few equations. Emission reduction of air pollutants can be achieved by fuel substitution (non-energy for energy or within-energy inputs), by efficiency improvement in power generation, and by the energy user. The potential for emission reduction can focus on energy use per unit of production or on emissions per kWh. Stages of the techno-economic development have to model incentives and costs of R&D, implementation costs (information and operating costs), commercialization, wide-scale diffusion, appropriability, barriers to market penetration, the technological infrastructure and the scope for future efficiency improvement of established versus novel products. For reducing greenhouse gas emissions, for example, there are many technologies or means which could be introduced in a model: fuel substitution to less carbon-intensive fuels, renewable energy, advanced power generation cycles, transmission improvements, end-user efficiency improvement or carbon sequestration (for example by biomass greening). It is obvious that it is not possible to model all those measures within a CGE framework. Bottom-up firm-specific models (for example the EU models MURE, MARKAL, EFOM) try to capture technological change by linking detailed technically oriented sub-models to economic models in order to endogenize technical change. However, in recent years there have been significant new developments in CGE modeling of endogenous technological change. Until recently, the following four main approaches were used to incorporate technical progress in CGE models:

- a partially endogenous treatment of technical progress initiated by Jorgenson and Wilcoxen;

- autonomous energy efficiency improvement (input-saving technical change);
- the vintage composition of the capital stock;
- the transition to backstop technologies.

In Jorgenson and Wilcoxen (1990a, b), and later in the G-Cubed model of McKibbin and Wilcoxen (1992a, b), technological development is partly endogenized by the specification of productivity growth as a function of the prices of all inputs of an industry. In this approach, substitution away from polluting inputs can affect the rate of productivity growth. A decrease in an industry's productivity level will raise the price of its output relative to its input prices; that is, the industry will become less competitive. If the bias of technical change is input of type i using and the price of such a pollution-intensive input increases (for example by a tax), then cost reduction due to productivity growth will be reduced.

The translog unit cost or price function of the prices of all the inputs of an industry j is

$$\ln c_j = \alpha_0^j + \sum \alpha_i^j \ln p_i + \alpha_T^j \cdot t + \frac{1}{2} \sum \beta_{ik}^j \cdot \ln p_i \cdot \ln p_k + \sum \gamma_{iT}^j \ln p_i \cdot t + \frac{1}{2} \gamma_{TT}^j \cdot t^2$$

where t is time and an index of technology. Input coefficients derived by Shephard's lemma are:

$$\frac{x_{ij}}{x_j} = \left(\alpha_i^j + \sum_k \beta_{ik}^j \ln p_k + \gamma_{iT}^j \cdot t \right) \frac{c_j}{p_i}$$

where γ_{iT} indicates the bias of technical change. The rate of cost reduction due to productivity growth is

$$\frac{\partial \ln c_j}{\partial t} = \alpha_T^j + \sum_i \gamma_{iT}^j \ln p_i + \gamma_{TT}^j \cdot t$$

and is expected to be negative. If the bias of technical change is input i using, that is, $\gamma_{iT} > 0$, and the price of this pollution-intensive input increases ($\Delta p_i > 0$, then cost reduction due to productivity growth $(\partial \ln c_j)/(\partial t)$ in industry j will become smaller, because $\gamma_{iT} \cdot \ln \Delta p_i$ is added to the negative cost reduction parameter α_T^j (in the base year all $p_i = 1$, $t = 0$). Technological development is treated only partially in this model because an autonomous trend is included which interacts with the prices of intermediate inputs. There is price-induced productivity growth in the model which affects input shares. But technological change is not endogenized in terms of reversing a bias, leading to new vintages of durable goods, to new products or to different qualities or major breakthroughs. The models by Glomsrød et al. (1992) or by Hazilla and Kopp (1990) endogenize fuel-specific technical change in a similar way, that is, as an incentive for substitution only.

Autonomous energy efficiency improvements (AEEIs) are more difficult to estimate than those that are induced by price increases. AEEI decouples resource demand and economic output, and so yields resource-saving technical change. In the dual cost function approach some input prices are multiplied by a function representing price-diminishing technical change, that is, $P_i(t) = P_i(t - 1) \cdot \exp(-\gamma_i \cdot t)$, $\gamma_i > 0$. Non-price-induced efficiency improvements may be induced by changes in public policy like a mandatory doubling of average fuel efficiency of automobiles during the course of ten years. Manne and Richels (1990) introduce those exogenous efficiency improvements, for example. They also include explicit carbon removal technologies if carbon tax rates are large. Their production function also allows for the possibility of 'autonomous (costless) energy efficiency improvements' which reduce the share of energy in GNP over time. A factor for autonomous energy efficiency improvement integrates all non-price-induced changes in energy intensity and therefore represents the efficiency effect of technological, structural and political objectives (for example voluntary agreements). This approach emphasizes showing the *effect* of technical change but cannot model aspects like innovation, adaptation or diffusion. If an environmental policy induces technical change, for example triggers emission- or resource-saving technical change, it would reduce the cost of achieving a given abatement or resource conservation target. Most CGE models, however, assume no difference in the pattern of technical change between the base case and the policy case. This probably leads to an upward bias in the cost estimate of that policy.

An alternative approach to incorporate technical change is the use of capital vintages involving different technologies. The differentiation of technologies can have effects on the form of the production function, on the input structure, or on flexibility (different elasticities of substitution for the vintages). With new vintages, substitution possibilities among production factors are higher than with old vintages. In Bergman (1990b) the 'old' production units in steel or pulp and paper industries are assumed to have zero elasticities of substitution, whereas the elasticity of substitution of 'new' production units in these industries is positive. In GREEN's dynamic structure, two kinds of capital goods coexist in each period, 'old' capital installed in previous periods, and 'new' capital resulting from current-period investment. This putty/semi-putty technology also implies different substitution possibilities by age of capital.

A more formal presentation of the idea that the latest vintage, added to the aggregate capital stock, embodies innovation and technical improvement can be found in Conrad and Henseler-Unger (1986). The methodological approach is an integration of price-dependent input coefficients with input coefficients of the latest vintage, both derived from cost functions. The elasticity of substitution is the same for old and new vintages but the distribution parameters in the CES functions, that is the relative significance of the inputs, differs.

The integration of the 'jelly' capital concept with disembodied technical progress, used in the neoclassical approach to input–output analysis, with the vintage concept follows from adjusting, for example, an energy coefficient based on the new relative prices in $t + 1$ by the decay of old plants (δ is the rate of decay) and by adding the input coefficient of the new plant or vintage:

$$\frac{E_{t+1}}{X_{t+1}} = d_{E,t}^{\sigma} \left(\frac{PE_{t+1}}{PX_{t+1}} \right)^{-\sigma} (1-\delta) + (g+\delta) \cdot \theta_{E,t}^{\sigma} \left(\frac{PE_t}{PX_t} \right)^{-\sigma} \tag{2.26}$$

where d_E (θ_E) is the distribution parameter of the old (new) production process, and g is the growth rate of output.

The characteristic feature of this approach is that on the one side an input structure reacts to changes in relative prices by substitution on the basis of the jelly capital stock. On the other side, the input structure changes due to new energy-efficient plants (second term in (2.26)) for the retired worn-out energy-intensive installations.[17] A similar approach of a vintage recalibration has been used in the OECD model (Beghin et al., 1995). At the beginning of each new period, the parameters of the production structure are modified to reflect the changing composition of capital.

A further methodological approach to take into account the vintage concept is to replace capital K in a restricted cost or profit function by Solow's (1959) expression for an effective capital stock. In his article, Solow criticized the disembodied nature of technical change in aggregate production functions. He emphasized the fact that most improvements in technology need to be embodied in net capital formation, or in the replacement of old-fashioned equipment, before they can be made effective. Solow proposed to distinguish capital equipment of different vintages and formulated a Cobb–Douglas function for output produced with capital of a given vintage. Technical change is represented by a rate of embodied technical change as well as of disembodied technical change. His measure of effective capital incorporates the assumption that all technical progress is embodied in the improving quality of successive vintages of capital investment.[18] If technical progress is unembodied in capital plant and equipment, then its effects do not depend in any way on the rate of investment in those factors. An alternative notion is that technical progress is entirely embodied in the design and operating characteristics of new capital plant and equipment. According to this view, the energy-saving effects of embodied technical progress depend critically on the rate at which new investment goods diffuse into the economy, that is, on the vintage composition of the capital stock. For policy measures the nature of technical progress matters. If technical progress is embodied, tax credits for investments in new energy-efficient equipment provide an incentive to realize its effects more quickly than if technical change were unembodied. However, under embodied technical change energy-savings can be realized only by changing the energy using characteristics of the long-lived capital stock, whereas under unembodied technical change the effectiveness of the entire capital stock is augmented regardless of its vintage composition. One example of unembodied technical change is 'learning by doing', in which workers learn how to produce more efficiently. However, if technical progress were embodied, it augments only the most recent vintage of investment, and not any of the earlier vintages of surviving capital.[19] Berndt et al. (1993) have estimated the rates of embodied and disembodied technical change using a translog specification of a restricted cost function and data from the manufacturing sectors in the USA, Canada and France from 1970 to 1987. They found that embodiment played at best a modest role. From the total cumulative effects of technical progress, embodied technical progress was responsible for 0.5 percent in the USA, 3.6 percent in Canada, and 10.7 percent in France. They conclude that technical progress embodied in new equipment is responsible for only a surprisingly small proportion of productivity growth.

Energy-oriented CGE models introduce exogenously provided new technologies which are known but not yet implemented. These backstop technologies are already known today, but are options of commercial interest in the future. The introduction of these technologies depends on maturation (exogenous penetration time) as well as on the cost of production relative to competitive technologies. Backstop inputs are modeled to be available at an unlimited quantity for an exogenously given price. A precise knowledge of the technology in question is not necessary. For the design of carbon reduction policies Rutherford (1999) assumes that there exists a carbon backstop technology which can produce carbon-free energy at constant marginal cost. In simulations of carbon abatement policies costs of the carbon backstop are set equal to a future value per ton of carbon and then application of a carbon limit causes a gradual introduction of the backstop activity. The introduction of new alternative sources of fossil fuels depends on the exogenously given cost of the backstop.

The new generation of CGE models employs a more sophisticated treatment of endogenous technical progress by modeling explicitly the connection between R&D expenditure and knowledge growth. The models of Nordhaus (1999) and of Goulder and Schneider (1999) connect the rate of invention with resources spent on R&D. The Nordhaus model of induced innovation describes the impact of changes in prices or regulation on the innovations in different sectors. At a given time, there is an existing stock of general and sector-specific basic knowledge and engineering knowledge. Resources (research as an input) can be applied to improve the state of knowledge (called 'innovation') in order to raise the productivity of resources. The conclusion of the study based on the DICE model (Nordhaus, 1992, 1994) was that induced innovation seems to be a less powerful factor in implementing climate change policies than substitution. The reductions in CO2 concentrations and in global mean temperature due to induced innovation turned out to be approximately one-half of those due to substitution. Goulder and Schneider (1999) model induced technical change in greenhouse gas abatement by making R&D for lower-carbon technologies responsive to the economic incentives created by greenhouse gas policies. Firms employ labor, capital and two types of energy and materials to produce output. By distinguishing conventional (carbon-based) energy from alternative forms of energy, they can consider how a tax on carbon influences incentives to R&D in alternative fuels industries. And by distinguishing carbon-intensive materials from other materials, they can observe how the performance of other industries might depend on the extent to which carbon fuels are a significant input into production. In addition, they distinguish physical capital and knowledge capital. The former is expanded by investment in new physical capital, the latter by expenditure on R&D activities. Enlarging either capital stock raises the productivity of energy and non-energy inputs.[20] They apply the model to the US economy but concede that it is (not yet) possible to obtain precise data on the technology for producing R&D services or to identify precisely the relationship between R&D services and knowledge capital. These new models are inspired by the industrial organization literature or by macro-models of induced technological change (Romer, 1990). A CGE application of these approaches needs calibration of parameters which express the strength of substitution possibilities between knowledge capital and ordinary inputs or the spillover knowledge enjoyed by all industries. More econometric studies need to be carried out in order to provide an empirical background for the calibration of R&D-related parameters.

9.   ABATEMENT TECHNOLOGIES

If emission data are directly associated with the volume of output, that is abatement activities are not endogenously modeled, then the only way to reduce emissions is by reducing output. This is a rather unpleasant conclusion for countries troubled with unemployment as well as for developing countries. However, for an analysis of the impact of environmental regulation on international competitiveness and on growth, the inclusion of the operating costs of pollution control is of importance. Polluting firms can react to standards and/or emission taxes either by factor substitution or by abatement activities or both. They have abatement cost functions and determine the level of the abatement activity by equating marginal cost of abatement to the uniform tax rate on emissions. Abatement activities also imply demand for intermediate goods, for capital and for labor. Depending on the objective of the study, several approaches to imposing pollution control regulations on the technology can be found in the literature. The easiest way to deal with the problem of how to model abatement technologies is to study the economic impact of reducing CO_2 emissions. Since there are no carbon abatement technologies available at reasonable economic costs, this explains the popularity of modeling CO_2 reduction policies. Substitution and output effects are the only measures to reduce CO_2 emissions.

In determining the impact of environmental restrictions on economic growth, Jorgenson and Wilcoxen (1990a) simulated US economic growth with and without pollution control in effect. For eliminating the operating cost of pollution control for constructing their base case, they estimated the share of pollution abatement in total costs of each industry to compute the share λ_i of costs, pollution abatement excluded, in total costs. To simulate the effect of eliminating the operating costs associated with pollution controls for all industries, they insert the cost shares λ_i into the unit cost functions for these industries, that is,

$$\ln p_i = \ln\lambda_i + \ln c_i(w,t).$$

To simulate the impact of eliminating controls on motor vehicle emissions they reduced the price of motor vehicles in proportion to the cost of pollution control devices. Finally, mandated investment in pollution control equipment has been implemented as an increase in the price of investment goods.

Hazilla and Kopp (1990) also impose pollution control regulations directly on the technologies. They model their impact through modification of the derived input demand equations in each sector. The input structure of each industry is modified to account for increased input usage required by regulation. In Bergman (1990) total emissions of air pollutants (SO_2, NO_X, CO_2) can be reduced by means of separate cleaning activities that are available to all sectors. Technically the reduction of emissions is modeled as a central abatement unit, selling services to the different sectors. The price of these abatement services is equal to marginal cost of abatement. This price will then be determined on the market for emission permits, implying that marginal cost of abatement will be equal across sources of emissions.

In Conrad and Schröder (1991a, 1993) and in the GEM-E3 model (Capros et al., 1996) abatement activities are modeled so as to increase the user cost of the polluting inputs in terms of additional operating costs. Let d be a degree of abatement which is defined as the ratio of abated emission over potential emissions ($0 \leq d \leq 1$) and $c(d)$ are the costs of abatement measures per unit of emission or waste, measured in base-year prices. They depend on the degree of abatement with $c'(d) > 0$ and $c''(d) > 0$. Then the user cost of fossil fuel, for instance, is $\tilde{w}_F = W_F + W_M \cdot c(d) \cdot d \cdot e$, where W_F is the fuel price, W_M is the price of material or abatement technology and e is an emission or waste coefficient in terms of tons of an air pollutant per unit of energy input. User costs therefore consist of the fuel price W_F and of the additional costs due to environmental regulation when using one unit of the fuel input. This user cost of energy increases over-proportionally with an enforcement in environmental regulation.[21] On the production side this implies an increasing share of complementary material inputs. The change of the user cost of energy will also cause the firm to alter its input choices. A stricter environmental policy will have a substitution effect which will result in a reduced demand for energy and its price complements and in an increased use of its substitutes. This integration of abatement costs in a user cost concept can be used to model the impact of regulation on household and firm behavior; for the latter each sector should be treated separately.

The user cost approach can be extended to the case of several pollutants, either air pollutants, water pollutants, or land pollutants. Furthermore, if there is a tax on a pollutant, then there is also a cost component for the emissions released, that is,

$$\tilde{w}_F = W_F + W_M \cdot c(d) \cdot d \cdot e + t(1 - d) \cdot e.$$

Finally, if there is an energy tax and/or an emission tax on carbon dioxide, t_{CO}, where no convenient end-of-pipe measures exist, then d is equal to zero in this user cost of fuel.

This approach permits us to model the effect of alternative environmental policies. If there is a regulated degree of abatement, then users of furnaces must adhere to governmentally enforced limits of emissions which can be interpreted as a minimum degree of abatement $\bar{d}$. Then the degree of abatement is given and abatement costs increase the price of energy. If a tax on emission is introduced, the degree d is a decision variable of the firm.

Cost minimization with respect to the degree of abatement d yields the optimal degree.

Furthermore, future environmental regulations can be accounted for by modifying the emission coefficients for appropriate sectors. For instance, as new cars are equipped with catalytic converters, the emission of NO_x for a given amount of gasoline will fall gradually (see Glomsrød et al., 1992; Conrad and Schröder, 1991a).

In the user cost approach environmental regulation will have an impact on the composition of the energy aggregate, it will increase the price of the product produced with fuel, and it will reduce the demand for energy.

10.   DATA REQUIREMENTS

The sources of data for the multisectoral CGE models are the national accounts and input–output tables which can be comfortably combined in the framework of the Social Accounting Matrix (SAM). If yearly input–output tables are available, then the parameters of the unit cost functions and of the factor demand functions can be estimated econometrically (for example Hudson and Jorgenson, 1974, and Jorgenson and Wilcoxen, 1990a, 1990b). The econometric approach is very demanding in terms of data requirements but makes it possible to incorporate behavioral responses to changes in relative prices based on the behavior in the past. However, given the often poor data situation (the latest input–output table is often five years old), and the high degree of aggregation, the knowledge of an estimated elasticity of substitution between energy and capital or energy and material in the investment goods industry might not be worth the enormous effort required to explore the production structure from a set of yearly input–output tables. The common approach in CGE modeling is therefore to choose nested CES functional specifications which account for different degrees of substitutability between input factors on different nesting levels. The distribution parameters which indicate the relative significance of the inputs are calibrated (calculated) from benchmark data, but the substitution elasticities have to be taken from other sources. A typical source is substitution elasticities presented in the econometric literature or own 'best-guess' estimates. Since sign and magnitude of those estimated elasticities differ, some model builders assume capital and energy to be complements and labor and energy to be weak substitutes. Those CGE modelers, who assume energy and capital to be substitutes rather than complements, face the problem that the adjustment to new relative prices will be complete and immediate. As the demand for energy reflects to a significant degree the properties of the existing stock of capital, this is hardly a satisfactory assumption. A reasonable alternative to the question about the true elasticity of substitution is to carry out different simulation studies. What we know is that a high degree of substitution among inputs implies that the cost of environmental regulation is low, while a low degree of substitutability implies higher costs of environmental regulation. The higher the substitution elasticity between labor and energy, the higher the chance that an ecological tax reform, which taxes energy and reduces non-wage labor cost, will raise employment. If we simulate the nature of substitutability among inputs by assuming a CES specification with first a low elasticity of substitution, and then with a higher one, we get an interval for the range of economic effects of an environmental policy. This is maybe more informative than getting a point-forecast under the econometric approach.

The response of an economy to changes in environmental regulation also depends crucially on assumptions made with respect to which variables are exogenous and what is their magnitude then. A standard assumption is exogenous technical change or population growth. In most models the price of crude oil is exogenous, as is the foreign exchange rate. It is not always desirable to endogenize each economic variable (for example the exchange rate), because this makes it harder to understand the outcome of a policy simulation due to the huge number of potential channels.

11.   ENVIRONMENTALLY RELATED SIMULATION ANALYSES USING CGE MODELS

11.1   The Double Dividend Policy

CGE analyses have played a key role in the evaluation of green tax reforms, the reorienting of the tax system to concentrate taxes more on 'bads' like pollution and less on 'goods' like labor input or capital formation. Before turning to an example of a double dividend analysis,[22] it is useful to comment on how the incidence of a tax reform should be measured. It can be assessed by looking at the equivalent variation (EV) associated with the tax change for each partici-pant in the economy. The EV provides a dollar measure of the impact of a given tax change on individual economic welfare. The EV gives the change in expen-diture at base prices P^0 that would be equivalent to the policy-implied change in utility. The EV may be computed as follows:

$$EV = e(P^0, U^1) - e(P^0, U^0) \qquad (2.27)$$

where $e(\cdot)$ is the expenditure function which depends on the consumer price vector P^0, and initial utility U^0 or post-tax utility U^1. If $EV < 0$, welfare after the policy measure is lower than in the base case. The consumer is willing to pay the maximum amount EV at the fixed budget level $e^0 = e(P^0, U^0)$ to avoid the decline of utility from U^0 to U^1. Similarly, if $EV > 0$, the consumer would be willing to pay the maximum amount EV to see the change in environmen-tal policy implemented. Alternatively, similar measures such as the compensating variation (CV) that replaces P^0 in (2.27) with the tax reform price vector given the initial utility level U^0, may be used in assessing tax reforms.

The question in the double dividend debate is whether the internalization of environmental externalities can be beneficial for other policy areas as well, since the revenues from pollution taxes could be used to cut other distortionary taxes. The non-environmental dividend can be defined in various ways. Given the important unemployment problem in the EU, priority has been given to the analysis of distortions in the labor market that might explain persisting unemployment.[23] The revenue from the pollution taxes is recycled to cut labor taxes. On the one side, the narrow base of an energy tax constitutes an inherent efficiency handicap. On the other side, the impact of the tax reform on pre-existing inefficiencies in taxing labor could offset this handicap and a double dividend arises. Therefore, in principle a double dividend can arise only if (i) the pre-existing tax system is significantly inefficient on non-environmental grounds and (ii) the revenue-neutral reform significantly reduces this prior inefficiency. The double dividend actually arises only if the second condition operates with sufficient force. However, it could also arise if the burden of the environmental tax falls mainly on the undertaxed factor (for example immobile capital) and relieves the burden of the overtaxed factor labor.[24]

As an example of such a policy analysis we present results from the GEM-E3 project (Capros et al., 1996 or Conrad and Schmidt, 1998b). In that model CO_2 emissions have been reduced by 10 percent in each country in the base year (the non-coordinated policy approach). For that purpose a CO_2 tax with a rate just high enough to achieve the 10 percent reduction in each country has been introduced. The revenue from this tax was used to reduce the contribution to social security by the employers. The carbon tax should affect the substitution of other inputs for energy and therefore contribute to reducing global warming (first dividend).[25] This substitution effect could have a positive impact on the demand for labor if output remained at the pre-reform level. However, the recycling of the tax money to social insurance as a partial compensation for employers' contribution could definitely increase the demand for labor (second dividend). The hope of the advocates of the double dividend is that the substitution effect of labor for energy outweighs the negative output effect resulting from lower growth when the tax is imposed.

The model considers full competitive equilibrium in all markets, including the labor market. We have included leisure only of employed persons in our welfare measure EV. If a policy simulation results in more leisure, this is interpreted to be equivalent to an increase in the number of employed persons. We will use the double dividend terminology for policies resulting in less CO_2 emissions and in more employment irrespective of whether consumption has declined due to lower real wages. In principle, there could be a third dividend, because $EV > 0$ can imply more leisure (of newly employed persons) as well as more consumption in addition to a better environment. It can also imply less consumption dominated by more leisure, or less leisure dominated by more consumption. The first column of Table 2.1 shows the equivalent variations in ECU per capita. Since all signs are positive and the burden on the environment is reduced by 10 percent, there is a double dividend effect for all countries. A German, for example, is willing to pay at most 62 ECU to see such a policy implemented. The EV per capita is the highest for Denmark and The Netherlands and the lowest for Greece.[26]

The figures in column 2 show negative growth rates for gross domestic production. Since employment, in turn, increases (see column 4), labor productivity declines. If in addition to employment (that is leisure) consumption increases, EV will be positive in any case according to the formula for EV. Italy and Greece, with the lowest increase in real wages, show a negative change in consumption. In these two countries the reduced purchasing power from higher energy prices cannot be compensated by the increase in real wages. As leisure of employed persons enters our utility function, the growth in employment explains their positive EV. As investment declines (not shown in the table) for all countries but Belgium, the double dividend policy is not a strategy for more growth in capital formation. Also not shown in the table are the negative changes in exports and imports.

The growth in employment differs by country due to different CO_2 tax revenues. Countries with a high CO_2 tax rate have also high growth rates in employment (for example, Denmark and the UK), because a higher tax revenue can be used to reduce the cost of labor. Substitution of labor for energy, given the price of labor and the higher price of energy, induces more employment. But especially the lower cost of labor from the relief in non-wage labor cost enhances the substitution of labor for other inputs. Due to changes in relative output prices, output of industries where energy is a minor input will increase and output of energy-intensive industries will decline. This leads to an intersectoral mobility of labor from industries hit by CO_2 tax to industries which benefit from relative output change and reduction in non-wage labor cost. The negative output effect from lower production cannot offset the positive effects from substitution. This kind of argument explains why Italy, with the second highest CO_2 tax (33.75) has only moderate growth in employment (0.34 percent); its production declines by more (–0.43 percent) than the average rate in the EU (–0.36 percent). However, as we model a flexible wage rate, higher demand for labor will, in turn, increase the wage rate. A higher real wage rate will then partly offset the double dividend policy of reducing the cost of labor. The positive growth effect of a higher real wage rate on private consumption may, however, partly offset the labor cost effect. Column 6 finally shows an

Table 2.1 The impact of an environmental tax reform under a non-coordinated and under a coordinated (figures in brackets) environmental policy

	EV in ECU per capita	Production (%)	Priv. cons. (%)	Employ. (%)	Wage rate	CO$_2$ tax (ECU/ton CO$_2$)	CO$_2$ reduction (%)
Belgium	85 [151]	−0.22 [−0.36]	0.80 [1.14]	0.16 [0.29]	1.86 [3.30]	10.88 [21.8]	−10.00 [−16.0]
Germany	62 [67]	−0.43 [−0.49]	0.33 [0.34]	0.34 [0.39]	1.41 [1.55]	18.98 [21.8]	−10.00 [−11.2]
Denmark	155 [83]	−0.19 [−0.09]	1.07 [0.57]	0.87 [0.46]	2.21 [1.18]	45.37 [21.8]	−9.99 [−5.6]
France	56 [48]	−0.28 [−0.26]	0.36 [0.30]	0.21 [0.19]	0.83 [0.70]	24.92 [21.8]	−10.00 [−9.1]
Greece	5 [21]	−0.21 [−0.39]	−0.18 [−0.2]	0.18 [0.35]	0.19 [0.58]	9.76 [21.8]	−10.00 [−17.5]
Ireland	51 [55]	−0.19 [−0.24]	0.85 [0.84]	0.12 [0.15]	1.52 [1.53]	19.40 [21.8]	−10.00 [−11.0]
Italy	36 [24]	−0.43 [−0.29]	−0.03 [−0.02]	0.34 [0.23]	0.51 [0.34]	33.75 [21.8]	−9.99 [−7.3]
Netherlands	92 [91]	−0.24 [−0.26]	0.58 [0.56]	0.43 [0.44]	2.73 [2.73]	21.37 [21.8]	−9.99 [−10.1]
Portugal	27 [26]	−0.57 [−0.56]	0.39 [0.37]	0.48 [0.46]	2.79 [2.69]	22.71 [21.8]	−10.00 [−9.7]
Spain	42 [45]	−0.44 [−0.47]	0.36 [0.39]	0.37 [0.40]	1.70 [1.82]	20.20 [21.8]	−10.00 [−10.6]
UK	73 [59]	−0.36 [−0.30]	0.18 [0.12]	0.92 [0.79]	0.84 [0.64]	26.62 [21.8]	−10.00 [−8.5]
EU	56 [53]	−0.36 [−0.35]	0.28 [0.27]	0.44 [0.40]	–	23.51 [21.8]	−10.00 [−10.0]

Notes:
Compensation: rate of social security, fixed public deficit.
Reduction: 10% of carbon dioxide in each country (10% EU-wide reduction of carbon dioxide).

average tax rate of 23.51 per ton of CO_2 and a group of countries with a lower rate (for example, Belgium or Greece) and a group with a higher rate (for example, Denmark or Italy). The tax rate depends on country-specific emission coefficients, on the energy intensity, on the energy mix, and on the cost of avoiding CO_2, that is, the elasticities of substitution.

As for a global pollutant, marginal damage is about the same for each country, for efficiency reasons the tax rate should be the same. We have therefore lowered overall CO_2 emissions of all EU member states by 10 percent, irrespective of the source of CO_2 (the coordinated policy approach). In order to achieve this bubble concept, we have calculated an EU-wide CO_2 tax rate such that its level will guarantee the reduction of total EU CO_2 emissions by 10 percent. Again each country will collect the tax revenues from its domestic firms and will use the money to lower employers' contribution to the social security insurance. We expect that the CO_2 tax rate under the bubble concept will be somewhat lower than the average of the rates under an uncoordinated, country-by-country CO_2 policy. Because of the cost-effectiveness of a coordinated policy we also expect that the tax revenue from the CO_2 tax under the coordinated policy will be lower than the sum of the revenues collected under the single-country policy. The reasons for the national differences in the impacts of a CO_2 policy are the different structure of the economies in terms of different weights of the energy-intensive industries, of the service sector, of the composition of exports and imports or the difference in equipment with consumer durables. All these factors imply a different slope of the marginal cost curve of avoiding CO_2.

We next turn to the results obtained under the coordinated carbon reduction policy. In this case there is a uniform tax rate whereby the countries' contributions to the CO_2 reduction target of 10 percent for the EU can differ. Efficiency of this policy shows up in the lower overall tax rate of 21.8 ECU/ton CO_2 compared to 23.5 ECU/ton CO_2 as the average rate under the coordinated policy. As production declines somewhat less (–0.35) than under the non-coordinated policy (–0.36), a lower level of production cannot be an explanation for the lower tax rate. The labor market dividend is somewhat reduced under a coordinated policy because tax revenues are lower. Less leisure and somewhat less consumption explain why the *EV* for the EU is lower under a coordinated policy. Although the overall performance for the EU does not change very much, for some countries a coordinated CO_2 policy matters. The labor force in countries with a low CO_2 tax under the non-coordinated policy, like Belgium and Greece, is pleased to have a higher uniform CO_2 tax. The additional revenue of this tax supports the labor market dividend. The labor force in countries with a high CO_2 tax under the non-coordinated policy is in turn not so fond of the coordinated policy. For Italy, for example, employment now increases by only 0.23 percent compared to 0.34 percent under the non-coordinated policy.

Another measure of efficiency is labor productivity. The change in output minus the change in labor input is –0.75 under the coordinated policy and –0.80 under the non-coordinated policy; that is, labor productivity declines more under the non-coordinated policy. However, all those efficiency arguments are buried by the welfare effect of more employment and a higher real wage rate, and hence of more leisure from persons now being employed, and of more consumption.

Our numerical results indicate that the beneficial efficiency impact from the reduction of pre-existing inefficiencies in taxing labor in the EU seems to be large enough to overcome the efficiency handicap of the narrow tax base of the CO_2 tax. However, our findings can also be linked to the factor mobility assumption made in the GEM-E3 model. The putty-clay approach used in this recursively dynamic model is based on the assumption that sectoral capital stocks are fixed within a single period. In such a situation the burden of the environmental tax falls partly on capital as stocks can adjust only gradually over time by depreciation and gross investment. Another explanation for the double dividend outcome can be the foreign trade specification and its para-meterization (elasticities of substitution in the Armington function).[27]

11.2 Global Warming and the Cost of Greenhouse Gas Emissions Control

Most efforts to study energy–economy–environment interactions using (mul-tiregional) CGE models address the problem of global warming. Examples in this field are the Nordhaus models DICE (Nordhaus, 1992), the Global 2100 model of Manne and Richels (1990, 1992), the MERGE model of Manne et al. (1995), the OECD model GREEN of Burniaux et al. (1992a, b), the model G-Cubed of McKibbin and Wilcoxen (1992b), the LEAN model by Welsch and Hoster (1995), and the EU model GEM-E3 (Capros et al., 1996).[28] Since space does not permit us to describe all the features of these models, we will make only some brief comments. The GEM-E3 model (Capros et al., 1996; Conrad and Schmidt 1998a, 1998b) is based on a disaggregated representation (11 industries) of 14 EU member state economies linked by trade flow matrices for each of the 11 goods considered. The model addresses problems of global warming and of acidification. Emissions of pollutants CO_2, SO_2 and NO_X are differentiated by country, sector of origin, type of fuel, and by goods (producers and consumers durable goods, and non-durable goods). A variety of policy instruments are used to affect transboundary air pollution, deposition, additive (end-of-pipe) and integrated (substitution) abatement.

Recent CGE models address the importance of international trade and financial flows in evaluating greenhouse gas (GHG) control costs. The topic is crucial in understanding GHG control costs not just because international trade and financial linkages are important, but also because the 1997 Kyoto Protocol requires different proportionate emission control efforts by the industrialized countries and no controls at all by developing countries. McKibbin et al. (1999) use an econometrically estimated multiregion, multisector CGE model of the world economy to examine the effects of using a system of internationally tradable emission permits to control CO_2 emissions. Their results show that international trade and capital flows significantly alter projections of the domestic effects of emissions mitigation policy, compared with analyses that ignore international capital flows. Since the USA has relatively low GHG abatement costs within the OECD, it could even be a net supplier of permits. Bernstein et al. (1999) also find significant aggregate gains from international emissions trading, with winners and losers depending on the nature of the trading regime (that is, only industrialized countries vs a global system involving China and India as well). Their CGE world model focuses on the international trade aspects of climate change policy, which include the distribution of impacts on economic welfare, international trade and investment across regions, the spillover effects of carbon emission limits and the effect of international emissions trading.

In principle, CGE models could also be used to study optimal GHG policies under the possibility of an irreversible global catastrophe. As temperature increases up to a threshold value, marginal damage increases sharply. The models which analyse possible catastrophic outcomes arising from global warming are small theoretical or numerical models where a catastrophic event is assumed to reduce the utility of consumption (or production).[29] Since precise knowledge and empirical evidence on catastrophic occurrences are lacking, there is no need to employ a full-scale CGE model.

11.3   Environmental Regulation and Economic Growth

Environmental regulation affects the supply side (marginal costs) and the demand side (abatement expenditure). In assessing the impact of environmental regulations on growth, Jorgenson and Wilcoxen (1990a) modify their basic model which implicitly includes environmental regulation in the 1970s and early 1980s, because it is based on historical data. Thus, to determine the effect of regulation on the performance of the US economy, they conduct counter-factual simulations in which regulation is removed. They found that the long-run cost of regulation is a reduction of 2.6 percent in the level of the US gross national product during the period 1973–85. Over this period the annual growth rate of the US economy has been reduced by 0.19 percent. Since the stringency of pollution control differs substantially among industries, their model also assesses the impact of environmental regulation on individual industries. For example, they find that the long-run output of the automobile industry has been reduced by 15 percent, mainly as a consequence of motor vehicle emissions controls.

11.4   Tradable Permits for CO2

When permits for air pollutants are introduced, the supply of permits is exogenous and the endogenous permit price equilibrates demand and the fixed supply. Whereas for taxes the recycling of revenues is an important issue, for permits it is not because the initial endowment is based on the grandfathering principle and not on auctioning the permits. For reasons of cost-effectiveness, a permit system for the European Union should be introduced and not separate, non-coordinated, country-specific systems in order to curb global CO_2 emissions. This topic was pursued in Conrad and Schmidt (1998a, 1998b, 1998c). The main emphasis of the analysis was laid on the national and EU-wide economic impacts of such a policy. In the non-coordinated case each country reduces 10 percent of its baseline CO_2 emissions: the permits are traded between sectors and households within the country. In the coordinated policy, the permits are traded between all European sectors and households to realize a 10 percent reduction of the EU's total CO_2 emissions. Curbing SO_2 emissions by introducing coordinated or non-coordinated pollution permit systems is also of interest. An EU-wide permit system for the electricity sector that is operational and in line with the requirements of the Oslo Protocol (convention of Transboundary Air Pollution) was introduced and national and EU-wide economic impacts were studied.

11.5   The Costs of Environmental Standards

Although most countries use technical standards to curb air pollutants, modeling the effect of market-based instruments is very popular among CGE model builders because they favor allocation through relative prices. The command-and-control approach can be based on technical restrictions, on concentration of an emission or on the use of an input. They affect the technology and hence the cost of production. A different CGE application is to measure the inefficiency of the present regulation by air quality standards by introducing taxes which warrant the same air quality (Conrad and Schröder, 1993). For measuring the cost-effectiveness of such a change in environmental policy, first a base run is produced based on present emission standards given by the air quality acts. These emission standards can be converted into permitted emissions per unit of input. Emissions considered are SO_2, NO_X and particulates. Simulations then show the economic impact of an efficient environmental policy in which all industries are confronted with uniform emission tax rates which have been computed so as to guarantee exactly the air quality under the base run with standards. This minimizes abatement costs given the quality of the air from the base run. The result was that real GNP in 1996 would have been higher by 0.6 percent and unemployment lower by 14 percent if emission taxes instead of standards had been introduced in 1988. In Goulder et al. (1999) a simple CGE model is used to compare the costs of command-and-control and incentive-based environmental policy instruments in the presence and absence of distortionary taxes.

11.6   Forestation and Deforestation

As the forest is a carbon sink if it absorbs more carbon than it releases through felling and natural decay, implementing the forests as carbon sinks in a CGE model is another topic. Persson and Munasinghe (1995) simulate the effect of government policies on Costa Rican forests to reduce deforestation. The allocation of property rights to forests results in a dramatic decrease in defor-estation and an increase in the net import of logs. Activity in the forest sector increases significantly because of the increase in imports of logs. Forests are multiple-use assets because if forest is used as a carbon sink, it cannot be used as a raw material in the pulp and paper industry. CGE models can evaluate the efficient use of forests as an intertemporal allocation problem (Pohjola, 1996).

11.7   Environmental Policies for Developing Countries

CGE models for developing economies can be used to analyze the links between growth and environment and between trade policies and the environment. Of special interest are efficient economic policies which can readily be imple-mented in the context of a developing country. At the OECD Development Centre CGE models for three Latin America economies (Chile, Costa Rica, Mexico), and three Asia Pacific economies (China, Indonesia, Vietnam) have been developed to shed light on the importance of these links, or on the main mechanisms through which changes in trade regimes have impact on the envi-ronment (Dessus et al., 1996). In international trade, for example, countries with less stringent environmental regulations may have comparative advantage in dirty industries. This leads to the export of 'pollution services' embodied in goods made with technologies that do not meet the environmental standards of the importing countries. Using a CGE model for Indonesia, Lee and Roland-Holst (1997) show that a combination of trade liberalization and a cost-effective tax policy would not only raise the country's welfare, but might also improve the environmental quality. Their results indicate that unilateral trade liberal-ization by Indonesia would increase the ratio of emission levels to real output for almost all major pollution categories. When tariff removal is combined with a cost-effective tax policy, then, however, the twin objectives of welfare enhancement and environmental quality improvement appear to be feasible. CGE models have also been used to project the effects of trade liberalization on the economy and the environment, concentrating especially on the issues of fertilizers and transportation or on tropical deforestation. Beghin et al. (1995) combine environmental and trade policies for Mexico and show how they interact.[30] Contrary to the common fear, economic integration of Mexico in the regional economy will not exacerbate environmental degradation. The pollution elasticity with respect to growth is very stable in Mexico (near unity) and trade orientation does not have much impact on the elasticity.

Interaction between environmental policies and trade policies is of interest not only for developing countries but also for Eastern European countries which are going to join the European Union. For these countries environmental regulations equivalent to those already introduced in the EU may affect their competitiveness and patterns of trade. The approach to measure these effects could follow Ho and Jorgenson (1998), who examined the impact of environmental regulations enacted in the 1960s and 1970s by projecting the evolution of the US economy with and without these regulations. Their approach consists of first running a base-case simulation designed to mimic the actual evolution of the US economy. The base-case simulation is a regime with pollution controls mandated by the environmental laws in place. To assess the impact of the controls, they perform counterfactual simulations where they are removed. That is, they calculate the path of the economy, including how the sectors evolve and how the trade pattern changes, had there been no environmental regulation in the USA before 1980. For the Eastern European countries the base-case simulation could be a regime with lax pollution controls.

11.8 Joint Implementation

International treaties on climate protection allow, in addition to domestic actions, for the supplementary use of flexible instruments in order to exploit cheaper emission reduction possibilities elsewhere. One concrete option for industrialized countries would be to enter joint implementation with developing countries such as India or China where the industrialized country pays emission reduction abroad rather than meeting its reduction target solely by domestic action. Joint implementation allows for the reduction of domestic emission taxes without adverse effects on the environmental dividend. In addition, joint implementation is typically based on technology transfer where the host demands investment goods by the donor, triggering direct positive employment effects for the latter. Based on CGE models for Germany and India, Böhringer et al. (2000) compare employment and welfare effects under a revenue-neutral environmental tax reform versus a tax reform cum joint implementation. The open question was whether an environmental tax reform in Germany combined with joint implementation in the Indian electricity sector could improve the prospect for a double dividend: not only that joint implementation would lower the level of emission taxes in Germany and thus reduce adverse effects on labor demand; but also investment demand for energy-efficient power plants produced in Germany would trigger positive employment effects in the German manufacturing industries. From the Indian perspective, joint implementation would equip its electricity industry with additional capital goods, leading to a more efficient power production with lower electricity prices for the economy. In their model analysis, revenue-neutral carbon taxes have a negative impact on employment in Germany; however, joint implementation can help to diminish this effect through the associated cost savings and additional investment demand from joint implementation with host countries.

11.9   Environmental Policy in Agriculture

Issues like agricultural chemicals, food safety and water quality have brought agriculture and nonpoint-source pollution to the forefront of environmental attention. Significant crop yield increases over the last several decades have been associated with the adoption of pesticides and fertilizers. At the same time, agricultural chemicals may impose economic costs on the environment and human health. Using a CGE model of the US economy, Hrubovcak et al. (1990) weigh such trade-offs for assessing the benefits and costs from integrating agricultural, environmental and food safety policies. They found that public policies designed to simultaneously satisfy farm income and environmental objectives face some serious challenges. Efforts to achieve a reduction in agricultural chemical use through taxes should impact chemical use and reduce environmental residuals. But output price and production uncertainties, coupled with uncertainties about the elasticities of substitution between key inputs, generate significant uncertainties about the beneficial environmental impacts.

12.   CGE MODELS WITH A TWO-WAY LINK BETWEEN THE ENVIRONMENT AND THE ECONOMY

Many environmentally related CGE models take into account that emissions and the accumulation of pollutants negatively affect the quality of the environment. In those models there is a one-way link between the development of economic variables and their generation of environmental externalities (Glomsrød et al., 1992; Ballard and Medema, 1993; Boyd et al., 1995, or Brendemoen and Vennemo, 1996). However, the quality of the environment also has an impact on the performance of economic variables. Models with a two-way link include in their simulation studies environmental feedbacks on labor productivity, capital depreciation and on the welfare of the consumer. Noise, traffic accidents and reduced air quality affect the welfare of the consumer as well as his labor productivity. Capital depreciation is negatively affected by the increase in corrosion caused by sulfur emissions or infrastructure capital by heavy traffic. Acidification of forests leads to decreased growth in forests and reduced recreational value. The objective of these studies is to develop a measure of green net national product and to show that growth in GDP or consumption is not equivalent to growth in welfare because of the effect of deterioration of the environment on welfare. CGE models which include the two-way link have been developed by Nordhaus (1994), Vennemo (1997), or Bergman and Hill (2000). In Nordhaus, the accumulation of CO_2 emissions increases the temperature of the earth, which harms production. In Vennemo's DREAM model external effects of economic activity are evaluated in terms of their costs on the economy. Damage estimates have been produced for acidification of lakes and of forests, for health and annoyance from emissions of NO_X, SO_2, CO_2 and particulates, for corrosion, noise, traffic accidents, congestion and road depreciation. In his simulation experiment he finds that the feedback on environmental quality is much more significant for consumer welfare than the feedback in the form of increased depreciation and a decline in productivity. Bergman and Hill model productivity effects of environmental stock and flow pollution by including damage effects from pollution accumulation on production. To model the feedback effects, the resource endowments are included in the model and the externality is linked to these endowments. The model assesses the effects that the inclusion of feedback mechanisms and the use of defensive expenditure might have on GDP and on consumption. It turns out that the positive productivity effects of proposed emission reductions are smaller than the costs of attaining these emission reductions. The feedback of traffic and congestion on economic variables is another externality-related aspect which has been modeled by Conrad and Heng (2000) using a CGE model for Germany. In a baseline scenario it is shown how congestion and its costs will develop over time given the present bottlenecks in road infrastructure. The present stock of trucks and private cars deviates from the capacity-related stocks, which results in a congestion index. This index affects the efficiency of firm-owned trucks and of trucks owned by the transportation industry. The reduced efficiency raises the cost of transportation in the economy due to costs of the substitutes for truck transportation and labor cost paid during congestion. Congestion due to the insufficient provision of infrastructure and the negative externality effect from the growth in truck transportation raises the prices in the economy and generates a non-optimal allocation of resources. Given the necessity to act, the fuel tax is raised in the model partly to finance infrastructure investment. The costs of the addition in infrastructure are then compared with the savings in congestion costs in order to see whether such a policy measure is self-financing. It turned out that the savings in congestion costs exceed by 50 percent the costs of the addition in infrastructure investment.

The specifications chosen by the authors are very pragmatic and some features are given next.

12.1   Nordhaus

Environmental feedback on output X with D as the loss in output is

$$\frac{D(t)}{X(t)} = \theta_1 \cdot T(t)^{\theta_2},$$

where T is temperature change and θ_1, θ_2 are parameters. Abatement costs TC are:

$$\frac{TC(t)}{X(t)} = b_1 \mu(t)^{b_2},$$

where μ is the degree of abatement and b_1, b_2 are parameters. Combining the loss in output and cost relationships, a feedback relationship Ω of global warming on productivity can be derived:

$$\Omega(t) = \frac{\left(1 - b_1 \mu(t)^{b_2}\right)}{\left[1 + \theta_1 T(t)^{\theta_2}\right]}.$$

It comprises damage and cost effects in one term and enters a production function

$$X(t) = \Omega(t) \cdot A(t) \cdot K(t)^{\gamma} \cdot L(t)^{1-\gamma}.$$

12.2   Vennemo

There is a health-induced productivity index h:

$$h = h(F), \ h' < 0,$$

where F is fuel oil consumption.

A capital depreciation rate σ also depends on fuel consumption:

$$\sigma = \sigma(F), \ \sigma'(F) > 0.$$

An index of intertemporal utility U captures the two-way link:

$$U = \frac{P_0}{P}\left(W_{-1} - D\right) + D_0,$$

where $P(P_0)$ is an intertemporal price index of wealth (baseline scenario), W_{-1} is household wealth and $D(D_0)$ is value of negative externalities (baseline scenario).

12.3　Bergman and Hill

A link between the accumulated sulfur and nitrogen stock, S, and the forest endowment is expressed as:

$$NR_t = f_t(S_t) \cdot NR_{0,t},$$

where f_t is a linear function of the stocks and NR_t is the actual annual harvest from the forest resource at time t ($NR_{0,t}$ is the path from the baseline scenario).

Feedback on labor productivity is modeled as:

$$L_t^{Tot} = \bar{L} - \gamma^{NO_x} \cdot \left(F_t^{NO_x} - \bar{F}^{NO_x}\right) \cdot L_{0,t}^{Tot},$$

where L_t^{Tot} is aggregate efficient labor endowment at time t and $L_{0,t}^{Tot}$ is the baseline scenario path. $\bar{F}_t^{NO_x}$ is the pollution flow level of the pollutant below which there is no negative impact on aggregate labor productivity, and $F_t^{NO_x}$ the simulated pollution flow level ($\bar{L}$ is unadjusted labor endowment and γ^{NO_x} is a positive parameter chosen in the calibration process).

12.4　Conrad and Heng

The stock of transportation equipment by n firms and private households ($n + 1$) affects an index Z of congestion:

$$Z = \exp\left(\frac{\alpha}{KI^*}\right)\prod_{k=1}^{n+1}\left(\frac{KT_k^0}{\overline{KT}_k^0}\right)^{\beta_k}, \quad \alpha > 0.$$

KI^* is an optimal provision of infrastructure which minimizes transportation costs in the economy subject to a financial constraint. The exponential term measure the shortage in infrastructure capacity and converges to one from above if $KI \to \infty$. KT_k^0 is the stock of transportation capital in industry k and $\overline{KT}_k^0$ is the lower stock related to the present quality and quantity of the infrastructure network. The parameter β_k measure the contribution of trucks in industry k to the congestion externality which affects the cost of production of each industry. Each industry has transportation costs CT in its nested input structure which are expressed as a short-run, variable sub-cost function

$$CT = CT(T, PT_1, PT_2, PT_3, KT^e),$$

where PT_i are the prices of the substitutes for transport services from firm-owned trucks ($i = 1$: road transportation; $i = 2$: waterways; $i = 3$: railways). T is the transport volume and KT^e is the quasi-fixed transportation capital input in terms of firm-owned trucks defined as

$$KT^e = KT(KT^0, KI) \cdot Z^{\varepsilon}$$

where $\varepsilon < 0$ is the elasticity of effective transportation capital with respect to the index of congestion, Z. Infrastructure KI affects the utilization of the stock KT^0 and reduces congestion. Partial derivative of the cost function with respect to KT^0 measures as an *ex-post* or shadow price of capital the benefit of having one more unit of the stock KT^0. It expresses the savings in the variable cost of transportation by having one additional truck given the transportation volume T. Using this price, congestion costs caused by each industry can be calculated, which could then be reduced by investing in infrastructure.

13.   LIMITATIONS OF CGE MODELS AND OUTLOOK OF FUTURE RESEARCH

Given the challenge of more restrictive environmental regulation in the near future, it is becoming more and more important to quantify the costs of such a policy. CGE models are becoming a widely used tool for quantifying the costs and benefits of environmental policies. CGE models are not intended to forecast the values of economic variables, but rather to provide useful insights that may help policy-makers to undertake more informed policy actions. Since they cannot be used for forecasts, CGE modelers are not compelled to compare their results with outcomes of policy changes in the world. They use the current theory and produce results from changes in the structure of the economy or of a policy experiment which cannot be falsified. This problem results also from the fact that not many CGE models have a very solid empirical basis. Since CGE experiments analyze the results of actual reforms rather than hypothetical ones, it is important to improve the empirical assessment of these models. Since most CGE models are calibrated and not econometrically estimated, simulation experiments are required to check the robustness of the results given the limited quality of the deterministic calibration. Since CGE models are based on assumptions concerning the economic development (elasticities of substitution and transformation, technical change, exogenous variables), it would be misleading to base policy decisions on a specific numerical result. Stochastic simulation studies can be thought of as a statistical form of sensitivity analysis which can generate a distribution of possible outcomes through 'Monte Carlo' methods.

An extension often mentioned in survey articles is research on specifying alternative market structures in CGE models. With a few exceptions (Harris, 1984), most models assume that all markets are competitive. However, there is not one but many models of imperfect competition and eventually it becomes less obvious what has driven the model and its results. The same argument holds for modeling disequilibria in some markets of the economy. We know that disequilibria exist in the labor market and in the market for physical capital, and that changes in unemployment or in the utilization of capacities are often the short-run consequences of sudden changes in the magnitude of an environmental policy instrument. In such cases some model builders modify their approaches by allowing explicitly for partial disequilibria in the labor and capital markets by adopting theories on under- or over-utilization of the primary factors of production. In principle, economic theory offers a variety of possibilities for future research: imperfect competition; endogenous technical change; adjustment costs in the labor market and in capacity formation; the role of infrastructure; uncertainty in supply of non-renewable resources, and so on. However, the more complicated the model, the more it becomes a black box. Since no model can completely represent reality, a choice has to be made about what key features are to be included in any modeling approach.

NOTES

1. I wish to thank Henk Folmer, Larry Goulder, Sjak Smulders and Tom Tietenberg for their many suggestions on an earlier version of this paper.
2. See Krutilla (1999) on the usefulness of partial equilibrium models in the context of trade and the environment and Bovenberg and Goulder (2001) for a survey of the imp lications of general equilibrium interactions for environmental tax and regulatory policies.

3. See Ierland (1999) for a survey on macroeconomic modeling and the environment, and Duchin and Steenge (1999) for a survey on input–output analysis of the environment.
4. For a survey on the development of CGE modeling see Shoven and Whalley (1984), Robinson (1989), Bergman (1990a) or Conrad (1999).
5. I will also not discuss theoretical issues like uniqueness of a general equilibrium or externalities as a source of nonconvexity. Under concavity – convexity assumptions Pareto optimality in a basic general equilibrium model with externalities exists and is unique (see Baumol and Oates, 1988, ch. 4). The existence of a competitive solution that is consistent with any particular Pareto optimum has been explored in an extensive literature. The question is, however, whether in GE models calibrated on real-world data nonexistence is a serious problem. A proof of existence of, and computational procedure for finding, a general equilibrium with taxes was derived by Shoven and Whalley (1973). A more serious problem is that any detrimental externalities can produce nonconvexity. This breakdown in the concavity–convexity conditions may result in several local optima so that prices may give the wrong signals – directing the economy away from the social optimum.
6. For alternative closure rules see Dewatripont and Michel (1987).
7. See Bovenberg and Goulder (1991) on introducing intertemporal features in CGE models. For CGE models where investment decisions are based on maximizing the value of the firm see Goulder (1995), Goulder and Summers (1989), Keuschnigg and Kohler (1994) or Vennemo (1997).
8. Several assumptions are possible about the dividend and financing policy of a firm which we will not discuss here.
9. We assume that all tax rates on capital income are of equal size.
10. An example in this context is the issue whether capital is assumed to be perfectly mobile across sectors (as in Jorgenson and Wilcoxen, 1990b), or imperfectly mobile (because of adjustment costs, as in Bovenberg and Goulder, 1991)). This can be very important to how the economy responds to a policy shock, and to the welfare impacts.
11. This is only one (frequently used) way to model intertemporal consumer behavior.
12. Conrad and Schröder (1991b) developed an integrated framework of consumer demand for 20 non-durable goods like food and services, and for three durable goods: cars, heating and electric appliances.
13. The same concept is used in the GEM-E3 model.
14. The GEM-E3 model is not based on that assumption (see Capros et al., 1996 and Conrad and Schmidt, 1998c).
15. To simplify the notation we omit an index j for the industry.
16. In our presentation we omit taxes and customs duties.
17. The adjustment of the distribution parameter d_E for energy in the CES cost function after the decay of retired vintages and the inclusion of new vintages is then

$$d_{E,t+1}^{\sigma} = \frac{1}{1+g}\left[d_{E,j}^{\sigma}(1-\delta)+(g+\delta)\theta_{E,t}^{\sigma}\right].$$

18. For a CGE application see Conrad and Ehrlich (1993).
19. For the definition of the capital stock in efficiency units see Solow (1959) and Berndt et al. (1993).
20. For an extension of this model with two channels for knowledge accumulation (R&D and learning by doing) see Goulder and Mathai (2000). In this model a social planner chooses optimal paths of carbon abatement and carbon taxes taking into account the impact of taxes on technological progress and future abatement costs. The stock of technological knowledge enters the production function and, at the same time, affects the emission output ratio.
21. With $C(d) = c(d) \cdot d$, then $C'' = c''(d)d + 2c'(d) > 0$.
22. For a state-of-the art review on the double dividend issue see Goulder (1997) and Bovenberg and Goulder (2001).

23. For theoretical papers on the double dividend issue see Bovenberg and Goulder (1996); Goulder (1995). For empirical papers see Jorgenson and Wilcoxen (1992), Proost and van Regemorter (1995) and Welsch (1996).
24. See Bovenberg and Goulder (2001) on this point.
25. This dividend cannot be quantified by our model because our utility function underlying the *EV* (see section 5) does not include the amenities from the environment.
26. Favorable recycling results are also obtained by Jorgenson and Wilcoxen (1992). Recycling fails in Bovenberg and Goulder (1997), Goulder (1995) and Proost and van Regemorter (1995).
27. A detailed discussion on why GEM-E3 produces a double dividend is given in Conrad and Schmidt (1999).
28. For a more detailed summary of models for studying environmental policy effects see Jorgenson and Wilcoxen (1993).
29. See Gjerde et al. (1999) for such a model.
30. See Steininger (1999) for a survey on general models to analyze international trade aspects under environmental regulation.

REFERENCES

Armington, P.S. (1969), 'The Geographic Pattern of Trade and the Effect of Price Changes', FMF, *Staff Papers*, **58**, 179–201.
Auerbach, A.J. and L.J. Kotlikoff (1987), *Dynamic Fiscal Policy*, Cambridge: Cambridge University Press.
Ballard, C.L. and S.G. Medema (1993), 'The Marginal Efficiency Effects of Taxes and Subsidies in the Presence of Externalities – A CGE Approach', *Journal of Public Economics*, **52**, 199–216.
Baumol, W.J. and W.E. Oates (1988), *The Theory of Environmental Policy*, 2nd edn, Cambridge: Cambridge University Press.
Beghin, J., D. Roland-Holst and D. van der Mensbrugghe (1995), 'Trade Liberalization and the Environment in the Pacific Basin: Coordinated Approaches to Mexican Trade and Environment Policy', *American Journal of Agricultural Economics*, **77**, 778–85.
Bergh, J.C.J.M. van den (ed.) (1999), *Handbook of Environmental and Resource Economics*, Cheltenham, UK and Northampton, USA: Edward Elgar.
Bergman, L. (1990a), 'The Development of Computable General Equilibrium Modeling', in L. Bergman, D.W. Jorgenson and E. Zalai (eds), *General Equilibrium Modeling and Economic Policy Analysis*, Oxford: Basil Blackwell, pp. 3–30.
Bergman, L. (1990b), 'Energy and Environmental Constraints on Growth: A CGE Modeling Approach', *Journal of Policy Modeling*, **12**(4), 671–91.
Bergman, L. and M. Hill (2000), 'Productivity and Growth Effects of Acidification: A Dynamic CGE Modeling Study of Sweden', Discussion Paper, Stockholm School of Economics.
Berndt, E., C. Kolstad and J.-K. Lee (1993), 'Measuring the Energy Efficiency and Productivity Impacts of Embodied Technical Change', *Energy Journal*, **14**(1), 33–55.
Bernstein, P.M., W.D. Montgomery and T.F. Rutherford (1999),' Global Impact of the Kyoto Agreement: Results from the MS–MRT Model', *Resource and Energy Economics*, **21**, 375–413.
Böhringer, C., K. Conrad and A. Löschel (2000), 'Carbon Taxes and Joint Implementation – An Applied CGE Analysis for Germany and India', ZEW Discussion Paper, Mannheim.

Bovenberg, A.L. and L.H. Goulder (1991), 'Introducing intertemporal and open economy features in applied general equilibrium models', in F.J.H. Don et al. (eds), *Applied General Equilibrium Modelling*, Dordrecht: Kluwer, pp. 47–64.

Bovenberg, A.L. and L.H. Goulder (1996), 'Optimal Environmental Taxation in the Presence of Other Taxes: General Equilibrium Analysis', *American Economic Review*, **86**(4), 985–1000.

Bovenberg, A.L. and L.H. Goulder (1997), 'Costs of Environmentally Motivated Taxes in the Presence of Other Taxes: General Equilibrium Analyses', *National Tax Journal*, **50**(1), 59–88.

Bovenberg, A.L. and L.H. Goulder (2001), 'Environmental Taxation and Regulation in a Second-Best Setting', in A. Auerbach and M. Feldstein (eds), *Handbook of Public Economics*, 2nd edn, Amsterdam: North-Holland.

Boyd, R., K. Krutilla and W.K. Viscusi (1995), 'Energy Taxation as a Policy to Reduce CO_2-Emissions – A Net Benefit Analysis', *Journal of Environmental Economics and Management*, **29**, 1–24.

Brendemoen, A. and H. Vennemo (1996), 'The Marginal Cost of Funds in the Presence of Environmental Externalities', *Scandinavian Journal of Economics*, **98**, 405–22.

Burniaux, J.-M., J.P. Martin, G. Nicoletti and J.O. Martins (1992a), 'The Cost of Reducing CO_2 Emissions: Evidence from GREEN', OECD Working Paper No. 115.

Burniaux, J.-M., J.P. Martin, G. Nicoletti and J.O. Martins (1992b), 'GREEN: A Multi-Sector, Multi-Region General Equilibrium Model for Quantifying the Costs of Curbing CO_2 Emissions: A Technical Manual', OECD Working Paper No. 116.

Capros, P., G. Georgakopoulos, S. Zografakis, S. Proost, D. van Regemorter, K. Conrad, T. Schmidt and Y. Smeers (1996), 'Double Dividend Analysis: First Results of a General Equilibrium Model (GEM-E3) Linking the EU-12 Countries', in C. Carraro et al. (eds), *Environmental Fiscal Reform and Unemployment*, Dordrecht: Kluwer, pp. 193–227.

Carraro, C. and M. Galeotti (1994), 'WARM (World Assessment of Resource Management)', Technical Report, GRETA, Venice.

Conrad, K. (1999), 'Computable General Equilibrium Models for Environmental Economics and Policy Analysis', in J.C.J.M. van den Bergh, (ed.), *Handbook of Environmental and Resource Economics*, Cheltenham, UK and Northampton, USA: Edward Elgar, ch. 69.

Conrad, K. and M. Ehrlich (1993), 'The Impact of Embodied and Disembodied Technical Progress on Productivity Gaps – An AGE Analysis for Germany and Spain', *Journal of Productivity Analysis*, **4**, 317–35.

Conrad, K. and S. Heng (2000), 'Financing Road Infrastructure by Savings in Congestion Costs: A CGE Analysis', *The Annals of Regional Science*, forthcoming.

Conrad, K., and I. Henseler-Unger (1986), 'Applied General Equilibrium Modeling for Longterm Energy Policy in the Fed. Rep. of Germany', *Journal of Policy Modeling*, **8** (4), 531–49.

Conrad, K. and T. Schmidt (1998a), 'National Economic Impacts of an EU Environmental Policy – An AGE Analysis', in S. Proost and J. Braden (eds), *Climate Change, Transport and Environmental Policy*, Cheltenham, UK and Northampton, USA: Edward Elgar, pp. 48–77.

Conrad, K. and T. Schmidt (1998b), 'The International Policy Dimension of Sustainability – the Effect of Policy Harmonization within the EU using the GEM-E3 Model', in J. van den Bergh and M.W. Hofkes (eds), *Theory and Implementation of Economic Models for Sustainable Development*, Dordrecht: Kluwer, pp. 287–316.

Conrad, K. and T. Schmidt (1998c), 'Economic Effects of a Uncoordinated vs. a Coordinated CO$_2$-Policy in the EU – An AGE Analysis', *Economic System Research*, **10**(2), 161–82.

Conrad, K. and T. Schmidt (1999), 'Double Dividend of Climate Protection and the Role of International Policy Coordination in the EU – An AGE Analysis with the GEM-E3 Model', in O. Hohmeyer and K. Rennings (eds), *Man-Made Climate Change*, ZEW Economic Studies, Heidelberg: Physica.

Conrad, K. and M. Schröder (1991a), 'An Evaluation of Taxes on Air Pollutants Emissions: An AGE-approach', *Schweizerische Zeitschrift für Volkswirtschaft und Statistik*, **127**, 199–224.

Conrad, K. and M. Schröder (1991b), 'The Control of CO$_2$-emissions and its Economic Impact', *Environmental and Resource Economics*, **1**, 289–312.

Conrad, K. and M. Schröder (1991c), 'Demand for durable and non-durable goods, environmental policy and consumer welfare', *Journal of Applied Econometrics*, **6**, 271–86.

Conrad, K. and M. Schröder (1993), 'Environmental Policy Instruments using General Equilibrium Models', *Journal of Policy Modeling*, **15**, 521–43.

Dessus, S., D. Roland-Holst and D. van der Mensbrughe (1996), 'General Equilibrium Modelling of Trade and the Environment', Technical Paper No. 116, OECD Development Centre, Paris, September.

Dewatripont, M. and G. Michel (1987), 'On Closure Rules, Homogeneity and Dynamics in AGE models', *Journal of Development Economics*, **26**, 65–76.

Duchin, F. and A.E. Steenge (1999), 'Input–Output Analysis, Technology and the Environment', in J.C.J.M. van den Bergh, (ed.), *Handbook of Environmental and Resource Economics*, Cheltenham, UK and Northampton, USA: Edward Elgar, ch. 68.

Gjerde, J., S. Grepperud and S. Kverndokk (1999), 'Optimal Climate Policy under the Possibility of a Catastrophe', *Resource and Energy Economics*, **21**, 289–317.

Glomsrød, S., H. Vennemo and T. Johnsen (1992), 'Stabilization of Emissions of CO$_2$: A Computable General Equilibrium Assessment', *Scandinavian Journal of Economics*, **94**(1), 53–69.

Goulder, L.H. (1995), 'Effects of Carbon Taxes in an Economy with Prior Tax Distortions: An Intertemporal General Equilibrium Analysis', *Journal of Environmental Economics and Management*, **29**, 271–97.

Goulder, L.H. (1997), 'Environmental Taxation in a Second-Best World', in H. Folmer and T. Tietenberg (eds), *The International Yearbook of Environmental and Resource Economics*, Cheltenham, UK and Lyme, USA: Edward Elgar.

Goulder, L.H. and K. Mathai (2000), 'Optimal CO$_2$ Abatement in the Presence of Induced Technological Change', *Journal of Environmental Economics and Management*, **39**, 1–38.

Goulder, L.H. and S.H. Schneider (1999), 'Induced Technological Change and the Attractiveness of CO$_2$ Abatement Policies', *Resource and Energy Economics*, **21**, 211–53.

Goulder, L.H. and L.H. Summers (1989), 'Tax Policy, Asset Prices, and Growth: A General Equilibrium Analysis', *Journal of Public Economics*, **38**, 265–96.

Goulder, L.H., I.W.H. Parry, R.C. Williams and D. Burtraw (1999), 'The Cost-Effectiveness of Alternative Instruments for Environmental Protection in a Second-Best Setting', *Journal of Public Economics*, **72**, 329–60.

Harris, R. (1984), 'AGE Analysis of Small Open Economies with Scale Economies and Imperfect Competition', *American Economic Review*, **74**, 1016–32.

Hazilla, M. and R.J. Kopp (1990), 'Social Cost of Environmental Quality Regulations: A General Equilibrium Analysis', *Journal of Political Economy*, **98**(4), 853–73.

Ho, M.S. and D.W. Jorgenson (1998), 'Environmental Regulation and U.S. Trade', in D.W. Jorgenson (ed.), *Growth, Vol. 2: Energy, the Environment and Economic Growth*, Cambridge, MA: MIT Press.

Hrubovcak, J., M. Le Blanc and J. Miranowski (1990), 'Limitations in Evaluating Environmental and Agricultural Policy Coordination Benefits', *American Economic Review*, **80**, 208–12.

Hudson, E.A. and D.W. Jorgenson (1974), 'U.S. Energy Policy and Economic Growth, 1975–2000', *Bell Journal of Economic and Management Science*, **5**, 461–514.

Ierland, E.C. van (1999), 'Environment in Macroeconomic Modelling', in J.C.J.M. van den Bergh (ed.) *Handbook of Environmental and Resource Economics*, Cheltenham, UK and Northampton, USA: Edward Elgar, ch. 41.

Johansen, L. (1979), *A Multisectoral Study of Economic Growth*, Amsterdam: North-Holland.

Jorgenson, D.W. and P.J. Wilcoxen (1990a), 'Environmental regulation and U.S. economic growth', *The Rand Journal of Economics*, **21**, 314–40.

Jorgenson, D.W. and P.J. Wilcoxen (1990b), 'Intertemporal General Equilibrium Modeling of U.S. Environmental Regulation', *Journal of Policy Modeling*, **12**, 715–44.

Jorgenson, D.W. and P.J. Wilcoxen (1992), 'Reducing U.S. Carbon Dioxide Emissions: The Cost of Different Goals', in J.R. Moroney (ed.), *Energy, Growth, and Environment: Advances in the Economics of Energy and Resources*, **7**, JAI Press, pp. 125–58.

Jorgenson, D.W. and P.J. Wilcoxen (1993), 'Energy, the Environment and Economic Growth', in A.V. Kneese and J.L. Sweeney (eds), *Handbook of Natural Resources and Energy Economics*, Vol. 3, Amsterdam: North-Holland, ch. 27.

Keuschnigg, C. and W. Kohler (1994), 'Modeling Intertemporal General Equilibrium: An Application to Austrian Commercial Policy', *Empirical Economics*, **19**, 131–64.

Krutilla, K. (1999), 'Partial Equilibrium Models of Trade and the Environment', in J.C.J.M. van den Bergh (ed.), *Handbook of Environmental and Resource Economics*, Cheltenham, UK and Northampton, USA: Edward Elgar, ch. 27.

Lee, H. and D. Roland-Holst (1997), 'The Environment and Welfare Implications of Trade and Tax Policy', *Journal of Development Economics*, **52**, 65–82.

Manne, A.S. and R.G. Richels (1990), 'CO_2 Emission Limits: An Economic Analysis for the USA', *The Energy Journal*, **11**(2), 51–74.

Manne, A.S. and R.G. Richels (1992), *Buying Greenhouse Insurance – The Economic Costs of CO_2 Emission Limits*, Cambridge, MA: MIT Press.

Manne, A.S., R. Mendelsohn and R. Richels (1995), 'MERGE: A Model for Evaluating Regional and Global Effects of GHG Reduction Policies', *Energy Policy*, **23**, 17–34.

McKibbin, W.J. and P.J. Wilcoxen (1992a), 'The Global Costs of Policies to Reduce Greenhouse Gas Emissions', Brookings Discussion Papers, No. 97, The Brookings Institution, October.

McKibbin, W.J. and P.J. Wilcoxen (1992b), 'G-Cubed: A Dynamic Multi-Sector General Equilibrium Model of the Global Economy (Quantifying the Costs of Curbing CO_2 Emissions)', Brookings Discussion Papers, No. 98, Brookings Institution, November.

McKibbin, W.J. R. Shackleton and P.J. Wilcoxen (1999), 'What to Expect from an International System of Tradable Permits for Carbon Emissions', *Resource and Energy Economics*, **21**, 319–46.

Mercenier, J. (1995), 'Nonuniqueness of Solutions in Applied General Equilibrium Models with Scale Economies and Imperfect Competition', *Economic Theory*, **6**, 161–77.

Nordhaus, W.D. (1992), 'The DICE Model: Background and Structure of a Dynamic Integrated Climate – Economy Model of the Economics of Global Warming', Cowles Foundation Discussion Paper No. 1009, New Haven, Yale University.

Nordhaus, W.D. (1994), 'Rolling the "DICE": An Optimal Transition Path for Controlling Greenhouse Gases', *Resource and Energy Economics*, **15**, 27–50.

Nordhaus, W.D. (1999), 'Modeling Induced Innovation in Climate-Change Policy', paper presented at the IIASA Workshop on Induced Technological Change and the Environment, Laxenburg, 21–22 June.

Persson A. and M. Munasinghe (1995), 'Natural Resource Management and Economywide Policies in Costa Rica: A Computable General Equilibrium (CGE) Modeling Approach', *The World Bank Economic Review*, **9**(2), 259–85.

Pohjola, J. (1996), 'Integrating Forests as Carbon Sinks in a CGE Framework: A Preliminary Analysis for Finland', paper presented at the Meeting of the European Association of Environment and Resource Economists, Lisbon.

Proost, S. and D. van Regemorter (1995), 'The Double Dividend and the Role of Inequality Aversion and Macroeconomic Regimes', *International Tax and Public Finance*, **2**, 207–19.

Robinson, S. (1989), 'Multisectoral Models', in H. Chenery and T.N. Srinivasan (eds), *Handbook of Development Economics*, Vol. 2, Elsevier Science Publishers B.V., pp. 885–947.

Romer, P.M. (1990), 'Endogenous Technical Change', *Journal of Political Economy*, **98**, 71–102.

Rutherford, T.F. (1999), 'Carbon Abatement in Denmark: Technical Change and Intergenerational Burden Sharing', Discussion Paper, Mobi DK and University of Colorado.

Samuelson, P.A. (1951), 'Abstract of a Theorem Concerning Substitutability in Open Leontief Models', in T.C. Koopmans (ed.), *Activity Analysis of Production and Allocation*, New York: Wiley, pp. 142–46.

Samuelson, P.A. (1953), 'Prices of Factors and Goods in General Equilibrium', *Review of Economic Studies*, **21**, 1–20.

Shephard, R.W. (1953), *Cost and Production Functions*, Princeton, NJ.

Shoven, J.B. and J. Whalley (1973), 'General Equilibrium with Taxes: A Computation Procedure and an Existence Proof', *Review of Economics Studies*, **60**, 475–90.

Shoven, J.B. and J. Whalley (1984), 'AGE Models of Taxation and International Trade: An Introduction and Survey', *Journal of Economic Literature*, **22**, 1007–51.

Solow, R.M. (1959), 'Investment and Technical Progress', in K.J. Arrow et al. (eds), *Mathematical Methods in the Social Sciences*.

Steininger, K.W. (1999), 'General Models of Environmental Policy and Foreign Trade', in J.C.J.M. van den Bergh (ed.), *Handbook of Environmental and Resource Economics*, Cheltenham, UK and Northampton, USA: Edward Elgar, ch. 28.

Tobin, J. (1969), 'A General Equilibrium Approach to Monetary Theory', *Journal of Money, Credit, and Banking*, **1**, 15–29.

Vennemo, H. (1997), 'A Dynamic Applied General Equilibrium Model with Environmental Feedbacks', *Economic Modeling*, **14**, 99–154.

Welsch, H. and F. Hoster (1995), 'A General Equilibrium Analysis of European Carbon/Energy Taxation: Model Structure and Macroeconomic Results', *Zeitschrift für Wirtschafts- und Sozialwissenschaften*, **115**, 275–303.
Welsch, H. (1996), 'Recycling of Carbon/Energy Taxes and the Labor Market – A General Equilibrium Analysis for the European Community', *Environmental and Resource Economics*, **8**, 141–55.
Whalley, J. and R. Wigle (1991), 'Cutting CO_2 Emissions: the Effects of Alternative Policy Approaches', *The Energy Journal*, **12**, 109–24.
Willenbockel, D. (1994), *Applied General Equilibrium Modeling – Imperfect Competition and European Integration*, Chichester, UK: Wiley.

3. The use of hedonic property value techniques for policy and litigation

Raymond B. Palmquist and V. Kerry Smith*

1. INTRODUCTION – 'EVERYTHING HAS A PRICE'

Surely, an economist promoted this perspective on life. Nonetheless, if 'price' is defined as the opportunity cost of a decision, few observers would debate the fact that choice in the presence of scarcity has always implied dealing with trade-offs. There have been many efforts to quantify (in monetary terms) the trade-offs people are willing to make and to use that information in both the policy-making process and in public litigation. This chapter focuses on applications of hedonic methods to this quantification. We will show that economic analysis has had an impact on the evaluation of environmental policy, as well as a marked effect on litigation. This view is somewhat different from the more guarded conclusions developed recently by two prominent economists. The first of these is closer to ours. Oates (2000) recently reviewed the role of economics on policy design and noted:

> it is difficult to lay out neatly the ways in which economic research has influenced environmental policy. I can find no well-defined process of diffusion here, but there surely has been an important impact. (p. 153)

Writing a little earlier, Hahn (1999) judges a less dramatic effect:

> In sum, the impact of economists on environmental policy to date has been modest. Economists can claim credit for having helped change the terms of the debate to include economic instruments – no small feat. They can also claim some credit for legislation that promotes greater balancing of costs and benefits. But specific victories of consequence are few and far between. (pp. 22–3)

No economist would argue that economic criteria should be the exclusive basis for public policy decisions. Instead, most would probably suggest that economic analysis, whether of policy instruments (including incentive-based approaches) or of the net benefits of a new regulation, should have a 'place at the table.' In most cases today, it has! To be sure, at times economists are struggling to deliver useful information, but we are not in the days when economic evaluations were conducted long after policies were promulgated. Environmental economists provide a somewhat different viewpoint on policy evaluation. Consideration of the details of how economics contributes to measuring the benefits and costs of proposed policies and the indirect influence such analyses have in 'feeding back' to the redesign of the policies can reveal the contributions of economists. This paper does not address all aspects of this issue. Instead, we hope to examine some specific cases where hedonic methods have been used and made a contribution, and to discuss the reasons that the methods have had less impact in some other areas.

The hedonic price model is one of the most widely accepted methods for estimating the monetary trade-offs for quality attributes of private goods and spatially delineated environmental amenities. This framework maintains that the prices of closely related heterogeneous goods are associated with measures of the attributes distinguishing those goods. A visit to the Bureau of Labor Statistics' (BSL) website confirms the widespread use of this logic in evaluating the prices for everything, from different hairdryers to diverse camcorders or DVD players.[1] Hedonic price functions are a part of the routine quality adjustment practices of the BLS in developing cost-of-living indexes such as the Consumer Price Index.

The hedonic method has enjoyed wide acceptance in environmental applications as well. While most of these studies have been associated with air pollution (see Smith and Huang, 1995 for a summary and meta-analysis), a range of site amenities has been studied. Hedonic theory and techniques have been widely discussed.[2] With these available summaries of the theory and practice of hedonic models, it is not clear we 'need' another review of the literature.

Our focus is on how the hedonic method has been used in practice, outside the scrutiny of publication, in policy evaluations as well as in public litigation. To provide this perspective, we combine published articles along with unpublished sources – government and expert reports along with personal experience. We also include some of the 'behind-the-scenes' stories of how hedonic modeling has been used to 'price' the outputs of policy or to estimate the monetary damages of environmental injuries.

Section 2 provides some historical context for the diverse origins of the model. Section 3 outlines the various property value techniques to set the stage for the rest of the chapter. Our emphasis is on benefit measurement with these models since that is the element most relevant to policy or litigation. Section 4 discusses how the method has been part of policy evaluations and selects two examples to describe the issues that can arise when hedonic analysis is selected to evaluate environmental policy. Section 5 follows a comparable strategy and selects two examples where hedonic results have been part of experts' damage assessments in public litigation. In these profiled examples, our objective is to show how the uses and interpretation of hedonic results differ from what can be found published in studies. The sixth section describes how hedonic techniques have evolved in response to the need to study new environmental issues, and the last section provides a summary and some speculations about the future.

2. THE CONTEXT FOR ENVIRONMENTAL APPLICATIONS OF HEDONIC METHODS

Hedonic price functions have occurred in economics for at least 70 years. Most observers credit Waugh (1929) as the first to introduce them in his Ph.D. thesis research on methods to adjust the prices of various vegetables (for example, asparagus, tomatoes and hothouse cucumbers) for those characteristics that were presumed to be related to quality.[3] Their role in price indexes became more widely appreciated through the 1959 Stigler Commission that included in its subsequently published report Griliches's (1961) proposal to use hedonic price indexes to adjust for quality change.[4]

It took some time before this approach would be used to measure the role of positive and negative site attributes for residential locations through property markets. In the mid-1960s, before the existence of the US Environmental Protection Agency and before major federal environmental legislation, research on using property values to reveal the willingness to pay for air quality was under way, funded by federal agencies. The Division of Air Pollution in the US Public Health Service supported a research effort on the costs of air pollution headed by Ronald Ridker with the assistance of several other economists.[5] Arguably the most important part of that project was the property value study that provided the basis for the influential article by Ridker and Henning (1967). This article considered the effect of air pollution on property values in St Louis. It generated a significant literature and debate on the interpretation of the results. Despite the controversy, the idea of using real-estate prices to reveal the value placed on environmental quality became firmly entrenched in the environmental economist's toolbox.[6]

The use of property value studies to provide information in developing environmental policy was accepted almost from the beginning. In a report to the National Air Pollution Control Administration within the US Department of Health, Education, and Welfare, Barrett and Waddell (1970) offered a status report on air pollution damages. One of the techniques they used for estimating air pollution's cost was residential property value studies. Using estimates from four studies,[7] they generated national annual estimates of the cost of sulfate air pollution of $5.2 billion.

In the three decades since this beginning, applications have considered almost every type of environmental problem and every geographical area.[8] Given the number and diversity of the applications supporting use of the hedonic framework for valuing site-specific amenities, one might reasonably ask whether the results have been influential. Our answer is that while they have had little *direct* role in designing public policy, they have been used as evidence supporting policy decisions. This distinction does not imply they have not influenced the policy debate. Environmental policy can no longer be designed without considering its full economic consequences – both costs and benefits.

Hedonic estimates of damage have been an important method of damage appraisal for hazardous waste contamination in private litigation. Their role in public litigation seems to stand between the extremes. They are certainly more than the source for a 'cross-check,' but they are also less than the exclusive basis for someone to 'write the check' for damages. This distinction stems, in part, from the objectives of the two types of litigation. Damage claims in private cases are made based on injuries (and resulting monetary losses) to one or more private parties as a result of the actions of another private party. For example, suppose a plant disposes of industrial residues within its own property in a properly designed and maintained landfill. Nonetheless, there may be an accidental breach of the liner and a release of hazardous materials into the groundwater. Eventually, if undetected, the groundwater contamination can migrate to another property owner's site and affect their ability to assure the site has a clean and safe water supply. If the causality is readily established, a private claim would focus on the diminution in the property value of this other person's land due to the environmental problem. The focus of hedonic methods on market prices makes the monetization of this loss relatively easy to establish and understand.

The same situation would be viewed differently in public litigation, where the groundwater would be interpreted as a resource held in trust for the public. Use and non-use values would need to be considered in evaluating monetary losses experienced by the public. Hedonic models would not capture the non-use values.

Because this chapter is about how hedonic applications have been developed and used in these types of applications, it is important not to get ahead of our story in elaborating these conclusions. Nonetheless, some further explanation is warranted. Our conclusion for policy applications is based on distinguishing whether hedonic estimates provided the primary basis for the evaluation of gains (or losses) due to an action. As a rule, they did not. Instead, they served as a 'check' (hence our use of 'cross-check' earlier). For example, in the case of air quality, analysts would compare the benefits due to an air quality improvement that were derived by summing various types of health improvements and materials damage reductions with the benefits that were estimated using hedonic techniques.[9] A finding that the hedonic estimate exceeded the monetized sum of the other damage-specific effects was viewed as a 'plausibility check.' The opposite outcome, with a large discrepancy, was often a source of anxiety.

In the case of public litigation the role was different. The objective was to estimate the value of services lost due to injury of natural resources, and the hedonic model was viewed on the plaintiff's side as providing a measure for a small component of the losses. For sites regarded as important to a region or a state, losses measured by the hedonic were considered a small component of the total and difficult to separate from the losses that might be subject to private litigation.

3. A BRIEF OVERVIEW OF THE EVOLUTION PROPERTY VALUE TECHNIQUES

At the most basic level, a hedonic property value model is based on the premise that it is possible to establish a statistical relationship between a home's sale price and its characteristics.[10] These attributes include the structural features, the neighborhood characteristics, the accessibility of the location, and environmental characteristics usually delineated by location. The earliest hedonic studies used census data with tract averages for the characteristics and the average of the owners' estimates for the property value. In the last two decades most studies have used actual sales prices for individual houses. In the early work, relying on the tract averages, initial findings were greeted with concerns about the prospects for 'omitted factors' that might be the actual source of the effects attributed to approximate measures of the site disamenities. However, as the research record accumulated, these concerns have largely disappeared from the literature.[11] Another source of controversy and stimulus for research stems from early studies' desire to go beyond using the estimates an indication of 'concern.' Instead, users of the studies' estimates proceeded to calculate the benefits of eliminating air pollution within a city or throughout the country. For example, almost immediately after the Ridker and Henning (1967) study was published, debate ensued about these types of conclusions based on their estimates.[12] Soon the conceptual focus became directed to whether it was possible to infer anything about the willingness to pay for environmental quality from a hedonic regression. If so, what was revealed and under what conditions?

Fortunately, in 1974 two important papers were published that considered the theory that provided a justification for the hedonic regressions being estimated. Rosen (1974) continues, even today, to provide the basis for most of the environmental research on property values. An equally important, but less extensively cited, paper by Freeman (1974b) raised some of the same issues, but was more concerned with addressing the issues associated with measuring willingness to pay from hedonic models. One conclusion that comes from both of these papers is that the estimated hedonic price schedule provides an estimate of the marginal willingness to pay for environmental quality for each household at the location they have chosen. Equally important, these authors suggested, and a significant amount of subsequent research further clarified, a second conclusion. In general, estimates of willingness to pay for non-marginal environmental changes or estimates of marginal willingness to pay at other locations are not available directly from the hedonic regressions.

At about the same time,[13] Polinsky and Shavell (1976) used an urban model to analyze the conditions under which land rents could be used to infer aggregate willingness to pay. They showed that if the city was 'small' (so that changes in that city did not influence prices in other cities) and 'open' (so there was free in- and out-migration), the change in aggregate land values due to an amenity change would measure aggregate willingness to pay.

As a rule, we are unwilling to assume that migration between cities is costless. Nonetheless, the logic has merit. One can use it for a given urban area. That is, Palmquist (1992a) showed that willingness to pay for non-marginal environmental changes can be derived from the hedonic regression if the environmental change is 'localized' (that is, causes the prices of some houses to change but does not change the overall hedonic equation in the city). For some types of environmental problems, such as hazardous waste sites or highway noise, this assumption of a localized impact is appropriate. The willingness to pay for non-marginal changes can be estimated by predicting the change in property values at the affected houses.[14]

If an externality is not localized, the hedonic equation can continue to provide some useful information. It had been known since Rosen (1974) and Freeman (1974b) that, for any given household, the prediction of the change in property value at the original house (predicted from the *ex-ante* hedonic price equation) would be greater than the willingness to pay of that household if they stayed in the original house. However, in response to a major environmental change, there will be household relocations that make the benefit measurement more complex.[15] Bartik (1988) argued that when all possible adjustments were considered, the original hedonic equation still provided an upper bound for the benefits under almost all circumstances. He also suggested reasons why the bound might be fairly tight.[16]

Interpreting the marginal price (that is, partial derivative of the hedonic function with respect to a site-specific amenity or disamenity) as a benefit measure relies on a condition describing household adjustment at the intensive margin of choice. That is, assuming a full array of choice alternatives and costless adjustment, households will search over the available homes until their marginal willingness to pay for increasing each attribute that varies with location is equal to the incremental price they must pay to get it. This logic suggests that a hedonic price function describing how prices in equilibrium vary with site characteristics also reveals a point on the marginal willingness to pay schedule. It does not reveal the full marginal willingness to pay schedule.

Rosen (1974) suggested a second-step approach could be used to develop this function, based on estimates of hedonic price models. Under his proposal, after estimating the hedonic price equation, the second stage would use the point estimates of the marginal prices to recover the underlying behavioral equations. This process is actually more complex than his suggestion implied. Identification of the marginal willingness to pay function requires that there be sufficient information to distinguish the behavioral functions of individuals based on their preferences for homes and site characteristics from both the equilibrium price schedule and the supply functions for these characteristics. A variety of restrictions have been proposed, such as pooling information from multiple independent markets (Palmquist, 1984) or maintaining that household preferences follow a specific functional form with nonlinear restrictions on the role of site amenities as influences to marginal willingness to pay (Epple, 1987; Mendelsohn, 1985; Chattopadhyay, 1998).

In the first case, independent variation in the marginal prices across different markets serves to distinguish the marginal willingness to pay function from differences in equilibrium conditions. In the second, the analysis assumes how marginal willingness to pay will vary with factors that constrain household choice.[17] The complexity and data requirements of both strategies have limited the number of examples available in the literature. As a result, it is fair to say that few of the available second-stage models have had an influence on policy or litigation. There is, nonetheless, important information that would be generated in successful second-stage analysis. Obviously, refined estimates of willingness to pay for non-marginal environmental changes could be important. Perhaps equally important is the fact that second-stage estimates would generate information about the effect of income on the demand for environmental quality and thus the equilibrium hedonic schedule. The relationship between income and hedonic prices is important in aggregating benefit measures and in benefits transfer.[18]

With second-stage estimates of the bid functions or demand functions, one could estimate the willingness to pay of the households that received a change in environmental quality, if there were no adjustments made, such as relocation (see Bartik, 1988). To take the adjustments fully into account would require knowledge of the hedonic price schedule after the improvement had taken place and all adjustments had been made. This would preclude *ex-ante* benefit measurement unless one were able to use a reliable general equilibrium model to predict the new price schedule.[19] However, even without knowledge of the new hedonic price schedule, it is possible to consider all the adjustments and develop a lower-bound estimate of the benefits (Palmquist, 1988).

A related technique that has had some impact on policy and litigation uses houses that have been sold more than once during the period being studied. If there has been an environmental change during that time and if not all the houses have experienced the change or at least not the same change, then it may be possible to use the repeat sales to estimate the environmental effect on property values without using the hedonic characteristics of the houses.

Griliches's work noted earlier generated interest in the use of regression techniques instead of conventional index number procedures to construct real-estate price indexes. This literature developed independently from the literature on the use of hedonic models to measure the effects of amenities and also dates to the early 1960s. In this context, Bailey et al. (1963) developed a technique for using repeated sales of houses to develop a real-estate price index. The objective of their study was to develop a price index to track the movement of prices for constant quality housing units over time. Thus the prospect of basing a price index on the sales prices of the same property at different times offered the opportunity to control for quality differences that might arise by comparing different properties over time.

A second use of time can be found in work that recognized that environmental variables and time may be interrelated, as they would be in 'event studies' in finance. The analyst then observes prices over time for a treatment group (that is, a portion of the market area with some environmental distinction) and compares it to a control group. Nourse (1967) is an example of this type of study. It attempted to consider how an environmental problem affected the trends in the property value indexes in a study area when compared with a control. The use of study areas and control areas was well established at that time, but the technique required finding a control area where all the real-estate price effects were identical to the study area, except for the development of the environmental problem.

Palmquist (1982) showed how the environmental variable could be incorporated in the regression to avoid the need for a control area. The alternatives developed in this early literature have a direct parallel in more recent discussions of the requirements for control groups in the literature on program evaluation (see Heckman et al., 1997). As Palmquist noted, with proper adjustment for depreciation and any modifications to a structure, a repeat sales method can help in the task of matching the conditioning variables that may influence how the treatment (that is, area experiencing some environmental effect) affects market prices. This judgment relies on the absence of a selection effect that conditions the homes with repeated sales in some way relevant to the measurement of the effect of the environmental measure (see Gatzlaff and Haurin, 1997).[20]

Another modification of the hedonic method takes account of the fact that there is evidence that wages as well as property values are affected by environmental quality.[21] Following Rosen (1979), Roback (1982) and Hoehn et al. (1987), among others, have combined hedonic wage and hedonic property value studies to estimate amenity values. Most of these studies have included an air pollution measure and climate measures, and some have included hazardous waste sites. These studies have assumed nationwide markets for both employment and real estate. To this point, these types of studies have not, to our knowledge, had an effect on either policy or litigation.[22]

4. THE USE OF HEDONIC STUDIES IN POLICY

As we suggested at the outset, the role of property value studies in policy evaluation has been indirect, confirming that environmental problems are a source of concern for the public. Moreover, that concern is displayed in more tangible terms than would be the case with an opinion poll that can change with developments on the evening news broadcast. People are demonstrating a willingness to pay for locations with higher levels of amenities or cleaner air. They may simply be paying to avoid the problems resulting from the pollution or to enhance the environmental amenities where they live. It does not matter. We measure their incremental values through the market revelation of these trade-offs in the prices (and rents) for homes.

This section reviews three areas where publicly funded hedonic research has provided information to policy-makers – air pollution, water pollution and hazardous waste. In two of them (air quality and hazardous waste), we are able to use our own personal experiences to describe how and why research contributed (or failed to contribute) to the policy-making process. This is done by highlighting our two examples as 'Panel' inserts and summarizing the key features in the text.

4.1 Air

The early research on the use of hedonic models to study air pollution developed along two lines: (a) technical guidance on how these studies should be interpreted; and (b) efforts to evaluate, in general terms, improvements in air quality. Both lines of research were not tied to a specific regulation. However, the second category did contribute to the general motivation for air pollution policy.

As noted earlier, the first environmental property value study was done as part of a research project funded by the US Public Health Service (see Ridker, 1967).

It sought to contribute to both lines of inquiry. An early example relevant to evaluating air pollution policy was Barrett and Waddell's (1970) report to the National Air Pollution Control Administration. It surveyed eight categories of damages and developed estimates of damages for health, materials, vegetation, and residential property values. They concluded that '(t)he property value approach ... has provided the soundest basis for estimating pollution costs.' By 1974 Waddell (1974) had released a similar report, although by then it was a report to the US Environmental Protection Agency, and the number of property value studies increased from four to ten.

Another early example focused on developing guidance was the 1974 *The Costs and Benefits of Automobile Emission Control*, issued as volume 4 of *Air Quality and Automobile Emission Control* by the National Academy of Science and the National Academy of Engineering. Chapter IV was on 'Economic Benefits of Air Quality Data as Estimated from Market Data' (Polinsky, et al., 1974). It contained research that would later appear in Polinsky and Shavell (1976) and Polinsky and Rubinfeld (1977), and research by Harrison that foreshadowed Harrison and Rubinfeld (1978). It also provided some early theoretical guidance on the measurement of benefits from property value studies.

The focus of property value research changed in the early 1980s during the development of evaluations for EPA's proposed secondary standards for sulfur dioxide and total suspended particulates. Mathtech (1981), under contract to the EPA, did the benefit analysis. This work provides the basis for our first panel summary of research that has not found its way into the mainstream of the published literature in environmental economics. We devote specific attention to it here because, despite the fact that 20 years have elapsed since it was finished, the results are still in use today![23]

This particular set of research was organized in Allen Basala's Benefit Analysis Program. It was conducted by a variety of consulting firms and we were retained as outside reviewers for the research throughout its development. As a result, we can provide insiders' perspectives on the work. Economists at Mathtech (primarily Drs Robert Horst and Ernest Manuel) conducted original research on the effects of air pollution on households and firms. In the first set of work (for households) their analysis considered how individuals reallocate their budgets in response to changes in air pollution. The logic of their analysis followed the linear expenditure system, which was frequently used at that time to estimate the full set of consumer demand parameters. The application of the logic for measuring the contribution of amenities had been pioneered by Shapiro and Smith (1981), but that analysis had not attempted a full-scale application to commodities, such as cleaning services, likely to be impacted by a change in air pollution.

This strategy was selected because the original objective had been to measure what EPA had labeled the benefits due to the secondary standards for the criteria pollutants. These secondary benefits were non-health-related because the primary standards were to 'eliminate' any damages people might experience due to health effects. Thus this approach, by relating levels of air pollution to specific commodities, permitted the isolation of the non-health consequences.

Previously estimated property value studies were essential because the household method was new to everyone. It relied on using the expenditure data for specific types of commodities to reveal a seemingly weak 'signal' of the effects on household adjustments. As a result, it was argued that the hedonic model's upper bound could be relied upon to reflect the more complete adjustment a household would make to improve the air quality conditions they experienced. Estimates of the incremental change in the annualized housing price could be developed for each city and compared with measures of benefits from reductions in air pollution in that city, based on the expenditure model. It then offered a 'cross-check' of the plausibility of the Mathtech model's results. Using the theoretical developments of Rosen and Freeman, the Mathtech economists interpreted the results of existing studies to define this upper bound. There were 11 hedonic studies that were judged appropriate, and benefit measures were developed from them to compare with estimates from the expenditure model for alternative secondary standards.

Mathtech was to measure the avoided losses from reductions in soiling and materials damage. These were the main non-health or what the legislation referred to as 'welfare effects' from the policy. These measures were to provide the basis for the secondary national ambient standards. The household model estimates the non-health damages associated with air pollution by linking pollution measures to the minimum or threshold expenditures a household was hypothesized to undertake in activities associated with cleaning or materials damage. The preference specification in the model was a Stone–Geary utility function. This formulation is often interpreted as implying some threshold level of consumption that is an estimated parameter for each category of expenditures. This threshold amount must be consumed before there is a positive contribution to utility. By hypothesizing that air pollution increased these thresholds their model targeted the non-health effects. Four aggregate categories were targeted in the model: shelter (including home repair and utilities); home operations (including laundry and cleaning); furnishings and equipment; and transportation. Both sulfur dioxide and total suspended particulates were considered potentially to affect these expenditures. Hedonic estimates of the incremental benefits from reduced air pollution were assumed to reflect all the related gains for an equivalent reduction in air pollution. Thus, in principle, they should be larger. They would include expenditures households would be willing to make to avoid health impacts and other aesthetic effects that were omitted from the expenditure model.

Table 3.1 summarizes the per household (in 1980 dollars) benefits measure for TSP (total suspended particulate) and SO_2 secondary standards. The model's estimates of benefits from meeting the secondary standard at the household level were recognized as incomplete. The model would not reflect aesthetic dimensions (for example, enhanced visibility) of reduction in air pollution or any additional health-related gain experienced by households from improvements beyond the primary standard.

Table 3.1   *Mathtech secondary benefit analysis – household versus hedonic analysis, per household estimates*

Pollutant	Household model	Hedonic cross-check[*]
TSP	$16.25	$120.00–289.00
SO_2	$16.50	$48.00–69.00

[*] These estimates were derived by evaluating the most likely property value/air pollution elasticities from past literature. The Mathtech study reports the likely range for sulfur dioxide as –0.07 to –0.10 and –0.05 to –0.12 for TSP. The measures for ambient concentrations were expressed in terms of the average of the second high values.

Comparing these benefit measures to those derived using a linear approximation from a hedonic property value model should have a clear inequality. That is, we expect the hedonic estimates (for example, marginal willingness to pay times the change in the relevant air pollutant) to exceed those from the household model. This inequality follows from both the fact that the approximation is generally an upper bound and from the fact that we would expect the hedonic to capture more sources of benefits from air pollution reductions.

At one level, this is not an especially demanding plausibility check. It is difficult to specify, without further detailed assumptions, how much of a difference to expect. As a result, some observers have suggested these types of comparisons add little to the policy analysis. We believe this argument misses a more fundamental aspect of the comparison. Each model uses quite different economic data and describes, at very different levels, how air pollution affects behavior. Yet, when the results are evaluated, the benefit measures follow the ordering that we expect and they are in a plausible range in relation to household income. This is not a discriminating test at one level, but it is a general endorsement of the logic, underlying the fact that there are behavioral responses to air pollution and that we can use them to estimate benefits.

Two years later, as part of Mathtech (1983), the same economists made a similar study of alternative primary standards for particular matter, including a move to a new format for measuring particulate matter and defining the standard. The change was from total suspended particulate (TSP) matter to one based on small particles (10 microns or less), PM10. This second set of activities provides the information for Panel 3.1.

When the scope of the regulatory analysis was expanded to consider a new primary standard for these pollutants, all the health and the welfare effects of a new standard could be considered. In this case, the hedonic estimates should serve as a more discriminating cross-check, because the categories of benefits now considered were more complete and, thus, much closer to the full range of issues assumed to be considered influences on property values. Indeed, the issue of double counting was identified as a clear possibility as the various effects were separately estimated and then simply added together.

Panel 3.1 summarizes the aggregate analysis.[24] Aggregation procedure A limited consideration of morbidity studies to those reviewed as part of the development of EPA's Criteria Document for the standard. It omitted some morbidity effects, because the health effects were regarded as not reliably measured. Procedure C includes these effects, along with measures of the benefits from soiling and materials effects.

The panel illustrates one of the difficulties with relying on the first stage of the hedonic model. We know in advance that using the marginal wilingness to pay (WTP) from the hedonic model as a 'price' for pollution improvement is incorrect. We also know that there will be double counting when we add across categories of benefits from other benefit measurement strategies, as if they are independent. Given the potential errors in the same direction with both estimation strategies, it is not possible to predict unambiguously their relationship.

Our conclusion, as reviewers of the Mathtech study, could not, as a result, be especially discriminating. Rather, we were forced to focus on the 'glass half-full' dimensions of the findings. That is, as we noted earlier, these largely independent strategies produced estimates that were within the same 'order of magnitude' (for example, comparing aggregation procedure C with the midpoint and maximum of the hedonic results). As such, it offered a broad-based confirmation of the plausibility of behavioral responses to air pollutants that partially reflect the health consequences of pollution and, as a result, provide an approximate estimate of the benefits.

Because the standard was motivated by health concerns, no one involved in the process, and especially not the health scientists involved in the risk assessments that led to the standards, was prepared to accept the assumption that the hedonic 'magically' reflected all of these concerns. It was accepted as a 'cross-check' based on the revealed 'actual' spending decisions of households!

About this same time, the EPA was also funding important work by Brookshire et al. (1982a) on benefits measurement. The main thrust of that research was advancing contingent valuation methods. However, as part of the project they developed a hedonic property value study of air pollution in the

Panel 3.1   Hedonic property studies as a 'cross-check'

Benefit category	Aggregation procedure[*]	
	A	**C**
Mortality	1.12	1.12
Acute morbidity	0.00	10.65
Chronic morbidity	0.12	0.12
Household sector soiling and materials	0.00	0.73
	1.24	12.63

	Minimum	**Midpoint**	**Maximum**
Property value cross-check	3.43	6.85	11.42

[*] Present values in billions of 1980 dollars for 7-year period (1989–95). Several 'aggregation' procedures were considered. These refer to judgments about studies of the effects of air pollution that would be considered admissible. Six were done for this possible evaluation. The two reported here represent the most restrictive. (A) applies the CASAC standard from the health criteria document. Adjustments were made in (C) to allow for acute morbidity and soiling effects but to attempt to avoid double counting.

Context: EPA Analysis of Primary National Ambient Air Quality Standard for Particulate Matter

Source: Benefit Analysis Program Office of Air Quality Programs and Standards EPA (March 1983) conducted by Mathtech

Task: Measure present value of discounted benefits for ambient air quality standards for PM10 and TSP; with implementation date of 1989; benefits are present value in 1980 dollars computed in year 1982 for time span covering 1987 to 1999 or 1989 to 1995; discount rate was 10 percent in real; all counties in compliance.

South Coast Air Basin surrounding Los Angeles. They were using the established hedonic method as a comparable type of 'cross-check' on the newer contingent valuation method. This was Appendix A of the report and became Brookshire et al. (1982b). However, in this case the check was on a new method and not an attempt to construct composite estimates of the benefits from a policy.[25]

Clearly, the opportunities to observe a multiplicity of household choices – all motivated by a desire to obtain improved air quality – was recognized. What evolved from the process, ultimately, were the joint estimation strategies we now take for granted. The logic of 'cross-checks' initiated in the early Mathtech comparisons and independently used by Brookshire et al. to evaluate contingent valuation estimates were rudimentary steps in a process that was taken to a new level in Cameron's (1992) breakthrough article proposing a joint estimator combining revealed preference and contingent valuation estimates for recreation demand. It is clear that the logic was being used prior to her paper in a range of different ways – including this 'cross-check' role for the hedonic.

4.2 Visibility

Basala's program also led efforts to introduce benefit measures for visibility effects on Class I (or pristine) areas. The program contracted with Rowe and Chestnut (1981) to develop the *Visibility Benefits Assessment Guidebook*. While the guidebook emphasized survey methods, it also discussed the use of property value studies to estimate willingness to pay for visibility. The desire to use more than one method and provide plausibility checks through comparison was clearly a part of the recommendations. Most of the early visibility studies were at recreation areas in the west, so estimates from hedonic methods were not well adapted to address the issues involved.[26] However, there was recognition that hedonic models could serve as cross-checks in this context. This lead EPA to contract for a study of visibility in the eastern USA, and Tolley et al. (1986) did use hedonic techniques as one part of the research.

This hedonic research was headed by Glenn Blomquist and sought to value 'view-oriented' amenities and compare the values to those derived by contingent valuation methods. While visibility was the purpose of the research, the hedonic effort considered 'views' rather than visibility. The comparison of hedonic and contingent valuation results for 'views' was then used as partial justification for relying on the latter for visibility estimates. The data came from 'view-oriented' residences near the shore of Lake Michigan in Chicago. They interviewed residents of ten high-rise buildings, obtaining 208 responses. They asked three contingent valuation questions about a view of the lake and the height of the unit in the building. They also obtained information on the characteristics of the unit and monthly housing expenditure from the survey. For the most part, the comparison of hedonic and contingent valuation methods was as expected. The willingness to pay for a lake view by those that had a lake view exceeded the increase in market rent for a lake view. The willingness to pay to be on a higher floor was less than the increase in equilibrium rent to live on the higher floor, as one would expect since the residents had not chosen to live on the higher floor.

An anomalous result from the study was that those without a lake view said they would be willing to pay more to get the lake view than the hedonic results said they would have to pay for the view, implying they should have moved and be enjoying the views. This result could have been a reflection of incomplete information available to existing renters about the premium required for a view. Overall, since the study obtained the expected results in all cases but this last one, the authors interpreted their overall findings as support for the survey methods, which they then used to value improvements in visibility.

4.3   Water Pollution

One of the earliest property value studies funded by the US Environmental Protection Agency was for water pollution control (Dornbusch and Barrager, 1973). Their study identified areas that experienced a significant change in water quality between 1960 and 1970. This strategy was comparable to efforts initiated for air pollution by Nourse (1967) to define environmental events and use hedonic methods to estimate their effects on people's willingness to pay. Dornbusch and Barrager included both residential and recreational areas in their selection process. Their final choices were six sites on four rivers.[27] One of the sites was rural, while the others were in developed areas. They used actual sales in the later period. These were linked to an adjusted assessed value at the earlier time. The adjustment was based on the average ratio of assessed value to market value. They regressed the change in property values from before to after a water quality change on the initial value of the house, other (non-water quality) changes that took place in the area, and distance from the water body. In addition to this absolute property value change, they estimated a percentage change model. They interpreted the changes in property values on the river as being attributable to the water quality improvement. For houses located back from the rivers, the regressions suggested that the appreciation was reduced with distance from the river, but the water quality improvement had effects as far as 4000 feet (1219m) back from the river. The regressions were considered successful in only four of the six study areas. As with other early studies, the results from the few study areas were used to generate national estimates of water pollution damages, although with a number of caveats.

Today it would be easy to point out shortcomings with the Dornbusch and Barrager study, but as an early hedonic study it was thoughtfully done. Moreover, the problems they encountered also help to explain the relative paucity of hedonic models using water quality. The residential effects of water quality only extend back from the water body a short distance, which limits the areas that can be considered. There are no objectively measurable effects of the water quality that vary with distance. Proximity to water can be desirable or undesirable depending on the condition of the water body. At any particular time there is likely to be relatively little variation in the water quality experienced by different houses in a single market area.[28] This feature differs sharply from air pollutants, and so on. Thus, one has to use water quality changes over time, but to do so requires a relatively clear basis for controlling how other factors influenced property values during the time period being studied. This point is another reflection of the 'event study' feature that is implicit in the design of some hedonic studies involving environmental amenities. We return to this issue in our second Panel on the use of hedonic models in hazardous waste policy evaluations. All of these reasons may account for the paucity of government-funded hedonic water quality studies.[29]

4.4 Transportation Noise

The effect of disamenities, particularly noise, from transportation facilities on surrounding property values has been a concern since the 1960s. By the early 1970s government agencies were funding studies using what would become known as hedonic techniques. The Federal Highway Administration (FHWA) within the US Department of Transportation funded many of the studies that focused on highway noise. Because of the nature of the externality involved, these studies were some of the first to use disaggregate data.

While there were limited studies on highway noise and property values (Colony, 1966, 1967; Towne, 1966; Brinton and Bloom, 1969) before Gamble et al. (1973), this was the first major study funded by FHWA. They considered both beneficial and adverse effects from interstate highways in four communities in New Jersey, Virginia and Maryland. The areas were selected primarily to analyze the adverse effects of both noise and air pollution. They had some information on the characteristics of the houses and the occupants, although some important variables such as square feet of living space were not available. They used stepwise regression techniques to arrive at 'final' specifications.[30] Because of this strategy for model specification, the model for one area had only two independent variables other than noise, while another had seven. Ideally, one would like to be able to compare the effects of the noise variable with approximately comparable specifications. There was also a limited number of observations, with noise levels above ambient conditions in two of the areas. In spite of these problems, the noise variable's estimated coefficient was consistently negative and had a plausible value (in terms of overall magnitude) in all the areas. In addition to the hedonic-type regression, as part of this study Langley compared real-estate price indexes next to the highway and further back using the Bailey, Muth and Nourse technique. He found that houses next to the highway appreciate more slowly, although there were some problems with his interpretation.[31]

Nelson (1975), in the next major study, attempted to distinguish the hedonic equation and the demand curves for environmental quality of both air pollution and noise. Unfortunately, rather than using data on individual sales, Nelson used census tract data. Census data would be subject to the shortcomings discussed for air quality above, but there is a further problem with using them with highway noise. Noise effects are quite localized and cover an area much smaller than a census tract. A noise prediction program was used for each census tract, but even if it provided an accurate measure (which was unlikely), that measure would represent an average of the noise near and further back from the highway. Similarly, the owner-estimated property values would be an average of properties with and without highway noise. Thus we might expect little ability to detect an effect for noise. Nonetheless, Nelson's estimates were very close to those of Gamble et al.

One of us (Palmquist) initiated his long-standing interest in hedonics through an FHWA-funded research project. In Palmquist (1980) it was possible to use much better data to consider the link between highway noise and property values. In each of three areas bordering interstate highways in Washington State, data on a large number of sales of individual houses were collected, and extensive noise monitoring was also done. The three areas represented three different types of neighborhoods that could be classified as upper-middle class, lower-middle class, and lower class. As expected, the effects of highway noise increased with the average income in the neighborhoods.[32]

Related research has been conducted in Canada. The Ontario Ministry of the Environment supported Hall et al. (1978). They used areas where there were rows of houses parallel to a highway to assist with the noise monitoring and where the houses were fairly homogeneous. They did include some of the major characteristics of the houses to control for differences. They found that in an area with a high noise level, property values next to the highway were discounted, but in areas with more moderate noise levels this was not the case. A follow-on study using a large data set (Taylor et al., 1982) found a significant noise discount for both arterial and expressway sites.

Surprisingly, few of the studies of airport noise have been sponsored by government agencies, so they will not be covered in much detail here.[33] It is worth noting that a majority of the airport noise studies have used census data. However, with airplane noise, wide areas experience comparable noise levels so the problems identified for highway studies with accurately gauging the noise level do not arise. Census data in this case are not subject to the problem of being too aggregated to capture the effect. An interesting study of airport noise using both disaggregate and aggregate data (O'Byrne et al., 1985) obtained comparable results with the alternative data sources.

4.5 Hazardous Wastes

The Superfund legislation (CERCLA – the Comprehensive Environmental Response, Compensation, and Liability Act – in 1980 and RCRA – Resource Conservation and Recovery Act – in 1983) raised the profile of studies evaluating the economic consequences of land disposal of hazardous substances.

The US Environmental Protection Agency funded the first major study on this topic, Adler et al. (1982). As in the Dornbusch and Barrager (1973) study, the work accepts the premise that site selection must be used as a means to establish control over the additional influences on the property values. This was considered key to measuring the amenity or disamenity effects. In the Adler et al. study, the researchers screened 150 sites and selected two as being promising for further analysis. They sought relatively homogeneous areas that were primarily residential and had no other major sources of disamenities. They also wanted the hazards of the site to be known to the public. Finally, adequate data had to be available. The overall requirements implied that the analyses were *retrospective* studies, where it was possible to characterize contamination as an event, and evaluate the effects on property values once it was recognized.

It is interesting to note that the hedonic analysis can become an event that may influence property values! That is, a detailed analysis of how current property values have been influenced by a contamination episode from an existing waste site might be interpreted as a signal that public action was about to take place. We expect that asset prices would reflect new information about conditions that impact the services provided by those assets in the future and a cleanup of the site might lead to a change in those services. Thus we might expect knowledge that the analysis was taking place to influence subsequent sale prices in the area, perhaps making it difficult to replicate the negative effects of the existing waste site. That is, if households' expectations were that the cleanup would be successful, then one might argue this would reduce the likelihood of capturing the negative effects of the disposal site in subsequent studies.

This concern is not speculation. It was, in fact, a key consideration in the decisions about how to report and use hedonic results that were part of a Regulatory Impact Analysis (RIA). This occupied a substantial amount of the attention of the Environmental Economics Committee of EPA's Science Advisory Board when one of us (Smith) co-chaired this committee. We return to it below as part of describing our second policy panel.

For now, considering Adler et al., by all measures it was regarded as reasonably successful. However, to our knowledge, it was never published and is rarely cited in the hedonic literature on the effects of hazardous waste sites. The authors were able to develop a fairly complete specification of housing characteristics in both locations (Andover, Minnesota and Pleasant Plains, NJ). They used dummy variables for quarter-mile rings up to 2½ miles from dumpsites in some specifications, and distance gradients in others.

The nature of the environmental problems differed at the two sites that were used. The first (Pleasant Plains, NJ) was a case of illegal dumping of benzene, ketones and the like during 1971, which resulted in groundwater contamination. About 1974 the problem was discovered and quick action taken, including closing of wells used for some of the water supply, extending wells deeper to an uncontaminated aquifer, and providing municipal water. In this area there was fairly clear evidence that property values generally increased with distance from the site once the problem was known. Sales prior to the dumping did not show the same trend.

The second site (Andover, MN) included a waste site with somewhat less toxic wastes and a landfill that had received some hazardous wastes in the distant past and where the lining was beginning to deteriorate. However, there was little contamination at the time of the study, even though there was a future threat. There was no evidence that property values were reduced near either of the sites. Since both sites had been used for a long time, there was no opportunity for a before-and-after comparison. While hedonic techniques have been refined in the years since these studies were done, the results in both areas seem plausible.

After the Adler et al. study, the EPA funded a series of additional studies of the effects of hazardous waste sites on property values. Harrison and Stock (1984) identified two important issues that had not received much consideration in the Adler et al. study. When there are multiple hazardous waste sites in a given housing market, how does one characterize the disamenity effects? When information about a hazard is made available, what effect does this have on property values? The former issue has not been addressed much in later research. Michaels and Smith (1990) used the Harrison and Stock data to investigate the definition of the extent of the housing market for hedonic price functions. Stock (1991) proposed nonparametric kernel estimates for evaluating hedonic price functions with hedonic data. However, neither study addressed the multiple site/distance issue identified in the initial unpublished effort.[34]

In some respects, this issue is similar to a current issue in hedonic modeling of the value of open space and distribution of public and private land uses that contribute to this positive externality. An important issue raised by Bockstael and Irwin (2000) in that context is the endogeneity in some of the land use measures, reflecting proxies for amenity effects and other attributes that are relevant to competing demands for the sites involved.

The second effort funded by EPA, Schulze et al. (1986), used both survey and property value methods. This study sought to apply the insights of economics and psychology to evaluate people's reactions to the risks posed by living near hazardous waste sites. They selected three sites that were in homogeneous, populated areas, where the disamenity was clearly perceived. The first area was a large landfill where the build-up of methane gas had caused an evacuation of nearby residents. There were odors and some contamination of groundwater off-site but no contaminated wells at that time. There was some vinyl chloride on the site. They ran hedonic specifications using, in turn, proximity to the site (within 1000 feet (305 m)), the inverse of distance from the site, and these variables combined with variables that incorporated the timing of the evacuation of homes near the site. All of the coefficients implied negative effects for proximity and were significant. The magnitude of the damages was much greater than that implied by the objective health risks.

The second site was also a landfill with both hazardous and municipal wastes. There was methane build-up but no evacuation. At the time of their analysis, the site had been recently closed. The estimates were not as significant as in the first location, although they were larger in magnitude. Within 1000 feet (305 m) of the site there was a negative effect, and if anything, closing the site raised concerns. For this second site, the researchers also combined survey results on residents' subjective risk perceptions with the property value data. For a series of small areas around the site, they assigned the average risk ranking given by residents in that area. Based on these subjective risks, closing the landfill increased property values by an average of $5000, but the proximity of the site still reduced the value by about $4800. These results are also reported in McClelland et al. (1990).

The third site was not as well suited for this type of study, and the results were inconclusive. The bottom-line conclusion to be drawn from these three case studies is the difficulty in characterizing how landfills posing hazards are perceived by consumers. The specific details of each situation seem to preclude broad generalizations about the effectiveness of distance-based measures for the perceived risk in all cases. Equally important, they support our observation that a hedonic analysis, conducted in a policy context, can itself become an 'event' that triggers a market response.

In October 1992, EPA issued several draft studies intended to be used in Regulatory Impact Analysis for the Corrective Action Rule for RCRA sites that had accidentally leaked or released hazardous substances. An important part of one of the studies involved the use of a contingent valuation survey to estimate the nonuse benefits from the site cleanups envisioned under the rule. The evaluation was very high profile for a number of reasons. Foremost among them was the controversy about contingent valuation that was dominant in discussions of researchers involved in non-market valuation. The Exxon-sponsored Symposium on Contingent Valuation had earlier (April 1992) raised issues with the method (see Hausman, 1993 for the published versions of the papers presented at that symposium). This study reported one of the largest publicly available contingent valuation (CV) surveys at the time. As a result, most of the evaluation of the RIA focused on the CV effort.

What has been largely overlooked from the economic analysis in the RIA is a detailed hedonic study of the effects of events involving releases of hazardous substances from these sites on residential property values near the sites. Greg Michaels of Abt Associates (and of the Michaels and Smith, 1990, paper described earlier), conducted the hedonic analysis (Michaels et al., 1992). It considered each of three sites and sought to use them in the evaluation of the benefits from the proposed rule. Panel 3.2 provides a summary of the hedonic property value analysis for one of the three treatment, storage, and disposal facilities (TSDF). This specific study of properties around what was identified as facility No. 1, was included in the draft RIA, and benefit measures were computed based on the estimates. Very short summaries of the estimated values (based on the increased property values) of the one-mile intervention scenarios for the other two sites were included in the RIA.

Several aspects of this analysis are important to our example. First, the facilities were never identified in the benefit analysis for the RIA. In all supporting documents, the names and identifying information were redacted. The reason was direct. As we noted, the policy analysts recognized that the decision to undertake the analysis of these specific aspects offered the prospects of 'creating an event' that could have a short-term influence on property values. As noted earlier, the policy analysts involved (and presumably EPA's lawyers) were concerned it could be interpreted as signaling to private homeowners that corrective action would be undertaken.

Second, the analysis did not attempt to identify how the specific facilities related to the set of all TSDFs likely to be covered by the corrective action rule. The draft report noted that:

> The property value results may contribute to an improved understanding of the economic damages impacted by TSDFs, but the analysis should be viewed as a work-in-progress ... They derive from housing market behavior at three TSDFs only and are not intended to represent the entire universe of TSDFs. (pp. 11–18)

The section on hedonic models concludes by noting that the range of benefits estimated in these cases is likely to encompass benefits experienced at TSDFs.

Finally, the analysis, as identified in the panel, indirectly isolated an issue with the hedonic approach. The policy must be converted into the format used to capture the effects of the undesirable facility. All of the hedonic studies for the effects of hazardous facilities have used some function of distance. To gauge the marginal benefits from a policy, the analyst must define the policy's anticipated effects in terms of some change in the distance measure used in the hedonic function. When the hedonic study involves evaluating a site-specific amenity, like air pollution or noise, the environmental variable is measured in units of pollution. The translation to a measure of the marginal benefits for an environmental improvement is reasonably straightforward. For hedonic studies of hazardous waste sites that use distance as a proxy for the site-specific environmental attribute, defining the benefits of a cleanup is more complex. Unless the site is completely cleaned up and there are no residual effects on property values, it is necessary to translate the actual reduction in perceived risk at a given site into an effective increase in distance from the site.[35]

Panel 3.2   Hedonic property value where analysis creates an 'event'

Results from hedonic model for facility 1 (1983–91)[*]		
	Simple linear	Linear with rental variables
Period indicator	−63.35	−91.99
(=1 after 1986.5)	(−4.15)	(−5.46)
(=0 before 1986.5)		
Distance (miles)	15.62	37.16
from facility ×	(2.79)	(4.40)
period indicator		
Distance (miles)	−3.83	−35.73
from facility	(−0.77)	(−3.48)
Number of rental	−	−185.33
homes	−	(−3.44)
Distance × rental	−	77.17
homes	−	(3.55)

Benefit measures (Facility 1, $1,000)[**]

Move each house 1 mile		
Aggregate	25 002	33 761
Per house	7.20	9.71
Move each house 4 miles		
Aggregate	39 351	48 993
Per house	11.32	14.10
Event reversal		
Under pre-event conditions	829 019	775 037
Under post-event conditions	738 764	711 912

[*] Estimates were computed for 1992 by using time trend to adjust for price movements. Results from hedonic models are derived from a linear specification of the hedonic price equations with actual sales prices. The numbers in parentheses are the t-ratios for the null hypothesis of no association.

[**] Benefit measures are in 1000 of 1992 dollars. Eighty percent of housing transitions were 2 to 4 miles from facility.

Context: Resource Conservation and Recovery Act (RCRA) Corrective Action Rule – cleanup of solid waste management units – at RCRA facilities; analysis applied to a sample of 79 facilities – 70 non-federal and 9 federal facilities.

Panel 3.2   (cont.)

Source: Regulatory Analysis Branch Office of Solid Waste EPA (March
          1993) conducted by Abt, ICF Industrial Economics Inc.
          Hedonic analysis was led by Dr R.G. Michaels (Michaels et al.,
          1992)

Task: Under the proposed rule EPA regions or states were expected
          to select corrective action remedies at RCRA Facility Investi-
          gation (RFI) and corrective measures study (CMS) reports
          submitted to the owners. EPA's draft RIA projected that out of
          a universe of 5800 facilities, 2100 would conduct a CMS private
          implementation of corrective action. Of these, 2200 were
          projected to have released above the action levels to at least one
          environmental medium, i.e., groundwater, surface water, air or
          soil. The analysis expected that groundwater remedies and soil
          cleanups would be most prevalent remediation activities.
          The draft Regulatory Impact Analysis sought to measure
          benefits associated with human health risks, ecological threats,
          water use costs, groundwater nonuse values, residential property
          values and hazardous waste facility values for the corrective
          action requirements.

Panel 3.2 shows how the sample analysis for Facility 1 interprets the
corrective action rule as equivalent to moving each house different distance
increments away from the facility. The definition of these distance increments
is the way that the policy is translated into terms consistent with the estimated
model. The study also considered a policy alternative as the equivalent to
returning to the pre-event conditions. The overall benefits from each interpretation of the policy are quite different. With the policy treated as equivalent to
a reversal of the events associated with contamination to the pre-event
conditions, the hedonic model yields aggregate benefit estimates for the homes
around Facility 1 that are 20 times larger than in the case of a distance increment
of 4 miles. Thus it is possible to have a dramatic effect on the benefits attributed
to policy through the process used to link the results of the policy to the proxy
variables characterizing how the negative effects of a hazardous waste site
influence private properties.[36] As research in hedonic models has expanded to
consider a wider range of site-specific amenities and disamenities, experience
is growing in how to address these issues. Nonetheless, we are not at a stage
where it is possible to prescribe answers to the issues implicitly raised in this
RIA's evaluation of cleanup alternatives. The logic stemming from the cross-

check use of hedonics may offer an approach to accelerate the learning process. There is no reason why the Cameron joint estimation logic could not be applied using a hedonic framework. By focusing a stated preference study on the relationship between distance to landfills (as well as other proxies) and an individual's perceived risk or disamenity and then estimating the risk perception model jointly with a behavioral model consistent with the hedonic framework, it may be possible to test the logic that has been used to represent policies.[37]

5. THE USE OF HEDONIC STUDIES IN LITIGATION

Property value studies have also been used in litigation. We distinguished two types of litigation: (a) public litigation where some designated agent becomes the trustee for a public interest and seeks compensation under a liability statute; and (b) private litigation where individuals bring civil law suits under the common law or a private liability statute. The most visible examples where hedonic models have been used in litigation are those pursued under a liability statute that involves a public interest. However, even in these cases the exact record of the analysis undertaken is often not readily available. The majority of the cases have been settled before they go to court and the record can be sealed as a condition of settlement.

To illustrate how hedonic models can be used in different ways in these settings, we relied on the information available to us from one or another form of participation in the process involving public litigation.[38] There is no specific discussion of uses of hedonic methods in private litigation. We identified these potential applications because the use of hedonic methods, especially in activities associated with site-specific disamenities associated with hazardous waste, has evolved to the point where pragmatic guidance is now routinely published in practitioner journals (see Patchin, 1994 and Roddewig, 1996 as examples). Thus our summary will not represent the full extent of uses that have been made of hedonic models in litigation.

Most of the public litigation involving residential properties and liability for environmental effects stems from the Comprehensive Environmental Response, Compensation, and Liability Act (CERCLA) of 1980, its amendments, and the Oil Pollution Act (OPA) of 1990. Natural resource damage assessments (NRDAs) under these statutes have used a variety of techniques to estimate damages arising from injuries to natural resources that stem from releases of hazardous substances (CERCLA) or oil (OPA). We selected two cases and prepared panel summaries for each to organize this discussion.

Panel 3.3 summarizes the hedonic components of one of the earliest NRDA cases to use property value methods. It concerned contamination of a stretch of the Eagle River with hazardous substances from the mine tailings of an abandoned silver mine, the Eagle Mine. Figure 3.1 provides a map of the affected area, which is not too far from the Vail Ski Area in the Colorado Mountains. The map is included to locate the town with most home sales in relation to the mine site and the river. Metals and other contaminants from the mine and its tailings ponds were entering the Eagle River with alleged adverse effects. Energy and Resource Consultants, Inc. (with the research team led by Robert Rowe and William Schulze) conducted the economic analysis in support of the state's case (Rowe and Schulze, 1985). They conducted two surveys, one in Eagle County where the mine was located and one statewide. Both contained contingent valuation questions about the damages. The local survey also obtained information on the residence of the respondent. The data included the location of the residence and its characteristics, the rent paid or the purchase price and date, and an estimate of its current value on the real-estate market. These data were supplemented with an index of the distance to the ski areas.

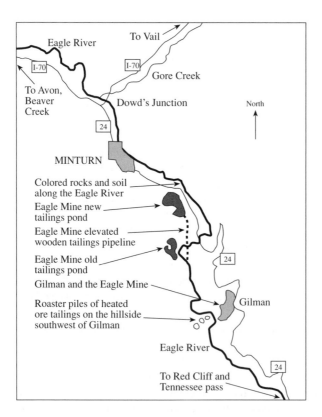

Figure 3.1   Location of the Eagle Mine and Eagle River

The purchase price adjusted to 1985 dollars was used for the hedonic regressions. The researchers were able to use data on 151 homes within a 25-mile radius of the mine.

Panel 3.3 summarizes a few key features of the hedonic models described in the plaintiff expert's report. We report a few of the estimated coefficients from the linear specification. Proximity refers to a dummy variable indicating the property was within six miles of the site. Qualitative variables are given for structural characteristics of the homes. The ski access measure sums (with equal weight) ski acres at Vail relative to driving distance and a comparable measure for Beaver Creek (two well-recognized nearby ski areas).

The analysis described in the expert report is the equivalent of a 'cross-check' on the environmental amenities values of local residents who were affected by the river's contamination. The report suggests that using the hedonic to estimate willingness to pay would provide an overestimate.

A different use for the analysis arose after the defendant's expert report became available. One component of the injuries due to the releases of hazardous substances involved documented contamination of at least one homeowner's private well. The defense estimated the loss using what was suggested to be a perfect substitute – bottled water. In this context, if we interpret proximity to the site as a proxy for increased likelihood of experiencing contamination of a home's drinking water supply, we have a direct basis for comparing computed private mitigation costs with one measure of willingness to pay.

At the bottom of the panel we develop just this comparison using the defendant's discount rate. This type of comparison is extremely effective in this setting. A 'market' estimate of the loss was found to be over two and a half times larger than the computed mitigation cost, the only cost the defense was willing to acknowledge. This made the defense estimates seem implausibly low and thereby indirectly may have raised questions about other components of the defense's work.

The second natural resource damage case, described in Panel 3.4, involves a long-standing case involving New Bedford Harbor in Massachusetts. Polychlorinated biphenyls (PCBs) were released over a long period, but their presence was unknown until 1976, and the seriousness of the problem was probably not widely appreciated until late 1979 when public health restrictions were announced. Debate about the risks continued throughout 1980–81. The pollution was greatest near the site of the release in the inner harbor. Pollution levels were high throughout the inner harbor, and the pollution migrated outside the barriers of the inner harbor although the levels were lower. Far enough out, the levels were undetectable. Three zones of restricted harbor use were defined by the Massachusetts Department of Public Health. Houses in zone I, identified in Figure 3.2, were associated with the inner harbor, where swimming,

Panel 3.3   Hedonic property value in public litigation – challenging lower bounds

---

Summary of hedonic analysis

Sample includes 151 properties with a reported sales price; qualitative variable (0,1) indicating homes within six miles of Eagle Mine site (proximity) measures the effect of the injury. It was argued that these households experienced 'most dramatic perceived water quality effects.' Selected parameters from linear hedonic price function are given below, with t-statistics in parentheses.

Independent variables	Parameter estimate
Proximity	−26 162.6
	(−2.44)
Index of distance to ski areas	27 480.8
	(6.29)
Condo	−30 514.5
	(−2.30)
Townhouse	−29 886.4
	(−2.18)
Duplex	11 682.7
	(0.61)
Trailer	−54 445.1
	(−3.91)

Summary of mitigation cost

Potable water needs for a household can be met with bottled water. These are estimated as $60 per month – $15 per month for the hot/cold water dispenser and $5 per bottle with nine bottles estimated per month. Annual cost estimated at $720 per year per household.

Per household comparison – annual cost (1985 dollars)

Hedonic property value[*]	$1808
Mitigation cost	$720

[*] This annual cost estimate uses the discount rate proposed by the defendant's expert report: 6.91 percent.

Context: State of Colorado Analysis of natural resource damages due to contamination of stretch of Eagle River and groundwater with hazardous waste from mine tailings.

Panel 3.3 (cont.)

Source:	Expert reports for case: Energy and Resource Consultants, Inc. conducted by Drs Robert Rowe and William Schulze for plaintiff (State of Colorado) and NERA, Inc. conducted by Dr Charles Cicchetti for defense (Gulf and Western Industries Inc.).
Task:	Measure the losses to homeowners due to problems with drinking water and blowing dust from Eagle River Mine tailings ponds. Plaintiff used hedonic property value model with owners' recall of sales price for properties within 25 miles of mine. Defense used cost of bottled water to replace well water for households that had contaminated wells.

lobstering and all fishing were precluded. In zone II (also on the map in Figure 3.2), the restrictions on the neighboring waters were not as limiting. This area extends from the hurricane barrier to a point four miles out from the harbor. In this area lobstering and bottom fishing were prohibited. The last restrictive area, the waters adjacent to zone III, had prohibitions only on lobster fishing. Zone IV on the map was associated with no PCB contamination and is free of restrictions.

The challenge posed in this case was to describe how the injuries to natural resources affected people. In the case of swimming, fishing and lobstering, the restrictions have direct impacts on the costs of undertaking these activities. Provided there are substitute facilities, there are clear connections between the restrictions and constraints. Because the injuries motivated the restrictions on private choice, we have a reasonably clear line of causation.

However, it is also reasonable to expect that the injuries affected others who lived in the area, regardless of their decisions to undertake specific water-based activities. The hedonic analysis was an attempt to capture these impacts. The issue that arises is the same one we discussed with respect to the hedonic analysis of the RCRA corrective action rule and the Eagle River case – how one represents the effects of contamination.

The New Bedford case used a carefully structured hedonic analysis for three towns – Fairhaven (652 observations on repeated sales), Dartmouth (389), and New Bedford (189) – with efforts to collect information on modifications to the structures and to evaluate local site attributes that might affect sales prices. Sales within two miles of the harbor were collected.

This study used a variant of the repeat sales techniques discussed earlier. Properties that sold more than once were included in the data set, and since only changes in price were used, characteristics of the houses were not

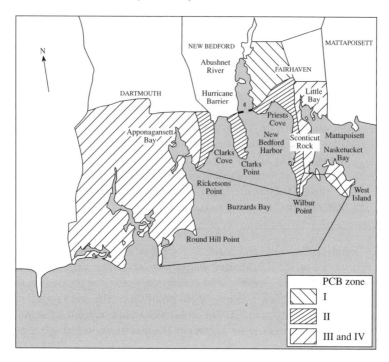

Figure 3.2   Acushnet Estuary study area

necessary. The expert developing the analysis, Robert Mendelsohn, did not use the techniques discussed above simultaneously to generate a local real-estate price index and a measure of the environmental effect. Instead he sought to deflate the prices by the GNP non-farm deflator or a statewide real-estate price index, and he controlled for mortgage interest changes over time. He also included variables representing different lengths of time between sales and changes in census variables. He considered both linear and log differences for the prices. His preferred specification had two dummy variables. One indicated that the pair of sales spanned 1980 (the time the information became available) and the closest water was the polluted inner harbor. The other indicated that the sales spanned 1980 and the closest water was the polluted part of the outer harbor. Both of the dummy variables had the expected negative signs and were significant at the 10 percent level or better. The coefficient on the outer harbor dummy was larger and more significant. Some variations in the census variables included did not seem to alter the results substantially. Using distance to the release site did not indicate as consistent an impact.

The issue considered in Panel 3.4, and central to this analysis for the litigation, was the process of detecting when the event was known. The examples

Panel 3.4   Repeat sales – injury as an event

Repeat sales results for linear model[*]

Year	Improve	Event	EVPCBZ1	EVPCBZ2
1974	1 092	–12 400	4 111	6 990
	(6.63)	(–6.06)	(1.26)	(2.14)
1975	1 068	–15 150	5 482	11 640
	(6.52)	(–7.45)	(1.86)	(4.05)
1976	1 079	–17 850	9 234	13 596
	(6.86)	(–9.22)	(2.91)	(4.79)
1977	1 095	–13 870	9 290	10 160
	(6.67)	(–7.59)	(2.98)	(3.62)
1978	1 071	–9 606	10 500	7 565
	(6.41)	(–5.04)	(3.34)	(2.70)
1979	1 014	7 952	7 953	–1 729
	(6.07)	(3.82)	(3.82)	(–0.64)
1980	1 076	16 920	–5 616	–6 338
	(6.69)	(8.90)	(–1.94)	(–2.43)
1981	1 047	14 060	–8 609	–7 843
	(6.45)	(8.05)	(–3.07)	(–2.96)
1982	996	15 800	–11 664	–8 160
	(6.18)	(9.13)	(–4.09)	(–3.17)
1983	976	19 330	–13 660	–7 080
	(6.13)	(9.56)	(–4.24)	(–2.40)

[*] The figures in parentheses below the estimated parameters are the t-rates for the null hypothesis of no association. The models are distinguished by the timing of the event, as reflected by when it is assumed homeowners knew about the PCB contamination in the harbor. The variables presented are a subset of those in the model. Housing sale prices were deflated to constant dollars before computing the difference in prices between sales (1985 dollars). The independent variables in the model reported here are:

Improve –   value in thousands of 1985 dollars of improvements between the first and the second home sale based on building permit records.

Events –   qualitative variable (0,1) indicating the sale dates involved in the repeat sale bracket the date hypothesized for the event.

EVPCBZ1 –   qualitative variable (0,1) that requires sales in the repeat sales bracket the date hypothesized as the event and property lies in the nearest PCB zone – that is, property's nearest rate lies in zone.

EVPCBZ2 –   qualitative variable (0,1) that requires sales in the repeat sales bracket the date hypothesized as the event and property lies in area of harbor with lowest traces of PCBs from hurricane barrier to four miles out (see Figure 3.2).

Panel 3.4   (cont.)

Context:	National Oceanic and Atmospheric Administration (NOAA), US Department of Justice and State of Massachusetts Analysis of Natural Resource Damages due to PCB contamination of New Bedford Harbor.
Source:	Expert Report for case by Dr Robert Mendelsohn.
Task:	Measure losses to homeowners, due to injuries to resource from contamination of harbor with PCBs. Hedonic model assumes injuries due to PCBs will be reflected in residential property values for access once it is known that the harbor is contaminated.

involving studies of hazardous waste sites used in policy relied on the development of site history and the maintained assumption that the injury was known by a predefined date. The New Bedford case investigated this issue by systematically studying the impact of sales that bracketed each potential date assumed for the event. The change in the pattern of signs displayed in the panel shows that a change in the effects of the most severe PCB zones interacted with the dates for the repeated sales that corresponds to the 1979 announcement – quite striking support for the framework's ability to isolate an effect.[39] While one might question the ability to use this estimate and approximate the loss by assuming it was experienced by all homes in the zone, the role of the model in documenting a loss to private homeowners was direct and convincing.

6.   HEDONIC MODELS FOR OTHER ENVIRONMENTAL EFFECTS

A large number of other environmental issues have generated hedonic studies. To some degree, past success has made analysts 'bolder' in their willingness to search for more subtle effects. It has also re-focused attention on innovative mixes of time and indirect measures of environmental effects. To organize a diverse array of research, we have separated them into groups by the nature of the problem studied. We have chosen to categorize them along two dimensions. The first has to do with whether the environmental effect is current or in the future. By this we mean, is the effect actually observed currently? For example, air pollution is currently observed in various locations and improvements in air quality can take place over a relatively short horizon. On the other hand, some effects may not be realized until far into the future. For example, with an environmental hazard such as radon the health effects may not be realized for many years. Nonetheless, this future realization may influence decisions today and thus affect property values. Another example is global warming, where the effects would be in the distant future, yet land values today may reveal information about those future effects.

The second dimension on which we stratify the studies relates to whether the environmental effects are fairly certain or not, at least when averaged over relatively short time periods. For example, the noise levels at a house from a nearby highway are quite predictable and thus fairly certain. On the other hand, some environmental effects are very difficult to predict. For example, it is impossible to predict that an earthquake will strike at a particular location within a particular time period. However, seismologists can provide forecasts of the probability of an earthquake at a given location. The environmental effect is a probability rather than a certain event, but that probability can affect property values.

The studies discussed here are categorized by both timing and uncertainty, although we have not discussed all four cells. The case of current and certain has largely been covered in our discussion of policy analyses involving hedonics. If an environmental effect will not take place until the distant future, we assume that there is also uncertainty involved. The newest area of work with a significant and growing number of studies involves current and uncertain issues. Far fewer hedonic studies have dealt with future environmental events.

6.1 Current and Uncertain Environmental Effects

This category involves environmental risks where the risk is immediate but there is a high level of uncertainty concerning the actual outcome. Two examples may clarify our classification of these studies. A landfill that accepts non-hazardous household waste may have external effects such as heavy truck traffic and flocks of seagulls. These effects are quite predictable. They are current and certain and thus would fit in that group.[40] On the other hand, there is usually a great deal of uncertainty about the effects that may result from a hazardous waste site. Residents may be aware that one exists, but there is uncertainty about the effects that may result. It may not be known where the waste has migrated off-site. It may not be known what the effects on the surrounding population will be. There may even be questions about when and how the residents become aware of the risk and when and how they revise their risk perceptions in the face of new information. These issues are critical for estimating the willingness to pay for reductions in environmental risk.

The first major hedonic study to incorporate risk in a hedonic model was Brookshire et al. (1985), which was an outgrowth of work funded by the US Geological Survey. The researchers studied the effect of a 1972 California law that required that the purchasers of houses be informed if the house was located in an area that was prone to earthquakes. They found that after the Act, houses located in those zones sold at a discount, although before the information was available (before the Act) there was no statistically significant discount. They used the estimate and their expected utility model to evaluate if there was evidence that people's self-insurance by location accorded with the implications of the expected utility framework. Their conclusion was that the hedonic results supported the model.

While this study of earthquake risk was done quite early, most of the subsequent developments in incorporating risk in a hedonic framework have come from research on hazardous waste sites. Some of the innovations discussed here are related specifically to the uncertainty, while others have more general application. These innovations have not yet played a direct role in policy. Nonetheless, they have been influential and may well play a larger role in the future. We have discussed studies of hazardous waste sites funded by the EPA during the early 1980s. Here we will focus on the innovations in methodology. Michaels and Smith (1990) used disaggregate housing data from the Boston area and 11 hazardous waste sites in their study. They analyzed whether the entire suburban Boston area could be considered a single market and used realtors to stratify their sample by the quality of the housing and area. This type of segmentation was an alternative to the previous debate on segmentation by location. They found that the effect of distance to the nearest hazardous waste site was of the expected sign and statistically significant after the waste site was known when the area was treated as a single market. When the submarkets were used, they obtained the expected signs (except in the below-average market), but they were not always statistically significant. They also examined whether the impact varied with the time from the announcement of the site, an issue that has been examined a great deal since then and, as we noted, was an important component of both the policy and litigation uses of hedonic models with this class of effects.[41]

A study by Stock (1991) used the same data as Michaels and Smith (1990)[42] but very different techniques. He developed nonparametric estimates of the benefits of cleanup at two of the sites. The nonparametric methodology had not been used previously for environmental property value studies. He also developed risk measures that were based on the sum of the inverse of the distance squared to each of the sites and in one case weighted the inverses by the area of the sites. Considering multiple sites and their characteristics was one of his contributions. Unfortunately, both the parametric and nonparametric techniques yielded imprecise estimates.

At about the same time, Kohlhase (1991) was considering the National Priority List hazardous waste sites in Houston. She used distance and distance squared to the nearest toxic waste site, but did not consider the characteristics of the sites or sites further away. Her study considers the effect of Superfund legislation on the perceptions of hazardous waste sites and, in turn, the perceptions' effect on property values. Three time periods were used: before the legislation was passed; after it was passed but before most of the sites had been listed; and after all sites were listed. While the sites existed before the legislation, they did not have an effect on property values. Some of the hedonic results in the middle period were anomalous. However, after all sites were listed, the expected effect for distance was statistically significant.

Thayer et al. (1992) did a comparison study of a non-hazardous waste site and a hazardous waste site. As expected, distance from the hazardous waste site was more valuable. They also found that the price gradient with distance for the sites seemed to level off.

Kiel and McClain (1995) considered a related environmental problem – the siting, construction and operation of a hazardous waste incinerator. They used hedonic estimation in five time periods from before the site was rumored to after it had been operating a number of years. Their plausible results show that there is no effect on property values before the site is rumored or during the rumor stage. However, during construction and the beginning of operation, property values increase significantly with distance from the plant. After the plant was operating several years, the effect was reduced in magnitude although it was still significant. Kiel (1995) conducted a similar timing study for a single hazardous waste site in the Boston area. Before there had been any news accounts, the site had no significant effect on property values, even though the site was operating. After that there was a significant effect that remained even through the EPA's acceptance of cleanup plans.

Recently there have been some new results on residents' learning about risk and its effect on property values. It is a common view that people's perception of the risk from hazardous wastes sites is significantly greater than experts' opinions of that same risk. Gayer et al. (2000) use a Bayesian updating model for risk perceptions and hedonic regressions to address this question. The information comes from the release of EPA's Remedial Investigation. Once this information is available, they argue that the perceived health risk is substantially reduced. The hedonic results imply that the value of avoiding a statistical cancer case is reduced from about $50 million to about $4 million, which is in line with other estimates. This provides some evidence that the information in the Remedial Investigation is used by the residents to update their risk perceptions so the perceptions are more in line with objective risks. The study makes several improvements on previous studies. In addition to objective risk measures, they include National Priorities List (NPL) ranking of the nearest site, the time since the nearest site was placed on the NPL, the area and the type of operations there, and the number of non-NPL sites within different distances from the house.

In a related paper, Gayer (2000) considers the potential endogeneity of the hazardous waste site risk measures. We would expect that property values may be reduced by the risks associated with proximity to hazardous waste sites. On the other hand, he suggests that when decisions are made about the location of a hazardous operation, surrounding property values are likely to be considered because of potential liability. Thus he argues that the risk measure is likely to be endogenous. Using a Hausman (1978) test, his estimates reject the null hypothesis of exogeneity. Moreover, there are fairly dramatic differences between the estimated effects of risk and the risk interactions with income (in the census block group), education (proportion with college education in the block group), and the proportion of nonwhites. While the empirical evidence is certainly supportive of his argument, the basic facts of the sources of the risk are not.

The risk measures included in the model are lifetime excess cancer risks estimated based on EPA risk assessments. These rely on soil and groundwater exposure models. While these estimates will be a function of the location of the site in relation to the households that could be exposed, the decisions about site location were made years before the decisions of current households to live in the area.[43] It seems unlikely that firms could have anticipated these patterns or the processes that led to the risks.

Thus we find that the earlier Gayer, Hamilton and Viscusi analysis is more convincing. It uses the logic of an event study to evaluate how information about sites, combined with the same technical risks, can be used to measure an individual's incremental valuation of risk reductions.[44]

6.2   Distant-future Environmental Effects

Our final category of property value studies considers environmental events that are far in the future. Because of the time involved, one cannot observe the effect currently. There is also a great deal of uncertainty about the environmental events that may take place, the physical effects that may result from the environmental effects, and the human response to these events. However, it may be possible to infer something about the various possible scenarios from data we can observe today. Such effects form our third category. The main example we will consider is global warming and using agricultural land values to estimate the economic effects.

This is not to suggest that the lines between this category and the previous one are always clear. For example, the probability of experiencing an earthquake at a particular location is quite low and may not occur until far in the future. Nonetheless, the probabilities assigned by the experts are accepted by most individuals, and the risk, however slight, seems immediate. For these reasons, we put earthquake risk in the second category. With global warming, it is doubtful that the expected changes from global warming are being capitalized in current land prices. However, we observe varying climatic conditions today, and these conditions may affect land prices. The land price differentials that are due to climate differences may provide insights into the effects if climates change.

This insight is the basis of Mendelsohn et al. (1994)'s analysis of the effect of global warming on agriculture. They used the average farmland price per acre for each county in the contiguous 48 states in the USA. They explained these prices using data on the characteristics of the land, including 30-year average temperature and rainfall in each of the four seasons. Because the data were county averages, they weighted by cropland acres and by crop revenue. Their predictions of the contribution of current climate to current land prices did not differ much between the two weighting schemes. However, when they applied a uniform doubling of CO_2 with a resultant 5° F increase in temperature and an 8 percent increase in precipitation across all land and seasons, the results differed by weighting. With the cropland weighting, land rents were reduced throughout the southern parts of the country. However, with the crop-revenue weighs, the warming was beneficial to much of the country and was only harmful in the mountain regions.

The Mendelsohn et al. (1994) paper attempted a new approach to valuing the economic effects of global warming. Effectively, they are estimating a hedonic equation for agricultural land throughout the country. However, in their predictions of land values after global warming, they are assuming the price schedule will not change. A change in climate throughout the country (and the world) is a major event that will have ramifications for the relative prices of the various crops. In turn, this will change the price of land with a particular vector of climate characteristics. Once the hedonic price schedule changes, the forecast of Ricardian rent changes is more complex. For example, if citrus crops could be grown throughout the southern half of the country, rather than just in California and Florida, the value of land where citrus crops could be grown would probably fall.

Subsequent authors (see Quiggin and Horowitz, 1999, and Darwin, 1999) have raised questions about the specification and interpretation of this work. In their response to Darwin, Mendelsohn and Nordhaus (1999b) highlight what they interpret as the 'take away messages' of their paper

it was one of the first studies to demonstrate that cross sectional evidence could provide quantitative estimates of the economic effects of climate.

it was one of the first empirical studies to demonstrate that warming could be beneficial.

The MNS [Mendelsohn, Nordhaus and Shaw] study also revealed, however, that cross sectional analyses are demanding and can profit from constructive criticism. (Mendelsohn and Nordhaus, 1999, p. 1053)

In this vein we believe this line of research on detecting long-term signals in hedonic models is promising but just a beginning! It is especially important to consider the same range of issues raised with short-term effects about what is being measured and how it relates to consumers' willingness to pay or farmers' profits.

7.   IMPLICATIONS AND NEXT STEPS

Hedonic models are one of the 'success stories' of modern applied microeconomic analysis. They have gone from concept to practical tool in the evaluation of quality adjustments for new varieties of private commodities. Their role in environmental policy has been equally substantial but more indirect. Even in cases where the link between the policy (for example, changes in specific air pollutants) and the measurement of attributes in a hedonic model is clear, their role in policy has remained indirect – as a cross-check to methods with links to policy that seem more tangible. This characterization is especially true for evaluating the health effects of air pollution policy. As our discussion of Panel 3.1 suggested, the health risk orientation of US air pollution regulations has required an evaluation of the health risks associated with different air quality standards. Rather than 'disconnect' the benefit measures for these avoided health effects, most policy analysts have sought to monetize either the risk or the set of health effects associated with air pollution separately and to assume that they can be added. A hedonic model offers a composite measure because the air pollution measure enters the model directly and the analyst does not attempt to evaluate the reasons for seeking improved air quality.

In other areas where the connection between the proxy used to reflect an attribute in the hedonic model and the objective of policy are not easily related, the results from hedonic models have not had a direct role. Their contribution is to offer suggestive evidence of a behavioral linkage. Even in situations where the connection between measures and policy outcomes is clear (for example, water quality) and the regulatory mandate does not identify some effects as dominant (for example, health effects with the criteria air pollutants), efforts to use hedonic findings in policy evaluation are largely confined to cases where they serve as checks. We believe the reason stems from concern that the hedonic models' estimates may not fully reflect all the ways the resources influence people. Here we are not referring to nonuse values but rather to a diverse array of uses that may not be fully captured by the locational choices.

This concern is a commentary on the range of substitutes assumed available and the detail with which locational choice models are specified. Progress in integrating hedonics into these policies must await integrated models that address squarely the extent of overlap in benefit measurement methods, rather than offering simple statements that there are prospects for overlaps in estimates. This progress will only come through a willingness to develop specific structural models. Cameron's (1992) joint estimation strategy that we discussed earlier is an example of what we have in mind.

Structural models must provide as part of the specification of the objective function and constraints a means to resolve the interrelationship between different estimates of the effects of disamenities. That is, when a behavioral model specifies several different avenues for household adjustment, each is a potential source of a marginal willingness to pay estimate. In short, the model is spelling out how individuals can acquire substitutes for environmental amenities. If air quality around one's residence is poor, does this imply the household takes more weekend trips to the mountains, is more likely to operate air conditioning before temperature and humidity conditions might imply it is needed, or simply avoids going outside on bad days? To the extent we can specify these adjustments and incorporate them consistently into a formal model of choice, it is possible to establish a direct relationship between hedonic and other methods for non-market valuation.

Smith et al., (2002) have demonstrated that hedonic, travel cost, and contingent valuation estimates of water quality improvements can be combined consistently. This is the logic Cameron used to derive her joint estimator and could be applied to help resolve estimates derived from hedonic models with those for health risks. Indeed, Portney's (1981) early computation of the value of a statistical life (VSL) from a hedonic property value model is an example of an application where a VSL estimate is derived from housing market evidence. It was based on the assumption that reducing the risk of premature death was the only reason for avoiding air pollution around one's home.

Hedonic analyses have had more success in litigation. Property values change in response to an environmental problem because people are willing to pay to avoid the problem. Judges and juries are more convinced when people actually pay to avoid environmental disamenities or experience losses when they are discovered. The tangible evidence of an effect on people and their property has been convincing in litigation. Hedonic work for litigation involves *ex-post* estimation of damages at a specific location, whereas policy uses of hedonic results often involve *ex-ante* application of results derived under different circumstances. The 'hidden literature' we discussed raised some new issues worthy of further research. A few of the most promising include:

- When do hedonic models actually provide a credible cross-check? And are they upper or lower bounds? Can we do a better job at specifying what the relationship should be between the hedonic cross-check and the other (effect-specific) estimates being used? We have presented results where they were interpreted both ways.

- What is the influence of the socio-economic characteristics of neighborhoods or urban areas on the hedonic estimates obtained in those locations?
- When an agency undertakes analysis of a significant environmental policy issue, is it really a 'signal' in housing markets? This was clearly a concern of policy-makers and would undermine our ability to publicly evaluate significant spatial amenities or disamenities. Will full disclosure of the decision process help mute these effects?
- Can hedonic models help to identify environmental events through carefully designed repeat sales models or are selection effects too important a limitation?
- What are the conditions for using hedonics to estimate values with very long-term events?

Economists maintain a fundamental confidence in a 'law of one price.' That is, there are incentives that assure different people will pay the same price for the same commodity in well-functioning markets. When we observe this is not happening, it usually tells us something about restrictions on the markets, limitations in the information, or subtle differences in the commodities recognized by the people involved, but not the analysts trying to describe their behavior. The hedonic framework is statistical detective work and has been very successful. Because many of its successes never make it into profession journals, we have tried to combine some less known examples with more recognized cases to gauge where we stand in valuing site-specific environmental amenities. The record is remarkable, and the techniques have considerable promise for enhancing what we can learn about consumer preferences for spatially delineated externalities as housing sales price data become routinely available to researchers.

NOTES

* As this paper was being prepared, Sherwin Rosen died prematurely of cancer. We would like to acknowledge his significant contribution to hedonic models and the profession in general through his research by dedicating this paper to his memory. Thanks are due to the series editors Henk Folmer and Tom Tietenberg as well as Shelby Gerking, Bengt Kriström and an anonymous referee for most helpful comments on an earlier draft of this paper. Partial support for Smith's research was provided by the US Environmental Protection Agency under grant # R-826609–01.
1. The Bureau of Labor Statistics web site includes a number of working papers with hedonic price functions; see http://www.bls.gov/cpihome.htm.
2. Bartik and Smith (1987); Palmquist (1991); Freeman (1993); and Palmquist (forthcoming) are examples of surveys that are oriented to the theory and methodology of property value studies.
3. Berndt (1991) credits Waugh with the first empirical hedonic study. For a discussion of the historical antecedents to the hedonic approach for dealing with quality attributes of goods, see Banzhaf (forthcoming).

4. As Banzhaf notes, Griliches's initial proposal viewed the hedonic function as an empirical, rather than a theoretical, relationship. He offered two perspectives on the function. In one price was a function of the characteristics. The sample to estimate the relationship was varieties of the commodity. In the second, developed to account for changing attributes over time, he included dummy variables along with the characteristics to account for the base and subsequent years when new varieties were introduced.

5. The research is summarized in Ridker (1967).

6. It is interesting to note that the Public Health Service project also included another property value study. Hugh Nourse compared the trends in real-estate price indexes near a metal-fabricating plant emitting noxious odors and a nearby control area. (See Ridker, 1967, chapter 7 or Nourse, 1967.) While the results were not entirely satisfactory, they foreshadowed the use of repeat sales to measure environmental effects, which will be discussed later.

7. Ridker and Henning (1967) St Louis; Anderson and Crocker (1969) St Louis, Washington, DC, and Kansas City; Peckham (1970) Delaware Valley; and Zerbe (1969) Toronto. The latter three studies are cited in Barrett and Waddell (1970). Part of the Anderson and Crocker work was later published in Anderson and Crocker (1971).

8. In the case of air quality as measured by total suspended particulates, Smith and Huang (1993, 1995) found 37 empirical studies generating 86 estimates that were usable in their meta-analysis.

9. The scaling of an individual point estimate of marginal willingness to pay must address whether the change is large enough to induce a shift in the market equilibrium represented in the hedonic function. As noted by a variety of authors (for example, Bartik, 1988, Palmquist, 1988, and Smith and Huang, 1995), such computations are also approximations at the individual level. A single hedonic price function does not, except with additional restrictive assumptions such as identical preferences across individuals, allow estimation of the marginal willingness to pay function.

10. Hedonic studies have been done for an extremely diverse set of differentiated products and factors of production. Environmental applications have almost always used real-estate prices or wages. Hedonic wage studies involving spatially delineated measures of pollution have had little use in the policy arena. Wage hedonic models with information about job risks have been extremely influential to a wide range of areas in US regulatory policy. The concept of the value of a statistical life, a measure of the incremental compensation required to accept the increased risks of a fatal accident, is the primary focus of these studies. See Viscusi (1993) for a review of this literature and Mrozek and Taylor (2002) for a meta-analysis of the available estimates. The emphasis in this chapter is on property value studies.

11. Graves, et al. (1998) do note concern with the magnitude of estimates of the marginal willingness to pay, noting that:

> estimates of the marginal valuations of nonmarket commodities, generated with the hedonic method, would change substantially with alternative estimating techniques ... [O]ur findings cast doubt on the results of studies that have utilized the hedonic-based marginal prices to evaluate the validity of other nonmarket methods. (pp. 220–21)

12. The debate began with Freeman (1971) and was soon joined by Anderson and Crocker (1972), Freeman (1974a), Polinsky and Shavell (1975) and Small (1975).

13. The work was first reported as part of a National Academy of Sciences/National Academy of Engineering report on *Air Quality and Automobile Emission Control* in 1974.

14. This measure is exact if there is free mobility within the urban area. If there are transactions and moving costs, bounds on willingness to pay are possible (Palmquist, 1992b).

15. Sieg et al. (2001) use a locational equilibrium model to evaluate how the new computed equilibrium assignment of heterogeneous households and associated vector of housing prices (across communities) in response to an exogenous change in air pollution affects welfare measures.

16. In unpublished research Smith et al. (2001) have shown that empirical measures of the Bartik upper and lower bounds for air pollutants in Southern California do not fall within a narrow band.

17. For an overview of the theoretical, econometric and empirical work on second stage models, see the hedonic surveys cited in note 2.

18. It is important to recognize the constraints on income elasticities that are imposed when we make assumptions that allow revealed preference methods, such as the hedonic model, to recover the marginal willingness to pay schedule. Smith (2001) has shown, for example, that the assumptions of weak complementarity and the Willig (1978) condition imply the income elasticity of the willingness to pay will equal the income elasticity of the private good that is the weak complement. Earlier it was also shown that it is possible to obtain some information about the effects of income on hedonic schedules without the second stage (see Palmquist, 1992a, for this discussion and Smith et al., 2002 for discussion of how they can be used in benefit transfer).

19. Cropper et al. (1988, 1993) use an assignment model for simulations addressing estimation issues. Such models may prove useful in forecasting the *ex-post* hedonic price schedule for use in benefit measurement. In a different type of model, Sieg et al. (2000) forecast the price gradient after the equilibrium adjustment occurs.

20. Poulos and Smith (2001) apply propensity scores to evaluate whether it is possible to construct a spatial experiment with a repeat sales model that combines sales in an area experiencing impacts from a new interstate road with other areas that have not.

21. See, for example, Smith (1983).

22. The early work by Mathtech (1982), discussed below, did explore the feasibility of using wage hedonic models for plausibility checks, but none accounted for the jointness discussed in the Rosen–Roback framework.

23. EPA's (1997) recent retrospective study of the benefits and costs from the Clean Air Act regulations from 1970 to 1990 bases the estimates of household soiling damages avoided on the Mathtech research (see Table J-2, Appendix I, pp. 1-15 – 1-19 for discussion).

24. There are no separate reports of the per household benefit measures, in part due to the complexity of the national policy evaluations.

25. The EPA also funded a series of projects on developing the hedonic method. McConnell (1984) headed a project devoted to the problems and prospects for estimating the second stage of the hedonic model. The most important work in that project was on the identification problem in the second stage. Certain aspects of this work were reported in McConnell and Phipps (1987) and Mendelsohn (1985). Graves et al. (1985), on the other hand, concentrated on the issues involved in estimating the first stage hedonic equation. They considered the specification of the hedonic equation, variable selection, measurement error, functional, and non-normal errors. A summary is contained in Graves et al. (1988). The EPA has continued to fund research on air pollution and property values today (Sieg et al., 2001).

26. In Brookshire et al. (1982a), discussed above in the air quality section, the contingent valuation survey used several techniques to present air quality including photographs showing visual range. However, the hedonic study used objective pollution measures for nitrogen dioxide and total suspended particulate matter. Later hedonic studies in the South Coast Air Basin (for example, Murdoch and Thayer, 1988) did use visual range.

27. Smith was a reviewer for EPA for one of the versions of their efforts. A key argument in the proposal was the need for site investigations – visits by research staff of each area to determine whether the changes taking place could actually be attributed to water quality. In many respects, their logic was consistent with the search for natural experiments and instruments so common in literature on policy evaluation commonly used in labor economics and most recently proposed by Chay and Greenstone (2000) for hedonic applications involving air quality. To our knowledge, no one has suggested this connection to this early work.

28. With air pollution there may be little variation within a given neighborhood, but for many air pollutants there is variation throughout an urban area and air pollution is a consideration at all locations. With water pollution, once you get back a short distance from the water, the water pollution may have no relevance. However, see the next note.

29. This does not mean that there have not been interesting property value studies done in recent years. Two innovative recent studies have considered water quality. Leggett and Bockstael (2000) take advantage of a high irregular coastline in Maryland to obtain significant water quality variation within a single residential market for coastal properties. In several related

studies (Lawson 1997; Boyle et al., 1999; Michael et al., 2000), differing water qualities on several lakes in Maine have provided spatial, in addition to temporal, variation. A second-stage hedonic model has been estimated (Boyle et al., 1999). If one broadens the category from water pollution to water-related effects, other interesting papers emerge. Lind (1967) modeled the relationship between flood control and land values, and his model had a significant effect on early property value work. Shoreline erosion is considered in Kriesel et al. (1993). Parsons (1992) uses a repeat sale model to evaluate coastal land use restrictions. Smith and Palmquist (1994) consider temporal substitution, coastal rental property, and amenities.

30. They eliminated all variables that were not significant at the 10 percent level. They do not report their results with the full model.
31. This work was later published as Langley (1976).
32. This research provides early support for the logic underlying the locational equilibrium models recently proposed by Epple and Sieg (1999) for evaluating spatially delineated public goods.
33. For an overview of the early studies, see Nelson (1980).
34. Michaels's thesis (1987) did investigate the implications of different distance-based measures of the effect of hazardous waste sites in both hedonic models and in a linked random utility analysis.
35. Distance from a site is not the only way the hedonic equation could be estimated. Dichotomous variables for proximity to the site or different distances from the site can be used. Which specification is better depends on the way the site is perceived by nearby residents. Recent developments in spatial econometrics may broaden the range of choices here.
36. This conclusion is independent of the issues that would also be associated with the size of the impact in relation to the scale of the market and the plausibility of marginal approximations in these cases.
37. The McClelland et al. (1990) study took a first step toward this process by using average risk perceptions of respondents in different areas around a landfill as attributes in their hedonic model.
38. Our access to documents from the two cases described here stem from the second author's role in each case. In the first (the Eagle River case), he was hired to 'play' the plaintiff's expert in a mock trial. As a condition of participation, he was given access to all documents from both sides of the case and allowed to write about the research. In the second case (New Bedford Harbor), he was a member of a peer review panel providing plaintiff attorneys' comments and guidance on the research activities undertaken as part of the litigation.
39. Mendelsohn et al. (1992) repeat a portion of this analysis in their published paper. They altered the deflator used and several aspects of the specification so the numerical estimates are not comparable, but support the same general conclusion.
40. It is interesting to note that by 1971 there was a property value study of a solid waste disposal site (Havlicek et al., 1971).
41. Another study of hazardous waste sites (Smith and Desvousges, 1986) used the hedonic framework to motivate the research. Since the data came from a survey about willingness to pay for increases in the distance from a hazardous waste site rather than real-estate data, we have not included it here, although it has been influential.
42. The data were developed by Harrison and Stock (1984) as part of an EPA project.
43. Gayer (2000) acknowledges that there is a wide disparity between siting decisions and the sales data he has available, but argues that the elements of a dynamic process reinforcing an initial site location can be uncovered from the more recent data. He does provide information on how this judgment can be supported, aside from the exogeneity test itself. Thus, in fairness, the issue requires further work within a more complete dynamic framework.
44. Schulze et al. (1986) also used the framework of an event study to investigate how the amount of time after an announcement was made affected the sales price/distance relationship. Michaels and Smith (1990) found similar sensitivity, supporting the view that these asset markets can also signal the effects of information.

REFERENCES

Adler, K.J., R.C. Anderson, Z. Cook, R.C. Dower, A.R. Ferguson and M.J. Vickers (1982), *The Benefits of Regulating Hazardous Waste Disposal: Land Values as an Estimator*, Washington, DC, Public Interest Economics Center, for US Environmental Protection Agency.

Anderson, R.J., Jr and T.D. Crocker (1969), 'Air Pollution and Housing: Some Findings', Institute for Research in the Behavioral, Economic, and Management Sciences, Krannert Graduate School of Industrial Administration, Purdue University.

Anderson, R.J., Jr and T. D. Crocker (1971), 'Air Pollution and Residential Property Values', *Urban Studies*, **8**, 171–80.

Anderson, R.J., Jr and T.D. Crocker (1972), 'Air Pollution and Property Values: A Reply', *Review of Economics and Statistics*, **54**, 470–73.

Bailey, M.J., R.F. Muth and H.O. Nourse (1963), 'A Regression Method for Real Estate Price Index Construction', *Journal of the American Statistical Association*, **58**, 933–42.

Banzhaf, H.S. (forthcoming), 'Quantifying the Qualitative: Quality-Adjusted Price Indexes in the US, 1915–1961', *History of Political Economy, Annual Supplement*.

Barrett, L.B. and T.E. Waddell (1970), *The Cost of Air Pollution Damages: a Status Report*, Raleigh, NC, National Air Pollution Control Administration, Public Health Service, US Department of Health, Education, and Welfare.

Bartik, T.J. (1988), 'Measuring the Benefits of Amenity Improvements in Hedonic Price Models', *Land Economics*, **64**, 172–83.

Bartik, T.J. and V.K Smith (1987), 'Urban Amenities and Public Policy', in E.S. Mills (ed.), *Handbook of Regional and Urban Economics*, vol. 2., Amsterdam: North-Holland, pp. 1207–54.

Berndt, E.R. (1991), *The Practice of Econometrics: Classic and Contemporary*, Reading, MA: Addison-Wesley.

Bockstael, Nancy E. and Elena G. Irwin (2000), 'Economics and the Land Use–Environmental Link', in Tom Tietenberg and Henk Falmer (eds), *International Yearbook of Environmental and Resource Economics 2000/2001*, Cheltenham, UK and Northampton, USA: Edward Elgar.

Boyle, K.J., P.J. Poor and L.O. Taylor (1999), 'Estimating the Demand for Protecting Freshwater Lakes from Eutrophication', *American Journal of Agricultural Economics*, **81**, 1118–22.

Brinton, J.H. and J.N. Bloom (1969), *Effect of Highway Landscape Development on Nearby Property*, National Cooperative Highway Research Report, No. 75.

Brookshire, D.S., R.G. Cummings, M. Rahmatian, W.D. Schultze and M.A. Thayer (1982a), *Experimental Approaches for Valuing Environmental Commodities*, US Environmental Protection Agency.

Brookshire, D.S., M.A. Thayer, W.D. Schultze and R.C. d'Arge (1982b), 'Valuing Public Goods: A Comparison of Survey and Hedonic Approaches', *American Economics Review*, **72**, 165–78.

Brookshire, D.S., M.A. Thayer, J. Tschirhart and W.D. Schultze (1985), 'A Test of the Expected Utility Model: Evidence from Earthquake Risks', *Journal of Political Economy*, **93**, 369–89.

Cameron, T.A. (1992), 'Combining Contingent Valuation and Travel Cost Data for the Valuation of Nonmarket Goods', *Land Economics*, **68**, 302–17.

Chattopadhyay, S. (1998), 'An Empirical Investigation Into the Performance of Ellickson's Random Bidding Model, With an Application to Air Quality Valuation', *Journal of Urban Economics*, **43**, 292–314.

Chay, K.Y. and M. Greenstone (2000), 'Does Air Quality Matter? Evidence From the Housing Market', Working Paper.

Colony, D.C. (1966), *Study of the Effect, If Any, of an Urban Freeway upon Residential Properties Contiguous to the Right of Way*, University of Toledo.

Colony, D.C. (1967), *Expressway Traffic Noise and Residential Properties*, University of Toledo.

Cropper, M.L., L. Deck and K.E. McConnell (1988), 'On the Choice of Functional Forms for Hedonic Price Functions', *Review of Economics and Statistics*, **70**, 668–75.

Cropper, M.L., L. Deck, N. Kishor and K.E. McConnell (1993), Valuing Product Attributes Using Single Market Data: A Comparison of Hedonic and Discrete Choice Approaches', *Review of Economics and Statistics*, **75**, 225–32.

Darwin, R. (1999), 'The Impact of Global Warming on Agriculture: A Ricardian Analysis: Comment', *The American Economic Review*, **89**, 1049–52.

Dornbusch, D.M. and S.M. Barrager (1973), *Benefit of Water Pollution Control on Property Values*, report to Office of Research and Monitoring, US Environmental Protection Agency, EPA-600/5–73–005.

Epple, D. (1987), 'Hedonic prices and implicit markets: estimating demand and supply functions for differentiated products', *Journal of Political Economy* 95:59–80.

Epple, D. and H. Sieg (1999), 'Estimating Equilibrium Models of Local Jurisdictions', *Journal of Political Economy*, **107**, 645–81.

Freeman III, A.M. (1971), 'Air Pollution and Property Values: A Methodological Comment', *Review of Economics and Statistics*, **53**, 415–16.

Freeman III, A.M. (1974a), 'Air Pollution and Property Values: A Further Comment', *Review of Economics and Statistics*, **56**, 554–6.

Freeman III, A.M. (1974b), 'On Estimating Air Pollution Control Benefits from Land Value Studies', *The Journal of Environmental Economics and Management*, **1**, 277–88.

Freeman, A.M., III (1993), *The Measurement of Environmental and Resource Values*, Washington, DC: Resources for the Future.

Gamble, H.B., C.J. Langley, Jr, R.D. Pashek, O.H. Sauerlender, R. D. Twark and R.H. Downing (1973), *Community Effects of Highways Reflected by Property Values*, report to the Federal Highway Administration, US Department of Transportation.

Gatzlaff, Dean H. and Donald R. Haurin (1997), 'Sample Selection Bias and Repeat-Sales Index Estimates', *Journal of Real Estate Finance and Economics*, **14**, 33–50.

Gayer, T. (2000), 'Neighborhood Demographics and the Distribution of Hazardous Waste Risks: On Instrumental Variables Estimation', *Journal of Regulatory Economics*, **17**, 131–55.

Gayer, T., J.T. Hamilton and W.K. Viscusi (2000), 'Private Values of Risk Tradeoffs at Superfund Sites: Housing Market Evidence on Learning About Risk', *Review of Economics and Statistics*, **82**, 439–51.

Graves, P., J.C. Murdoch, M.A. Thayer and D. Waldman (1985), *Improving the Accuracy of Hedonic Price Methods: Econometric Analysis of Existing Data Sets*, volume VI of *Improving the Accuracy and Reducing the Costs of Environmental Benefit Assessments*, US Environmental Protection Agency.

Graves, P., J.C. Murdoch, M.A. Thayer and D. Waldman (1988), 'The Robustness of Hedonic Price Estimation: Urban Air Quality', *Land Economics*, **64**, 220–33.

Griliches, Zvi (1961), 'Hedonic Price Indexes for Automobiles: An Econometric Analysis of Quality Change', in *The Price Statistics of the Federal Government*, General Series No. 73, New York: Columbia University Press for the National Bureau of Economic Research, pp. 137–96. Reprinted in Ziv Griliches (ed.), *Price Indexes and Quality Change: Studies in New Methods of Measurement*, Cambridge, MA: Harvard University Press, 1971, pp. 55–87.

Hahn, Robert W. (1999), 'The Impact of Economics on Environmental Policy', working paper 99–4, AEI–Brookings Joint Center for Regulatory Studies (May).

Hall, F.L., B.E. Breston and S.M. Taylor (1978), 'Effects of Highway Noise on Residential Property Values', *Transportation Research Record*, No. 686, pp. 38–43.

Harrison D., Jr, and D.L. Rubinfeld (1978), 'Hedonic Housing Prices and the Demand for Clean Air', *Journal of Environmental Economics and Management*, **5**, 81–102.

Harrison, D., Jr and J.H. Stock (1984), *Using the Hedonic Housing Method to Estimate the Benefits of Hazardous Waste Cleanup*, Volume I, part 1 of *Research and Demonstration of Improved Methods for Carrying Out Benefit–Cost Analyses of Individual Regulations*, Report to the US Environmental Protection Agency.

Hausman, Jerry A. (1978), 'Specification Tests in Economics', *Econometrica*, **46**, 1252–71.

Hausman, J.A. (ed.) (1993), *Contingent Valuation, A Critical Assessment*, Amsterdam: North-Holland.

Havlicek, J., Jr, R. Richardson and L. Davies (1971), 'Measuring the Impacts of Solid Waste Disposal Site Location on Property Values', *American Journal of Agricultural Economics*, **53**, 869.

Heckman, J., H. Ichimura and P. E. Todd (1997), 'Matching as an Econometric Evaluation Estimator: Evidence from Evaluation of a Job Training Programme', *Review of Economic Studies*, **64**, 605–29.

Hoehn, J.P., M.C. Berger and G.C. Blomquist (1987), 'A Hedonic Model of Interregional Wages, Rents, and Amenity Values', *Journal of Regional Science*, **27**, 605–20.

Kiel, K.A. (1995), 'Measuring the Impact of the Discovery and Cleaning of Identified Hazardous Waste Sites on House Values', *Land Economics*, **71**, 428–35.

Kiel, K.A. and K.T. McClain (1995), 'House Prices During Siting Decision Stages: The Case of an Incinerator from Rumor Through Operation', *Journal of Environmental Economics and Management*, **28**, 241–55.

Kohlhase, J.E. (1991), 'The Impact of Toxic Waste Sites on Housing Values', *Journal of Urban Economics*, **30**, 1–26.

Kriesel, W., A. Randall, and F. Lichtkoppler (1993), 'Estimating the Benefits of Shore Erosion Protection in Ohio's Lake Erie Housing Market', *Water Resource Research*, **29**, 795–801.

Langley, C.J., Jr (1976), 'Adverse Impacts of the Washington Beltway on Residential Property Values', *Land Economics*, **52**, 54–65.

Lawson, S.R. (1997) *Estimating the Benefits of Water Quality in Maine's Lakes: A Hedonic Property Value Model*, master's thesis, University of Maine.

Leggett, C. and N.E. Bockstael (2000), 'Evidence of the Effects of Water Quality on Residential Land Prices', *Journal of Environmental Economics and Management*, **39**, 121–44.

Lind, R.C. (1967), 'Flood Control Alternatives and the Economics of Flood Protection', *Water Resources Research*, **3**, 345–57.

McClelland, G. H., W. D. Schulze, and B. Hurd (1990), 'The Effect of Risk Beliefs on Property Values: A Case Study of a Hazardous Waste Site', *Risk Analysis*, **10**, 485–97.

McConnell, K.E. (ed.) (1984), *Identification of Preferences in Hedonic Models*, volume 1 of *Implicit Market Methods for Benefit Estimation*, report to the US Environmental Protection Agency.

McConnell, K.E. and T.T. Phipps (1987), 'Identification of Preferences in Hedonic Models: Consumer Demands With Nonlinear Budget Constraints', *Journal of Urban Economics*, **22**, 35–52.

Mathtech (1981), *Benefit Analysis of Alternative Secondary National Ambient Air Quality Standards for Sulfur Dioxide and Total Suspended Particulates*, Benefit Analysis Program, Office of Air Quality Planning and Standards, US EPA, Research Triangle Park, draft final analysis.

Mathtech (1982), *Benefit Analysis of Alternative Secondary National Ambient Air Quality Standards for Sulfur Dioxide and Total Suspended Particulates, Volume II*, Benefit Analysis Program, Office of Air Quality Planning and Standards, US EPA, Research Triangle Park, Final Analysis.

Mathtech (1983), *Benefit and Net Benefit Analysis of Alternative National Ambient Air Quality Standards for Particulate Matter, Volume I*, Economic Analysis Branch, Office of Air Quality Planning and Standards, US EPA, Research Triangle Park.

Mendelsohn, R. (1985), 'Identifying Structural Equations With Single Market Data', *Review of Economics and Statistics*, **67**, 525–9.

Mendelsohn, R., D. Hellerstein, M. Huguenin, R. Unsworthy and R. Brazee (1992), 'Measuring Hazardous Waste Damages With Panel Models', *Journal of Environmental Economics and Management*, **22**, 259–71.

Mendelsohn, R., W.D. Nordhaus and D. Shaw (1994), 'The Impact of Global Warming on Agriculture: A Ricardian Analysis', *American Economic Review*, **84**, 753–71.

Michael, H.J., K.J. Boyle and R. Bouchard (2000), 'Does the Measurement of Environmental Quality Affect Implicit Prices Estimated From Hedonic Models?', *Land Economics*, **76**, 283–98.

Michaels, R.G. and V.K. Smith (1990), 'Market Segmentation and Valuing Amenities With Hedonic Models: The Case of Hazardous Waste Sites', *Journal of Urban Economics*, **28**, 223–42.

Michaels, R.G., R. Barnes, P. Giordano, W. Lin and M. Wojcik (1992), 'Hazardous Waste Facilities and Residential Property Values', in Abt Associates, *Preliminary Results in Support of Benefits Estimation for the Corrective Action Rule*, US Environmental Protection Agency.

Mrozek, J. and L.O. Taylor (2002), 'What Determines the Value of Life? A Meta-Analysis', *Journal of Policy Analysis and Management* (forthcoming).

Murdoch, J.C. and M.A. Thayer (1988), 'Hedonic Price Estimation of Variable Urban Air Quality', *Journal of Environmental Economics and Management*, **15**, 143–6.

Nelson, J. P. (1975), *The Effects of Mobile-Source Air and Noise Pollution on Residential Property Values*, report to the US Department of Transportation.

Nelson, J.P. (1980), 'Airports and Property Values', *Journal of Transport Economics and Policy*, **14**, 37–52.

Nourse, H.O. (1967), 'The Effect of Air Pollution on House Values', *Land Economics*, **43**, 181–9.

Oates, Wallace E. (2000), 'From Research to Policy: The Case of Environmental Economics', *University of Illinois Law Review*, 135–54.

O'Byrne, P.H., J.P. Nelson and J.J. Seneca (1985), 'Housing Values, Census Estimates, Disequilibrium, and the Environmental Cost of Airport Noise: A Case Study of Atlanta', *Journal of Environmental Economics and Management*, **12**, 169–78.

Palmquist, R.B. (1980), *Impact of Highway Improvements on Property Values in Washington*, Washington State Department of Transportation, report to the Federal Highway Administration, US Department of Transportation.

Palmquist, R.B. (1982), 'Measuring Environmental Effects on Property Values Without Hedonic Regressions', *Journal of Urban Economics*, **11**, 333–47.

Palmquist, R.B. (1984), 'Estimating the Demand for the Characteristics of Housing', *Review of Economics and Statistics*, **66**, 394–404.

Palmquist, R.B. (1988), 'Welfare Measurement for Environmental Improvements Using the Hedonic Model: The Case of Nonparametric Marginal Prices', *Journal of Environmental Economics and Management*, **15**, 297–312.

Palmquist, R.B. (1991), 'Hedonic Methods', in J.B. Braden and C.D. Kolstad (eds), *Measuring the Demand for Environmental Quality*, Amsterdam: North-Holland, pp. 77–120.

Palmquist, R.B. (1992a), 'Valuing Localized Externalities', *Journal of Urban Economics*, **31**, 59–68.

Palmquist, R.B. (1992b), 'A Note on Transactions Costs, Moving Costs, and Benefit Measures', *Journal of Urban Economics*, **32**, 40–44.

Palmquist, R.B. (forthcoming), 'Property Value Models', in Karl-Göran Mäler and Jeffrey Vincent (eds), *Handbook of Environmental Economics*, Elsevier: North-Holland.

Parsons, G.R. (1992), 'The Effect of Coastal Land Use Restrictions on Housing Prices: A Repeat Sales Analysis', *Journal of Environmental Economics and Management*, **22**, 25–37.

Patchin, Peter J. (1994), 'Contaminated Properties and the Sales Comparison Approach', *The Appraisal Journal*, **62**(3), 402–10.

Peckham, B.W. (1970), Division of Economic Effects Research, National Air Pollution Control Agency, Raleigh, NC.

Polinsky, A.M. and D.L. Rubinfeld (1977), 'Property Values and the Benefits of Environmental Improvements: Theory and Measurement', in L. Wingo and A. Evans (eds), *Public Economics and the Quality of Life*, Baltimore, MD: Johns Hopkins University Press, pp. 154–80.

Polinsky, A.M. and S. Shavell (1975), 'Air Pollution and Property Value Debate', *Review of Economics and Statistics*, **57**, 100–105.

Polinsky, A.M. and S. Shavell (1976), 'Amenities and Property Values in a Model of an Urban Area', *Journal of Public Economics*, **5**, 119–29.

Polinsky, A.M., D.L. Rubinfeld and S. Shavell (1974), 'Economic Benefits of Air Quality Improvements As Estimated From Market Data', *Air Quality and Automotive Emissions, NAS/NAE*, vol. 4 ch. 4, sections 3–5, Washington, DC: National Academy of Science/National Academy of Engineers.

Portney, Paul R. (1981), 'Housing Prices, Health Effects and Valuing Reductions in Risk of Death', *Journal of Environmental Economics and Management*, **8**, 72–8.

Poulos, Christine and V. Kerry Smith (2001), 'Transparency and Takings', unpublished working paper, Center for Environmental and Resource Economics, North Carolina State University, August.

Quiggin, J. and J.K. Horowitz (1999), 'The Impact of Global Warming on Agriculture: A Ricardian Analysis: Comment', *The American Economic Review*, **89**, 1044–5.

Ridker, R.G. (1967), *Economic Costs of Air Pollution: Studies in Measurement*, New York: Praeger.

Ridker, R.G. and J.A. Henning (1967), 'The Determinants of Property Values With Special Reference To Air Pollution', *Review of Economics and Statistics*, **49**, 246–57.

Roback, J. (1982), 'Wages, Rents, and the Quality of Life', *Journal of Political Economy*, **90,** 1257–78.

Roddewig, Richard (1996), 'Stigma, Environmental Risk and Property Value: 10 Critical Inquiries', *The Appraisal Journal* **64**, 375–87.

Rosen, S. (1974), 'Hedonic Prices and Implicit Markets: Product Differentiation In Pure Competition', *Journal of Political Economy*, **82,** 34–55.

Rosen, S. (1979), 'Wage-based Indexes of the Quality of Life', in P. Mieszkowski and M. Straszheim (eds), *Current Issues in Urban Economics*, Baltimore, MD: Johns Hopkins University Press, pp. 74–104.

Rowe, R.D. and L.G. Chestnut (1981), *Visibility Benefits Assessment Guidebook*, Abt\West, for Office of Air Quality Planning and Standards, US Environmental Protection Agency.

Rowe, R.D. and W.D. Schulze (1985), *Economic Assessment of Damage Related to the Eagle Mine Facility*, Energy and Resource Consultants, Inc.

Schulze, W., G. McClelland, B. Hurd and J. Smith (1986), *A Case Study of a Hazardous Waste Site: Perspectives from Economics and Psychology*, US Environmental Protection Agency.

Shapiro, Perry and Terence Smith (1981), 'Preferences for Nonmarket Goods Revealed Through Market Demands', *Advances in Applied Microeconomics*, **1**, 105–22.

Sieg, H., V.K. Smith, H.S. Banzhaf and R. Walsh (2001), 'Estimating the General Equilibrium Benefits of Large Changes in Spatially Delineated Public Goods', working paper, North Carolina State University.

Small, K.A. (1975), 'Air Pollution and Property Values: Further Comment', *Review of Economics and Statistics*, **57,** 105–7.

Smith, V.K. (1983), 'The Role of Site and Job Characteristics In Hedonic Wage Models', *Journal of Urban Economics*, **13,** 296–321.

Smith, V.K. (2001), 'Do Revealed Preference Methods Predetermine the Estimate for the Income Elasticity of WTP?', working paper, North Carolina State University (January).

Smith, V.K. and W. H. Desvousges (1986), 'The Value of Avoiding a *LULU*: Hazardous Waste Disposal Sites', *Review of Economics and Statistics*, **68,** 293–9.

Smith, V.K. and J.C. Huang (1993), 'Hedonic Models and Air Pollution: Twenty-Five Years and Counting', *Environmental and Resource Economics*, **3**, 381–94.

Smith, V.K. and J.C. Huang (1995), 'Can Markets Value Air Quality? A Meta-Analysis of Hedonic Property Value Models', *Journal of Political Economy*, **103**, 209–27.

Smith, V.K. and R.B. Palmquist (1994), 'Temporal Substitution and Recreational Value of Coastal Amenities', *Review of Economics and Statistics*, **76,** 119–26.

Smith, V.K., Holger Sieg, H. Spencer Banzhaf and Randy Walsh (2001), 'Do the Bartik Kanemoto Bounds Really Work?', unpublished paper under revision, CEnREP, North Carolina State University, April.

Smith, V.K., George van Houtven and Subhrendu Pattanayak (2002), 'Benefit Transfer Via Preference Calibration: "Prudential Algebra" for Policy', *Land Economics* (forthcoming, February).

Stock, J.H. (1991), 'Nonparametric Policy Analysis: An Application To Estimating Hazardous Waste Cleanup Benefits', in W.A. Barnett, J. Powell and G.E. Tauchen (eds), *Nonparametric and Semiparametric Methods id Econometrics and Statistics*, Cambridge, Cambridge University Press, pp. 77–98.

Taylor, S.M., B.E. Breston and F.L. Hall (1982), 'The Effect of Road Traffic Noise On House Prices', *Journal of Sound and Vibration*, **80,** 523–41.

Thayer, M., H. Albers and M. Rahmatian (1992), 'The Benefits of Reducing Exposure to Waste Disposal Sites: A Hedonic Housing Value Approach', *Journal of Real Estate Research*, **7**, 265–82.

Tolley, G., A. Randall, G. Blomquist, M. Brien, R. Fabien, G. Fishelson, A. Frankel, M. Grenchik, J. Hoehn, A. Kelly, R. Krumm, E. Mensah and T. Smith (1986), *Establishing and Valuing the Effects of Improved Visibility in Eastern United States*, University of Chicago, for Office of Policy, Planning and Evaluation, US Environmental Protection Agency.

Towne, R.M. and Associates, Inc. (1966), *An Investigation of the Effect of Freeway Traffic Noise on Apartment Rents*, report to the Oregon Highway Commission.

US Environmental Protection Agency (1997), The Benefits and Costs of the Clean Air Act, 1970 to 1990, Office of Policy, Planning and Evaluation and Office of Air and Radiation.

Viscusi, W. Kip (1993), 'The Value of Risks to Life and Health', *Journal of Economic Literature*, **31**, 1912–46.

Waddell, T.E. (1974), *The Economic Damage of Air Pollution*, Economic Analysis Branch, Washington Environmental Research Center, Office of Research and Development, USEPA, EPA-600/5–74–012, Socioeconomic Environmental Studies Series.

Waugh, F.V. (1929), *Quality as a Determinant of Vegetable Prices: A Statistical Study of Quality Factors Influencing Vegetable Prices in the Boston Wholesale Market*, New York: Columbia University Press. Reprinted by the AMS Press, Inc., New York, 1968.

Willig, Robert (1978), 'Incremental Consumer's Surplus and Hedonic Price Adjustment', *Journal of Economic Theory*, **17**(2), 227–53.

Zerbe, R.O., Jr (1969), *The Economics of Air Pollution: A Cost–Benefit Approach*, Ontario Department of Public Health.

4. Progress and problems in the economics of sustainability

John C.V. Pezzey and Michael A. Toman*

1. INTRODUCTION

Concerns about the sustainability of industrial civilizations are old and new. 'Old' concerns stretch back over at least two centuries. As landmarks, they include concerns about Britain's balance of food output with a rising population (Malthus, 1798), about Britain's coal supplies (Jevons, 1865) and about US mineral supplies (the President's Materials Policy Commission, 1952); and concerns about possible *Limits to Growth* of the whole planet's industrial system because of pollution and resource depletion (Meadows et al., 1972). The 'new' wave of concern dates from the publication of *Our Common Future* (WCED, 1987). This highlighted new environmental threats – such as deforestation, desertification, biodiversity loss, the enhanced greenhouse effect, and the effects of poverty on pollution – that were especially relevant to developing countries, or to the global environment. WCED's explicit focus on 'sustainability' and 'sustainable development' as development goals also challenged many articles on the economics of sustainability.

Our basic aim here is to evaluate how far work by economists since 1987 has advanced our understanding of sustainability, broadly defined (as in WCED, 1987) as the problem of ensuring that future generations are no worse off than today's. (Sections 2 and 3 have more detailed discussions of sustainability concepts.) What progress has been made, and what problems remain? Our format is thus a synthesis, not a review: we ask where are we now, rather than who said what on the way here.[1] Much of the literature has been concerned with the extent to which there *is* a sustainability problem. This question can in turn be subdivided into two broad parts. One deals with technical or physical limits (or lack thereof) to maintaining satisfactory economic and ecological conditions over time. The other deals with the nature of possible obligations to future generations – if there are potential limits to maintenance of satisfactory economic and ecological conditions into the future, to what extent should this be an object of concern?

If one concludes that there is a sustainability problem, then the natural follow-up question concerns policy: what should be done about it? This branch of the sustainability literature is much skimpier than the branch on the nature of a sustainability problem. Moreover, while empirical considerations surely loom large in determining both the nature of the problem and the usefulness of different responses, much of the recent work on sustainability economics has remained theory-rich and data-poor.[2] Thus our synthesis here, as a rough reflection of the literature, emphasizes conceptual treatments of the nature of the sustainability problem. The challenge we face here is to make something of the few existing data, and consolidate the often confusing theories in order to highlight the most important empirical questions that remain. The umpteenth theoretical variant based on hallowed but empirically unsupported assumptions will be of no interest for its own sake, but we will point to remaining conceptual puzzles which are relevant to real-world policy-making.

'Sustainability' now includes a vast range of topics. Almost any current government or corporate document on environmental issues contains multiple S-words (sustainability, ecological sustainability, sustainable development, environmentally sustainable development, sustainable cities/forestry/industry/ transport, and so on). So despite the length of this chapter, we have in fact severely limited the ways in which we approach sustainability. These limits are spelt out in the next section, which also serves as an extended non-technical introduction to sustainability economics. The formal 'road map' of the rest of the chapter's structure comes at the end of this.

Before proceeding, we wish to make a more personal observation. While writing this chapter, we, like the rest of the environmental and natural resource economics profession worldwide, were saddened by the death of Allen Kneese. We note Allen's passing here because in our view he was not only a giant in the field of environmental economics; he also was an often unsung intellectual father in the areas of ecological economics and the economics of sustainability. Two seminal articles suffice to make the case: his article on materials balance with Robert Ayres (Ayres and Kneese, 1969), and his brief 1973 article on the intergenerational equity dilemmas surrounding nuclear power (reprinted as Kneese, 1999; see also Kneese and Schulze, 1985). We therefore dedicate this essay to Allen's memory and the inspiring example he set for all of us.

2.   DEFINING THE ECONOMICS OF SUSTAINABILITY

The 'economics of sustainability' is taken here to include any work with some concern for intergenerational equity or fairness in the decision-making of a whole society over many generations; some recognition of the role in this of finite environmental resources; and some recognizable, if perhaps unconven-

tional, use of economic concepts such as cost, production, momentary (instantaneous) utility, or some kind of aggregating of utility over time into
(intertemporal) welfare.[3] (More precise definitions of sustainability, sustainable development, sustainedness, and so on, are given in section 3.1.) We
include work in which no S-word is used, or in which the focus is on ecological
or physical feasibility of continued economic expansion with finite resources,
rather than on any welfare consequences. We make two key exclusions:

- We exclude the common use nowadays of 'sustainable' to mean just
'environmentally desirable or responsible', since this makes no distinction, for example, between momentary and cumulative pollution. (So in
our language, traffic noise and congestion could be quite undesirable in
a city, yet sustainable.)
- We also exclude intra*generational equity from the definition of sustainability. This will disappoint readers who see it as philosophically
inseparable from inter*generational equity. However, it can still appear
as an influence on production (through disruption and social breakdown)
or utility. A future with rising consumption but sharply rising inequity
may be seen as one in which 'society's' quality of life is not sustained.

In addition to these exclusions, further restrictions or clarifications emerge
when we consider when, why, where and for whom well-being is to be
sustained, and we turn to these next.

2.1 Sustainability When? The Choice of Time Horizon

It is impossible for this planet's civilization to be sustained forever, given a
finite life for our sun. So some finite time horizon is present in almost all sustainability writing, but it is usually not explicit. A horizon of, say, ten years is
a very long one for macroeconomic management, but far too short to address
the full range of issues that 'sustainability' raises in most people's minds. Our
choice of several generations (at least 100 years, which takes us into the 'far
future') reaches a time when there will be many descendants of an average
person now, but when the vast majority of each descendant's genes will come
from many other, unknown people alive now. It also reaches well beyond the
most far-seeing futures and insurance markets in the world. Because of this,
we will also look at what physical rather than economic measures of scarcity
can say about marketed resource availability in the far future. And for assessing
the role of non-marketed resources, physical measures are a vital complement
to the limited availability of non-market valuations of environmental effects
on both utility and production.

2.2 Sustainability Why?

As defined in the Introduction, sustainability is a goal that in principle very few people would oppose. It is hard to find someone who openly thinks it acceptable for future generations to be worse off than today.[4] But the rationale for being concerned about sustainability is still hotly debated, and needs to be addressed.

Some participants in the debate take the view that whatever one might think about intergenerational responsibility in concept, the issue is moot in practice because there is good reason to expect technical and economic progress to continue, leaving future generations better off than today (see for example Weitzman, 1997). Others (ourselves included) take the view that economic progress and ecological protection over several centuries are not so automatically assured. But within this body of opinion, there are several different strands; and the 'why' of sustainability cannot be entirely separated from the 'how', which we discuss in the next subsection.

There have recently been many papers on the philosophical rationales for intergenerational concern (see for example Pezzey, 1992, 1997; Toman, 1994; Norton and Toman, 1997; Howarth, 1997; and Page, 1997). Very broadly, one can discern two lines of rationalization in this literature. The first comes from classical utilitarianism (see for example Broome, 1992). This is concerned with ends – individual welfare – but rejects the notion that individuals should be regarded differently just because of the time when they are alive, as occurs when future welfare is discounted in a typical intergenerational optimization problem. This approach can throw up some challenging incentive compatibility issues. If individuals in fact do experience some intergenerational concern (altruism), but do not weigh the welfare of (unknown potential) future generation equally with their own, then they will not accept the intertemporal resource allocation implied by classical utilitarianism.

A second view is based on a more explicitly rights-based or entitlements-based view of intergenerational obligation. Rawls's (1971) now-classical construction of a rationale for maximizing the well-being of least well-off (across space, and at least to some extent across time) is a relatively familiar example of this approach in the sustainability literature. Another variant is the notion of Kantian imperative, a kind of Golden Rule in which we seek to treat others as we would wish to be treated. This approach also could lead to inconsistency with an individual utilitarian preference ordering, in which people value the well-being of future generations, but less than their own well-being. In some sense, the problem can be circumvented if one accepts the notion that individuals have dual natures animated by different factors, for example, consumers and citizens, with moral considerations of citizenship having the capacity to trump more selfish individual interests.[5] Economists tend stoutly to resist this bifurcation in the treatment of human motivations, and we return to this point in section 3.2 below

2.3 Sustainability How? Substitutability, Technical Progress, and Weak versus Strong Sustainability

Incompatible and often polarized views on the issue of substitutability are held with some passion, as we will discuss in section 4. The mainstream neoclassical view has come to be known as 'weak sustainability'.[6] This view is that substitutability of built (that is, human-made) capital for environmental resources is more or less unlimited.[7] In this view, degradation of specific natural resources (often called 'natural capital' in the literature) is not in itself cause for concern, so long as there are offsetting increases in other forms of capital such that overall well-being can be maintained or increased over time. In short, people can become better off over time, though the composition of the input and consumption bundles will change. This view is very much focused on utilitarian objectives, and is common in models of intertemporal growth that are used to study sustainability, as synthesized in section 3.

As already noted above, some would go further to assert that substitutability, technical progress (whether caused by investment or just by time passing), and conventional policy measures to internalize environmental externalities will together be enough to make conventionally optimal development sustainable. There is then no need for a sustainability policy as such. A less confident view about the future is that, while there is enough substitutability to make neoclassical methods of marginal analysis meaningful and rising utility feasible, policy intervention – over and beyond correction of conventionally defined externalities – may still be needed to achieve the intergenerational distributional objectives embodied in sustainability.

At the pessimistic end of the spectrum are variants of the broad 'strong sustainability' view, supported by some economists and many non-economists, that capital–resource substitutability is either a self-evidently impossible concept, or subject to strict and fairly imminent limits. This view implies that economic growth over a few centuries inevitably requires higher material throughput, not just improved efficiency in the generation of disembodied economic value from the same menu of material inputs. Since these inputs (including available energy and waste-holding capacity) are inherently limited in their availability, strong sustainability leads to both a positive and normative problem in balancing the aspirations of the population for more output as a way to improve living standards with binding physical limits.[8]

Perhaps the best-known summary of this view is due to Daly (1990), who regarded it as self-evident that sustainability requires (a) ecological services critical to life support to be maintained, and pollution stocks to be prevented from increasing beyond certain critical loads; (b) renewable resource stocks (or at least aggregates of these stocks) to be used no faster than they are renewed; and (c) depletion of non-renewable resources to be offset by investment in the production of comparable services from renewable resources (for example in the switch from fossil to renewable energy sources). Daly's perspective is a strong version of a broader perspective that the *combination* of technical/physical substitution limits and moral obligations to future generations (the rights-based approach discussed above) implies the need for strong measures to protect or replace specific natural resources. This view is amplified by concerns about largely unknown risks from future environmental degradation that would compromise the rights of future generations. From this perspective flow different variants of the *precautionary principle* (Howarth, 1997) – a priori constraints on resource degradation or depletion, distinct from what might be justified on cost–benefit grounds, to limit such risks.

Our own view is that there is still scope for plenty of capital–resource substitutability, especially over the medium term when technology is endogenous, but some physical limits on the availability of resource or environmental services could exist on a multigenerational timescale. The key question – which is empirical, not theoretical – is if, when, where and how those limits might show themselves. This perspective ultimately forces those interested in sustainability to abandon ideology, be it cornucopian or catastrophist, and confront difficult, inherently empirical questions.

2.4   Sustainability Where, and for Whom? The Choice of Geographical and Human Scales

As well as a time scale, sustainability needs a geographical scale (sustainability where?) and a human scale (sustainability for whom?) to be well defined. Our geographical focus in this chapter, reflecting the literature, is a mixture between the national and the global. The neoclassical approach in section 3 formally allows the ultimate physical and ecological requirements for sustainability to be treated as items in a nation's financial balance sheet, using values defined on world markets. Any one nation may largely deplete its natural resources now, become a 'knowledge nation' reliant on human capital, import most of its resources in the far future, and perhaps remain sustainable. (The 'perhaps' cautions about both the harm that resource depletion may do to national environmental quality, and the inherent uncertainty of resource prices that far ahead.) But this is not an option for the global economy: not every nation can be a resource importer (Pezzey, 1998). Nevertheless, decision-making power rests largely with nation states and regional trading blocs, and sustainability measurements have been applied to national economies (mainly using closed-economy theory, despite the high degree of openness of all modern economies). To be both intellectually coherent and relevant to policy, we try to consider both global and national perspectives on sustainability here, though we sometimes fall short of this ideal.

There are still some striking omissions in our topical coverage. We will not address the many special problems of sustainability in *poor countries*, such as how to avoid open-access overuse of living resources; how to escape from poverty traps; and how to develop institutions to collect relevant data and apply effective policy instruments – even though it was these problems that largely revived interest in sustainability in the late 1980s. We also do not consider sustainable production within specific *resource sectors* (agriculture, forestry, and so on). Sustainability rhetoric may play a vital political role in achieving better management of such resource sectors, but from our substitutability-with-limits perspective, it is rare that sustaining an economy requires any particular sector's output to be sustained.

We further ignore *population growth* below. As well as to save space, this is because of the philosophical difficulty of choosing weights for the utility of future populations whose size is partly predetermined and partly chosen (Koopmans, 1977, p. 270). Given the importance of population in determining total impact of civilization on the environment in the far future, this remains a major shortcoming in what follows. Finally, our outlook is firmly anthropocentric, and owes little to 'deep ecology' thinking.

2.5 Economic, Environmental and Social Sustainability

Countless government and corporate documents now mention separate notions of economic sustainability, environmental (or ecological) sustainability, and social sustainability, while treating all these together as essential components of an integrated sustainability policy. The origin of this 'triple sustainability' approach can be traced to at least as far back as a much-cited article by Barbier (1987), but this does not help much in interpreting its often very fuzzy modern meanings. In our formal analysis in section 3, one could perhaps interpret 'economic' sustainability as a narrow focus on sustaining marketed production and consumption only; 'environmental' sustainability as a wider approach that includes also (or instead) the effect of environmental quality on current well-being; and 'social' sustainability as a focus on intragenerational inequality as an important negative influence on well-being, the importance of which we recognize, but have chosen to ignore. However, it is hard to find any clear theoretical basis in the triple sustainability literature for how these three concepts of sustainability are meant to interrelate: for example, how substitutable are they for each other? So having noted these popular labels, we largely set them aside for notions of sustainability which we can relate more precisely to economic analysis.

2.6   The Structure of the Chapter

Despite our above concern to avoid entrenching the divide between weak and strong sustainability, these two viewpoints form the simplest way to structure the rest of this chapter, and we investigate their basic foundations more thoroughly than in TPK or Pezzey and Toman (forthcoming). The pervasive smoothness (differentiability) of mathematical functions assumed by the neoclassical or 'weak' sustainability approach, combined with a common unit of value, has allowed an impressively sophisticated theory to develop about the role of environmental resources in an economy's growth and development. However, less of it is directly linked to sustainability than is sometimes claimed. We summarize this theory in most of section 3, and discuss how it has been applied empirically to sustainability measurement (but unfortunately, not to sustainability policy). Section 4 develops 'strong' sustainability themes by probing the boundaries of neoclassicism, to see what physical and ecological science can say about the limits to substitutability and technical progress in the far future as strategies for ameliorating limits to growth.

Section 5 uses climate change to illustrate some of the points considered up till then. This is a dauntingly good example, involving the far future (because of the slow removal of CO_2 from the atmosphere and thermal response of the ocean), and hence discounting over several generations; ultimate limits to substitutability and technical progress (in using capital and knowledge to reduce net greenhouse gas emissions or otherwise reduce climate change risks); profound scientific uncertainty about many aspects of climate change and its effects; global versus national policy perspectives; and so on. Finally, as befits our title, section 6 summarizes the considerable progress in the economics of sustainability in the last decade or so, and then summarizes the problems remaining.

The emphasis on finding some relationship between sustainability, and observable prices and quantities, puts section 3 at the heart of what most authors mean by *sustainability accounting*. *Green accounting* can variously mean the same thing, or a focus on only finding 'correct' (that is, socially optimal) measures of welfare, or a blend of the two (for example, contrast Vincent, 2000 and Cairns, 2000). Compared to our predecessors in this *Yearbook* (Aronsson and Lofgren, 1998; see also Aronsson et al., 1997), our overall focus is both narrower, because we look solely at sustainability accounting, and yet wider in other ways. We use recent results to include non-constant discounting and exogenous changes in technology or world prices in our analysis from the start; we look more closely at the philosophical foundations and empirical applications of neoclassical theory; and we counterbalance the neoclassical approach by our detailed discussion of strong sustainability ideas in sections 4 and 5.

3. THE NEOCLASSICAL ('WEAK') ECONOMICS OF SUSTAINABILITY

The neoclassical approach to sustainability combines two main characteristics, already discussed separately above. One is a willingness to assume unlimited substitutability: of one type of productive input for another, of one source of instantaneous utility for another, and of utility at one time for utility at another time (though with some discount factor applied). This assumption allows a rich set of mathematical results, littered with partial derivatives which are the 'exchange rates' of these substitutions. The other main characteristic is a willingness to ignore intragenerational equity, by most often using a representative agent (RA) to represent the human population alive at any one time; though overlapping generation (OLG) models are sometimes used to provide insights into trade and transfers among different age groups.

We have subdivided our presentation of neoclassical sustainability as follows. Section 3.1 gives several alternative, formal definitions of sustainability. Section 3.2 discusses the paradox of why and how these definitions are combined with results from 'optimal' paths: for such paths are themselves defined by maximizing some intertemporal objective, a maximization which at first blush leaves no room for any further intertemporal concerns like sustainability. Section 3.3 gives key theoretical results from the neoclassical approach, most importantly about measuring sustainability on an optimal development path. Section 3.4 considers the policies that might theoretically achieve sustainability, if unsustainability has been detected by the results of section 3.3; unfortunately, these results have yet to be explored empirically. Section 3.5 looks at various empirical studies of measuring sustainability, starting with their practical problems. Notation and abbreviations are listed in the Appendix.

3.1 Definitions of Sustainability which Ignore Intragenerational Equity

Since we ignore population change, we need not distinguish total from per capita levels of 'consumption', (instantaneous) utility or (intertemporal) welfare in our models. These levels will be denoted respectively by $\mathbf{C}(t)$ (a vector which includes dimensions of environmental quality as well as market consumption goods), $U(\mathbf{C}(t))$ and $W\{U(\cdot)\}$ in (infinitely lived) representative agent (RA) models which ignore intragenerational equity.[9] But in overlapping generations (OLG) models, which also ignore intragenerational equity, we use i to label one of several generations alive at one time: thus $\mathbf{C}_i(t)$, $U_i(\mathbf{C}_i(t))$, and $W_i\{U_i(\cdot)\}$ which is called 'lifetime welfare' in the OLG context. Sustainability can be defined in dozens of ways (Pezzey, 1989), but here we choose to highlight one general approach to intertemporal equity, and then three sets of sustainability definitions that can be used within a neoclassical framework:

1. By assuming various axioms that utility distributions over time must satisfy, one can justify a range of intertemporal equity criteria in RA models. One well-known criterion, explored by Solow (1974) after Rawls's (1971) idea of the 'maximin', is to keep utility *constant* from time t onwards at its *maximum sustainable level* $U_m(t)$ then (which depends on the economy's stocks at t), formally defined as

$$U_m(t) := \max U \text{ s.t. } U(s) \geq U \text{ for all } s \geq t; \qquad (4.1)[10]$$

A number of alternative criteria, and the axioms which can be proved to lead to them, can be seen from Asheim et al. (2001) and the works they cite. The ethics of intergenerational equity criteria can then be debated in terms of the appeal of the underlying axioms. Koopmans (1960) showed that a set of five axioms (continuity, sensitivity, period independence, stationarity, and the existence of a best and worst path) lead to the criterion that society should always aim to maximize welfare defined as *present value* (*PV*):

$$W^P(t) := \int_t^\infty U(s)e^{-\rho(s-t)}ds = e^{\rho t}\int_t^\infty U(s)e^{-\rho s}ds, \rho > 0 \text{ constant} \qquad (4.2)$$

We will call the development path that results from maximizing (4.2) *PV-optimal*, assuming the integral converges and can be maximized. Thanks to Koopmans's axiomatic foundation, many economists defend a (utility) discount factor $e^{-\rho t}$ as a perfectly good reflection of 'intergenerational equity'; while many others just use an $e^{-\rho t}$ factor with little comment (Barro and Sala-i-Martin 1995, p. 61).[11] Many others, though, see the remorseless discounting of the future at rate ρ in *PV* optimality as being very inequitable to the far future. Such critics must then, implicitly or explicitly, reject at least one of Koopmans's underlying axioms.

A source of semantic misunderstanding here is to call the PV-optimal path *efficient*. It is (intertemporally Pareto-) efficient, but so too are most of the alternative, non-PV-optimal paths we consider. In fact, if the negative exponential discount factor $e^{-\rho s}$ in (4.2) is replaced by a general discount factor $\phi(s) > 0$, $\phi(0)=1$, $\dot{\phi} < 0$,[12] and the $e^{\rho t}$ factor (which corrects for the integral starting at t rather than 0) is replaced by $1/\phi(t)$, we call the maximizing path *GPV-optimal*, since we are then maximizing a *generalized present value* (*GPV*)

$$W(t) := \int_t^\infty U(s)[\phi(s)/\phi(t)]ds = [1/\phi(t)] \int_t^\infty U(s)\phi(s)ds, \qquad (4.3)$$

and it is a fundamental result of welfare economics that *any* efficient path must be the result of maximizing GPV for some discount factor $\phi(t)$. However, GPV maximization is not the 'primitive problem' in many cases. For example, if the primitive problem is to find a constant utility path, there is little ethical significance in the form of $\phi(t)$ which happens to give constant utility when maximizing GPV.

2. Sustainability can be intuited from political rhetoric as a *constraint on utility over time* (Pezzey, 1992, 1997). Possible variants are constant utility ($\dot{U}(t) = 0$ for all t), non-declining utility ($\dot{U}(t) \geq 0$ for all t, also called 'sustained-ness'), and stopping current utility exceeding the current maximum sustainable level ($U(t) \leq U_m(t)$ for all t). We choose the third (which is generally implied by the second) as a fairly natural definition to use in the theory set out in sections 3.3–3.4. That is, we will use as our main sustainability criterion,

$$\text{an economy is } \textit{sustainable at time } t \Leftrightarrow U(t) \leq U_m(t). \qquad (4.4)$$

The corresponding general concept in an OLG model would be constraints on the change in generational welfare, $W_i(t)$, from an older to a younger generation. Constraints on $W(t)$ could be used in RA models too.

3. Sustainability can instead be defined as a *constraint on changes in opportunities over time* (rather than on future outcomes, that is, utility). The constraint most frequently suggested is non-declining wealth or aggregate capital, instead of non-declining utility. There is a difference in underlying political philosophy here, depending on whether it is future generations' opportunities (the resource set they inherit) or outcomes (the welfare they enjoy) which is regarded as the proper focus of public policy. However, within the deterministic, optimizing framework of this section, the two approaches can be linked with each other, though by no means equated, as we will see in Proposition 4.5 in section 3.3.

4. A sustainability *concern* could be built into welfare $W(\cdot)$ in various ways. One could use a utility discount rate (or 'rate of impatience') $-\dot{\phi}/\phi$ which declines over time, rather than staying constant. One could add some multiple of asymptotic utility ($\lim_{t\to\infty} U(t)$) to $W(\cdot)$ from (4.2), and maximize the sum (Chichilnisky, 1996).[13] Or one could incorporate a preference for the *growth* as well as the *level* of consumption into instantaneous utility $U(\cdot)$, for example by assuming $U(C,\dot{C}/C)$ rather than just $U(C)$ when C is scalar (Pezzey, 1997). The last of these seems psychologically realistic, but is mathematically difficult and has been little used so far. Stepping outside

the RA framework, psychological realism could also demand that one add concerns about intragenerational inequity to $U(\cdot)$, as perhaps measured by the Gini coefficient or some other measure of the spread of individual consumption levels about the mean.

3.2   The Practical and Philosophical Basis of the Neoclassical Approach: Optimization, Externalities and Sustainability Constraints

Despite its mathematical fineries set out below, the neoclassical approach to sustainability contains some key approximations and apparent paradoxes, which may limit its use as a practical tool for policy-makers. The approximations stem from two unavoidable facts about prices *and* quantities. First, because of significant externalities, *current* prices and quantities observed in the market, including those estimated with non-market valuation techniques for the externalities, are significantly different from *optimal* prices and quantities that would be observed after policy intervention shifted development to the (GPV-)optimal path. Second, if sustainability imposes any significant constraint on optimality, then the *sustainability* prices and quantities that would apply after further intervention achieves the constraint (presumably with minimum loss of GPV) are different again.

The neoclassical approach to sustainability below, then,

(i)   *assumes* that current prices and quantities adequately approximate optimal prices;

(ii)   *proves* a theoretical inequality relationship (Proposition 4.5) between measures with optimal prices and quantities, and sustainability. The relationship is only an inequality, because optimal prices do not 'know' anything exact about sustainability;[14]

(iii)   *assumes* that the goal of policy intervention is GPV maximization, subject to a sustainability constraint or modified by a public sustainability concern, even though individuals are not assumed to seek sustainability, only GPV optimality, in their private actions.

Assumption (i) will not be explored further in this chapter, though much of modern environmental economics can be read as calling it into question. However, we will now comment on the apparent paradox at the heart of assumption (iii) (although it is usually hidden and hence not discussed, since most literature focuses on measuring rather than implementing sustainability). Why should the government be interested in sustainability if private agents maximize GPV? Maximizing GPV in general has nothing to do with sustainability, and gives a complete and unique prescription for the time paths of every decision that ever has to be made in the economy. So there is no apparent motive for using result (ii) to measure sustainability on a GPV-optimal path! Likewise, if unsustainability is thus found, there is no apparent justification for the policy intervention which will in general be needed to make the economy depart from its optimal path to achieve sustainability.[15]

The resolution of this paradox has to lie in some kind of split between private and public concerns about the far future. We must assume that the individual chooses his or her own actions to maximize some form of present value, but votes for a government which applies a sustainability concern, both by measuring sustainability, and taking action to achieve it if necessary. People are thus in some sense schizophrenic, treating private economic decisions as the domain of Economic Man, and governmental decisions as the domain of the Citizen (Marglin, 1963, p. 98).[16] One good reason for this is that individuals cannot provide personally for their distant descendants, because of the mixing of bequests that occurs over several generations (Daly and Cobb, 1989, p. 39; Pezzey, 1995).

The philosophical basis of neoclassical sustainability economics is thus distinct from three other main philosophical approaches to social choice over time, the first and third of which were discussed in section 2. It rejects classical utilitarianism, which prohibits any discounting; it rejects neoclassical utilitarianism, which sees maximizing PV (with a constant ρ) as a complete prescription for intertemporal equity; and it rejects the purely rights-based view that it is future generations' resource opportunities, not utility outcomes, that matter.

We see clear roots of this somewhat schizophrenic approach to sustainability in the long discussion in mainstream economics about the purpose and methods of calculating *income*. The most general economic concept of income is some measure of what the economy is now doing or enjoying that includes an adequate provision for the future, just as individuals make provision for the future by investing some of their current money income rather than consuming it all. Asking what an 'adequate' provision for the future should be immediately returns us to the philosophical debate about intergenerational equity. And, to risk controversy with scholars of the work, one can see a certain degree of schizophrenia in the classic discussion of income in Hicks (1946, ch. 14). He sees income there as a guide to 'prudent' behaviour that will avoid 'impoverishment', but also as something that, held constant, is equivalent to the present value of future receipts. The profusion of different fundamental measures of income below is further testimony to the schizophrenia. Below we will be defining *sustainable income*, *wealth-equivalent income* and *green net national product*; and these have been shown to be strictly different from each other, and from two further measures (welfare-equivalent income, as defined by Asheim, 2000, p. 30, and Sefton–Weale income), in a specific example with a non-constant utility discount rate (Pezzey, 2002).

3.3   The Neoclassical Theory of Income and Sustainability Measurement

This is technically the most demanding subsection of our essay, which merits introduction in its own right. In section 3.3.1 we set out a theoretical model of development in an RA economy, with a general consumption vector **C** and utility $U(\mathbf{C})$, where the elements of **C** can include measures of environmental quality as well as of goods and services consumed; and a vector **K** of productive stocks such as built (human-made) capital or natural resources. To provide both historical background and illustration, section 3.3.2 then gives results from classic 1970s theoretical papers about optimal development in simple 'capital–resource' economies, where **K** comprises K, a single built capital, and S, a non-renewable natural resource stock, and consumption is a single number C. Back with the general model, section 3.3.3 develops various price and production or income concepts, especially green net national product (GNNP). This is the sum of consumption expenditures and net investments, $Y := \mathbf{P}.\mathbf{C} + \mathbf{Q}^{\dagger}.\dot{\mathbf{K}}^{\dagger}$. Here, **P** and $\mathbf{Q}^{\dagger}$ are real price vectors; and $\mathbf{K}^{\dagger} := (\mathbf{K},t)$ is the vector of *all stocks*, including time t seen as a productive (but not 'physical') stock because of the progress in production techniques that may result exogenously just from time passing.[17] Section 3.3.4 gives six general theoretical results using GNNP, the most important of which is a 'one-sided' test, denominated in 'real dollars', of whether the economy is unsustainable at any given time. All results up to here are both theoretical and very general, and leave unexplained how certain concepts like the 'value of time' might be measured.

Section 3.3.5 moves towards results which can be applied practically. It uses a more detailed, but hence less general, model to show how GNNP is computed when there are realistic features such as resource renewal, discovery and extraction, transient and cumulative pollution with abatement, and trade in both resources and consumption goods. Finally, section 3.3.6 discusses to what extent recent developments in mainstream growth economics, which emphasize the role of endogenous technical progress, can be applied to the sustainability question. None of this says what policy actions could and should be taken to avoid unsustainable development, if measurement detects it; that is the topic of section 3.4. Throughout, we try to explain the intuitive meaning and purpose of all results presented, and we put all new proofs in the Appendix.

3.3.1   A general model

We consider an economy as in Asheim and Weitzman (2001) (hereafter AW), though augmented by the treatment of time t as a stock, and allowing for a general utility discount factor $\phi(t)$ rather than the conventional exponential factor $e^{-\rho t}$. A vector $\mathbf{C}(t)$ represents a consumption bundle containing everything, including environmental amenities, that influences current well-being, which is denoted by instantaneous utility $U(\mathbf{C}(t))$. A vector $\mathbf{K}(t)$ (of maybe different dimension to $C(t)$) represents stocks of built capital, natural resources, environmental assets, human capital from education, and knowledge produced by R&D. At any time, the combination of consumption $C(t)$ and all *net* investments $\dot{K}(t)$ is constrained by the convex production possibilities set $\Pi\{\cdot\}$, in which there is exogenous technical progress, as shown by the dependence of $\Pi\{\cdot\}$ on t as well as K:

$$[C(t),\dot{K}(t)] \in \Pi\{K(t),t\} \qquad (4.5)$$

We assume (crucially but controversially, as discussed above in section 3.1) that the economy acts as to maximize the generalized present value (GPV) of utility defined in (4.3), subject to an appropriate constraint to prevent unlimited household borrowing (for example condition (19) in Vellinga and Withagen, 1996). We further develop concepts and results for this model, focusing especially on the measurement of income, in section 3.3.3. However, we first mention three simple versions of this model in famous papers published in 1974, and inspired by the debate following the publication of *The Limits to Growth* (Meadows et al. 1972).

3.3.2   Classic results about optimal paths with non-renewable resources

All three papers studied the optimal consumption path of special cases of the above economy, and made the innovation of including a non-renewable resource stock, $S(t)$, as well as a built capital stock $K(t)$, as part of the economy's overall stocks $K(t)$; though consumption remained just a single number $C(t)$. The papers made little reference to income or sustainability concepts, but their results form an essential foundation for later work on sustainability. However, we have summarized these carefully in TPK and Pezzey and Toman (forthcoming), so we give only concise results here. For all three papers the production possibilities relations [15] are

$$\dot{K} = F(K,R) - C, \quad K(0) = K_0 > 0; \quad \dot{S} = -R, \quad S(0) = S_0 > 0, \qquad (4.6)$$

where $R(t)$ is the rate of resource extraction and depletion, and $F(K,R)$ shows how inputs of capital stock and resource flow produce output of a good which is divided linearly between consumption and investment. We also define *maximum sustainable consumption or maximum constant consumption*, $C_m(t)$, as

$$C_m(t) := \max C \text{ s.t. } C(s) \geq C \text{ for all } s \geq t. \qquad (4.7)$$

Results are:

Dasgupta and Heal (1974): With $\phi = e^{-\rho t}$, $\rho > 0$ constant, PV-optimal consumption obeys the Ramsey rule

$$\dot{C}/C = [F_K(K,R) - \rho]/[-U_{CC}C/U_C], \qquad (4.8)$$

and under a range of precise conditions (see Pezzey and Withagen, 1998), the interest rate F_K eventually falls below the discount rate ρ, so that long-run consumption tends asymptotically towards zero. This represents unsustainable development by any reasonable definition.

Solow (1974): Under assumptions as for Dasgupta and Heal, but with Cobb–Douglas production $F(K,R) = K^\alpha R^\beta$ and $\beta < \alpha < \alpha + \beta \le 1$, constant consumption ($\dot{C}/C = 0$) is possible, and the maximum constant consumption level is $C_m(0) = (1-\beta)\{K_0^{\alpha-\beta} [(\alpha - \beta)S_0]^\beta\}^{1/(1-\beta)}$. This is not PV-optimal; in fact the utility discount factor that makes $\{C(t) = C_m(0)$ for all $t\}$ optimal is hyperbolic, $\phi(t) = (1 + \theta t)^{-\eta}$ for some parameters θ and η.

Stiglitz (1974): Under assumptions as for Dasgupta and Heal, but with exogenous technical progress at rate $\nu > 0$ added to Cobb–Douglas production, $F(K,R,t) = K^\alpha R^\beta e^{\nu t}$, the asymptotic, PV-optimal rate of consumption growth obeys $\{\dot{C}/C \gtrless 0\} \Leftrightarrow \{\nu/\rho \gtrless 1-\alpha\}$. That is, if the progress ν is big enough in comparison to 'impatience' (the discount rate ρ), PV-optimal consumption eventually grows, and so does not conflict with sustainability (by any reasonable definition) in the long run.

3.3.3   Concepts of prices, national income and product

Before we can discuss results for the general economy which maximizes welfare (4.3) subject to production possibility constraints (4.5), that is, solves

$$\text{Max}_{C,\dot{K}} \; W(t):= \int_t^\infty U[C(s)][\phi(s)/\phi(t)]ds \text{ s.t. } [C(s),\dot{K}(s)] \in \Pi\{K(s),s\}, \quad (4.9)$$

we must first define several further measures of prices and production. Associated with the development path that solves (4.9) are $(\partial U/\partial C)(t)$ and $\Psi(t)$, respectively the shadow utility prices of consumption goods and of net investments,[18] but these are unobservable. What can actually be observed are nominal prices $\mathbf{p}(t)$ and $\mathbf{q}(t)$ denominated in money like dollars. They are proportional to utility prices, formally $\mathbf{p}(t):= [(\partial U/\partial C)(t)]/\lambda(t)$ and $\mathbf{q}(t):= \Psi(t)/\lambda(t)$, where $\lambda(t)$ is the marginal utility of a dollar at time t. If we further deflate the nominal prices by some (yet-to-be-calculated) price index $\pi(t)$, we get *real dollar* prices $\mathbf{P}(t) := \mathbf{p}(t)/\pi(t)$ and $\mathbf{Q}(t) := \mathbf{q}(t)/\pi(t)$, hence

$$\mathbf{P}(t) := [(\partial U/\partial \mathbf{C})(t)]/\lambda(t)\pi(t) \text{ and } \mathbf{Q}(t) := \Psi(t)/\lambda(t)\pi(t), \qquad (4.10)$$

where $\pi(t)$ is chosen to satisfy the Divisia property that defines the sense in which the overall real price level is constant:

$$\dot{\mathbf{P}}(t).\mathbf{C}(t) = 0 \text{ at all times on the optimal path.} \qquad (4.11)$$

Since consumption is now a vector, the concept of maximum sustainable consumption level becomes sustainable income, which is the constant level of consumption expenditures on the maximum sustainable utility path:

sustainable income $:= \mathbf{P}_m(t).\mathbf{C}_m(t)$ where $\mathbf{P}_m(t)$, $\mathbf{C}_m(t)$ are price
and consumption levels on the maximum sustainable utility path (4.1).
$$(4.12)^{19}$$

The real consumption discount factor $\Phi(t)$ is defined as the utility discount factor, times the marginal utility of money, times the price index:

$$\Phi(t) = \phi(t)\lambda(t)\pi(t) \qquad (4.13)$$

and we define *real wealth* $\Theta(t)$ as consumption expenditures $\mathbf{P}.\mathbf{C}$ discounted by the real consumption discount factor:

$$\Theta(t):= \int_t^\infty \mathbf{P}(s).\mathbf{C}(s)[\Phi(s)/\Phi(t)]ds. \qquad (4.14)$$

Just as the utility discount rate is defined as $-\dot{\phi}/\phi$, the (real) *consumption discount rate*, which in a perfectly informed and maximising economy is the (real) *interest rate* $r(t)$, is defined as

$$r(t) := -\dot{\Phi}(t)/\Phi(t) = -\dot{\phi}(t)/\phi(t) - \dot{\lambda}(t)/\lambda(t) - \dot{\pi}(t)/\pi(t). \qquad (4.15)$$

An expression to be used later is found by integrating $\dot{\Phi}/\Phi = -r$ between times t and s and applying the exponential function:

$$\Phi(s)/\Phi(t) = \exp[-\int_t^s r(z)dz] \ (= e^{-r(s-t)} \text{ if } r \text{ is constant}). \qquad (4.16)$$

Green net national product (GNNP) $Y(t)$ is then a measure of national income and output, defined here as the real value of consumption plus investment expenditures:

$$Y(t) := \mathbf{P}(t).\mathbf{C}(t) + \mathbf{Q}(t).\dot{\mathbf{K}}(t). \qquad (4.17)$$

Augmented GNNP is GNNP plus an amount $Q'(t)$ which we call the 'value of time' and will define below. Intuitively, $Q'(t)$ measures the real value to the economy at t of time passing, just as each element of $\mathbf{Q}(t)$ measures the value at t of another stock growing:

$$Y(t) := Y + Q' = \mathbf{P}.\mathbf{C} + \mathbf{Q}^{\dagger}.\dot{\mathbf{K}}^{\dagger} \text{ where } \mathbf{Q}^{\dagger} := (\mathbf{Q}, Q'). \qquad (4.18)[20]$$

Finally, we define *wealth-equivalent income*, $Y_e(t)$, as the consumption level which, if held constant from t to ∞, gives the same present value as wealth on the optimal path:

$$Y_e(t) := \int_t^{\infty} \mathbf{P}(s).\mathbf{C}(s)\Phi(s)ds / \int_t^{\infty} \Phi(s)ds \Rightarrow \int_t^{\infty} Y_e(t)[\Phi(s)/\Phi(t)]ds = \Theta(t). \quad (4.19)[21]$$

3.3.4   General results about income and sustainability

Proposition 4.1: The time derivative of augmented GNNP (after Asheim and Weitzman, 2001)

Our first result is a very general theorem. It is neither easy to explain intuitively, nor immediately relevant to sustainability, but it forms the foundation of everything that follows.

Result: The time derivative of augmented GNNP $Y(t)$ is always the interest rate $r(t)$ times augmented net investment $\mathbf{Q}^{\dagger}(t).\dot{\mathbf{K}}^{\dagger}(t)$:

$$\text{For all } t,\ \dot{Y}^{\dagger}(t) = r(t)\mathbf{Q}^{\dagger}(t).\dot{\mathbf{K}}^{\dagger}(t) = r(t)[Y^{\dagger}(t) - \mathbf{P}(t).\mathbf{C}(t)] \text{ by } (4.18). \qquad (4.20)$$

Proposition 4.2: The value of time

Our second result is a formula derived from Proposition 4.1 that shows the value of time Q' as the sum of its effects on GNNP for the rest of time. It will take on a more precise form in Proposition 4.7 in section 3.3.5, where it shows what Q' adds to GNNP as a result of exogenous technical progress and changes in world resource prices.

Result: The value of time Q' is the generalized present value of the partial time derivative of GNNP:

$$Q'(t) = \int_t^{\infty} [\partial Y(s)/\partial s] \exp[-\int_t^s r(z)dz]ds$$

$$(= \int_t^{\infty} [\partial Y(s)/\partial s] e^{-r(s-t)}ds \text{ if } r \text{ constant}) \qquad (4.21)$$

Q' is thus forward looking, and likely to be much harder to calculate than other elements of $\mathbf{Q}^{\dagger}$, which are based on current values only.

Proposition 4.3: The present-value equivalence of GNNP (after Sefton and Weale, 1996)

Our third result uses Proposition 4.1 to find an expression for augmented GNNP Y which is closely related to wealth. It allows the terms of trade and the interest rate to vary (as do Sefton and Weale in their equation (8)) and also for exogenous technical progress (which they do not).

$$\text{Result (a): } Y^\dagger(t) = \int_t^\infty r(s)\mathbf{P}(s).\mathbf{C}(s)\exp[-\int_t^\infty r(z)dz]ds. \quad (4.22)$$

Extra assumption: The interest rate r is constant. Using (4.19) then gives:

$$\text{Result (b): } Y^\dagger(t) = r\int_t^\infty \mathbf{P}(s).\mathbf{C}(s)e^{-r(s-t)}ds = r\Theta(t) = Y_e(t). \quad (4.23)$$

So in the special case of a constant interest rate, augmented GNNP $Y^\dagger$ is the same as wealth-equivalent income Y_e, and both can be seen as a return (at rate r) on wealth Θ. This *PV-equivalence* property of NNP was first shown by Weitzman (1970, 1976) and further developed by Asheim (1997).

Proposition 4: The time premium (Weitzman, 1997)

This is a simplification of Proposition 4.3(b) that is important if one hopes to arrive at a better estimate of wealth-equivalent income in an economy with exogenous technical progress. The growth rate $\chi(t)$ in (4.26) below is the result of any change in production possibilities caused by time alone, whether this is due to technical progress in the economy or a change in the terms of trade with the rest of the world, though obviously the latter will not appear in a closed (that is, global) economy. Hence we call $Q^t/Y = (Y_e/Y)-1$ the 'time premium', rather than Weitzman's more specific 'technological progress premium'. The proof comes directly from Weitzman (1997, p. 9), so is not listed in the Appendix.

Extra assumption: The interest rate r is constant, as for Proposition 4.3(b).

Result: The augmented GNNP (or the wealth-equivalent income) equals GNNP Y increased by a 'time premium' Q^t/Y:

$$Y^\dagger(t) = Y_e(t) = Y(t)[1 + Q^t(t)/Y(t)] = Y\{1 + \chi(t)/[r-\Gamma(t)]\} \quad (4.24)$$

where $\quad \Gamma(t) := \int_t^\infty \dot{Y}(s)e^{-rs}ds / \int_t^\infty Y(s)e^{-rs}ds \quad (4.25)$
is the time-averaged overall growth rate of GNNP

and $\quad \chi(t) := \int_t^\infty [\partial Y(s)/\partial s]e^{-rs}ds / \int_t^\infty Y(s)e^{-rs}ds \quad (4.26)$
is the time-averaged growth in GNNP due to time alone.

Proposition 4.5: A one-sided sustainability test

This is the most important neoclassical result of the paper, since our focus is more on knowing about sustainability than on the more general question of 'greening national income' by having a fully inclusive measure of GNNP, even when sustainability is of no interest.

Extra assumptions: The utility discount rate $-\dot{\phi}/\phi$ is a constant, say ρ; and the optimal utility path is unique and non-constant.

Result: A non-rising augmented GNNP (or non-positive augmented net investment, non-rising wealth at constant prices $\mathbf{Q}^\dagger$) at t means the economy is *un*sustainable at t. That is:

$$\{\dot{Y}^\dagger(t) \leq 0 \text{ or } \mathbf{Q}^\dagger(t).\mathbf{K}^\dagger(t) \geq 0\} \Rightarrow \{U(t) > U_m(t)\} \tag{4.27}$$

or equivalently (from (4.18))

$$\{\dot{Y}(t) + \dot{Q}^I(t) \leq 0 \text{ or } \mathbf{Q}(t).\dot{\mathbf{K}}(t) + Q^I(t) \leq 0\} \Rightarrow \{U(t) > U_m(t)\} \tag{4.28}$$

Corollary 1: If the growth rates Γ and χ defined in Proposition 4.4 are constant, *and* the interest rate r is constant, then $Q^I(t) = \chi Y(t)/(r-\Gamma)$ and $\dot{Y}^\dagger/Y^\dagger = \dot{Y}/Y$, so

$$\{\dot{Y}(t)/Y(t) = \Gamma \leq 0 \text{ or } \mathbf{Q}(t).\dot{\mathbf{K}}(t)/Y(t) \leq -\chi/(r-\Gamma)\} \Rightarrow \{U(t) > U_m(t)\} \tag{4.29}$$

Comments:

(a) Positive augmented net investment, $\mathbf{Q}^\dagger.\dot{\mathbf{K}}^\dagger > 0$, does not necessarily mean the economy is sustainable. No general test *for* sustainability is known. For example there is no known generalization of the $\beta < \alpha$ condition that Solow (1974) discovered to be necessary for maximum sustainable utility U_m to exist in the economy of section 3.3.2.

(b) If the interest rate is constant, then $Y^\dagger = Y_e = r\Theta$ from Proposition 4.3(b). Relation (4.27) then includes the striking result that $\dot{\Theta}(t) = 0$, that is, *constant* wealth at t, implies *un*sustainability at t, contrary to some well-known but rather informally worded claims to the contrary (Pearce et al., 1989; Solow 1986, 1993). At the instant of constant wealth on an optimal path, consumption expenditures are the same as wealth-equivalent income, but this exceeds sustainable income because optimal consumption expenditures are not constant.[22]

(c) However, in the case of any economy where the welfare-maximizing path is not unique, the first two inequalities in each of (4.27), (4.28) and (4.29) must be strict ($\mathbf{Q}^{\dagger}.\dot{\mathbf{K}}^{\dagger} < 0$, and so on) to be able to conclude that the economy is unsustainable.

(d) Moreover, *in a small, open economy*, where all prices are exogenous world prices, and with just one consumption good, wealth-equivalent income Y_e equals sustainable income C_m (Asheim, 2000, p. 38). The sustainability test is then *two-sided*, that is, $\mathbf{Q}^{\dagger}.\dot{\mathbf{K}}^{\dagger} \gtrless 0 \Leftrightarrow C \gtrless C_m$, and so on, and comment (a), which underlay the concern expressed in Asheim (1994) and Pezzey (1994) that there was no direct connection between GNNP and sustainability, then no longer applies. However, with multiple consumption goods, this deduction cannot be made, because the Divisia price index defining prices $\mathbf{Q}$ is generally different on the PV-optimal and maximum sustainable paths. Also, the result obviously cannot work for the sum of all open economies (that is, the world economy), for prices are then no longer exogenous.

(e) $\mathbf{Q}.\dot{\mathbf{K}}/Y \leq 0$, that is, net investment (as a proportion of GNNP) without the time premium Q^t/Y, is the test used for most empirical measurements of sustainability. Weitzman (1997) and Vincent et al. (1997) are the only papers we know that include part of the time premium $\chi/(r-\Gamma)$ in their calculations. Relation (4.29) shows that, if $\chi > 0$, sustainability is more likely than indicated by the $\mathbf{Q}.\dot{\mathbf{K}}/Y \leq 0$ test that applies when $\chi = 0$, while the $\dot{Y}(t)/Y(t) \leq 0$ test is formally unaffected! Weitzman estimated $\chi/(r-\Gamma)$ to be about 0.4 for the USA, while the natural resource components of $\mathbf{Q}.\dot{\mathbf{K}}$ make up only about 0.03 of Y. However, some of $\chi/(r-\Gamma)$ could be endogenous technical progress (see section 3.3.6 below) and some of it could be changes in the terms of trade

(f) Of the two tests in (4.28) or (4.29), the $\mathbf{Q}.\dot{\mathbf{K}}$ ones should be easier to compute than the $\dot{Y}$ ones in the time-autonomous ($Q^t = 0$) case, because $\mathbf{Q}.\dot{\mathbf{K}}$ does not need estimation of the comprehensive consumption vector $\mathbf{C}$ and its associated price vector $\mathbf{P}$. If $Q^t \neq 0$, the comparison is not so simple.

(g) With constant production possibilities ($Q^t = 0$), our net investment $\mathbf{Q}.\dot{\mathbf{K}}$ is what Hamilton (1996, p. 27) and others call 'genuine saving'. But since his 'welfare' is our GNNP, Y, AW's result, that negative net investment means negative GNNP growth at any instant, is stronger than his claim (p. 28) that 'persistently negative genuine savings are not sustainable – eventually welfare must decline'.

Proposition 4.6: Constant net investment and constant utility (after Hartwick, 1977)

Result: If $\mathbf{Q}^{\dagger}(t).\dot{\mathbf{K}}^{\dagger}(t)$, net investment ($\mathbf{Q}.\dot{\mathbf{K}}$) in an economy's stocks plus the value of time (Q^t), is zero forever, then utility $U(t)$ is constant forever.[23]

Comments:

(a) The result is obviously not true without the 'forever'. At time t, $\{\mathbf{Q}^\dagger(t).\dot{\mathbf{K}}^\dagger(t)$ $= 0\} \Rightarrow \{\dot{H}^\dagger(t) = 0$ and $H^\dagger(t) = U(t)\} \not\Rightarrow \{\dot{U}(t) = 0\}$. Moreover, it is possible to have $\mathbf{Q}^\dagger(t).\dot{\mathbf{K}}^\dagger(t) > 0$ while the economy is unsustainable, $U(t) > U_m(t)$ (Asheim, 1994; Pezzey, 1994).

(b) Hartwick's rule is usually restricted to the autonomous case with no exogenous time-dependency, and also a single consumption good. The value of time is then zero and the price of the consumption good is 1, giving the familiar 'zero net investment forever means constant consumption forever' form first shown by Hartwick (1977). Our Proposition 4.6 shows that these restrictions are not necessary; and that the rule still holds when there is capital depreciation, despite the contrary statement by Hartwick (1977, p. 974), which was derived with an inappropriate Hotelling rule.

(c) The constant-utility path on which Hartwick's rule holds is, like any efficient path, optimal for *some* utility discount factor $\phi(t)$. However, for a *general* discount factor $\phi(t)$ at a general time t, there is no reason why $\mathbf{Q}^\dagger(t).\dot{\mathbf{K}}^\dagger(t) = 0$. So '$\mathbf{Q}^\dagger(t).\dot{\mathbf{K}}^\dagger(t) = 0$ forever' cannot be added as a constraint on a GPV-optimal path, contrary to suggestions in Solow (1986, p. 147), Hartwick (1997, p. 511), Aronsson et al. (1997, p. 101) and Aronsson and Lofgren (1998, p. 213). Hartwick's rule (in all its many variants since the seminal, simple version in Hartwick, 1977) thus can have no direct, general connection with measuring sustainability on a GPV-optimal path; for this we must use Proposition 4.5.

3.3.5   Results for a more specific economy, as an illustration

How can we calculate augmented GNNP $Y^\dagger$ in a real economy, in order to make practical use of the one-sided sustainability test in Proposition 4.5, or any other theorems above? We need to know $\dot{\mathbf{K}}^\dagger$, the changes in the economy's stocks, which is straightforward in theory, if often very difficult in practice. But how, even in theory, do we find $\mathbf{Q}$, the optimal prices of stocks, and Q^t, the value of time, in terms of familiar variables such as the costs of resource extraction and pollution abatement? We answer these questions below for a detailed version of the above general RA economy, which is an amalgam and extension of the examples in Vellinga and Withagen (1996).[24] It has two 'consumption' goods (material consumption and environmental quality); investment and depreciation in both productive and abatement capital; instantaneous and cumulative forms of environmental pollution; discovery, extraction and renewal of n different natural resource stocks; and foreign trade in resources and consumption, resulting in a stock of foreign capital. Such features can occur in endless different ways. For example, can the stock (environmental concentration) of a cumulative pollutant be abated by human action, or only the flow (emissions)?

Is abatement effort the result of current spending, or of capital equipment which is the result of past spending? Are extraction costs affected by the extraction rate, the remaining stock, or both? Hence the economy defined below is just an arbitrary, illustrative example. Indeed, the results found show that some accepted methods of accounting for pollution or resource depletion in GNNP measurement are often far from general.

We designate the example economy's stocks of the n renewable and non-renewable resource stocks by the n-vector $S(t)$. They are discovered at rate $D(t)$, grow naturally at a stock-dependent rate $G(S)$, and are depleted at rate $R(t)$, all n-vectors, so:

$$\dot{S} = D + G(S) - R; \; S(0) = S_0, > 0, \text{ given; } S(t) \geq 0 \qquad (4.30)$$

Two capital stocks in the domestic economy are productive capital $K(t)$ and abatement capital $K_a(t)$. They each increase at the rate of investment (respectively $I(t)$ and $I_a(t)$) minus depreciation ($\delta K(t)$ and $\delta K_a(t)$):

$$\dot{K} = I - \delta K; \qquad K(0) = K_0, > 0, \text{ given; } K(t) \geq 0 \qquad (4.31)$$
$$\dot{K}_a = I_a - \delta K_a; \quad K_a(0) = K_{a0}, > 0, \text{ given; } K_a(t) \geq 0 \qquad (4.32)$$

Production $F(\cdot)$ depends positively on inputs of capital $K(t)$, domestic resource use (extraction $R(t)$ minus net exports $R_x(t)$) and time t (exogenous technical progress). The sum of production, plus net imports $M(t)$ of the consumption/investment good, is distributed among (material) consumption $C(t)$, productive and abatement investments $I(t)$ and $I_a(t)$, abatement current expenditure $a(t)$, discovery costs $V(D,S,t)$ with $V_D > 0$, $V_S < 0$, $V_t < 0$, and extraction costs $X(R,S,t)$ with $X_D > 0$, $X_S < 0$, $X_t < 0$ (note the flow and stock dependences in the last two costs, and the allowance for exogenous technical progress in both of them):

$$F(K,R - R_x,t) + M = C + I + I_a + a + V(D,S,t) + X(R,S,t). \qquad (4.33)$$

To calculate net national rather than net domestic product, we must include terms for the economy's trade. The economy owns a stock $K_f(t)$ of foreign capital (or foreign debt, if $K_f < 0$) which earns a return at the exogenous world interest rate $r(t)$; and its net resource exports $R_x(t)$ are sold at exogenous world prices $Q^x(t)$ (x signifies exports, while X is the resource extraction cost). The foreign capital stock then changes as follows (where only exogenous dependences on time t are shown):[25]

$$\dot{K}_f = r(t)K_f + Q^x(t).R_x - M; \; K_f(0) = K_{f0}, \text{ given.} \qquad (4.34)$$

Instantaneous utility U depends on consumption $C(t)$ and environmental quality or amenity $B(t)$ (so the 'consumption vector' is $\mathbf{C} = (C,B)$):

$$U(t) = U[C(t),B(t)]; \; U_C, U_B > 0, \; C(t) \geq 0 \qquad (4.35)$$

Environmental quality $B(t)$ is, in this particular model, assumed to be some pristine level of quality B_0, minus ε^B times the quality lost from flow pollution $E^B(t)$ (which depends on output, abatement expenditure, abatement capital and time), and minus ε^Ω times the quality lost from stock pollution, as measured by the drop in some environmental absorption capacity $\Omega(t)$ below its pristine, pre-industrial level Ω_1:

$$B = B_0 - \varepsilon^B E^B \left[F(K, \mathbf{R} - \mathbf{R}_x, t), a, K_a, t \right] - \varepsilon^\Omega (\Omega_1 - \Omega); \; \varepsilon^B, \varepsilon^\Omega > 0 \quad (4.36)$$

To aid comparison with other authors it will be convenient to denote:

$$b(t) := 1 \,/(\partial B/\partial a) \text{ as the marginal cost of improving}$$
$$\text{environmental quality by abating emissions.} \qquad (4.37)$$

Finally, absorption capacity $\Omega(t)$ – say the gap between the current average environmental concentration in the economy of a long-lived pollutant and a maximum acceptable concentration – rises at assimilation rate $\gamma(\Omega)$, $\gamma' < 0$, and falls with emissions E^Ω which depend positively on domestic resource use $\mathbf{R} - \mathbf{R}_x$. Emissions can be abated only by reducing $\mathbf{R} - \mathbf{R}_x$:[26]

$$\dot{\Omega} = \gamma(\Omega) - E^\Omega(\mathbf{R} - \mathbf{R}_x); \; \Omega(0) = \Omega_0, \text{ given}; \; \Omega(-\infty) = \Omega_1 > \Omega_0 \qquad (4.38)$$

All functional forms are assumed to be as smooth and convex as is needed for generalized present value $W(t)$ in (4.3) to converge, and for partial derivatives below (denoted by subscripts) to exist. As before, we make the heroic assumption that society chooses its control variables, which here are $C(t)$, $I_a(t)$, $a(t)$, $D(t)$, $R(t)$, $R_x(t)$ and $M(t)$, with $I(t)$ being given by (4.33), to maximize $W(t)$. Augmented GNNP $Y^\dagger$ is then as follows:

Proposition 4.7: A detailed formula for GNNP in a specific case

Result: $\quad Y^\dagger = P^C \{ C + bB + \dot{K} + \dot{K}_a + \dot{K}_f + (bB_R + F_R - Q^x); \, (\gamma - E^\Omega)/(E_R^\Omega)$
$$+ (Q^x - X_R).[D + G(S) - R]\} + Q^t, \text{ where} \qquad (4.39)$$

$$Q^t(t) := \int_t^\infty P^C(s) \, \{ bB_t + F_t - V_t - X_t + \dot{r}K_f + \dot{Q}^x.R_x \}(s) \, \exp[-\int_t^s r(z)dz] \, ds, \qquad (4.40)$$

and

$$(GB_R + F_R - Q^x)_i(\alpha - E^\Omega)/(E_R^\Omega)_i \qquad (4.41)$$

has the same value for all $i = 1, ..., n$.

Comments:

(a) GNNP $Y^\dagger$ is thus the value sum of: the 'consumption' vector, $C = (C,B)$; the changes in the three capital stocks, $\dot{K}$, $\dot{K}_a$ and $\dot{K}_f$, where the price is the same as for consumption; the change in the absorption capacity, $\dot{\Omega} = \gamma - E^\Omega$, valued at a price $(bB_R + F_R - Q^x) =; / (E_R^\Omega)$ which reflects the various roles in the economy played by the resource flow R; and the change in the resource stocks, $\dot{S} = D + G(S) - R$, valued at their prices Q^x minus marginal extraction costs X_R; plus the value of time Q^t. Q^t is in turn the discounted present value of the various sources of exogenous technical progress, as represented by the pure time derivatives $bB_t + F_t - V_t - X_t$ plus the 'capital gains' from exogenously changing world prices. These gains, a specific example of the more general analysis in Asheim (1996), are here the change in interest rate $\dot{r}$ times the economy's foreign capital K_f, and the changes in world resources prices 188^x times the economy's resource exports R_x.

(b) Note how (4.39) clarifies which 'defensive' expenditures to abate pollution should be explicit parts of green net national product. Abatement net investment $\dot{K}_a$ should be included, but abatement current spending a should not, because it is already accounted for in the value bB of environmental quality. Note also that only the capital gains in resource exports R_x, not in resource extractions R, are counted in GNNP.

(c) With no technical progress, $B_t = F_t = V_t = X_t = 0$, and Q^t becomes

$$Q^t = \int_t^\infty [\dot{r}(s)K_f(s) + \dot{Q}^x(s).R_x(s)] \exp[\int_t^s r(z)dz] \, ds, \qquad (4.42)$$

which makes (4.39) similar to the open economy results of Sefton and Weale (1996, section 4). If we also exclude domestic capital K, environmental quality B (hence $P^c \equiv 1$), abatement capital K_a, domestic production F, domestic resource use $R - R_x$ (so $R_x = R$), discoveries D and resource growth G, and assume a constant interest rate r, (4.39) then becomes

$$Y^\dagger = C + \dot{K}_f - (Q^x - X_R).R + \int_t^\infty \dot{Q}^x(s).R(s)e^{-r(s-t)}ds, \qquad (4.43)$$

which with [20] rapidly gives the main result (8) of Vincent et al. (1997).

(d) The problem of translating results from utility units to consumption units, which was bypassed in Hartwick (1990) with an approximate 'linearization of the Hamiltonian', is here transformed to finding how $P^C(t)$, the real price of consumption, changes over time. This must be inferred using $P^B = bP^C$

from the Appendix, and the Divisia property (4.11) which defines the price level,

$$\dot{\mathbf{P}}.C = \dot{P}^C C + \dot{P}^B B = \dot{P}^C C + (b\dot{P}^C + \dot{b}P^C)B = 0$$
$$\Rightarrow \dot{P}^C/P^C = -\dot{b}B/(C + bB). \tag{4.44}$$

Unless marginal abatement cost $B(t)$ is constant, the problem is transformed rather than solved, because of the difficulties of calculating both $b(t)$ and environmental quality $B(t)$. However, we now have a precise formula (4.44) to aim at, rather than an unknown linearization error.

3.3.6 Endogenous technical progress and sustainability

Since the mid-1980s there has been a huge revival in mainstream economics of interest in sustainable growth, though it is usually called the economics of *endogenous growth* (for an excellent overall survey see Aghion and Howitt, 1998). The name of this new growth economics comes from its focus on how technical progress arrives not just exogenously, like 'manna from heaven' with time passing, as modelled above. Endogenous technical progress results from people's and firms' economic (though often suboptimal) decisions to invest in accumulating human capital (from education) and knowledge or improved product quality (from research and development). Despite their parallel timing, there has been only limited cross-fertilization between the endogenous growth and sustainable development literatures. This has mainly come from neoclassical (new) growth economists injecting pollution or resource depletion into their production or utility functions. For examples, see Bovenberg and Smulders (1995); Stokey (1998); Aghion and Howitt (1998, ch. 5); Hamilton et al. (1998); Smulders (2000); and Pemberton and Ulph (2000).

However, almost without exception, such modelling has assumed unlimited substitutability of human capital or knowledge (as well as of physical capital) for environmental resources in production, and (where relevant) of consumption for environmental quality in utility. The conclusions are then essentially unchanged from the classic results in section 3.3.2 about optimal growth with and without exogenous technical progress. If endogenous progress is absent or bounded, optimal development is not sustainable.[27] If endogenous progress is unbounded and big enough in relation to the utility discount rate, optimal development is sustainable, at least on the balanced-growth path, which is usually the long-run trend. So endogenous growth economics can add important new terms to net investment $\mathbf{Q}.\dot{\mathbf{K}}$ in weak sustainability calculations.[28] But thus far, it sheds no new light on the ultimate limits to neoclassical substitutability assumptions.

3.4 The Theory of Sustainability Policy (as Distinct from Environmental Policy)

We now consider the theory of what can be done not to measure, but to *correct* unsustainability using government policy intervention, though the available literature is much sparser than for sustainability measurement, and more based on the overlapping generations (OLG) framework. Our context is economies with non-renewable resources or cumulative pollution, where environmental amenity or productivity decreases as the resource is depleted or as pollution accumulates. Here it is important to bear in mind our purely intertemporal definition of sustainability set out in sections 2 and 3.1(b). 'Sustainability policies' (those designed to achieve some kind of intertemporal equity) may thus be quite separate from 'environmental policies' (those designed to internalize environmental externalities, and hence achieve PV-optimality). Applying the two policy types together gives an *optimal sustainability* approach, which achieves sustainability with minimum loss of PV (Pezzey, 1994).

In the OLG context, sustainability policies are typically transfers of income or resource rights from or to generations, in order to meet an ethical goal (most often equality, or maximizing the undiscounted sum) for the intergenerational distribution of each generation's lifetime welfare. Environmental policies are typically taxes or other disincentives applied to emissions of a cumulative pollutant, which affects generational distribution only as a side effect. Howarth and Norgaard (1992) did not analyse constant welfare policies as such. However, they found that consumption decline decreases, and the marginal social value of cumulative pollution (effected by the environmental policy of an emissions tax) increases, as the ethical goal gives increased weight to future generations' welfare (effected by the sustainability policy of income transfers from old to young). Mourmouras (1993) calculated the income transfers and resource flow taxes which do achieve constant lifetime welfare across generations, though this required the assumption of an exponentially growing rather than non-renewable resource, and a capital stock which decays completely in one generation.

In an OLG model of climate change, Howarth (1998) showed how a policy of maximizing the undiscounted sum of welfare across generations, rather than having no intergenerational policy at all, requires much more abatement of greenhouse gas emissions, whether or not intergenerational transfers are possible. In Gerlagh and Keyzer (2001), environmental policy is achieved by creating a public corporation which makes producers and consumers pay (effectively Pigouvian taxes) for resource use and environmental services. Two alternative intergenerational policies are then 'grandfathering' control of the corporation entirely to the first generation, or the sustainability policy of establishing a trust fund which ensures that every generation receives an income sufficient to buy a minimum bundle of environmental services. Not surprisingly, the trust fund results in higher steady-state welfare in the long run than under grandfathering, but lower welfare for the first generation, so that the trust fund 'can only come into play through empathy of the present generation with future generations'. This brings to mind the possible schizophrenia of social objectives discussed in section 3.2. (Other papers in this line of literature are Marini and Scaramozzino (1995), and Bovenberg and Heijdra (1998)).

A similar division between environmental and sustainability policies occurs in infinitely lived, representative-agent (RA) versions of such economies. Pezzey (1989, 2001) considered policies to achieve constant utility in a range of models where individual PV-optimizing makes utility fall over time. A consistent result is that while environmental policies often slow the decline in utility, a further sustainability policy may be needed to achieve constant utility, and always lowers agents' effective rates of utility discount. In a simple capital–resource model as in section 3.3.2, but with utility $U(C,S)$ including the environmental amenity of S, the non-renewable resource stock, Pezzey (2001) showed that a nearly optimal sustainability policy together comprises specific taxes $\tau_S(t)$ on the resource stock and τ_C (t)on consumption, where

$$\tau_S(t) = -U_S(t)/U_C(t) \; (<0, \text{ hence a subsidy}), \text{ and} \qquad (4.45)$$
$$\dot{\tau}_C/(1 + \tau_C) = -[(\rho - F_K) + R(U_{CS} - U_S U_{CC}/U)/U_C]. \qquad (4.46)$$

Here, $-\tau_S$ can be seen as the environmental policy needed to internalize the resource stock externality, even if there is no sustainability goal. The consumption tax τ_C (which eventually falls over time, giving an incentive to save) achieves the sustainability policy objective. It may be needed even if the environmental effect U_S is zero, and may approach a 100 per cent subsidy for far-distant consumption, reflecting the schizophrenia between individual discounting and the collective goal of constant utility (see section 3.2).

Of the two modelling approaches, the OLG approach connects to the fact that some small nations, mostly those reliant on extracting a non-renewable resource like oil or guano, have set up trust funds to save general financial wealth for future generations. In contrast, the idea in (4.46) of using falling consumption taxes to lower impatience is a long way from policy-makers' agendas. What theory does not say, in either case, is how accurately the numbers needed for sustainability policies can be estimated from current market or shadow prices. In the RA example above, the conundrum is that τ_S and τ_C need to be measured on a sustainable path, that is, using 'sustainability prices'; but currently observed prices are, by assumption, 'unsustainable'.

3.5 Empirical Results Based on Neoclassical Theory

We survey here the application of the theory of section 3.3 to measuring sustainability in many countries. As far as we know, no one has attempted any empirical estimation of the theory-based sustainability policies just analysed in section 3.4. Perhaps it is the variety of these policies that accounts for this. After all, the impossibility of measuring 'sustainability prices' in an unsustainable economy is a problem not just for quantifying sustainability policies, but also for measuring sustainability, as noted in section 3.2, and the literature on the latter is extensive, as our survey now shows. In section 3.5.1 we review the measurement problems that are already evident from the theory. In section 3.5.2 we look at the empirical results themselves. Lastly, in section 3.5.3 we consider a popular though very variable and much-debated extension of GNNP measurement, to a so-called index of sustainable economic welfare (ISEW).

3.5.1 Reminder of problems in applying the theory

Most measurements of sustainability estimate (by heroically wrestling with serious data deficiencies) the growth rate of GNNP, $\dot{Y}/Y$, or net investment as a proportion of GNNP $\mathbf{Q}.\dot{\mathbf{K}}/Y$. If the assumptions needed for Corollary 1 of Proposition 4.5 (forever constant, positive rates of interest, GNNP growth and exogenous progress in production) hold, then only the sign of the first estimate, but not of the second, is useful, since it is $\dot{Y}/Y \leq 0$ but $\mathbf{Q}.\dot{\mathbf{K}}/Y \leq -\chi/(r-\Gamma)$ which is the condition for unsustainability. The problem arises because most authors ignore technical progress and shifts in world prices of traded goods, both of which cause exogenous shifts in production possibilities. Papers like Weitzman (1997), focusing on exogenous technical progress in the USA, and Vincent et al. (1997) focusing on exogenous shifts in oil export prices facing Indonesia,[29] are the exception rather than the rule. In addition to this problem, there are two others that are worth mentioning:

1. We already noted in section 3.2 that any real economy is not on its (socially) PV-optimal path because of significant environmental externalities. How big its uninternalized externalities are depends on how strong are its environmental policies, and these do not spring into existence overnight. Social and political pressures grow gradually, in reaction to growing environmental degradation, before institutions and laws evolve to enact control policies. This growing degree of internalization is captured by hardly any theory, but it is captured by empirical studies of how growth affects the environment. These are often (though perhaps misleadingly) labelled as environmental Kuznets curve (EKC) studies. (For development to follow an EKC usually means that overall environmental quality first gets worse, and then improves, as per capita income increases. This feature is by no means

always found in practice; see Barbier, (1997) and Rothman and de Bruyn (1998), for survey issues.) As far as we know, the connection between EKC studies and sustainability measurement remains unexplored.

2. All the theory is deterministic, and cannot allow for pure uncertainty. The downside uncertainties (for example of ecosystem collapse) are unlikely to be balanced with the upside uncertainties (for example of sudden innovations in pollution abatement).

Estimating how big all these errors may be, about which theory says very little, is a key topic for future research. As an illustration, Figures 4.1 and 4.2 show how much effect two related parameters can have on the spread between four different income measures in the capital–resource economy of Pezzey and Withagen (1998, section V). In Figure 4.1, both the importance of resource flow R in the production function F is much greater, with a power of 0.4 instead of 0.15, and the elasticity of marginal utility is much lower, at 0.6 instead of 0.85, than in Figure 4.2. (The two parameters are constrained to add to 1, so it is impossible to disentangle their separate effects.) The combined effect is to make the income measures much wider apart in Figure 4.1, and so they give much more variable signals about sustainability. (The discount rate ρ is the same in both figures, and the different initial values K_0 and S_0 merely shift and stretch the time scale, not the dispersion of income measures.)

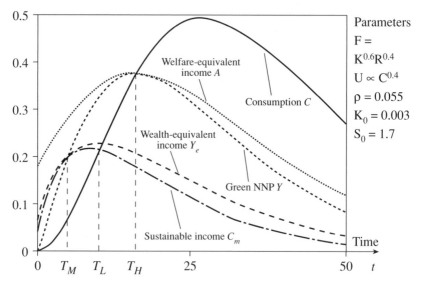

Note: Welfare-equivalent income $A(t) := U^{-1}\{\int_t^\infty \phi(s)U[C(s)]ds\}$ (Asheim, 2000).

Figure 4.1   Optimal paths of consumption and income variables

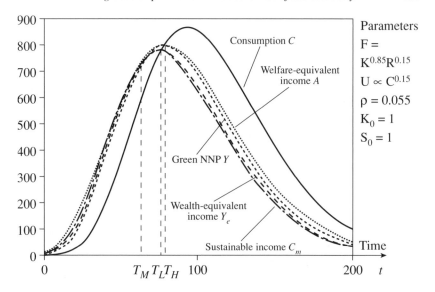

Figure 4.2   Optimal paths of consumption and income variables

About the only problem not faced by our utility-based, neoclassical sustainability test is any *extra* operational difficulty in comparison to a wealth-based definition of sustainability. In the specific model of section 3.3.5, both approaches need a dollar estimate of U_B/U_C, the marginal value of environmental quality; the division by U_C avoids the problem of the non-measurability of utility suggested by Pearce et al. (1989, p. 49). Moreover, non-declining wealth can be an inaccurate theoretical indicator of sustainability, as noted in comment (b) to Proposition 4.5.

3.5.2   Empirical sustainability results
We report here only empirical results for the sustainability of whole economies. These results mainly deal with the time-autonomous case, so that net investment in the one-sided sustainability test in Proposition 4.5 is $\dot{\mathbf{Q}}.\mathbf{K}$ rather than $\mathbf{Q}^{\dagger}.\dot{\mathbf{K}}^{\dagger}$; and mainly ignore trade, despite most of the countries being very small and open relative to the world economy. We ignore the plethora of sector-based, micro-indicators of 'sustainability', precisely because they are 'micro' and therefore hard to aggregate into an overall view of sustainability (see for example Levett, 1998 and Pannell and Glenn, 2000, who come from the very different perspectives of UK policy-making and Australian agricultural economics).

Measuring sustainability has often been done using just the $\mathbf{Q}.\dot{\mathbf{K}}$ measure, for example by Pearce and Atkinson (1993), Pearce et al. (1993), Hamilton

(1994), Atkinson et al. (1997) and Neumayer (1999), of which we report just on the first, seminal paper. Few authors have tried both the parallel calculations (of $\dot{Y}$ and $\mathbf{Q.\dot{K}}$) suggested by the one-sided sustainability test, and we report on one, Hanley et al. (1999).[30] Finally, we report an explicit attempt to bring trade into sustainability calculations, Proops et al. (1999), and a very different approach to resource scarcity by Weitzman (1999).

Pearce and Atkinson used data for 18 countries, from the USA to Burkino Faso, to estimate a 'variant' of $\mathbf{Q.\dot{K}}/Y$ in which savings instead of investment is used when calculating the net increase $\dot{K}$ in built capital. All the European countries and Japan came out as definitely sustainable, essentially because of high savings rates and low resource depletion rents (the latter perhaps being because these countries have relatively few resources left to deplete). By contrast, all the African countries were judged to be definitely unsustainable, because of low savings rates and high depletion rents. The USA was only marginally sustainable, because of a much lower savings rate than Europe or Japan. The study thus focused empirical attention on savings-funded investment in built capital, as well as natural resource depletion, being an important influence on sustainability, if one 'believes' in the substitutability of these two inputs to production.

In heroically estimating and comparing seven sustainability measures for Scotland during the period 1980–93, Hanley et al. (1999) helped to highlight both progress and problems in sustainability empiricism. The two economic sustainability indicators, GNNP (Y) and genuine savings (GS = $\mathbf{Q.\dot{K}}$) yielded fairly different results. GNNP showed Scotland to be increasingly sustainable over the period; GS showed it to be unsustainable, but becoming less so. It is hard to draw any conclusion from this, because GNNP used investment data, while (like Pearce and Atkinson) GS used savings data, which come from a different administrative source. More generally, there was no coherent accounting for Scottish trade in goods, resources and financial capital, the last of which for example allows savings to diverge widely from investment.

The main focus of Proops et al. (1999) was to show that one way or another, trade in both resources and resource-intensive goods is significant in analyses of sustainability for most countries. They gave an analytically and empirically clear (though debatable) development of the idea of 'exporting unsustainability' suggested by Pearce et al. (1989, pp. 45–7). This states that rich, industrialized countries, which import large amounts of resources (or resource-intensive goods ultimately derived) from countries which are depleting their resources unsustainably, bear some responsibility for this unsustainability. Proops et al.'s calculations for various countries centred on the difference between 'closed-economy sustainability', analogous to Pearce and Atkinson's measure, and 'open-economy' sustainability, which replaces calculations of the capital and resources used 'by' an economy with the capital and resources used 'for' or 'attributable to' an economy. The latter are calculated by matrix algebra derived from an input–output analysis of world trade flows.

Their most important single empirical finding was that moving from the closed measure to the open measure dramatically increases the calculated sustainability of resource-rich regions like the Middle East, and reduces it for industrial regions like Western Europe and the USA. However, despite their contention (p. 77) that 'industrialised countries appropriate the carrying capacity of other countries (e.g. by importing natural resources), therefore benefiting at the expense of their trading partners,' Proops et al. drew no conclusions from their calculations for either national or international policy-making. Also absent was any explicit discussion of how and to what extent trade can be unfair and exploitative.

Weitzman's (1999) analysis of resource scarcity asked a seemingly complicated question: what is the cost to the US economy of minerals being non-renewable resources, so that eventually the economy will have to do without at least some of its currently provided minerals inputs? Weitzman showed that *if* one accepts the premises of his 1976 article, then the answer to the question posed is simple. The present-value 'scarcity premium' relative to total social wealth is just the current value of the resource rent, divided by the current flow of conventionally measured national income (that is, income without deduction for depletion rent). Using some admittedly rough calculations, Weitzman found that according to this formula, the relative cost of resource depletability is quite low: on the order of only 1 per cent of total wealth.

This result has an intuitive appeal, since a resource-scarcity rent, as indicated by the unit price of *in situ* reserves, is in fact the present value of future benefits from an additional unit of resource stock today. What is striking about the model, and not necessarily so general, is the application of this reasoning to *non-marginal* changes in resource stock (a question which recurs in valuing climate change in section 5). This can lead one to question Weitzman's interpretation of his results as 'pricing the limits to growth'. If resource substitution and innovation do not provide large cushions against scarcity, and some depletion is of critical and non-substitutable resources, then there is every reason to expect the cost of such non-marginal scarcity to be huge. However, this kind of scarcity will not be picked up in Weitzman's model. As elsewhere, one's judgements about the prospects for sustainability are strongly coloured here by one's assumed underlying worldview.

This is as good a place as any to comment on what has become a notorious paper in *Nature* by Costanza et al. (1997), because of the methodological connection with Weitzman through non-marginal valuation, but stark contrast in worldview. Costanza et al. sought to calculate the total dollar value of ecosystem services, using a set of calculations which combined many dissimilar things. As many critics have noted, the combining of component values using so many different methods and so many untested assumptions is a stretch. But the bigger problem with this strategy is that the calculation is not just operationally dubious, but also logically meaningless. Life cannot survive without ecosystem services, so their *total* value to us must be infinite! But that says nothing about the highly relevant question of how to value partial changes in ecosystem service flows, or states of being.

3.5.3   An *ad-hoc* extension of neoclassicism: the Index of Sustainable Economic Welfare (ISEW)

The ISEW (also called the Genuine Progress Indicator or GPI) was popularized by Daly and Cobb (1989). It has been developed by many other authors, including Hanley et al. (1999), as reviewed above. Its declared purpose is generally to adjust GNP per capita to get a better measure of 'welfare'. But is 'welfare' meant to be a better dollar-equivalent measure of instantaneous utility U, to reflect valid concerns that people have for (say) environmental quality and intragenerational equity? Or of sustainable utility, U_m; or of utility which is PV-equivalent to intertemporal welfare, W? There is no clear answer, given that Daly and Cobb's measure took consumption divided by an index of distributional inequality, and then added or subtracted nearly twenty separate expenditures for household labour services, public health and education services, pollution clean-up costs, as well as the environmental resource components of net investment $Q.\dot{K}$. So many of these adjustments are *ad hoc*, with arbitrary weights, that the ISEW cannot be regarded as having a clear theoretical foundation. For example, the empirical basis for the heavy negative weight often given to inequality (which drags the ISEW down over periods like 1980–2000) is often shaky; and unlike our income measure in (4.39) in section 3.3.5, there is no consistent accounting for the net effects of current versus capital spending on pollution abatement.

This allows critics like Neumayer (1999, p. 190) to form 'the impression that [ISEWs] are constructed with the very intention of producing the desired result of decreasing "sustainable economic welfare".' To the extent this is true it is unfortunate, since intragenerational equity, other aspects of civic life, and environmental quality all do affect social well-being. Arguably it is better to be roughly right by including these features in a broader assessment of sustainability, than to be precisely wrong by omitting them altogether. In theory the features to include, and the weights to give them, could be guided by an intelligent combination of social valuation studies, and the income theory from section 3.3. An example is the Atkinson measure of empirical (rather than the writers') preferences for income equality, used by Hamilton and Denniss (2000, p. 24). As an alternative, one could pursue the currently popular approach of developing multi-criteria indicators that do not add up to a single measure, and include public values and perceptions in a variety of ways (Froger and Munda, 1998; Toman, 1999).

4.   STRONG SUSTAINABILITY: STUDIES OF LIMITS TO SUBSTITUTABILITY AND TECHNICAL PROGRESS

The models of neoclassical (weak) sustainability in section 3 assumed neoclassical properties of input substitution that make it feasible to sustain well-being across generations despite finite resource constraints (Solow, 1974). And as shown by Stiglitz (1974), for a sustainable path to be not just feasible but also PV-optimal, production must typically exhibit both unlimited substitutability and technical progress, and the future must not be discounted too rapidly.

In this section we address some of the conceptual underpinnings and empirical applications of the contrasting, strong sustainability perspective. Adherents of this view are also greatly concerned with intergenerational distribution. Indeed, strong sustainability advocates often criticize a more utilitarian perspective on intergenerational distribution, and emphasize rights-based theories of intergenerational justice that result in stewardship obligations for the current generation to preserve options over time. These obligations assume particular importance when there is uncertainty about the future resilience or viability of natural systems. Strong sustainability advocates also tend to put more emphasis on concepts of community, as opposed to the more individualistic concepts underlying utilitarian analysis.

Strong sustainability proponents are also concerned with whether sustainable time paths of consumption or utility are even possible. That is, they question the assumptions of substitution and technical advance that undergird the neoclassical approach to the subject. There is a range of reasons for this found in the literature, which implies a range of possible limits on substitution. After reviewing this range of ideas in section 4.1, we will consider in section 4.2 different empirical approaches for assessing strong sustainability, and in section 4.3 the policy imperatives that derive directly or indirectly from the strong sustainability perspective.

We noted in section 2 that strong sustainability puts emphasis on maintaining specific components of society's productive stocks, rather than just maintaining or increasing the overall value of consumption, utility, or wealth. To be sure, no advocate of strong sustainability argues for preserving *all* stocks. This would lead to the absurd implication that no depletable resource should ever be diminished. Rather, advocates of strong sustainability argue for maintaining the key *functions* of natural resource stocks (a development of Daly's 1990 call for preventing assimilative capacities and renewable resources from declining, and investing in renewable substitutes for inevitable declines in non-renewables; see also Common and Perrings, 1992; Ekins, 1996). The emphasis is thus on physical measures of resources and functions, in contrast to section 3's emphasis on economic concepts of sustainable income, utility, and wealth (see also Sollner, 1997).

Before developing these themes in more detail, we briefly discuss how strong sustainability analysis might be connected to the more formal analytical apparatus erected in section 3. This connection is often not made in the literature, in particular because of broader objections to a utilitarian framework by many strong sustainability advocates. Consider the welfare maximization problem for an economy in which utility $U(C,B)$ depends on consumption C and environmental quality B, and the economy's production possibilities are summarized by a neoclassical production function $F(K,R,t)$ depending on built capital stocks K, natural resource flows R, and time t. Weak sustainability analysis involves maximizing the generalized present value of the utility integral, subject to the production possibilities, and to constraints implying that utility never rises to an unsustainable level and subsequently declines.

Here, given the emphasis on particular components or functions of natural capital, we could replace the sustainable utility constraint with constraints that limit environmental degradation or preserve other critical natural capital service flows (components of R). In effect, the analysis then tells us how to maximize a utilitarian welfare measure subject to more 'hard' ecological constraints. For those constraints that are binding, the analysis tells us how to achieve them in the most cost-effective manner (that is, with the least loss of welfare). This is an important consideration that deserves more recognition in strong sustainability analyses.

We could also manipulate the production and utility functions in various ways to capture features seen to be important by strong sustainability advocates. For example, the production function could be written implicitly (assuming single capital and resource stocks, and suppressing the time component, for simplicity) as

$$F(K,R) = K^{\alpha}(R - \mu F)^{\beta} \qquad (4.47)$$

where μ is the minimum resource content needed per unit of output (expressed in units of, for example, tonnes per dollar). Note that with this formulation production will be very similar to Cobb–Douglas if R is large relative to μF, but if R declines relative to μF (as with a non-renewable resource) then substitution possibilities are circumscribed.

One other point worth making in this context is that while much of the discussion of substitutability in sustainability analysis focuses on production, the utility function can also capture substitution constraints. For example, the Stone–Geary function

$$U(C,B) = (C - C_{min})^{\alpha}(B - B_{min})^{\beta} \qquad (4.48)$$

captures the idea that there are minimum threshold levels C_{min} of 'basic needs' consumption, and B_{min} of environmental quality.

4.1 Rationales for Limited Substitution

Various views about limits to substitution can be arrayed along a continuum. An extreme view is that because of thermodynamic constraints, decline (not just stagnation) is ultimately inevitable. Less extreme views incorporate limits to growth, but see these limits as manageable in varying degrees. For example, a high steady-state standard of living may be possible through the further economic development of renewable substitutes for depletable resources. Or, significant consumption growth may be possible, but at the cost of increasing damage to the 'environmental sinks' that absorb the residuals of economic activity. Since our understanding of natural processes is still so poor, the argument goes, the risk of serious damage to them poses a potential limit to growth.

4.1.1 The structure of production

One argument for the existence of substitution limits is that the actual process of production offers fewer chances for altering inputs than is assumed in neo-classical constructs. This is the underlying premise of the neo-Austrian approach described by Faber et al. (1999). Its key features include an activity analysis approach to production in the short term. For a given choice of technique, input proportions are largely fixed. Moreover, since capital goods production must precede the adoption of a different technique and production takes time, input proportions cannot be readily switched in the short term. In the longer term, however, input proportions become more variable through changes in the choice of technique. Therefore, without additional features, an activity analysis framework cannot itself explain limits on substitutability over the longer term. Such limits in effect circumscribe the set of possible techniques.[31]

4.1.2 Thermodynamic limits to production technique

This complex subject has been the source of much contention and no small amount of misunderstanding in debates over ecological economics and sustainability. In this review we can hope only to give a flavour of some of the arguments.[32]

Natural scientists often criticize economic models of production for not adhering to basic laws of nature. One of these basic principles is the first law of thermodynamics (the conservation law), which indicates that matter can only be transformed, not created or destroyed. An immediate corollary of this principle is that there is a minimum material input required to produce any *material* output; we cannot create something from nothing. In addition, the first law implies that production inevitably creates material by-products: we cannot return something back into nothing. To the extent that these by-products are harmful to people or their environment, and the neutralizing capacity of the natural environment is limited, the adverse effects of such residuals could constitute a limit to growth.

But such a limit could also be overcome, in principle at least, by the application of other inputs (including significant energy) to expand the environment's carrying capacity for residuals (through storage, neutralization, or reduced exposure). If only because people remain dependent on material substances for physical sustenance, there is some minimum material throughput required. But this in itself need not inherently be a critical constraint. Moreover, limits on *material* outputs need not limit the value of economic activity, as highlighted by the increase in value added in the service sector. Ausubel (1996) claimed that we are observing significant dematerialization of the modern economy, and that this trend can be expected to continue in the future. Ayres (1998) disputed the positive interpretation of such calculations. He argued that while material throughput per unit of GDP has shrunk because of productivity increases (greater embodiment of 'information' in final output), total material throughput – and thus the stress on natural environments – has not shrunk, and is not likely to in the future without a more deliberate conservation policy.

The relevance of the first law is widely accepted in principle among resource and environmental economists (see Ayres and Kneese, 1969), though the extent to which materials balance is considered in practice in neoclassical analyses is more limited. Also, when harmful by-products are considered they are not always explicitly modelled as joint products. Nor is there agreement about how much the harm from residuals is a limit to growth. Much greater controversy and confusion attends the application of the second law of thermodynamics (the entropy law), however. Invoking this principle in the context of economic activity starts with observing that transformations of the physical environment involve the use of more highly concentrated or otherwise better organized energy and materials, while generating wastes that are more dissipated or otherwise less well organized (for example, waste heat or diluted materials). Moreover, no degree of technical progress can drive down the minimum energy input for a particular materials transformation process below a certain threshold (Daly, 1994; Cleveland and Ruth, 1997).

The fact that there are minimum energy and material requirements for material output starts to call into question the basic tenets of unlimited substitution that undergird much weak sustainability theory. In particular, the

Cobb–Douglas production function with isoquants asymptotic to the axes in input space (see section 3.3.2) fails to satisfy these conditions. The model of exponential resource-augmenting technical progress advanced there by Stiglitz (1974) also fails this test.

Minimum energy and materials requirements mean that the ultimate scale of the economy is bounded above by the product of the average product of energy or materials and the long-term capacity of renewable energy or materials recycling (see TPK for elaboration). These constraints may be very loose, in that the implied capacities may be very large, but this is an empirical question.[33] Minimum energy requirements also have implications at the micro-level for optimal patterns of resource depletion (see in particular Ruth's 1995 study of the copper extraction sector). In particular, very low-quality materials, that would ultimately be exploited in a standard depletion model, are not economic when these constraints on production feasibility are taken into account.[34]

Ayres (1996, 1998, 1999) also advocated strong sustainability, and he shared the concern with the adverse consequences of excessive material throughput, but he rejected the notion that entropic dissipation of materials is an inherent limit to growth. He argued that while a large flow of energy is available from the sun, this energy (along with natural biological processes that already act to concentrate material like nutrients) can be used to recycle dissipated materials. Such dissipation is never complete; at worst the materials are dissipated to their average concentration in the earth's crust (though this may be pretty low, as noted above). Ayres's analogy is that materials dissipated in production can be thought of as collecting in a wastebasket; and while energy is available to empty the wastebasket and sort it on to the work table, the materials can be reclaimed.

In this perspective, the key challenge is not materials conservation, but the rapid development of more efficient solar energy, so that the necessary energy potential is available to work with more dilute materials streams. To that end, Ayres argued that some of the fossil energy endowment should be used for constructing the large-scale capital infrastructure for deploying solar energy, rather than for satisfying current demands. He would also support materials conservation as a way to take stress off natural systems (including the human species) that are adversely affected by the propagation of harmful residuals. We return to this point below.

It is useful briefly to compare this view with more conventional economic analysis of energy and materials scarcity. Ayres's argument can be reinterpreted as implying that there is a Ricardian sustainability user cost (shadow price) of materials use, since use implies an increased future energy expenditure for materials recovery. If this shadow price of dissipation (or equivalently the full marginal cost of recycling) were built into the price of materials, and fossil energy carried a price premium that reflected its full scarcity, then a market system would be capable of generating a sustainable pattern of energy and materials use. There would be no need for a separate conservation policy for energy and materials to achieve sustainability. In particular, the private sector would deploy large-scale solar energy as it became economic in the long term and would generate efficient materials conservation and recycling.

In practice, however, there would still be a need to confront both conventional environmental externalities, and long-term sustainability concerns related to the accumulation of damaging residuals in the environment. Could society organize the correct shadow-pricing system to address both materials and environmental sink scarcity? Would it be adequately motivated by long-term concerns of intergenerational fairness? This approach would not put to rest the concerns of those who criticize weak sustainability as not being adequately concerned with large-scale future harms, that either cannot or will not be properly evaluated by conventional economic techniques.

4.1.3   Substitution limits due to uncertainty, ecological degradation and bounded rationality

The above discussion of thermodynamic limits concentrates on substitution between energy and other inputs. A broader view of strong sustainability is that there may be other limits, at least at the macro scale, on the substitution between capital and resources generally and on the capacity of innovation to stretch these limits.

These arguments boil down to the already discussed view that human beings cannot live, or at least cannot thrive, in highly degraded natural environments, even with a high degree of material wealth. This wealth, the argument goes, cannot undo the direct threats to well-being through illness or injury, the disruptions of natural systems and processes on which all life depends, or the loss of humanistic or spiritual values in such a situation (see O'Connor, 1993; Ayres, 1996; Norton and Toman, 1997; and the survey in Neumayer, 1999, ch. 4).

We can connect these arguments to the previous discussion of thermodynamic limits in the following way. Following Ayres, a degraded environment is one with a high presence of dissipated materials that are harmful to its biological organisms and processes. If we understood how these processes operated, we could use the huge well of potential solar energy for various environmental restoration activities, just as this energy can be used to re-concentrate dissipated materials. It is our lack of understanding of underlying biological processes that limits our capacity to do so. Whether this constraint can ever be overcome in practice depends on one's view about whether nature ever really is 'knowable'. But given current uncertainties about natural processes, concern about their long-term degradation can be a reason for specific action to prevent further degradation, even with offsetting investment in built capital (see also Woodward and Bishop, 1997).

One last possible constraint that has been noted only rarely (for example by Pezzey, 1992, p. 339) is the finite amount of human information processing capacity. The degree and speed of knowledge acquisition needed to stay abreast of materials and energy dissipation by adopting new technologies (and assumed by models of endogenous growth) may ultimately exceed what the human brain is adapted by evolution to accomplish. This can be seen as an example of Herbert Simon's concept of 'bounded rationality', which would also question the ability of the neoclassical representative agent to act as if maximizing complex integrals over a perfectly foreseen, infinite time horizon (see Lipman, 1995 for a survey).

Before moving on to more empirical issues, we note that the concept of *scale* is ubiquitous in the debate over substitution possibilities. On the one hand, a larger overall scale of throughput should imply more possibilities, because the range of possible activity types increases. On the other hand, a larger throughput for a particular process may make substitution more difficult by further damaging fixed ecological factors.

Who is right in the weak-versus-strong debate? Neumayer (1999) argued that there is no compelling empirical evidence for or against either view. Econometric evidence on energy–capital substitution versus complementarity suggests that some of both has happened at various times. Other kinds of analyses (such as engineering process analyses) consider only a limited range of inputs and outputs. Up until now, the weak sustainability view of substantial substitution and innovation possibilities seems to have been borne out by history. Whether it will be in the far future remains an open empirical question, that will require big advances in data and methodology to answer. Putting this to the side for now, we turn next to some current empirical measures of sustainability inspired by, or consistent with, strong sustainability views.

4.2   Measures of Strong Sustainability

Given concerns with the seemingly overoptimistic numbers coming out of neoclassical sustainability analysis, critics of that approach have argued that physical calculations can reveal truths that markets do not fully apprehend. As suggested in section 4.1.3, this is at least plausible where non-owned, large-scale ecological resources are concerned. Physical indicators may also be useful for traditional market resources if there is reason to suspect market failures in the efficient allocation of these resources, or that there could be large divergences between the PV-optimal and sustainable use of these resources. Nevertheless, physical indicators also have serious shortcomings, as described below for several of the main indicators.[35]

4.2.1   Sustainability gaps

If one concludes that certain critical resource stocks are in peril, then there is clearly a need to take action to preserve them. *Sustainability gaps*, as discussed for example by Ekins and Simon (1999, 2001), try to measure the 'distances' between current practice, and protective and restorative efforts sufficient to bring critical stocks back above (or pollution loads below) *prespecified* threshold levels. The units can either be physical measures (for example, tonnes of excess pollution), or as in Ekins and Simon (2001), a 'years to sustainability' measure of how long it would take, given current trends in environmental improvement, for the thresholds to be met.

Clearly the gap sizes depend on how the sustainability thresholds are defined relative to current resource stocks or conditions. To achieve the kind of strong sustainability outcome sketched in section 2.3 (pollution below critical loads, renewables maintained, depletion of resources compensated by new alternatives) usually implies quite substantial sustainability gaps. For example, Ekins and Simon (2001) showed that it may take many decades to meet specified environmental norms in the UK and the Netherlands, given current trends.

Such calculations are usually taken to show how much more effort is needed to reach sustainability. But because the baselines are defined in physical terms, their incremental benefits cannot be readily compared to their incremental costs in making such adjustments; nor does sustainability gap analysis generally compare what benefits other uses of these protective and restorative outlays might achieve. As Ekins and Simon said, making monetary calculations of a sustainability gap is very difficult, given uncertainties about the costs and synergies among different environmental remediation strategies.

Faucheux et al. (1998) described a modelling platform applied to the French and Dutch economies in which one can combine analysis of production and household demand for goods and environmental amenities with identification of and constraints on degradation of critical natural resources. With this approach, one can measure the relative reduction in household consumption required by different environmental constraints. These authors presented preliminary figures in which the only limiting environmental factor is CO_2 emissions. These results are somewhat difficult to interpret in that they require a comparison of scenarios that differ in several respects, for example, technology and social attitudes toward consumption. Extending this approach to a more comprehensive analysis of environmental constraints and multiple response options would be a formidable task.

4.2.2 Human appropriation of net primary production, and ecological footprints

One of the most commonly cited 'folk statistics' in the ecological limits to growth debate is that human beings already use about half of all the solar energy gathered by photosynthesis planet-wide. The implication is that humans are already dangerously crowding natural processes at the current scale of economic activity. If we already use this much, the argument goes, what happens when the population doubles and human usage rises to 80 per cent or more as per capita incomes rise?

The source of this statistic is in Vitousek et al. (1986), who defined and calculated figures for successive levels of human appropriation of the world's net primary production (NPP) from photosynthesis by plants. Their first figure (Table 2), including only direct caloric consumption by humans and domestic animals, was about 3 per cent of NPP. A second figure also accounted for human activities that reduce NPP through replacement of natural ecosystems with simpler managed systems. While the authors in no way attempted to relate their calculations to human welfare measures used by economists, NPP could ultimately be a constraining resource for sustainability, and the reduction could be thought of very loosely as a kind of user cost. By comparing Tables 3 and 4 of Vitousek et al., one can see that this reduction accounts for about 15 per cent of NPP.

The rest of the NPP appropriation calculated in Table 3 of Vitousek et al. came from assuming that the energy flow in *any* ecosystems 'co-opted' by humans is in effect debited from NPP. So this assumed that none of this energy is available to any other organisms, such as butterflies or songbirds that inhabit agricultural land. This seems greatly to overstate the practical draw on NPP made by the human species, especially when these debits are added to the NPP appropriations already mentioned above.

We conclude that calculations of NPP appropriation could in principle be useful indicators of some kind of macro-scale sustainability problem. However, the figures often encountered in the literature appear to overstate the current problem; and more modest figures for appropriation are still difficult to interpret, since the connections among current levels of NPP appropriation, ecological stability or resilience, and human welfare are unclear and poorly understood.

Various other physical indicators have been constructed for various purposes. One currently popular approach is the *ecological footprint*, which seeks to measure the total land area of ecosystems required to produce a population's consumed resources and assimilate its wastes, both locally and elsewhere (see Wackernagel and Rees, 1996, and the March 2000 special issue of *Ecological Economics* for many articles on this indicator). For example, one can calculate the land area needed to make all the food and fibre used (including grain fed to livestock); the amount of land needed to assimilate greenhouse gas emissions or provide renewable substitutes for fossil fuels; the amount of land paved over or otherwise 'lost' due to human settlement; and so forth. Typically these calculations sound an alarm by showing that the imputed 'land use' by rich people far exceeds the effective land available on a global scale. For example, Wackernagel and Rees (1996) found an ecological footprint of about 5 hectares per capita in North America, as against about 1.5 hectares per capita of available land worldwide. In many of these calculations, moreover, the production and accumulation of greenhouse gases is a major culprit, though not the only factor.

Our own view is that such indicators provide only limited insight even into the issue of scale, let alone into issues of natural system constraints. The definitions and boundaries of such physical indicators (what is included or excluded, and how meaningfully to add together widely different types of hectares or tonnes) are unclear or arbitrary. As the proponents readily acknowledge, the indicators are not robust to changes in technology (for example, advances in biological carbon sequestration or waste treatment), and thus they are also not robust to changes in policy that induce such responses. Nor do the aggregates provide insight into the degree of environmental risk incurred. They do not for example distinguish between a hectare of paved road in an industrial zone and a hectare of paved road in Amazonia, or between a kilogram of biologically inert material and a kilogram of toxic heavy metal. Without a firmer grounding in some broad notion of relative risk or opportunity cost that can be used to weigh the significance of these measures, it is difficult to use them for assessing sustainability or redirecting policy (Ayres, 1995, 2000).

4.2.3   Energy return on investment

Broadly speaking, the energy return on investment (EROI) seeks to reveal how much direct and embodied energy has to be invested to produce a unit of useful output or energy. If there are significant biophysical limits to growth, one would expect both that this energy requirement will rise over time, and that technical innovation will do little to offset this. A specific application of the concept is in the extraction of energy itself, where one measures how much available energy is yielded per unit of energy used for extraction, and physical limits are manifested in an inexorable decline in this energy yield. Cleveland et al. (1984) drew much attention to these issues, and subsequent work includes Cleveland and Kaufmann (1991, 1997), Faucheux and O'Connor (1998) and Kaufmann and Cleveland (2001).

While EROI indicators can provide general information about pressure of ecological systems, they, like NPP appropriations or ecological footprints, have a number of shortcomings as measures of aggregate scarcity or sustainability. We have already noted reservations with the concept of thermodynamic limits that lies behind some energy indicators. In addition, one cannot develop an aggregate measure with output-based EROIs unless energy requirements are expressed per unit value of economic output. But then the energy requirement measure will be affected by changes in prices, confounding measurement of the physical intensity of energy demands. Similarly, the apparent energy intensity of activity would change if the composition of that activity changed (for example, from manufacturing to services), making it impossible to separate out real changes in energy efficiency.

These operational problems are less serious when the concept is applied more narrowly to net energy yield in the energy sector. However, simple models of physical scarcity still do not explain observed behaviour. Cleveland and Kaufmann (1997) and Kaufmann and Cleveland (2001) considered the case of oil and gas extraction in the USA. For natural gas they found that yield per unit effort has declined over time, and that technical advances in discovering and recovering gas resources have not kept pace with resource depletion. However, they acknowledged that their analysis is circumscribed by data limitations that complicate the separation of depletion and innovation influences, and they noted that occasional technical advances have significantly offset depletion effects. For oil the effects of depletion seem even more equivocal. The cost of resource production has not risen monotonically; it has been affected in particular by technical innovation and episodes of higher prices.[36] Production, cost, prices, and regulatory institutions are a complex 'co-evolving' system in their analysis. Moreover, if great progress is made in developing renewables, as Ayres (1998) envisaged is possible, then rising fossil energy scarcity – measured in economic or physical terms – is clearly less of a concern.

4.3   Strong Sustainability Policy

We have already noted that the underlying philosophy of strong sustainability embraces concepts such as critical loads and thresholds that establish absolute limits on how much resource or system depletion or degradation is acceptable. This is a version of the 'precautionary principle', a kind of ecological Hippocratic oath to do no wrong. When looked at from this perspective, strong sustainability gives rise to a couple of policy conundrums with which we end this section.

The first and most general one is the question of whether an absolute limit itself, with no prospect for trade-off, is tenable. Even if one takes the view (highly controversial among economists) that there may be great difficulty in comparing some environmental values with individual consumption values, one is not automatically led to a strong precautionary principle. There is no easy way to decide when possible ecosystem effects could be so large and uncertain that attempts at calculating trade-offs between the costs and benefits of standards should be replaced with a more precautionary approach. Variants of constrained trade-off approaches, such as a safe minimum standard, are more flexible alternatives to a strict precautionary principle (Toman, 1994; Norton and Toman, 1997; Woodward and Bishop, 1997; Farmer and Randall, 1998).

Second, if substitution of man-made for natural inputs is limited, then why aren't ever-rising prices (and thus weak sustainability indicators) signalling this scarcity? And if they are, weak sustainability indicators would be signalling a problem too. One view among many analysts and practitioners who think sustainability is both important and undervalued is that long-term discounting trivializes the problem. This may emphasize the wrong point, however. Unless future resource scarcity is severe enough for properly measured opportunity costs (not necessarily observed costs) to be rising faster than an appropriately specified efficient discount rate, then in a real sense there is no threat to sustainability, provided resources are at least somewhat fungible. In themselves, policies to promote sustainability-enhancing activities by applying especially low discount rates to project assessment make investment inefficient and run counter to private actor incentives.

It may be more effective to uncover why a real scarcity problem, or a problem of limited substitution capacity, is not being reflected in current prices. Once the problem is identified, appropriate corrective action at the microeconomic level can be taken. A fundamental problem is obviously the lack of markets for a variety of waste sinks and other environmental attributes, including macro-scale concerns with ecosystem resilience. The analysis of weak sustainability makes clear, however, that simply internalizing conventionally identified externalities will not in itself resolve a sustainability problem, if the resulting externality-corrected prices imply an unacceptable intergenerational distribution of well-being. The strong sustainability perspective goes further, to argue that even sustainability prices will not be an adequate policy response if such prices are not reliably measurable – because of irreducible long-term uncertainties, in particular – or if resources are at some scale not adequately fungible. There are then thresholds beyond which degradation of specific elements of natural capital inexorably lead to unacceptable intergenerational distributions.

5.   ILLUSTRATION OF SUSTAINABILITY ECONOMICS: CLIMATE CHANGE POLICY

Climate change policy well illustrates two key sustainability issues: intergenerational equity; and the technical capacity to use substitution and innovation to offset environmental degradation. The intergenerational equity issue arises because of the long-lived impacts of climate change as well as from the scale of potential investment and social change needed to arrest changes in the atmosphere.

Many scientists have emphasized that the accumulation of greenhouse gases (GHGs) in the atmosphere is ultimately likely to alter global climate both beyond levels, and at much faster rates, than any experienced for the past thousands of years. Scientific assessments also have emphasized the potentially large response of natural systems to such stresses. Major changes in patterns of rainfall, and dieback of forest areas and other natural habitats are just two examples (IPCC, 1996a, 1996b). At least implicitly, and often explicitly, these changes are seen as leading to large damages to critical natural resources.

Substitution and innovation are central in defining and measuring the cost of a changed climate. The conventional economic analysis of climate change impacts is well illustrated by the work of Nordhaus (1994) and Mendelsohn and Neumann (1999), though many other experts have ploughed the same ground. To model the cost of climate change simply in his simulation model, Nordhaus used a power function to link changes in GHG concentration to changes in average temperature, and changes in average temperature to changes in potential economic activity. The power function allows for the marginal cost of increased GHG concentration to increase, remain constant, or decline, depending on one's views about the relevant science. But in any case, the cost is treated as a smoothly differentiable function of a single climate indicator, which allows for neither the impact of increased climate variability, nor for the possibility of catastrophic climate change beyond some threshold (both discussed further below).

Putting numbers into the cost function relies on empirical evidence of the cost of a particular degree of temperature increase relative to baseline, and this evidence is very sketchy (see IPCC, 1996c, ch. 6). Nordhaus, and many other climate cost analysts, use figures that imply a fairly small GDP loss (under 3 per cent, and maybe under 1 per cent) for advanced industrialized countries if there is a doubling of atmospheric GHG concentration given the current economic structure. The reason given for the small impact is that relatively little added value in these countries is really vulnerable to climate change. There may be some local harm to agriculture and forestry, and some adverse health effects and impacts on coastal areas, but at current prices these do not constitute the bulk of value added in the economy.

Much of the judgement that the potential impact of climate change is limited is based on the possibility of *adaptation*, the focus of Mendelsohn and Neumann's volume, and adaptation in turn depends on the prospects for substitution and innovation. Potential costs of climate change can be curbed, the argument goes, by developing new plant varieties, strengthening health care, gradually moving coastal infrastructure inland, and the like. The contrast between this comforting marginalist view, and the view that the climate is a critical natural system whose perturbation could cause massive damage and even catastrophe, is stark.

Marginalist studies lead fairly robustly to a strong conclusion: to maximize the present value (PV) of intertemporal well-being, assuming a constant discount rate as always, short-term curbs on GHG emissions should be very limited; and global emissions should continue to rise until well into the twenty-first century, if not longer (Manne, 1996). The damage cost assumptions underlying this conclusion have been criticized as both understating expected costs, and downplaying the chance of extreme events (Roughgarden and Schneider, 1999). Climate cost modellers have explored the robustness of their analyses in several respects. One way to model rising climate risk is to assume that marginal cost rises more rapidly (Peck and Teisberg, 1993). Or one can posit the possibility of a catastrophe if climate change continues unabated (Manne, 1996; Gjerde et al., 1999). However, it turns out these factors are of little significance in assessing the *PV-optimal* GHG policy. The reason is that climate damages occur far in the future, so their expected value today is low, unless they are very severe or the discount rate is extraordinarily low.

The standard PV-optimality criterion, ubiquitous in the economics literature on climate change cost–benefit analysis, puts more weight on the near-term costs of reducing GHGs in relation to the long-term costs of a changing climate. It is arguably an appropriate criterion *if* the effects of climate change can be more than offset by other forms of economic progress, so that future generations can be better off than the present even with a changed climate (Schelling, 1995). Indeed, if damages grow linearly with increased GHG concentrations, but economic activity grows geometrically because of technical change, then even with climate change, the future will be better than the present in terms of overall utility.

However, even if the cost of significant climate change were to become unmanageable in the future, this would be of little consequence under PV-optimality. Howarth (1996, 1998) illustrates the distributional implications of PV-optimality, by using a contrasting, overlapping-generations approach to show that greater concern for long-term equity implies more aggressive GHG abatement than implied, for example, by Nordhaus's work. And in Howarth (2000), by dividing the utility of consumption into half from absolute consumption and half from *relative* consumption (that is, status), he shows the optimal GHG emissions control rises from 9–14 per cent to 37–47 per cent in Nordhaus's own model. So the pure psychology of status (which, along with other psychological realities noted in section 3.1(d), is rarely included in growth modelling) can have a significant effect on GHG control policy, by making continuing consumption growth socially less desirable.

Those concerned with limited substitution and adaptation capacities favour using a precautionary principle or safe minimum standard in setting and achieving a clear limit on GHG concentrations. One common approach is to establish long-term concentration goals deemed a priori to be adequately protective, and then to pursue these goals in the most intertemporally cost-effective fashion (Manne and Richels, 1997). This approach can reduce premature capital obsolescence and take advantage of technological progress, though the least-cost timing is also sensitive to the rate of discount. Taking into account both intertemporal distributional concerns and cost-effectiveness (not to mention political credibility) remains one of the major challenges in designing and assessing climate policy (see Shogren and Toman, 2000 for further discussion).

6. CONCLUSIONS

6.1 Progress in the Economics of Sustainability

What can we say about the accomplishments of economic research on sustainability over the past few years? Obviously there is no consensus yet about the importance of the topic. This is partly because theoretical work has vastly outstripped empirical work, and judgements about the importance of sustainability ultimately are empirical. That said, there have been a number of real advances of understanding in the field. These include:

1. A greatly improved understanding of the theoretical differences among income measures, and the relationships among income, utility and wealth. Also important has been an improved understanding, derived from unified, general results, of how to include changes in technology, interest rates and prices, trade in resources, goods and capital, and many different types of natural resource depletion and environmental pollution, into a consistent theory of income accounting and sustainability measurement. Work here by Asheim and Weitzman has been particularly notable.

2. A greatly improved understanding of theory of 'sustainability prices', sustainability policies, environmental policies, and the connections (and disconnections) among them. In particular, work by Asheim, Howarth, Pezzey and others has shown the logical incompatibility of Hartwick's rule for sustainable investment with policies and measures based on observed prices, since the latter are not generated by an underlying sustainability objective function. These authors have also added considerably to understanding the more basic question of when sustainable outcomes can be achieved; but in so doing, they have underscored how difficult it is robustly to define and measure sustainability prices or sustainable income.

3. Empirically, the efforts stimulated by Pearce and Atkinson (1993) have begun to flesh out sustainability measurement based on 'weak' assumptions of capital–resource substitutability. Despite their theoretical and practical shortcomings, these studies have undoubtedly stimulated collection and codification of data, without which progress will be impossible. There are now many more raw data, if of often unknown quality, available on estimated resource quantities and values for many countries (see for example *World Development Indicators*, World Bank, 2001). The studies have also pointed up some gross disparities between different countries' sustainability measures, disparities that are likely to remain, even after many of the known shortcomings in the empirical work are identified and corrected. It should even be possible in time crudely to test the implicit prediction that

the social wellbeing of an economy that was measured as severely unsustainable will eventually fall.

4. The debate between weak and strong sustainability proponents, while little more settled than a decade ago, has again drawn valuable attention to what physical limits to growth may exist because of limited substitutability, in concept or in practice. It has helped stimulate a new examination of the powers and limits of technical change as a means of relaxing these limits, as well as focus attention on how physical laws interact with economic principles.

6.2   Problems in the Economics of Sustainability

As our synthesis has shown, many important problems still remain, and we would highlight the following.

1. There are five major practical flaws in what we have described as the neo-classical ('weak') theory of sustainability measurement:

    (a) We don't actually know if people want to maximize PV (present value of future utility using a constant discount rate).

    (b) If they want PV-optimality, we know that they cannot achieve it while significant externalities (environmental and otherwise) remain.

    (c) Even if PV-optimality is achieved, it tells us nothing precise about sustainability, because of the chicken-and-egg problem that 'sustainability prices' are observed only once sustainability has already been achieved. The closest we can get is an inequality (our one-sided test of *un*sustainability in Proposition 4.5).

    (d) The philosophical tension ('schizophrenia') between assuming that people seek to maximize PV, and yet support government efforts to measure and achieve sustainability, remains inadequately explored.

    (e) On a more practical note, the construction of models of resource depletion and environmental pollution is sufficiently complex that detailed formulae for GNNP (such as our equation (4.39)) can vary quite widely from one study to another.

2. Expanding first on problem (d), there is a need to make the justification for sustainability policy intervention in a PV-optimal economy more coherent. What sustainability criteria is society's intervention trying to accomplish, and why? How do these criteria relate to individual preferences and values? There are different ways that this argument could be developed. One is to try to make something formal of the intergenerational public-good argument, or of the contrast between representative agent and overlapping generations views of economies. Another is to continue as at present: presume that

members of society do have some morally based concerns about the inter-generational distribution of well-being, and capture the implications of these concerns as constraints on PV-maximization in RA models of society, or as intergenerational objectives added to OLG models. But this does little to address or close the 'credibility gap' which we think exists between general policy declarations in favour of sustainability, and day-to-day economic management in response to short-run political pressures.

3. Problems (b) and (c) set an important double agenda for the mass of empirical work that needs to be done to test and guide further development of the theory, and that we hope this essay helps to motivate. We need current observations not just to put into formulae for green net national product, but at the same time to estimate the gap that theory shows to exist between GNNP based on current-market observations or environmental valuations, and sustainable income. How accurately can we frame sustainability policies (like a reinvestment rule) under market conditions that do not reveal sustainability prices? Thus, the extent to which weak sustainability approaches can be empirically substantiated and operationalized remains an open question.

4. In addition to estimating the inaccuracies in income calculations caused by significant environmental externalities, empirical work is also needed to measure the importance of other errors or shortcuts in applying neoclassical sustainability theory. These include the impacts of uncertain future world price changes and capital market adjustments, and the measurement of exogenous versus endogenous technical progress.

5. Theoretical models of sustainability and economic development would benefit from a number of extensions. Areas of particular interest that we have ignored in this paper are the question of sustainability in poor countries, a prime inspiration for popularizing the idea of sustainability, and the connections between sustainability and the development process. Much of this debate has recently been wrapped up in discussions of the meaning and reliability of environmental Kuznets curves (EKCs). At the conceptual level, there is a clear need to explain EKCs and their connections to existing institutions better. The aim would be to blend something of the relatively theory-rich but data-poor neoclassical approach with the theory-poor but data-rich tradition of EKC enquiries.

6. Another important ignored area is endogenous population change. This gives rise to theoretical questions about the emphasis on per capita versus total utility, and the intragenerational distribution of income. Opening up this issue leads in turn to important questions about how people's utility depends on their quality of life not just absolutely, but also relative to their peers and to their past experiences. It highlights the possibility that growing inequality can undercut both individual and social utility, an issue of much

concern in a globalizing world. It would also be useful to include preferences for environmental quality, and a subsistence requirement, more systematically into utility functions. Finally, the whole question of uncertainty, which pervades real-life sustainability decisions, needs to be included more often in theoretical work.

7. Just as our centuries-long timescale requires realistic psychology to be built into the utility function, it also needs realistic physics, biology and engineering to be built into the production function. The whole question of what biophysical limits to growth might exist needs a great deal more work, and one approach would be to use forms of production functions that have built-in (but not immediate) limits to substitution. This may mean much more reliance on numerical methods, and less stress on mathematically elegant but empirically questionable paths of balanced growth. Efforts to this end would also reinvigorate empirical work in the strong sustainability tradition, by more clearly identifying where resource availability and substitutability constraints stretch thin the neoclassical paradigm, rather than by just making blanket applications of the precautionary principle to justify setting standards on purely scientific grounds.

In all these areas, only a suitable balance of theory and data, and a reduced role for ideological preconvictions, will move us towards what we take to be a common goal: a better economic science of sustainability.

APPENDIX

Proof of Proposition 4.1

Result (4.20) is a minor generalization of Proposition 3 in AW. Unlike them, we assume a general discount factor $\phi(t)$ rather than $e^{-\rho t}$, and we include exogenous changes in the production possibility set, so that time t is treated as a productive stock, with its own co-state variable Ψ^t. AW's proof then still carries through, as long as the capital stock and associated price vectors are suitably augmented. That is, $\mathbf{K}$ is replaced by $\mathbf{K}^\dagger := (\mathbf{K},t)$; Ψ by $\Psi^\dagger := (\Psi,\Psi^t)$; and $\mathbf{Q}$ by $\mathbf{Q}^\dagger := (\mathbf{Q},Q^t)$.

Proof of Proposition 4.2

$Y^\dagger(\mathbf{K}^\dagger,\mathbf{Q}^\dagger)$ is defined as max $\mathbf{P.C} + \mathbf{Q}^\dagger.\dot{\mathbf{K}}^\dagger$ for $(\mathbf{C},\dot{\mathbf{K}}^\dagger) \in \Pi(\mathbf{K}^\dagger)$. Hence from Proposition 4.1,

$$\begin{aligned} r\mathbf{Q}^\dagger.\dot{\mathbf{K}}^\dagger &= (d/dt)[Y^\dagger(\mathbf{K}^\dagger,\mathbf{Q}^\dagger)] \\ &= (\partial Y^\dagger \partial/\mathbf{K}^\dagger).\dot{\mathbf{K}}^\dagger + (\partial Y^\dagger/\partial \mathbf{Q}^\dagger).\dot{\mathbf{Q}}^\dagger \\ &= (\partial Y^\dagger/\partial \mathbf{K}^\dagger).\dot{\mathbf{K}}^\dagger + \dot{\mathbf{Q}}^\dagger.\dot{\mathbf{K}}^\dagger, \end{aligned}$$

and since this is true for any general $\dot{\mathbf{K}}^\dagger$, for all components with $\dot{K}^\dagger_i \neq 0$,

$$rQ^\dagger_i - \dot{Q}^\dagger_i = \partial Y^\dagger/\partial K^\dagger_i. \tag{4A.1}$$

Since $\dot{t} = 1$, $\dot{K}^\dagger_i \neq 0$ for the time component of (4A.1), which is

$$rQ^t - \dot{Q}^t = \partial Y^\dagger/\partial t = \partial Y/\partial t = Y_t \tag{4A.2}$$

because $Q^t = Y^\dagger - Y$ has no exogenous time dependence. Equality (4A.2) can be integrated from time t to ∞ to give

$$Q^t(\mathrm{t}) = \int_t^\infty [\partial Y(s)/\partial s]\exp[-\int_t^s r(z)dz]ds \quad \text{which is (4.21)}.$$

Proof of Proposition 4.3(a)

This follows directly by integrating $\dot{Y}^\dagger(s) = r(s)[Y^\dagger(s) - \mathbf{P}(s).\mathbf{C}(s)]$ from (4.20) from time t to ∞, and assuming that the integral converges.

Proof of Proposition 4.5

Thanks to $-\dot{\phi}/\phi = \rho$, constant, we can use augmented versions of propositions 2 and 3 from AW:

$$\dot{W}^\rho(t) = \Psi^\dagger.\dot{\mathbf{K}}^\dagger = \lambda\pi\mathbf{Q}^\dagger.\dot{\mathbf{K}}^\dagger = \lambda\pi\dot{Y}^\dagger/r \tag{4A.3}$$

so that the change of welfare has the same sign as the utility value of net invest-ments. Then, the current-value Hamiltonian of our welfare-maximization problem (4.9) is

$$H = U + \Psi^\dagger.\dot{\mathbf{K}}^\dagger. \qquad (4A.4)^{37}$$

Combining (4A.4) with an augmented version of AW's equation (5),

$$\dot{H} = \rho\Psi^\dagger.\dot{\mathbf{K}}^\dagger \qquad (4A.5)$$

and (4A.3) then gives

$$\dot{W}^\rho = \dot{H}/\rho = H - U. \qquad (4A.6)$$

Hence from (4A.3) and (4A.6), at any time t,

$$\dot{Y}^\dagger \le 0 \text{ or } \mathbf{Q}^\dagger.\dot{\mathbf{K}}^\dagger \le 0 \Rightarrow \dot{W}^\rho \le 0 \Rightarrow H \le U. \qquad (4A.7)$$

Now, integrating (4A.6) from time t to ∞ gives

$$H(t) = \rho\int_t^\infty U(\mathbf{C}(s))e^{-\rho(s-t)}ds = \int_t^\infty U(\mathbf{C}(s))e^{-\rho(s-t)}ds / \int_t^\infty e^{-\rho(s-t)}ds. \qquad (4A.8)$$

so the non-constancy and uniqueness of the optimal path means that

$$H(t) > U_m(t). \qquad (4A.9)$$

Otherwise, following the feasible constant utility path $U(s) = U_m(t)$ for all $s \ge t$ would, using the PV-equivalence result (4A.8), give at least the same PV as the optimal utility path, a contradiction of a unique optimum. Combining (4A.7) and (4A.9) gives the result that current $U(t)$ is unsustainable:

$$U(t) \ge H(t) > U_m(t) \qquad \text{as in (4.29).}$$

Proof of Proposition 4.6

Using (4A.5) and (4A.6),

$$\{\mathbf{Q}.\dot{\mathbf{K}} + Q^t = \mathbf{Q}^\dagger.\dot{\mathbf{K}}^\dagger = 0 \text{ forever}\}$$
$$\Rightarrow \{\rho\lambda\pi\mathbf{Q}^\dagger.\dot{\mathbf{K}}^\dagger = \rho\Psi^\dagger.\dot{\mathbf{K}}^\dagger = \dot{H} = \rho(H - U) = 0 \text{ forever}\}$$
$$\Rightarrow \{\dot{U} = \dot{H} = 0 \text{ forever}\}, \quad \text{as required.}$$

Proof of Proposition 4.7

The current-value Hamiltonian of the dynamic optimization problem of maximizing wealth (and hence welfare W) is

$$Y^\dagger(t) := Y(t) + Q^t = P^C C + P^B B + \mathbf{Q}^\dagger . \dot{\mathbf{K}}^\dagger \tag{4A.10}$$

where

$\mathbf{K}^\dagger := (K, K_a, K_f, \Omega, S, t)$ is the vector of all state variables; $\quad$ (4A.11)
$\mathbf{Q}^\dagger := (Q^K, Q^a, Q^f, Q^\Omega, Q^S, Q^t)$ is the vector of corresponding co-state
$\quad$ variables (shadow consumption prices of stocks) $\quad$ (4A.12)

The prices and investment flows defined by (4.30)–(4.38) then make

$$Y^\dagger(t) = P^C C + P^B B + Q^K \dot{K} + Q^a \dot{K}_a + Q^f \dot{K}_f + Q^\Omega \dot{\Omega} + Q^S . \dot{S} + Q^t \tag{4A.13}$$

$$= P^C C + P^B \{B_0 - \varepsilon^B E^B [F(K, \mathbf{R} - \mathbf{R}_x, t), a, K_a, t] - \varepsilon^\Omega (\Omega_1 - \Omega)\}$$
$$+ Q^K [F(K, \mathbf{R} - \mathbf{R}_x, t) + M - C - \delta K - a - I_a - V(D, S, t) - X(\mathbf{R}, S, t)]$$
$$+ Q^a [I_a - \delta K_a] + Q^f [r(t) K_f + \mathbf{Q}^x(t).\mathbf{R}_x - M]$$
$$+ Q^\Omega [\gamma(\Omega) - E^\Omega (\mathbf{R} - \mathbf{R}_x)] + Q^S . [D + G(S) - R] + Q^t \tag{4A.14}$$

so the first-order conditions with respect to the control variables are

$$\partial Y^\dagger / \partial C = P^C - Q^K = 0 \qquad \Rightarrow Q^K = P^C \tag{4A.15}$$
$$\partial Y^\dagger / \partial a = P^B B_a - Q^K = 0 \qquad \Rightarrow P^B / P^C = 1/B_a = b \tag{4A.16}$$
$$\partial Y^\dagger / \partial I_a = -Q^K + Q^a = 0 \qquad \Rightarrow Q^a = Q^K = P^C \tag{4A.17}$$
$$\partial Y^\dagger / \partial D = -Q^K V_D + Q^S = 0 \quad \Rightarrow Q^S / Q^K = V_D \tag{4A.18}$$

$$\partial Y^\dagger / \partial \mathbf{R} = P^B B_R + Q^K (F_R - X_R) - Q^\Omega E^\Omega_R - Q^S = 0$$
$$\Rightarrow Q^\Omega E^\Omega_R / Q^K = (P^B / P^C) B_R + F_R - X_R - Q^S / Q^K$$
$$\Rightarrow Q^\Omega / Q^K = (bB_R + F_R - X_R - V_D)_i / (E^\Omega_R)_i \tag{4A.19}$$

$$\partial Y^\dagger / \partial M = Q^K - Q^f = 0 \quad \Rightarrow Q^f = Q^K = P^C \tag{4A.20}$$
$$\partial Y^\dagger / \partial \mathbf{R}_x = -P^B B_R - Q^K F_R + Q^f \mathbf{Q}^x + Q^\Omega E^\Omega_R = 0; \text{ then use (4A.16), (4A.20),}$$
(4A.18):

$$\Rightarrow P^B B_R + Q^K F_R - Q^\Omega E^\Omega_R = P^C \mathbf{Q}^x = Q^K X_R + Q^S \tag{4A.21}$$
$$\Rightarrow bB_R + F_R - (Q^\Omega / Q^K) E^\Omega_R = \mathbf{Q}^x = X_R + V_D \tag{4A.22}$$

For Q^t, first use (4A.10) and (4A.14) to get

$$\partial Y / \partial t = P^B B_t + Q^K (F_t - V_t - X_t) + Q^f (\dot{r} K_f + \dot{\mathbf{Q}}^x . \mathbf{R}_x)$$

which, after using (4A.15), (4A.16) and (4A.20) becomes

$$Y_t = P^C(bB_t + F_t - V_t - X_t + \dot{r}K_f + \dot{Q}^x.R_x)$$

hence from (4.21),

$$Q^t(t) := \int_t^\infty P_C(s) \{bB_t + F_t - V_t - X_t + \dot{r}K_f + \dot{Q}^x.R_x\}(s) \exp[-\int_t^s r(z)dz]ds,$$

which is (4.40).

Inserting (A4.15)–(A4.22) into a cross between (A4.13) and (A4.14) then gives

$$Y^\dagger = P^C C + P^C bB + Q_K\{\dot{K} + \dot{K}_a + \dot{K}_f\} + Q^\Omega[\gamma(\Omega) - E^\Omega(R - R_x)]$$
$$+ Q^S.[D + G(S) - R] + Q^t$$

which using (4.21), (4.A18) and (4.A22) gives

$$= P^C \{C + bB + \dot{K} + \dot{K}_a + \dot{K}_f + (bB_R + F_R - Q^x)_i(\gamma - E^\Omega)/(E_R^\Omega)$$
$$+ (Q^x - X_R).[D + G(S) - R] \} + Q^t \qquad \text{which is (4.39).}$$

If the problem is autonomous, time is 'unproductive', so its value Q^t, the last term of (4.39), disappears.

Notation and Abbreviations

(Bold type denotes vectors; a subscript may be either a partial derivative or just a label; := means 'is defined as'; * means 'this definition is used only in the example economy of section 3.3.5'.)

$a(t)$	= direct expenditure on abating emissions*
a	denotes 'abatement'
AW	= Asheim and Weitzman (2001)
$b(t)$	:= $1/(\partial B/\partial a) = 1/B_a$ = marginal abatement cost*
$B(F,a,K_a,t,\Omega)$	= environmental quality*
B_0	= pristine level of environmental quality*
$C(t)$	= 'consumption' flow vector (including all environmental amenities)
$C(t)$	= consumption flow when scalar
$C_m(t)$	= maximum sustainable consumption from t onwards, when C is sole component of C
$D(t)$	= rates of discovery of resources*
$E^B(F,a,K_a,t)$	= emissions of (instantly dispersed) flow pollutant*

$E^{\Omega}(\mathbf{R} - \mathbf{R}_x)$	= emissions of cumulative pollutant*
EROI	= energy return on investment
^{f}	denotes 'foreign'*
$F(K,\mathbf{R} - \mathbf{R}_x,t)$	= domestic production of consumption/investment good*
$G(S)$	= amounts of natural growth per unit time of resources*
GNNP	= green net national product
GPV	= generalized present value (using general discount factor $\phi(t)$)
GS	= genuine savings := net investment $\mathbf{Q}.\dot{\mathbf{K}}$ here
$I(t)$	= investment flow in production capital*
$I_a(t)$	= investment flow in abatement capital*
$K(t)$	= stock of production capital, of which K_0 = initial stock
$K_a(t)$	= stock of abatement capital, of which K_{a0} = initial stock*
$K_f(t)$	= stock of foreign capital, of which K_{f0} = initial stock*
$\mathbf{K}(t)$	= stocks of capital and resources = (K,K_a,K_f,Ω,S)*
$\mathbf{K}^{\dagger}(t)$	:= $(\mathbf{K},t)$ = augmented stocks, (that is, including time)
$M(t)$	= net imports of consumption/investment good*
^{m}	denotes 'maximum sustainable level'
NPP	= net primary [photosynthetic] production
OLG	= overlapping generations
$P(t)$	= real prices of consumption vector = $(P^C(t),P^B(t))$*
$P^B(t)$	= real price of environmental quality*
$P^C(t)$	= real price of consumption*
PV	= present value (using a constant discount rate ρ)
$\mathbf{P}.\mathbf{C}$	= real consumption expenditures
$\mathbf{Q}(t)$	:= $\Psi(t)/\lambda(t)\pi(t)$ = shadow real consumption prices of stocks = $(Q^K,Q^a,Q^f,Q^{\Omega},Q^S)$*
$\mathbf{Q}(t).\dot{\mathbf{K}}(t)$	= net investment in consumption units
$Q^t(t)$	:= $\Psi^t/\lambda(t)\pi(t)$ = value of time (shadow real consumption price of time as stock)
$\mathbf{Q}^{\dagger}(t)$	:= $(\mathbf{Q},Q^t)$ = shadow real consumption prices of augmented stocks
$\mathbf{Q}^{\dagger}(t).\dot{\mathbf{K}}^{\dagger}(t)$	= augmented net investment in consumption units
$Q^x(t)$	= world prices of resource exports*
$r(t)$	:= $\dot{\phi}(t)/\Phi(t)$ = current real interest rate
$\mathbf{R}(t)$	= extraction rates of resources*
$\mathbf{R}_x(t)$	= net exports of resources (so $\mathbf{R} - \mathbf{R}_x$ = domestic resource use)*
RA	= representative agent
s	= variable of integration
$S(t)$	= stocks of resources = $D + G(S) - \mathbf{R}$ *
t	= time; also seen as a productive stock, with $\dot{t} = 1$
TPK	= Toman, Pezzey and Krautkraemer (1995)
$U(\mathbf{C}(t))$	= utility of representative agent = $U(C(t),B(t))$*

$U_m(t)$ = maximum sustainable utility level from t onwards

$V(\mathbf{D},\mathbf{S},t)$ = total cost of discovering resources*

$W(t)$ = $[1/\phi(t)] \int_t^\infty U(s)\phi(s)ds$ (GPV of utility using utility discount factor)

$W_i(t)$ = generational welfare (GPV of utility of one generation i over its lifetime, for use in OLG context)

$_x$or ^{x} denotes 'exports'*

$X(\mathbf{R},\mathbf{S},t)$ = total cost of extracting resources*

$Y(t)$ = green net national product (GNNP), $\mathbf{P.C} + \mathbf{Q.\dot{K}}$

$Y^\dagger(t)$ = augmented GNNP, $\mathbf{P.C} + \mathbf{Q.\dot{K}}^\dagger = Y + Q^t$

$Y_e(t)$ = wealth-equivalent income

α = power of capital K in Cobb–Douglas production function

β = power of resource flow R in Cobb–Douglas production function

$\gamma(\Omega)$ = amount of pollution assimilated per unit time*

$\Gamma(t)$ = time-averaged growth rate of GNNP

δ = rate of depreciation of productive or abatement capital*

ε^B = loss of environmental quality per unit of flow pollution*

ε^Ω = loss of environmental quality per unit of cumulative pollution*

$\Theta(t)$ = wealth (GPV of real 'consumption' expenditures using consumption discount factor)

$\lambda(t)$ = marginal utility of nominal money (dollars)

υ = rate of exogenous technical progress, $(\delta F/\delta^t)/F$

$\pi(t)$ = Divisia price index

$\Pi\{\mathbf{K}(t),t\}$ = production possibility set

ρ = utility discount rate, when constant

$\tau_S(t)$ = tax rate on resource stock

$\tau_C(t)$ = tax rate on consumption

$\phi(t)$ = general utility discount factor (so $\dot{\phi}/\phi$ = utility discount rate)

$\Phi(t)$ = $\phi(t)\lambda(t)\pi(t)$= general consumption discount factor (so $\dot{\Phi}/\Phi$ = consumption discount rate)

$\chi(t)$ = time-averaged growth of GNNP due to time alone

$\Psi(t)$ = shadow utility prices of stocks

$\Psi^t(t)$ = shadow utility price of time as productive input

$\Psi^\dagger(t)$:= $(\Psi(t),\Psi_t(t))$ = shadow utility prices of all productive stocks

$\Omega(t)$ = absorption capacity of the environment*

Ω_0 = initial absorption capacity*

Ω_1 = pristine (pre-industrial) absorption capacity*

$\dagger$ denotes 'augmented': that is, including a term that relates to time viewed as a productive stock denotes time derivative, d/dt

$\cdot$ denotes time derivative, $\dot{\chi} = \delta\chi/\delta t$

NOTES

* We thank Tom Tietenberg and Henk Folmer for their encouragement, guidance and great patience. We are especially grateful to Geir Asheim for detailed technical advice on section 3.3, and we also thank Giles Atkinson, Bob Ayres, Steve Dovers, Rich Howarth, Martin O'Connor, John Proops, Cees Withagen and two anonymous referees for generous and helpful comments. None of them bears any responsibility for the final product.

1. We have given a review of sorts, though necessarily uneven and including literature before 1987, in Pezzey and Toman (forthcoming), an introduction to 23 reprinted journal articles on sustainability.

2. Our earlier synthesis (Toman, Pezzey and Krautkraemer, 1995, hereafter TPK) also reflected this.

3. We almost always use the *instantaneous* meaning of utility $U(t)$ at time t, and the *intertemporal* meaning of welfare $W(t)$, being the integral of discounted utility from time t onwards. (Our notation is set out in full later.) However, many writers use 'welfare' to mean instantaneous utility, U.

4. Open critics of sustainability, like Beckerman (1994), are mainly opposed to concepts of strong sustainability, as defined below.

5. O'Connor (1997) discusses a view attributed to John Stuart Mill that a lasting 'decent' society, in which individual freedom and competition thrive, requires a broader social agreement on reciprocity and humanitarianism. Broadly similar ideas are expressed in Norgaard (1988) and Arrow (1999), and can be traced back at least to Marglin (1963).

6. We use established terminology here; but 'weak' and 'strong' views are really views about the facts of *substitutability*, not about the goals of sustainability

7. Unlimited and perfect substitutability are not the same. Using notation developed later, in the Cobb–Douglas production function $F = K^{\alpha}R^{\beta}$ the capital stock K is an *unlimited* substitute for resource flow R, because however small a positive R is, there is always some K which will produce a given F. By contrast, in the linear production function $F = \alpha K + \beta R$, a unit of K is a *perfect* substitute for α/β units of R.

8. For a recent survey of these considerations see O'Connor (1998).

9. In keeping with our intergenerational motivation, one could instead think of an infinite sequence of representative agents, each alive for just an instant of time, though this is hardly any more realistic than the notion of an infinitely lived single agent.

10. s is used throughout as a variable time, for example within integrals.

11. Some go further, and call PV-optimal paths loosely sustainable, particularly if they have asymptotic paths which preserve a positive level of resource stocks (Heal, 1998). However, it seems inconsistent with current policy interests in the subject to call 'sustainable' a future where utility could decline forever, even if it stays above some minimum.

12. Also known as 'non-constant discounting', since the general utility discount rate $-\dot{\phi}(t)/\phi(t)$ need not be constant over time.

13. Working in a discrete-time framework, Chichilnisky proposed two extra axioms that any intertemporal welfare function $W(\cdot)$ of a utility stream $\{U_t\}$ should satisfy in order for maximizing $W(\cdot)$ to provide an acceptable criterion for optimally sustainable development. The axioms are that $W(\cdot)$ should also satisfy both 'no dictatorship of the present' and 'no dictatorship of the future'. Such a $W(\cdot)$ yields a very different intergenerational distribution than maximizing PV does. It remains to be seen if this rigorous development of sustainability theory will be any more operational or politically acceptable than more frequently suggested options in current debates.

14. Moreover, even if the 'right' (that is, sustainability) prices could be calculated, combining them with current or optimal quantities would not say anything exact about sustainability, despite suggestions in Solow (1993) and Hartwick (1997) that this is so.

15. The apparent paradox is not as direct in an OLG context. Society may have a view on distributing resources across generations to achieve an intergenerational sustainability objective, but this need not imply a constraint on any generation's maximization of its own GPV.

16. We would not go as far as Marglin in saying that 'The Economic Man and the Citizen are for all intents and purposes two different individuals,' since Economic Man can still maximize self-interest (seek optimality) within the bounds (sustainability) that the Citizen lays down. However, recent protests over fossil fuel prices in many Western countries, despite those countries having recently signed the Kyoto Protocol which aims to limit greenhouse gas emissions, may perhaps be seen as a sign that the schizophrenia is real and can lead to quite disconnected behaviour.

17. The device of treating time as a stock is mentioned by Aronsson et al. (1997, p. 54) and used by Pemberton and Ulph (2001).

18. Formally, Ψ is the vector of current-value co-state variables of the dynamic optimization problem of maximizing (4.3) subject to the constraints (4.5).

19. If utility depends on just one consumption good, sustainable income is the maximum sustainable consumption level, $C_m(t)$, defined above in (4.7).

20. Recall that $\mathbf{K}^{\dagger} := (\mathbf{K}, t)$, so that $\dot{\mathbf{K}}^{\dagger} = (\dot{\mathbf{K}}, 1)$.

21. For wealth-equivalent income Y_e to be well defined, the utility function $U(\mathbf{C})$ has to be homothetic. Otherwise, the Divisia index $\pi(t)$ is path-dependent, and cannot be used to compare expenditure $\mathbf{P.C}$ on different development paths. This is not a problem when we assume a constant interest rate, since we then effectively assume a constant utility discount rate ρ, and a linear homogeneous utility function $U(.)$ which is a stronger restriction than homotheticity. We thank Geir Asheim for these insights.

22. A different illustration of this phenomenon is that along Solow's (1974) constant consumption path for a capital-resource economy, wealth is not constant but *rising*. It is the product of wealth and a *falling* interest rate that gives constant consumption.

23. The converse of this result has been proved by Withagen and Asheim (1998).

24. Seminal models here are Hartwick (1990) and Mäler (1991). Other notable models are Hamilton (1994, 1996) and Vincent et al. (1997).

25. There is no distinction here between private or government ownership of foreign capital (or debt). For a large open economy, the interest rate r would depend also on the level of capital K_f, and the resource price Q^x would depend also on net exports R_x.

26. We model absorptive capacity rather than cumulative pollution so all stocks in the model are goods, and so can satisfy the 'free disposal' assumption of Asheim (1997). We ignore the complication that total emissions of the most important pollutants, greenhouse gases in the global atmosphere, can in reality be controlled only by the global economy, not by our example, open, economy.

27. Note the distinction between sustainable development (defined in section 3.1.1) and sustainable growth, which many writers (for example Aghion and Howitt, 1998, p. 166) equate with just consumption growth, even when utility depends on both consumption and environmental quality.

28. Hamilton et al. (1998) reckoned that endogenous growth accounts for most of the technical progress premium reported in Proposition 4.4, which greatly reduces the economy's sustainability measure.

29. The need for such a calculation is underscored by the fact that resource prices have typically been flat or falling, not rising as in most theoretical models.

30. As far as we know, no one has tried to cross-check measures of $[\dot{Y}]$ and $r\mathbf{Q}.[\dot{\mathbf{K}}]$.

31. It is interesting to note the outcomes of neo-Austrian and neoclassical growth models have similar properties (Faber et al. 1999, ch. 6).

32. See also our earlier discussion in TPK. Other useful syntheses include Stern (1997), Beard and Lozada (1999) and Neumayer (1999).

33. The most extreme adherents to the thermodynamic perspective take this line of argument much further than is credible in our view. Georgescu-Roegen (1971) was one of its strongest advocates, holding that a principle he called the 'fourth law of thermodynamics' implied the inescapable loss of production opportunity through material dissipation, just as entropy unavoidably degrades available energy. This principle has been refuted (see Beard and Lozada, 1999), but the prospect of thermodynamic limits is still frequently invoked by advocates of strong sustainability.

34. Moreover, much of the world's resource base may be found in low-concentration forms (Skinner, 1976). This implies the possibility of rapidly rising real costs as higher-quality resources are depleted, though technical advance in resource identification and recovery (Simpson, 1999) and development of new materials can mitigate this.
35. One indicator we have not analysed is materials intensity per unit of service, or MIPS (see for example Hinterberger et al., 1997), but similar remarks would apply.
36. An example of an influence that would increase yield with little additional energy cost or effort is the refinement of computer-assisted seismic mapping techniques that can help pinpoint smaller resource deposits and avoid dry holes (Bohi, 1999).
37. The relevant transversality condition is then $\lim_{t\to\infty}[e^{-\rho t}H(t)] = 0$.

REFERENCES

Aghion, Philippe and Peter Howitt (1998), *Endogenous Growth Theory*, Cambridge, MA: MIT Press.

Aronsson, Thomas and Karl-Gustaf Lofgren (1998), 'Green accounting: what do we know and what do we need to know?', in T. Tietenberg and H. Folmer (eds), *The International Yearbook of Environmental and Resource Economics 1998/99*. Cheltenham, UK and Northampton, USA: Edward Elgar.

Aronsson, Thomas, Per-Olov Johansson and Karl-Gustaf Lofgren (1997), *Welfare Measurement, Sustainability and Green National Accounting: A Growth Theoretical Approach*, Cheltenham, UK and Lyme, USA: Edward Elgar.

Arrow, Kenneth J. (1999), 'Discounting, morality and gaming', in P.R. Portney and J.P. Weyant (eds), *Discounting and Intergenerational Equity*, Washington, D.C.: Resources for the Future.

Asheim, Geir B. (1994), 'Net National Product as an Indicator of Sustainability', *Scandinavian Journal of Economics*, **96**(2), 257–65.

Asheim, Geir B. (1996), 'Capital gains and net national product in open economies', *Journal of Public Economics*, **59**, 419–34.

Asheim, Geir B. (1997), 'Adjusting green NNP to measure sustainability', *Scandinavian Journal of Economics*, **99** (3), 355–70.

Asheim, Geir B. (2000), 'Green National Accounting: Why and How?', *Environment and Development Economics*, **5**, 25–48.

Asheim, Geir B. and Martin L. Weitzman (2001), 'Does NNP growth indicate welfare improvement?', *Economics Letters*, **73**, 233–9.

Asheim, Geir B., Wolfgang Buchholz and Bertil Tungodden (2001), 'Justifying sustainability', *Journal of Environmental Economics and Management*, **41** (3), 252–68.

Atkinson, Giles et al. (1997), *Measuring Sustainable Development: Macroeconomics and the Environment*, Cheltenham, UK and Lyme, USA: Edward Elgar.

Ausubel, Jesse (1996), 'Can technology spare the earth?', *American Scientist*, **84**, 166–78.

Ayres, Robert U. (1995), 'Life Cycle Analysis: A Critique', *Resources, Conservation and Recycling*, **14**, 199–223.

Ayres, Robert (1996), 'Limits to the growth paradigm', *Ecological Economics*, **19**, 117–34.

Ayres, Robert (1998), 'Eco-thermodynamics: Economics and the second law', *Ecological Economics*, **26**, 189–210.

Ayres, Robert (1999), 'The second law, the fourth law, recycling, and limits to growth', *Ecological Economics*, **29**, 473–84.

Ayres, Robert U. (2000), 'Commentary on the Utility of the Ecological Footprint Concept', *Ecological Economics*, **32**(3), 347–50.

Ayres, Robert U. and Allen V. Kneese (1969), 'Production, Consumption, and Externalities', *American Economic Review*, **69**, 282–97.

Barbier, Edward B. (1987), 'The Concept of Sustainable Economic Development', *Environmental Conservation*, **14**(2),101–10.

Barbier, Edward B. (1997), 'Introduction to the Environmental Kuznets Curve special issue', *Environment and Development Economics*, **2**(4), 369–81.

Barro, Robert J. and Xavier Sala-i-Martin (1995), *Economic Growth*, New York: McGraw-Hill.

Beard, T. Randolph and Gabriel Lozada (1999), *Economics, Entropy, and the Environment: The Extraordinary Economics of Nicholas Georgescu-Roegen*, Cheltenham, UK and Northampton, USA: Edward Elgar.

Beckerman, Wilfred (1994), 'Sustainable development': Is It a Useful Concept?', *Environmental Values*, **3**(3), 191–209.

Bohi, Douglas (1999), 'Technological improvement in petroleum exploration and development', in R. David Simpson (ed.), *Productivity in Natural Resource Industries: Improvement Through Innovation*, Washington, DC: Resources for the Future.

Bovenberg, A. Lans and Sjak Smulders (1995), 'Environmental quality and pollution-augmenting technological change in a two-sector endogenous growth model', *Journal of Public Economics*, **57**, 369–91.

Bovenberg, A. Lans and Ben J. Heijdra (1998), 'Environmental tax policy and intergenerational distribution', *Journal of Public Economics*, **67**, 1–24.

Broome, John (1992), *Counting the Cost of Global Warming*, Cambridge: White Horse Press.

Cairns, Robert D. (2000), 'Sustainability accounting and green accounting', *Environment and Development Economics*, **5**(1–2), 49–54.

Chichilnisky, Graciela (1996), 'An axiomatic approach to sustainable development', *Social Choice and Welfare*, **13**, 231–57.

Cleveland, Cutler and Robert Kaufmann (1991), 'Forecasting ultimate oil recovery and its rate of production: incorporating economic forces into the models of M King Hubbert', *Energy Journal*, **13**, 199–211.

Cleveland, Cutler and Robert Kaufmann, (1997), 'Natural gas in the US: How far can technology stretch the resource base?', *Energy Journal*, **18**, 89–108.

Cleveland, Cutler and Matthias Ruth (1997), 'When, where, and how much do biophysical limits constrain the economic process? A survey of Georgescu-Roegen's contribution to ecological economics', *Ecological Economics*, **22**, 203–24.

Cleveland, Cutler et al. (1984), 'Energy and the US economy: A biophysical perspective', *Science*, **225**, 890–97.

Common, Mick and Charles Perrings (1992), 'Towards an ecological economics of sustainability', *Ecological Economics*, **6**, 7–34.

Costanza, Robert et al. (1997), 'The value of the world's ecosystem services and natural capital', *Nature*, **387**, 253–60.

Daly, Herman E. (1990), 'Toward Some Operational Principles of Sustainable Development', *Ecological Economics*, **2**(1), 1–6.

Daly, Herman (1994), 'Operationalizing sustainable development by investing in natural capital', in A. Jansson, M. Hammer, C. Folke and R. Costanza (eds), *Investing in Natural Capital: The Ecological Economics Approach to Sustainability*, Washington, DC: Island Press.

Daly, Herman E. and John B. Cobb (1989), *For the Common Good: Redirecting the Economy Toward Community, the Environment and a Sustainable Future*, Boston, MA: Beacon.

Dasgupta, Partha S. and Geoffrey M. Heal (1974), 'The Optimal Depletion of Exhaustible Resources', *Review of Economic Studies, Symposium on the Economics of Exhaustible Resources*, pp. 3–28.

Ekins, Paul (1996), 'Towards an economics for environmental sustainability', in R. Costanza et al., *Getting Down to Earth: Practical Applications of Ecological Economics*, Washington, DC: Island Press.

Ekins, Paul and Sandrine Simon (1999), 'The Sustainability Gap: A Practical Indicator of Sustainability in the Framework of the National Income Accounts', *International Journal of Sustainable Development*, 2(1), 24–58.

Ekins, Paul and Sandrine Simon (2001), 'Estimating Sustainability Gaps: Methods and Preliminary Applications for the UK and Netherlands', *Ecological Economics*, 37(1), 5–22.

Faber, Malte, John Proops, Stefan Speck with Frank Jost (1999), *Capital and Time in Ecological Economics: Neo-Austrian Modeling*, Cheltenham, UK and Northampton, USA: Edward Elgar.

Farmer, Michael C. and Alan Randall (1998), 'The Rationality of a Safe Minimum Standard', *Land Economics*, 74(3), 287–302.

Faucheux, Sylvie and Martin O'Connor (1998), 'Energy Measures and their Uses', in Sylvie Faucheux and Martin O'Connor (eds), *Valuation for Sustainable Development*, Cheltenham, UK and Northampton, USA: Edward Elgar.

Faucheux, Sylvie, Martin O'Connor and Sybille van den Hove (1998), 'Toward a Sustinable National Income?', in Sylvie Faucheux and Martin O'Connor (eds), *Valuation for Sustainable Development*, Cheltenham, UK and Northampton, USA: Edward Elgar.

Froger, Geraldine and Guiseppe Munda (1998), 'Methodology for Environmental Decision Support', in Sylvie Faucheux and Martin O'Connor (eds), *Valuation for Sustainable Development*, Cheltenham, UK and Northampton, USA: Edward Elgar.

Georgescu-Roegen, Nicholas (1971), *The Entropy Law and the Economic Process*, Cambridge, MA: Harvard University Press.

Gerlagh, Reyer and Michiel A. Keyzer (2001), 'Sustainability and the intergenerational distribution of natural resource entitlements', *Journal of Public Economics*, 79, 315–41.

Gjerde, Jon, Sverre Greppud and Snorre Kverndokk (1999), Optimal Climate Policy under the Possibility of a Catastrophe', *Resource and Energy Economics*, 21(3–4), 289–317.

Hamilton, Clive and Richard Denniss (2000), 'Tracking well-being in Australia: the Genuine Progress Indicator 2000', *Australia Institute Discussion Papers*, No. 35, Australia Institute, Canberra.

Hamilton, Kirk (1994), 'Green adjustments to GDP', *Resources Policy*, 20(3), 155–68.

Hamilton, Kirk (1996), 'Pollution and pollution abatement in the national accounts', *Review of Income and Wealth*, 42(1), 13–33.

Hamilton, Kirk, Giles Atkinson and David Pearce (1998), 'Savings rules and sustainability: selected extensions', 1st World Congress of Environmental and Resource Economists, Venice, Italy, June.

Hanley, Nick et al. (1999), Measuring Sustainability: A Time Series of Alternative Indicators for Scotland', *Ecological Economics*, 28, 55–74.

Hartwick, John M. (1977), 'Intergenerational Equity and the Investing of Rents from Exhaustible Resources', *American Economic Review*, **67**(5), 972–74.

Hartwick, John M. (1990), 'Natural Resources, National Accounting and Economic Depreciation', *Journal of Public Economics*, **43**, 291–304.

Hartwick, John M. (1997), 'Paying down the environmental debt', *Land Economics*, **73**(4), 508–15.

Heal, Geoffrey (1998), *Valuing the Future: Economic Theory and Sustainability*, Columbia University Press.

Hicks, John R. (1946), *Value and Capital*, 2nd edn, Oxford: Oxford University Press.

Hinterberger, F., F. Luks and F. Schmidt-Bleek (1997), 'Material flows vs. "natural capital": What makes an economy sustainable?', *Ecological Economics*, **23**(1), 1–14.

Howarth, Richard B. (1996), 'Climate Change and Overlapping Generations', *Contemporary Economic Policy*, **14**, 100–111.

Howarth, Richard B. (1997), 'Sustainability as Opportunity', *Land Economics*, **73**(4), 569–79.

Howarth, Richard B. (1998), 'An Overlapping Generation Model of Climate–Economy Interactions', *Scandinavian Journal of Economics*, **100**(3), 575–91.

Howarth, Richard B. (2000), 'Climate change and relative consumption', in E. Jochem, D. Bouille and J. Sathaye (eds), *Society, Behaviour and Climate Change Mitigation*, Dordrecht: Kluwer.

Howarth, Richard B., and Richard B. Norgaard, (1992), 'Environmental Valuation under Sustainable Development', *American Economic Review*, **82**(2), 473–7.

IPCC (Intergovernmental Panel on Climate Change) (1996a), *Climate Change 1995: The Science of Climate Change*, contribution of Working Group I to the Second Assessment Report of the Intergovernmental Panel on Climate Change, New York: Cambridge University Press.

IPCC (1996b), *Climate Change 1995: Impacts, Adaptations, and Mitigation of Climate Change: Scientific–Technical Analysis*, contribution of Working Group II to the Second Assessment Report of the Intergovernmental Panel on Climate Change, New York: Cambridge University Press.

IPCC (1996c), *Climate Change 1995: Economic and Social Dimensions of Climate Change*, contribution of Working Group III to the Second Assessment Report of the Intergovernmental Panel on Climate Change, New York: Cambridge University Press.

Jevons, Stanley, (1865/1977), 'The Coal Question: An Inquiry Concerning the Progress of the Nation and the Probable Exhaustion of our Coal Mines', in E. Cornish et al. (eds), *The Study of the Future*, Washington, DC: World Future Society.

Kaufmann, Robert K. and Cutler J. Cleveland (2001), 'Oil Production in the Lower 48 States: Economic, Geological, and Institutional Determinants', *Energy Journal*, **22**(1), 27–49.

Kneese, A. V. (1999), 'The Faustian Bargain', in W. Oates (ed.), *The RFF Reader in Environmental and Resource Management*, Washington, DC, Resources for the Future.

Kneese, A. V. and W.D. Schulze (1985), 'Ethics and Environmental Economics', in A.V. Kneese and J.L. Sweeney (eds) *Handbook of Natural Resource and Energy Economics*, Amsterdam: North-Holland.

Koopmans, Tjalling C. (1960), 'Stationary Ordinal Utility and Impatience', *Econometrica*, **28**, 287–309.

Koopmans, Tjalling C. (1977), 'Concepts of optimality and their uses', *American Economic Review*, **67**(3), 261–74.

Levett, R. (1998), 'Sustainability indicators: Integrating quality of life and environmental protection', *Journal of the Royal Statistical Society Series A – Statistics in Society*, **161**, Part 3, 291–302.

Lipman, B.L. (1995), 'Information-processing and bounded rationality – a survey', *Canadian Journal of Economics*, **28**(1), 42–67.

Mäler, Karl-Göran (1991), 'National accounts and environmental resources', *Environmental and Resource Economics*, **1**(1), 1–17.

Malthus, Thomas R. (1798/1976), *An Essay on the Principle of Population*, New York: Norton.

Manne, Alan S. (1996), 'Hedging Strategies for Global Carbon Dioxide Abatement: A Summary of the Poll Results EMF 14 Subgroup – Analysis for Decisions under Uncertainty', in Nebojsa Nakicenovic et al. (eds), *Climate Change: Integrating Science, Economics, and Policy*, Laxenburg, Austria: International Institute for Applied Systems Analysis.

Manne, Alan S. and Richard Richels (1997), 'On Stabilizing CO_2 Concentrations – Cost-Effective Emission Reduction Strategies, *Environmental Modeling and Assessment*, **2**(4), 251–65.

Marglin, Stephen A. (1963), 'The social rate of discount and the optimal rate of investment', *Quarterly Journal of Economics*, **77**, 95–111.

Marini, Giancarlo and Pasquale Scaramozzino (1995), 'Overlapping generations and environmental control', *Journal of Environmental Economics and Management*, **29**,(1), 64–77.

Meadows, Donella H. et al. (1972), *The Limits to Growth*, New York: Universe Books.

Mendelsohn, Robert and James E. Neumann (eds) (1999), *The Impact of Climate Change on the United States Economy*, Cambridge, UK: Cambridge University Press.

Mourmouras, Alex (1993), 'Conservationist Government Policies and Intergenerational Equity in an Overlapping Generations Model with Renewable Resources', *Journal of Public Economics*, **51**(2), 249–68.

Neumayer, Eric (1999), *Weak versus Strong Sustainability: Exploring the Limits of Two Opposing Paradigms*, Cheltenham, UK and Northampton, USA: Edward Elgar.

Nordhaus, William D. (1994), *Managing the Global Commons: The Economics of Climate Change*, Cambridge, MA: MIT Press.

Norgaard, Richard (1988), 'Sustainable Development: A Co-Evolutionary View', *Futures*, 606–20.

Norton, Bryan G. and Michael A. Toman (1997), 'Sustainability: Ecological and Economic Perspectives', *Land Economics*, **73**(4), 553–68.

O'Connor, Martin (1993), 'Entropic irreversibility and uncontrolled technological change in economy and environment', *Journal of Evolutionary Economics*, **3**, 285–315.

O'Connor, Martin (1997), 'J.S. Mill's Utilitarianism and the Social Ethics of Sustainable Development', *European Journal of the History of Economic Thought*, **4**, 478–506.

O'Connor, Martin (1998), 'Ecological–Economic Sustainability', in Sylvie Faucheux and Martin O'Connor (eds), *Valuation for Sustainable Development*, Cheltenham, UK and Northampton, USA: Edward Elgar.

Page, Talbot (1997), 'On the Problem of Achieving Efficiency and Equity, Intergenerationally', *Land Economics*, **73**(4), 580–96.

Pannell D.J. and N.A. Glenn (2000), 'A framework for the economic evaluation and selection of sustainability indicators in agriculture', *Ecological Economics*, **33**(1), 135–49.

Pearce, David W. and Giles D. Atkinson (1993), 'Capital Theory and the Measurement of Sustainable Development: an Indicator of "Weak" Sustainability', *Ecological Economics*, **8**(2), 103–8.

Pearce, David, Anil Markandya and Edward B. Barbier (1989), *Blueprint for a Green Economy*, London: Earthscan.

Pearce, David W. et al. (1993), *Blueprint 3: Measuring Sustainable Development*, London: Earthscan.

Peck, Stephen C. and Thomas J. Teisberg (1993), 'Global Warming Uncertainties and the Value of Information: An Analysis Using CETA', *Resource and Energy Economics*, **15**(1), 71–97.

Pemberton, Malcolm and David Ulph (2000), 'Technical progress and the measurement of national income', typescript, Department of Economics, University College London, UK.

Pemberton, Malcolm and David Ulph (2001), 'Measuring income and measuring sustainability', *Scandinavian Journal of Economics*, **103**(1), 25–40.

Pezzey, John (1989), 'Economic Analysis of Sustainable Growth and Sustainable Development', Washington DC: World Bank. Environment Department Working Paper No. 15. Published as *Sustainable Development Concepts: An Economic Analysis*, World Bank Environment Paper No. 2, 1992.

Pezzey, John (1992), 'Sustainability: An Interdisciplinary Guide', *Environmental Values*, **1**(4), 321–62.

Pezzey, John (1994), 'The Optimal Sustainable Depletion of Non-renewable Resources', AERE Workshop, Boulder, Colorado, and EAERE Annual Meeting, Dublin, Ireland.

Pezzey, John (1995), 'Concern for sustainable development in a sexual world', *Discussion Paper* 95–02, Department of Economics, University College London.

Pezzey, John C.V. (1997), 'Sustainability Constraints versus "Optimality" versus Intertemporal Concern, and Axioms Versus Data', *Land Economics*, **73**(4), 448–66.

Pezzey, John C.V. (1998), 'Stripping resources and investing abroad: a path to sustainable development?', in M. Acutt and P. Mason (eds), *Environmental Valuation, Economic Policy and Sustainability*, Cheltenham, UK and Northampton, USA: Edward Elgar.

Pezzey, John C.V. (2001), 'Sustainability policy and environmental policy', typescript, Centre for Resource and Environmental Studies, Australian National University, Canberra.

Pezzey, John C.V. (2002), 'Exact measures of income in a hyperbolic economy', typescript, Centre for Resource and Environmental Studies, Australian National University, Canberra.

Pezzey, John C.V. and Michael A. Toman (forthcoming), 'The economics of sustainability: Introduction', in J. Pezzey and M. Toman (eds), *The Economics of Sustainability*, Aldershot: Ashgate.

Pezzey, John C.V. and Cees A. Withagen (1998), 'The Rise, Fall and Sustainability of Capital–Resource Economies', *Scandinavian Journal of Economics*, **100**(2), 513–27.

President's Materials Policy Commission (1952), *Resources for Freedom*, Washington, DC: Government Printing Office (June).

Proops, John L.R. et al. (1999), 'International trade and the sustainability footprint: a practical criterion for its assessment', *Ecological Economics*, **28**(1), 75–98.

Rawls, John (1971), *A Theory of Justice*, Cambridge, MA: Harvard University Press.

Rothman, Dale S. and Sander M. de Bruyn (1998) 'Probing into the environmental Kuznets curve hypothesis', *Ecological Economics*, **25**(2), 143-5.

Roughgarden, Tim and Stephen H. Schneider (1999), 'Climate Change Policy: Quantifying Uncertainties for Damages and Optimal Carbon Taxes', *Energy Policy*, **27**, 415–29.

Ruth, Matthias (1995), 'Thermodynamic implications for natural resource extraction and technical change in US copper mining', *Environmental and Resource Economics*, **6**, 187–206.

Schelling, Thomas C. (1995), 'Intergenerational Discounting', *Energy Policy*, **23**, 395–401.

Sefton, J.A. and M.R. Weale (1996), 'The net national product and exhaustible resources: The effects of foreign trade', *Journal of Public Economics*, **61**, 21–47.

Shogren, Jason and Michael A. Toman (2000), 'Climate Change Policy', in Paul Portney and Robert Stavins, (eds), *Public Policies for Environmental Protection*, 2nd edn, Washington, DC: Resources for the Future.

Simpson, R. David (ed.) (1999), *Productivity in Natural Resource Industries: Improvement Through Innovation*, Washington, DC: Resources for the Future.

Skinner, Brian J. (1976), 'A New Iron Age Ahead?', *American Scientist*, **64**,158–69.

Smulders, Sjak (2000), 'Economic growth and environmental quality', in H. Folmer and L. Gabel (eds), *Principles of Environmental Economics*, 2nd edn. Cheltenham, UK and Northampton, USA: Edward Elgar.

Sollner, Fritz (1997), 'A re-examination of the role of thermodynamics for environmental economics', *Ecological Economics*, **22**, 175–202.

Solow, Robert M. (1974), 'Intergenerational Equity and Exhaustible Resources', *Review of Economic Studies, Symposium on the Economics of Exhaustible Resources*, pp. 29–46.

Solow, Robert M. (1986), 'On the Intergenerational Allocation of Natural Resources', *Scandinavian Journal of Economics*, **88**(1), 141–9.

Solow, Robert M. (1993), 'An Almost Practical Step Toward Sustainability', *Resources Policy*, **19**(3), 162–72.

Stern, David I. (1997), 'Limits to Substitution and Irreversibility in Production and Consumption: A Neoclassical Interpretation of Ecological Economics', *Ecological Economics*, **21**(3), 197–216.

Stiglitz, Joseph E. (1974), 'Growth with Exhaustible Natural Resources: Efficient and Optimal Growth Paths', *Review of Economic Studies, Symposium on the Economics of Exhaustible Resources*, pp. 123–37.

Stokey, Nancy L. (1998), 'Are there limits to growth?', *International Economic Review*, **39**(1).

Toman, Michael A. (1994), 'Economics and "Sustainability": Balancing Trade-offs and Imperatives', *Land Economics*, **70**(4), 399–413.

Toman, Michael (1999), 'Sustainable Decision Making: The State of the Art from an Economics Perspective', in Martin O'Connor and Clive Spash (eds), *Valuation and the Environment*, Cheltenham, UK and Northampton, USA: Edward Elgar.

Toman, Michael A., John Pezzey and Jeffrey Krautkraemer (1995), 'Neoclassical Economic Growth Theory and "Sustainability"', in D. Bromley (ed.), *Handbook of Environmental Economics*, Oxford: Blackwell (TPK).

Vellinga, Nico and Cees Withagen (1996). 'On the concept of green national income', *Oxford Economic Papers*, **48**, 499–514.

Vincent, Jeffrey R. (2000), 'Green accounting: from theory to practice', *Environment and Development Economics*, **5**(1–2), 1–12.

Vincent, Jeffrey R., Theodore Panayotou and John M. Hartwick (1997), 'Resource Depletion and Sustainability in Small Open Economies', *Journal of Environmental Economics and Management*, **33**(3), 274–86.

Vitousek, Peter M. et al. (1986), 'Human appropriation of the products of photosynthesis', *BioScience*, **36**(6), 368–73.

Wackernagel, Mathis and William Rees (1996), *Our Ecological Footprint: Reducing Human Impact on the Earth*, Gabriola Island, BC, Canada: New Society Publishers.

Weitzman, Martin L. (1970), 'Aggregation and disaggregation in the pure theory of capital and growth: a new parable', Cowles Foundation Discussion Paper No. 292. New Haven: Yale University.

Weitzman, Martin L. (1976), 'On the Welfare Significance of National Product in a Dynamic Economy', *Quarterly Journal of Economics*, **90**(1), 156–62.

Weitzman, Martin L. (1997), 'Sustainability and Technical Progress', *Scandinavian Journal of Economics*, **99**(1), 1–13.

Weitzman, Martin L. (1999), 'Pricing the limits to growth from mineral depletion', *Quarterly Journal of Economics*, **114**(2), 691–706.

Withagen, Cees and Geir B. Asheim (1998), 'Characterizing sustainability: the converse of Hartwick's rule', *Journal of Economic Dynamics and Control*, **23**, 159–65.

Woodward, Richard T. and Richard C. Bishop (1997), 'How to Decide When Experts Disagree: Uncertainty-based Choice Rules in Environmental Policy', *Land Economics*, **73**(4), 492–507.

World Bank (2001), *World Development Indicators*, Washington, DC: World Bank. Also available on CD-ROM: see http://publications.worldbank.org/ecommerce.

World Commission on Environment and Development (WCED) (1987), *Our Common Future*, Oxford: Oxford University Press.

5.   Valuing the health effects of pollution

Anna Alberini and Alan Krupnick

1.   INTRODUCTION

Prolonging people's lives and improving their health are arguably the most important effects underlying environmental laws to protect the air and drinking water. We know this, not only because of the prominent role they play in debates over these laws, but because the public places a very high value on such improvements. In recent assessments of the Clean Air Act (USEPA, 1999) and of regulations to reduce ground-level ozone and airborne particulate matter (USEPA, 1998), for example, reductions in deaths were estimated to constitute the lion's share (70–80 percent) of the monetary benefits to be gained, with most of the remaining benefits gained through chronic health improvements. These findings are by no means restricted to the USA. Mortality and morbidity benefits dominated a recent major cost–benefit assessment performed in Canada for reducing the sulfur content in diesel fuel and gasoline (Health Canada, 1997), and similar studies can be found in Europe and in some developing countries. Indeed, estimates of the so-called 'ancillary' benefits[1] of climate change mitigation focus almost entirely on the value of health improvements from reductions in conventional air pollutants, and in many studies exceed the costs of CO_2 mitigation (Davis et al., 2000).

   In spite of the interest in and use of estimates of the value people place on health improvements, there are comparatively few original studies placing a monetary value on such improvements. The ones that are available tend to be used in benefit transfer exercises in settings that take one far from those underlying the original studies. Therefore, the purpose of this chapter is to acquaint the reader with the conceptual underpinnings for estimating values for reducing mortality and morbidity and to present and critique many of the primary studies in the literature. These studies are generally chosen for their applicability to the context of reducing conventional air pollutants (that is, respiratory and cardiovascular effects from particulates, ozone, and the like), although we occasionally refer to cancer as an endpoint and water pollution as a cause. In addition, we critique this literature and point to future directions it might take if its current limitations are to be addressed.

Finally, owing to the increased attention of NGOs and leaders in developing countries to the linkage between health and pollution, we review some of the health valuation literature and special issues specific to developing countries. Because the literature on children's health valuation is in an embryonic state, we ignore this literature, referring the reader to recent work by Agee and Crocker (1994), Dickie (1999), Dickie and Ulery (2001), Navrud (1997), Schulze et al. (1999), and Tolley (1999).

The remainder of this chapter is organized as follows. In section 2, we present a taxonomy of health endpoints and of the value of avoiding these health effects. In section 3, we list and discuss some of the actual values used in the policy arena. In section 4, we take up the value of avoiding acute health effects, deriving the willingness to pay measure, reviewing measurement approaches in the literature, and discussing benefit transfers for these endpoints. Models of investment in health are classified under acute health effects because this type of effect is most applicable to such models. The valuation of chronic health effects is similarly discussed in section 5. Section 6 is dedicated to the issues and literature on the value of avoiding mortality outcomes, and section 7 to valuation efforts for or in developing countries, with an extensive discussion of benefit transfers. Section 8 concludes.

2.   HEALTH EFFECTS OF POLLUTION AND THEIR VALUE

The morbidity literature may be classified in several ways: by whether the values are consistent with welfare economics principles or not; by the duration of the effect; by the type of medical intervention associated with the effect; and by the functional limitations caused by the effect (or other severity measures). To be consistent with principles of welfare economics means that the values are derived from studies asking for or revealing willingness to pay from an *ex-ante* and risk-based perspective. Based on these criteria, concepts other than willingness to pay (such as medical costs), asking people to report their willingness to pay to avoid a certain, rather than a probabilistic,[2] effect, and taking an *ex-post* perspective would be judged as inconsistent with welfare economics. In practice, however, for simplicity much valuation work is done exactly in these ways.

Considering duration, *acute* effects last for a limited number of days, and have well-defined beginnings and endings. A mostly older literature exists to provide values for acute effects. *Chronic* morbidity typically lasts over a long period. Chronic disease may feature recurrent attacks, as in the case of asthma, or entail permanently reduced functions, as in breathing with emphysema. The literature valuing reductions in this type of effect is exceedingly thin.

The most commonly valued morbidity effect is a symptom day avoided with certainty. The use of this concept, however, is fraught with difficulty, since many illnesses, especially respiratory illnesses, often present themselves as a multi-symptom complex. In addition, illness is usually experienced as an episode, and empirical research (see below) has found that the value of avoiding consecutive days of an episode of illness is not constant, but falls with additional sick days and depends on many illness attributes.

Values for avoiding chronic respiratory effects (and mortality effects) are generally appropriately derived in the literature, that is, they are *ex ante* and assume the event occurs probabilistically. However, to our knowledge there are only two studies available on this endpoint (Viscusi et al., 1991; Krupnick and Cropper, 1992).

Both acute and chronic illnesses have been valued based on medical costs associated with the symptoms of these effects. Chronic illness has been valued according to the life-cycle of medical costs associated with a disease (Hartunian et al., 1981).

By functional limitations, we mean limitations in normal daily activities. A *restricted activity day*, for instance, implies that an individual has reduced some, but not all, of his normal activities, but is not bedridden and does not miss work. A *work loss day* implies that the individual was sick enough to have to stay home from work. A *bed disability day* implies that the individual was confined to bed for all or most of the day. Estimates of values for these measures have been taken from a mixture of welfare-consistent studies and medical cost and wage loss estimates, as will be discussed below.

In valuing the morbidity effects of environmental pollution, values should take into account the fact that exposure to toxicants does not result necessarily in immediate morbidity. In many case, long-term exposure to even relatively modest doses results in the development of cancer (or other chronic disease), usually many years after the beginning of the exposure.

A death is a death, but the literature valuing mortality risk reductions makes distinctions between deaths to children (valued through examining altruism of parents through the family) and deaths to adults, with almost all research focused on the latter and very recent attention paid to the age and health status of the adults being affected. There is also a very small literature on values people hold for avoiding deaths to others outside the family. Within the adult mortality risk valuation literature, distinctions are made between immediate deaths, caused by accidents or other reasons, and deaths in the future. Conjectures are also made that the type of death matters: it seems reasonable to hypothesize, for instance, that changes in risk of dying from cancer might be perceived, and valued, differently than an equivalent change in the risk of dying from food poisoning or an accident in the home. However, almost no research investigates the impact of such distinctions on value.

To estimate the benefit of a policy that saves lives, economists now generally rely on the concept of a value of a statistical life (VSL), which is expected to measure what society is willing to pay in order to avoid one death in a population of specified size. This is an *ex-ante* concept, since the identity of the person saved is not known, and is appropriate in policy analyses.

Whether the values at issue refer to mortality or morbidity, most attempts to estimate the benefits of a particular policy, project or program use the damage function approach. This approach involves determining the change in concentration of a pollutant from the policy, converting this change to health effects using concentration–response functions and estimates of the population at risk, and converting these effects to values using unit values or valuation functions. What is often forgotten with this approach is that individuals may take steps to avoid exposures and would be willing to pay something to avoid this averting behavior. Not counting such averting behavior misses social value even if the concentration–response functions perfectly capture the effects of pollution on health (net of the averting behavior).

Concentration–response functions are estimated when the ambient concentration is known at a specified locale. This is typically the case in field studies. One example is studies that attempt to explain daily counts of some health effect in a city over a period of a year or more with pollution concentrations and weather variables. The health effects could be counts of hospital admissions or doctor visits of people experiencing specified symptoms generally associated with pollution exposures, or deaths where the cause of death could be potentially linked with pollution exposures (Thurston et al., 1994; Schwartz, 1997). Another example is prospective cohort studies. This type of study follows large numbers of individuals for a period of time to gauge their health and relates these measures to individual characteristics, pollution concentrations, weather, and other time-varying characteristics.

One of the most important studies in the air pollution context is Pope et al. (1995), which followed over 500 000 individuals living all over the USA for up to eight years to ascertain whether and when they died and found strong and significant effects of fine particulate concentrations on the probability of death. Specifically, Pope et al. estimate that a 1 $\mu g/m^3$ reduction in fine particulate concentrations would lower death rates by about 0.7 percent. Assuming these reduced rates of death are proportional to age, over 75 percent of the deaths 'avoided' would be concentrated among persons of age 65 and older.

3.   HEALTH VALUES USED IN COST– BENEFIT ANALYSES

Table 5.1 provides the best or midpoint values typically used by practitioners of health benefits analyses, as well as ranges of these values (where available), for selected morbidity endpoints and for mortality. We picked the unit values for health endpoints chosen by four major studies or models in the USA, Canada and Europe, ordered from highest to lowest based on the first of these studies – the US study on the costs and benefits of the 1990 Clean Air Act Amendments (USEPA, 1999) – and put them in common currency (using purchasing power parity) and constant dollars.

The willingness to pay for reducing risks of mortality and chronic morbidity is expressed, for convenience, in terms of the value of a statistical life (VSL) and the value of a statistical case of chronic disease (VSC).

The table shows quite close agreement on the size of the best or midpoint VSLs and VSCs. Any differences that do exist may be explained partly by currency conversions and partly by researchers not always adjusting values over time for inflation. The relative ordering of values (for example, whether illness A is valued more or less than illness B) is consistent across studies, even though not all studies consider the same set of health endpoints.

The low VSLs for the tracking and analysis framework (TAF) (Bloyd et al., 1996) and air quality valuation model (AQVM) (Stratus, 1999) result from adjusting VSL for age effects. ExternE (1996, 1999) takes the VSL and converts it to a value of a life-year for subsequent analysis.[3] In other analyses, US EPA (1999) and TAF have done the same thing. These efforts have yielded values ranging from $50 000 to $300 000 per life-year.

In general, the close agreement between the health values shown in Table 5.1 is the result of several factors, including replicability of findings in original studies in different locations (that is, independent choices made by different research teams), and the consensus reached by research teams on a common pool of studies, results and interpretations (see Lee et al., 1995 and ExternE, 1996, 1999). In addition, the Canadian studies have been informed by the AQVM model (Hagler Bailly, 1995) and other models developed for the debate in the USA on the social costs of electricity. However, many studies in the USA pre-date these efforts (for example, Rowe, et al., 1986; USEPA, 1985).

The ranges around these estimates are all somewhat different, seemingly without pattern, possibly because there is no treatment of uncertainty that is universally accepted. The low and high estimates of VSL used by EPA are based on one standard deviation from the distribution (the Weibull) that best fits the mean WTP estimates from 26 studies. The Canada results are based on a representation of uncertainty as a probability distribution defined over three possible values, which includes expert judgment. The TAF distributions are Monte Carlo-based, assuming, unless otherwise indicated by the original studies, that errors about mean estimates are normally distributed, with variances given in the concentration–response and valuation studies relied upon for the underlying estimates. Bounds are defined as 5th and 95th percentile. Error

Table 5.1 Comparison of unit values used in several major studies or models (1990 dollars)

Values	US EPA[a]			US TAF[b]			Canada AQVM[c]			Europe ExternE[d]
	Low	Central	High	Low	Central	High	Low	Central	High	Central
Mortality	1 560 000	4 800 000	8 040 000	1 584 000	3 100 000	6 148 000	1 680 000	2 870 000	5 740 000	3 031 000
Chronic bronchitis	–	260 000	–	59 400	260 000	523 100	122 500	186 200	325 500	102 700
Cardiac hosp. admissions	–	9 500	–	–	9 300	–	2 940	5 880	8 820	7 696
Resp. hosp. admissions	–	6 900	–	–	6 647	–	2 310	4 620	6 860	7 696
ER visits	144	194	269	–	188	–	203	399	602	218
Work loss days	–	83	–	–	–	–	–	–	–	–
Acute bronchitis	13	45	77	–	–	–	–	–	–	–
Restricted activity days	16	38	61	–	54	–	26	51	77	73
Resp. symptoms	5	15	33	–	12	–	5	11	15	7
Shortness of breath	0	5.3	10.60	–	–	–	–	–	–	7
Asthma	12	32	54	–	33	–	12	32	53	36
Child bronchitis	–	–	–	–	45	–	105	217	322	–

Notes:
a   The Benefits and Costs of the Clean Air Act Amendments of 1990–2010 (USEPA, 1999). Low and high estimates are estimated to be 1 standard deviation below and above the mean of the Weibull distribution for mortality. For other health outcomes they are the minima and maxima of a judgmental uniform distribution.
b   Air Quality Valuation Model Documentation, Stratus Consulting for Health Canada. Low, central, and high estimates are given respective probabilities of 33 percent, 34 percent, and 33 percent. (RCG/Hagler, Bailly, 1995).
c   Tracking and analysis framework (Lee et al., 1995), developed by a consortium of US institutions, including RFF. Low and high estimates are the 5 percent and 95 percent tails of the distribution. See also Bloyd et al. (1996) for details on the framework.
d   ExternE report (1999). Uncertainty bounds are set by dividing (low) and multiplying (high) the mean by the geometric standard deviation (2).

bounds in the latest ExternE report are established as one-half (low) and twice (high) the geometric mean.

It is worth noting that the endpoints shown in Table 5.1 are not all comparable to one another. The unit values for mortality risk, chronic lung disease risk, and acute symptoms all are derived from a willingness to pay (WTP) approach that may be thought of as capturing, however imperfectly, the full value to the individual of reducing the risk or the symptom. The other values are only partial, mainly relying on cost-of-illness (COI) techniques. They are meant to capture the most severe manifestations of either acute events or chronic states and may, without proper adjustments, double-count WTP benefits or provide significant underestimates of the WTP to reduce such effects. Indeed, it is fairly common practice to adjust such COI estimates by a factor to bring them up to a WTP estimate, so as to eliminate such underestimation. The AQVM model (Stratus, 1999), for instance, recommends using a factor of 2–3 to make this adjustment, even though there is limited empirical evidence in support of using the same adjustment factor for all endpoints.

4.   VALUING ACUTE MORBIDITY

The appropriate concept to value health endpoints is 'total' willingness to pay (WTP) – the amount an individual is willing to pay to avoid the health endpoint in question. Note that by total WTP, we mean total *social* WTP, that is, a measure that includes the real resource costs of medical expenditures, even though the individual may be compensated for these costs by insurance, and the real loss to the economy of lost work days, even though the individual may get paid sick leave.

In the remainder of this section, we derive WTP to avoid illness, and review approaches that measure WTP, or parts thereof. We discuss the advantages and disadvantages of each of these approaches and describe the empirical literature applying these methods.

4.1   Theory

The household production framework is used to derive the health benefits of a proposed policy reducing pollution or imposing workplace environmental regulation. In the simplest model, which is suited for minor, acute symptoms, an individual's well-being increases with aggregate consumption (X) and leisure (L), but is negatively affected by sick days, D:

$$U = U(X,L,D;Z_u) \tag{5.1}$$

where Z_u is a vector of individual characteristics capturing preferences for income, leisure and health.

In this model, pollution, P, does not influence utility directly, but only indirectly by triggering illness. The relationship between pollution and health outcomes is summarized in a dose–response function: $D = D(P;Z_D)$. The dose–response function can be amended to accommodate for averting activities, A, undertaken by the individual to reduce exposure to pollution, and hence illness:

$$D = D(P,A;Z_D) \qquad (5.2)$$

where it is assumed that $fD/fA < 0$ and $fD/fP > 0$. A vector of individual characteristics, Z_D, is usually included among the arguments of the dose–response function to allow for individual predisposing factors and baseline health, and because the ability to offset exposure to pollution through averting behavior is likely to vary across individuals.

The individual chooses the levels of L, X and A to maximize utility, subject to the budget constraint:

$$y + w[T - L - W(D(P,A))] = X + p_M \cdot M(D(P,A)) + p_A \cdot A \qquad (5.3)$$

Equation (5.3) assumes that the individual must allocate his time between work and leisure, and spend income on aggregate consumption and medical care, M, which in turn depends on the number of sick days, and on the averting activity. The prices of M and of A are equal to p_M and p_M, respectively, whereas the price of a unit of the aggregate consumption good is normalized to one. Sick time enters in the budget constraint because it reduces work time available to the individual. In equation (5.3), work time lost to illness is denoted by $W(\cdot)$.

An individual's willingness to pay (WTP) for a reduction in pollution is the amount that must be taken away from the individual's income while keeping his or her utility unchanged:

$$V^*(y - WTP, w, p_m, p_a, P_1) = V^*(y, w, p_m, p_a, P_0) \qquad (5.4)$$

where V^* is the indirect utility function, and P_0 and P_1 are the initial and final levels of pollution ($P_0 > P_1$, that is, environmental quality is improved).

Harrington and Portney (1987) show that WTP for a small change in pollution can be decomposed into:

$$WTP = w\frac{dW}{dP} + p_m \frac{dM}{dP} + p_a \frac{dA^*}{dP} - \frac{U_D}{\lambda} \cdot \frac{dD}{dP}, \qquad (5.5)$$

where A^* is the demand function for A, and dA^*/dP gives the optimal adjustment of A to a change in pollution. Equation (5.5) states that marginal willingness to pay comprises marginal lost earnings and medical expenditures, and the marginal cost of the averting activity. In addition, willingness to pay includes the disutility (discomfort) of illness, converted into dollars through dividing by the marginal utility of income.

Equation (5.5) can be rearranged to produce:

$$WTP = \frac{dD}{dP} \cdot \left[w\frac{dW}{dD} + p_m \frac{dM}{dD} + p_a \frac{dA^*}{dD} - \frac{U_D}{\lambda} \right], \qquad (5.6)$$

showing that marginal *WTP* can be expressed as the product of the slope of the dose–response function times the marginal value of illness (the quantity in brackets).

This has an important implication for valuation work. Following equation (5.6), WTP for a reduction in pollution could be computed by asking individuals to report their WTP to avoid illness *per se* (without implicating pollution), and then blending such WTP figures with epidemiological evidence, summarized into *dD/dP*.

In practice, however, researchers following this approach have often focused on estimating only *some* of these components of WTP using revealed preference data, due to the obvious difficulty of measuring the value of the disutility of illness. This is termed the cost-of-illness approach (see Tolley et al., 1994), where attention is limited to the loss of work income plus mitigation expenditures (that is, the first and second component of (5.6)). It is also possible to focus on averting expenditures, the third component of (5.6). Unless individuals increase averting expenditures as pollution decreases (which is unlikely), averting expenditures underestimate willingness to pay and provide a lower bound for it (Harrington and Portney, 1987; Courant and Porter, 1981). In general, both the cost-of-illness and the averting-expenditure approaches neglect the value of the discomfort caused by illness, and can do no better than producing a lower bound for WTP.

Even if one uses the approach suggested by equation (5.6), there is still the necessity to link the health effect being valued to the response being estimated in the available concentration–response functions. This has proved challenging to researchers as the epidemiological and clinical literatures have developed largely independently from the economics valuation literature. The clinical literature, for example, has estimated dose–response functions for lung function, but individuals are probably more comfortable valuing common manifestations of lung function reductions (for example, shortness of breath, getting tired easily, greater risk of developing emphysema, and so on) than a lung function reduction itself.

Another valuation approach – the hedonic approach – is more in the spirit of equation (5.5), except it does not explicitly link pollution to the various terms in brackets. The hedonic property value approach, for instance, uses housing price, housing attribute, and neighborhood attribute (including pollution concentration) data to estimate the implicit price discount associated with the market for houses in areas with higher pollution concentrations than houses located in other areas. Concentration–response functions in this model are those implicitly perceived by buyers and sellers in the housing market, and may include non-health, as well as both morbidity and mortality relationships. As a given type of pollution may also be highly correlated with other neighborhood characteristics, such as crime rates, and other types of pollutants (different types of air pollutants; closeness to dumps or toxic waste sites), it may be difficult to isolate the WTP for reduction of a given pollutant. Also, such estimates would be conditional on general knowledge (and, more importantly, perhaps misconception) about the concentration–response relationships.

4.2   Empirical Literature

4.2.1   CV studies

The most straightforward way to obtain WTP to avoid pollution-related illness is to use survey-based methods to ask people to place a value on avoiding illness, and to combine these values with dose–response or concentration–response functions as shown in equation (5.6).

Contingent valuation (CV) is one such survey-based method.[4] In a contingent valuation survey that elicits WTP to avoid illness, the researcher must address the definition of the illness that the respondent is to value. In many studies, the illness is described by the researcher to the respondent, and is defined as a complex of attributes, such as the duration of the illness (in days), the type of symptoms (for example, headache, respiratory symptoms), their severity and the restrictions that they cause to the individual's normal activities, plus, if appropriate, whether mitigating behavior should be taken into consideration.[5]

The advantages of this approach are clear. The commodity to be valued – (the recurrence of) an illness with specified severity and other attributes – can be interpreted as an 'experimental treatment' assigned to the respondent. If the illness description is varied across respondents, the attributes of the commodity can be treated as exogenous regressors in a regression relating WTP to the attributes of the illness. This regression allows the researcher to determine how illness attributes influence WTP.

In practice, however, respondents who are not familiar with the illness or do not think the illness applies to them might find this exercise meaningless or confusing, and report zero WTP or otherwise unreliable WTP amounts.

This difficulty has led to the development of an alternative approach, where respondents are asked to recall an episode of illness they have previously experienced, describe it to the enumerator by answering structured questions, and report their WTP to avoid a recurrence of this episode. This approach eliminates the problem of unfamiliarity with the disease. Provided that the sample is sufficiently large, the distribution of illnesses and their attributes in the sample should be similar to that in the population.

One potential problem, however, is that the description of the commodity to be valued by the respondent may be subject to recall problems.[6] It is also difficult for the researcher to control for all of the attributes of the illness that would presumably affect WTP. This is akin to the problem of independent variables observed with error in a regression model: the presence of observation errors results in biased estimates of the regression coefficients.

In addition, it is likely that the illnesses that are best recalled by the respondents and the respondent's WTP share characteristics that are unobserved by the researcher, effectively making WTP endogenous with the illness attributes. Finally, the survey instrument may place a relatively heavy burden on the respondent.

Since the effects of air pollution on acute illness are uncertain, ideally, respondents should be asked their WTP to reduce the *probability* of experiencing a given illness. In practice, this is not done, partly out of the added complications of communicating probabilities, partly out of a judgment that the values are too small to warrant such a sophisticated treatment. Rather, it is common practice to ask respondents to consider a *certain* recurrence of the illness (that is, the probability of experiencing the described illness, as an example). Researchers have also simply asked respondents their WTP for eliminating a recurrence of multiple illness episodes over a given time period to ascertain how marginal WTP varies with numbers of illnesses (or symptom days) reduced.

Partly out of a judgment that WTP estimates for acute illness are relatively small and do not warrant much further research funding, much of the literature valuing minor, acute health effects is somewhat old, although a new wave has started in Europe and Asia.

In Loehman et al. (1979), and Loehman and De (1982), respondents were first asked a number of questions designed to elicit background information about their health and the annual episodes of respiratory illnesses, and then were asked whether they would be prepared to pay specified amounts to avoid episodes of specified severity and involving specified combinations of symptoms. Respondents were shown a payment card, and asked to circle the dollar amount of the payment card closest to their WTP. As later shown by

Cameron and Huppert (1988), payment card responses are correctly interpreted as bounding WTP between the amount circled by the respondent (lower bound) and the next amount on the card (upper bound), requiring interval-data maximum likelihood estimation. Loehman and De, however, treated the responses as simply providing a lower bound to WTP, much like a single-bounded, dichotomous-choice payment question would.[7] Their values per symptom day were in the $5 to $15 range (1979 dollars)

The most interesting result of the Loehman and De study, and one replicated in other studies, is that WTP grows with the severity and the duration of the spell of illness, but in a less than proportional fashion. Also, wealthier individuals are willing to bid more to avoid an episode, with the income elasticity of WTP ranging between 0.2 and 0.6, depending on the symptom complex.

Rowe and Chestnut (1985) utilized the approach in which respondents describe their own illnesses, and asked asthmatics in Los Angeles to report their WTP for a 50 per cent reduction in their number of bad asthma days, obtaining a $21 WTP for each bad day of asthma avoided (1985 dollars).

Tolley et al. (1986) estimated WTP of respondents after describing symptoms to them, but failed to mention whether mitigation of symptoms was possible, and whether WTP was to be before or after mitigation.

Using the approach in which the illness is described for the respondent, Dickie et al. (1987) focused on nine symptoms associated with ambient ozone exposure, including sinus pain, cough, being out of breath easily, experiencing pain when breathing, wheezing, and headache. One interesting feature of this study is that, concerned about respondents reporting unrealistically high WTP values, the researchers attempted to correct such large values by pointing out to the respondent that if his WTP for a specified symptom-day was X, and he experienced Y such days a year, annual WTP would be a total of X^*Y. This prompted many respondents to revise their announced WTP figures dramatically downward. After revisions, mean WTP to avoid one day of symptoms ranged from $1.161 (cough) to $4.67 (could not breathe deeply) (1987 dollars).

A recent study by Desvousges et al. (1996) uses conjoint analysis, asking respondents which situation they find better between two states of illness described by several attributes, such as the type of symptoms, the number of episodes experienced, the limitation in daily activities that they imply, and costs.[8] The responses provided by the respondents are then used to estimate rates of trade-off between various attributes, and WTP to avoid each state of illness. Both morbidity and mortality were covered in this study, which drew from a pilot survey taken of residents of Quebec and Ontario, Canada. The study was self-administered by the respondents using the computer. The pilot study found WTP to avoid stuffy, runny nose and sore throat of $143 if only mild limitations to daily activities are involved, and of $683 with more severe restrictions. Shortness of breath is worth $1443 and $1816, depending on the severity of the limitations it causes (all figures are expressed in 1996 Canadian dollars). These estimates are far larger than those typically found in other studies or used in cost–benefit analyses. A more recent study using conjoint analysis with 400 subjects in Toronto (Johnson et al., 2000) found somewhat lower estimates of WTP for mild symptoms that increased more than proportionally for five days relative to one day of such symptoms. WTP increased significantly for more severe restrictions.

An example of the new wave of CV studies for acute illness is a series of studies by Navrud, Ready and others. For instance, Navrud (1997) interviewed in person 1000 Norwegians to ascertain their WTP to avoid a variety of acute health effects (one more day over their usual annual frequency, and 14 days over their usual annual frequency). The values for avoiding symptoms are slightly smaller than those found in the older US studies (in constant dollars), but WTP to avoid asthma attacks is much larger.

Following up this study, Ready et al. (1999) developed a new CV instrument to compare WTP estimates in Norway, the Netherlands, England, Portugal and Spain for avoiding some standard, if severe, acute health endpoints for one day as well as for a respiratory emergency room visit, a respiratory hospital admission, and three days in bed.

WTP for the standard acute health endpoints is high for all of the five countries relative to the older US studies (over $75 for a cough-day that is serious enough to reduce strenuous activity), with WTP higher for the more serious episodes described. Yet, WTP for hospitalization and emergency room visits is relatively low compared to US values, which are strictly based on medical cost and lost time. This may reflect responses that consider only pain and suffering, failing to include medical costs. Holding income and other respondent characteristics the same, Spanish and Portuguese respondents had the highest WTP values, and British respondents had the lowest WTP values.

4.2.2 Comparison between WTP and cost of illness

The cost-of-illness (COI) approach has been used extensively in the medical and public health literature and the values it has produced have been applied to the health effects of pollution. Equation (5.5) shows that medical expenditure and work income losses are only two of the components of total WTP for pollution control. The question is: how small or large a fraction of total WTP is measured by the cost of illness?

The few studies that have directly queried individuals about their willingness to pay to avoid illness, and have compared WTP with averting expenditures and cost-of-illness figures, have found that WTP is about 1.6 to 4 times larger that the sum of mitigating expenditures and income loss, suggesting that the cost of illness (COI) substantially underestimates true WTP to avoid illness (Rowe and Chestnut, 1985; Chestnut et al., 1998). As shown below, there is a rough consistency in the available evidence, although one should not extrapolate such estimates to diseases or disease severity beyond those studied.

These comparisons are useful for two reasons. First, they act as validity checks for the WTP figures reported by the respondents in the contingent valuation survey. As seen earlier, economic theory posits that WTP to avoid illness should be greater than cost-of-illness measures, which represent a lower bound for WTP. Assuming that the CV study has been correctly designed and implemented, one would then expect estimated WTP to be greater than cost-of-illness figures.

Second, since cost-of-illness figures may in some instances be obtained from official statistics, and may be easier and less expensive to obtain than survey-based WTP data, if one knew – at least approximately – what fraction such costs represent of total WTP, one would be able to obtain a rough estimate of the health damages of air pollution by multiplying the cost of illness by the inverse of that fraction.

The approach by Dickie and Gerking (1991a) is particularly interesting. Invoking the assumption of weak complementarity between demand for medical care and pollution levels, they fit a probit model to explain demand for a doctor visit as a function of the ambient levels of ozone, CO, SO_2, and NO_2 at the respondent's place of residence, while controlling for the price of a doctor visit, respondent baseline health, occupation, occupational exposure, age and education.

WTP for a change in ambient ozone readings from y_1 to the level specified in the US National Ambient Air Quality Standards (y_0; $y_1 > y_0$) is $(1/\lambda) \int_{y_0}^{y_1} \Phi(y) dy$, where Φ is the standard normal cumulative distribution function and λ is the marginal utility of income. The estimates derived in this fashion are then compared with the change in the (medical) cost of illness, computed as the price of a doctor visit times $[\Phi(y_1) - \Phi(y_0)]$. Dickie and Gerking find that, depending on the specification of their random effects probit model, the former are two to four times the latter.

Alberini and Krupnick (2000) report on the findings of a study in Taiwan that combines a prospective cohort study and a contingent valuation survey designed to elicit WTP to avoid minor respiratory illnesses. They find that the ratio of WTP to COI ranges from 1.48 at very low levels of particulate matter to 2.26 at the highest PM10 readings (350 $\mu g/m^3$). The ratio increases with particulate matter levels, because as pollution worsens, people experience more symptoms, but their doctor visits, prescription medication expenses and lost earnings do not increase proportionally. Despite economic, cultural, and institutional differences between the USA and Taiwan, the WTP/COI ratios for the Taiwanese are, therefore, in line with (if somewhat smaller than) similar ratios computed for the USA.

4.2.3 Averting expenditures

Bartik (1988) examines the role of averting behavior in recovering WTP to reduce pollution, spelling out the two conditions required for averting expenditures to provide a lower bound for WTP. The first is that there is no joint output: the averting behavior must not affect utility directly (as when air conditioning is run to filter pollution out of the air, but also because it makes the home more comfortable during hot days). The second is that the averting activity must not require investment in durable goods entailing sunk costs.

Harrington et al. (1989) estimate upper and lower bounds for economic losses from a giardiasis outbreak in the drinking water for some communities in Luzerne County, Pennsylvania in 1983, including losses from averting behavior and from illness, accounting for a range of estimates for the value of time. Using survey data and county records, they find that losses from averting behavior range between \$170 and \$2300 per household, with average losses per confirmed case of about \$1000.

Abdalla et al. (1992) surveyed a sample of residents of Perkasie, PA, where in 1987 one of the wells supplying water to the town was found to be contaminated with trichloroethylene (TCE). Averting behaviors were found to be more likely among people who reported higher concern for the cancer risks associated with TCE in water, more information received about TCE, and who had children of ages 3–17 at home.

Dickie and Gerking (1991b) use the household production function approach to show how WTP to avoid symptoms associated with pollution exposures can be obtained if sufficient information is available about the averting activities and the cost of all inputs into the household production function. They focus on two health symptoms which are assumed to depend on the individual's health stock and other characteristics, pollution levels, and the extent of averting activity, and show that marginal willingness to pay is

$$\frac{\partial WTP}{\partial P} = -\sum_1 \left[\frac{\partial U}{\partial S_i} \cdot \frac{1}{\lambda} \right] \cdot \frac{\partial S_1}{\partial P}$$

where P is pollution, S is symptom, U is the utility function, which is positively affected by income and negatively affected by symptoms, λ is the marginal utility if income, and $i=1,2$ indexes the symptoms. The first-order conditions for utility maximization imply that marginal WTP can also be computed as

$$\left(-\tau_j / S_j^1 \right) = \frac{\partial S_1}{\partial P}$$

with τ the price of a unit of averting activity j, and $S^1{}_j$ the derivative of symptom 1 with respect to averting activity j.

In practice, the difficulty lies in identifying the averting behaviors and in their relationship with symptoms. Dickie and Gerking show that the marginal value of the avoided symptoms (the term in parentheses in the equation above) can be determined using exclusively prices and parameters of the household production function only if the number of averting activities is at least as great as the number of symptoms, and the columns of the household technology matrix are linearly independent.[9] Complications arise in the presence of joint outputs, where an averting activity both influences health symptoms *and* utility directly. For instance, if there is one symptom with two averting activities, and the second of these activities influences both the symptom and utility directly, marginal WTP can still be calculated as

$$\left(\tau_1 / S_1^1\right) = \frac{\partial S_1}{\partial P}$$

but cannot be calculated correctly using the second averting activity as the basis.

Dickie and Gerking use a longitudinal dataset following 226 residents of Los Angeles over time, focusing on one aggregate outcome of the household production function (all acute respiratory symptoms), and two averting activities: use of air conditioning in the car (ACCAR) and presence of central air conditioning system (ACCEN) in the home for respondents who do not suffer from chronic respiratory ailments, and ACCAR plus the presence/absence of a gas cooking range in the home for healthy respondents.[10] Clearly, each of these averting activities or goods may directly affect utility, and the authors caution the readers that the marginal WTPs are approximations. WTP to avoid one respiratory symptom for a day ranges from 75 cents to $1.12 (1985 dollars).

While in the case of contaminated water it is relatively straightforward to identify averting behaviors and their prices, this task appears more difficult in the context of air pollution, due to the possible joint output problem and to the fact that some of these behaviors may not necessarily be linked by the individual with pollution and health outcomes. Dickie and Gerking chose to work with the use of air conditioning in the car but here the joint output problem is significant. Another measure of averting behavior to air pollution could be time spent outdoors. Presumably, individuals should curtail time spent outdoors on high-pollution days. Krupnick et al. (1990) use time spent outdoors to adjust ambient readings of pollutants in the Los Angeles area, producing pollution levels corrected for actual exposure.

Bresnahan et al. (1997) examine how time spent outdoors varies with pollution levels, controlling for individual characteristics and health stock and for weather, using the panel dataset previously used by Dickie and Gerking (1991a, 1991b). They find that Los Angeles residents do – all else remaining the same – curtail outdoor time as smoggy conditions arise, but they do not do so in a fashion that is linear with pollution levels.

Analyses of three possible averting behaviors (cutting down time spent outdoors; changing planned leisure activities when smoggy; and running air conditioners when smoggy) suggest that individuals who suffer from chronic respiratory conditions and individuals who experience symptoms on highly polluted days are more likely to undertake averting behaviors. Because these data were collected several years ago, when pollution control efforts in the LA area were not quite as well developed and perhaps information on the health effects of pollution was not so readily available, it would be interesting to see how these results would compare with a new, similar study in the same areas. For comparison, Alberini and Krupnick (1997, 1998) find little evidence of averting activities in their Taiwan study.

4.2.4 Investment in health

Equation (5.5) implies that the value of reduced pollution can be computed by predicting the health effects of a change in pollution, and multiplying by the value of avoiding the health endpoint. The model, however, is not adequate when individuals invest in their health, thus affecting the time they spend ill.

If people in polluted areas engage in activities – such as changes in diet, exercise, and use of medical products – meant to build up their stock of health (resistance to illness), an improvement in environmental quality not only reduces their ill time, but also reduces the investment required to maintain their health stock. Traditional approaches that would only consider the former would thus be missing a component of this person's WTP for an improvement in environmental quality.

Cropper (1981) shows that omission of the latter component can result in gross underestimation of WTP. She proposes a type of human capital approach to model health, which postulates that individuals have a stock of health H, and they invest time and medical services or products to maintain H. Investment is $I_t = TH_t^{1-\zeta} M_t^{\zeta}$, where TH is time spent investing in health and M represents the medical products or services. Health stock depreciates at rate δ, so that $dH_t/dt = \dot{H} = I_t - \delta_t H_t$, with δ influenced by pollution. Health stock influences time spent ill TL (hence providing the main reason to invest in health): $\ln TL_t = \gamma - \alpha \ln H_t$. The model is appropriate for acute illness, such as minor respiratory illnesses, colds and the flu, which are influenced by the individual's resistance to illness but are unlikely to have long-lasting effects on one's stock of health.

Cropper shows that the value of a small change in pollution comprises two components. The first is the elasticity of sick time with respect to pollution, multiplied by time spent sick and the wage rate. The second component is the change in health investment costs caused by the change in pollution. Cropper points out that the traditional approach is approximately equal to only the first of these components, and uses data from the Michigan Panel Study of Income Dynamics to produce WTP values that account for such behaviors.

She first fits an equation where log sick days (measured as work loss days) are regressed on log air pollution, an occupational dummy, a dummy for chronic illness, and other individual characteristics using a tobit equation. This yields an estimate of the elasticity of sick days with respect to pollution. Combined with the value of a sick day and the second component mentioned above, this implies that WTP for a 10 percent decrease in mean SO_2, the measure of air pollution, is \$7.20, twice as much as the figure one would get if the change in investment in health were ignored.

4.2.5   Benefit transfers

Benefit transfer is a technique (see Desvousges et al., 1992) whereby values obtained at certain locations/populations under certain conditions are extrapolated or adjusted to produce values applicable to other locations and populations (or under different conditions). The technique has been widely used in the USA and other countries whenever it was not possible – due to budget or time constraints – to conduct original valuation studies in the location in question.

The most basic technique for a benefit transfer is to adjust a WTP estimate for one country for the income differentials between the study and the application country (Krupnick et al., 1996). Early benefit transfer efforts from US studies to Eastern European countries beginning their transition from communist regimes to market economies relied on correcting WTP from the USA for the income differential between the two countries. Specifically, these exercises relied on the equation:

$$WTP_T = WTP_{US}\left(\frac{\text{income of household in target country}}{\text{income of US household}}\right)^{\alpha}. \quad (5.7)$$

where α is the income elasticity of WTP, generally set equal to 1, and the subscripts T and US denote the target country and the USA, respectively.

Most of the literature has addressed transfers from developed to developing countries, which will be discussed in section 7. A very small literature has attempted to examine the validity of transferring benefit estimates for acute morbidity between developed countries. The tentative conclusion from this specific literature, as well as from the bulk of the benefit transfer studies, is that adjusting WTP estimates taken from the study country based on income differentials (and with an assumed income elasticity of WTP equal to 1) between the study country and the transfer country is unlikely to lead to very accurate estimates of value for the latter. The Ready et al. (1999) study, which was discussed in section 4.2.1, is probably the best example of a benefit transfer validity test among developed countries.

5.   VALUING CHRONIC ILLNESS

To our knowledge, there is only a handful of primary studies in the literature that attempt to value chronic illness in ways consistent with welfare economics, all of them using a concept analogous to the value of a statistical life (VSL), that is, the value of avoiding a statistical case of chronic disease (VSC). The VSL is the WTP to reduce one's probability of dying divided by that probability reduction, while the VSC is the WTP to reduce one's probability of getting a chronic disease, divided by that probability reduction.

Viscusi et al. (1991) devised a computerized self-administered questionnaire in which respondents are asked to choose between two cities: city A has a given risk of chronic bronchitis and a certain cost of living, while city B has a lower risk of chronic bronchitis, but a higher cost of living. Individuals are asked to choose a city, and the program alters the attributes of the two cities until indifference is reached between them, which gives WTP for a given risk reduction. This is, effectively, a variant of conjoint analysis.

Krupnick and Cropper (1992) used the same instrument in one part of their study but, to test whether familiarity with the disease matters, applied it to a sample of individuals whose family members have chronic respiratory disease. They found that familiarity did matter, in that their sample was willing to pay more to avoid a given probability of getting the disease (in a risk–cost of living trade-off question) than a sample without familiarity with the disease (although when the trade-off was chronic respiratory disease and auto-death, no differences were observed). They also modified the program to ask respondents for their WTP to avoid chronic respiratory disease with symptoms just like those of their relatives. The resulting regression equation used to predict WTP as a function of disease severity and other factors proved useful to modify the Viscusi et al. results for use in cost–benefit analyses, as it was widely suggested that the description of the disease used by Viscusi et al. was far more severe than that in the general population. The subsequent value used in the cost–benefit literature is about \$260 000 per statistical case (1990 dollars).

Because Viscusi et al. intercepted shoppers in a mall, and Krupnick and Cropper recruited their respondents using a newspaper advertisement, both studies rely on samples that are not representative of the population at large.

Indeed, EPA was criticized for adopting the figures produced by these studies in its key cost–benefit analyses, on the grounds that these were mere 'pilot' studies (of around 300 persons each), that the samples of respondents were unrepresentative of the populations at risk, and that the studies had not been replicated (OMB memo, 1999).

Dickie and Gerking (1996) use a household production function model to address WTP to avoid skin cancer. The model postulates that people combine consumption goods, goods to reduce the harmful effects of sunlight, and time spent in the sun to produce utility. The model allows for risk perceptions to influence averting behavior, which in turns influences WTP. A contingent behavior survey of 300 people involving a sunscreen produces a value of $6160 for a statistical case (when risks are set equal to true risks).

Finally, it is possible to obtain a lower bound for the value of avoiding chronic illness using the cost-of-illness approach. Although this approach fails to capture the value of pain and suffering, productivity loss and fear of an illness, it has nevertheless been used in Hartunian et al. (1981) and Oster (1984) for the progress of cancer and respiratory disease.

We are unaware of any studies that have attempted to examine the validity of benefit transfers for the WTP to reduce risks of developing chronic disease.

6.   MORTALITY

6.1   The Value of a Statistical Life

To illustrate the concept of value of a statistical life (VSL), consider the following example. Suppose each member of a group of 10 000 people is willing to pay $30 for a 1/10 000 (or 0.0001) reduction in the risk of death. Then the group as a whole is willing to pay $30/0.0001, or $300 000, to avoid one death. The $300 000 computed in this fashion is the value of a statistical life (VSL) within this group.

The concept of the VSL is used to quantify the life-saving benefits of proposed environmental policies and regulations. The risk reduction brought about by the proposed policy is multiplied by the population exposed to estimate the number of lives saved by the policy. The mortality reduction benefits of the proposed policy are then obtained by multiplying the number of lives saved times the VSL. VSL is the appropriate concept to use in *ex-ante* cost–benefit analyses, because it refers to an unidentified 'statistical' person in the affected population.

The original way of obtaining a VSL was to compute the present value of the stream of earnings that would have been realized by the individual in the remaining years of his life – called the human capital approach. This approach is still in use in the food safety area (Buzby et al., 1996), but generally not for valuing mortality risk reductions from pollution. Clearly, the human capital approach produces a higher value of life for individuals in better-paid occupations, in their prime age, and in better health (if individuals in compromised health are forced to lower-paying occupations or can devote fewer hours to working than healthier individuals) relative to older persons, retirees, housewives and the unemployed. Indeed, retirees and the unemployed, in a strict application of the approach, would be assigned a zero value, even though in principle these persons *are* willing to pay for a reduction in the risk of death.

The appropriate, welfare-theoretic measure to use to compute the VSL is a person's willingness to pay for a reduction in the risk of death – that is, the income they are willing to give up for an increase in the probability of surviving – divided by the reduction in risk. Ideally, the individual whose WTP is being observed would base his or her WTP on the difference in their survival curve with and without the change being contemplated.[11]

The WTP for a risk reduction, and the corresponding VSL, has been estimated using both revealed preference and stated preference approaches. Most revealed preference studies rely on behaviors and choices made by workers in the labor market or consumers in product markets (for example, automobiles, seatbelts, smoke detectors, bike helmets) to infer the rate at which individuals are willing to trade off income for reduced risks of death. Revealed preference studies where mortality risks are from causes other than environmental pollution include Atkinson and Halvorsen (1990), who relate car prices to the car safety level, and Blomquist (1979), who uses the time spent by motorists buckling up to infer the implied VSL. Ippolito and Ippolito (1984) derive VSL by observing people's smoking decisions. These studies rely on the assumption that individuals are perfectly aware of the health risks implied by the ambient levels of pollution at different locations or by different models of automobile, and that the objective risks are reflected in the market price of houses and cars.

Some revealed preference studies have examined directly mortality risks from pollution exposures. Examples include hedonic housing studies relating house values to structural and locational characteristics of a house, and to pollution levels, proxies for such levels (such as distance from a hazardous waste site), or implied death risks. Examples are Portney (1981) for the risk of death associated with air pollution and Gayer et al. (2000) for the risk of cancer in the vicinity of Superfund sites in the Grand Rapids area, Michigan. The latter study implies a VSL of $4.5 million.

The majority of the available VSL figures, however, come from observing trade-offs between income and risk made from compensating wage (labor market) studies. These studies reason that workers are willing to give up income for improved workplace safety, and that firms are willing to pay higher wages to workers willing to accept jobs with higher risks of death and non-fatal injuries, as improved workplace safety investments are costly. Labor market data correspond to the tangency between the wage–risk trade-off loci of workers (that is, the combinations of risks p and wage rates w that keep expected utility constant: $Z = (1-p)U(w)+pV(w)$, where Z is a specified constant level of utility, $U(\cdot)$ is the utility in the healthy state and $V(\cdot)$ is the utility in the injured state) with the market opportunity curve provided by firms.

Using individual worker data, the income–risk trade-off at market equilibrium is thus estimated by fitting the econometric equation:

$$w_i = \alpha + \beta p_i + \gamma q_i + \delta q_i WC_i + \sum_{m=1}^{M} x_m \lambda_m + \varepsilon_i, \tag{5.8}$$

where w is the wage rate of worker i, p and q are the risks of occupational death and the risk of non-fatal injury for worker i, and WC is worker compensation paid to worker i in the event of a non-fatal injury. The equation also controls for other individual characteristics (such as age, education, experience, gender, union status and region of residence) and attributes of the occupation likely to influence wage rates.

The coefficient β allows one to recover the value of a statistical life.[12] Viscusi (1993) notes that it is important to control for both the risks of a fatal and a non-fatal injury in the estimated compensating wage equation. Failure to do so will typically overestimate the coefficient β.[13] Additional complications occur when in the sample being studied risks only vary across industries,[14] and not across individuals. This is problematic when one wishes to include industry dummy variables in the right-hand side of (5.8) to control for inter-industry wage differentials (widely documented to exist since Krueger and Summers, 1988). Leigh (1995) reports that the coefficient of the fatal risk variable, measured at the industry level, becomes insignificant when industry dummies are also included in the equation to reflect industry-specific wage differentials. Shogren and Stamland (2000) suggest that accounting for diversity in skill for reducing risks is likely to bias VSLs upwards.

A raft of studies has sought to bring order to this literature by considering groups of labor market and other studies together. For instance, Viscusi (1993) reports the VSL from 24 compensating wage studies, which ranges from $4 million to $9 million (converted to 1998 dollars). Other noteworthy efforts include Fisher et al. (1989) and Miller and Guria (1991). A very recent study (Mrozek and Taylor, forthcoming) uses meta-analysis techniques on over 40 labor market studies to estimate the factors contributing to the VSL estimates, including baseline risks, demographic sample characteristics, and researcher judgments on equation specification and sample selection. The researchers particularly focus on the 'Leigh effect' noted above. They conclude that an appropriate range of VSLs is from $1.3 to $2.5 million (in 1998 dollars) when evaluated at average workplace death risks of 1 in 10 000.

All compensating wage studies rely crucially on the assumption that workers know their objective risks of fatalities and non-fatal risks, and that the objective risks faced by worker i are the same as that of all other workers in his industry (or in his occupation), without ever testing these assumptions. The only study that used subjective, as opposed to objective, risk as the determinant of wage rates is Gegax et al. (1988). This study revealed that the risks workers believed to face were much larger than the industry-wide averages. Unfortunately, it is unclear how much credence should be lent to this finding, because workers' subjective risk estimates were elicited by asking them to pick a risk figure out of several figures displayed on a card, but the figures on that card were disproportionately large relative to the objective risks.

Stated preference studies, while less numerous than labor market studies, can, at least in theory, address many of the shortcomings of labor market studies. In a CV study, for instance, individuals can be educated about their baseline risks rather than having to assume they know them.

Starting with Jones-Lee et al. (1985), who conducted one such study in the context of transportation safety, CV studies for risk reductions have, however, suffered from their own share of problems. One is that relatively large fractions of respondents are not willing to pay any positive amount of money for a risk reduction, a problem that could be due to inexperience with (small) risks and probabilities, with trading off income for risk reductions, or to a rejection of the scenario delivering the risk reduction (Smith and Desvousges, 1987). Another is that WTP is often found to be insensitive to the size of the risk reduction, violating the expectation from economic theory that people should be willing to pay more for a greater quantity of the good (Hammitt and Graham, 1999; Beattie et al., 1998).

Finally, under relatively restrictive assumptions, the life-cycle model of consumption predicts that WTP will be approximately proportional to the size of the risk reduction. In practice, several CV studies (reviewed in Hammitt and Graham, 1999) reject the hypothesis that WTP is proportional to the size of the risk reduction, and find that VSL varies with the size of the risk reduction valued. Hammitt and Graham report that near-proportionality is observed when the analysis of the WTP responses is restricted to those persons who claim to be more confident about their willingness to pay. Carson and Mitchell (forthcoming) find that WTP for a program that reduces trihalomethanes in the drinking water supply, and hence the risk of a certain type of colon cancer, is a concave function of the risk reduction.

6.2   VSL and Environmental Policy Analyses

Because of the dearth of studies estimating WTP for a reduction in the risk of death due to environmental threats, in practice the USEPA has relied on a number of compensating wage studies and a few CV studies for estimates of VSL. Because these studies produced different VSL amounts, EPA analysts have treated them as draws from a Weibull distribution. The mean of this distribution for VSL is $6 million (1998 dollars) which has been used as the central value for VSL in recent EPA regulatory and other cost–benefit analyses.

Is it appropriate to use the VSL from compensating wage studies to quantify the avoided mortality benefits of environmental regulations? For this 'transfer' to be appropriate, one is forced to assume that VSL is independent of the size of the risks, although the risk of workplace fatalities is of the order of 10^{-4}, while some environmental risks are frequently much smaller (10^{-6} to 10^{-8} or less) and others, say from large reductions in particulate pollution, may be larger. Even when attention is restricted to the VSL estimated from compensating wage studies, however, Mrozek and Taylor (forthcoming) find that there is a quadratic relationship between VSL and risk, which would seem to raise questions about the appropriateness of this assumption. (If VLS were a constant, the meta-analysis would not find any statistically significant relationships between VSL and the size of the risk reduction.)

Moreover, the population from which the VSL is estimated from labor market studies is likely to be completely different from the beneficiaries of environmental regulation, whose WTP should be used in computing the mortality benefits of environmental regulations. The former includes mostly males in their prime age and health, while the latter includes older persons, small children, and persons in compromised health. Without further documentation, there is no reason to believe that the tastes of workers are similar to the income–risks trade-offs in other strata of the population.

Finally, workplace risks differ from the risks associated with environmental exposures in still other respects: the former are undertaken voluntarily, while the latter are usually not undertaken voluntarily by victims; and the former imply immediate death, while the latter imply that the effects may arise later in life, perhaps with death following a period of suffering and pain. All of these factors represent differences as to the nature of the risk that could result in a different WTP for an equivalent magnitude reduction in that risk. In fact, economic theory predicts that the value of a future risk reduction should be equal to the value of an immediate risk reduction at the later age, discounted back to the present, and multiplied by the probability of surviving to the later age.

6.3 Addressing Limitations of VSL Transfers: Age, Baseline Risks, Latency and Dread

Two responses have been made to deal with these criticisms of the use of the labor market literature. The first attempts to adjust estimates of VSLs from labor market studies for age, latency and other factors using assumptions or factors taken from various other studies. For instance, to address the fact that average ages of workers are much lower than those (adults) at risk from air pollution, one can, under strong assumptions, convert the VSL from a labor market study or other source into a value per life-year saved (Moore and Viscusi, 1988). The value of a life-year can then be multiplied by discounted remaining life expectancy to value the statistical lives of persons of different ages.[15] To illustrate this calculation, suppose that the VSL based on compensating wage differentials is $5 million, and that the average age of people receiving this compensation is 40. If remaining life expectancy at age 40 is 35 years and the interest rate is zero, then the value per life-year saved is approximately $140 000. If, however, the interest rate is 5 percent, then *discounted* remaining life is only 16 years, and the value per life-year saved rises to approximately $300 000.[16]

The relationship between WTP for a risk reduction (and hence VSL) and age and health is best illustrated with the aid of a life-cycle model. In a continuous-time version of the model (Shepherd and Zeckhauser, 1982), the individual maximizes the discounted flow of utility over his or her lifetime:

$$\int_0^T u(X_t)e^{rt}\theta(t)dt \qquad (5.9)$$

where $u(\cdot)$ is the utility function, X is consumption, r is the discount rate, and θ is the probability of surviving period t. In different variants of this model the individual is (a) liquidity constrained (that is, cannot be a borrower), or (b) can borrow and lend at an actuarially fair rate. The model is completed by the requirement that the individual cannot borrow indefinitely; that is, the discounted value of lifetime expected consumption equal the present value of lifetime earnings plus initial wealth.

Shepherd and Zeckhauser (1982) make specific assumptions about the functional form of $u(\cdot)$ and select values for the parameters of the model, showing that – under these assumptions – WTP is a quadratic function of age, with WTP peaking around 40 years of age. It should be emphasized, however, that this prediction follows from the specific assumptions employed by Shepherd and Zeckhauser.

Cropper and Sussman (1990) present a discrete-time version of the model, deriving expressions for WTP when borrowing is and is not allowed, respectively. When the individual can never be a net borrower, *WTP* at age *j* for a small change in the conditional probability of dying at age *j* is:

$$WTP_{i,j} = \frac{1}{(1-D_j)} \sum_{t=j+1}^{T} (1+\rho)^{j-t} q_{j,t} \frac{u(X_t)}{u'(X_t)}, \qquad (5.10)$$

where D is the conditional probability of dying at time t, ρ is the rate of time preference, and q is the probability that the individual dies at time t, just before his or her $(t + 1)$ birthday. If the individual can lend and borrow at an actuarially fair rate, then

$$WTP_{i,j} = \frac{1}{(1-D_j)} \sum_{t=j+1}^{T} (1+\rho)^{j-t} q_{j,t} \frac{u(X_t)}{u'(X_t)} + (y_t - X_t), \qquad (5.11)$$

where y is income in period t. Equations (5.10) and (5.11) show that the effect of age on WTP for a small change in risk is ambiguous: On the one hand, the likelihood of surviving this period reduces the conditional probability of survival (the first term), which would raise WTP. On the other hand, age should decrease remaining lifetime (which is, effectively, the sum of the q terms), which would lower WTP.

In addition, age could influence the rate at which individuals are prepared to trade off income for longevity, and (in (5.11)) individuals may reason that if their life is extended, the consumption that they can afford in the future is less (which should reduce WTP). The net effect of all of these factors is unclear a priori.

Similarly, it is not clear if and how WTP depends on health status: persons in poor health may have a higher baseline risk (which should raise WTP), but value survival less if it entails poor quality of life.

Johannesson and Johansson (1996) investigate the relationship between WTP for a mortality risk reduction that lasts only one year, and age in a telephone survey of Swedes. Their sample includes adults of ages 18 to 74. They find that VSL has an inverted-U shape with respect to age, providing empirical support for the theoretical results of Shepherd and Zeckhauser. Additional evidence of the internal validity of the WTP responses, is, however, limited: 'quality of life,' income and size of the household are not statistically significant predictors of WTP, and education – while statistically significant – is *negatively* related to WTP.

Krupnick et al. (forthcoming) conducted CV studies in Canada and the US specifically designed to explore the relationship between age and WTP, health status and WTP, and to compare WTP for an immediate risk reduction with that of a risk reduction of the same size to be incurred at a later age. Their samples included adults of ages 40 to 75 (in Canada) and to over 90 (in the USA).

The Canada study resulted in VSL values ranging between $1 and $3 million, depending on whether VSL is calculated on the basis of WTP for a larger (5 in 10 000) or smaller (1 in 10 000) risk reduction. Respondent-reported WTP increased, as predicted by economic theory, with the size of the risk reduction, but not in a proportional fashion. Age was found to have little effect on WTP. However, after age 70 WTP declined by about one-third. Physical health was found to have no effect on WTP, with one exception: persons who have or have had cancer reported about a 30 percent higher WTP.

However, this finding should be interpreted with caution for two reasons. First, only 26 people in the sample had or had had cancer. Second, the study required respondents to travel to a centralized facility to take a self-administered computerized questionnaire. These 26 respondents, therefore, would have had to be well enough to travel, and may not be representative of the population with cancer. Perhaps the most novel finding of the study is that mental health – a measure of psychological distress, or absence thereof – is strongly related to WTP, with people that are calm, report fewer symptoms of psychological distress, and have a better outlook on life willing to pay more for an increase in the chance of survival. Finally, as expected, people reported being willing to pay about one-third less if the 5 in 10 000 annual risk reduction was to be incurred later in life, between age 70 and 80. WTP for the future risk reduction increased with the respondent-reported probability of surviving to age 70, and implies a discount rate of 12 percent, which is similar to the discount rate calculated by Moore and Viscusi from revealed preferences under restrictive assumptions.

The US counterpart of the study took place in August 2000, with respondents recruited from a national panel representative of the US population for age, race and income compiled and maintained by Knowledge Networks, Inc. Respondents took the survey questionnaire over 'Web TV.' Preliminary analyses of the data (Alberini et al., 2001) reveal that the WTP values held by this sample are very similar to those from the Canada study, but indicate that WTP is not sensitive to age, and *is* sensitive to health status. Individuals with certain chronic respiratory and cardiovascular illness were willing to pay a greater amount, all else remaining the same, than individuals of similar characteristics but not suffering from those ailments. The difference between the two countries can probably be ascribed to two reasons. First, there were more chronically ill people in the US study, since participants could take the survey in their homes, whereas in Canada they would have to be well enough to travel to a centralized facility to take the survey. Second, the health status questions were revised for the US survey, resulting in more precise information about the presence of diagnosed chronic illnesses.

Another response to the criticisms of the labor market literature has been to conduct original CV studies with the context and sample for valuation characterized to better match that relevant for pollution reductions. Johannesson and Johansson (1996) (noted above) were the first to test for WTP for an increased life expectancy. They asked a sample of Swedes to report their WTP for an increase of one year in their life expectancies, added between ages 75 and 85. The resulting VSL was $70 000–$110 000. These figures are very low when compared with the VSL used by EPA in their policy analyses and with the VLS implied by WTP for a future risk reduction in the Krupnick et al. Canada and US studies.

However, the study was problematic in many respects. It was conducted over the telephone, precluding the use of visuals in depicting life expectancy and probabilities. The commodity being valued is also not clear: based on the English translation of the payment question, one wonders whether the extension of life expectancy may have been interpreted by the respondents as an extension of one year to their life span that takes place with probability 1. Finally, the article is silent about debriefing questions to find out whether respondents had fully understood the scenario they were asked to consider.

Johannesson et al. (1996) also investigate the matter of WTP for a private risk reduction versus WTP for a risk reduction delivered by a public program. Surprisingly, they find that WTP for a private risk reduction device is greater than WTP for a uniform, public-program risk reduction of the same magnitude.

Current research, however, has not addressed the issue of dread – in other words, are death risks associated with cancer (a major concern for environmental policy) valued differently than non-cancer death risks?[17]

Finally, some researchers have attempted to adjust VSL not only for the remaining years of life, but also for the *quality* of life in those remaining years. The so-called QALY approach uses survey data to assign an index to various health conditions. The index ranges between 0 (death) and 1, and higher index values indicate quality of life that is preferred over that implied by lower score values (Tolley et al., 1994). Although common in the medical literature, the QALY approach is only supported by economic theory under very restrictive assumptions about how health and consumption enter in the utility function of a life-cycle model.

Carrothers et al. (1999) use a QALY approach to estimate a VSL appropriate for the time-series studies documenting the short-term mortality effects of air pollution. They discount the life-years lost because the people who die prematurely are not in good health; they also assume that only 'days to years' are lost because of exposure to air pollution. Each life-year lost is assigned a QALY value of $50 000, a commonly accepted benchmark for medical interventions, although not necessarily the appropriate figure in the air pollution context. The resulting VSL is less than 10 percent of the $4.8 million (1990 dollars) used by EPA.

7. DEVELOPING-COUNTRY ISSUES

For many years, only economists in developed countries performed studies valuing health benefits of environmental improvements. This situation is beginning to change as governments and other organizations become increasingly aware of the usefulness of such estimates in building support for and prioritizing environmental policies,[18] and as valuation techniques become increasingly portable and standardized.[19] In the remainder of this section, we highlight the issues concerning research in this area and review some of the studies in the literature.

7.1 Issues

Probably the most controversial aspect of health valuation in developing countries concerns the use of income differentials across countries as a means of adjusting WTP values from a developed country. Some feel that using income as a means of adjusting demand for health improvements would disadvantage the low-income countries, but thus far all available empirical evidence suggests that preferences for health do not fall in proportion with income.

For a number of reasons, valuation of health improvements in developing countries is more challenging than in developed countries. Indigenous valuation studies are in very short supply, basic data are limited, exchange processes are constrained, growth is (it is hoped) rapid, and a number of broader social development concerns are more vexing and severe, such as providing living conditions of the poor and institutional capacity. Markandya (1998) argues that health valuation in developing countries faces the following difficulties:

- Reliance on valuation studies performed in developed countries (or the unit values arising from such studies) will introduce more than the usual amount of uncertainty into valuation estimates. These uncertainties could be based, for instance, on cultural differences, such as differences in respect for the elderly, and in access to medical care and in health status.
- Limited basic data, such as data on wage rates in manufacturing, make application of some valuation approaches problematic, or altogether impossible.

- Medical cost information may not reflect social opportunity costs and, therefore, may need adjustments.
- Hedonic labor market studies, which presume that labor and goods markets are competitive and workers have reasonable information on death and injury risks, may carry more uncertainties than those relying on developed country labor markets.
- Valuation of health of household members – particularly children – may be quite different from what is inferred for comparable persons in developed countries because of the more central role played by children in the economy and the household.
- Rapid economic growth may imply that the applicability of indigenous studies several years hence is questionable.

Perhaps the most pressing issue when attempting to estimate WTP to avoid morbidity and mortality endpoints in developing countries is the lack of suitable data. Should one wish to use revealed preference methods, it must be borne in mind that observing purchases of medical services or averting expenditures might be very difficult in countries with non-institutional health care and medicine, liquidity constraints and barter-based economies. Labor markets may be restricted, resulting in unreliable estimates of wage premiums for taking occupational risks. In addition, subsidized housing and the absence of a mortgage market may result in too few house sales and purchases for researchers to be able to see if and how housing prices are influenced by pollution levels.

One way to circumvent these problems might be to conduct original contingent valuation studies in developing countries. Whittington (1998) discusses the difficulties associated with the design and implementation of such studies. One problem is that it is difficult, if not impossible, to select households using the most desirable sampling frames (such as random sampling or stratified sampling) for lack of listings of households and other census information. In addition, local community leaders in some cases interfere with the regular administration of interviews, and attempt to influence individual responses in hopes of increasing the likelihood that a specified good is provided to the community.

The concept of 'maximum willingness to pay' and the hypothetical nature of such a survey may conflict with social and cultural convention. When Whittington et al. (1990) conducted a CV study in Nigeria to obtain WTP for improved water supply in the dry season, they found that WTP was extremely low, despite the fact that households spent considerable fractions of their income on water purchases during that season. The researchers blamed this result on the fact that during the dry season agricultural employment was virtually non-existent, and people were reluctant to commit to regularly scheduled payments. While economic theory predicts that WTP for improved water supply should be greater for those persons who bear higher costs of securing alternative water sources (the female members of the household), in practice in several cases women did *not*, after all, announce higher WTP amounts than male respondents, perhaps due to cultural and social conventions.

7.2 A Sampling of Literature from Developing Countries

7.2.1 Vaccinations against malaria

Cropper et al. (1999) estimate the WTP to protect against malaria for a year using the contingent valuation (CV) approach and compare results to cost-of-illness (COI) measures. The COI measures include treatment and drug costs, transportation costs, work-days lost and losses associated with household labor substitution. They arrive at a cost of $4–$24 (1997 dollars) per episode, and $9–$31 per household annually. In contrast, annual household WTP for preventing malaria is $36 (median of $25), which is about 15 percent of annual income. Under a range of assumptions, WTP is two to three times larger than COI. The income elasticity of vaccine demand is 0.4. The authors also estimate the WTP for bednets, which provide partial protection from malaria. They find that WTP for bednets is about 70 percent of WTP for a vaccine promising complete protection. The comparison, however, may be a bit misleading, because the bednets would normally provide protection over several years.

7.2.2 WTP for improved quality of drinking water

Households in Korea were found to be willing to pay $3.28 per month for a device on their public water supply to provide early warning of chemical contamination. A somewhat different approach to valuing safe drinking water is presented in McConnell and Rosado (2000), who identify a number of options, such as filtering the water or boiling it, each of which implies a certain cost and time requirement, for residents of an urban agglomeration in the state of Espirito Santo, Brazil. A nested logit model is then fit to predict the option selected by the respondent as a function of the cost and time requirement for each alternative, interacted with respondent socio-demographic characteristics. The value of safer drinking water is then computed as the compensating variation of eliminating one of the possible water disinfection options (Freeman, 1993). McConnell and Rosado find that willingness to pay for filters that make drinking water safer is about $10 per month per household.

7.2.3 WTP for air pollution reductions

Wang and Whittington (undated) surveyed 514 people in Sofia, Bulgaria, to assess their WTP for reductions in air pollution. The respondents were told that most air pollutants would be reduced by approximately 75 percent. They were told that respiratory illness would be reduced (without providing a specified amount), that 700 lives per year would be saved for every 1000 who die from health problems related to air pollution), and a variety of other improvements would occur, such as reduced materials damage, improved visibility, and lower damage to trees and plants, and that these benefits would be realized 'in a few years' time.' Various estimates of mean WTP are reported, the highest being about 4.2 percent of income. Income elasticity of WTP was about 0.27, in line with other studies. The complexity of the commodity being valued and the large benefits resulting from this study make comparison with other studies on related environmental policies difficult. The bid elicitation method used in this study was somewhat unusual, in that it asked respondents to indicate the probability with which they feel they would make the proposed payments, rather than simply asking whether the respondent would make or not make the payment.

7.2.4   Demand for improved water supply

Numerous studies, summarized in Alberini and Cooper (2001), document that people in developing countries are generally willing to pay for improved drinking water supply. Some exceptions are noted at locales where people are very disappointed by the provision of infrastructure, in places where there are large fluctuations in the supply of water, and in places where seasonal employment in agriculture does not allow people to make the commitment to regularly scheduled payments (for example, monthly) as typically required by the water supply agency.

7.2.5   WTP to avoid illness

In three cities of Taiwan, Alberini et al. (1997) asked respondents to describe their most recent episode of illness by (a) checking which of the symptoms listed on a card they had experienced; (b) reporting the duration (in days) of each symptom on a time line; (c) answering questions to further identify the nature of the illness and its seriousness (for instance, was the illness a cold, or the flu?); and (d) reporting medical visits and expenditures, as well as restrictions in daily activities and the related costs. Pollution was not mentioned to the respondents.

Finally, respondents were asked to imagine that they were about to experience, in a few days, a similar illness. How much – the questionnaire asked them – would they be willing to pay completely to avoid a recurrence of such an episode of illness? To facilitate their answers, the question was rephrased using a dichotomous-choice format and two follow-up questions.

WTP to avoid an episode of illness is well predicted by the episode's (a) duration, (b) number of symptoms and (c) nature (a cold or otherwise), and by the respondent's (d) education, (e) income and (f) baseline health. The income elasticity of WTP is approximately 0.4; respondents suffering from a serious respiratory illness hold WTP values that are 39 percent higher than those of healthier respondents, and respondents with a chronic non-respiratory condition have WTP that are 46 percent greater than those of non-chronic subjects.

Median WTP to avoid an average illness (one that lasts 5.3 days, entails 2.2 symptoms) is NT$980, or US$39.20 (1992 dollars). There is a considerable degree of variation in WTP, depending on the length and seriousness of the episode one considers. Specifically, WTP increases with the duration of the episode, but at a decreasing rate: avoiding the first day of a cold is worth $20.45, but avoiding the entire 5.3-day episode is worth $34.62, for an average WTP per day of $6.53. These values are not out of line with US estimates for similar endpoints, suggesting that the income elasticity of WTP is quite low.

This contingent valuation survey was preceded by a prospective cohort study that asked participants to monitor their respiratory symptoms on a daily basis. These records were matched with daily pollution levels at a nearby pollution monitor, and concentration–response equations were fitted to complete the estimation of the morbidity benefits of pollution control. Alberini and Krupnick (1997, 1998) combine the illness rates predicted by the epidemiological concentration–response function for Taiwan with WTP to avoid illness estimated from the CV part of the study, showing that the benefits of reducing particulate matter levels from an initial $150\mu g/m^3$ to $135\ \mu g/m^3$ would entail expected benefits of $265 476 (1992 US dollars) to the adult populations of Taipei, Kaohsiung and Hualien (for a total adult population of about 3 million). A larger reduction to $120\ \mu g/m^3$ would imply morbidity benefits of $519 177, while lowering PM10 from $300\ \mu g/m^3$ to $150\ \mu g/m^3$ would produce health benefits worth $3.393 million.

Chestnut et al. (1998) interviewed respondents in Bangkok, Thailand, in April 1996, about their WTP to avoid respiratory symptoms of varying severity. Chestnut et al. followed the traditional approach of querying individuals about their WTP to avoid a 'symptom day' (which created no particular restrictions to work or other daily activities), a 'restricted activity day' (during which subjects curtailed some of their activities, but did not necessarily miss work or spent the day in bed), and a 'work loss day' using the payment card elicitation method. WTP to avoid each of the endpoints was relatively high: mean WTP for a symptom day was $16 (1996 US dollars), for a restricted activity day $30 and for a work loss day $63. Median WTP was $4, $12 and $24, respectively.

7.2.6 WTP for reduced mortality risks

VSL in developing countries has been estimated using labor market data. Simon et al. (1999) take a broad, comprehensive look at Indian labor markets, examining blue-collar workers, both male and female, in all of India's manufacturing industry and at the three-digit level, along with risk data at the industry level. They find that the implied VSL is between $150 000 and $360 000 on an exchange rate basis ($1990). They compare the VSLs across countries by computing the ratio of the VSL to the present value of foregone earnings implied by a unit change in occupational death risk – that is, to the values derived using the human capital approach. They find that, using their original study, the VSL is from 20 to 48 times larger than the value of foregone earnings. The implication is that a benefit transfer assuming a unitary income elasticity of WTP would greatly underestimate the VSL for India.

In a compensating wage study conducted with Taiwan labor market data, Hammitt et al. (2000) find that the 'longitudinal' income elasticity of VSL is 2 to 3. Hammitt et al.'s finding is based on samples of workers and their wage rates and fatality risks for each of the years between 1982 and 1997. They estimate the usual compensating wage equations separately for each year, and derive the corresponding VSLs (16 values, one for each year), the logarithmic transformations of which are then regressed on log GNP (controlling for the average risk in each of the annual samples). This illustrates the differences between the predictions based on cross-section income elasticities of WTP (and VSL) and the time-series income elasticities.

Hammitt and Zhou (2000) conducted a CV survey of 3600 individuals to obtain VSLs for three sites in China, estimating a VSL of only $3000–$4000 for either a 1/1000 or a 2/1000 risk change. While some internal consistency was found, the results did not pass a scope test.

7.3   Benefit Transfers

Most benefit transfers have been from developed to developing countries because of the lack of original studies in the latter. At least two recent studies, by Alberini and Krupnick (1997) and Chestnut et al. (1998), have questioned whether this approach is satisfactory, showing that willingness to pay to avoid illness can be higher in Taiwan and Thailand than one would expect from extrapolations from US studies based strictly on income differentials. In practice, available estimates of income elasticity of WTP for risk reductions or avoiding acute illness symptoms are very low (usually on the order of 0.2 to 0.3), implying that very little adjustment for income is necessary, and that WTP in the target developing country is much closer to the US figure than the income differential would imply.

To assess the appropriateness of benefit transfer procedures, Alberini and Krupnick select two studies from the USA by Tolley et al. (1986) and Loehman et al. (1979), and extrapolate the dollar figures from these studies, focusing on a one-day head cold, and adjust these figures for income to produce predictions for Taiwan, using equation (5.7) for two alternative values of α: 0.4, the income elasticity of WTP in the Taiwan sample, and 1.

If the illness day here considered causes restrictions in daily activities, the dollar figures from the original US studies and for Taiwan can be summarized as shown in Table 5.2.

Table 5.2   Benefit transfer comparisons for WTP for one-day head cold (all figures are expressed in 1992 US dollars)

	WTP in original study	Prediction for Taiwan ($\alpha=1$)	Prediction for Taiwan ($\alpha=0.4$)	Actual WTP from Taiwan study
Tolley et al. (1986)	40.32	28.07	34.88	20.45 (95% confidence interval: 16.31, 27.29)
Loehman et al. (1979)	19.23	16.37	18.06	

Source: Alberini and Krupnick (1997).

This shows that the WTP figure from Tolley et al.'s study would overpredict WTP for Taiwan, while the WTP figure from Loehman et al.'s study under-predicts WTP for Taiwan, but falls within the 95 percent confidence intervals around the point estimate for the latter. One can also reverse the comparison, using the WTP from Taiwan to predict WTP for the USA. This approach yields a prediction for the Tolley et al. sample of $62.12, with 95 percent confidence interval of $26–$98. The confidence interval thus covers the point estimate from the Tolley study, which is $40.32. Based on these comparisons, one can neither confirm nor rule out the appropriateness of benefit transfers.

In the Bangkok study (Chestnut et al., 1998) mean WTP for a symptom day was $16 (1996 US dollars), for a restricted activity day $30 and for a work loss day $63. Median WTP was $4, $12 and $24, respectively. Chestnut et al. compare these figures with those provided by selected studies in the USA, and find that even without adjusting for income differential across the two countries the pairs of WTP figures are remarkably similar, since mean WTP for a comparable endpoint in the USA is (in order) $11, $26, and $99 to $189. Since household and per capita incomes in Bangkok are approximately one-quarter to one-third of their US counterparts, these findings suggest that Bangkok residents place a relatively high value on avoiding respiratory symptoms. The figures obtained in the study also compare well to those obtained by Alberini et al. for a typical episode of respiratory symptoms.

Because of the lack of microdata for many of the original valuation studies, some benefit transfers studies have used the predictions or estimates from the valuation studies in a meta-analysis. By treating each study's results as an observation, group data (average education levels in the country where the study was performed) can be used to estimate the effect of specified factors on WTP. Bowland and Beghin (1998), for instance, use 33 labor market studies to estimate the marginal effect of risk differences, income, education, age, and various labor market descriptors on WTP for mortality risk reductions and apply the estimated equation to predicting the benefits of fine particulate reductions in Santiago, Chile. They find that the implied VSL is about $740 000 (1992 US dollars), adjusted for PPP (purchasing power parity). This figure can be compared to the standard VSL figure of $4.8 million (1990 dollars).

This study, however, has a number of problems. Key variables to help explain differences in WTP (such as health status) are missing, and the studies used in the meta-analysis are mostly from the USA, and have insufficient variation in the independent variables. One of the most important results of the study is that the income elasticity of WTP is well over 1.0, which is at odds with the rest of the literature. Finally, while the authors realize that they are using a regression to make predictions for levels of income (about one-half of income in the USA) well outside of the sample, and check carefully the quality of the predictions under these circumstances, it is important that future exercises based on meta-analyses validate their predictions by comparing them with actual VSL estimated from the target country.

On balance, though, the main conclusion of these comparisons is that benefit transfers assuming an income elasticity of WTP of 1.0 or even making other adjustments do not appear to be reliable for valuing mortality and morbidity risks in developing countries. Perhaps this should not be surprising. Health status, family size, the availability and cost of medical care and insurance, average life expectancies, and a host of cultural factors may be operating to alter WTP in ways that counteract the effect of lower income.

8.   CONCLUSIONS

We have reviewed the state of the art in the literature valuing the health effects of (primarily) air pollution, seeking to cover theoretical and empirical work, the limitations and the advantages of the various approaches used, and the actual values used in the policy arena.

We have surveyed the literature for both morbidity and mortality outcomes, with the caveat that at the present time much of the debate in the USA and abroad seems to be focused on the value of reducing the risk of death. Although there is reason to believe that the type of risk (voluntary or involuntary), the type of death (caused by cancer or of an accidental nature) and the timing of the risk reduction are important determinants of the value of reducing death risks, the figures used in the environmental policy arena have been largely based on transferring estimated values from contexts other than environmental policy. It is our hope that future work will address these shortcomings.

The values of morbidity endpoints are much smaller, but of sufficient interest to warrant a recent wave of studies in Europe and in developing countries. A particularly important need is for studies providing values for a statistical case of chronic disease. The high values suggested by the two pilot studies in the literature suggest that the value of new information here would be large.

With a handful of exceptions, the valuation literature has focused on adults. It is important to determine values for reducing death risks and morbidity for children and to treat the household, rather than the individual, as the key decision unit. The recent wave of interest in conducting original valuation studies outside of the USA needs to continue and spread to developing countries, as the literature shows that benefit transfers across countries can be unreliable.

NOTES

1. Ancillary benefits are those benefits brought about by pollution control measures in addition to or jointly with the main benefits of concern.
2. To make this point perfectly clear, as will be explained in more detail later, epidemiological studies predict the expected number of cases of adverse health effects by estimating the probability that a person will experience such effects at pollution level P and multiplying that probability by the population exposed. We do not know, however, which individuals *will* become sick. From the perspective of an individual member of the population, the illness is a probabilistic event, and not a certain one, and the correct commodity to be valued should be the probability of experiencing the health effect. However, it is difficult to explain probabilities to people and to obtain values for reduced probabilities of becoming sick. In addition, for certain illnesses, such as minor respiratory illness (for example, a cold or a cough) or headaches, it is reasonable to assume that a person will indeed experience them again during their lifetime.
3. Subsequent analyses by the European Commission – DGXI Environment (1998, 1999) have adopted the methods and monetary figures developed by ExternE. Conversion from a VSL to a life-year is discussed below.
4. Contingent valuation is a method of estimating the value that a person places on a good. The approach asks people to directly report their willingness to pay (WTP) to obtain a specified good, or willingness to accept (WTA) to give up a good, rather than inferring them from observed behaviors in regular marketplaces. Because it creates a hypothetical marketplace in which no actual transactions are made, contingent valuation has been successfully used for commodities that are not exchanged in regular markets, or when it is difficult to observe market transactions under the desired conditions. Applications include public goods such as improvements in water or air quality, amenities such as national parks, and private non-market goods, such as reduction of risks or illness.
5. The value attached by the respondent to avoiding a headache, for instance, should be lower if the respondent is assumed to engage in mitigating behavior (for example, taking an aspirin).
6. To mitigate this problem, surveys conducted in the public health and medical literature often limit the time period within which the illness was experienced to two weeks or the last 30

days. This approach, however, implies that no description of the commodity and no valuation exercise can be conducted by people unless they experienced the illness. Alberini and Krupnick (1998, 2000) attempt to address some of these issues by first conducting a daily diary survey of health symptoms over six months and then returning to the participants to ask them their WTP to avoid a new episode like the last episode they described in their diary.

7.   The most widely used approach to eliciting information about the respondent's WTP is the so-called dichotomous-choice format. A dichotomous-choice payment question asks the respondent if he would pay $X to obtain the good. A frequently used wording of the payment question is whether the respondent would vote in favor of the proposed plan or policy if approval of the plan would cost his household $X (in the form of extra taxes, higher prices of products, and so on). There are only two possible responses to a dichotomous-choice payment question: 'yes,' and 'no' (or 'vote for' and 'vote against'). The dollar amount $X is varied across respondents, and is usually termed the bid value. The dichotomous-choice approach mimics behavior in regular markets (at least, in Western countries), where people usually purchase, or decline to purchase, a good at the posted prices. It also closely resembles people's experience with political markets and propositions on a ballot. The dichotomous-choice approach has also been shown to be incentive-compatible: provided that respondents understand that provision of the good depends on the majority of votes, and the respondent's own vote in itself cannot influence such provision, truth-telling is in the respondent's best interest (Hoehn and Randall, 1987). It is important to note that the dichotomous-choice approach does not observe WTP directly: at best, we can infer that the respondent's WTP amount was greater than the bid value (if the respondent is in favor of the program) or less than the bid amount (if the respondent votes against the plan), and form broad intervals around the respondent's WTP amount. Mean WTP is estimated by fitting special statistical models of the responses. To improve the precision of the WTP estimates, in recent years researchers have introduced follow-up questions to the dichotomous choice payment question (for example, Hanemann et al., 1991).

8.   Conjoint analysis and 'choice experiments' are becoming increasingly popular techniques to value environmental quality and natural resources. In a typical choice experiment study, respondents are asked to choose between two or more commodities (or 'policy packages') each of which is defined by a set of attributes, one of which is usually the cost to the respondent, or a related financial concept. Attributes are varied across 'packages,' and the packages are usually matched in such a way that the choice between them is not straightforward, and trading off between attributes is required. For the purpose of statistically modeling the respondent's choices, it is typically assumed that the respondent will choose the alternative that gives the highest utility. Utility is a function of the alternative's attributes and of residual income (income net of the cost of alternative under consideration), plus a random error term. The statistical model of the choices among alternative depend on the assumption the analyst is prepared to make about the error terms. For instance, if the error terms are independent and identically distributed and follow the type I extreme value distribution, the resulting statistical model is a conditional logit. A conditional logit model is easily estimated, but it imposes the restrictive assumption of independence of irrelevant alternatives. If the error terms are jointly normally distributed across alternatives, the resulting model is a multinomial probit. The marginal values of each attribute and the welfare changes associated with changes in the level of the attributes are easily derived (Freeman, 1993).

9.   The household technology matrix comprises the first derivatives and cross-derivates of symptoms with respect to the averting activities.

10.   Gas cooking ranges may elevate indoor nitrogen oxides (NO_x). Hence, avoiding a gas cooking range is interpreted by Dickie and Gerking as an avoidance behavior.

11.   The survival curve provides the probability that a person of age t will survive to age $t+1$ for all ages.

12.   To illustrate how the VSL is calculated from (5.8), suppose risk p is expressed in the number of deaths per 10 000 workers in a year, while w is annual wages paid to a worker. Then $\partial w_1 / \partial p_i$ is the WTP for a 1 in 10 000 risk change, and VSL is equal to $\beta/0.0001$.

13. In practice, however, the risks of fatal and non-fatal injuries, p and q, are highly correlated, so that collinearity in the right-hand side of the econometric equation makes it difficult to interpret the estimated coefficients and their standard errors.

14. If the workers whose wages are analyzed are US residents, one can rely on several sources of data for p and q, the probabilities of a fatal and a non-fatal workplace injury. The Bureau of Labor Statistics documents death risks data at the three-digit SIC level until 1971, publishing only death risks at the one-digit SIC level after 1971. Death risks at the two-digit SIC level remain available from this agency, while the National Institute for Occupation Safety and Health (NIOSH) compiles death risk data at the one-digit level for each of the states. The Society of Actuaries fatality data are based on occupational risks rather than industry risks, and use 37 occupational categories. Effectively, one estimates the regression equation

$$w_{ij} = \alpha + \beta p_j + \gamma q_j + \delta_{qj} WC_i + \sum_{m=1}^{M} x_m \lambda_m + e_{ij},$$

where j indexes the worker's industry (or occupation, if the study relies on the Society of Actuaries fatality risk data).

15. Assuming that the value of each remaining life-years is constant, VSL $= \int_{t=1}^{T} VSLY \cdot (1 + \delta)^{-t}$ where *VSLY* is the value of a statistical life-year, and d is the discount rate.

16. In a new study, Smith et al. (2001) apply a hedonic wage model to data for people aged 51–60 in the Health and Retirement Survey. They find WTP increases for older workers and, overall, the VSLs are over \$10 million.

17. See USEPA (2000) for a discussion of factors that might be used to adjust typical VSLs for cancer.

18. See Ostro et al. (1996a, 1996b), Cropper et al. (1997) and Sanchez (1996) for some recent examples of epidemiological studies linking pollution and adverse health outcomes in less developed countries.

19. See Pearce (1996) for another assessment of the state of the art in the valuation of the health effects of pollution in developing countries. Also, for an example of such work in countries in transition, see Larson et al. (1999) and for Turkey, see Zaim (1997).

REFERENCES

Abdalla, Charles W., Brian A. Roach and Donald J. Epp (1992), 'Valuing Environmental Quality Changes Using Averting Expenditures: An Application to Groundwater Contamination,' *Land Economics*, **68**(2), 163–9.

Agee, M.D. and T.D. Crocker (1994), 'Parental and Social Valuations of Child Health Information,' *Journal of Public Economic*, 55, 89–105.

Alberini, Anna and Joseph Cooper (2001), 'Applications of the Contingent Valuation Method in Developing Countries: A Survey,' FAO Economic and Social Development Paper 146, Food and Agriculture Organization of the United Nations, Rome, Italy.

Alberini, Anna and Alan Krupnick (1997), 'Air Pollution and Acute Respiratory Illness; Evidence from Taiwan and Los Angeles,' *American Journal of Agricultural Economics*, **79**, December.

Alberini, Anna and Alan Krupnick (1998). 'Air Quality and Episodes of Acute Respiratory Illness in Taiwan Cities: Evidence from Survey Data,' *Journal of Urban Economics*, **44**(1), 68–92.

Alberini, Anna and Alan Krupnick (2000), 'Cost of Illness and WTP Estimates of the Benefits of Improved Air Quality in Taiwan,' *Land Economics*, **76**(1) 37–53.

Alberini, Anna, Maureen Cropper, Tsu-Tan Fu, Alan Krupnick, Jin-Tan Liu, Daigee Shaw and Winston Harrington (1997), 'Valuing Health Effects of Air Pollution in

Developing Countries: The Case of Taiwan,' *Journal of Environmental Economics and Management*, **34**(2), 107–26.

Alberini, Anna, Maureen Cropper, Alan Krupnick and Nathalie Simon (2001), 'The Willingness to Pay for Mortality Risk Reductions in the United States and Canada,' paper presented to the Summer Workshop on Public Economics and the Environment, National Bureau of Economic Research, Cambridge, MA, July.

Atkinson, S.E. and Robert Halvorsen (1990), 'The Valuation of Risks to Life: Evidence from the Market for Automobiles,' *The Review of Economics and Statistics*, **72**(1), 133–6.

Bartik, Timothy J. (1988), 'Evaluating the Benefits of Non-Marginal Reductions in Pollution Using Information on Defensive Expenditures,' *Journal of Environmental Economics and Management*, **15**, 111–27.

Beattie, Jane, Judith Covey, Paul Dolan, Lorraine Hopkins, Michael Jones-Lee, Graham Loomes, Nick Pidgeon, Angela Robinson and Anne Spencer (1998), 'On the Contingent Valuation of Safety and the Safety of Contingent Valuation: Part 1 – *Caveat Investigator*,' *Journal of Risk and Uncertainty*, **17**(1), 5–25.

Blomquist, Glenn (1979), 'Value of Life Saving: Implications of Consumption Activity,' *Journal of Political Economy*, **96**(4), 675–700.

Bloyd, Cary et al. (1996), *Tracking and Analysis Framework (TAF) Model Documentation and User's Guide*, ANL/DIS/TM-36, Illinois: Argonne National Laboratory.

Bowland, Brad J. and John C. Beghin (1998), 'Robust Estimates of Value of a Statistical Life for Developing Economies: An Application to Pollution and Mortality in Santiago,' draft paper, North Carolina State University, Raleigh, NC, February.

Bresnahan, Brian W., Mark Dickie and Shelby Gerking (1997), 'Averting Behavior and Urban Air Pollution,' *Land Economics*, **73**(3), 340–57.

Buzby, Jean C. Tanya Roberts, C.-T. Jordan Lin and James M. MacDonald (1996), *Bacterial Foodborne Disease: Medical Costs and Productivity Losses*, ERS, USDA, Agricultural Economic Report No. 741.

Cameron, T.A. and D.D. Huppert (1988), 'OLS versus ML Estimation of Non-market Resource Values with Payment Card Interval Data,' *Journal of Environmental Economics and Management*, **17**, 230–46.

Carrothers, T. J., John D. Graham and John Evans (1999), 'Valuing the Health Effects of Air Pollution,' *Risk in Perspective*, **7**(5).

Carson, Richard T. and Robert C. Mitchell (forthcoming), 'Public Preferences Toward Environmental Risks: The Case of Trihalomethanes,' in A. Alberini, J. Kahn and D. Bjornstad (eds), *Contingent Valuation Handbook*, Cheltenham, UK and Northampton, USA: Edward Elgar.

Chestnut, L.G., B. Ostro, N. Vichit-Vadakan, K.R. Smith and Feng C. Tsai (1998), 'Final Report. Health Effects of Particulate Matter Air Pollution in Bangkok,' prepared for the Air Quality and Noise Management, Pollution Control Department, Royal Thai Government, Bangkok, Thailand, under grant from the World Bank.

Courant, P.N. and R.C. Porter (1981), 'Averting Expenditures and the Costs of Pollution,' *Journal of Environmental Economics and Management*, **8**, 321–29.

Cropper, Maureen L. (1981), 'Measuring the Benefits from Reduced Morbidity,' *American Economic Review Papers and Proceedings*, 71(2), 235–40.

Cropper, Maureen and Francine Sussman (1990). 'Valuing Future Risks to Life,' *Journal of Environmental Economics and Management* **19**(2) 160–74.

Cropper, Maureen L., Nathalie B. Simon, Anna Alberini and J.P. Sharma (1997), The Health Benefits of Air Pollution Control in Delhi,' *American Journal of Agricultural Economics*, **79**(5), 1625–9.

Cropper, Maureen L. and Frances Sussman (1990), 'Valuing Future Risks to Life', *Journal of Environmental Economics and Management*, **19**(2), 160–70.

Cropper, Maureen L., Mitiku Haile, Julian A. Lampietti, Christine Poulos, and Dale Whittington (1999), 'The Value of Preventing Malaria in Tembien, Ethiopia,' Draft paper, The World Bank, Washington, DC.

Davis, Devra, Alan Krupnick and George Thurston (2000), 'The Ancillary Health Benefits and Costs of GHG Mitigation: Scale, Scale, and Credibility,' paper presented at the Expert Workshop on Ancillary Benefits and Costs of Greenhouse Gas Mitigation Strategies, Washington, DC, March.

Desvousges, W.H. et al. (1992), 'Benefit Transfer: Conceptual Problems in Estimating Water Quality Benefits Using Existing Studies,' *Water Resources Research*, **28**(3), 675–83.

Desvousges, W. H., F. Reed Johnson, S. P. Hudson, S. R. Gable and M.S. Ruby (1996), 'Using Conjoint Analysis and Health-State Classifications to Estimate the Value of Health Effects of Air Pollution,' Research Triangle Park, NC.

Dickie, Mark (1999), 'Willingness to Pay for Children's Health: A Household Production Approach,' paper presented at the EPA, ORD workshop, Valuing Health for Environmental Policy with Special Emphasis on Children's Health Issues, Silver Spring, MD, March.

Dickie, Mark and Shelby Gerking (1991a), 'Willingness to Pay for Ozone Control: Inferences from the Demand for Medical Care,' *Journal of Environmental Economics and Management*, **21**, 1–16.

Dickie, Mark and Shelby Gerking (1991b), 'Valuing Reduced Morbidity: A Household Production Function Approach,' *Southern Economic Journal*, **57**(3), 690–702.

Dickie, Mark and Shelby Gerking (1996), 'Genetic Risk Factors and Offsetting Behavior: The Case of Skin Cancer' University of Wyoming Discussion Paper, Laramie, WY.

Dickie, Mark, and Victoria Ulery (2001). 'Valuing Health in the Household: Are Kids Worth More than Parents?', paper presented at the Association of Environmental and Resource Economists 2001 Workshop: Assessing and Managing Environmental and Public Health Risks (June).

Dickie, M. et al. (1987), 'Reconciling Averting Behavior and Contingent Valuation Benefit Estimates of Reducing Symptoms of Ozone Exposure (draft),' in *Improving Accuracy and Reducing Costs of Environmental Benefit Assessments* (Washington, DC: US Environmental Protection Agency, February).

European Commission – DGXI Environment (1998), *Economic Evaluation of Air Quality Targets for Sulphur Dioxide, Nitrogen Dioxide, Fine and Suspended Particulates and Lead*, Final Report, Luxembourg: Office for Official Publications of the European Communities (ISBN 92–828–3063–2).

European Commission – DGXI Environment (1999), *Economic Evaluation of Air Quality Targets for Tropospheric Ozone: Part C: Economic Benefit Assessment*, Final Report, Luxembourg: Office for Official Publications of the European Communities (ISBN 92–828–7797–3).

ExternE (1996), 'Externalities of Energy,' prepared by ETSU, UK and Metroeconomica, Ltd, UK for European Commission, DG XII EUR 16521 EN.

ExternE (1999), 'Externalities of Energy, Volume 7: Methodology 1998 Update,' Brussels: European Commission.

Fisher, Ann., Lauraine G. Chestnut and Dan Violette (1989). 'The Value of Reducing Risks of Death: A Note on New Evidence,' *Journal of Policy Analysis and Management*, **8**(1), 88–100.

Freeman, A. Myrick, III (1993). *The Measurement of Environmental and Resource Values: Theory and Methods*, Washington, DC: Resources for the Future.

Gayer, Ted, James T. Hamilton and W. Kip Viscusi (2000), 'Private Values of Risk Tradeoffs at Superfund Sites: Housing Market Evidence on Learning About Risk,' *The Review of Economics and Statistics*, **82**(3), 439–51.

Gegax, Douglas, Shelby Gerking, and William Schulze (1988), 'Perceived Risk and the Marginal Value of Safety,' *The Review of Economics and Statistics*, **73**(40), 589–96.

Hagler Bailly Consulting, Inc. (1995), *The New York State Externalities Cost Study*, Dobbs Ferry, NY: Oceana Publications.

Hammitt, James K. and John D. Graham (1999), 'Willingness to Pay for Health Protection: Inadequate Sensitivity to Probability,' *Journal of Risk and Uncertainty*, **18**(1): 33–62.

Hammitt, James K. and Ying Zhou (2000), 'Economic Value of Reducing Health Risks by Improving Air Quality in China,' in *Proceedings of the Sino–U.S. Research Workshop on Economy, Energy and Environment*, Tsinghua University, Beijing, People's Republic of China (January).

Hammitt, James K., Jin-Tan Liu, and Jin-Long Liu (2000), 'Survival is a Luxury Good: The Increasing Value of a Statistical Life,' paper presented at the NBER Summer Institute Workshop on Public Policy and the Environment, Boston, MA, July.

Hanemann, Loomis and Barabara Kanninen (1991), 'Statistical Efficiency of Double-Bounded Dichotomous Choice Contingent Valuation,' *American Journal of Agricultural Economics*, **73**(4), 1255–63.

Harrington, Winston and Paul R. Portney (1987), 'Valuing the Benefits of Health and Safety Regulation,' *Journal of Urban Economics*, **22**, 101–12.

Harrington, Winston, Alan Krupnick, and Walter Spofford (1989), 'The Economic Losses of a Waterborne Disease Outbreak,' *Journal of Urban Economics*, **25**(1), 116–37.

Hartunian, Nelson S. et al. (1981), *The incidence and economic costs of major health impairments: a comparative analysis of cancer, motor vehicle injuries, coronary heart disease, and stroke*, Lexington, MA: Heath.

Health Canada (1997), *Health and Environmental Impact Assessment Panel Report*, Joint Industry/Government Study on Sulphur in Gasoline and Diesel Fuels, June.

Hoehn, J.P. and A. Randall (1987), 'A Satisfactory Benefit Cost Indicator from Contingent Valuation,' *Journal of Environmental Economics and Management*, **14**, 226–47.

Ippolito, P.M. and R.A. Ippolito (1984), 'Measuring the Value of Life Saving from Consumer Reaction to New Information,' *Journal of Public Economics*, **25**, 53–81.

Johannesson, Magnus and Per-Olov Johansson (1996), 'To Be, or Not to Be, That Is the Question: An Empirical Study of the WTP for an Increased Life Expectancy at an Advanced Age,' *Journal of Risk and Uncertainty*, **13**, 163–74.

Johannesson, Magnus, Per-Olov Johansson, and Richard M. O'Conor (1996), 'The Value of Private Safety versus the Value of Public Safety,' *Journal of Risk and Uncertainty*, **13**(3), 263–76.

Jones-Lee, M.W., M. Hammerton and P.R. Phillips (1985), 'The Value of Safety: Results of A National Sample Survey,' *The Economic Journal*, **95**, 49–72.

Johnson, F. Reed, Melissa R. Banzhaf and William H. Desvousges (2000), Willingness to Pay for Improved respiratory and Cardiovascular Health: A Multiple-Format, Stated Preference Approach,' unpublished paper, Triangle Economic Research, Inc. (June),

Krueger, Alan B. and Lawrence H. Summers (1988), 'Efficiency Wages and the Inter-Industry Wage Structure,' *Econometrica*, **56**(2), 259–93.

Krupnick, Alan J. and Maureen Cropper (1992), 'The Effect of Information on Health Risk Valuation,' *Journal of Risk and Uncertainty*, **5**, 29–48.

Krupnick, Alan, Winston Harrington and Bart Ostro (1990), 'Ambient Ozone and Acute Health Effects: Evidence from Daily Data,' *Journal of Environmental Economics and Management*, **18**, 1–18.

Krupnick, Alan J. et al. (1996), 'The Value of Health Benefits from Ambient Air Quality Improvements in Central and Eastern Europe: An Exercise in Benefit Transfer,' *Environmental and Resource Economics*, **7**(4), 307–32.

Krupnick, Alan, Anna Alberini, Maureen Cropper, Nathalie Simon, Bernie O'Brien, Ronald Goeree and Martin Heintzelman (forthcoming), 'What Are Older People Willing to Pay to Reduce Their Risk of Dying?' *Journal of Risk and Uncertainty*.

Larson, B.A. et al. (1999), 'The Economics of Air Pollution Health Risks in Volgograd,' *World Development*, **27**(10), 1803–19.

Lee, et al. (1995), *The External Costs and Benefits of Fuel Cycles*, Study by the US Department of Energy and the Commission of the European Communities, prepared by Oak Ridge National Laboratory and Resources for the Future, McGraw-Hill, Utility Data Institute, New Jersey, December.

Leigh, J. Paul (1995), 'Compensating Wages, Value of a Statistical Life, and Inter-Industry Differentials,' *Journal of Environmental Economics and Management*, **28**(1), 83–97.

Loehman, Edna and Vo Hu De (1982), 'Application of Stochastic Choice Modeling to Policy Analysis of Public Goods: A Case Study of Air Quality Improvements,' *The Review of Economics and Statistics*, **LXIV**(3), 474–80.

Loehman, E.T., S.V. Berg, A.A. Arroyo, R.A. Hedinger, J.M. Schwartz, M.E. Shaw, W. Fahien, V.H. De, R.P. Fishe, D.E. Rio, W.F. Rossley and A.E.S. Green (1979), 'Distributional Analysis of Regional Benefits and Costs of Air Quality Control,' *Journal of Environmental Economics and Management*, **6**, 222–43.

Markandya, Anil (1998), 'The Indirect Costs and Benefits of Greenhouse Gas Limitation. Economics of GHG Limitations,' Handbook Series, UNEP Collaborating Centre on Energy and Environment, Risø National Laboratory Denmark.

McConnell, Kenneth E. and Marcia A. Rosado (2000), 'Valuing Discrete Improvements in Drinking Water Quality Through Revealed Preferences,' *Water Resources Research* **36**(6), 1575–82.

Miller, Ted R. and J. Guria (1991), *The Value of Statistical Life in New Zealand*, Wellington, NZ, Land Transport Division, New Zealand Ministry of Transport.

Moore, Michael J. and W. Kip Vicusi (1988), 'The Quantity-Adjusted Value of Life,' *Economic Inquiry*, **26**, 369–88.

Mrozek, Janusz R. and Laura O. Taylor (forthcoming), 'What Determines the Value of a Life? A Meta-Analysis,' *Journal of Policy Analysis and Management*.

Navrud, Stale (1997), 'Valuing Health Impacts From Air Pollution in Europe: New Empirical Evidence on Morbidity,' Discussion paper D-15/97, Department of Economics and Social Sciences, Agricultural University of Norway.

OMB Memo to US EPA, RE: 812 Report Comments (Sept. 1999).

Oster, Gerry (1984), *The economic costs of smoking and benefits of quitting*, Lexington, MA: Lexington Books.

Ostro, Bart J., Gunnar Eskeland et al. (1996a), 'Air Pollution and Health Effects: A Study of Medical Visits Among Children in Santiago, Chile,' *Environmental Health Perspectives*, **107**, 69–73.

Ostro, Bart J., J.M. Sanchez et al. (1996b), 'Air Pollution and Mortality: Results from Santiago, Chile,' *Journal of Exposure Analysis and Environmental Epidemiology*, **6**, 97–114.

Pearce, David (1996), 'Economic Valuation and Health Damage from Air Pollution in the Developing World,' *Energy Policy*, **24**(7), 627–30.

Pope, C., M.J. Arden, M.M. Thun, D.D. Namboodiri, J.S. Dockery, F.E. Evans, Speizer and C.W. Health, Jr (1995). 'Particulate Air Pollution as a Predictor of Mortality in a Prospective Study of U.S. Adults,' *American Journal of Respiratory Critical Care Medicine*, **151**, 669–74.

Portney, Paul R. (1981), 'Housing Prices, Health Effects, and Valuing Reductions in the Risk of Death,' *Journal of Environmental Economics and Management*, **8**(1), 72–8.

RCG/Hagler Bailly (1995), *New York Environmental Externalities Cost Study*, Report prepared for ESSERCO, EP 91–50.

Ready, Richard et al. (1999), 'Benefit Transfer in Europe: Are Values Consistent Across Countries?', paper presented at the Environmental Valuation in Europe EU Workshop on Benefit Transfer, Lillehammer, Norway, October.

Ready, Richard et al. (2000), 'Contingent Valuation of Ill-health Caused by Pollution: Testing for Context and Ordering Effects,' under review for the *Journal of Health Economics*.

Rowe, Robert D. and Lauraine G. Chestnut (1985), 'Valuing Changes in Morbidity: WTP versus COI Measures,' Energy and Resource Consultants, Inc., Boulder, CO.

Rowe, R.D., L.G. Chestnut, D.C. Peterson and C. Miller (1986), *The Benefits of Air Pollution Control in California*, Prepared for the California Air Resources Board by Energy and Resource Consultants, Inc., Boulder, CO. Contract No. A2–118–32.

Sanchez, R.A. (1996), 'Health and Environmental Risks of the Maquiladora in Mexicali,' *Natural Resources Journal*, **30**(1), 163–86.

Schulze, W., L. Chestnut, T. Mount, W. Weng and H. Kim (1999), 'Valuing Reduced Risk for Households with Children or Retirement,' paper presented at EPA, ORD workshop, Valuing Health for Environmental Policy with Special Emphasis on Children's Health Issues, Silver Spring, MD, March.

Schwartz, Joel (1997), 'Health Effects of Air Pollution From Traffic: Ozone and Particulate Matter', in *Health at the Crossroads: Transport Policy and Urban Health*, T. Fletcher and A.J. McMichael (eds), New York: John Wiley & Sons.

Shepherd, D.S. and R.J. Zeckhauser (1982), 'Life-cycle Consumption and Willingness to Pay for Increased Survival,' in M.W. Jones-Lee (ed.), *The Value of Life and Safety*, Amsterdam: North-Holland.

Shogren, Jason F. and Tommy Stamland (2000), 'Skill and the Value of Life,' unpublished paper, Department of Economics and Finance, University of Wyoming, Laramie (January).

Simon, Nathalie B., Maureen L. Cropper, Anna Alberini and Seema Arora (1999), 'Valuing Mortality Reduction in India: A Study of Compensating Wage Differentials,' draft paper, The World Bank, Washington, DC.

Smith, V. Kerry and William Desvousges (1987), 'An Empirical Analysis of the Economic Value of Risk Change,' *Journal of Political Economy*, **95**(1), 89–113.

Smith, V. Kerry, Hyun Kim and Donald H. Taylor, Jr (2001), 'Do the "Near" Elderly Value Mortality Risks Differently?', unpublished paper, CEnREP, Department of Agricultural and Resource Economics, North Carolina State University (June).

Stratus Consulting, Inc. (1999), 'Air Quality Valuation Model Documentation,' prepared for Health Canada, Boulder, CO.

Thurston, George. D., K. Ito, Morton Lippmann and David V. Bates (1994), 'Respiratory hospital admissions and summertime haze air pollution in Toronto, Ontario: Consideration of the role of acid aerosols,' *Environmental Research* **65**, 271–90.

Tolley, George (1999), 'Contingent Valuation and Children's Health,' paper presented at EPA, ORD workshop, Valuing Health for Environmental Policy with Special Emphasis on Children's Health Issues, Silver Spring, MD, March.

Tolley, George et al. (1986), *Valuation of Reductions in Human Health Symptoms and Risks*, Final Report for the US Environmental Protection Agency, Grant #CR-811053–01–0, University of Chicago, January.

Tolley, George, Donald Kenkel and Robert Fabian (eds), (1994), *Valuing Health for Policy: An Economic Approach*, Chicago, IL: University of Chicago Press.

US Environmental Protection Agency (1985), *Costs and Benefits of Reducing Lead in Gasoline*, Office of Policy Analysis, Washington, D.C. EPA-230–05–85–006.

US Environmental Protection Agency (1998), *Regulatory Impact Analysis for Ozone and Particulate National Ambient Air Quality Standards*, Washington, DC.

US Environmental Protection Agency (1999), *The Benefits and Costs of the Clean Air Act Amendments of 1990–2010. Report to the U.S. Congress*, Washington, DC, November.

US Environmental Protection Agency (2000), 'Valuing Fatal Cancer Risk Reductions', Scientific Advisory Board Draft, Washington, DC, March.

Viscusi, W. Kip (1993), 'The Value of Risks to Life and Health,' *Journal of Economic Literature*, **XXXI**, 1912–46.

Viscusi, W. Kip, Wesley Magat and Joel Huber (1991), 'Pricing Environmental Health Risks: A Survey Assessment of Risk–Risk and Risk–Dollar Trade-offs for Chronic Bronchitis,' *Journal of Environmental Economics and Management*, **21**, 32–51.

Wang, Hua and Dale Whittington (undated), 'Willingness to Pay for Air Quality Improvement in Sofia, Bulgaria,' draft paper, The World Bank, Washington, DC.

Whittington, Dale (1998), 'Administering Contingent Valuation Surveys in Developing Countries,' *World Development*, **26** (1), 21–30.

Whittington, D., A. Okarafor, A. Okore and A. McPhail (1990), 'Strategy for Cost Recovery in the Rural District Sector: A Case Study of Nsukka District, Anambra State, Nigeria,' *Water Resources Research*, **26**(9), 1899–913.

Zaim, K.K. (1997), 'Estimation of health and economic benefits of air pollution abatement for Turkey in 1990 and 1993,' *Energy Policy*, **25**(13), 1093–7.

6. The economics of carbon sequestration in agricultural soils

John M. Antle and Bruce A. McCarl

1. INTRODUCTION

Science has established conclusively that concentrations of greenhouse gases (GHGs) in the earth's atmosphere have been rising rapidly since the Industrial Revolution (for example, see IPCC, 1996). While these increasing concentrations are associated primarily with fossil fuel consumption, a significant share (estimated in the range of 12 to 42 percent) is believed to be caused by changes in land use, including deforestation and the expansion of agriculture (Watson et al., 2000, p. 5). While the consequences of increasing atmospheric GHG concentrations remains the subject of intensive scientific study and debate (see the US National Assessment US Global Change Research Program, 2000 and IPPC, 1996, 2001 for current literature reviews), there is growing national and international momentum to implement policies to reduce GHG emissions. The most obvious – but not necessarily least costly – way to do that is to reduce fossil fuel consumption. However, GHGs can also be removed from the atmosphere by reversing some of the processes associated with land use changes.

International negotiations to reduce and offset emissions are being led by the United Nations Framework Convention on Climate Change (UNFCCC). The first quantitative goals for GHG emission reductions were set in the Kyoto Protocol (KP) of the UNFCCC (1998), where it was agreed that the industrialized countries would reduce emissions 6 to 8 percent below 1990 levels by the period 2008–12. The KP recognized carbon (C) sequestration as a means by which countries could offset emissions of GHGs. The USA insisted that GHG emissions trading be included in the KP mechanisms to reduce GHG emissions, based on the successful SO_2 emissions trading system developed in the USA (Joskow et al., 1998). However, in the KP it was recognized that technical details needed to be resolved before C sequestration could provide measurable, verifiable offsets. In addition to these international activities, individual countries and non-governmental organizations have undertaken policies and programs to manage emissions, some of which encourage C sequestration. Some firms in GHG-emitting industries such as electricity generation have begun to enter into contracts for afforestation and soil C sequestration even before they are required to meet GHG emission standards, presumably in anticipation of such standards (CAST, 2000). Agriculturalists in some countries, notably in Canada and the USA, have entered into contracts to adopt management practices that would increase soil C, and at least 20 bills related to C sequestration were introduced for consideration by the US Congress in 2001. Yet ratification of the Kyoto Protocol by the USA has always been in doubt, and is even more so with the position against the Protocol taken by the Bush Administration in early 2001. However, the administration ran on a platform that declared carbon dioxide (CO_2) to be a pollutant, and the fossil fuel and electric utility industries continue to express support for reducing emissions through sequestration. Sequestration is thus a topic of considerable current and future interest.

Scientists estimate that about 80 percent of global C is stored in soils (Watson et al., 2000, p. 4), and that a substantial proportion of C that was originally in soils has been released due to human land use, implying that there is a large technical potential to sequester C in soils (Lal et al., 1998). However, it is less clear what the economic potential is for increasing soil C. Important questions need to be addressed: what economic incentives would be required to induce farmers to undertake the necessary actions to increase soil C? Could C be sequestered in soil at a cost that would be competitive with other sources of GHG emissions reductions?

The goal of this chapter is to survey the emerging economics literature that is beginning to answer these questions. We begin with a brief review of the literature on agriculture and GHG emissions, including the technical feasibility to sequester C in agricultural soils, a topic that has received considerable attention in the recent literature related to climate change mitigation. The following sections address various issues related to assessing the economic feasibility and competitiveness of soil C sequestration, including: the on-farm economics of the adoption of practices that increase soil C; the design of incentive mechanisms and contracts for soil C sequestration; the issue of soil C sequestration in developing countries as a mechanism to fund sustainable agricultural development; recent empirical evidence on the cost of sequestering C in agricultural soils; and a comparison to the costs of competing sinks such as industrial emissions reductions and afforestation.

2. GHG MITIGATION AND AGRICULTURAL SOIL C

Agriculture and forests are mentioned as both emitters of GHGs and as a sink for GHGs in the KP. Annex A of the KP lists agriculture as an emission source in terms of enteric fermentation, manure management, rice cultivation, soil management, field burning and deforestation. The KP also lists agriculturally related sinks of afforestation and reforestation. Additional sources and sinks are under consideration, including agricultural soil C, and were important topics of discussion at the November 2000 Conference of the Parties in The Hague. McCarl and Schneider (1999, 2000) provide surveys of the ways agriculture may participate in or be influenced by greenhouse gas mitigation efforts. Here we briefly review the principal interactions between agriculture and climate change mitigation.

First, agriculture is a significant emitter of GHGs, particularly methane, nitrous oxide, and CO_2. Thus policies designed to reduce emissions may be targeted at these agricultural sources. The IPCC (1996) estimates that globally, agriculture emits about 50 percent of total methane, 70 percent of nitrous oxide, and 20 percent of CO_2. Sources of methane emissions include rice, ruminants and manure. Nitrous oxide emissions come from manure, legumes and fertilizer use. CO_2 emissions arise from fossil fuel usage, soil tillage, deforestation, biomass burning and land degradation. Contributions across countries vary substantially, with the greatest differences between developing and developed countries. Deforestation and land degradation mainly occur in developing countries. Agriculture in developed countries uses more energy, more intensive tillage systems, more fertilizer, resulting in fossil-fuel-based emissions, reductions in soil C and emissions of nitrous oxides. In addition, animal herds emit methane from ruminants and manure (IPCC, 1996; McCarl and Schneider, 1999, 2000).

Second, agriculture may enhance its absorption of GHGs by creating or expanding sinks. This may be achieved through a variety of changes in land use and management practices. The Kyoto Protocol allows credits for emission sinks through afforestation and reforestation. Until recently most studies of C sequestration focused on the conversion of cropland to forest land (Adams et al., 1993; Parks and Hardie, 1995; Platinga et al., 1999; Stavins, 1999). In these studies producers are assumed to convert land to trees if they are compensated for the agricultural rents of the land, where the rents reflect regional or county-level estimates of net returns to agricultural land. The costs of C sequestration are based on converting the forested land to C storage units using a representative time path of C sequestration for a given forest management regime. The KP also allows for consideration of additional sources and sinks for C, including agricultural soils, the focus of this review.

Third, agriculture may provide products that substitute for GHG-emission-intensive products, thus displacing emissions. Agriculture may provide substitute products that replace fossil-fuel-intensive products. One such product is biomass for fuel usage or production. Biomass can be used directly in fuelling electrical power plants or may be processed into liquid fuels. Burning biomass reduces net CO_2 emissions because the photosynthetic process of biomass growth removes about 95 percent of CO_2 emitted when burning the biomass. Fossil fuel use, on the other hand, releases 100 percent of the CO_2 in it. Substitute building products can be drawn from forestry, reducing fossil-fuel-intensive use of steel and concrete (Marland and Schlamadinger, 1997).

Finally, agriculture may find itself operating in a world where commodity and input prices have been altered by GHG emission policies. The need to reduce emissions and the implementation of emissions trading will likely affect fossil fuel prices. For example, diesel fuel distributors might need to purchase an emissions permit, effectively raising fuel prices. Similarly the USA might implement a fuel tax. The tax and corresponding transportation cost increases might influence the cost of petrol-based agricultural chemicals and fertilizers as well as on-farm fuel prices and off-farm commodity prices (McCarl et al., 1999; USDA, 1999; Antle et al., 1999; Konyar and Howitt, 2000).

2.1 Technical Feasibility of Sequestering C in Agricultural Soils

When undisturbed soil is put into cultivation, the associated biological and physical processes result in a release of 20 to 50 percent of the soil C over a period of about 50 years, with the amount varying by soil type, agricultural practices and other site-specific conditions (Tiessen et al., 1982; Mann, 1986; Rasmussen and Parton, 1994). Therefore in most cultivated soils there is a potential to rebuild the soil C stock up to the level that existed before the land was used for agricultural purposes. Some scientists believe that with improved management, the stock of soil C could be brought to a higher level than existed before the soil was first disturbed by agriculture.

Increases in soil C can be achieved through the adoption of various land use and management practices (Lal et al., 1998; CAST, 1992). Management practices that can increase soil C sequestration include land retirement (conversion to native vegetation or reversion to wetlands), afforestation, residue management, less intensive tillage, changes in crop rotations, conversion of cropland to pasture and restoration of degraded (that is, highly eroded) soils. Lal et al. (1998) estimate that 49 percent of agricultural C sequestration can be achieved by adopting conservation tillage and residue management, 25 percent by changing cropping practices, 13 percent by land restoration efforts, 7 percent through land use change and 6 percent by better water management.

It is important to note that practices to enhance soil C storage can change agricultural productivity. Soil scientists argue that improved soil management improves soil quality and ultimately increases crop yields in many cases (Lal et al., 1998). However, such changes are not without their costs, and as we shall discuss further below, farmers face an opportunity cost associated with changing to practices that increase soil C. The literature also acknowledges that these practices may, under some conditions, actually reduce agricultural productivity or the size of the agricultural cropland base (IPCC, 1996, 2000; Marland et al., 1998; McCarl and Schneider, 1999, 2000).

While some changes in land use and management practices can increase the stock of C in the soil, they can only do so up to a new equilibrium state that depends on management and the biophysical conditions of the site. As the soil C level increases, the rate of soil absorption of C eventually decreases, and the soil's potential to become a future emission source increases because subsequent alteration of the management regime (for example, reversion to conventional tillage after the use of reduced tillage) can lead to a release of C. This latter point is an important one that we will discuss below in the context of what has become known as the permanence issue in the international debate over inclusion of soil C as an allowable sink under the Kyoto Protocol.

As with the process of disinvestment, the rate at which the soil C stock can be rebuilt will be a function of various site-specific biophysical conditions, as well as the types of land use and management practices that are followed. For most changes in agricultural practices, soil scientists estimate that the equilibrium level of soil C will be achieved after a period of 20–30 years following the change in practices. West et al. (2000) reviewing over 30 experiments show this occurs after approximately 20 years. Thus, on a land unit where the ith practice has been followed for a long period of time, the stock of soil C reaches an equilibrium level C^i. If the sth practice is then adopted and followed continuously thereafter, the time path of soil C typically follows a logistic path, eventually reaching a new equilibrium level C^s (Figure 6.1). This time path can be approximated with the annual average rate of soil C increase $\Delta c^{is} \equiv (C^i - C^s)/N$. However, it must be emphasized that these rates are an approximation to the generally nonlinear path of soil C accumulation or decumulation, and it also must be emphasized that actual rates vary spatially as a function of biophysical conditions (soil type, depth, climate), land use history and the current practices that are followed, a key point discussed further below.

Due to the long periods of time over which soil C stocks change, it is relatively difficult to measure such changes directly in the soil, although such methods do exist and have been applied at long-term study sites (Watson et al., 2000). Therefore, in order to estimate such changes over a wide range of locations, it is more practical to use models to estimate potential changes in soil C. With available data on site-specific soil and climate conditions, land use history, and other relevant parameters, the changes in the stocks of soil C can be simulated over the long periods of time using biophysical process models (Parton et al., 1994; Paustian et al., 1996).

The spatial variability exhibited by resource endowments and climate means that a single land use or management practice will not be effective at sequestering C in all regions and thus different management practices will be efficient

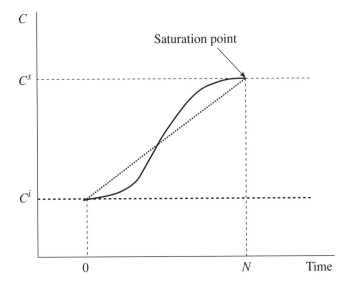

Figure 6.1   Time path and saturation point for soil C in response to a change in land use or management practices

Table 6.1   Annual increase in soil C from management changes: Iowa and Montana

Change in management	Additional carbon[a] (tonnes/ha/yr)
Iowa – change in tillage practice	
Intensive tillage to moderate tillage	0.19
Intensive tillage to no-till	0.52
Montana – change in cropping system	
Spring wheat fallow to continuous spring wheat	0.38
Spring wheat fallow to continuous winter wheat	0.44
Permanent grass to continuous spring wheat	0.06
Permanent grass to continuous winter wheat	0.13

[a]   Estimates were calculated using Century (Parton et al., 1987; Paustian et al., 1992, 1996) and provided by the Natural Resource Ecology Laboratory, Colorado State University.

Source: Antle et al. (2001c).

Table 6.2   Rates of potential carbon gain under selected practices for cropland (including riceland) in various regions of the world

Practice	Country/ region	Rate of carbon gain	Time[a] (yr)	Other GHGs and Impacts
Improved crop production				
and erosion control	Global	0.05–0.76	25	+N$_2$O
Partial elimination of	Canada	0.17–0.76	15–25	
bare fallow	USA	0.25–0.37	8	±N$_2$O
Irrigation water management	USA	0.1–0.3		
Fertilization, crop rotation, organic amendments	USA	0.1–0.3		+N$_2$O
Yield enhancement, reduced bare fallow	Tropical and subtropical China	0.02	10	
Amendments (biosolids, manure, or straw)	Europe	0.2–1.0	50–100	
Forages in rotation	Norway	0.3	37	
Ley-arable farming	Europe	0.54	100	
Conservation tillage	Global	0.1–1.3	25	±N$_2$O
	UK	0.15	5–10	
	Australia	0.3	10–13	
	USA	0.3	6–20	
		0.24–0.4		
	Canada	0.2	8–12	
	USA and Canada	0.2–0.4	20	
	Europe	0.34	50–100	
	Southern USA	0.5	10	
		0.2	10–15	
Riceland management				
Organic amendments (straw, manure)		0.25–0.5		++CH$_4$
Chemical amendments				–CH$_4$, +N$_2$O
Irrigation-based strategies				–CH$_4$

[a]   Time interval to which estimated rate applies. This interval may or may not be time required for ecosystem to reach new equilibrium.

Source: Watson et al. (2000), Table 4–5.

in different areas. For example, in the intensively cropped cornbelt states, soil C can be increased by reducing tillage intensity. In the Great Plains a large amount of cropland is in a crop–fallow rotation, and soil C can be increased under those conditions by increasing cropping intensity (that is, reducing the frequency of fallow) as well as by reducing tillage. Conversion of cropland to permanent trees or pasture can also increase soil C.

To illustrate, Table 6.1 presents estimates of the biophysical potential to increase soil C with changes in tillage practices in Iowa and with increased cropping intensity in Montana. A change from conventional tillage to no-till can sequester an additional 0.52 tonnes C per hectare per year in Iowa, compared to the estimated potential in Montana from changing from fallow to continuous cropping of 0.44 tonnes C per hectare per year.[1] The 1997 Census of Agriculture reports 11 million hectares of cropland in Iowa and 7 million hectares of cropland in Montana. The data in Table 6.1 indicate that if Iowa and Montana producers were to change their practices this could result in about 9 million tonnes or about 1.5 percent of the US Kyoto accord commitments. Using a nationwide estimate of about 120 million hectares at a rate of 0.5 tonnes per hectare per year would offset about 10 per cent of the US commitment to Kyoto.

Table 6.2 presents a wide range of estimates of rates of potential C gain for a variety of practices derived from a number of studies around the world. One can see that the rates in Table 6.1 are within the bounds of Table 6.2. Table 6.2 also indicates the time period over which these rates are applicable. Note that in most cases the periods range from 5 to 30 years, depending on the type of practice.

The spatial variability evidenced by the data in Tables 6.1 and 6.2 has important implications for the design of contracts for soil C sequestration, and for issues such as the monitoring of compliance with contracts. These are topics that we shall address in detail later in this chapter.

3.   ECONOMIC FEASIBILITY AND COMPETITIVENESS OF SEQUESTERING C IN SOIL

Soil scientists suggest that the most suitable land for C sequestration is where the potential gain in C is highest (for example, Lal et al., 1998). However, the potential C gain estimates for soils (as in Tables 6.1 and 6.2) indicate only the technical potential to increase the stock of C in agricultural soils. These data do not provide the basis to determine at what cost agricultural producers are willing to adopt practices that increase soil C. In the following section we show that the economic feasibility and competitiveness of soil C sequestration depend on the opportunity cost per tonne of C, that is, the opportunity cost per hectare of changing land use or management practices, divided by the rate of soil C accumulation.

We know from various data that there is great spatial variability in the productivity of agricultural land, and thus in the opportunity cost associated with changing land use and management practices. One measure of this economic variability is provided by the different rates at which farmers voluntarily bid to remove land from crop production and place it in conserving uses in the Conservation Reserve Program (CRP) in the USA. These data show that the highly productive cropland in Iowa is bid into the CRP for about $36 per hectare, whereas the lower productivity land in Montana is bid in for about $14 per hectare (USDA, 2000). Thus even though the technical potential to sequester C in soil is higher in Iowa than in Montana, it does not follow that soil C can be sequestered at a lower cost per tonne of C. We show below that indeed the opportunity cost per tonne in Montana is lower than in Iowa for some levels of C sequestration.

3.1   Economic Analysis of Agricultural Soil C Sequestration at Farm and Regional Scales

The atmosphere is a public good – everyone benefits from it without having to 'pay' for it. This fact means that private individuals and firms, and even individual countries, have little incentive to take actions to prevent the accumulation of GHGs in the atmosphere. Therefore the demand for individuals to reduce emissions must derive primarily from collective action, that is, from government policy. As of this writing, the Kyoto Protocol has not been ratified by the USA or enough other countries to put it into force. Any perceived incentive to sequester carbon therefore must be based on private entities' anticipation of future policies requiring reductions in GHG emissions.

Two provisions of the Kyoto Protocol illustrate policies that may be implemented by individual governments or through international agreements. One provision is the clean development mechanism (CDM), an institution that would channel funds from industrialized countries to pay for investments in cleaner production technologies in developing countries. The other likely future institution is a carbon trading system modeled after the sulfur dioxide emissions trading system now in operation in the USA (Joskow et al., 1998). A carbon emissions trading system would be used by a country like the USA to meet a *net* emissions target established through its own policies or through an international agreement. This net emissions target could be met either by emissions reductions or by increasing the use of sinks such as forests and cropland. Thus, in contrast to a 'cap-and-trade' system in which the total emissions are fixed, under a system that includes sinks *gross* emissions would not be fixed, and could in fact increase as long as the size of sinks was sufficient to offset emissions increases. The inclusion of sinks in the Kyoto Protocol was controversial because some countries argued that it would allow the USA and other countries with large sink potentials to avoid reducing overall emissions.

In addition to market-based mechanisms, GHG emissions could also be reduced through direct government interventions. There are many examples of government policies designed to reduce environmental impacts of human activity. In the USA, for example, the Conservation Reserve Program provides payments to farmers who take actions that reduce soil erosion. In a similar way policies could be designed to sequester soil C.

Private entities may also be motivated to take individual or collective actions to mitigate GHG emissions. Interest groups may organize concerned individuals to raise funds to purchase C credits, or to enter directly into contracts with individuals or groups to sequester C. Business firms wanting to demonstrate environmental concern also may be motivated to buy C, whether or not their emissions are constrained by government policy. Business firms also may buy C contracts in anticipation of emissions standards or to pre-empt the possibility of emission standards being imposed. This type of behavior may explain recent transactions involving C even though most countries do not have policies requiring firms to reduce GHG emissions (CAST, 2000).

From an economic perspective, soil C provides value in three dimensions, first as an essential component of soil that affects agricultural productivity, second as a way to offset CO_2 emissions from other sources, and third as an indirect source of benefits involving improved environmental quality. The first component of soil C's value is a private benefit to the farmer, hence a farmer who understands the productive value of soil C will make management decisions to optimize the soil C stock. Soil C is not detectable visually, and at least some soil scientists argue that many farmers do not understand the role of soil C in production or how to manage it, and thus tend to use practices that result in a smaller-than-optimal soil C stock in terms of private benefits. The second and third dimensions of soil C involve external benefits; hence farmers will not optimally manage soil C from a social point of view – and can be expected to maintain a smaller stock than socially optimal – unless some mechanism exists to induce farmers to equate the marginal social benefit with the marginal social cost.

Our goal is to assess the role that economic incentives play in inducing farmers to adopt practices that would increase the amount of C in the soil. To analyze soil C from an economic perspective, we shall assume that agricultural producers are economically rational and thus utilize those land and management practices that they believe yield the highest economic returns (the analysis can be generalized to account for risk, and other non-economic objectives). Thus economically motivated producers will adopt alternative practices that increase soil C if and only if there is a perceived economic incentive to do so, but we do not assume farmers are necessarily managing the stock of soil C optimally from either a private or a public perspective. If indeed farmers are underinvesting in the stock of soil C from either a private or public perspective, then a policy that provides additional incentive to increase the stock of soil C should move them towards a more efficient resource allocation.

3.2   Incentives and Contract Design

Farmers could be given economic incentives to sequester C in soil through direct government payments or private markets. Direct government programs would include efforts such as the Conservation Reserve Program or other government conservation programs where the government pays farmers to provide environmental services or reduce off-site damages. Alternatively, private markets would arise if the government imposed GHG emissions standards on industry and permitted trading of emissions credits from farmers. In either case, contracts between buyers (emitters) and sellers (farmers) would specify the payment mechanism and other terms for either a government program to sequester soil C or for sales in a market for C credits. Following Antle et al. (2001b), there are two classes of costs associated with implementing contracts for the provision of an environmental amenity through changes in agricultural practices – farm opportunity costs and contract costs. The first is the opportunity costs of resources expended on the farm to produce the amenity; the second is the costs associated with implementing contracts and involves brokerage fees, and monitoring of compliance with the C accumulation or practice execution terms of the contract, as well as other transactions costs.

For the purposes of this discussion we assume that contracts for soil C are designed and implemented using an approach that is similar to existing conservation programs (below we discuss whether this is an efficient way to design contracts). Antle et al. (2001b) describe two ways in which these incentive payments could be made. The first type of incentive gives producers a fixed payment per hectare of land switched from a cropping system with a relatively low equilibrium level of soil C to a system that produces a higher equilibrium level of soil C. This per-hectare payment mechanism is similar to existing programs such as the CRP that provide payments on an area basis to producers who adopt land use or management practices designed to reduce environmental damages or enhance environmental quality. As with the CRP, the per-hectare payments could vary by region, although what criteria would be used for this is less clear than in the CRP case, where farmers' bids are used to establish payment levels. The second policy is a per-tonne payment mechanism that pays farmers for each tonne of C sequestered when they change land use or management practices. We assume that C rates are established through a combination of field measurements and modeling. For example, agroecozones (areas with relatively homogeneous soils and climate) could be used as the basis for designing a statistically based sampling strategy for field measurements to establish soil C levels, and models of soil C dynamics could be coupled with those measurements to estimate soil C rates for each combination of land use and management practice. These estimated soil rates could be verified by periodic field measurements.

Per-hectare contracts would specify management practices that the farmer agrees to follow, and the farmer would receive this payment regardless of the amount of C that is sequestered on the contracted land unit as long as the specified practices are followed. A per-tonne contract would be based on the agreed price per tonne of C and the established annual C rate for that agroeco-zone and the practices the farmer uses. Both types of contracts would involve similar conventional transaction costs for contract negotiation, legal fees and so on. The per-hectare contract would require monitoring to ensure that the farmer follows the practices specified in the contract, whereas the per-tonne contract would require establishing the soil C rates for each type of contract and monitoring C accumulation. Thus assuming that the costs of monitoring compliance with practices under the per-hectare contract are less than the costs of measuring and monitoring C under the per-tonne contract, the total contracting costs required to implement the per-hectare contracts would be lower than for the per-tonne contracts. If the per-hectare contracts were used to satisfy an international agreement such as the Kyoto Protocol or were traded in a carbon market, then some type of measurement and monitoring system would be needed, similar to what would be needed to implement the per-tonne contracts. Consider a contract for n periods that pays a farmer g^{is} dollars per time period for each hectare that is switched from system i to system s. We assume that farmers have static price expectations for future real expected returns under each practice. For the producer to switch management practices, the present value of system s must be greater than the present value of system i. Letting D be the present value of 1 at interest rate r for n periods, and letting π^i be the returns to the ith system, the present value of expected returns for the the ith system is $V^i = \pi^i D(r,n)$, and the present value of a payment of g^{is} dollars each year is $G^{is} = g^{is} D(r,n)$. Thus the producer will switch from system i to system s for n years if $V^i < V^s + G^{is}$, which implies $\pi^i < \pi^s + g^{is}$ or $(\pi^i - \pi^s) < g^{is}$ each period. Defining $h^{is} = \pi^i - \pi^s$ as the opportunity cost of changing from practice i to practice s, it follows that a producer will agree to switch practices if $h^{is} < g^{is}$, otherwise the producer will continue to use practice i.

Now consider a policy that offers producers a payment for each tonne of sequestered soil C. The farmer is offered a price, P ($ per tonne of C), so if the farmer switches from system i to system s and produces an additional Δc^{is} tonnes of C per hectare each period, the payment per hectare will be $P\Delta c^{is}$. Following the logic of the previous paragraph, the farmer will agree to switch from system i to system s if and only if $\pi^i < \pi^s + P\Delta c^{is}$ or if $(\pi^i - \pi^s)/\Delta c^{is} = h^{is}/\Delta c^{is} < P$, that is, if and only if the opportunity cost per tonne $h^{is}/\Delta c^{is}$ is less than or equal to the price per tonne.

As noted earlier, the rate of soil C change varies with time. Also price expectations may not be static. Under these conditions one cannot simplify the present-value expressions to expressions for payments per time period, but the opportunity cost per tonne per year remains a useful approximation.

3.3 Spatial Heterogeneity and the Marginal Cost of Soil C at the Field and Agroecozone Scales

Agricultural land is generally spatially heterogeneous with respect to physical, climatic and economic characteristics. This means that each agroecozone has distinct environmental and economic characteristics. To account for the physical and climatic heterogeneity we introduce a site-specific vector of environmental characteristics e_j, for $j = 1, \ldots, J$ land units in the region. To account for economic heterogeneity we index prices and capital services by land unit. Letting p be crop price, w input prices, and z fixed factors, the profit function for each land unit can now be represented as $\pi^i(p_j^i, w_j^i, e_j, z_j^i)$, indicating that profit varies spatially. The opportunity cost for switching the jth land unit from system i to system s is now $h_j^{is} = \pi^i(p_j^i, w_j^i, e_j, z_j^i) - \pi^s(p_j^s, w_j^s, e_j, z_j^s)$ and is also spatially variable. For input quantity x the equilibrium soil C per hectare is expressed as $C_j^i = C^i(x_j^i, e_j, z_j^i)$, and the average rate of C sequestration for a change from practice i to practice s over N years is $\Delta c_j^{is} = [C^i(x_j^i, e_j, z^i) - C^s(x_j^i, e_j, z^i)]/N$. Thus in a spatially heterogeneous region, the opportunity cost per tonne, $h_j^{is}/\Delta c_j^{is}$, varies across land units.

At the level of the individual land unit (the field), farmers make discrete land use decisions involving tillage system choices, land retirement choices and so on. Antle and Mooney (2002) provide a detailed analysis of these discrete land use decisions and how they are affected by spatial heterogeneity. They define the per-hectare and per-tonne switch prices as the marginal opportunity cost at which farmers enter into a contract to sequester soil C. In the case in which there is one alternative management practice, the marginal cost curve for C production is perfectly inelastic at a zero quantity for all payment levels or C prices below the switch price, and then is perfectly inelastic at the quantity of soil C produced on that land unit for all payments or C prices greater than the switch price. Antle et al. (2001a, 2001b) show that when individual land units are aggregated, the resultant regional marginal cost curve is upward sloping. This mapping can be constructed by ordering all land units according to their switch price or marginal opportunity cost, and then aggregating the quantity of soil C produced at each marginal opportunity cost.

Note that the total quantity of C sequestered is a stock accumulated over time. This raises the issue of how to compare C accumulated at different points in time to a marginal cost at a point in time. Some studies (for example, Stavins, 1999) discount the flows of C into a stock in the same manner that the financial flows were discounted in the discussion above. This type of procedure can be justified by assuming that P, the real value per tonne of C, is constant. Then the total value can be expressed as $V = \Sigma_t P \Delta c_t (1+r)^{-t} = P \Sigma_t \Delta c_t (1+r)^{-t} = P \cdot C$, so the term C can be interpreted as the aggregate discounted quantity. However, there is no reason to believe that the real value of C will be constant, calling the logic of this procedure into question. An alternative approach is to simply aggregate C changes undiscounted, recognizing that discounting (if deemed appropriate) would reduce the estimated C stock commensurately.

3.4 Spatial Heterogeneity and Policy Efficiency

The literature on design of environmental policies for agriculture has noted that, ignoring contracting costs and market imperfections, existing policies are inefficient in the sense that they pay farmers for the adoption of alternative practices rather than per unit of environmental benefit provided by the practices, and thus do not account for the spatial variability in benefits and costs associated with the adoption of improved management practices (see Babcock et al., 1996; Helfand and House, 1995; Fleming and Adams, 1997). Efficient incentive mechanisms would account for the spatial heterogeneity in the environmental benefits produced and the costs of providing these benefits. Explanations for the use of existing policies include: the cost of information required to implement site-specific policies; information asymmetries between government agencies and farm decision-makers; and political considerations (see Wu and Boggess, 1999). In an analysis of C sequestration in forests, Stavins (1999) suggests that a payment mechanism based on tonnes of C sequestered would be prohibitively expensive to implement. Pautsch et al. (2000) suggest that it is useful to investigate efficient sequestration mechanisms because they provide a lower bound on costs.

Antle et al. (2001b) show that for each quantity of C sequestered, the marginal opportunity cost of the per-hectare payment mechanism (MC_H) is greater than or equal to the marginal opportunity cost of the per-tonne mechanism (MC_T), that is, $MC_H \geq MC_T$, as illustrated in Figure 6.2, with equality holding at the saturation point C_S. In addition they show that the efficiency of the per-hectare payment mechanism relative to the per-tonne mechanism, (MC_T/MC_H), is a decreasing function of the spatial heterogeneity of the opportunity cost per tonne of C. This result derives from the fact that the opportunity cost per tonne is equal to the ratio of the opportunity cost divided by the C rate. When spatial heterogeneity is high, farmers with very low C rates can participate under a per-hectare payment contract, yielding a higher cost for each amount of C sequestered than with a per-tonne payment contract. In their analysis of the marginal cost of soil C sequestration in Montana, Antle et al. (2001b) find that a per-hectare payment scheme is as much as four times more costly than the per-tonne payment mechanism. They conclude that there could be high payoffs to implementing C contracts that account for spatial variability in biophysical and economic conditions.

3.5   Saturation, Permanence, Contract Duration and Price Equivalence

Soil science has established that there is an upper bound on the amount of soil C that can be stored in the soil (see Figure 6.1 and West et al., 2000). This saturation of the soil means that the time period over which soil C may be removed from the atmosphere through changes in agricultural land use and other management practices is limited. For this reason agricultural soil C has been described as providing a near-term method to offset GHG emissions while longer-term options are being developed (CAST, 2000).

A related issue is the permanence of C in the soil. Soils research has shown that sequestered C is volatile and it has been found that if practices sequestering soil C (such as reduced tillage) are discontinued the C stored in the soil can be released back into the atmosphere in a short period of time. One way to

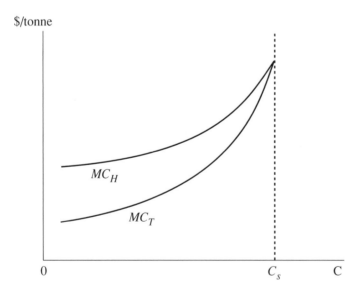

Figure 6.2   Marginal cost functions for per-hectare and per-tonne payments

address the permanence issue is to view farmers who enter into soil C contracts as providing a service in the form of accumulating and storing soil C. During the time period in which C is being accumulated, the farmer is providing both accumulation and storage services. Once the soil C level reaches the saturation point, the farmer is providing only storage services. However, the key point is that both accumulation and storage services depend on the farmer continuing to maintain the land use or management practices that make the accumulation possible. This means that if saturation is reached in N_S years but society wants to store the C for $N_D > N_S$ years, the duration of the contract will have to be for N_D years. Clearly if society wants to sequester soil C and this takes $N_S = 20$ years, but wants this C to remain in the soil for $N_D = 50$ years, farmers will have to be paid for 50 years. This implies a much higher cost than if farmers only have to be paid during accumulation. For example a payment of $1 per hectare over 20 years has a present value (at 5 percent interest) of about $12.50, whereas the present value of $1 for 50 years is about $18.30, roughly 50 per cent higher.

A similar result has been derived by McCarl and Murray (2001). They evaluate the price for C that renders the net present value of a stream of C-equivalent offsets equal to the costs incurred under a carbon project. They solve the following equation for the breakeven C price P:

$$\sum_{t=0}^{T}(1+r)^{-t}PE_t = \sum_{t=0}^{T}(1+r)^{-t}C_t$$

where r is the discount rate, T the number of years in the planning horizon, E_t the emissions offset generated by the prospective project in year t, and C_t the cost of operating the emissions offset project in year t including initial investment, operation and maintenance terms as they vary over project life. They compute the price discount for various scenarios, ranging from an emissions offset which costs one dollar per year generating one unit of C per year, to scenarios in which soil saturates in 20 years, at which time the practice may be reversed and the C volatilized. The analysis shows that the saturating/volatile soil C can be worth one-third to one-half of the value of an emissions offset for plausible values of the parameters.

Another way to approach the permanence issue in designing contracts is to impose a penalty for failure to comply with the terms of the contract, including penalties for subsequent release of the C after the contract expires. But this would increase the cost to the farmer of complying with the contract, farmers would demand greater compensation, so this contract provision would also have the effect of raising the cost of the contract.

Some have referred to soil C as a 'commodity' that farmers can produce and sell like conventional agricultural commodities (USDA et al., undated). The issues of saturation and permanence show that contracts between buyers and sellers of environmental services are different from contracts for conventional agricultural commodities. The buyer never actually takes delivery of the commodity; rather, the commodity is stored in the soil that belongs to the land owner. The discussion above shows it is more accurate to describe the farmer as providing a service for a specified period of time.

4.   OTHER GREENHOUSE GASES: GLOBAL WARMING POTENTIAL

As noted earlier, agriculture is both a sink for C as well as a major emitter of CO_2 and two other potent greenhouse gases, nitrous oxide and methane (McCarl and Schneider, 2000; Robertson et al., 2000). Ideally policies to mitigate GHG emissions would reward sinks and tax sources according to some index of their global warming potential (GWP). For example, scientists estimate the 100-year GWP for methane to be about 21 times more potent than a unit of CO_2, and nitrous oxide is estimated to be about 310 times more potent (IPCC, 1996). Indeed, compliance with the Kyoto Protocol was defined in terms of an index of GWP of six greenhouse gases (Tietenberg et al., 1998).

Both methane and nitrous oxide are also likely to be influenced by land use and other management practices. An efficient GHG policy would provide incentives according to GWP that accounted for the total mixture of emission and sequestration fluxes of GHG caused by a farmer's altered land use and management practices. To do so one could simply replace the C rate in the earlier analysis of farm opportunity cost with a measure of GWP and provide a positive payment for a reduction in GWP and impose a tax on actions that increase GWP. While this generalization is straightforward in principle, implementing it poses formidable measurement problems because methods and models to quantify nitrous oxide and methane emissions are not as well developed as those for C. Nevertheless, this does appear to be the direction that policy will move as the needed science and data are developed.

4.1   Co-benefits and Costs

Many of the potential soil-sequestering practices have been previously encouraged in US government programs designed to achieve environmental improvements and agricultural income support. Conservation titles involving reduced tillage have been included in recent agricultural farm bills in an effort directed toward achieving environmental improvement while at the same time supporting agricultural income. Water quality and soil erosion programs have also been undertaken to encourage practices which change tillage intensity and land use, retire fragile croplands to grass or trees, preserve or re-establish wetlands, improve wildlife habitats and provide chemical- and erosion-retaining stream buffers but which also increase soil C. Thus a number of the soil-sequestering practices can have positive co-benefits providing net GHG emission reductions along with farm income support and environmental quality improvements. Co-costs of practices that sequester soil C may also arise through increased pesticide use with reduced tillage.

The benefits of a number of these activities arise external to the farm producer who is employing them. This raises an important economic issue of inventorying and valuing benefits that accrue above and beyond net GHG reductions as well as the economic issue of determining how the incentive system might be designed to reflect the value of these other effects. An efficient policy designed to encourage beneficial agricultural practices would need to account not only for C sequestration but also for all other co-benefits and costs. Concepts such as an environmental benefits index have been developed for use with existing programs and could be generalized to include soil C sequestration or greenhouse warming potential (Feather et al., 1999).

5. CONTRACTING COSTS, INCENTIVE COMPATIBILITY, AND PROGRAM ELIGIBILITY

Above we noted that if a buyer were to enter into a contract to pay a farmer to use specified practices, the farmer's compliance with the terms of the contract would have to be monitored. When the practices are easily observable, for example changing from a crop–fallow rotation to continuous cropping, compliance can be monitored at relatively low cost, as shown by experience with the Conservation Reserve Program (the US Department of Agriculture has substantial human resources already monitoring compliance with other programs). Alternatively, changes in land use over large areas can be monitored at relatively low cost using remote sensing technology (CAST, 2000). However, if contracts specify other changes in management, such as tillage practices, and use of fertilizer and pesticides, the cost of monitoring compliance may be substantially higher.

The other component of contracting costs is measuring the quantity of soil C sequestered. A significant part of this measurement involves determining soil and climatic variables on a site-specific basis. Farmers know their management practices, and also typically have considerable knowledge of their soil quality and climatic conditions, but buyers of the contracts can only obtain that information at a cost, so there is an information asymmetry between sellers (farmers) and the buyers. One solution to the monitoring and measurement problems is to design contracts so that farmers voluntarily participate and have an incentive to follow the practices designed for their circumstances.

Wu and Babcock (1996) address this issue in a simple model in which use of an environmentally damaging input and an index of land quality determine environmental outcomes, and input use is a function of land quality. They show that farmers will self-select a suitable contract (one that is designed for their land quality) when environmentally damaging input use is non-decreasing in land quality, and when per-acre payments to reduce environmental damages are non-increasing in land quality. In the case of payments for soil C sequestration, the potential to sequester soil C is highest on degraded lands, hence there is the required inverse relationship between payments (either per hectare or per tonne) and land quality. However, note that farmers with high-quality (non-degraded) land are those farmers who are using the management practices that maintain soil C (for example reduced tillage), whereas farmers with low-quality land are those using practices that cause soil C to be lost (for example conventional tillage). This means that the first part of the Wu–Babcock incentive compatibility conditions is not likely to be satisfied in the case of soil C sequestration contracts. Farmers who have been using soil C-preserving practices such as reduced tillage before a soil C contract is offered will have an incentive to claim their land is degraded so that they can receive payments even though their soil may be already saturated so that its potential to sequester additional C may be limited or zero.

This incentive compatibility issue is closely related to the question of who would be eligible for payments under a government program to sequester soil C. A program that pays farmers to increase soil C on land that has been degraded can be viewed as penalizing those farmers who had adopted environmentally beneficial land use and management practices before the program began. Some observers have argued that programs with this type of design would create the perverse incentive for producers using reduced tillage to plow their land, release the C, and then enter the program. A solution in the case of a government program would be to provide payments to those who could document that they had changed practices previously and sequestered soil C. In the case of a private market for C that was driven by an international agreement requiring increases in soil C from a fixed baseline, credit for prior actions might not be acceptable. In that case, governments could prevent the perverse incentive problem by purchasing and holding credits from those farmers who had already adopted soil C-increasing practices.

Another way to look at the perverse incentive problem is suggested by the above discussion of incentive compatibility. Those farmers who adopted improved practices presumably did so because it was in their economic interest. Therefore, their land must exhibit the properties that violate the incentive compatibility conditions. By this logic, those producers should not receive payments for doing what they already had deemed to be in their economic self-interest. Some may counter this argument by claiming that producers are motivated by more than economic self-interest. That may well be true; it is then a public policy decision whether the taxpaying public should reward those individuals for their voluntary private acts that yield social benefits.

6.   INCENTIVES FOR ADOPTION OF SUSTAINABLE PRACTICES IN DEVELOPING COUNTRIES

Sustainable agricultural development is widely acknowledged as a critical component in a strategy to combat both poverty and environmental degradation. Yet sustainable agricultural development remains an elusive goal, particularly in many of the poorest regions of the world (World Bank, 2000). While there have been successes, more typically investments in soil conservation and other sustainable practices have been adopted as part of a development project, and then abandoned after the project is completed.

There are various possible explanations for the failed attempts to promote the long-term adoption of more sustainable land use and management practices. While more research is no doubt needed, this situation does not appear to be due to a lack of either research or development efforts, since in many cases technically feasible, appropriate sustainable practices are available.

The other principal explanations for the continuing trend towards land degradation are related to the lack of economic incentives to prevent degradation and encourage conservation. On-farm benefits from investments in soil conservation or other sustainable practices often accrue too far in the future to be valuable to farmers who strongly discount future benefits due to low and uncertain incomes and imperfect capital markets. These on-farm disincentives may be magnified by high transport costs and other market imperfections, adverse government policies, insecure property rights, limited availability of fodder for grazing or fuel for cooking and heating. In many cases the benefits from more sustainable management practices are external to the farm. We should not be surprised if poor farmers in the developing world, often existing at the margin of subsistence, are not willing to forgo some of their income to mitigate environmental problems they may not even realize exist or which will occur well beyond their planning horizon (Heerink et al., 2001).

As we noted earlier, an important provision of the Kyoto Protocol was the clean development mechanism (CDM), a process whereby the developing countries would be encouraged through subsidies from industrialized (Annex I) countries to adopt 'clean' development strategies that would emit lower rates of GHGs than they might otherwise.

These considerations have generated interest among the development community in the potential to use payments for soil C sequestration – either through a policy such as the CDM or through a C emissions credit market – as a mechanism to provide farmers in developing countries with the economic incentives needed to adopt more sustainable land use and management practices (Antle, 2000). Due to the fact that farmers in degraded environments are some of the world's poorest people, this type of mechanism could simultaneously contribute to the goals of alleviating rural poverty, enhancing agricultural sustainability and mitigating GHG emissions.

A number of the issues discussed above provide insight into the economic potential to use soil C sequestration as a mechanism to help fund sustainable agricultural development. First, we noted earlier that the buyer of a C contract never actually takes delivery of the commodity; rather, the commodity is embodied in an asset (the soil) that belongs to the land owner. The creation of C contracts with farmers in developing countries may be impeded by a number of property rights issues, including uncertain tenure and land ownership, and weak legal institutions that may limit enforceability of contracts, and widespread political and legal corruption. Second, we noted that the total cost of providing soil C services is equal to the farm opportunity cost plus contracting costs (measurement, monitoring and transactions costs). The contracting costs per tonne of C associated with negotiating contracts will decline with the size of contract, and a market for C credits is likely to operate for large, standardized contracts (for example, 100 000 tonnes). Considering that a typical farmer may be able to sequester 0.5 tonne per hectare per year, it follows that transactions costs per tonne will be high for individual small farms in developing countries. For small farms to enter into C contracts, some form of institution (such as a cooperative or marketing intermediary) will be needed to organize farmers into groups so as to lower transactions costs, or governments will need to subsidize contracting costs.

A significant component of the estimated global technical potential for C sequestration is severely degraded lands, especially in densely populated tropical regions. In some cases severe degradation is caused by mismanagement, but in many cases lands are degraded because of economic incentives to 'mine' soil fertility. In such cases the required level of investment both to alter management and cause actions to be undertaken to reverse the degradation or cause cessation of current degrading practices in favor of more sequestration-friendly practices is likely to be high. Time lags and lost productivity while the land is recovering are also likely to be substantial. Thus sequestering soil C on severely degraded lands is likely to be more costly than on more productive lands where more marginal, less expensive changes are required. There are likely to be additional benefits to land restoration, including food security and other environmental benefits (see the above discussion of co-benefits).

7.   ESTIMATING THE ECONOMIC FEASIBILITY OF SOIL C SEQUESTRATION IN AGRICULTURE

We now survey recent empirical studies that provide evidence of the economic feasibility of agricultural soil C sequestration in two regions of the USA and for the USA as a whole.

7.1   A Comparison of Two Recent Regional Studies

Antle et al. (2001a, 2001b) examine the regional economic potential for C sequestration on approximately 3 million hectares of cropland soils in Montana using a site-specific econometric-process model coupled with output from Century, an ecosystem model of soil C dynamics (Parton et al., 1987; Paustian et al., 1992, 1996). The econometric-process model approach uses site-specific data from a production survey to estimate econometric production models for each crop, and then uses these data to parameterize a simulation model that represents the farmer's discrete land use and continuous management decisions (Antle and Capalbo, 2001). This simulation model is executed using the site-specific production data, with C rate data obtained from simulations of the Century ecosystem model parameterized for agroecozones used in the policy analysis. Simulations were conducted for per-hectare and per-tonne payments for six agroecozones in Montana. The marginal cost curves for these agroeco-zones show that there is substantial spatial variation in the amount and cost of C that can be produced by changing from crop–fallow rotations to continuous cropping in the dryland grain production system in that region.

Pautsch et al. (2001) use a discrete-choice econometric model in conjunction with soil C estimates from the EPIC model (Williams et al., 1989) to estimate the costs of soil C sequestration in Iowa. This model estimates the probability of adoption of conservation tillage in Iowa, using data from the National Resources Inventory, combined with county-level yield data and state-specific price data. This model is used to estimate the average annual cost of purchasing soil C for a government program that would provide payments targeted to those producers adopting conservation tillage. They consider a policy that 'perfectly discriminates' across land units – this is simply a per-hectare policy based on soil C rates for each individual land unit rather than for an agroecozone. They justify this type of analysis by noting that it provides a lower bound on the cost of sequestering soil C.

To compare the results of these two studies, Antle et al. (2002) showed how the cost estimates from these two studies can be converted into common units. Figure 6.3 shows this comparison of the marginal cost per tonne C in Montana (MC_M) and Iowa (MC_I) for C prices ranging from \$10 to \$700 per tonne C. The location of these marginal cost curves illustrates both the regional differences in the marginal costs of sequestering soil C and the differences in the crop acreages and C rates in the two regions. At prices greater than \$340 per tonne, MC_M is almost vertical, implying that any further price increases will not result in appreciably more soil C since all the cropland has been switched to the most productive means for sequestering soil C. Iowa producers can sequester a greater total amount of soil C at higher prices, due to the larger area of cropland available (9 million hectares in Iowa vs 3 million hectares in Montana), the higher soil C rates in Iowa (Table 6.1), and the possibility of inducing more farmers to adopt reduced tillage with a sufficiently large economic incentive.

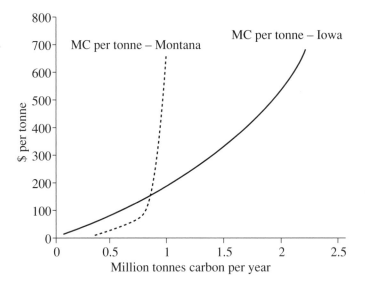

Source: Antle et al., 2001c

Figure 6.3   *Marginal cost of soil C sequestration under a per-tonne payment scheme in Iowa for conservation tillage and Montana for cropping intensification*

These analyses – and others like them that will no doubt be forthcoming in the future – impose a number of assumptions and parameter estimates that should be subjected to sensitivity analysis. Both studies measure only farm opportunity costs, and assume efficient per-tonne payments are made and are targeted only to those farmers changing practices; no payments are made to those who previously adopted C-storing practices. Also these studies ignore the permanence issue in the sense that they do not include payments required to store C after saturation occurs. Antle et al. (2001a) compute costs for less efficient per-hectare payments for increasing cropping intensity and for conversion of crops to permanent grass, and find the costs may be several times higher due to spatial heterogeneity and due to the higher opportunity costs of converting crops to grass. Antle et al. (2002) assess the effects of uncertainty in the measured C rates used in the Antle (2001a) and Antle (2001b) studies. They find that errors in measured C rates are magnified in estimates of marginal costs, due to the nonlinear relationship between C rates and marginal cost. Further research should address the effects of uncertainties in other key parameters that affect farm opportunity cost, such as the possible effects of C sequestration practices on crop productivity.

8. AN ANALYSIS OF C SEQUESTRATION IN US AGRICULTURE

McCarl and Schneider (2001) and McCarl et al. (2001b) investigated C seques-tration for the USA as a whole using a mathematical programming, sector-wide modeling approach to develop information on the marginal abatement cost curve describing how much GHG emissions can be offset for different effective C prices considering a number of emission and sequestration possibilities. Their analysis considered changes in US agriculture and forestry (AF) including afforestation, biofuel production, changes in crop management (mix, input use, tillage, irrigation), livestock management and manure management. They examined the relative role of AF sequestration efforts in the total portfolio of potential agricultural responses at alternative C price levels.

The McCarl and Schneider (2001) modeling approach involves simulation of the amount of GHG net emission reduction produced in the AF sectors and the choice of strategies under alternative C prices. They used the agricultural sector model (ASM) (McCarl et al., 2001a) modified by Schneider (2000) to include GHGs (hereafter called ASMGHG) coupled with data from a forestry sector model (Adams et al., 1996). ASMGHG depicts production, consump-tion and international trade in 63 US regions of 22 traditional and 3 biofuel crops, 29 animal products and more than 60 processed agricultural products.

Environmental impacts such as levels of greenhouse gas emission or absorption for CO_2, methane and nitrous oxide plus chemical use, and soil erosion were included. ASMGHG simulates the market and trade equilibrium in agricultural markets of the USA and 28 major foreign trading partners. The model incorporates domestic and foreign supply and demand conditions, as well as resource endowments. The market equilibrium provides: commodity and factor prices; levels of domestic production; export and import quantities; management adoption; resource usage; and environmental impact indicators. ASMGHG was subjected to C prices from $0 per tonne to $500 per tonne, using 100-year global warming potentials of 21 for methane and 310 for nitrous oxide to put them on a tonne C equivalent basis.

Analysis using ASMGHG shows that AF provides cost-effective emissions offsets, particularly through soil sequestration. Figure 6.4 shows the amount of C offsets gained at C prices ranging from $0 to $500 by broad category of strategy. Low-cost strategies involve afforestation, soil C sequestration, fertilization and manure management. Another finding is that a portfolio of AF strategies seems to be desirable, including biofuels, forests, agricultural soils, methane- and nitrous-oxide-based strategies. Figure 6.4 also shows that different strategies take on different degrees of relative importance depending on the C price level. Reliance on individual strategies appears to be cost increasing. For

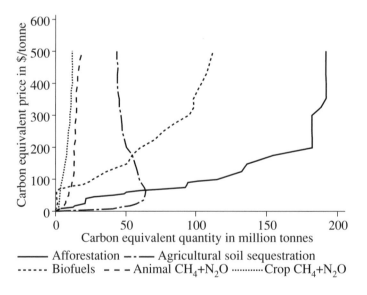

Figure 6.4   Agricultural mitigation potential at $0 to $500 per tonne carbon equivalent prices

example, reliance solely on agricultural soil C shows it would cost about $30 per tonne to achieve 60 million tonnes, whereas by using the total portfolio leads to a cost below $15 (adding all the contributions from Figure 6.4).

The analysis also shows that there are important differences between technical, economic and competitive economic potential. As argued earlier, estimates of the technical potential to sequester C in soils ignore the factors of cost and resource competition. Lal et al. (1998), for example, compute a total agricultural soil C potential but do not specify the cost of achieving such a potential level of sequestration. The total technical potential in the ASMGHG model if only C is maximized and other resource constraints are ignored is 75 million tonnes annually, but relying only on soils a maximum of 70 million tonnes can be produced at a price approaching $300 per tonne. When sequestration strategies are considered simultaneously along with other strategies, the maximum rate of sequestration is 94 per cent of the single strategy amount and declines at prices above $60 per tonne due to resource competition.

The ASMGHG model also shows that mitigation-based offsets are competitive with food and fiber production. Achieving net GHG emission offsets requires changes in the AF sector. For example, the results show that corn prices more than double at C prices above $300 as land competition rises due to afforestation and biofuel usages of croplands.

Finally, this model shows that there can be substantial co-benefits. McCarl and Schneider (2001) found as much as 25 per cent reductions in nitrogen and phosphorous runoff and in erosion. At higher prices, environmental co-benefits stabilize as a result of increased biofuel production.

9. MARKETS FOR C: CAN AGRICULTURE COMPETE?

Trading emissions allowances can be an efficient mechanism to implement an emissions reduction policy, because the regulated firms have an incentive to allocate emissions allowances so that the marginal costs of emissions reductions are equated across all sources (Tietenberg, 1985). Market trading schemes also are desirable because they encourage innovation and faster adoption of more efficient technology as compared to command-and-control approaches to regulation (see Joskow et al., 1998). A trading scheme for sulfur dioxide emissions was authorized in the Clean Air Act of 1990, with the first trades taking place in 1992 (see Petsonk et al., 1998; Joskow et al., 1998). US farmers are participating in emerging markets for other environmental goods such as water and for nutrient emissions (see Colby et al., 1993; Landry, 1996; Schleich and White, 1997). GHG allowance trading was incorporated into the Kyoto Protocol, and could provide the mechanism for the implementation of a soil C sequestration policy in which farmers would sell C credits to industries that emit GHGs.

In a C market, C credits would be supplied by firms that could reduce emissions at relatively low cost, or by entities that sequester C if they can do so at a cost that is competitive with emissions reductions. There is a variety of estimates of the cost at which emissions reductions could be obtained and thus of the probable price of C if a market were to emerge. These as well as other complications associated with large sectoral models are involved in estimating the likely price of a tonne of C. Wiese and Tierney (1996) used a model of the US economy to estimate the effects of meeting C emissions goals of the KP through taxes on the C content of energy. They considered two scenarios, a $110 (1987 dollars) per-tonne C tax that stabilized emissions at 1990 levels by 2020, and a $162 (1987 dollars) per-tonne C tax that reduced emissions by 20 per cent from their 1990 levels by 2020. These taxes were levied on the production of coal and on the production and imports of crude oil and natural gas. In another model-based analysis the Clinton Administration estimated that under a global emissions trading system, US compliance with the Kyoto Protocol would require a 3 to 5 percent increase in energy prices for US households in the period 2008–12, corresponding to a C emissions tax in the $14 to $23 per-tonne range (Yellen, 1998; Council of Economic Advisers, 1998). Also Weyant and Hill's report (1999) that a multi-model, Energy Modeling Forum sponsored study of non-agricultural Kyoto compliance found costs that averaged from $44 to $89 per tonne depending on the trading assumption and, in the individual model results, as high as $227.

Experience with the SO_2 trading program that was initiated under the 1990 clean air legislation suggests that the cost of reducing C emissions may be less than what economic models predict. Before SO_2 trading began, economists estimated that an emissions credit would trade for over $300 per tonne. Since the market was implemented the price has been in the range of $100 per tonne on the Chicago Board of Trade (Joskow et al., 1998). It seems likely that the input–output models and econometric models overestimated the cost of abating SO_2 emissions because they use aggregate historical data and because they fail to account for the abatement opportunities that can be created when economic agents are rewarded for reducing emissions efficiently. Sandor and Skees (1999) used this logic and evidence on the cost of reducing industrial CO_2 emissions to estimate that a market in tradable C emissions credits could price C in the range of $20 to $30 per tonne.

Kopp and Anderson (1998) argue that C prices as low as those estimated by the Clinton Administration and by Sandor and Skees (1999) are not likely given the various practical considerations that may limit the effectiveness of a global emissions trading system. They also note that, if such trading were to take place under the Kyoto Protocol, only emissions trading among the developed countries whose emissions are restricted would be allowed. A similar analysis to the Clinton Administration's with trading only among the developed countries showed that C emissions costs would be at least $72 per tonne. Under the assumption that the USA would meet a larger share of its emissions reductions commitments through reductions in energy consumption, the estimated costs of compliance are even higher, as indicated by the Wiese and Tierney (1996) study discussed above.

These data suggest that at least the lowest-cost producers of soil C could compete with forestry and with industrial emissions reductions in a market for C credits. However, the marginal cost curves in Figure 6.2 also indicate that for agriculture to be a major player in the provision of C credits, the price per tonne of C would probably have to be at least $50 or higher. Alternatively, if farmers received credit for the various co-benefits of environmentally positive practices, including increasing soil C, then the amount paid for the C component alone would not have to support the adoption of the improved practices. Under these conditions soil C sequestration appears to have considerable potential in a broader green payment program such as has been proposed in recent US legislation.

10. CONCLUSIONS

This chapter has reviewed the literature on the technical feasibility of soil C sequestration and the emerging economics literature on the economic analysis of soil C sequestration. The key economic question to be answered is whether C can be sequestered in agricultural soils at a cost that is competitive with industrial emissions reductions and other sinks for C such as forests. We surveyed the issues that arise in designing contracts for soil C sequestration, and reviewed the empirical evidence to date.

The economic cost of sequestering soil C depends on both the on-farm opportunity costs of sequestering soil C and contracting costs. The farm opportunity costs are highly spatially variable, raising issues of how to design contracts that take this spatial variability into account in an efficient manner. Soil C is not easily observable like trees; therefore the cost of measuring soil C stocks and changes over time is a key issue that needs to be addressed. Similarly, monitoring compliance with land use and management practices specified in contracts raises issues of incentive compatibility. The fact that C stored in soil can be released if practices are not maintained over time raises the issue of permanence of soil C. By viewing soil C contracts as contracts for accumulating and storing C in soil for a specified period of time, the permanence issue can be resolved. Practices that sequester soil C may produce important environmental co-benefits, such as reduced soil erosion, that should also be counted if farmers are to be given appropriate incentives for adopting practices that sequester soil C and produce other benefits.

Empirical studies for Iowa, Montana and the USA as a whole provide estimates of the marginal cost of sequestering C in soil that range from near zero to hundreds of dollars per tonne C, depending on how much C is to be sequestered. The US-wide analysis indicates that the most efficient policy would utilize a mix of greenhouse gas mitigation methods, including soil C sequestration. All of these studies show substantial potential for agriculture to play a role at low carbon prices (below $50 per tonne). Further research to develop the marginal abatement curves for agricultural sources is needed to assess the best greenhouse gas strategy for each region of the USA and for other regions of the world.

Payments for soil C sequestration have been promoted as a way to encourage farmers in the developing countries to adopt more sustainable land use and management practices. While many regions in the developing world do appear to have a high technical feasibility to sequester soil C, the costs of rehabilitating highly degraded lands may be high, and it remains to be seen where soil C sequestration would be economically feasible. Lack of well-defined property rights, fragmented land use, and related incentive problems may limit the feasibility of soil sequestration in many regions.

NOTE

1. We use the word tonne to mean 1000 kilograms or one metric ton.

REFERENCES

Adams, R.M., D.M. Adams, J.M. Callaway, C.C. Chang and B.A. McCarl (1993), 'Sequestering Carbon on Agricultural Land: Social Cost and Impacts on Timber Markets', *Contemporary Policy Issues*, **11** (January), 76–87.

Adams, D.M., R.J. Alig, J.M. Callaway and B.A. McCarl (1996), *The Forest and Agricultural Sector Optimization Model (FASOM): Model Structure and Policy Applications*, USDA Forest Service Report PNW-RP-495.

Antle, J.M. (2000), 'Economic Feasibility of Using Soil Carbon Sequestration Policies and Markets to Alleviate Poverty and Enhance Sustainability of the World's Poorest Farmers', paper presented at the Expert Workshop on *Carbon Sequestration, Sustainable Agriculture, and Poverty Alleviation* held at the World Meteorological Organization (WMO), Geneva, Switzerland, 31 August.

Antle J.M. and S.M. Capalbo (2001), 'Econometric-Process Models for Integrated Assessment of Agricultural Production Systems', *American Journal of Agricultural Economics*, 83, 389–401.

Antle, J.M. and S. Mooney (2002), 'Designing Efficient Policies for Agricultural Soil Carbon Sequestration', in J. Kimble (ed.), *Agriculture Practices and Policies for Carbon Sequestration in Soil*, Boca Raton FL: CRC Press.

Antle, J.M, S.M. Capalbo, J.B. Johnson and D. Miljkovic (1999), 'The Kyoto Protocol: Economic Effects of Energy Prices on Northern Plains Dryland Grain Production', *Agricultural and Resource Economics Review*, **28**, 96–105.

Antle, J.M., S.M. Capalbo, S. Mooney, E. Elliott and K. Paustian (2001a), 'Economic Analysis of Agricultural Soil Carbon Sequestration: An Integrated Assessment Approach', *Journal of Agricultural and Resource Economics*, 26, 344–67.

Antle, J.M., S.M. Capalbo, S. Mooney, E. Elliott and K. Paustian (2001b), 'Spatial Heterogeneity and the Efficient Design of Carbon Sequestration Policies for Agriculture', research discussion paper, www.climate.montana.edu.

Antle, J.M., S.M. Capalbo, S. Mooney, E. Elliott and K. Paustian (2002), 'Sensitivity of Carbon Sequestration Costs to Soil Carbon Rates', *Environmental Pollution*, 116, 413–22.

Antle, J.M., S.M. Capalbo, S. Mooney and E. Elliott (2002), 'A Comparative Examination of the Efficiency of Sequestering Carbon in US Agricultural Soils', *American Journal of Alternative Agriculture*, in press.

Babcock, B.A., P.G. Lakshminarayan, J.J. Wu and D. Zilberman (1996), 'The Economics of a Public Fund for Environmental Amenities: A Study of CRP Contracts', *American Journal of Agricultural Economics*, **78**, 961–71.

CAST (Council for Agricultural Science and Technology) (1992), *Preparing US Agriculture for Global Climate Change*, Task Force Report No. 119, Ames, Iowa: Council for Agricultural Science and Technology.

CAST (Council for Agricultural Science and Technology) (2000), 'Storing carbon in agricultural soils to help mitigate global warming', Issue Paper No. 14, April.

Colby, B.G., K. Crandall and D.B. Bush (1993), 'Water Right Transactions: Market Values and Price Dispersion', *Water Resources Research*, **29**(6), 1565–72.

Council of Economic Advisers (1998), *The Kyoto Protocol and the President's Policies to Address Climate Change: Administration Economic Analysis*, Executive Office of the President, Washington DC, July.

Feather, P., D. Hellerstein and L. Hansen (1999), *Economic Valuation of Environmental Benefits and the Targeting of Conservation Programs: The Case of the CRP*, Agricultural Economic Report No. 778, Resource Economics Division, Economic Research Service, Washington, DC: US Department of Agriculture.

Fleming, R.A. and R.M. Adams (1997), 'The Importance of Site-specific Information in the Design of Policies to Control Pollution', *Journal of Environmental Economics and Management*, **33**, 347–58.

Heerink, N., H. van Keulen and M. Kuiper (eds) (2001), *Economic Policy and Sustainable Land Use: Recent Advances in Quantitative Analysis for Developing Countries*. New York: Physica-Verlag.

Helfand, G.E. and B.W. House (1995), 'Regulating Nonpoint Source Pollution under Heterogeneous Conditions', *American Journal of Agricultural Economics*, **77**(4), 1024–32.

IPCC (1996), *Climate Change 1995: The IPCC Second Assessment Report, Volume 2: Scientific–Technical Analyses of Impacts, Adaptations, and Mitigation of Climate Change*, R.T. Watson, M.C. Zinyowera and R.H. Moss (eds), Cambridge and New York: Cambridge University Press.

IPCC (2000), *Land Use, Land-use Change, and Forestry*, Geneva, Switzerland: Cambridge University Press.

Joskow, P.L., R. Schmalensee and E.M. Bailey (1998), 'The Market for Sulfur Dioxide Emissions', *American Economic Review*, **88** (September), 669–85.

Konyar, K. and R.E. Howitt (2000), 'The Cost of the Kyoto Protocol to US Crop Production: Measuring Crop Price, Regional Acreage, Welfare and Input Substitution Effects', *Journal of Agricultural and Resource Economics*, **25**(2), 347–67.

Kopp, R.J. and J.W. Anderson (1998), 'Estimating the Costs of Kyoto: How Plausible Are the Clinton Administration's Figures?', Washington DC: Resources for the Future, 12 March.

Lal, R., J.M. Kimble, R.F. Follett and C.V. Cole (1998), *The Potential of US Cropland to Sequester Carbon and Mitigate the Greenhouse Effect*, Chelsea, MI: Ann Arbor Press.

Landry, C.J. (1996), 'Giving Color to Oregon's Gray Water Market: An Analysis of Price Determinants for Water Rights', unpublished MS thesis, Department of Agricultural and Resource Economics, Oregon State University, Corvallis, Oregon.

Mann, L.K. (1986), 'Changes in Soil C Storage after Cultivation', *Soil Science*, **142** (November), 279–88.

Marland, G. and B. Schlamadinger (1997), 'Forests for Carbon Sequestration or Fossil Fuel Substitution A Sensitivity Analysis', *Biomass and Bioenergy*, **13**, 389–97.

Marland, G., B.A. McCarl and U. Schneider (1998), 'Soil and Carbon Policy and Economics', in N.J. Rosenberg, R.C. Isaurralde and E.L. Malone (eds), *Carbon Sequestration in Soils: Science Monitoring and Beyond*, Columbus, OH: Battelle Press, pp. 153–69.

McCarl, B.A. and B.C. Murray (2001), 'Harvesting the Greenhouse: Comparing Biological Sequestration with Emissions Offsets', unpublished paper, Department of Agricultural Economics, Texas A&M University, College Station, TX.

McCarl, B.A. and U. Schneider (1999), 'Curbing Greenhouse Gases: Agriculture's Role', *Choices*, First Quarter, 9–12.

McCarl, B.A. and U. Schneider (2000), 'Agriculture's Role in a Greenhouse Gas Emission Mitigation World: An Economic Perspective', *Review of Agricultural Economics*, **22**(1), 134–59.

McCarl, B.A. and U. Schneider (2001), 'Harvesting Gasses from the Greenhouse: Economic Explorations Regarding the Role of Agriculture and Forestry', unpublished paper, Department of Agricultural Economics, Texas A&M University, College Station, TX.

McCarl, B.A., M. Gowen and T. Yeats (1999), *The Impact of Carbon Permit Prices on the US Agricultural Sector*, final report for EPA Climate Change Policies and Programs Division.

McCarl, B.A., C.C. Chang, J.D. Atwood and W.I. Nayda (2001a), 'Documentation of ASM: The U.S. Agricultural Sector Model', unpublished report, Texas A&M University, http://agecon.tamu.edu/faculty/mccarl/asm.

McCarl, B.A., U. Schneider, B.C. Murray, J. Williams and R.D. Sands (2001b), 'Economic Potential of Greenhouse Gas Emission Reductions: Comparative Role for Soil Sequestration in Agriculture', presented at DOE First National Conference on Carbon Sequestration, Washington DC, 14–17 May.

Parks, P.J. and I.W. Hardie (1995), 'Least-cost Forest Carbon Reserves: Cost-effective Subsidies to Convert Marginal Agricultural Land to Forests', *Land Economics*, **71** (February), 122–36.

Parton, W.J., D.S. Schimel, C.V. Cole and D.S. Ojima (1987), 'Analysis of Factors Controlling Soil Organic Matter Levels in Great Plains Grasslands', *Soil Science Society of America Journal*, **51**, 1173–9.

Parton, W.J., D.S. Schimel, D.S. Ojima and C.V. Cole (1994), 'A General Model for Soil Organic Matter Dynamics: Sensitivity to Litter Chemistry, Texture and Management', in R.B. Bryant and R.W. Arnold (eds), *Quantitative Modeling of Soil Forming Processes*, SSSA Special Publication 39. Madison, WI: Soil Science Society of America, pp. 147–67.

Paustian, K., E.T. Elliott, G.A. Peterson and K. Killian (1996), 'Modeling Climate, CO_2 and Management Impacts on Soil Carbon in Semi-arid Agroecosystems', *Plant and Soil*, **187**, 351–65.

Paustian, K., W.J. Parton and J. Persson (1992), 'Modeling Soil Organic Matter in Organic Amended and Nitrogen Fertilized Long-term Plots', *Soil Science Society of America Journal*, **56**, 476–88.

Pautsch, G., L. Kurkalova, B. Babcock and C. Kling (2000), *The Efficiency of Sequestering Carbon in Agricultural Soils*, Working Paper 00-wp 246, Center for Agricultural and Rural Development, Ames: Iowa State University.

Pautsch, G.R., L.A. Kurkalova, B. Babcock and C.L. Kling (2001), 'The efficiency of sequestering carbon in agricultural soils', *Contemporary Economic Policy*, in press.

Petsonk, A., D.J. Dudek and J. Goffman (1998), 'Market Mechanisms and Global Climate Change: An Analysis of Policy Instruments', Environmental Defense Fund in cooperation with the Pew Center on Global Climate Change.

Platinga, A.J., T. Mauldin and D.J. Miller (1999), 'An Econometric Analysis of the Cost of Sequestering Carbon in Forests', *American Journal of Agricultural Economics*, **81** (November), 812–24.

Rasmussen, P.E. and W.J. Parton (1994), 'Long-term Effects of Residue Management in Wheat Fallow: I. Inputs, Yield and Soil Organic Matter', *American Journal of Soil Science*, **58** (March–April), 523–30.

Robertson, G.P., E.A. Paul and R.R. Harwood (2000), 'Greenhouse Gases in Intensive Agriculture: Contributions of Individual Gases to the Radiative Forcing of the Atmosphere', *Science*, **289** (September), 1922–4.

Sandor, R.L. and J.R. Skees (1999), 'Creating a Market for Carbon Emissions: Opportunities for US Farmers', *Choices*, Third Quarter, 13–17.

Schleich, J. and D. White (1997), 'Cost Minimisation of Nutrient Reduction in Watershed Management Using Linear Programming', *Journal of the American Water Resource Association*, **33**(1), 135–42.

Schneider, U. (2000), 'Agricultural Sector Analysis on Greenhouse Gas Emission Mitigation in the United States', Ph.D. dissertation, Texas A&M University, December.

Stavins, R.N. (1999), 'The Costs of Carbon Sequestration: A Revealed-preference Approach', *American Economics Review*, **89** (September), 994–1009.

Tiessen, H., J.W.B. Stewart and J.R. Bettany (1982), 'Cultivation Effects on the Amounts and Concentration of Carbon, Nitrogen and Phosphorous in Grassland Soils', *Agronomy Journal*, **74**, 831–5.

Tietenberg, T.H. (1985), 'Emissions Trading: An Exercise in Reforming Pollution Policy', Washington, DC: Resources for the Future.

Tietenberg, T., M. Grubb, A. Michaelowa, B. Swift, Z.-X. Zhang and F. Joshua (1998), *International Rules for Greenhouse Gas Emissions Trading: Defining the Principles, Modalities, Rules and Guidelines for Verification, Reporting and Accountability*, Geneva: United Nations. UNCTAD/GDS/GFSB/Misc 6.

United Nations Framework Convention on Climate Change (UNFCCC) (1998), *Kyoto Protocol*, Climate Change Secretariat, http://www.unfccc.de/resource/convkp.html, March.

US Department of Agriculture (1999), *Economic Analysis of US Agriculture and the Kyoto Protocol*, Office of The Chief Economist, Global Change Program Office, http://www.usda.gov/oce/gcpo/Kyoto.pdf, May.

US Department of Agriculture (2000), *2000 Agricultural Statistics*, Washington, DC: National Agricultural Statistics Service.

US Department of Agriculture, Environmental Defense, and Soil and Water Conservation Society (undated), 'Growing Carbon: A New Crop that Helps Agricultural Producers and the Climate Too.'

US Global Change Research Program (2000), *Climate Change Impacts on the United States: The Potential Consequences of Climate Variability and Change*, Report of the National Assessment Synthesis Team, http://www.gcrio.org/nationalassessment.

Watson, R.T., I.R. Noble, B. Bolin, N.H. Ravindranath, D.J. Verardo and D.J. Dokken (eds) (2000), *Land Use, Land-Use Change, and Forestry*, a special report of the IPCC, Cambridge, UK: Cambridge University Press.

West, T., M. Post, J. Amthor and G. Marland (2000), 'Review of Task 2.1, National Carbon Sequestration Assessment', presentation at DOE Center for Research on Enhancing Carbon Sequestration in Terrestrial Ecosystems (CSITE) Program Review, Oakridge National Laboratories, TN, November.

Weyant, J. and J. Hill (1999), 'Introduction and Overview', in J. Weyant (ed.), *The Costs of the Kyoto Protocol: A Multi-Model Evaluation*, *The Energy Journal*, Special Issue, vii.

Wiese, A.M. and B. Tierney (1996), 'The Cost Impacts of a Carbon Tax on US Manufacturing Industries and Other Sectors', Research Study No. 081, Policy Analysis and Strategic Planning Department, Washington, DC: American Petroleum Institute, June.

Williams, J.R., C.A. Jones, J.R. Kiniry and D.A. Spaniel (1989), 'The EPIC Crop Growth Model', *Transactions of the American Society of Agricultural Engineers*, **32**, 497–511.

World Bank (2000), *World Development Report 2000/2001: Attacking Poverty*, a co-publication of the World Bank and Oxford University Press, Herndon, VA, September.

Wu, J. and B.A. Babcock (1996), 'Contact Design for the Purchase of Environmental Goods from Agriculture', *American Journal of Agricultural Economics*, **78**(4), 935–45.

Wu, J. and W.G. Boggess (1999), 'The Optimal Allocation of Conservation Funds', *Journal of Environmental Economics Management*, **38**(3), 302–21.

Yellen, J. (1998), Testimony Before the House Commerce Subcommittee on Energy and Power on the Economics of the Kyoto Protocol, 4 March.

7. Tradable permits for air quality and climate change

David Harrison, Jr[1]

1. INTRODUCTION

The use of tradable permits to lower the cost of achieving environmental targets has emerged over the last two decades as an important policy tool for improving air quality. Building on a conceptual foundation provided by economists as well as on the accumulating experience with actual programs, the tradable permits approach is increasingly being included in air quality policies and policy proposals. Most of the existing tradable permit programs are in the USA, although there are significant programs in other countries as well.

The tradable permits approach is receiving a great deal of attention throughout the world in part because of its prominence in proposals to deal with climate change. As discussed below, the Kyoto Protocol – a proposed international agreement to control carbon dioxide and other greenhouse gases – includes various tradable permit mechanisms that would be implemented at the international level. In addition, many countries are considering developing a tradable permits scheme as a domestic tool to limit their greenhouse gas emissions.

The increasing experience with tradable permits means that one can evaluate how such programs work in practice, not just how they might work in theory. The key objective of a tradable permit program is to reduce the cost of meeting an environmental target compared to the 'command-and-control' approach of setting individual emission standards for various sources. Allowing sources to buy and sell emission permits (that is, the right to emit a ton) provides incentives for emission reductions to be concentrated on relatively low-cost sources. The bulk of the early empirical literature deals with the *potential* savings from the tradable permits approach, assuming that all cost-reducing trades take place.[2] The applicability of these results to actual policy situations is limited both by uncertainties in the marginal cost information for sources that lie behind the calculations of potential cost savings and by the inability to take into account transactions costs and other practical considerations that limit the trades that actually take place.

While it is difficult to assess actual cost savings, experience does provide some indications of the likely gains from tradable permit programs in practice. It also gives some indication of their environmental impacts. The traditional assumption is that marketable permit programs are environmentally neutral – a less expensive means of achieving a given environmental target. Environmental goals might be affected, however, if tradable permit programs in practice lead to differences in emissions or if the pattern of emission increases affects environmental quality.[3] Moreover, as discussed below, tradable permit schemes may encourage more ambitious environmental goals because of their flexibility and cost-saving potential.

This chapter focuses on the practical experience with tradable permits.[4] In particular, it summarizes the main features of these programs and provides information on their results, both environmental and economic. These results furnish the bases for some inferences on the elements of program design that appear to be important for successful implementation – that is, significant cost savings without compromising environmental targets – as well as some implications for additional research. The chapter also discusses various new applications of the tradable permits approach, including those designed to provide cost-minimizing control of greenhouse gases. Although experience is encouraging about the usefulness of the tradable permits approach in practice, it is clear that these applications raise new challenges as well as new opportunities.

The chapter is organized as follows. The next section provides a brief overview of the three major types of tradable permit programs and their key differences as well as a summary of the programs that have been adopted. This background section also reviews some major decisions that influence the economic and environmental results of implementing tradable permit programs. The next – and largest – section reviews experience with major previous and existing tradable permit programs. The following section describes some potential programs, including those proposed to deal with climate change. The final section offers concluding remarks and implications for additional research.

2.   BACKGROUND

The basic rationale for tradable permits is straightforward and well established.[5] Allowing firms the flexibility to buy and sell emission rights or emission reduction credits can reduce the overall cost of meeting environmental objectives and provide gains to both buyers and sellers (Harrison, 1999a). Under a typical tradable permit system, an aggregate cap on emissions is set and allocated initially to covered sources. Each source must hold permits to cover its emissions, with sources free to buy and sell permits from each other. In a well-functioning market for allowances (that is, rights to emit), an equilibrium price will emerge that reflects the value of the allowance to all sources. Each firm managing a source faces the choice of buying an allowance or reducing emissions. Firms tend to cut back on emissions if it is cheaper to do so, with the result that each firm equates its marginal cost to the allowance price. Because all sources face the same allowance price, marginal costs are equal for all sources, thereby minimizing the overall cost of meeting the aggregate cap.

By establishing a market price for the right to emit, the tradable permit approach also could encourage firms to find cost-effective and innovative means of reducing emissions below existing levels because they can profit from these innovations.[6] The approach thus provides incentives for dynamic efficiency in meeting emission targets over time.

2.1 Broad Types of Tradable Permit Programs

The description of the marketable permit approach given above relates specifically to the cap-and-trade type. There are two other types, credit-based programs and emission-averaging programs. Although they share the feature of tradability, the three differ in the nature of the commodity that is traded. Because the experiences are somewhat different – as discussed below – it is useful to distinguish the three types of tradable permit programs. These three types are not, however, mutually exclusive. As discussed below, several cap-and-trade programs include credit-based programs as well.

2.2.1 Cap-and-trade programs

Under a cap-and-trade system, as noted above, an overall allowable level of emissions is established for a given set of emission sources. The allowable emissions typically are allocated initially to these sources, although they could be auctioned or distributed to other groups. The commodity under a cap-and-trade program is an allowance to emit. The program requires that each participating source hold enough permits to cover its emissions. Pre-certification of permits typically is not required because the allowances that are allocated effectively are certified when initially distributed. Sources can buy and sell permits, so that in any given year some sources will have more permits than their initial allocations (buyers of permits) and others will have fewer (sellers of permits). In a well-functioning market, a price will be established for the allowance. In equilibrium, each profit-maximizing firm equates its marginal cost to the allowance price. Because all sources face the same allowance price, marginal abatement costs will tend to be equalized across sources and the overall cost of meeting the cap on emissions will be minimized.

Although a cap-and-trade approach traditionally is viewed as achieving the same environmental benefits as the emission standards approach, the cap can provide greater certainty that emission targets are met because emission standards – that is, limits on emissions per unit of input or output – by themselves do not cap total emissions. Moreover, as noted above, there can be differences in environmental performance in practice due to changes in the spatial or temporal patterns of emissions due to trading.

2.1.2   Credit-based programs

Under credit-based programs, emission reduction credits (ERCs) are created when a source reduces emissions below a baseline level. Pre-certification of credits typically is required to determine how many ERCs have been created. These credits can be used by the same source in other periods or by another source to meet an emission standard. The commodity under a credit-based program, the ERC, has a right to emit one ton per year of the emission for as long as the ERC is valid. Credit-based programs can reduce the total cost of meeting multiple emission standards. Moreover, as a supplement to cap-and-trade programs, they can reduce the cost of meeting the cap by bringing other potentially low-cost compliers into the program.

Credit-based programs, however, could in practice compromise environ-mental objectives because of the difficulty of determining the baseline for calculating credits, that is, the emissions that would have occurred absent the credit-generating control (for example, installation of emission controls on a stack). Instituting a credit-based program, therefore, can create a trade-off between cost savings and environmental performance if the credits do not represent actual emission reductions; that is, they would have been achieved without the incentives provided by the credit-based program.

2.1.3   Emissions-averaging programs

Emissions averaging represents somewhat of a hybrid between the credit-based and cap-and-trade approaches.[7] Averaging caps the average emission rate (that is, emissions per unit of input or output) rather than the total level of emissions from the covered sources. Pre-certification of the traded commodity typically is not required under an emission-averaging approach because no baseline deter-mination is necessary. The commodity is a right to emit a ton, as in the cap-and-trade approach, and firms buy and sell the right to emit a ton. However, firms are not constrained in the total number of tons they can emit. The program can be seen as equivalent to a cap-and-trade program in which the initial allowances each source receives are changed each period to reflect the overall input or output (that is, the factor used to calculate the emission rate). Averaging programs provide firms with the opportunity to reduce the cost of meeting emission rate standards. The key difference between a cap-and-trade program and an averaging program is that participants in the latter do not face an opportunity cost for producing additional output (or using additional inputs) and thus the opportunity costs of permits are not reflected in product prices. Moreover, it is difficult to integrate sources in different sectors into a single rate-based program. (Consider what output or input measure could be used to calculate a common rate for electric generators, oil refineries and steel mills.)

The environmental effects of averaging are generally assumed to be equivalent to the emission standards they supplement. (Note that overall emissions are not capped under either alternative.) The possibility of cost savings from averaging may, however, indirectly affect environmental performance if the cost reductions lead to more ambitious targets.

2.1.4 Summary

Table 7.1 summarizes the major differences between the three types of tradable permit programs. As noted, the three types can differ in the unit of exchange, in whether pre-certification is required before units can be bought and sold, and in whether overall emissions from the covered sources are subject to an overall cap.

Table 7.1   Major features of the three types of marketable permit programs

Type	Unit of trade	Pre-certification required	Cap on total emissions
Cap-and-trade	Right to emit	Not necessarily	Yes
Credit-based	Emission reduction credit	Yes	Not necessarily
Averaging	Right to emit	Not necessarily	No

2.2   Overview of Prior and Existing Tradable Permit Programs

Table 7.2 summarizes tradable permit systems that actually have been implemented.[8] The list is dominated by experience in the USA, although there are prominent examples in other countries (notably programs to implement the Montreal Protocol, as noted below).[9] As discussed below, there is increasing interest in Europe and the rest of the world in adopting this approach, particularly to deal with possible restrictions on carbon and other greenhouse gas emissions.

Table 7.2 Major implemented tradable permit programs for air quality and climate change

Country	Program	Regulated pollutant	Permit program type	Period of operation
Canada	Montreal Protocol	Various ODS	Cap-and-trade	1993–present
Chile	Santiago Air Emissions Trading	Particulates	Cap-and-trade	1995–present
European Union	Montreal Protocol	Various ODS	Cap-and-trade	1991–94
Germany	Offsets	Various conventional	Credit-based	1974–present
Singapore	Montreal Protocol	Various ODS	Cap-and-trade	1991–present
USA	Emissions trading programs	Various conventional	Credit-based	1974–present
	Lead-in-gasoline program	Lead	Average	1982–7
	Montreal Protocol	Various ODS	Cap-and-trade	1987–present
	RECLAIM (Los Angles Air Basin)	NO_x and SO_2	Cap-and-trade	1994–present
	Acid rain program	SO_2	Cap-and-trade	1995–present
	Ozone Transport Commission Budget (Northeast)	NO_x	Cap-and-trade	1999–present
	Heavy-duty engines	HC and NO_x	Average	1999–present
	Marine engines	HC and NO_x	Average	1999–present
	Lawnmower engines	HC and NO_x	Average	1999–present
	Small utility engines	HC and NO_x	Average	2000–present
	Emissions Reduction Marketing System (Illinois)	VOM	Cap-and-trade	2000–present

Notes: ODS: Ozone-depleting substances. HC: hydrocarbons. NO_x: nitrogen oxides. VOM: volatile organic materials.

Sources: Stavins (2000); Klaassen (1999); Harrison (1999a); Illinois Environmental Protection Agency (2001).

3. EXPERIENCE WITH MAJOR PRIOR AND EXISTING PROGRAMS

The previous and existing allowance programs include all three of the broad types discussed above. As noted, these programs have been developed over more than two decades. This section provides descriptions of the programs – emphasizing their key features – and information on their success in promoting cost savings and achieving environmental objectives.[10] The programs are described in the chronological order in which they were initially developed.

3.1 US Emissions Trading (ET) Programs

Starting in the mid-1970s, the United States Environmental Protection Agency (EPA) and the states developed four programs designed to increase flexibility and reduce the costs of achieving air quality standards.

1. *Netting*. Netting allows large new sources and major modifications of existing sources to be exempted from certain review procedures if existing emissions elsewhere in the same facility are reduced, so that the net addition from the new source is below the level triggering new source review.
2. *Offsets*. The offset policy allows a major new source to locate in an area that does not attain a given national ambient air quality standard – a 'non-attainment area' – if emissions from an existing source are reduced by at least as much as the new source would contribute (after installation of stringent controls). The offset ratio, that is, the relationship between the offsets that must be acquired and the new source emissions, varies depending upon the degree of non-attainment of the area. (For example, the offset ratio in ozone non-attainment areas varies between 1.1 and 1.5 to 1, according to the seriousness of the area's non-attainment problem.[11])
3. *Bubble*. The bubble policy allows firms to combine the limits for several different sources into one overall emissions level. The name refers to placing a 'bubble' over several sources and measuring the sum of their emissions, rather than measuring emissions from each source individually.
4. *Banking*. Under banking, firms that take actions to reduce emissions below the relevant standard can 'bank' the credits for future internal use or sale.

These four programs – collectively referred to as emissions trading or ET – are related by the common objective of providing sources with additional flexibility to comply with traditional command-and-control standards while maintaining environmental objectives. The programs are credit-based, that is, they involve the development and trading of ERCs.[12]

The ET programs cover all significant stationary sources of pollution for five principal conventional air pollutants (hydrocarbons, nitrogen organic gases, particulate matter, sulfur oxides, and carbon monoxide).[13] Programs authorized under the EPA framework include those in California, Colorado, Georgia, Illinois, Louisiana and New York (Stavins, 2000). Trades typically involve stationary sources, such as electricity generation units and pulp and paper plants, although credits for certain mobile sources (for example, cars) are allowed in specific circumstances (see Foster and Hahn, 1995).

The EPA developed detailed regulations to implement the ET program that take up 47 pages of multi-column fine print in the *Federal Register* (51 Fed. Reg. 43814, September 1986). In general, the regulations substantially restricted the applicability of the programs because of concerns that their use would compromise environmental objectives by providing 'paper credits' rather than legitimate emission reductions. The ERCs must meet detailed criteria to be certified as eligible for trading. In addition, as noted, offsets require greater than 1:1 trades and also are restricted in the geographic areas in which the trades can take place. Potential applications of the bubble policy initially faced even greater hurdles because they had to be approved as a revision to an applicable State Implementation Plan (SIP), a lengthy administrative process that thus discouraged their use (US Environmental Protection Agency, 2001). These and other EPA regulations largely eliminated the risk of paper credits but at the cost of a cumbersome system that makes trades expensive and uncertain and thus discourages many potential trades (Hahn and Hester, 1989).

Brokers and other intermediaries have evolved to provide ERCs in some jurisdictions. In the Los Angeles region, the area with the most active offset market, one broker has dealt with about 40 percent of trades – typically representing sellers of ERCs – and several attorneys also operate as intermediaries (Foster and Hahn, 1995). Although reducing search costs, brokers charge fees that can vary between 4 percent and 25 percent of the value of the trade, depending on the complexity of the transaction. Administrative fees to government agencies in Los Angeles can total about $25 000 per trade, with the approval process taking from 5 to 12 months. Moreover, only about 20 percent of proposed trades are fully approved as proposed (Foster and Hahn, 1995). In summary, certification of ERCs can be time-consuming, expensive and uncertain.

The performances of the bubble program and the other ET programs generally have fallen short of their cost-reducing potential as a result of these large transactions costs, delays and uncertainties. The programs have, however, provided some cost savings and, in the case of the offset program, have improved flexibility for new sources to locate in non-attainment areas. Moreover, experience with the ET programs has offered insights into the factors that can limit the performance of emissions trading programs as well as experience with some of the institutions of emissions trading.

Table 7.3 summarizes the cost savings estimated for each ET program based upon the period up to 1986. Relative to the hundreds of billions of dollars spent on air pollution control over the period, the overall cost savings of the early trading program were small. The bulk of these savings came from the netting program, which may have saved as much as $12 billion. Since offsets allow firms to build new sources in a non-attainment region by keeping overall emissions the same, no control-cost savings estimates can be developed for that program. Savings from the other two programs were modest.

Table 7.3   Emissions trading through 1986

Activity	Cost savings (millions of 1986 dollars)	Number of trades
Netting	$525–$12 000	5000–12 000
Offsets	Not applicable	2000
Bubble	$435	132
Banking	Very small	100

Source: Hahn and Hester (1989).

Foster and Hahn (1995) provide more recent information on the offset and netting programs in the Los Angeles air basin, the area that accounts for the large majority of overall transactions. From 1985 to 1992, more than 10 000 tons of various emissions were traded in the offset program. Based upon information from the leading private broker involved in offset trades, the average price over the course of a year ranged from $81 to $435 per ton, depending upon the year and the emission. There was, however, wide dispersion in the price at any point during the year. This suggests that ERC markets are not in a classical equilibrium, with a set of well-defined prices. The authors note that ERCs differ substantially in terms of their method of creation, their geographic location, whether they have been banked, and the risk-sharing arrangements embodied in the exchange contracts – all of these factors are likely to affect the price at which the credit is exchanged. Foster and Hahn point out that large transactions costs appear to have had a major effect on the incentive to engage in external trades. In many cases, the transactions costs exceeded the market value of the credits exchanged. In addition to the financial considerations, transactions tended to require lengthy periods and were subject to considerable uncertainty. Perhaps the greatest uncertainty concerned the possibility of the *ad hoc* devaluation of banked credits. Moreover, the requirement for offset ratios greater than 1:1 provided another transactions cost and thus disincentive to trade.

In sum, the primary obstacle to more widespread participation in – and therefore greater savings from – the ET programs seems to have been the high transactions costs and uncertainties associated with ERC trades. Indeed, as noted above, Foster and Hahn find that the transactions cost exceeded the market value of the credits in many cases. Other factors also contributed to the relative lack of success, including requiring trading ratios greater than one, administrative requirements and restrictions that made trading unattractive, and the novelty of the concept (Council of Economic Advisers, 2000).

Despite their limited success, EPA's experience with the ET programs has provided valuable experience and insight into the design of subsequent programs. The ET programs also gave federal and state agencies experience with developing credit-based programs and brokers experience with trading in emission reduction credits.[14] Moreover, some states recently have expanded their credit-based programs to include credits for premature retiring of cars and other mobile sources (see Stavins, 2000).

3.2   German Offset Program

German regulations allow for the transfer of emission reduction obligations for air pollution under two rules developed in the 1970s (see Klaassen, 1999):

1. Plant renewal clause
2. Compensation rule.

The plant renewal clause is similar to the offset rule under the US emissions trading program. Under this clause, new plants can be constructed in areas where air quality standards are exceeded if the new plant replaces an existing plant of the same kind in the same area. Guidelines developed in 1983 allowed renovation of an existing plant to provide offsets as long as the new plant has state-of-the-art emission controls and there is a net reduction in pollutant concentration in the area. The clause can only be used if the additional impact of the plant on ambient concentrations is less than 1 percent, if the offsets are in the same area, and if the new plant starts operating after the improvements at existing plants become effective.

The compensation rule was added in 1986 to provide flexibility for the requirement that existing plants meet strict emission standards. The compliance period can be extended from five to eight years if emission reduction measures at existing plants as a group provide greater emission reductions than the application of the technical guidelines for each individual plant. The application of this rule is limited to facilities within the same geographic area. Moreover, renewal plans had to be compiled within one year and all pollutants have to be covered.

Both of these elements have had relatively little effect on the overall cost or cost-effectiveness of the air quality program, largely because of their limited geographic applicability (Klaassen, 1999). Air quality standards are only exceeded in a few areas and thus the plant renewal clause is not relevant to many geographic areas; the clause is not applicable to new plants located in attainment areas, even if the new plant would result in exceedences. The compensation rule also is constrained by the stringency of the limits, leaving relatively little room for some units to over-control in exchange for relaxed requirements at other units.

Although the limited use of these provisions means that the environmental effects are modest, the overall effects are judged to be neutral to positive (Klaassen, 1999). The renewal clause prevents increases in emissions in non-attainment areas. The compensation rule can only be used if total emissions are reduced further than the source-by-source regulations.

3.3   US Lead-in-Gasoline Program

The tradable permit program used to regulate lead in gasoline during the mid-1980s provides a clearer example of a successful trading program than the early US or German emissions trading programs. The lead-in-gasoline program was an averaging program; that is, the program regulated the average lead content of gasoline rather than the total amount of lead in gasoline. Refiners could trade (both internally and externally) rights to include lead in the gasoline they produced, with the net sales or purchases of lead rights reflected in their demonstrations of compliance with the average limit.

The tradable permit program grew out of EPA's efforts to reduce the lead content of gasoline starting in the early 1970s.[15] Through 1982, lead limits were enforced on a refiner-by-refiner basis, with each refinery allowed to average lead concentration across its total production. In the language of the ET programs, such averaging was equivalent to an intra-plant bubble. In 1982, the rules were changed to allow trading across refineries and refining firms (47 Fed. Reg. 49322). Under the new rules, a refinery could use lead in its gasoline above the usual limit if it purchased an equivalent number of rights from other refineries that had reduced their own lead content. Lead credits were created by refiners, importers, and ethanol blenders (who reduced the lead content of gasoline by adding ethanol) (US Environmental Protection Agency, 2001). The 1982 regulations also significantly narrowed the definition of 'small' refineries that would be entitled to meet a less stringent limit (47 Fed. Reg. 38078).

The 1982 rules also shifted the basis for lead-in-gasoline regulation from all gasoline to leaded only. That is, refiners had to achieve the average limit per leaded gallon of gasoline, rather than per gallon of gasoline. This shift provided an advantage to refineries producing a higher percentage of leaded gasoline.

The shift to 'leaded only' was designed to help small refineries – which tended to produce more leaded gasoline because they had less sophisticated refineries – and thus partly cushion the end of their special treatment (Nichols, 1997a).

In 1985, EPA promulgated a new rule to reduce further the lead limit more than tenfold in two steps: in mid-1985, from 1.1 grams per leaded gallon (gplg) to 0.5 gplg, and then, in January 1986, to 0.1 gplg (50 Fed. Reg. 9400). As part of the new rule, EPA allowed refiners to 'bank' lead reductions: if they reduced ahead of schedule during 1985, they could save the excess rights for use or sale in 1986 and 1987.

The lead program was widely regarded as a success, both when trading was initially permitted in the 1983–85 period and when banking was added in the 1985–87 period. Figure 7.1 shows the development of the lead trading market for gasoline. From mid-1983 (when the new rules took effect) until early 1985 (when the further phase-down began), an increasingly vigorous market in lead rights developed. In a typical quarter, over half of all refineries participated in the market, and up to one-fifth of the lead rights were traded. In 1985, when provisions for banking were added, an even larger fraction of lead was bought and sold in the market.

Refiners were enthusiastic about the program as reflected in the high percentage of lead traded. Basing the averaging program only on leaded gasoline

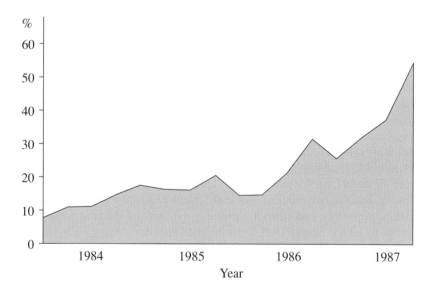

Source: Hahn and Hester (1989, p. 387).

Figure 7.1   Lead rights traded as percentage of all lead, 1983–87

– rather than all gasoline – did provide an advantage to refineries that produced higher than average shares of leaded gasoline (typically the smaller refineries). But as noted above, the change to leaded only was designed partly to compensate for the phase-out of special treatment for smaller refineries.

No estimates are available of the cost savings from the program, although the fact that so many trades took place suggests the gains were considerable. Moreover, the program appeared to provide incentives for cost-saving technology diffusion (Kerr and Newell, 2001). There is some evidence, however, that not all of the potential cost savings from permit trading were achieved (Kerr, 1993). Nearly one-half of all lead traded was between refineries owned by the same firm, suggesting that some profitable interfirm trades were not made either because of higher transactions prices or a preference to avoid revealing potentially valuable information to competitors.

The banking components of the lead trading appear to have been particularly successful. EPA predicted that refiners would bank 7 to 9 billion grams of lead, resulting in savings of up to $226 million (in 1985 dollars, discounted at a 10 percent real rate) over two and one-half years, or about 20 percent of the estimated cost of the rule over that period. Although no new estimates of the cost savings were made after banking occurred, the level of banking was even higher than predicted: refineries banked a total of 10.6 billion grams, almost 17 percent higher than the upper end of the predicted range. Thus, it seems likely that the actual savings were higher than the estimate. The large increase in trading after the banking program was put in place suggests the importance of temporal flexibility to a trading program.

The lead trading program also appears to have been an environmental success. There was some evidence of fraud – in which some small refiners and ethanol blenders sold many more credits than they earned – and thus some partial compromise of intermediate environmental objectives (US Environmental Protection Agency, 2001). But on balance the trading program allowed EPA to phase out the use of lead in gasoline more rapidly than otherwise would have been feasible (US Environmental Protection Agency, 2001).

3.4 US and European Programs for Ozone-Depleting Chemicals[16]

An international negotiating team in 1987 signed the Montreal Protocol, an international plan to curtail substantially the release of stratospheric ozone-depleting substances (ODSs). (The Protocol called for a 50 percent reduction in the production of certain chemicals from 1986 levels by 1998 and froze production and consumption of other chemicals at 1986 levels beginning in 1992.) The Protocol allowed for trade in the quotas assigned to individual countries in order to minimize the costs of this phase-out, which was implemented through a series of declining international caps over the period 1989 to

2000. Trading programs exist at both the international and domestic levels, although the rules, procedures and institutions differ. International trade was enabled through provisions allowing 'industrial rationalization' of production, where multiple countries can jointly meet their production target. Domestic or regional trading between firms, however, must be enabled by legislation in individual countries (or in regional groups such as the European Union).

3.4.1   US Program

As part of the US implementation of the Protocol – agreed to on 21 April 1988 – EPA set up a system of fully tradable production quotas to phase down the use of chlorofluorocarbons (CFCs), halons, and several other ODSs (58 Fed. Reg. 65018). This phase-out was extended to hydrochlorofluorocarbons (HCFCs) – identified as transitional substitutes for CFCs and other more destructive ODSs – in 1992 at the fourth meeting of the Parties to the Montreal Protocol.

Under the transferable permit system set up by the EPA, firms were allocated quotas on the basis of historical data on domestic production and imports. Each quota is good for a specific year, and the number has declined over time. The number of quotas required to produce or import a unit of chemical is proportional to that chemical's potential to deplete ozone.

Firms are free to trade quotas. Beyond the pre-existing ban on certain 'non-essential' aerosol uses of CFCs imposed in 1978, there are no restrictions on the use of CFCs produced under the quota limits. In contrast, if a command-and-control approach had been taken, EPA would have had to determine which uses should be banned and which restricted.

Trading in ODSs has been substantial in the USA, with firms trading a total of 321 million kilograms (in 561 trades) from 1989 to 1995. The 171 million kilograms traded in 1992, the most active trading year, represented about 13 percent of the total allowances in that year. International trading has been relatively limited, with only 20 trades over the period 1992 to 1995 totaling 36 million kilograms of ODSs.

The EPA recognized when it imposed the transferable quota system that it was creating potentially large gains to the relatively small number of CFC manufacturers, because limiting the supply of quotas would drive up the price of CFCs to the point at which demand would be driven down to the available supply. The value of the quotas is equal to the difference between the price that buyers – typically manufacturers of products that used CFCs, such as auto air conditioners – were willing to pay for the quantity and the price at which producers were willing to supply that quantity. Each firm to which the quotas were allocated received this value.

A 'windfall-profit' tax to prevent private firms from retaining the scarcity rents created by the cap-and-trade program eventually was passed by Congress (Merrill and Rousso, 1990, as cited in Stavins, 2000). The tax may have become the binding (effective) instrument after it was introduced.

No estimates of the cost savings from ODS trading under the US program have been developed. However, an earlier study estimated that a marketable quota scheme to reduce CFC emissions would cost about 49 percent less than a system of mandatory controls designed to achieve the same reductions (Palmer et al., 1980). Moreover, administrative costs appear to have been reduced relative to an alternative approach. The EPA needed just four staffers to oversee the program, rather than the 33 staffers and $23 million in administrative costs it anticipated (US Environmental Protection Agency, 2001). Industry estimated that a traditional regulatory approach to end uses would cost more than $300 million for record keeping and reporting, versus only $2.4 million for the allowance trading approach (US Environmental Protection Agency 2001).

The US trading program for ODSs appears to have been an environmental success in reducing ODS levels. For a variety of reasons, the USA reduced ODS production more quickly than required under the Montreal Protocol. It is not clear whether the use of a marketable permits approach promoted this faster timetable. Early reductions appear to have been primarily the result of tech-nological changes and the development of substitutes – both of which led to cost savings – rather than trading. Trading may have spurred innovation, however, by setting a price for ODS emissions reductions and sending a price signal to firms.

There is some evidence, however, that the difference between the treatment of CFCs in the USA and abroad has created difficulties. The US tax and permit approach leads to substantially greater prices for CFCs produced in the USA than in developing countries where production is still unregulated. The EPA reports that smuggling of these chemicals has become a serious problem, although no quantitative information is presented (US Environmental Protection Agency 2001). Smuggling of CFCs would mean that their overall decline is smaller than calculated on the basis of US and developed-country production, due to 'leakage' from regulated to unregulated producers.

3.4.2 The European Union Program

The European Commission (EC) has developed a transferable quota system for the European Union (EU) similar to that established in the USA (Klaassen, 1999). Quotas are allocated to producers on the basis of base year production levels (1986 or 1989, depending upon the substance). The phase-out of CFCs and halons was originally scheduled for 1998, but was accelerated to 1995 and 1994, respectively, in EC amendments in 1992 and 1994 (Klaassen, 1999). These later amendments also expanded the system to include other ODSs. The EU producers are allowed to transfer quotas domestically, within the EC, or with any other parties to the Protocol, provided that the overall targets are met. International transfers, however, require that both the EC and the member states involved agree beforehand. For national transfers, only the member state has to agree and only the EC has to be notified.

No estimates of the cost savings from the EU system are available (Klaassen, 1999). Table 7.4 reports transfers of CFCs involving EU companies from 1991 to 1994. A total of 19 transfers took place, representing about 13 percent of the allowable production. Most transfers were between EU companies and were intrafirm rather than interfirm. The principal reason for the transfers was the cost savings involved in concentrating the production, because CFC production is subject to considerable economies of scale (Klaassen, 1999). Initially transfers faced high transactions costs because the interpretation of EU rules was disputed. After the rules were clarified in 1993, transfers were usually accepted and transactions costs were low because the number of firms involved was small and pre-approval of the transfers involved little administration.

Table 7.4   Transfers of CFCs involving EU companies

Year	Allowable production (tons)	Amount transferred (tons)	Number of transfers				
			Total	EU internal	With non-EU	Intrafirm	Interfirm
1991/92	644 069	27 100	4	4	0	4	0
1993	214 690	53 645	7	7	0	6	1
1994	64 407	42 715	8	5	3	7	1
TOTAL	923 166	123 460	19	16	3	17	2

Note: 1991–92 pertains to 1 July 1991 – 31 December 1992.

Source: Klaassen (1999).

The trading program appears to have had a significant positive impact on the achievement of the Protocol's environmental goals in Europe (Klaassen, 1999). The system allowed parties to agree to a rapid phase-out since it enabled chemical companies to concentrate production in certain facilities and shift to substitutes. There were, however, problems with transfers to developing countries similar to those in the US program. Because developing countries do not have a cap, the baseline for transfers was unclear. In practice, many of these potential transfers were rejected (Peaple, 1993, as cited in Klaassen, 1999). Similarly, trades with the USA were restricted because the USA used a more stringent criterion than the EU (the lower of either allowed or actual production, in contrast to allowed production in EU legislation).

3.5   US Mobile Source Averaging, Banking and Trading (ABT) Programs

The US EPA has allowed certain sources of mobile emissions (for example, trucks and engines used in lawn-mowers) to meet emission standards using averaging, banking and trading (ABT). This approach was first provided for heavy-duty trucks and has been extended to several other categories of mobile sources regulated under Title II of the 1990 Clean Air Act Amendments. The mobile source categories with ABT programs now include the following: [17]

- Heavy-duty truck engines
- Large non-road diesel engines used in construction, agriculture and other activities
- Locomotive engines
- Marine outboard engines and personal watercraft
- Small utility engines (used in various lawn and garden and other applications).

The EPA has developed emissions standards from these sources, expressed as allowable emissions per unit of energy input (for example, emissions per horsepower-hour).

The ABT provisions provide flexibility to engine manufacturers in complying with the standards. The regulations allow the manufacturers to use credits for emission rates *below* the standard for some engine families to offset emission rates *above* the standard for other emission families (averaging), to put in an account to offset future year emissions (banking), or to be sold to another firm to offset emissions from its engine families (trading).

The specific provisions of the programs differ for the various engine types. The ABT program for marine engines, for example, involves trading of credits and debits for emissions from different engine families.[18] The calculation of credits and debits is based upon the following factors: the difference between the applicable emission standard and the engine family emission limit (FEL); sales in the relevant model year; average annual use in hours; the power output of the engine family; the future survival probabilities of the engines; and a discount factor used to calculate the net present value of the credit or debit. The regulations also permit early banking, which allows manufacturers to earn partial credit for emissions before the program is put in place. There are some temporary restrictions on allowable trades between manufacturers, prohibiting manufacturers from averaging across outboard motors and personal watercraft (for example, JetSki). (These restrictions represent implicit regulations concerning the initial allocation under an averaging program.) The restrictive provisions reflected concerns among manufacturers with small numbers of product lines that the averaging gains would be greater for companies with large numbers of product lines in both outboard motors and personal watercraft. Although in theory trading across manufacturers would provide the same gains to the small manufacturers, there were concerns that inter-manufacturer trading would be less common than intra-manufacturer averaging.

The ABT programs have not been the subject of detailed *ex-post* evaluations. The various manufacturers involved encouraged the development of the programs, although as noted there were some concerns about the relative gains to different manufacturers. The program for heavy-duty trucks and buses has been in place for the longest period. There has been considerable averaging and banking, but only one trade between firms, a 1996 exchange of credits for 5 tons of particulate matter from Navistar to Detroit Diesel (US Environmental Protection Agency, 2001).

Several *ex-ante* evaluations indicated that the ABT provisions would provide substantial potential cost savings for marine engines and various small utility engines.[19] These same studies suggest that the ABT provisions resulted in more ambitious environmental targets than if the flexibility were not available. In the case of the standards for marine engines, the EPA set the average emission standard in part on the basis of the marginal cost curve based upon emission trading.[20] If the ABT provisions had not been included, it seems likely that the average emission standard would have been less stringent.

3.6   US Acid Rain Trading Programs

The SO_2 allowance trading program is the best-known marketable permit program. The program was established under Title IV of the 1990 Amendments to the Clean Air Act, which calls for the creation of a national emission trading program for SO_2 emissions from fossil-fuel electric generating plants. As discussed below, Title IV also provides for voluntary SO_2 credit-based programs.[21]

3.6 SO_2 Cap-and-trade program[22]

The Title IV program created a national cap on SO_2 emissions from electric generating plants of roughly 9 million tons per year, effective in 2000 and beyond, which was advertised as requiring a 10 million-tons-per-year reduction from 1980 SO_2 levels (Ellerman et al., 2000). The emissions cap was to be achieved in two phases. During Phase I, a cap was established for the 263 largest electric generating emitters of SO_2 that involved reducing emissions by roughly 3.5 million tons per year, beginning in 1995. In 2000, the program entered Phase II, in which the program was expanded to include virtually all fossil-fuel electricity-generating units. Emission allowances were allocated initially to the relevant sources, with sources free to buy and sell the allowances. At the end of each year, each relevant source had to have sufficient allowances to cover its emissions. Excess allowances (that is, allowances greater than emissions) could be banked for future use or sale.

The Title IV program included several other provisions to implement the trading program. Continuous emission monitoring (CEM) equipment was required at each facility to check compliance. At the end of each year, units that were found to have emitted more SO_2 than their allowances covered would be given a grace period to acquire the necessary allowances. Facilities without sufficient allowances after the grace period are fined $2000 (adjusted for inflation) for every excess ton emitted. To provide maximum temporal flexibility, the trading program included provisions for unlimited banking of allowances. In addition, about 2.8 percent of the annual allowance allocations are withheld by EPA and distributed through an annual auction run by the Chicago Board of Trade; the revenues from the auction are returned to the original owners of the allowances. The auction provision responded to the concerns of independent power producers and utilities in growing regions that an active market would not emerge, perhaps because utilities would hoard initial allowances and not sell at any price (Ellerman et al., 2000).

As the acid rain trading program was implemented, contemporary commentators expressed considerable concern as to whether potential cost savings would be achieved (see, for example, Hausker, 1992). Potential concerns included the dampening effects of cost-of-service regulation on the incentives of participants to engage in cost-minimizing trades, uncertainties due to specific language in the legislation that an allowance was not a property right (and thus that allowances could be 'limited, revoked, or otherwise modified' without compensation in the future), the potential that state programs would limit trading, and uncertainties as to how the EPA would oversee the trading program. With regard to EPA oversight, for example, there were concerns that the EPA would require pre-approval of utility compliance plans, and thus hinder the development of viable markets for SO_2 allowances.

The environmental effects of trading also were challenged because of concerns that the geographic pattern of emissions after trading would reduce air quality, particularly in the Northeast. In 1993, the New York State Attorney General sued the US EPA to restrict allowance sales. The New York State legislature has passed legislation to constrain allowance sales between New York utilities and other entities (Burtraw and Mansur, 1999). This legislation – which has been subjected to legal challenges – reflects a concern that trading would result in increased emissions in areas downwind of New York and other Northeast regions and thus worsen air quality.

The SO_2 trading program appears to have avoided the pitfalls suggested by these concerns. The program is widely regarded as a success from both economic and environmental perspectives, although the actual performance of the program has been complex (see, for example, Ellerman et al. (2000) Burtraw, (1999) Schmalensee et al. (1998) and Swift (forthcoming).

An active and efficient market developed for SO_2 allowances, particularly in the period after 1994 (Ellerman et al., 2000). Despite fears, state agencies regulating electric utilities did not inhibit allowance trading.[23] As Ellerman et al. (2000) note, implementation of the SO_2 allowance program coincided with growing competitive pressures due to industry restructuring and deregulation,[24] which increased incentives for utilities to take advantage of the opportunities to reduce costs created by the allowance market. The EPA auction appears to have been successful in initially bringing parties to the market and establishing a range for market prices, although the vast majority of transactions have occurred in private markets (Ellerman et al., 2000). Trading volumes have grown with time and are a significant fraction of the total SO_2 allowed under the cap. Figure 7.2 shows the growth in trading among firms since the program's inception. (The estimates in Figure 7.2 exclude intra-company trades.) Table 7.5 shows the Phase I SO_2 emissions, as well as the cumulative number of allowances banked for future use or sale. Note that the total number of banked allowances currently exceeds the annual allotment.

Estimating the cost savings from the SO_2 trading program is complicated, although there seems little doubt that the savings have been substantial and promise to be even more so in the future. The complications in estimating the actual cost savings from trading include:

- uncertainty over the proper counterfactual comparison case (that is, what controls would have been put in place if an alternative approach had been adopted);
- banking and its effect on overall costs;
- effects of the voluntary programs on overall costs (see below); and
- uncertainty about the effects of trading on the development of cost-reducing innovations.

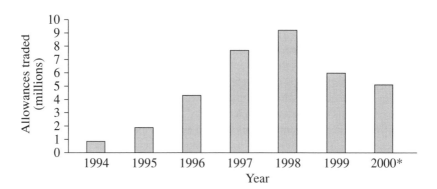

* Data are for the first half of 2000 only.

Source: US Environmental Protection Agency (2000a).

Figure 7.2   Interfirm trading of SO_2 allowances

Table 7.5   Phase I SO$_2$ emissions and allowances

	Phase I units total emissions (millions of tons)	Phase I units total allowances (millions of tons)	Cumulative total banked (millions of tons)
1980	10.9	–	–
1985	10.7	–	–
1990	10.0	–	–
1994	8.5	–	–
1995	5.3	8.7	3.4
1996	5.5	8.3	6.3
1997	5.5	7.1	8.0
1998	5.3	7.0	9.6
1999	4.9	7.0	11.6

Source: US Environmental Protection Agency Compliance Reports: 1995–99.

Several studies have estimated the cost savings from Phase I of the program and have used information on experience under Phase I to speculate about cost savings from banking and from Phase II. Researchers at the Massachusetts Institute of Technology (MIT) have produced careful studies covering both types of cost-savings estimates. Ellerman et al. (1997) conclude that the savings from Phase I emissions trading in 1995 were between $225 million and $375 million, or about 25 to 34 percent of the cost of abatement under the command-and-control approach (assuming the same initial distribution of allowances). Table 7.6 summarizes estimates from Ellerman et al. (2000) of the cost savings from the trading program, including the spatial flexibility in Phase I, the temporal flexibility from banking, and the spatial flexibility in Phase II. The MIT authors conclude that on average Phase I trading reduced costs by $358 million per year, a reduction of about 33 percent from the estimated cost of $1093 million per year under a non-trading regime. The authors estimate that the combination of Phase II trading and banking will reduce costs by about $2.3 billion per year, a reduction of over 60 percent from the total of about $3.7 billion per year. Over a 13-year period, costs are estimated to decline by a total of more than $20 billion, a cost reduction of about 57 percent from the assumed command-and-control alternative. Ellerman et al. (2000) present the results of various alternative estimates of cost savings due to trading, based upon different marginal costs of control and different periods over which the Phase I banked emissions are used in Phase II. In summary, Ellerman et al. (2000) conclude that emissions trading will reduce the cost of achieving the Phase II goal by about

Table 7.6 Abatement cost and cost savings from emissions trading

	Abatement cost with trading	Abatement cost without trading	Cost savings from emissions trading				
			Phase I spatial trading	Banking	Phase II spatial trading	Total cost savings	Savings as a percentage of cost without trading
Average Phase I year (1995–99)	735	1 093	358			358	33%
Average Phase II year (2000–07)	1 400	3 682		167	2 115	2 282	62%
13-year sum	14 875	34 925	1 792	1 339	16 919	20 050	57%

Note: All costs are in millions of present-value 1995 dollars.

Source: Adapted from Ellerman et al. (2000).

50 percent. This percentage cost saving is similar to that developed by other researchers as the MIT authors point out.[25]

The environmental effects of the SO_2 trading program also appear to be favorable. Burtraw and Mansur (1999) evaluate the concern that trading would lead to worse air quality, particularly in the Northeast. The authors assess the effects of trading and banking on overall utility emissions of SO_2, atmospheric concentrations of sulfates and deposition of sulfur, and public health benefits from reduced exposure to SO_2 and particulate matter (sulfates). The authors conclude that trading and banking have led to sizable geographic and temporal shifts in emissions. But contrary to the concerns discussed above, the authors conclude that the shifts due to trading lead to lower pollutant concentrations and greater health benefits in the East and Northeast. The authors also found that deposition of sulfur in the eastern regions decreased by a slight amount due to trading, even in New York State.

Although the acid rain trading program apparently has been successful both in lowering compliance costs and producing environmental benefits, its performance has not been perfect. With regard to cost savings, the full potential cost savings were not realized – at least initially – because of overinvestment in scrubbing (Ellerman et al., 2000). The allowance markets took some time to develop, and investment decisions on scrubbers and boiler modifications were based on price expectations for low-sulfur coal that proved to be high (Ellerman et al., 2000 and Burtraw and Mansur 1999). Phasing in of the sources subject to the program complicated the program's administration and also undermined the achievement of the emission reduction goals (McLean, 1997).[26] Moreover, the apparent advantageous environmental effects of trading are due to happenstance rather than program design, since the program does not differentiate SO_2 allowances based upon location. Despite these caveats, it seems safe to conclude that the major economic and environmental promises of the SO_2 acid rain trading program have been realized.

3.6 Voluntary programs

Title IV of the 1990 Clean Air Act Amendments also established three programs to allow sources voluntarily to enter the SO_2 trading program. These programs are:

1. Substitution Provision (including the Compensation Provision), which allows Phase II units to substitute for Phase I units. (Note that this was a temporary program that was not relevant after Phase II began.)
2. Opt-in Provision, which allows units to enter the trading program that were not included in the program under the 1990 Clean Air Act Amendments.

3. The Conservation and Renewable Energy Reserve (CRER), which provided additional allowances for utilities that adopted energy conservation programs or introduced additional renewable energy sources into their system.

Although the first two programs involve the trading of allowances rather than ERCs, they share with credit-based programs the importance of setting an emissions baseline, that is, the level of emissions that would have taken place without the program.

3.6.2.1 Substitution provision   Under the Substitution Provision, Phase II units could enter the program during Phase I and be awarded allowances equal to their baseline emissions.[27] Procedurally, the provision allowed Phase I units to submit a Substitution Plan that expands the number of units under compliance to include the opting-in Phase II units. Thus, Phase II units effectively were able to opt in to Phase I of the program. Because allowances awarded to sub- stitution units were equal to baseline emissions, in principle the Substitution Provision did not lead to increases in SO_2 emissions. A related Compensation Provision allowed utilities to reduce generation in Phase I units in a way that does not simply involve shifting production (and SO_2 emissions) to a Phase II unit.

The rules surrounding the Substitution Provision are relatively complicated because of compliance differences between Phase I and Phase II units. Many units voluntarily participating through the Substitution Provision receive regulatory benefits in addition to allowances. In particular, Phase II units vol- untarily opting in during Phase I are subject to less stringent Title IV NO_X standards (known as 'NO_X grandfathering'). A substitution unit may opt out of the program at any time so long as allowances are surrendered to the US EPA, and thus the decision to participate does not lock the unit into Phase I compliance standards.

Registration costs appear to have been low, despite the complex rules (Montero, 1999). They included the cost of baseline determination and admin- istrative costs. The baseline method involved information available for all units and a simple formula, making the cost of constructing the baseline very low.[28] Administrative costs also appear to be low, particularly since utilities that might participate are already required to do so through their designated Phase I units.

Title IV required that all affected utility units, including potential substitution units, have Continuous Emissions Monitoring (CEM) equipment installed and operating by 1995. Thus the cost of the CEM equipment – which is substantial – is not an additional cost incurred by a unit that enters the substitution program (Atkeson, 1997). Put another way, owners of potential substitution units were not deterred from entering the program by additional monitoring costs.

Participation in the Substitution Provision was high, with about 30 percent of eligible Phase II units opting in and adopting Phase I restrictions.[29] Table 7.7

provides data on participation in the program. In 1995, substitution units represented 175 of 445 units under Phase I requirements (Ellerman et al., 1997).[30] Emissions from these units were significantly lower than allowances received, with the remaining allowances being used to offset emissions at other Phase I units owned by the utility, sold on the allowance market, or banked for future use. The excess allowances received by these units (that is, the difference between allowances received and actual emissions) range from 0.40 to 0.55 million tons over the period 1995 to 1998. These excess allowances are the equivalent of emission credits. The final two rows provide information on the value to generating units of these excess allowances. In 1995, for example, the value of the excess allowances was about $72 million – assuming an allowance price of $150 per ton – or about $400 000 per participating generating unit. These values, however, do not take into account abatement costs. Ellerman et al. (2000) estimate that the 'net' value (that is, total value minus abatement costs) represented between 45 percent and 60 percent of the net allowances for two counterfactual cases and between 85 percent and 100 percent for a third counterfactual cost constructed specifically for these units. Assuming that the 'net' value was about 50 percent of the value, for example, the net value of the 1995 excess allowances would be $36 million, or about $200 000 per generating unit.

Table 7.7   Results of substitution provision

Statistic	1995	1996	1997	1998
Generating units[a]	182	161	153	135
Total allowances (million tons)	1.33	1.18	1.04	0.95
Total emissions (million tons)	0.85	0.63	0.62	0.55
Excess allowances				
Quantity (million tons)	0.48	0.55	0.42	0.40
Value (millions)[b]	$72.0	$82.5	$63.0	$60.0
Average value per unit (millions)	$0.40	$0.51	$0.41	$0.44

[a] Includes generating units from the Compensation Provision. There were seven compensation units in 1995. Note that the number of generating units in the program changed over time because the program allowed units the choice of entering or exiting the program in each year.
[b] The value of the net allowances is calculated as the quantity times the assumed allowance price ($150 per ton). As noted in the text, this value excludes the cost of reducing emissions.

Source: US Environmental Protection Agency (1999).

The voluntary nature of the Substitution Provision raises the question of whether some of the participation reflected allocations of 'extra' emissions, that is, allocations greater than the true baseline emissions. As Montero (1999) points out, information asymmetry (that is, greater information among owners of potential substitute sources than the regulator) leads to a potential problem of 'adverse selection,' in which sources receiving excess emissions under a given formula are more likely to participate. The effect of the adverse selection is to increase overall emissions, rather than hold emissions constant as the program assumes.

Montero (1999) provides a careful and detailed analysis of the Substitution Provision and concludes that adverse selection was a problem in practice.[31] Many units entering the trading program under the Substitution Provision appear to have 'actual' baseline emissions below the baseline used in the program. Montero (1999) also found that units whose baselines were lower than the formula were more likely to participate than those units whose baselines were higher than the formula; indeed, the likely 'baseline errors' were the most significant factor affecting utility decisions to opt in units under the Substitution and Compensation Provisions.[32] Many units appear to have received net allowances by taking few or no control actions. This systematic pattern resulted in emissions that were greater than predicted on the basis of average values.

Montero (1999) concludes that baseline formulas in the Substitution Provision overstated the 'actual' baseline SO_2 emissions for many eligible units. Baseline formulas were based on historical data that did not reflect recent changes in emissions. Heat input data were based on data from 1985 to 1987, and emission rates were based on data from no later than 1990 (five years before the units could opt in). These estimates did not reflect changes in fuel use that occurred as a result of decreases in the cost of low-sulfur coal from the Powder River Basin due to deregulation of railroad transport (see Ellerman et al., 2000). Increasing the use of low-sulfur coal reduced baseline SO_2 emissions.

In sum, the Substitution Provision produced mixed results. The program led to high levels of voluntary participation and undoubtedly reduced utility compliance costs. The transactions, however, appear to have resulted in substantial 'paper credits' and thus higher utility SO_2 emissions than presumed under Phase I.

3.6.2.2 Opt-in provision   The Opt-in Provision allows non-Phase II units to enter the SO_2 trading program. Eligible sources include electric generation units smaller than 25 MW (the cutoff in Title IV for inclusion in the acid rain trading program), simple combustion turbine units (built before 1990), industrial boilers, and non-affected municipal solid waste incinerators. Some sources, such as mobile sources and particular exempt units, are not eligible to opt in under this program.

Use of the Opt-in Provisions was limited, with only seven generation units (representing two facilities) entering during 1996 and three additional units entering during 1998. Table 7.8 provides data on participation in this program. Low participation appears to be due to the expensive monitoring requirements. Opt-in facilities had to install CEM equipment to comply with the monitoring requirements of the program. The CEM equipment can cost several million dollars (Atkeson, 1997). Relatively few firms found that the net value of the excess allowances – that is the value of the excess allowances minus the costs of control – warranted the investment in monitoring equipment (Atkeson, 1997).

Table 7.8 Results of Opt-in provision

Statistic	1995	1996	1997	1998
Generating units	0	7	7	10
Total allowances (million tons)	0.00	0.096	0.096	0.098
Total emissions (million tons)	0.00	0.040	0.079	0.080
Excess allowances				
Quantity (million tons)	0.00	0.056	0.017	0.018
Value (millions)[a]	$0	$8.4	$11.9	$12.0
Average value per unit (millions)	$0	$1.2	$1.7	$1.2

[a] The value of the net allowances is calculated as the quantity times the assumed allowance price ($150 per ton). As noted in the text, this value excludes the cost of reducing emissions.

Source: US Environmental Protection Agency (1999).

With regard to the environmental effects of the Opt-in Provision, there is no direct evidence that opt-in units resulted in 'paper credits,' although the baseline formulas potentially suffered from the same problems encountered in the Substitution Provision. All Opt-in Provision participants appear to have undertaken some emission reduction activities that resulted in emission reductions (Atkeson, 1997). Whether or not credits were awarded in excess of these reductions, however, is unclear.

3.6.2.3 Conservation and renewable energy reserve   The Conservation and Renewable Energy Reserve (CRER) is a pool of 300 000 total allowances that was reserved by the EPA for distribution to utilities or other organizations that undertake conservation or renewable energy activities that reduce SO_2 emissions. The program applied to activities undertaken from 1995 to 1999. To receive allowances, utilities (or other power producers) had to demonstrate that the conservation measures produced energy savings or that the addition of renewable sources reduced utilization of non-renewable units.

Utilities had to meet several eligibility requirements for the potential projects. These requirements included: (1) the utility must own either a Phase I or Phase II unit; (2) the activity producing the allowances must be undertaken within an integrated resource planning (or other least-cost planning) regulatory framework; and (3) the utility must be subject to a 'rate making process that does not make energy efficiency measures unprofitable,' a requirement referred to as 'net income neutrality' (US Environmental Protection Agency 1999).

Utilities applied for allowances based on activities undertaken during the previous year. Emission reductions were calculated according to a formula based upon multiplying energy savings (that is, kilowatt-hours saved) by an emission rate (that is, SO_2 emissions per kilowatt-hour). A standard emission rate was used, rather than a value specific to the individual utility or generating unit in order to reduce the complexity of the calculation (Morgan, 1999, as cited in Harrison and Schatzki, 2000). This rate (0.5 pounds of SO_2 per megawatt-hour) represented a relatively 'clean' mix of energy sources when the rate was included in the 1990 Clean Air Act.

The major complexity in the demonstration of SO_2 reductions concerned the estimate of energy savings. This had to be demonstrated to the EPA as part of the application procedure using one of two main methods:

1. *Public Utility Commission (PUC) approved method.* Projects implemented within an Integrated Resource Plan (IRP) or demand-side management (DSM) process could use the level of energy savings estimated in the process for the CRER.
2. *EPA Conservation Verification Protocol (CVP).* Other projects required the use of the protocol that the EPA developed. This protocol provided utilities with two approaches for estimating energy savings: (a) monitored energy use, which was the preferred approach, uses a comparison group to determine the level of energy consumption that would have occurred without the conservation program; and (b) stipulated energy use, which consists of basic engineering algorithms and conversion factors to estimate savings for 15 conservation measures.

Applications for the conservation allowances had to be submitted to the EPA for review. The EPA's review consisted of confirming PUC approval if that was the means of developing baselines or reviewing the baseline estimates submitted. The use of the PUC-approved methodologies involved lower administrative costs, both for the utility applicant and for the EPA. The EPA was sensitive to the costs of using the monitored energy approach, and allowed the stipulated savings approach to be used when verification costs were not cost-effective.[33]

The initial applications related to energy savings in the first year of the programs. Energy savings in subsequent years were adjusted, with the adjustment dependent on the type of verification chosen. Three options were available:

1. *Monitoring and inspection* – to receive the same level of credit for energy savings in later years, utilities had to continue to meet the statistical requirements for verified energy savings estimated using the Monitored Energy Use approach.
2. *Inspection only* – a utility could receive credit for up to 75 percent of the energy savings for half of the measure's lifetime. (Passive conservation measures (for example wall insulation) can receive up to 90 percent.)
3. *Default* – a default value for energy savings was chosen. Energy savings in subsequent years were 50 percent of the first year for half of the lifetime of the measure.

The higher credit given to the more accurate verification approaches provided some incentive for utilities to undertake these more costly approaches.

Activity in the CRER was relatively limited, with most of the reserve going unutilized. Table 7.9 summarizes the results of the CRER. As of January 1999, a total of 34 638 allowances had been awarded through 31 different applications, far short of the 300 000 allowances reserved in the CRER (US Environmental Protection Agency, 1999).[34] About 25 of the applications have used baselines and energy-saving estimates that have been approved by PUCs. Only six applications to the CRER have used the EPA's CVP, with five of these using a mix of stipulations and monitored energy savings and one using only solely stipulated savings estimates (Morgan, 1999, as cited in Harrison and Schatzki, 2000).

Table 7.9   Results of Conservation and Renewable Energy Reserve Program

Total transactions[a]	Quantity certified per unit			Market value/permit	Market value/transaction		
	Min.	Avg.	Max.		Min.	Avg.	Max.
31	4	1,083	4,144	$150	$600	$162 489	$621 600

[a] The number of allowances associated with the transactions equaled 12 percent of total allowances available.

Source: US Environmental Protection Agency (1999).

Several factors explain the relatively low participation in the CRER. The eligibility requirements clearly eliminated some potential projects. The relatively low value of allowances compared to the administrative and registration costs appear to have played a large role in the low participation (Morgan, 1999 as cited in Harrison and Schatzki, 2000). Even utilities that had already implemented eligible DSM programs participated at a low level. More stringent EPA reporting requirements and the cost of gaining explicit PUC approval are factors that would raise the registration costs, and might help explain the low participation.

The greater use of PUC-approved procedures in comparison to procedures based on EPA's more complex CVP does seem to suggest that higher transaction costs dampen program participation. As noted above, transaction costs were substantially higher for the CVP because new analyses of energy savings had to be developed. The use of stipulations can reduce these costs significantly, although they are still likely to be much larger than simply relying on estimates already developed under the PUC approach. Another potential factor is that the registration of energy savings estimates developed with the CVP may be subject to greater uncertainty than estimates that have already been approved by a PUC. Greater uncertainty over registration of energy savings estimates would reduce the expected payoff to utilities participating in the program.

In addition, for many eligible projects the potential financial gain was relatively limited. For example, at \$200 per SO_2 allowance (which is near historic highs, and more than double prices over much of the period from 1996 to 1998), 10 of the 31 approved projects are worth less than \$40 000, while a total of 14 are worth less than \$100 000 (US Environmental Protection Agency, 1999).

There is some evidence that utilities using the CVP took advantage of the flexibility it provided in choosing methodologies for estimating energy savings. Most of the applications using the CVP had a mix of stipulations and measured savings, suggesting that stipulations may allow utilities to take credit for programs where measurement may be costly (Morgan, 1999, as cited in Harrison and Schatzki, 2000). This flexibility may have allowed utilities to trade off higher monitoring costs against the value of additional allowances gained through greater accuracy.

In sum, the CRER had little overall effect on either the cost savings or the environmental effects of the acid rain program. The number of projects approved was small – far smaller than the amount allocated – and it is not clear that the projects represented new additions. Although the CRER provided some additional incentive for utilities to make conservation or renewable energy investments, it is not clear that utility decisions to undertake these activities were based on obtaining allowances through the CRER.

3.7 US (Los Angeles Air Basin) RECLAIM Program[35]

Regulators in the Los Angeles air basin developed a cap-and-trade emissions program in the early 1990s at the same time as the national SO_2 allowance program was being formulated (South Coast Air Quality Management District, 1993). The Los Angeles program, called the Regional Clean Air Incentives Market (RECLAIM), was significant both in some of its provisions and as the first major example of a tradable permit program developed by a local juris-diction, rather than a federal authority.

RECLAIM was designed to achieve emission reductions for NO_X and SO_2 equivalent to those projected to be achieved by a set of command-and-control regulations affecting relatively large stationary sources. The NO_X and SO_2 caps for these sources were set to decline by 8.3 percent and 6.8 percent per year, respectively, from 1994 to 2003, after which the caps remain constant. The program includes sources emitting over four tons of either NO_X or SO_2 with a few exceptions. The South Coast Air Quality Management District (SCAQMD) approved the program in October 1993 after a regulatory development period that lasted more than three years. RECLAIM began operation in January 1994. As discussed below, SCAQMD in May 2001 instituted a substantial mid-course correction to deal with dramatic increases in the price of NO_X permits, which are called RECLAIM Trading Credits (RTCs).

The design of the RECLAIM cap-and-trade program is distinctive for several reasons. Since it covers emitters in many sectors with a relatively low threshold, RECLAIM includes a far more heterogeneous mix of participants than the national SO_2 allowance program for electric power plants. As a result, it provides an indication of the possibilities of expanding the range of emissions trading to include multiple sectors. Considerable attention was paid to the initial allocation of RECLAIM trading credits in order to provide a program that was administratively feasible and politically salable (see Harrison, 1999a). The decision to base allocations on sources' peak activity over a certain period, for example, avoided concerns that an unrepresentative year was used to determine the initial allocation.

The RECLAIM program does not allow banking of permits because of concerns that banking would allow emissions to exceed mandated levels in some future year, and thus delay compliance with the ozone standard. RECLAIM does provide some temporal flexibility, however, by grouping sources into two 12-month reporting periods, one from January through December and the other from July through June. Sources can trade with other sources in either period and apply permits to their own period.

Another distinctive feature of the RECLAIM program is its division of the Los Angeles basin area into two zones, coastal and inland. The inland zone is downwind of the coastal zone, so emissions from the coast generally travel inland, but not vice versa. In developing the program, there was concern that trading might shift emissions to the coast, and thus worsen air quality inland. To guard against this problem, sources on the coast are prohibited from acquiring emissions permits from inland sources, but inland sources can acquire RTCs from both coastal and other inland sources. This two-zone system allows RECLAIM to address the different air quality effects of emissions in different areas of the Basin without creating an unworkable scheme.[36]

Experience with RECLAIM suggests both the advantages and some of the limitations of the tradable permit approach in dealing with uncertain demand for permits. Figures 7.3 and 7.4 show the reported emissions and total RTC supply for NO_X and SO_2 respectively. The total RTC supply declines in keeping with the trajectories established in the programs. Reported emissions generally decline over the period, coming very close to the total RTC supply by 1999. These figures illustrate that RECLAIM was successful in capping total NO_X and SO_2 emissions from the sources in the program.

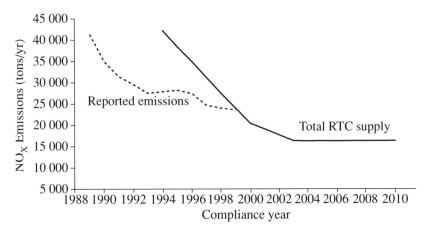

Source: South Coast Air Quality Management District (2001a).

Figure 7.3   RECLAIM NO_X emissions and RTC supply (tons/year)

RECLAIM also appears to be a success in facilitating an active market in RTCs. Its trading activity has been substantial. Figures 7.5 and 7.6 show how trading has developed in the seven years the RECLAIM program has been in effect. (The figures show both the number of RTCs 'traded' internally within firms, that is, without a price, and the number of RTCs traded between firms at the market price, and the total value of these market transactions.) As of 2000, permits for 265 000 tons of NO_X and 93 000 tons of SO_2 had been traded.

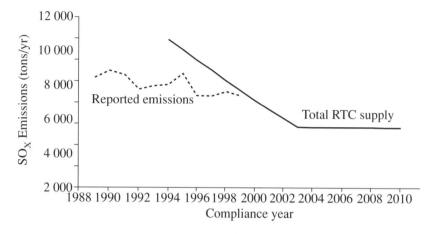

Source: South Coast Air Quality Management District (2001a).

Figure 7.4   RECLAIM SO$_X$ emissions and RTC supply (tons/year)

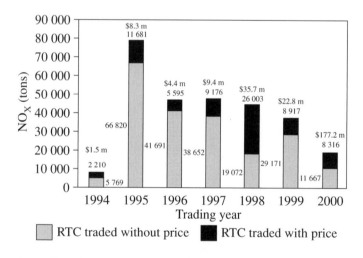

Source: South Coast Air Quality Management District (2001a).

Figure 7.5   NO$_X$ Trading under RECLAIM

No *ex-post* estimates have been prepared of the cost savings from RECLAIM. When the program was being developed, the cost savings were estimated to be about 40 percent compared to the cost of achieving the same emission reductions using the traditional regulatory approach (see Harrison and Nichols, 1992, and Johnson and Pekelney, 1996).

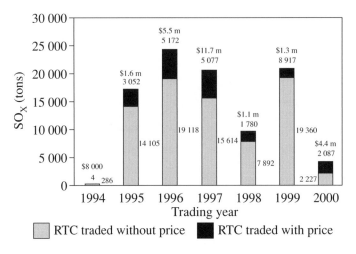

Source: South Coast Air Quality Management District (2001a).

Figure 7.6   SO$_X$ Trading under RECLAIM

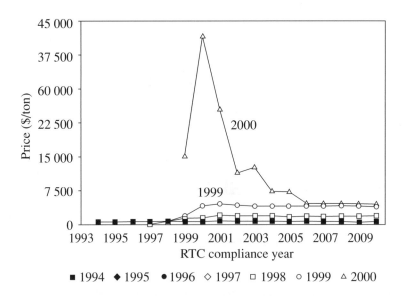

Source: South Coast Air Quality Management District (2001a).

Figure 7.7   Average NO$_X$ RTC prices

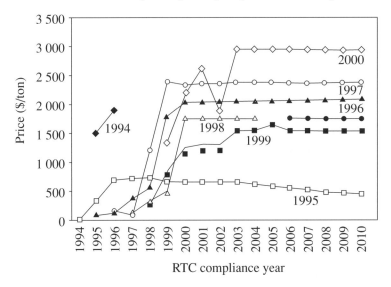

RTC compliance year

Source: South Coast Air Quality Management District (2001a).

Figure 7.8   Average SO$_2$ RTC Prices

The RECLAIM program in 2000 experienced a dramatic increase in the market price of NO$_X$ RTCs. Figures 7.7 and 7.8 show the average NO$_X$ and SO$_2$ RTC prices over time. (Note that because RTCs for future compliance years are subject to trade, the graph shows the average prices over time for RTC compliance years.) Between 1994 and 1999, the price of NO$_X$ RTCs remained relatively stable, ranging from $1500 to $3000 per ton. Beginning in June 2000, however, RECLAIM participants experienced a sharp and sudden increase in NO$_X$ RTC prices for both 1999 and 2000 compliance years (South Coast Air Quality Management District 2001a). The average price of 1999 NO$_X$ RTCs traded in 2000 was $15 377 per ton, which is almost ten times higher than the average price of $1827 per ton for NO$_X$ RTCs traded in 1999 for the 1999 compliance year. The increase for 2000 NO$_X$ RTCs was even more dramatic. The price increased from $4284 per ton for trades in 1999 to more than $45 000 per ton for trades in 2000. The average monthly price of NO$_X$ RTCs reached more than $70 000 per ton.

The high NO$_X$ RTC prices triggered a backstop provision in RECLAIM that requires the executive officer of SCAQMD to submit an evaluation and review within six months of the determination that the average RTC price has exceeded $15 000 per ton. The executive officer is also required to propose that the governing board amend the program as appropriate to address specific problems. On 11 January 2001, the SCAQMD released a White Paper evaluating the increases in NO_X RTC prices and presenting near-term and long-term options to stabilize NO_X RTC prices (South Coast Air Quality Management District, 2001a). This document reflected public input from an advisory committee. The staff concluded that increased demand by electric generation sources was the major cause of the abrupt change in NO_X RTC prices.[37] There also is evidence that the high NO_X RTC prices contributed substantially to the high electricity prices in California during this period.[38] The authors of the report concluded that substantial lower-cost control alternatives were available for RECLAIM sources, but that these controls would take some time to be put in place. The staff recommended various changes to the RECLAIM program.

The governing board of the SCAQMD on 11 May 2001 approved the following changes to RECLAIM (South Coast Air Quality Management District, 2001b):

- Power plants are separated from the rest of RECLAIM until at least 2002;
- Power plants will be subject to plans that require them to install pollution control equipment over the next two to three years;
- Power plants will pay into a mitigation fund for any excess emissions at the rate of $7.50 per pound ($15 000 per ton); and
- The SCAQMD will use the mitigation fund to reduce pollution from other sources, including diesel trucks and equipment at the ports.

The SCAQMD also developed a pilot RECLAIM Air Quality Investment Program (AQIP), allowing access to mobile and area source credits.

The dramatic increase in NO_X RTC prices in 2000 illustrates one of the key features of a cap-and-trade tradable permits program – uncertainty over allowance prices. This uncertainty is exacerbated when the program does not allow for banking, and thus provides no temporal flexibility. The mitigation fee adopted by the SCAQMD is similar to the 'safety-valve' mechanism that has been considered for greenhouse gas trading programs as a means of limiting the potential costs of the program.[39]

In sum, RECLAIM has been successful in limiting emissions and providing cost-saving flexibility. The recent short-term price increases suggest the need for temporal flexibility to reduce near-term spikes in prices. These price increases also suggest the usefulness of developing credit-based supplements – such as mobile source and area source credits – that provide the possibility of additional low-cost emission reductions.

3.8   US Northeast NO_X Budget Program

A NO_X budget program was developed by a group of Northeast states in the mid-1990s to deal with regional tropospheric ozone concerns. The cap-and-trade program is significant in part because it represents the first major example of a multi-jurisdictional program; the program was not imposed by the federal government but rather was jointly developed and implemented by the several states. These states were included within the Ozone Transport Region, established by Section 184 of the 1990 Clean Air Act Amendments. This multilateral creation is due partly to the fact that the EPA does not have statutory authority to implement a multi-state program for NO_X under the Clean Air Act. (In contrast, Title IV of the 1990 Clean Air Act Amendments specifically provides authority for the SO_2 acid rain trading program.)

The NO_X Budget Program applies to electric generating units greater than 15 megawatts and similar-sized industrial boilers (such as process boilers and refineries). It covers NO_X emissions from May through September in eight states.[40] The Budget Program has three phases, the last two of which involve cap-and-trade programs. (The first phase was essentially a re-labeling of existing technology-based requirements.) The second and third phases provide caps that reduce NO_X emissions by 55 to 65 percent (compared to uncontrolled levels) for 1999–2002 and by at least 65 to 75 percent starting in 2003.

The states involved in the NO_X Budget Program developed a 'model rule' via two multi-state groups. The model rule has several prominent features, one of which relates to initial allocations to each state. These are based upon 1990 emission rates, with allocations to individual boiler units to be determined by the individual states. As noted, the compliance period runs during the summer months from May through September, when NO_X effects on ozone concentration are most significant. There are relatively strict penalties for non-compliance, with each excess ton counting against three tons for the following year. There are no explicit plans to develop auctions or bulletin boards for permit trading.

The NO_X Budget Program includes banking, but limits the extent to which regulated boilers can use permits banked in previous years. When the NO_X Budget Program was being designed, environmental regulators were concerned that many allowances would be banked, creating the possibility of a 'NO_X spike' of higher-than-anticipated emissions. To deal with this possibility, the model rule provides for 'progressive flow control (PFC).'[41] Under PFC, if the total number of banked permits exceeds 10 percent of the allowances for that year, some of the banked allowances will have a discount factor of 50 percent (that is, two banked allowances have to be redeemed for each ton of NO_X emitted). The proportion of discounted allowances grows with the size of the bank. This provision complicates the incentives for sources to bank emissions (see Farrell, 2000).

The NO_X Budget Program provides for differences in the emission reductions for different broad areas within the multi-state region, to reflect the different likely effects of emissions on air quality and exposure. The fewest allowances are allocated to sources in an inner zone (the corridor from Washington, DC to

Portsmouth, New Hampshire), more to sources in the outer zone, and the most to sources in the northern zone (the Adirondack region and northern New Hampshire).[42] Note that these differences do not take into account the fact that emissions will have different effects on air quality on different days within the summer period, due to differences in peak demand for electricity and climate conditions. Several ideas to control emission during peak demand days were considered, but none was considered feasible (Farrell, 2000).

The NO_X Budget Program in the OTR has not been in operation long enough to evaluate its effectiveness or cost savings thoroughly, although a recent review suggests the program is operating effectively (Farrell, 2000). An early study estimated that a regional NO_X cap-and-trade program could lead to a 30 percent savings (or about $80 million in annualized cost savings) relative to a traditional emission standards program (NESCAUM/MARAMA 1996 as cited in Harrison, 1999a). In practice, phase-in of the program was somewhat hurried, but market participation has been broad and trading levels high (Farrell, 2000). During 1999, the first year of the program's implementation, eight states participated. With over 110 distinct firms and organizations receiving initial allocations and more than 50 others participating in the NO_X budget market, the program has reached a variety of sources. In 1999, almost 32 000 vintage 1999 NO_X allowances were traded by distinct economic entities in 643 transactions through the end of November, representing about 15 percent of all allowances allocated (Farrell, 2000). Power companies remain the largest participants, representing 98 percent of all trades. The market trades represent a total value of about $100–$120 million (Farrell, 2000). Even more allowances (42 000 tons) were transferred within firms, but this figure largely represents corporate reorganization in response to restructuring of the electricity generation sector.

The speed with which the NO_X market developed is due in part to the participation of marketing and brokerage firms that participate in power, emissions, fuel and other markets simultaneously, and to whom generating companies are turning for risk management services (Farrell, 2000). The NO_X market involved greater use of derivative products (for example, options) than the SO_2 market, because of greater volatility in price. These derivatives were traded in the first year of the NO_X Budget Program; in contrast, it took several years for options to develop in the SO_2 allowance market.

With regard to environmental performance, emissions from power plants in the NO_X Budget Program clearly have decreased. The 1999 NO_X emissions represent about a 25 percent decrease from 1998 emissions (US Environmental Protection Agency, 2000). No study has been done on the effects of the apparent reductions in emissions on ozone levels (or exposure levels) in areas within the region. Moreover, it is not clear whether the NO_X Budget Program in the Northeast results in 'leakage,' that is, increased emissions in areas outside of the region covered by the cap-and-trade program. Preliminary evidence suggests that concerns about the direction of trading in the Northeast have not materialized.[43]

In sum, the preliminary evidence suggests that the NO_X Budget Program is working to decrease the overall cost of reducing NO_X emissions in various Northeast states. At least where state interests and experiences are similar, multi-jurisdictional trading does appear to be feasible.

4.   POTENTIAL FUTURE PROGRAMS

The success of existing permit programs – notably the SO_2 acid rain trading program – has led to interest in extending the approach to other pollutants and, indeed, other media.[44] It is useful to include some of these applications here to provide an indication of the opportunities for extending the approach as well as some of the additional issues that are likely to be raised in these new applications. Indeed, it is clear from the previous experience as well as from the complexities of some of the potential applications that one cannot assume that a marketable permits approach will necessarily succeed in any particular application.

This section considers three potential applications, all of which raise novel issues. The first is a cap-and-trade program to deal with visibility in the West if other controls are not sufficient to meet visibility standards. The second is a proposal that would use trading to regulate mercury emissions from electricity generators. The third category is the use of marketable permits programs – both domestic and international – to reduce CO_2 and other greenhouse gas emissions. The primary objectives in this section are to illustrate some potential applications of marketable permits that are being considered and to indicate some of the additional issues that are likely to arise.[45] All of the applications – particularly those related to climate change – raise many complications beyond those included in this review article.

4.1   US Potential Program for Western Visibility

The states and tribes in the Western USA are developing a backstop cap-and-trade program for regional SO_2 emissions that would come into force if other voluntary provisions were not sufficient to achieve visibility-related emissions milestones (Western Regional Air Partnership, 2000). Both the voluntary program and the potential cap-and-trade program were developed by the Western Regional Air Partnership (WRAP), a group that includes representatives from Western states, tribes and federal agencies. WRAP is administered by the Western Governors' Association and the National Tribal Environmental Council. The WRAP recommendations were submitted to the US EPA for inclusion in an existing rule aimed at reducing regional haze and improving visibility in 16 national parks and wilderness areas on the Colorado Plateau, among other national parks and wilderness areas (64 Fed. Reg. 35715, 1999).

The trading program would reduce SO_2 emissions to a level at or below that achieved with the installation of 'best available retrofit technology' on various existing stationary sources that emit more than 100 tons per year of SO_2. These sources include smelters, refineries, cement kilns, lime plants, paper pulp mills and boilers. The allocation formulas being developed include regional set-asides for tribes and new sources. The details of the allocations to existing units are as yet underdetermined, as are many of the additional details of the program. The program, however, is intended to include the major features of the existing cap-and-trade programs, notably the acid rain program, RECLAIM, and the NO_X Budget Program.

The potential trading program for the Western states and tribes constitutes another interjurisdictional program. The WRAP program has the advantage of an existing legal and institutional framework, and thus presumably would encounter fewer difficulties of coordinating trading rules among the various jurisdictions. The program does face substantial challenges, however, such as the development of allocation formulas that are acceptable to the many different sources and the integration of the new cap-and-trade program with two other cap-and-trade programs that cover SO_2 emissions in the West (the acid rain trading program and RECLAIM).

4.2   US Potential Mercury Trading Programs

The USA may develop a cap-and-trade program to control mercury emissions from power plants. The EPA announced in December 2000 that it intends to regulate mercury from coal- and oil-fired power plants and that it would develop proposed regulations over the next three years (65 Fed. Reg. 13490, December 20, 2000). One possibility is that the proposed regulations would include a cap-and-trade program.[46] In addition, the US Congress is considering several bills that would require simultaneous reductions of multiple power plant emissions, including mercury (Energy Information Administration, 2001). These bills might allow for a cap-and-trade program for mercury.

The EPA has developed information on the potential costs of a cap-and-trade approach for mercury compared to a command-and-control approach that would require that given technology be applied to control mercury (US Environmental Protection Agency, 1999). This information indicates that the potential gains from a mercury emissions trading program will depend in large part on what other emissions are controlled at the same time. The EPA study considered the potential gains from trade under three alternative baselines:

1. Baseline with already-promulgated regulations;

2. Baseline with an additional SO_2 reduction of 50 percent; and
3. Baseline with an additional SO_2 reduction of 50 percent and a carbon cap.

The costs of reducing mercury – under both the command-and-control approach and the emissions trading approach – are lowest when the carbon cap is included and highest when only the already-promulgated regulations are assumed. Costs are lower for cases 2 and 3 because controlling carbon and SO_2 provides some mercury control as well.

The EPA results suggest that the gains from trading in the case of mercury are smaller than for other pollutants. The percentage gain from trading – versus the command-and-control approach – ranges from 6 percent under the baseline with SO_2 reductions (case 2), 10 percent under the baseline with already-promulgated regulations (case 1) and 23 percent under the baseline with SO_2 reductions and a carbon cap (case 3). These percentages are substantially smaller than those for the SO_2 acid rain trading program (as noted above) or for NO_X controls.[47] The EPA speculates that the relatively small gains reflect the limited control technologies for mercury and the high level of control assumed, leaving few opportunities for some sources to over-control and provide allowances to high-cost sources.[48] The gains from a mercury cap-and-trade program are greater when a carbon cap also is included for several reasons. For one thing, the lower electricity demand – due to higher electric rates from the carbon permit price – creates greater freedom for generators to select coals with lower mercury rather than lower sulfur content. In addition, lower electricity demand provides greater freedom to change the mix of units used to meet demand (US Environmental Protection Agency 1999). The EPA analysis emphasizes, however, that these results are based upon data that are limited and preliminary.

One of the biggest concerns under a cap-and-trade approach for mercury is the potentially uneven regional distribution of emissions.[49] The EPA concluded, however, that the cap-and-trade approach would not affect substantially the regional distribution of mercury emissions (US Environmental Protection Agency, 1999), a conclusion that was also reached by the Energy Information Administration (2001). Moreover, a cap-and-trade approach may be preferable from an environmental standpoint to a command-and-control approach requiring a given percentage removal; specifying a percentage removal standard could cause a shift to high-mercury coal to facilitate compliance, since with the available technology high percentage removal is significantly harder when the coal has a relatively low percentage of mercury.

A cap-and-trade program for mercury represents another potential application of the marketable permits approach. The cap-and-trade approach seems sensible from an environmental perspective; potential environmental concerns that a cap-and-trade approach would affect regional patterns of mercury emissions appear not to be borne out by the evidence. The cost analyses suggest that a cap-and-trade approach could be less costly than a command-and-control approach, although the potential cost savings appear to be substantially less than for other programs. The potential cost savings from mercury trading may be limited if the requirements turn out to be so stringent that few possibilities are available for relatively inexpensive over-control.

4.3   Potential International and Domestic Greenhouse Gas Trading Programs

The growing interest in tradable permits is due in large part to a growing concern about climate change and to interest in limiting emissions of carbon dioxide (CO_2) and other greenhouse gases (GHGs). The tradable permit approach seems ideally suited to the control of CO_2 and GHGs for several reasons (Ellerman, 2000). GHG emissions quickly become uniformly mixed in the atmosphere so that, unlike other issues, the location of the emissions does not matter. Moreover, because the residence time for various GHGs is long, the timing of abatement is not very important, providing a rationale for the cost-saving flexibility over time that banking and borrowing can offer.[50] The tradable permit approach also figures prominently in current proposals to address climate change. The major current international proposal – the Kyoto Protocol[51] – provides for use of the tradable permits approach, including both a cap-and-trade approach and a credit-based approach.[52] In addition, many individual countries – as well as the European Union – are considering the use of a tradable permits approach to control CO_2 and GHGs domestically.[53] Thus, in addition to its conceptual appeal, the tradable permits approach is receiving substantial attention in international and domestic discussions of climate change policy.

Many empirical studies have evaluated the potential costs of achieving GHG targets under different assumptions regarding both domestic carbon trading and international carbon trading (see, for example, Weyant and Hill, 1999; Toman et al., 1999; OECD 1999). All studies show that the cost of meeting carbon targets would be dramatically reduced if an international GHG trading program were in place to take advantage of relatively cheap emission reductions in developing countries. Trading only among developed countries – such as the Annex B countries specified in the Kyoto Protocol – also could reduce overall costs, although by substantially less than under a full international trading regime. Studies also show that domestic carbon trading can reduce substantially the cost of achieving a given domestic GHG target, compared to an alternative approach that would rely on command-and-control regulations on individual sectors to achieve GHG emission reductions (see Council of Economic Advisers, 2000, and Capros et al., 2001). The overall cost savings from a purely domestic trading program of course are smaller than if international trading also were available.

These studies suggest the usefulness of establishing domestic and international tradable permit programs if binding targets ultimately are required under domestic legislation in individual countries or under the Kyoto Protocol or some other international agreement. There are, however, many issues that would need to be addressed to develop workable programs. The following is a brief description of some of the key issues that have been raised regarding domestic GHG tradable permit programs:[54]

- *Upstream versus downstream compliance.* This issue concerns the point at which trading would occur and thus compliance would be measured. Commentators differentiate between an upstream system – in which trading participants would include coal and other fossil-fuel producers – and a downstream system that would regulate emissions from electric power plants and other fuel users (see, for example, Shogren and Toman, 2000). An upstream system presumably would be easier to administer because the number of participants would be smaller. Critics of this approach point to the potential large profits that would accrue to participants if they were initially allocated permits.[55]
- *Initial permit allocation.* Allocating permits inevitably is contentious, since it involves an assignment of rights and associated scarcity rents. The specific formula used to allocate permits generally does not affect the overall cost savings from a tradable permit program, although it does affect the gains of the participants.[56] The basic distinction is between auctioning the permits and grandfathering, that is, granting the permits to facilities. One of the arguments in favor of auctioning is that the auction revenue can be recycled to reduce inefficient taxes, thereby producing a 'double dividend.'[57] There are no examples of auctioning, due to the practical necessity of gaining agreement among those affected by the control program.[58]
- *Comprehensiveness of the emission cap.* A downstream cap-and-trade program raises the issue of which sectors to include. There is a trade-off between potential cost savings and administrative feasibility and costs; including more sectors provides greater diversity in marginal cost and thus more opportunities for cost-reducing trades, but monitoring and enforcement costs may overwhelm the cost savings for smaller sources. Several proposed programs attempt to strike a balance.[59]
- *Integration of other GHGs and sinks.* The Kyoto Protocol includes gases other than CO_2 and the possibility of carbon sinks. Including these other sources in a trading program offers the possibility of substantial economic gains, but questions of practicality arise at least in the near term (Ellerman,

2000). Relatively few data (with considerable variability) exist on non-CO_2 GHGs and on sinks, and thus measuring and monitoring them would be difficult. As Ellerman (2000) notes, most proposals start with CO_2 and then provide for possible expansion to other gases and sinks.

• *Banking and borrowing.* Because the timing of emissions has relatively little effect on the environmental consequences, as noted above, there is an economic argument for allowing both banking and borrowing in a GHG tradable permits program. Concerns have been raised, however, about whether borrowing would be enforceable.

• *Linkage with other domestic GHG policies.* Most domestic proposals assume that the tradable permits program would not cover all of a country's CO_2 or GHG emissions. Several problems arise when a cap-and-trade program for some sectors is combined with other policies in other sectors. These problems include uncertainty regarding whether the overall country target will be achieved, differential effects of the various policies on different sectors, inefficient arbitrage between policies (and thus overall compliance costs that are greater than necessary), and adverse effects on individual domestic sectors in the context of an international permits program (Ellerman, 2000).

• *Permit price cap or escape valve.* The possibility that capping domestic GHG emissions could be costly has created interest in a hybrid approach in which a cap-and-trade program is accompanied by a 'safety valve,' that is, a price at which the government would provide unlimited additional permits (see Kopp et al., 1999). Such a program limits the overall cost of the cap-and-trade program, but raises questions of compliance with the national cap and consistency with an international permits program (Pizer, 1999, and Ellerman, 2000).

The difficulties would be even greater to develop an international GHG trading program, as suggested by many studies and by the complicated negotiations over the tradable permit provisions of the Kyoto Protocol.[60] These implementation issues – which generally have not been addressed in previous programs – include the following:

• *International allocations and developing-country participation.* Allocating the overall cap to individual countries clearly is an important feature of an international system. The Kyoto Protocol represents an international allocation of permits for the period from 2008 to 2012 for the industrialized countries (although of course the Kyoto Protocol has not been ratified). The European Burden Sharing Agreement provides an additional example of reaching agreement on allocations. Determining an appropriate allocation for developing countries, however, promises to be substantially more difficult. One possible solution is to set targets indexed to economic growth, as reflected in the emissions commitment announced by Argentina in 1999 (Council of Economic Advisers, 2000).

- *Penalties and liability rules for trading.* In contrast to current domestic programs – in which credible penalty systems have been developed – a credible penalty system is difficult to consider at the international level. The problem is sometimes referred to as 'overselling,' that is, the sale of more permits than are excess to the country's emissions. Overselling could be dealt with under the traditional 'seller liability' arrangements if international sanctions were credible; concerns that such sanctions would not be credible have led to proposals for 'buyer liability.' (Ellerman, 2000 and Nordhaus et al., 2000 provide detailed analyses of the various liability options proposed.)
- *'Leakage' of emissions to countries or sectors outside the program.* This problem arises if emission controls in one country or sector are offset by increased emissions in countries or sectors that are not regulated. Although not peculiar to tradable permits, this problem would arise if the international program were not global.
- *Interaction between international GHG tradable permit program and domestic GHG programs.* Most empirical estimates of cost savings from an international program implicitly assume that all countries adopt domestic tradable permit programs. As Hahn and Stavins (1999) point out, if some countries use non-trading approaches, cost minimization would not be assured. Achieving cost savings would require some form of project-by-project credit program, such as joint implementation, which may be less likely to facilitate cost savings because of large transactions costs.
- *Integration of cap-and-trade and credit-based approaches.* The Kyoto Protocol includes both approaches. Under the Kyoto mechanisms, use of the credit-based approach is the only means of taking advantage of the cost savings from low-cost reductions in developing countries. The major difficulty with developing the credit-based approach is in developing credible baselines.[61]

These lists of problems[62] – which could be extended to include many other issues and much more complete treatments – should not obscure the fact that the tradable permits approach is well suited to control of GHG emissions, at both the domestic and international level. Although it is difficult to predict how international and domestic policies might evolve in the future, it seems likely that the tradable permits approach will figure prominently in discussions of policy instruments to achieve whatever goals ultimately are set.[63]

5. CONCLUSIONS AND RESEARCH AGENDA

The experience with tradable permits includes programs that appear to have achieved substantial cost savings while maintaining environmental goals as well as those whose performance has been less successful. Although necessarily somewhat subjective, several conclusions might be drawn from this experience. This experience also suggests several areas for additional applied research.

5.1 Conclusions

This section provides general conclusions regarding the various tradable permit types as well as conclusions regarding the elements of successful program design.

5.1.1 Overall evaluations of tradable permit types

5.1.1.1 Cap-and-trade schemes have been successful in meeting emission targets and reducing compliance costs A large number of studies have estimated the potential cost-saving gains from cap-and-trade programs. Experience confirms that these gains can be substantial in practice. The most comprehensive evidence is for the SO_2 acid rain trading program. As discussed above, trading appears to have reduced costs by about one-third in the first five years of the program (Phase I) and appears poised to reduce costs by about one-half when the effects of banking and Phase II controls are taken into account. These cost savings are in comparison to estimates of the costs that would have been incurred if the same emission reductions had been achieved under a command-and-control regime. The CFC tradable production/import allowance system appears vastly superior to a command-and-control alternative that would have established use-specific regulations or bans. Although it is not possible to provide estimates of cost savings, the NO_X Budget Program for the Northeast appears to be another promising application.

   These cost savings generally have not come at the expense of environmental protection. Emission caps have been met in the SO_2 acid rain trading program, the CFC program in the USA and Europe, and in RECLAIM. (As noted, however, recent high prices for RECLAIM NO_X trades suggest the usefulness of introducing some flexibility to modify the cap, at least in cases in which banking is restricted and a relatively small number of sources are involved.)

5.1.1.2 Credit-based schemes have had more varied performances
Experience with credit-based programs shows more variable results. EPA's long-standing, credit-based ET program has provided important flexibility in some cases, primarily for new sources in non-attainment areas, but for the most

part has served as a relatively minor adjunct to traditional emission standards. The same caveats appear relevant for the equivalent German programs.

One of the key factors in determining the success of trading programs appears to be the clarity with which the commodity is defined. Clear definitions minimize the obstacles to trading and increase the likelihood that potential cost savings will be achieved. If the commodity is not clear, time and resources are wasted trying to determine what is available for sale or purchase. The need to set a baseline to determine what can be sold as an ERC can lead to substantial transactions costs and thus fewer cost-reducing transactions. In addition, where participation is voluntary, as with the supplementary programs for the acid rain trading program, the problem of 'adverse selection' may mean that participation increases emissions rather than reduces costs of meeting a given environmental target.

5.1.1.3 Averaging schemes have lowered costs and may have increased environmental protection Clear allocations can be developed without setting an overall cap by establishing an averaging program. The lead in gasoline averaging program is widely regarded as a successful application of the tradable permits approach, with costs that are lower than if command-and-control standards were set. Although emissions are not capped, the presence of the averaging flexibility probably allowed lead to be phased out more quickly. Similar flexibility in the mobile source ABT (averaging, banking and trading) programs also may have allowed more ambitious environmental targets.

5.1.2 Elements of successful design for cap-and-trade programs
This section summarizes the implications of the existing experience for the design of successful tradable permit programs. We concentrate on the cap-and-trade program.

5.1.2.1 Initial allocations are contentious but feasible if most parties gain from cost savings Cap-and-trade programs require the regulatory agency to determine the distribution of initial allowances. This process is invariably highly contentious because valuable property rights are being distributed. The process of determining initial allowances was complicated by many 'equity' considerations in both the SO_2 trading program and RECLAIM. Nevertheless, the process of determining initial allocations appears to be feasible as long as most parties gain relative to the alternative command-and-control requirements. Most parties would gain, either as buyers or sellers, as long as the initial allocations were grandfathered to existing sources rather than auctioned (revenues to the government). Indeed, auctioning does not appear to be an acceptable allocation method, at least as the principal basis for initial allocations.

Note that allocation is less of an issue under the credit-based or averaging approaches. There are, however, distributional issues that can arise in terms of how products are subdivided for averaging purposes. In the case of lead in gasoline, basing the program only on leaded gasoline rather than all gasoline provided an advantage to refineries that produced higher-than-average shares of leaded gasoline. The restrictions on averaging across outboard motors and personal watercraft represent another example of how distributional issues can arise. Restricting averaging may work to the disadvantage of firms that do not produce products in both markets, although trading across firms can reduce or eliminate the disadvantage.

5.1.2.2   Intertemporal trading (banking) provides important flexibility
Banking provides important flexibility for sources to undertake early reductions to accumulate allowances that can be used to ease compliance in the future. This flexibility is particularly important where reductions are phased in over time. For example, both the SO_2 allowance program and the lead-in-gasoline programs involved substantial phase-downs in allowable emissions. In the lead phase-down, participating sources undertook considerably more control than would have occurred in the early stages of the program, and the high level of banking in the SO_2 program partially reflects a similar strategy. Banking during phase-downs is likely to generate environmental benefits, because it leads to greater emission reductions when overall emissions are relatively high – and thus potentially more damaging at the margin, based upon decreasing marginal damages – and to smaller emission reductions when overall emissions are lower.

Banking can be important even when there is not a large phase-down. The need for allowances is likely to differ significantly from year to year, due to economic cycles and swings within given sectors. Banking allows sources to accommodate these swings without leading to large changes in allowance prices.

5.1.2.3   Geographic differences should be kept relatively simple to avoid small markets or excessive complexity   A tradable permit program in theory should take into account differences in the effects of emissions in different geographic regions. This effect is not relevant for CO_2 and other greenhouse gases, because climate change effects are due to overall global emissions. But for emissions such as NO_X and SO_2, the effects could be quite different depending upon their timing and location. Emissions upwind of major population centers would have greater effects on overall exposure than emissions far from population areas. These differential effects in theory could be taken into account by establishing different trading zones or setting up different trading ratios.

Experience suggests, however, that major simplifications may be better for workable programs. In the case of RECLAIM, for example, the region is divided into two zones rather than the set of 38 that was originally proposed. Similarly, the early discussions of the acid rain trading program contemplated dividing the USA into several trading regions; the final program was national. Although these broad geographic boundaries are crude, they may on balance be superior to more complicated programs that run the risk of excessive transactions costs or the possibility of inadequate market participants.

5.1.2.4 Private institutions can facilitate trades and provide market information Brokers are important elements of the trading program for the SO_2 allowance program, RECLAIM and the emerging NO_X Budget Program. Brokers lower the overall transaction costs for trades, increasing the volume of trades and overall cost savings. In the SO_2 program, for example, brokers and other private market transactions currently account for the bulk of allowance sales and purchases. In contrast, relatively few transactions are accounted for by the auction mechanism set up initially to provide market information and liquidity.

5.1.2.5 Government intervention in market transactions should be limited, although auctions can be useful to assist in market development The early US emissions trading programs appear to have suffered from excessive government involvement in the market transactions. The bubble policy represents perhaps the extreme example; requiring that every transaction be approved *ex ante* as a modification to the State Implementation Plan meant that virtually no transactions took place.

Government involvement in the SO_2 acid rain program and RECLAIM has been much more circumscribed. Government agencies monitor performance and provide registration functions. But market transactions do not require approvals and the government does not require specific control requirements. It will be important, however, to follow the recent changes in RECLAIM in response to high NO_X trading prices to determine if the compliance plan requirements being considered have the effect of reducing cost savings.

5.2 Research Issues

This review emphasizes the issues involved in translating the theory of tradable permits into a workable program. Many issues have arisen in the existing and prior programs, and even more will arise in new applications, particularly those related to climate change. Fortunately, the development of program details for GHG programs has become an important priority for government agencies, private parties and academic researchers. Indeed, the literature on GHG tradable permit programs is becoming voluminous. These studies are likely to prepare the way for policy initiatives, although the process of developing appropriate policies is likely to be a long one. One should expect similar – if less well studied – initiatives for tradable permit programs in other areas.

In addition to policy-specific studies, it is useful to consider what general studies might be encouraged. The following are three important topics for additional research.

5.2.1   Assessing 'actual' rather than hypothetical gains from marketable permit programs

Most analyses of the gains from marketable permit programs are based on hypothetical programs, in which the analyst implicitly assumes 'perfect' trading, that is, that all potential gains from trade are realized. This perspective is understandable, because it is difficult to know, *a priori*, how much the actual cost savings will differ from the ideal. With increasing experience with tradable permit programs, however, it is increasingly feasible to consider the factors that might cause 'actual' costs to differ from those under a perfect program.

The term 'actual' is put in quotation marks because it is not possible to know with certainty what actual compliance costs have been under a marketable permit program; market prices reflect marginal costs rather than the compliance costs. Nor is it possible to know what the compliance costs would have been if an alternative command-and-control regime had been in place. Nevertheless, efforts should be made to develop estimates of costs under tradable permit programs in practice in order both to assess the factors that make for successful (that is, cost-minimizing) programs and to use the research information to design better future programs.

5.2.2   Assessing dynamic gains from marketable permit programs

The dynamic gains from marketable permit programs are more difficult to assess than the more static compliance cost savings that are typically estimated in prospective studies. The dynamic gains include several components:

- Savings in compliance costs due to banking provisions.
- Reductions in costs due to innovations in control technology.
- Reductions in costs due to greater diffusion of existing lower-cost control technology.

Although these gains are more difficult to quantify, their quantification would be part of a complete evaluation.

5.2.3   Integrating a safety valve into a tradable permit program

Experience with the California RECLAIM program in 2000 – in which permit prices increased more than tenfold within several months and led to substantial cost increases for all electricity generators in California – suggests the practical usefulness of including a 'safety valve,' that is, a maximum permit price. Although research 25 years ago described the advantages of the 'safety-valve' approach, there was no such system in place until recently, when an equivalent element was added to RECLAIM. The topic has generated more interest lately because of its possible applicability to GHG tradable permit programs.

Research into this hybrid approach could build on the RECLAIM experience to investigate how the program works and the methods that might be used in practice. What bases should be used to set such a 'safety valve'? How should emissions increases beyond the cap be made up, if at all? What temporal flexibility is appropriate, given the likelihood of 'price spikes' accounting for much of the concern? What is the relationship between a 'safety valve' and a penalty for exceedences?

NOTES

1. Helpful comments were provided by Tom Tietenberg and Henk Folmer (the two editors of the *Yearbook*), Denny Ellerman, Howard Gruenspecht, Albert (Nick) Nichols, Daniel Radov, Byron Swift, Peter Zapfel and an anonymous referee. Research assistance was provided by Warren Herold, Michael Lovenheim and Olga Shurchkov. The author is grateful to these individuals for their comments and assistance but alone is responsible for any remaining errors or omissions.
2. See Tom Tietenberg's website (http://www.colby.edu/personal/t/thtieten/) for a comprehensive list of empirical studies.
3. The tradable quantity could in theory be redefined to focus on environmental quality – or at least something closer to environmental quality than emissions, such as exposure – but there are no examples of such complexities. See Nichols (1984) for a general treatment and Atkinson and Tietenberg (1982) for an early application of this approach.
4. There is a large and growing literature on various aspects of the tradable permit approach. The major conceptual and theoretical issues related to the economic efficiency of the approach are treated well in many textbooks and general treatises (see, for example, Tietenberg, 1985, 2000). As various authors note (for example, Tietenberg, 1985; Cropper and Oates, 1992; and Hahn and Stavins, 1992), there are other issues concerning tradable permits, including issues of why particular policy instruments are chosen. Svendsen (1998), Dijkstra (1999), Wallart (1999), and Daugbjerg and Svendsen (2001) discuss the political and administrative feasibility of tradable permits. Tietenberg (1998) and Soloman and Lee (2000) discuss ethical issues raised by the tradable permits approach. Various documents provide overviews of the issues involved in designing and implementing such permits in practice (see, for example, Harrison, 1999b; OECD 1999, 2001).
5. Dales (1968) is regarded as the first complete explanation of how tradable permits would promote environmental protection at lower cost than conventional standards. Many recent textbooks and studies summarize the cost-reducing aspects of tradable permit programs (see, for example, Harrison, 1999a; Stavins, 1998, Council of Economic Advisers, 2000; Tietenberg, 2000). Note that several terms have been used to describe these programs, including tradable permits, marketable permits, and emissions trading. Similarly, the commodity traded is variously referred to as a permit or an allowance. This chapter does not distinguish among terms used to describe the programs or the commodity traded, and uses the various terms interchangeably.
6. See Downing and White (1986), Milliman and Prince (1989), Jaffe and Stavins (1995), Fisher et al. (1998), and Kerr and Newell (2001). Maleug (1989), however, points out that the

incentives created by a marketable permit program to develop cost-saving technologies are different for buyers and sellers. Although sellers have clear incentives to develop cheaper means of reducing emissions, the situation is more complicated for buyers: buyers only gain if the change in cost-saving innovations switches them from buyers to sellers.

7. Most authors include averaging programs within the category of credit-based programs. Because averaging programs do not involve the trading of ERCs – and thus the difficult determination of the appropriate baseline – it seems useful to include averaging as a separate category. See Nichols and Harrison (1994).

8. This list is expanded from that developed in Stavins (2000).

9. Several other international programs might be included in this list. Belgium, Denmark, the Netherlands and the UK have instituted 'bubble' programs to provide flexibility to electricity generators to meet overall targets (see Klaassen, 1999). These programs, however, do not allow rights to emit to be bought and sold and thus do not appear to be full-fledged tradable permit programs. Several pilot programs have been developed that are not included in Table 7.2. Canada has a voluntary pilot program for ozone precursors in Ontario. Pilot programs for greenhouse gases also have been developed as 'activities implemented jointly' (AIJ) under the Framework Convention on Climate Change in which credits are developed for projects to reduce greenhouse gas emissions. In Europe, there is a small program in the Basel canton in Switzerland, an experimental program in Chorzow, Poland and several emerging programs for CO_2 emissions. See OECD (1999), Klaassen 1999, and Ellerman (2000) for information on these other programs. Sorrell and Skea (1999) provide studies of other pilot programs and unsuccessful efforts to establish emissions trading in various countries: see papers by Bailey and Jackson, Bohm, Cros, Dekkers, Denne, Godard, Hoibye, Schärer, Sorrell and Zylicz.

10. See Harrison (1999a) for descriptions of tradable permit programs based upon a categorization of their major design and implementation elements.

11. See Brownell (1997).

12. The bubble program is more properly considered an averaging program, because the various sources under the bubble effectively must achieve combined emission rates based on an overall group average.

13. See Foster and Hahn (1995) for a concise review of the major features of the emissions trading program.

14. In the mid-1990s, the US Environmental Protection Agency published a proposed policy statement and model rule for open market trading, which involves the trading of discrete emission reductions (DERs) (60 Fed. Reg. 39668, August 1995). This program differs in several respects from the ET program, although both are credit-based programs. Various states have developed discrete emission reduction trading programs (see Farrell, 1999).

15. Efforts to reduce lead in gasoline were motivated both by the adverse health effects of lead and the fact that lead was incompatible with the catalytic converters used by automotive manufacturers to meet emission standards for other emissions. See Nichols (1997a).

16. Marketable permit programs for ODS also have been developed in Singapore, Canada and New Zealand (see Stavins, 2000).

17. The EPA Office of Air and Radiation website has information on various ABT programs. See http://www.epa.gov/oar/oarhome.html

18. The regulations are promulgated in 61 *Federal Register* 52088 (4 October 1996). The ABT programs promulgated for other sources are similar in overall design, although as noted the specific elements differ.

19. See Harrison (1999a) and Rubin and Kling (1993).

20. See US Environmental Protection Agency (1996). The average emission standard was set to reduce emissions by 75 percent, based in part on information that showed that the marginal cost per ton increased dramatically beyond a 75 percent reduction. The marginal cost curve was based upon detailed information on emission control technologies and on the assumption of 'perfect' trading, that is, that all cost-reducing trades took place.

21. Title IV also includes an averaging program for NO_X emissions. See 60 Fed. Reg. 18751 (April 1995).

22. The EPA website for the acid rain trading program is http://www.epa.gov/airmarkets/arp/

23. See Bailey (1998) and Ellerman et al. (2000) for discussions of the regulatory treatment of SO_2 trading and evaluations of the potential and actual effects of state Public Utility Commission (PUC) regulation on trading activity. Although it was feared that state PUC regulation would not provide utility managers the incentive or even the ability to pursue cost-saving opportunities made possible by emissions trading, explicit state regulation of trading appears to have encouraged rather than discouraged allowance trading activity. Moreover, trading was not deterred by the lack of state guidance – as some had feared – suggesting that utilities were comfortable engaging in trades without a formal ruling on how allowances would be treated for rate-making purposes.

24. See Joskow (1997).

25. Burtraw and Mansur (1999) develop estimates of cost savings for Phase I and Phase II years. For 1995 (Phase I), the authors estimate gains from trade equal to 13 percent of the no-trading costs. In 2005 (Phase II), they estimate that overall compliance costs will be reduced by about 37 percent relative to no-trading costs. They also note that these estimates are similar to those based upon an econometric model in Carlson et al. (1998). The authors also conclude that the opportunity for banking in Phase I led compliance costs to be greater, because the possibility of banking encouraged the construction of scrubbers, which appear *ex post* to be cost-inefficient.

26. McLean (1997) points out that with interconnected electric grids, participating Phase I units could shift electrical load to non-participating Phase II units, whose emissions could increase and undermine the Phase I emission reduction goal.

27. Title IV also includes a Reduced Utilization Provision. This program is not evaluated since only one unit used it (Ellerman et al., 2000). This provision was developed to address emissions leakage that would occur during Phase I if generation were shifted from capped Phase I to uncapped Phase II units. Utilities could retain allowances that would need to be surrendered if a Phase I unit reduced utilization by voluntarily entering a Phase II unit into the program.

28. Montero (1997) finds that units whose owners have a higher proportion of Phase I units (and thus have gained more experience with the program's rules) are more likely to opt in to the trading program.

29. Estimates in this section include units opted in through the Compensation Provision.

30. Table 7.6 shows 182 units because it includes 7 units from the Compensation Provision. In 1995, these 182 units accounted for 41.6 gigawatts, or 32 percent of the total power enrolled in Phase I of the program. In terms of allowances, however, these units accounted for only 16 percent (1.33 million of 8.55 million) of 1995 allowances.

31. Montero is a co-author of Ellerman et al. (2000), which includes a discussion of the results of the voluntary programs, including the Substitution Provision. See also McLean (1997) and Environmental Law Institute (1997b).

32. Montero (1999) examines the importance of different incentives on an eligible unit's decision to become a substitution unit. These incentives include the potential to receive allowances through baseline errors ('paper credits'), the potential to achieve cost savings (that is, reduce emissions at a cost lower than the cost of an allowance), and NO_X grandfathering benefits. Montero finds that baseline errors are the most important factor affecting participation decisions.

33. The stipulated energy savings approach could be used when verification met one of the following criteria: (1) measurement costs would exceed 10 percent of program costs; (2) no customer accounts for more than 20 percent of total savings; and (3) energy savings are expected to be less than 5 percent of use of the smallest isolatable circuit (for example, residential lighting energy efficiency).

34. Energy conservation projects made up 24 projects, renewable energy 5 projects, and 3 projects involved a mix of both kinds of reductions.

35. The website for the RECLAIM program is
http://www.aqmd.gov/rules/reclaim/reclaim_home_page.html

36. The original RECLAIM proposal included 38 separate trading regions, corresponding to the regions used for the offset program. This detailed geographic division was abandoned as a result of the plausible fear that the trading markets would be too thin. See Harrison (1999b).

37. The increased demand for RTCs by electric generation sources in the Los Angeles basin likely reflects several factors, including increased electricity demand in California and restructuring of the California electricity market as well as electricity demand and supply conditions (for example, hydro availability) in areas outside California. See Joskow and Kahn (2001) for discussions of factors affecting pricing behavior in California's wholesale electricity market during summer 2000.

38. See Joskow and Kahn (2001) for a discussion of the role that high RTC NO_X prices played in electricity costs.

39. See Pizer (1999). This issue is discussed below in the context of issues related to tradable permit programs for greenhouse gases. For an early application, see Roberts and Spence (1976).

40. Not all of the Ozone Transport Commission states joined the NO_X Budget Program. Vermont and Maine decided to operate traditional permit-based programs because the small number of sources in their states (less than three in each) did not justify the administrative expenses of developing an emissions trading program. Maryland's program was delayed for a year by a lawsuit from a power company. Virginia did not join the NO_X Budget Program and has not taken any action to regulate sources. See Farrell (2000).

41. See Nichols (1997b) for an analysis of issues related to banking and the development of the concept of flow control in the context of the NO_X Budget Program.

42. See Nichols (1998) for a discussion of the differential effects of emissions in different states on air quality in non-compliance regions.

43. Farrell (1999) reports that 'wrong-way' trades (net allowance sales from New York and New Hampshire) account for only about 3 percent of the total allocation. Moreover, at the time of his report, many of these allowances were owned by brokers and speculators and thus the geographic location of the corresponding emissions was not determined.

44. See Stavins (2000) and OECD (forthcoming) for discussions of examples and proposals for marketable permits in media other than air.

45. See OECD (forthcoming) for discussions of other potential applications.

46. The use of a cap-and-trade program for mercury would require new legislation if the Title III requirement for Maximum Achievable Control Technology (MACT) were interpreted to preclude the cap-and-trade approach.

47. EPA estimated that a command-and-control approach would be 30 to 60 percent more expensive than a cap-and-trade approach for the EPA Call for State Implementation Plans to Reduce Nitrogen Oxides (EPA SIP Call). See US Environmental Protection Agency (1999).

48. EIA (2001) came to similar conclusions regarding the relatively modest cost savings from a cap-and-trade approach for mercury relative to the command-and-control approach.

49. The EPA noted this concern. 'Any regulatory scheme for mercury that incorporates trading or other approaches that involve economic incentives must be constructed in a way that assures communities near the sources of emissions are adequately protected.' (65 Fed. Reg. 123890, December 20, 2000)

50. Manne and Richels (1995) describe temporal and geographic flexibility as 'when' and 'where' flexibility. The authors show that both flexibilities are important in reducing the overall cost of GHG targets.

51. In December 1997, representatives of signatories of the United Nations Framework Convention on Climate Change – which includes virtually all nations – met in Kyoto, Japan. Based upon a prior agreement that only industrialized countries – so-called Annex B countries – would limit emissions during the first commitment period, the Annex B parties agreed to reduce their emissions of six greenhouse gases by about 5 percent, on average, between 2008 and 2012, relative to 1990 levels. The Kyoto Protocol would come into force only if ratified by 55 nations, and by Annex B nations that represent 55 percent of 1990 Annex B emissions. International negotiators have been meeting intensively since 1997 to develop specific aspects of implementation of the Protocol.

52. The Kyoto Protocol includes three major international emissions trading programs (see Hahn and Stavins, 1999): (1) trading of emission rights (assigned amounts) among Annex B parties; (2) project-by-project bilateral exchange of credits (joint implementation) among Annex B countries; and (3) credits for reductions accomplished in non-Annex B countries (Clean Devel-

opment Mechanism). These three programs collectively are referred to as 'flexible mechanisms' or 'Kyoto mechanisms.' In addition, the Kyoto Protocol allows two or more Annex B signatories to form a 'bubble' in which the amounts assigned to the parties can be reassigned among themselves, a form of emissions trading. The most prominent example is the burden-sharing agreement among the members of the European Union, commonly known as the EU bubble. This agreement reallocated the uniform limit at 8 percent below 1990 emissions set for all members of the European Union in Annex B; targets for individual countries range from –28 percent (relative to 1990 emissions) for Luxembourg to +27 percent for Portugal (Ellerman 2000). Because compliance under Kyoto is based on the average of emissions over the five-year period from 2008 to 2012, the Kyoto Protocol implicitly allows banking and borrowing within the five-year period. In addition, the Protocol allows banking of emissions credits to subsequent periods (that is, beyond 2012), although targets beyond 2012 are not specified.

53. See Ellerman (2000) and Kitamori (forthcoming) for a summary of various domestic GHG tradable permit programs and proposals. See European Commission (2000) for a discussion of the development of a GHG trading program within the European Union. European Commission (2001) provides a proposal for a draft directive that would establish a framework for greenhouse gas emissions trading within the European Community.

54. Many studies and reports provide lists of relevant issues. Recent examples include Heinz Center (1988), OECD (2001), Ellerman (2000), European Commission (2000), and Kolstad and Toman (2001).

55. As Ellerman (2000) points out, the permits would not have to be allocated to 'upstream' sources even if upstream sources were monitored for compliance. Indeed, there is no necessary connection between the sources that are initially allocated permits and those that are required to surrender them.

56. The distribution of permits can affect cost savings if the formula provides for updating, that is, allocating permits on the basis of future activity, as would be the case if allocations were provided to new facilities. See Harrison and Radov (forthcoming).

57. See Wiener (2000), Goulder et al. (1997) and Goulder et al. (1999) for discussions of the significance of tax distortions.

58. Bovenberg and Goulder (2000) analyze the effects of grandfathering and auctioning of permits on shareholder equity in various sectors.

59. The European Commission Green Paper, for example, notes that six large sectors would cover approximately 45 percent of EU CO_2 emissions.

60. Issues related to international GHG tradable permit programs have been discussed in many papers and reports. See, for example, Stewart et al. (2000), Harrison (1997), Stavins (1997) Hahn and Stavins (1999), Fischer et al. (1998), Council of Economic Advisers (2000), Ellerman (2000), Weiner (2000), Tietenberg et al. (1999), and Kolstad and Toman (2001). Tom Tietenberg's website provides a comprehensive list of relevant studies. In addition, many of the issues have been considered in the context of the ongoing international negotiations under the United Nations Framework Convention on Climate Change. Some of the issues noted in this list have been addressed in these negotiations. This chapter does not provide information on the details of these negotiations. See United Nations 2001 for a summary of the results of July (2001) meeting (second part of the sixth session of the Conference of the Parties).

61. See Environmental Law Institute (1997b). Harrison et al. (2000) provide information on previous experience with setting baselines – in environmental and non-environmental programs – and the implications for developing an appropriate system for GHG emissions.

62. As Weiner (2000) points out, many of the problems are not unique to the tradable permits approach and would be problems regardless of approach used to reduce GHG emissions. Indeed, he notes that the use of tradable permit programs may make some problems easier; for example, the formula used to allocate permits can encourage participation and discourage free-riding.

63. Ellerman (1999) provides some thoughtful speculation about how tradable permit programs might develop over time, beginning with isolated domestic programs, increasing to allow bilateral trades among specific countries, and expanding to grow eventually into an international permit trading system. See Harrison (1999c) for commentary.

REFERENCES

Atkeson, E. (1997), *Joint Implementation: Lessons from Title IV's Voluntary Compliance Programs* (WP-97003), Center for Energy and Environmental Policy Research, MIT.

Atkinson, S.E. and T.H. Tietenberg (1982), 'The Empirical Properties of Two Classes of Designs for Transferable Discharge Permit Markets,' *Journal of Environmental Economics and Management*, **9**(2), 101–21.

Bailey, Elizabeth M. (1998), 'Allowance Trading Activity and State Regulatory Rulings: Evidence from the U.S. Acid Rain Program,' Working Paper No. MIT-CEEPR 98–005 WP, Cambridge, MA: MIT Center for Energy and Environmental Policy Research.

Bailey, Peter and Tim Jackson (1999), 'Joint Implementation for Controlling Sulphur in Europe and Possible Lessons for Carbon Dioxide,' in Steve Sorrell and Jim Skea (eds), *Pollution for Sale: Emissions Trading and Joint Implementation*, Cheltenham, UK and Northampton, USA: Edward Elgar.

Bohm, Peter (1999), 'An Emissions Quota Trade Experiment Among Four Nordic Countries,' in Steve Sorrell and Jim Skea (eds), *Pollution for Sale: Emissions Trading and Joint Implementation*, Cheltenham, UK and Northampton, USA: Edward Elgar.

Bovenberg, A. Lans and Lawrence H. Goulder (2000), *Neutralizing the Adverse Industry Impacts of CO_2 Abatement Policies: What does it Cost?* NBER Working Paper No. W7654. Cambridge, MA: National Bureau of Economic Research.

Brownell, F. William (1997), 'Clean Air Act,' in Thomas P. Sullivan (ed.), *Environmental Law Handbook*, 14th edn, Rockville, MD: Government Institutes, Inc.

Burtraw, Dallas (1999), 'Cost Savings, Market Performance and Economic Benefits of the US Acid Rain Program,' in Steve Sorrell and Jim Skea (eds), *Pollution for Sale: Emissions Trading and Joint Implementation*, Cheltenham, UK and Northampton, USA: Edward Elgar.

Burtraw, Dallas and Erin Mansur (1999), 'Environmental Effects of SO_2 Trading and Banking,' *Environmental Science and Technology*, **33**, 3489–94.

Capros, Pantelis, Leonidas Mantzos, Matti Vainio and Peter Zapfel (2001), 'Economic Efficiency of Cross Sectoral Emission Trading in CO_2 in the European Union,' in Johan Albrecht and Marc De Clercq (eds), *Instruments for Climate Policy: Limited versus Unlimited Flexibility*, University of Ghent.

Carlson, Curtis P., Dallas Burtraw, Maureen Cropper and Karen Palmer (1998), *Sulfur Dioxide Control by Electric Utilities: What are the Gains from Trade?*, Discussion Paper 98–44. Washington, DC: Resources for the Future.

Council of Economic Advisers (2000), *Economic Report of the President*, Washington, DC: United States Government Printing Office.

Cropper, M.L. and W.E. Oates (1992), 'Environmental Economics: A Survey,' *Journal of Economic Literature*, **XXX**, 675–740.

Cros, Christine (1999), 'Public Policy and Institutional Trajectories: What About Introducing SO_2 Emissions Trading in France?', in Steve Sorrell and Jim Skea (eds), *Pollution for Sale: Emissions Trading and Joint Implementation*, Cheltenham, UK and Northampton, USA: Edward Elgar.

Dales, J.H. 1(968), *Pollution, Property and Prices*, Toronto: University Press.

Daugbjerg, C. and G.T. Svendsen (2001), *Green Taxation in Question*, London: Macmillan.

Dekkers, Chris (1999), 'Trading Emissions and Other Economic Instruments to Reduce NO_X in the Netherlands,' in Steve Sorrell and Jim Skea (eds), *Pollution for Sale:*

Emissions Trading and Joint Implementation, Cheltenham, UK and Northampton, USA: Edward Elgar.

Denne, Tim (1999), 'Implementation Issues in International CO_2 Trading,' in Steve Sorrell and Jim Skea (eds), *Pollution for Sale: Emissions Trading and Joint Implementation*. Cheltenham, UK and Northampton, USA: Edward Elgar.

Dijkstra, B.R. (1999), *The Political Economy of Environmental Policy*, New Horizons in Environmental Economics, Cheltenham, UK and Northampton, USA: Edward Elgar.

Downing, P.B. and L.J. White (1986), 'Innovation in Pollution Control,' *Journal of Environmental Economics and Management*, **13**, 18–29.

Ellerman, A. Denny (1999), 'Obstacles to Global CO_2 Trading: A Familiar Problem,' in C. Walker, M. Bloomfield and M. Thorning (eds), *Climate Change Policy: Practical Strategies to Promote Economic Growth and Environmental Quality*, Washington, DC: The American Council for Capital Formation Center for Policy Research, May.

Ellerman, A. Denny (2000), 'Tradable Permits for Greenhouse Gas Emissions: A Primer with Particular Reference to Europe,' MIT Joint Program Report No. 69.

Ellerman, A. Denny, Richard Schmalensee, Paul L. Joskow, Juan Pablo Montero and Elizabeth Bailey (1997), *Emissions Trading Under the U.S. Acid Rain Program: Evaluation of Compliance and Allowance Market Performance*, Cambridge, MA: MIT Center for Energy and Environmental Policy Research.

Ellerman, A. Denny, Richard Schmalensee, Paul L. Joskow, Juan Pablo Montero and Elizabeth Bailey (2000), *Markets for Clean Air: The U.S. Acid Rain Program*, Cambridge, UK: Cambridge University Press.

Energy Information Administration (2001), *Analysis of Strategies for Reducing Multiple Emissions from Electric Power Plants: Sulfur Dioxide, Nitrogen Oxides, Carbon Dioxide, and Mercury and a Renewable Portfolio Standard*, Washington, DC: U.S. Department of Energy, July.

Environmental Law Institute (1997a), *Establishing Carbon Trading Programs: Lessons from Emissions Reduction Credit Systems for Criteria Pollutants*, Washington, DC: Environmental Law Institute.

Environmental Law Institute (1997b), *Implementing an Emissions Cap and Trade Allowance Trading System for Greenhouse Gases: Lessons from the Acid Rain Program*, Washington, DC: Environmental Law Institute, September.

European Commission (2000), *Green Paper on Greenhouse Gas Emissions Trading Within the European Union*. Com (2000) 87 final, 8.3.2000. Brussels: Commission on the European Communities, August.

European Commission (2001), Proposal for a Directive of the European Parliament and of the Council Establishing a Framework for Greenhouse Gas Emissions Trading Within the European Community and Amending Council Directive 96/61/EC, COM(2001)581, 23.10.2001. Brussels: Commission of the European Communities.

Farrell, Alex (1999), 'NO_X Control Costs and Allowance Prices: Expectations and Outcomes,' Pittsburgh, Pennsylvania: Department of Engineering and Public Policy, Carnegie Mellon University, June.

Farrell, Alex (2000), 'The NO_X Budget: A Look at the First Year,' *Electricity Journal*, March, 83–92.

Fischer, Carolyn, Suzi Kerr and Michael Toman (1998), *Using Emissions Trading to Regulate U.S. Greenhouse Gas Emissions: An Overview of Policy Design and Implementation Issues*, Discussion Paper 98–40. Washington, DC: Resources for the Future.

Fisher, Carolyn, Ian W.H. Perry and William Pizer (1998), *Instrument Choice for Environmental Protection When Technological Change is Endogenous*, Washington, DC: Resources for the Future.

Foster, Vivien and Robert W. Hahn (1995), 'Designing More Efficient Markets: Lessons from Los Angeles Smog Control,' *The Journal of Law and Economics*, **38**, 19–48.

Godard, Olivier (1999), 'Economic Instruments and Institutional Constraints: Possible Schemes for SO$_2$ Emissions Trading in the EU,' in Steve Sorrell and Jim Skea (eds), *Pollution for Sale: Emissions Trading and Joint Implementation*, Cheltenham, UK and Northampton, USA: Edward Elgar.

Goulder, Lawrence H., Ian W.H. Parry, Robert C. Williams III and Dallas Burtraw (1997), 'Revenue-Raising vs. Other Approaches to Environmental Protection: The Critical Significance of Pre-Existing Tax Distortions,' *Rand Journal of Economics*, Winter.

Goulder, Lawrence H., Ian W.H. Parry, Robert C. Williams III and Dallas Burtraw (1999), 'The Cost-Effectiveness of Alternative Instruments for Environmental Protection in a Second Best Setting,' *Journal of Public Economics*, **72**(3): 329–60.

Hahn, Robert W. and Gordon L. Hester (1989), 'Marketable Permits: Lessons for Theory and Practice,' *Ecology Law Quarterly*, **16**, 361–406.

Hahn, Robert W. and Robert Stavins (1992), 'Economic Incentives for Environmental Protection: Integrating Theory and Practice,' *American Economic Review*, **82**, 464–8.

Hahn, Robert W. and Robert Stavins (1999), *What Has Kyoto Wrought? The Real Architecture of International Tradable Permits Markets*, Washington, DC: American Enterprise Institute Press.

Harrison, David, Jr (1997), *Considerations in Designing and Implementing an Effective International Greenhouse Gas Trading Program*, Cambridge, MA: National Economic Research Associates, October.

Harrison, David Jr (1999a), 'Tradable Permits for Air Pollution Control: The United States Experience,' in J.P. Barde and T. Jones (eds), *Domestic Tradable Permit Systems for Environmental Management: Issues and Challenges*, Paris: OECD.

Harrison, David Jr (1999b), 'Turning Theory into Practice for Emissions Trading in the Los Angeles Air Basin,' in Steve Sorrell and Jim Skea (eds), *Pollution for Sale: Emissions Trading and Joint Implementation*, Cheltenham, UK and Northampton, USA: Edward Elgar.

Harrison, David Jr (1999c), 'Commentary: International Greenhouse Gas Trading and the Kyoto Protocol,' in C. Walker, M. Bloomfield and M. Thorning (eds), *Climate Change Policy: Practical Strategies to Promote Economic Growth and Environmental Quality*, Washington, DC: The American Council for Capital Formation Center for Policy Research, May.

Harrison, David, Jr and Albert L. Nichols (1992), *An Economic Analysis of the RECLAIM Trading Program for the South Coast Air Basin*, Cambridge, MA: National Economic Research Associates, Inc., March.

Harrison, David, Jr and Daniel B. Radov (forthcoming), *Evaluation of Alternative Initial Allocation Methods in a European Union Greenhouse Gas Emissions Cap-and-Trade Program*, prepared for the European Commission, Cambridge, MA: National Economic Research Associates, Inc.

Harrison, David Jr and S. Todd Schatzki (2000), *Fueling Electricity Growth for a Growing Economy*, Washington, DC: Edison Electric Institute. December.

Harrison, David Jr, S. Todd Schatzki, Thomas F. Wilson and Erik Haites (2000), *Critical Issues in International Greenhouse Gas Emissions Trading: Setting Baselines for*

Credit-Based Trading Programs – Lessons Learned from Relevant Experience, Palo Alto, CA: Electric Power Research Institute, Inc.

Hausker, Karl (1992), 'The Politics and Economics of Auction Design in the Market for Sulfur Dioxide Pollution,' *Journal of Policy Analysis and Management*, 553–572.

Heinz Center (1998), *Designs for Domestic Carbon Emissions Trading*. Washington, DC: The H. John Heinz III Center for Science, Economics and the Environment.

Hoibye, Geir (1999), 'Designing a Scheme for SO_2 Trading in Norway,' in Steve Sorrell and Jim Skea (eds), *Pollution for Sale: Emissions Trading and Joint Implementation*. Cheltenham, UK and Northampton, USA: Edward Elgar.

Illinois Environmental Protection Agency (2001), *Annual Performance Review Report – 2000. Emission Reduction Market System*, Springfield, IL, May.

Jaffe, A.B. and R.N. Stavins (1995), 'Dynamic Incentives of Environmental Regulations: The Effects of Alternative Policy Instruments on Technology Diffusion,' *Journal of Environmental Economics and Management*, **29** (3 Suppl. Part 2), S43–S63.

Johnson, S.L. and D.M. Pekelney (1996), 'Economic Assessment of the Regional Clean Air Incentives Market: A New Emissions Trading Program for Los Angeles,' *Land Economics* **72**(3), 277–97.

Joskow, Paul L. (1997), 'Restructuring, Competition, and Regulatory Reform in the U.S. Electricity Sector.' *Journal of Economic Perspectives*, **11**(3), 119–38.

Joskow, Paul and Edward Kahn (2001), 'A Quantitative Analysis of Pricing Behavior in California's Wholesale Electricity Market During Summer 2000,' NBER Working Paper No. 8157. Cambridge, MA: National Bureau of Economic Research.

Kerr, Suzi C. (1993), 'The Operation of Tradable Rights Markets: Empirical Evidence from the United States Lead Phasedown,' *Papers and Proceedings* of the Air and Waste Management Association Meeting 'New Partnerships: Economic Incentives for Environmental Management,' 3–4 November 1993, Rochester, New York.

Kerr, S. and R. Newell (2001), 'Policy-Induced Technology Adoption: Evidence from the U.S. Lead Phasedown,' Washington, DC: Resources for the Future, May.

Kitamori, Kumi (forthcoming), 'Domestic GHG Emission Trading Schemes: Recent Developments and Current Status in Selected OECD Countries,' Prepared for Informal Experts Workshop on Domestic Tradable Permits: Lessons and Future Directions. Paris: OECD.

Klaassen, Ger (1999), 'Emissions Trading in the European Union: Practice and Prospects,' in Steve Sorrell and Jim Skea (eds), *Pollution for Sale: Emissions Trading and Joint Implementation*, Cheltenham, UK and Northampton, USA: Edward Elgar.

Kolstad, Charles D. and Michael Toman (2001), *The Economics of Climate Policy*, Discussion Paper 00–40REV, Washington, DC: Resources for the Future.

Kopp, Raymond, Richard Morgenstern, William Pizer and Michael Toman (1999), *A Proposal for Credible Early Action in U.S. Climate Policy*. Resources for the Future. http://www.rff.org/~kopp/popular_articles/feature060.html

Maleug, David A. (1989), 'Emission Credit Trading and the Incentive to Adopt New Pollution Abatement Technology,' *Journal of Environmental Economics and Management*, **16**, 52–7.

Manne, Alan and Richard Richels (1995), 'The Greenhouse Debate: Economic Efficiency, Burden Sharing and Hedging Strategies,' *The Energy Journal*, **16**(4), 1–37.

McLean, Brian (1997), 'Evolution of Marketable Permits: The U.S. Experience with Sulfur Dioxide Allowance Trading,' *International Journal of Environment and Pollution*, **8**, 19–36.

Milliman, Scott R. and Raymond Prince (1989), 'Firm Incentives to Promote Techno-
  logical Change in Pollution Control,' *Journal of Environmental Economics and
  Management*, **12**, 247–65.
Montero, Juan-Pablo (1997), 'Environmental Regulation and Technology Innovation,'
  Ph.D. Dissertation, Massachusetts Institute of Technology.
Montero, J.P. (1999), 'Voluntary Compliance with Market-Based Environmental Policy:
  Evidence from the U.S. Acid Rain Program,' *Journal of Political Economy*, **107**(5),
  998–1033.
Nichols, Albert L. (1984), *Targeting Economic Incentives for Environmental Protection*,
  Cambridge, MA: MIT Press.
Nichols, Albert L. (1997a), 'Lead in Gasoline,' in R. Morgenstern (ed.), *Economic
  Analyses at EPA: Assessing Regulatory Impact*, Washington, DC: Resources for the
  Future.
Nichols, Albert L. (1997b), *Accounting for Location and Timing in NO_X Emission
  Trading Programs*, Palo Alto, CA: Electric Power Research Institute, Inc.
Nichols, Albert L. (1998), *Accounting for Location in NO_X Emission Trading Programs:
  Empirical Results from the OTAG Region*, Palo Alto, CA: Electric Power Research
  Institute, Inc.
Nichols, Albert L and David Harrison (1994), *Key Issues in the Design of NO_X Emission
  Trading Programs to Reduce Ground-Level Ozone*, Palo Alto, CA: Electric Power
  Research Institute, Inc.
Nordhaus, Robert R., Kyle W. Danish, Richard H. Rosenzwig and Britt Speyer Fleming
  (2000), 'International Emissions Trading Rules as a Compliance Tool: What is
  Necessary, Effective, and Workable?', *Environmental Law Reporter* (30 ELR
  10837–10855).
OECD (1999), *Economic Instruments for Pollution Control and Natural Resources
  Management in OECD Countries: A Survey*, Paris: OECD.
OECD (2001), *Strategic Guidelines for the Design and Implementation of Domestic
  Transferable Permits*, Paris: OECD.
OECD (forthcoming), *Domestic Tradable Permits: Lessons and Future Directions*,
  Paris: OECD.
Palmer, Adele R., et al. (1980), *Economic Implications of Regulating Chlorofluoro-
  carbon Emissions from Non-Aerosol Applications*, Santa Monica, CA: Rand
  Corporation, June.
Pizer, William A. (1999), 'The Optimal Choice of Climate Change Policy in the Presence
  of Uncertainty,' *Resource and Energy Economics*, **21**(3–4), 267–76.
Roberts, M.J. and M. Spence (1976), 'Effluent Charges and Licenses Under Uncer-
  tainty,' *Journal of Public Economics*, **5**(3–4), 905–12.
Rubin, Jonathan and Catherine Kling (1993), 'An Emission Saved is an Emission Earned:
  An Empirical Analysis of Emission Banking for Light-Duty Engine Manufacturers,'
  Journal of Environmental Economics and Management, November, 257–74.
Schärer, Bernd (1999), 'Tradable Emissions Permits in German Clean Air Policy: Con-
  siderations on the Efficiency of Environmental Policy Instruments,' in Steve Sorrell
  and Jim Skea (eds), *Pollution for Sale: Emissions Trading and Joint Implementa-
  tion*, Cheltenham, UK and Northampton, USA: Edward Elgar.
Schmalensee, Richard, Paul L. Joskow, A. Denny Ellerman, Juan Pablo Montero and
  Elizabeth M. Bailey (1998), 'An Interim Evaluation of Sulfur Dioxide Emissions
  Trading,' *Journal of Economic Perspectives*, **12**(3), 53–68.

Shogren, Jason F. and Michael A. Toman (2000), 'Climate Change Policy,' in Paul R. Portney and Robert N. Stavins (eds), *Public Policies for Environmental Protection*, 2nd edn, Washington, DC: Resources for the Future.

Skea, Jim (1999), 'Flexibility, Emissions Trading and the Kyoto Protocol,' in Steve Sorrell and Jim Skea (eds), *Pollution for Sale: Emissions Trading and Joint Implementation*, Cheltenham, UK and Northampton, USA: Edward Elgar.

Solomon, B.D. and R. Lee (2000), 'Emissions Trading Systems and Environmental Justice,' *Environment*, **42**(8), 32–45.

Sorrell, Steve (1999), 'Why Sulphur Trading Failed in the UK,' in Steve Sorrell and Jim Skea (eds), *Pollution for Sale: Emissions Trading and Joint Implementation*, Cheltenham, UK and Northampton, USA: Edward Elgar.

Sorrell, Steve, and Jim Skea (1999), *Pollution for Sale: Emissions Trading and Joint Implementation*, Cheltenham, UK and Northampton, USA: Edward Elgar.

South Coast Air Quality Management District (1993), *RECLAIM: Development Report and Proposed Rules, Revised Volume 1*, Los Angeles, CA: SCAQMD.

South Coast Air Quality Management District (2001a), *White Paper on Stabilization of NO_X RTC Prices*, Diamond Bar, CA: SCAQMD.

South Coast Air Quality Management District (2001b), Notes from May 11, 2001 Board Meeting, Agenda No. 35.

Stavins, Robert N. (1997), 'Policy Instruments for Climate Change: How Can National Governments Address a Global Problem?', The University of Chicago Legal Forum, 293–329.

Stavins, Robert N. (1998), 'Market-Based Environmental Policies,' in Paul R. Portney and Robert N. Stavins (eds), *Public Policies for Environmental Protection*, 2nd edn, Washington, DC: Resources for the Future.

Stavins, Robert N. (2000), 'Experience with Market-Based Environmental Policy Instruments,' Draft prepared as Chapter 21 in Karl-Göran Mäler et al. (eds), *The Handbook of Environmental Economics*, Amsterdam: North-Holland/Elsevier Science, November.

Stewart, Richard, et al. (2000), *The Clean Development Mechanism: Building International Public–Private Partnership: Technical, Financial and Institutional Issues*, New York: United Nations.

Svendsen, G.T. (1998), *Public Choice and Environmental Regulation: Tradable Permit Systems in the United States and CO_2 Taxation in Europe*, New Horizons in Environmental Economics, Cheltenham, UK and Northampton, USA: Edward Elgar.

Swift, Byron (forthcoming), 'Assessing Firms' Responses to Environmental Regulation: An Analysis of NO_X and SO_2 Regulation of Electric Utilities Under the Clean Air Act,' *Tulane Environmental Law Journal* (forthcoming).

Tietenberg, Thomas (1985), *Emissions Trading: An Exercise in Reforming Pollution Policy*, Washington, DC: Resources for the Future.

Tietenberg, Tom (1998), 'Ethical Influences on the Evolution of the US Tradable Permit Approach to Air Pollution Control,' *Ecological Economics*, **24**, 241–57.

Tietenberg, Tom (2000), *Environmental and Natural Resource Economics*, 5th edn, Reading, MA: Addison Wesley Longman.

Tietenberg, T., M. Grubb et al. (1999), *International Rules for Greenhouse Gas Emissions Trading: Defining the Principles, Modalities, Rules and Guidelines for Verification, Reporting and Accountability*, Geneva: United Nations, UNCTAD/GDS/GFSB/Misc.6.

Toman, Michael, Richard Morgenstern and John Anderson (1999), *The Economics of 'When' Flexibility in the Design of Greenhouse Gas Abatement Polices*, Resources for the Future Discussion Paper 99–38-REV, Washington, DC: Resources for the Future, June.

United Nations (2001), *Report of the Conference of the Parties on the Second Part of its Sixth Session, Held at Bonn from 16 to 27 July 2001*, Bonn: United Nations Framework Convention on Climate Change.

US Environmental Protection Agency (1996), *Regulatory Impact Analysis: Control of Air Pollution Emissions Standards for New Nonroad Spark-Ignition Marine Engines*, Washington, DC: Office of Air and Radiation and Office of Mobile Sources.

US Environmental Protection Agency (1999), *Analysis of Emissions Reduction Options for the Electric Power Industry*, Washington, DC: Office of Air and Radiation.

US Environmental Protection Agency (2000a), *1999 OTC NO_X Budget Program Compliance Report*, Washington, DC: Office of Air and Radiation.

US Environmental Protection Agency (2001), *The United States Experience with Economic Incentives for Protecting the Environment*, Washington, DC: Office of Policy, Economics, and Innovation.

Wallart, N. (1999), *The Political Economy of Environmental Taxes*, New Horizons in Environmental Economics, Cheltenham, UK and Northampton, USA: Edward Elgar.

Western Regional Air Partnership (2000), *Voluntary Emissions Reduction Program for Major Industrial Sources of Sulfur Dioxide in Nine Western States and A Backstop Market Trading Program*, An Annex to the Report of the Grand Canyon Visibility Transport Commission. Submitted to the US Environmental Protection Agency, Denver, CO: Western Regional Air Partnership. September 29.

Weyant, John and Jennifer Hill (1999), 'Introduction and Overview,' *The Energy Journal*. Special Issue, *The Costs of the Kyoto Protocol: A Multi-Model Evaluation*.

Wiener, Jonathan Baert (2000), *Policy Design for International Greenhouse Gas Control*. Climate Change Issues Brief No. 6 updated from 1997. Washington, DC: Resources for the Future.

Zylicz, Tomasz (1999), 'Towards Tradability of Pollution Permits in Poland,' in Steve Sorrell and Jim Skea (eds), *Pollution for Sale: Emissions Trading and Joint Implementation*. Cheltenham, UK and Northampton, USA: Edward Elgar.

8. From environmental ethics to environmental public philosophy: ethicists and economists, 1973–future

Bryan Norton and Ben A. Minteer

1. INTRODUCTION: THE TWO HISTORIES OF ENVIRONMENTAL ETHICS

Environmental ethics has two histories, depending on one's understanding of the scope of ethics. If an ethic is interpreted inclusively as a collection of attitudes toward nature that can guide human actions, there is a long history of environmental ethics that goes back at least to Genesis 1, and even further into the oral traditions that shaped the dominant Western creation story. In this inclusive sense, environmental ethics has been with us, in some form, since the beginnings of human consciousness. Genesis 1 is, or at least conveys, an environmental ethic in this broad sense; it articulates the idea of human dominion, including the view that humans are made in the image of God, and incorporates the 'ethic' of human dominion over nature as an integral part of the Judaeo-Christian creation story. Chapter 2 of Genesis adds an obligation to act as stewards of God's creation, an idea that is elaborated elsewhere throughout the scriptures, so there may not be a single environmental ethic, but several, to be found there. The point is that in the broad, historical sense, and including varied cultures, many environmental ethics can be found in literature, myth, and religion. More directly, in the period running from the mid-nineteenth century to the middle of the twentieth century, we can see the elaborate and thoughtful environmental ethics developed by early conservationists, especially including Henry David Thoreau, George Perkins Marsh, John Muir and, above all, Aldo Leopold's eloquent and sophisticated land ethic.

In this chapter we are concerned mainly with a narrower sense of environmental ethics – of environmental ethics as a practice of professional philosophers. In this sense, environmental ethics began not so long ago, sometimes pinpointed as 1973–74, years in which there was a spate of articles and books published on the subject of environmental values (Routley, 1973; Passmore, 1974; Stone, 1974; Blackstone, 1974). A prominent event in the narrower and briefer history of environmental ethics as a subdiscipline of philosophy was the initiation of the journal *Environmental Ethics* in 1979 and subsequent growth of interest and publications, in books and in serials, of topics on environmental values.

When one thinks about environmental values and theories for understanding these values, one might ask four questions, each of these leading to four different types of theories of environmental evaluation: (1) What is the nature of environmental value? Answers to this question can be called *ontological* theories of environmental value. (2) How can one measure environmental values? (To be answered by a theory of *measurement*.) (3) How can/should environmental values be employed in justifying proposed environmental policies? Answers to this question can be called *epistemological* theories of environmental value. (4) How should we, given disagreements about environmental values, proceed toward satisfactory policies? Answers to this question might provide a theory of the *process* of policy formation based on environmental values.

Given this classification, environmental ethics has concentrated mainly on questions of ontology, focusing mainly on specifying the *nature* of environmental values. Economists, by contrast, have for the most part taken the nature of environmental value to be resolved by their broad commitments to a market-value approach to the analysis of welfare; they have therefore concentrated mainly on the measurement question. In doing so, they have bypassed the ontological question, treating environmental values as a type of commodity value, and offered means to measure environmental values in terms of individual and aggregated willingness to pay. Given that ontology is a core area of philosophical study, it is perhaps not surprising that ontological theories of value were among the earliest topics addressed by environmental ethicists. What is more surprising is the extent to which the field continues to be dominated by these questions, despite the existence of a number of alternative intellectual paths toward better understanding of environmental values, and despite the extreme difficulty of, and lack of progress in solving, these deep, ontological issues about environmental value. As a result of their preoccupation with such intractable problems, environmental ethicists have made few contributions to actual discussions about what to do to improve the environment. The specialized nature of philosophers' concerns can be appreciated if we look in detail at the intellectual seeds that sprouted and became the subdiscipline of environmental ethics; to do so, we must look back to a 1967 article, 'The Historical Roots of Our Ecologic Crisis,' written by the historian, Lynn White, Jr, and published in *Science* magazine (White, 1967). We believe this short paper has shaped the subject-matter of environmental ethics because a particular interpretation of White's argument has catalyzed the philosophical debate about environmental values, and has given environmental ethics a rather unidimensional quality so far.

In the remainder of this section we examine White's formulation of the 'ecologic' problem and the response of environmental ethicists to it. Section 2 examines the development of environmental ethics as a field from its beginnings in 1973 until 1996, a period in which most professional environmental ethicists were engaged in a program that sought to 'extend' traditional, human-based ethical systems to apply to nonhumans in some way. This work, often referred to as 'nonanthropocentrism,' generally assumes that human individuals, as beings who have moral standing, can be correctly described as having 'intrinsic' value. Extensionists broaden moral standing by attributing intrinsic value also to some nonhumans, such as individual animals or ecosystems. While nonanthropocentrists sometimes call themselves 'radical,' we go on in section 3 to consider a more radical conceptual innovation, the rejection of moral individualism and the recognition that important environmental values may unfold on the communal scale, a scale that cannot be reduced to individual goods. This more radical innovation encourages a shift in the way we think about environmental values and valuation, shifting attention from ontological questions regarding the nature and measurement of values toward a more politically oriented process approach; section 4 is devoted to exploring the possibility of an environmental ethic conceived as a practical contribution to an environmental public philosophy. This approach begins with the assumption that the society holds multiple and sometimes competing values and experiments with multiple ways of measuring and expressing human values, embedding a pluralistic and experimental value discussion within an action-oriented, adaptive framework which is presented in section 5. Finally, the chapter closes with recommendations for encouraging more innovative and interdisciplinary work involving philosophers and economists.

First, let us begin with White's influential paper. White offered a broadbrush historical account of the ideas and social forces – science, technology, and, especially, the melding of the two – that have shaped Western culture's view of the human relationship to nature, and suggested that these features may be responsible for the degradation of modern environments in the West. White offered several criticisms of Western ideas and culture, including, for example, a brief reference to the conception of time as directional – a Christian idea as absorbed from the Hebraic tradition – that saw creation as a beginning of history, which had also an end. White suggested that this linear conception of time, which differs from the Greek conception of nature as cyclical, with no beginning or ending, has instilled in Western consciousness a directionality and a sense of purpose – and also a form of unjustified optimism – that treats all technological change as progress. Westerners, he seemed to be saying, are poor critics of technological proposals because we tend to be technological optimists by default. If developed, this line of reasoning, which encourages more critical evaluation of new technologies and of technological change, might have led

376 The international yearbook of environmental and resource economics

environmental ethicists more toward the analysis of proposed technologies and their long-term and unintended effects on social values. Had this happened, environmental ethics might today be a specialized form of the philosophy of technology, one that would address important questions of human value, but it would do so in the more practical context of evaluating technologically induced environmental change and its impact on core moral and social values.

This line of reasoning, however, has not been very important in environmental ethics in the years since White wrote. Environmental ethicists, instead, responded to another line of criticism, White's statement that Western Christianity 'is the most anthropocentric religion the world has seen.' White was of course referring to the creation story in Genesis 1, which is clear because he notes especially the claim that humans are made in the image of God and in an important sense separate from nature, according to the creation story. It was the charge that Western culture is 'anthropocentric' that provoked the first dozen or so papers and books that are clearly within the professional philosophical tradition. Similarly, early papers in the new journal, Environmental Ethics, responded in one way or another to White's criticism. Indeed, most early environmental ethicists took White's criticism to be valid and compelling, and proceeded to respond by proposing 'nonanthropocentric' ethical positions, which argued that nonhuman elements of the environment – elements of many different types from individual animals to species and ecosystems – had intrinsic value; and hence these elements should be considered morally considerable in human decision making (see, for example, Routley, 1973; Rolston, 1975, 1988; Regan, 1981, 1983; Callicott, 1989). Minority forces, in particular, the Australian philosopher John Passmore, argued to the contrary that the Western tradition has adequate intellectual and moral resources to criticize and reform environmental practices, that there are good human reasons to change current destructive practices, and that introduction of non-Western and nonanthropocentric ethical principles is unnecessary to correct environmentally damaging behaviors (Passmore, 1974). Passmore therefore rejected nonanthropocentrist ethical theory as inconsistent with central moral principles of Western social thought, and unnecessary to support improved environmental policies. Much of the writing on environmental ethics since those early days has addressed this issue of anthropocentrism in one way or another. Indeed, some leading advocates of nonanthropocentrism define environmental ethics as simply the study of intrinsic value in nature (for example, Regan, 1981; Callicott, 1989).

The focus of environmental ethicists on anthropocentrism has had a deeply negative effect on interactions of environmental ethicists and environmental economists. As noted above, environmental ethicists concentrated on the nature of environmental value, hoping to articulate a new ontological theory; economists took it that environmental values must be a kind of commodity values, and proceeded to measure them as such. Since the discipline of economics – especially as represented by its mainstream interpretation of economics as an aggregative science of individual human welfare – was a ready-at-hand example of an unapologetically anthropocentric discipline, environmental ethics became, for most practitioners, a discipline defined by its opposition to economics as a means of measuring the value of natural objects and anthropogenic impacts on natural systems. The result was polarization along disciplinary lines, with environmental ethicists developing arguments on the inadequacy of environmental economics as an *ontology* of environmental values, but formulating these arguments in a vocabulary that precluded the arguments having much effect on economists, who mostly are happy with their ontology and are working on problems of measurement and aggregation. Meanwhile, environmental economists either dismiss environmental ethicists as talking nonsense, or as trying to impose their own, specialized preferences on consumers. Worse, economists represent environmental ethicists' endorsements of intrinsic value, offered as assertions of a new ontology of natural value, as dollars-worth of 'willingness to pay' to protect 'existence' values. To environmental ethicists, not surprisingly, this 'category mistake' of treating principles as measurable willingness to pay is even more insulting than the charge that they speak nonsense. It did not help that philosophers also viewed economists as unquestioning advocates of economic growth at any cost, and saw their models as inimical to reasoned deliberation about what really matters in environmental protection (Sagoff, 1988). The two disciplines most likely to offer increased understanding of how we do and should value nature are thus trapped in a bifurcated discourse, each rejecting the other's ontological position, but doing so in a language that is not understandable – or at least considered inappropriate – by their opponents. Consequently the two disciplines can often present a united front within disciplinary lines, but this united front simply reflects their differing viewpoints as they are ossified into different languages, languages through which they can communicate with their disciplinary allies, but languages that ensure they will not hear, or at least not interpret, the arguments of their opponents. To put it simply, they operate within different paradigms.

Was this polarization and lack of communication inevitable? Perhaps not. Environmental ethicists, as noted above, might have explored White's concerns about our technological optimism and failure to develop a sense of fairness to the distant future because of this optimism. Was the polarization inevitable once White had introduced the label 'anthropocentric' and made his charge of anthropocentrism against Western culture? No. With hindsight, we can see that White's general critique, and especially the charge of 'anthropocentrism' can be given two rather different interpretations. White might have meant, as environmental ethicists have taken him to mean, (a) that anthropocentrism is an *ontological theory of environmental value* – the theory that all and only human beings have intrinsic value and that only humans are morally considerable. But White never explicitly states this theoretical interpretation of the target of his criticism; in fact, the only explanation he gives of the term is by reference to the doctrine that humans are made in the image of God. White could as well be interpreted as simply (b) criticizing an *attitude* of human-centeredness, a kind of hubris about the importance of humans in the larger scheme of things. This charge of hubris ties nicely to White's other concerns about our optimism about technology and cultural progress, and requires no positing of intrinsic, onto-logical values in nature. The ancient Greeks – clearly anthropocentric in their beliefs and evaluations of nature – found the moral resources – in epic poetry, theatrical tragedies and in Aristotle's ethics – to criticize overweening pride, hubris, the temptation of humans to act on behalf of the Gods. They did so without broadening moral citizenship, nor by radically changing their ontology of values, as they saw no need to appeal to a moral anchor beyond the idea of living a worthy human life. Note that if one interprets White in the second way, no particular antidote, theoretical or otherwise, is predetermined; and on this reading agreement with him requires acceptance of no particular ontological theory of environmental value, except perhaps for a belief that human action taken in humility is more noble than action taken out of selfishness and over-weening pride. Anthropocentrism, in this attitudinal sense, can be rejected without embracing an ontological theory that opposes it.

Moreover, White might have been understood to be expressing an explicit *political* concern about the environmental implications of a modern, democra-tized culture – one where greater and greater numbers of citizens have increasingly powerful and ecologically pernicious technologies at their fingertips – rather than a narrow philosophical argument for the distinct moral status of nonhuman nature. Had this interpretation taken hold, we would have found ourselves asking very different questions in the field, questions more accurately described as ones of 'environmental political theory,' perhaps, than environmental ethics. This, too, might have turned philosophical attention toward more productive institutional and procedural issues rather than tenden-tious ontological questions about the moral standing of nature. And, if the value explorations of environmental ethicists had extended beyond an ontology inimical to environmental economics, there might have been far more oppor-tunities for collaboration across disciplines.

Early environmental ethicists, nonetheless, for reasons that were never made very explicit – and therefore are difficult to judge – chose to respond to White's charge of anthropocentrism as an attack on a *false theory*, the theory that (all and) only human beings have intrinsic value. Once the question was posed in this unfortunate manner, it is not surprising that environmental ethicists responded with an alternative, competing moral theory, one that claims some (or many) nonhuman entities have intrinsic value. As noted, this formulation of problems in environmental valuation leads to polarized rhetoric and little communication, as economists and intrinsic value theorists agree about the importance of the ontological question, but disagree about where to draw the line between entities that are intrinsically valuable and those that are merely instrumentally valuable. We see, then, that the disciplinary polarization of discourse about environmental values, the topic of this chapter, was engendered at the very inception of the field of environmental ethics as a 'distinct' discipline, and this polarization has hampered discourse between environmental ethicists and environmental economists.

2. THE PERIOD OF EXTENSIONIST ENVIRONMENTAL ETHICS, 1973–96

Having defined Western environmental problems as due to acceptance of an anthropocentric ontology of value – a theory that guided economic measurement of environmental values – environmental ethics cast itself as a critical response to the basic ideas of economics (see, for example, Sagoff, 1988; Callicott, 1989). It is not surprising that collaborations with economists during this period were limited. The journal *Philosophy and Public Affairs* provided an organ for discussion of public values and a few papers in this journal dealt with important environmental issues, such as population and obligations to the future. A Congressional Fellows program has brought philosophers into contact with other policy analysts and activists, but only a few of the Fellows have concentrated on environmental issues. Especially notable were several projects organized by the Center – later, the 'Institute' – for Philosophy and Public Policy at the University of Maryland. Several collaborations with economists at Resources for the Future, especially with Allen Kneese and Clifford Russell, resulted in cross-over publications. These early attempts were mainly exercises in expressing divergent viewpoints within the covers of an anthology or report (see, for example, MacLean and Brown, 1983). More recently, a few philosophers have attempted to build more positively some areas of common intellectual ground (see, for example, Norton and Toman, 1997; Sagoff, 1998) in the USA. The British journal *Environmental Values*, founded in 1991, has stimulated discussion on the boundaries of philosophy and economics and regularly publishes high-quality work by both philosophers and economists. This journal has produced special issues and generally encouraged interdisciplinary research that has led to an active group debating issues such as the nature of preferences and the use of contingent valuation techniques to value nonmarket values in UK policy analyses (O'Neill, 1993; Foster, 1997).

Perhaps because of the polarization across disciplinary lines just described, interactions between environmental ethicists and environmental economists have mainly involved sparring about the true nature of environmental values. Participants from both fields have defended a general theory of environmental values that is both complete and at the same time comprehensive, as both disciplines seek to legitimize their methods and defend their intellectual turf. Within disciplines, this focus has led to articulation of disciplinary orthodoxies rather than to a diversity of understandings or an experimental approach to describing and analyzing environmental values. Despite very similar conceptual assumptions about the nature of environmental value, these two disciplines have largely gone their own way, failing to establish an effective cross-disciplinary dialogue about environmental values. Worse, the extra-disciplinary discussion between economists and environmental ethicists has not really been engaged, as members of each discipline remain trapped within their own theoretical structures and interpretations. What is needed is a discipline-independent discussion of the entire subject of environmental values and methods of valuation. This has not occurred, we have suggested, because the particular disciplines have developed and used their own language and definitions to describe their subject-matter, creating a communicative chasm between environmental ethics and economics.

To explain this early, and lingering, divergence briefly we resort to caricature, identifying two theories that represent the concept of value characteristic of environmental economics and environmental ethics. For convenience of reference, we call them Economism and Intrinsic Value Theory (IV Theory, for short), adopting the convention of capitalizing their names to make it clear that they refer to a theory that, while representative of the viewpoint of many members of the associated disciplines, may not be accepted by every member thereof. So considered, Economism can be defined as the theory that *all* environmental value is a kind of consumer value among other types, to be compared and balanced against other purchases that might be made with the consumer's, presumably limited, economic resources. This theory – here initially stated as an ontological theory – would have quite general consequences for the study of environmental values.

Only IV Theory – the theory that environmental values are to be understood as values intrinsic to nature itself, values that exist independently of human values – represents an alternative theory of competing scope. Although IV Theory comes in many forms, IV Theorists share a claim that intrinsic value is distributed in nature itself, not just in human individuals; and IV Theorists also take it as an obligation to protect intrinsic value, as possible, wherever it occurs. According to this theory, nonhuman elements of nature have intrinsic value. Since it is usually believed that human individuals have intrinsic value, IV Theory essentially achieves a universal theory of value by *extending* concepts and principles from human ethics to include the nonhuman world or some elements of it.

We have identified these two competing theories as deserving of special consideration because of their importance in the current debate. Speaking technically, we can refer to these theories as claiming both *comprehensiveness* (or *completeness* in the vernacular of formal semantics) and the highest degree of *connectedness* (also known as *elegance* or *simplicity*). To say that a theory of environmental values is comprehensive is to say that it has sufficient semantic power to describe each and every type of environmental value that evaluators legitimately express. Economists thus tend to say that, if some proposed value cannot be expressed within the Economistic concepts and principles characteristic of their theory, then it is no environmental value at all. The Economistic theory is thus claimed to be complete with respect to the domain of environmental values. To say that a theory is, on the other hand, highly connected is to say that all of the types of values can be expressed and asserted by appeal to a very small number of basic principles and entities. The limiting case of connectedness has been referred to by environmental ethicists as 'moral monism,' the view that all moral quandaries have a uniquely correct solution according to a single, unifying principle. In monistic theories, the entire subject-matter recognized by the theory can be expressed in a single vocabulary and can be supported by a single unifying theory (Stone, 1987).

It is interesting that these two theories, Economism and IV Theory, espouse both comprehensiveness and the highest degree of connectivity – monism – in that these two goals for theory exist in a certain unavoidable tension. The more one insists on comprehensiveness over a subject-matter like environmental values, the greater the demands on one's ingenuity in reducing all experienced values to a single rubric. And, the more one insists on the reduction of all values to a given vocabulary, the more difficult is the task of capturing varied types of values as experienced by people with different viewpoints and worldviews. One of the interesting features of this conversation about the ontology and foundational languages, however, is that these two theories of value – and the languages that express them – have been evolved in differing academic disciplines, with differing vocabularies and conceptualizations of values and ethical concepts. Economism was developed in environmental economics, while IV Theory was constructed in the emerging field of environmental ethics; both offered comprehensive and connected theories, and they differed regarding the basic ontology of who or what is a 'morally considerable' individual, regarding, that is, who has standing to have their interests count.

In the 1970s and 1980s there were a few philosophers who turned their attention to ethical questions concerning inter-generational obligations (for example, Rawls, 1971; MacLean and Brown, 1983; Barry and Sikora, 1978; Partridge, 1981; Norton, 1982). John Rawls's treatment, in his influential book,

A Theory of Justice, is of perhaps special interest to economists. Rawls argued that all generations (choosing as rational choosers who stand behind a 'veil of ignorance' concerning their specific place (including temporal place) in a society, would bind themselves to maintain a 'fair savings rate,' an idea that is broadly similar to the ideas of weak sustainability theorists, such as Solow (1993) in mainstream economics. The philosopher Brian Barry (1978, p. 24; 1989) has also defended a highly aggregated approach to intergenerational moral comparisons. Aside from these exploratory works on intergenerational ethics, which mainly explore the application of concepts of equity to cross-generational contexts, most writings in the field of environmental ethics – from 1973 to the present – have dealt mainly with the extension of moral standing to nonhuman organisms and natural systems.

Early extensionism (for example, Routley, 1973; Rolston, 1975; Routley and Routley, 1979; Stone, 1974; see also Passmore, 1973, who dissented from this rush to extend the moral community to include nonhumans) simply addressed the question: is it intelligible – and perhaps true – to say that some elements of nature have intrinsic value? Also, the related question is asked: what does it mean to say that a natural object has intrinsic value? On the question of interpretation, it turned out under analysis that IV Theorists split roughly down the middle between 'strong' and 'weak' nonanthropocentrists. Strong non-anthropocentrists, represented by Rolston, Regan, and Paul Taylor, argued that the intrinsic value found in nature exists entirely independently of humans, human judgment, or human consciousness. For example, Rolston once said that natural objects 'generate' their own intrinsic value (Rolston, 1994). Weak IV Theory, on the other hand, espoused by J. Baird Callicott and a number of other ethicists, has explicitly recognized the need for a valuer to attribute value. Callicott therefore treats intrinsic value 'adverbially' – as a way in which humans value nature – a way that is analogous to the way a parent values a child 'for' itself, based on characteristics of the object – or the child – rather than according to selfish needs of the valuer (Callicott, 1989). It is not clear what difference this should make in policies advocated but, speaking theoretically and epistemologically, the difference is huge. Theoretically, strong intrinsic value would exist even if humans had never existed; it is a feature of natural objects that exists entirely independently of human cognition; it is therefore independent of human cultural differences and exists within nature itself. Strong intrinsic value is attractive to environmental ethicists because, if proved to exist, it would provide culturally independent arguments for environmental policies, arguments that would be persuasive even across cultures and worldviews. Weak intrinsic value, on the other hand, is attributed by human beings and these attributions cannot help but be affected by cultural and ideological differences across cultures. Whereas with strong intrinsic value, which is said to be 'discovered' in nature – a characteristic of nature overlooked by anthropocentric cultures and theorists – weak intrinsic value is in an important sense creative and dynamic. Callicott, for example, argued that this kind of value was only perceptible once the science of ecology allowed us to expand our sense of what could be a 'whole', worthy of moral considerability.

Epistemologically, both of these theories are problematic. Rolston's strong intrinsic value apparently achieves considerable moral authority because of its universality and apparent independence of actual human experience; but at the same time, this authority demands that Rolston embrace a most difficult epistemological task – to provide evidence of intrinsic value beyond any particular human experiences (which are all, of course, particular cognitive events, occurring in a context and highly charged with cultural and other background meanings) (Norton, 1992, 2002). Callicott, on the other hand, treats attributions of intrinsic value to nature as relative to culture and worldview. Appeals to weak intrinsic values as premises in protectionist arguments therefore lack scope; they would not apply to those who do not accept a worldview that countenances intrinsic values in nature. The appeal of these arguments is thus restricted to those who accept the premise asserting intrinsic value. Apparently, then, weak IV Theorists can offer no culture- or worldview-independent reasons to act to protect nature and natural objects; their theories, understood in this way, provide only an *explication*, not an independent *justification*, of nonanthropocentric principles. Nonanthropocentrism, then, if taken to include thinkers as diverse as Rolston and Callicott, is not really a single ontological theory of environmental value; it represents, rather, a label that in fact comprehends several kinds of value and a variety of methods of value analysis (Norton, 2002).

Cutting across this puzzling ambiguity about the nature of the independence that is asserted for natural intrinsic value is another question: what types of beings can have intrinsic value?

Because of the speculative and exploratory tone of early work on nonanthropocentrism, little attention was paid to the *exact* nature of the natural objects that could be said to have intrinsic value, and there was no definitive understanding whether only individual organisms could have intrinsic value (on analogy with intrinsic value as usually attributed to human beings), or whether some composites, such as species or ecosystems, might have intrinsic value. In these early days, then, the literature of environmental ethics was not sharply separated from the growing and somewhat complementary – at least in their arguments critical of anthropocentrism – literature on animal rights and animal liberation (Regan, 1983; Singer, 1975). At first the use of a common label, 'nonanthropocentrists' or 'biocentrists,' papered over important differences; eventually, however, differences regarding what kinds of objects might have intrinsic value led to open schisms among academic environmental ethicists.

In 1981, Callicott published an influential essay, 'Animal Rights and Environmental Ethics: A Triangular Affair,' in the two-year-old journal, *Environmental Ethics* (included in Callicott, 1989). This article first noted the attack on anthropocentrism mounted by animal liberationists, whom he called 'Humane Moralists', and who were characterized as expanding moral considerability to include nonhuman organisms, especially animals, and often domestic animals. Then, articulating a version of Aldo Leopold's land ethic, Callicott argued that fully capturing the concerns of environmentalists such as Leopold would require attribution of moral standing not to individual animals – certainly not to domestic animals – but rather to species, ecosystems, and communities. Callicott, casting his lot with Leopold and declaring individualism inadequate to the task of building a distinctively environmental ethic, endorsed a robust holism that claimed 'the separate interests of the parts [are] acknowledge[d] to be subordinate to the health and well-being of the whole.' In response, the staunch ethical individualist, Tom Regan, declared Callicott and Leopold to be 'environmental fascists', advocates of running roughshod over individual welfare of humans and animals in pursuit of a higher, corporate good lodged in composite entities such as ecological communities.

Actually, Callicott's famous triangle represents a truncated quadrangle. By considering anthropocentric individualism nonanthropocentric individualism, and nonanthropocentric holism, Callicott apparently missed the possibility of an *anthropocentric holism* – a theory that the broader good of the human species is so dependent upon whole systems of nature that we should seek policies that protect species and systems as a broad strategy for protecting present and future human interests and fulfilling commitments to live sustainably. This fourth viewpoint may prove the most productive because it inoculates environmental ethics from the unfortunate implication that policy-makers must always choose *between* human and nonhuman interests, allowing the creative search for convergent policies that serve both broad human interests for the present and future and the 'interests' of natural systems because they support those human interests. Norton (1991) has therefore proposed the 'convergence hypothesis,' a prediction that empirical examination will reveal that, if one takes all human interests into account (including the full breadth of human values in the present and in the future), and if one defines nonanthropocentric interests reasonably, then the policies required to comply with anthropocentric and nonanthropocentric values will converge. A recent study of public values and policy attitudes has offered some initial empirical support for this notion of convergence in the case of national forest management goals (Minteer and Manning, 2000).

Today, many environmental ethicists – disturbed by the apparent intractability and unclear policy implications of extensionism – whether individualist or holist, have begun to wonder whether the experiment of simply extending standard ethical concepts such as welfare and rights to broader classes of entities, and the associated question of identifying beings who are morally considerable, represents the best formulation of questions concerning environmental values. These environmental ethicists, sometimes called 'weak anthropocentrists' or 'broad anthropocentrists,' attempt to avoid oversimplifying the range of human values, and often appeal to the principles of the American pragmatist movement (especially C.S. Peirce and John Dewey) as a philosophical rallying point for a new, more contextual and problem-based philosophy of the environment (Light and Katz, 1996).

3.   BEYOND INDIVIDUALISM, HOLISM AND EXTENSIONISM

According to this emerging argument, the extensionist strategy fails not because it is too radical, but because it is not radical enough. Extensionists simply take traditional ethical theories and apply them to a broader reference class, without changing or refining those ethical principles. Since these principles were developed to characterize ethical relations among human individuals, it is at least worth asking whether they are likely to be appropriate for recognizing and describing all environmental goods. In the last section, we emphasized the difference between economists and most environmental ethicists regarding anthropocentrism; in this section we explore another assumption – one shared by economists and by many philosophers, including many environmental ethicists – that of ethical individualism. By individualism we mean the view that all goods must necessarily be goods accruing to individual, conscious beings. One specific, and highly influential version – familiar in the social sciences since World War II – is referred to as 'methodological individualism,' the theory that all benefits must be defeasible into goods of individuals, without remainder. Interestingly, ethical individualism, as defined here, is embraced by utilitarians, including economists, who measure units of individual human welfare, and it applies also to the two other two major strains of thought in moral theory, natural rights theories such as those of Kant, Locke and Jefferson, and contractual rights theories such as that of Rawls. Extensionist claims that nature has intrinsic value – nonanthropocentrism – can be seen either as an extension of utilitarianism (Singer, 1975) or of the tradition of rights theory (Taylor, 1986; Regan, 1983). The multiple forms of IV Theory, in other words, represent variations on either consequential ethics (when the focus is on happiness or suffering of individual, sentient beings, whether human or nonhuman), or extend the idea of obligations to individual persons to include obligations of moral agents to individual elements of nature. Because the concept of rights, correlative to moral obligations in human ethics, has been so strongly associated with requirements for the treatment of human persons, most extensionists have avoided use of the term 'rights.' Instead, they have preferred to speak of natural objects as having 'intrinsic value,' value analogous to that which confers rights on humans, but value that differs from full-blown individual rights in some respects (see, for example, Taylor, 1986). The important point for the concerns of this section is that both forms of extensionist, nonanthropocentric approaches to environmental ethics begin their extensions from a thoroughly individualist perspective: goods to be protected – benefits, welfare, rights – are universally considered to be goods of human individuals.

We turn now to the possibility of a more radical critique of both contemporary ethical and economic thought by examining whether environmental goods are appropriately interpreted as individual goods in the sense often shared by economists and philosophers. Some environmental ethicists, mainly pragmatists who are impatient with speculative extensions of traditional theories, have urged a new approach to the field, one that encourages a more community-based, pluralistic approach to environmental values. We refer to this approach as radical (intellectually) because it questions, even attacks, assumptions that unite economists, many other social scientists, and traditional ethical theorists, by considering the possibility that environmental values include goods that cannot be defeasible, without remainder, into goods enjoyed by individuals, human or otherwise. Presently, we explain why we think it appropriate to call these values 'communal' values.

In this discussion, some fine distinctions are necessary to avoid confusion. Economists, of course, have shown considerable interest in (a) *aggregated* goods, (b) *public* goods, (c) *collective action/choices* to maximize individual goods, (d) *multi-criteria analyses* of policy outcomes, and (e) *institutions* to maximize individual goods. Aggregated goods, as noted above, are calculations based on units of welfare of individual humans – a thoroughly individualistic concept. Public goods are defined by economists as goods that are nonexclusive and (sometimes) nonrival; but, again, these goods are measured as aggregated benefits of individuals. Economists have also embraced game theory, including, of course, iterative games and multi-actor models, extending rational behavior to apply to collective behavior in search of maximizing aggregated individual interests; and economists have experimented with some forms of multi-criteria analyses. One particularly popular form of multi-criteria analysis has arisen among the group of scholars who call themselves 'ecological economists.' The ecological economists insist on seeking both economic efficiency and protecting 'natural capital.' Proponents of this new subdiscipline, however, have for the most part left the individualistic conception of value unquestioned, as natural capital is characterized in terms of Hicksian income (Daly and Cobb, 1989) and the value of ecological systems is often represented in terms of 'ecological services' (Costanza et al., 1997; Dailey, 1997) which are in turn expressed in monetary units representing values experienced by consumers. A few ecological economists have gone further, insisting that true sustainability requires measurement of physical as well as economic trends; one interesting approach in this direction – ecological foot-printing – holds promise eventually to offer a useful physical measure of the impacts of consumptive practices on ecological systems (Wackernagel and Rees, 1996).

Finally, economists have greatly increased their interest in institutions lately, but it is important to divide economic work on institutions into phases. Early advocates of institutional economics (Veblen, 1919; Commons, 1934) questioned basic assumptions of the mainstream, individualistc economic paradigm – questioning, for example, the dominant use of partial equilibrium models and the assumption of consumer sovereignty as they emphasized that individual preferences change dynamically in context. This early work, which had important affinities with the work of the pragmatist philosopher John Dewey, understood economics within a context of dynamically forming and changing contexts of an evolutionary system. By challenging consumer sovereignty and the associated assumptions of fixed and well-ordered individual preferences, these Old Institutionalists called into question the existence of a single, aggregatable concept of the good. They also recognized the important role of institutions in affecting and changing attitudes, which meant they envisioned a kind of economics in which non-individual, emergent goods might be recognized. The Old Institutionalists, that is, avoided theoretical commitment to the view that the good of a society is the aggregated good of all individuals. This approach, however, has been eclipsed by economists who can be called New Institutionalists, who have accepted the assumption that the goal of institutions is to maximize aggregated welfare of the society which supports them, and who study institutions mainly to understand how to use them as instruments to this goal (see, for example, Williamson, 1987; North, 1990). Only a few economists (Nelson and Winter, 1985; Arthur, 1989) have begun to raise some of these questions in a more dynamic, evolutionary context in which individualism and consumer sovereignty become more problematic. In the sense defined here, all of these experiments except the Old Institutionalism and evolutionary economics remain individualistic – they explore alternative ways to describe, analyze and maximize individual welfare. So it seems fair to say that economics today is, with few exceptions, a thoroughly individualistic discipline.

What is interesting is that almost all writers on ethics, including many extensionists among environmental ethicists, have likewise accepted this individualistic theory about the nature of the good. Those who, like Callicott (1989), endorse ecosystem values as intrinsic and 'holistic', do so by essentially turning ecosystems and species into moral individuals (Norton, 1996). This shared acceptance of an ethical bias toward values that are values of whole individuals is important to both ethical and economic theorists because it holds open the possibility of commensurability among all types of values. This approach at least keeps alive the hope that all value can be measured in a single theoretical vernacular, a belief that, as noted above, is referred to as 'moral monism' (Stone, 1987; Callicott, 1990).

Pragmatist philosophers, whose thought is anchored in the work of Charles Sanders Peirce and John Dewey, have recently challenged this shibboleth of most economists, many social scientists and many ethical theorists; pragmatic environmental philosophers criticize all of these individualistic theoretical approaches as being inadequate to characterize or measure what we might call 'communal goods.' This is truly a radical proposal in that it requires modification in the basic understanding of value in both economics and philosophy.

As the terms of debate shift away from environmental ethics as having an exclusive focus on intrinsic value of natural objects, a new departure in environmental thought, one that is independent of the simple charge of anthropocentrism, opens up. Explorations of the limits of individualism – explorations of assumptions that have been shared by economists and environmental ethicists – may identify some common ground for shared concepts and at least productive disagreements between ethicists and economists. A good starting-point for this discussion is a reconsideration of Garrett Hardin's (1968) classic analogy of human population growth as a 'Tragedy of the Commons.' This paper, and its now-ubiquitous analogy, has been reprinted many times and, while it has been criticized on both historical and logical grounds, has nevertheless proved powerful because it highlights a recurring dilemma in environmental policy formation. Indeed, far from remaining simply a metaphor for human population growth, the mental model of a tragedy of the commons has been expanded as an explanatory device to account for all kinds of failures of decision-making and consequent negative impacts on social values in situations where individual choice leads to collective ruin. For economists, the tragedy of the commons can be cured, or at least significantly mitigated, by assigning property rights in resources, creating incentives for individuals to protect the productive capability of their own parcels. The economic treatment involves the privatization of the common resource as represented by the pasture. Private goods that were once derived from the commons are now derived from one's personal property; a public good has been transformed into private goods; in principle, this privatization provides a reason for private owners to protect the productive features of the resource. The economists' interpretation of the tragedy can be, and has been, questioned on a number of points. First, there is strong empirical evidence that privatization of the commons is not *necessary* in order to protect the public good of the pasture. Political scientists have shown through detailed case studies, including the management of the high pastures of the Swiss Alps, that cooperative management of common resources has been accomplished successfully for hundreds of years without deterioration of the resource (see, for example, Ostrom, 1991), suggesting that the problem is with *open access* to resources, rather than a problem caused by common *ownership*. The mathematical bioeconomist Colin Clark (1974) has shown that private ownership is not *sufficient* in all cases to protect productive resources; under reasonable assumptions regarding discount rates and opportunities for investment, Clark showed – by distinguishing between maximizing rent over indefinite time and maximizing income over given periods of time – that a private owner of a resource may maximize income and profits by extinguishing the resource by overexploitation and reinvestment of the larger profits in other high-return ventures. Clark concludes, 'In view of the likelihood of private firms adopting high rates of discount, the conservation of renewable resources would appear to require continual public surveillance and control of the physical yield and the condition of the stocks' (p. 634). The result that privatization is neither necessary nor sufficient for protection of common resources apparently follows within a standard, individualistic interpretation of public goods.

The economists' understanding of the tragedy as an ownership problem can also be questioned at a deeper level, however. The shift from public to private ownership of the pasture replaces public goods with private goods, a move that is justified if methodological individualism is true. The benefits of the resource are fully transferable, on the economists' assumptions about value, without remainder, into private accounts. On the assumption that all goods are defeasible into private goods, the privatization process is simply an execution of the principle of methodological individualism. Consider, however, the counter-argument that there are goods, what might be called 'communal' goods, involved in the protection of a resource. These, one might argue, are analogous to 'emergent qualities' in biological evolution, and cannot be understood or translated into an aggregation of individual goods. This topic, obviously, is too involved to be fully explored in this review chapter, and must be left for later discussion; the present point, however, is not to establish the existence of emergent community values, but only to establish that it is at least sensible to talk about goods that are not defeasible into individual goods – they are goods that emerge at the level of communities and cannot be adequately represented or measured as aggregations of individual goods.

One can also think of the tragedy of the commons in another way – one inspired by Aldo Leopold's (1949) brilliant simile of 'thinking like a mountain.' Leopold, who opened his essay criticizing his own failed wolf-and-deer policies, said, 'Only the mountain has lived long enough to listen objectively to the howl of a wolf.' He goes on to suggest that the mountain has an interest in having wolves because, ecologically, they protect against overgrazing of ranges by deer. What is interesting is that Leopold's personification of the mountain need only be metaphorical; the harm to the mountain translated, over time, into harm to humans. But humans, who tend to analyze situations in terms of individual self-interest, are likely to miss the communal good of maintaining the pasture (or the mountain) over generations of users. This good need not, that is, be interpreted as a nonanthropocentric good; but it is also not, Leopold argues, capable of being expressed on the same level, at the same scale, as are individual, economic values. Leopold's endorsement of nonindividualistic, but human, values illustrates an alternative to the economists' approach to the tragedy of the commons. One can argue that the good of protecting the commons for future generations of users is a good that is expressed and representable at the level of community; as an ecologist might say, it emerges at the level of multi-generational interactions of populations of species, including but not limited to the human species. This 'ecological-scaled' value is not, on this view, defeasible into individual values. It exists on a different level and a different temporal and spatial scale. The tragedy occurs, on this view, because it posits individual, selfish decision-makers in a context in which each of their interests causes them to act in a way that destroys a higher-level value that emerges only on a multi-generational, communal scale (Norton, 1995; 1996).

This communal interpretation of the tragedy of the commons therefore opens up a new fault line among theories of value, a fault line that separates not economists from environmental ethicists, but individualistic economists and individualistic environmental ethicists from ones who recognize incommensurable human values, including communal values. Such values can be identified, perhaps even measured precisely, but they cannot all, in principle even, be aggregated meaningfully with other values from other levels.

By thinking of environmental goods in communitarian terms, one strikes at the heart of both the economists' and monistic environmental ethicists' core commitments to a single, commensurable measure of value. One opens up the possibility of a truly pluralistic and multi-voiced discussion of environmental values, a discussion that, for example, avoids discounting future benefits by treating them as expressible in a noncommensurable vocabulary that includes reference to communal goods. According to this viewpoint, public goods have an irreducible communal or social aspect and economic calculations aggregating individual benefits cannot capture the nature of decisions that involve choices between aggregated individual goods and communally based goods. Here, critics of economics can find support within the literature of economics itself, since it can be shown that no calculation of individual goods that fulfills minimal conditions of 'rationality' can represent the freely chosen good of democratic participants in a free society (Arrow, 1963; Sen, 1970a, 1970b; Sager, 1997). This result, which means that the most interesting questions in environmental policy cannot be accurately treated as optimization problems, was corroborated in a classic paper in planning theory (Rittel and Webber, 1973). 'Wicked' problems – problems that require the balancing of competing social values – resist optimization solutions because the question of which values to prioritize cannot, itself, be solved optimally.

This line of reasoning, and its implied strategy for environmental ethicists, is to treat normative issues regarding the environment as those requiring cooperative action based on public deliberation, attention to fair democratic processes, and to the building of institutions. These issues open up a new frontier for discussions between ethicists and economists, especially regarding collective choices and ways in which communities can design institutions that help citizens with diverse values and goals decide, in cooperative fashion, how to protect goods that go beyond questions of individual self-interest. Environmental ethics, on this reading, is therefore a *political* pursuit, one focused on the public processes of communication and justification rather than the metaphysical probing of the fundamental nature of environmental values.

But if we are to move in this direction and view questions of environmental ethics in terms of the workings of democratic processes and deliberative institutions within which environmental values as communal goods may be advanced, it is clear that the political culture of liberalism – the philosophical backbone of Western industrial democracies – raises some serious concerns about the potential of this agenda. This is especially true if we believe that the classical liberalism associated with Kant, Locke and Bentham (and, in a somewhat more complicated fashion, J.S. Mill) is guilty of the accusation – made by both radical and reformist critics – that it has historically supplied little more than moral justification and cover for the *laissez-faire* economic order widely thought to be responsible for modern ecological degradation. Indeed, the near consensus view of noneconomic environmental theorists is that the Western liberal tradition, tied to the notion of individual preference satisfaction and linked with an unfettered industrial capitalism, is incapable of motivating and justifying the kind of cooperative social action required to achieve most environmentalist goals. This would seem to be particularly true, if one believes, as we do, that such goals hinge on considerations of communal value and politically coordinated behavior rather than on individual utility maximization and the satisfaction of preferences and desires formed exogenously from the political system. The liberal tradition thus appears to fall into the same pit as (neoclassical) environmental economics (which should be no surprise given the intellectual linkages between the two projects): it presupposes methodological individualism, both in its theory of preference formation and its model of political choice. And, as an ethical principle cast predominantly in the language and commitments of individual rights, it would seem to promise to support little more than an adversarial and atomistic politics of environmental concern, where notions of the common good are muffled, and often completely drowned out, by the clamor of private interests jockeying for social or economic position.

If this were the end of the story, the prospect of creating a liberal political culture capable of supporting environmental values as communal goods would indeed be quite dim. But fortunately that rich tradition has more promising philosophical resources available to work with than this. In particular, we would suggest that the 'reconstructed' liberalism developed by John Dewey in the first decades of the twentieth century provides a critical corrective to the moral and methodological individualism of the earlier classical versions. For Dewey, the notion of a fixed, 'ready-made' liberal self acting from the basis of previously formed preferences was a fallacy inasmuch as it discounted the social and cultural conditioning of citizens. In fact, Dewey saw the self as a 'moving thing,' an entity constantly growing and developing over time through intelligent interaction with the larger environments – both human and natural. In this understanding, and in concert with the Old Institutionalists discussed above, social arrangements and institutions therefore are not charged with merely satisfying 'given' individual preferences; rather, the *institutions and associations themselves* are powerful forces shaping the moral growth and development of the individual as an 'effectively' free self and democratic citizen (Dewey, 2000, pp. 46–7). Dewey termed his position 'Renascent liberalism,' a revamped liberal project propelled by his method of 'social intelligence,' or the directed means by which communities adapt to new areas of experience over time. This adaptation was to be accomplished by the deliberate adjustment and transformation of shared goals and values in the face of ever more inclusive experience. Dewey's reformed liberalism thus provided the grounds for social action by focusing on the open and evolving character of democratic communities. And by emphasizing their ability to learn to grapple with problematic situations in all areas of lived experience, Dewey empowered citizen action in the full sweep of technical, political, and, most significantly, moral contexts.

Dewey's most profound philosophical contribution may well have been his application of experimental intelligence to the moral realm. Committed to the amelioration of the problems of citizens rather than the problems of philosophers, Dewey sought to develop a process of social inquiry whereby individuals, as cooperative problem-solvers committed to democratic methods and values, would systematically work through the myriad problematic situations that arise in human experience, whether they be primarily moral or cognitive in nature. As a result of this move, ethics for Dewey was a thoroughly contextual, 'bottom-up' affair driven by specific social problems and dilemmas rather than abstract philosophical puzzles and indulgent speculations. Furthermore, he saw this moral inquiry as a thoroughly empirical business. By his lights, this was an enterprise that required a clearly articulated naturalistic method of logically testing moral goods by evaluating their experiential import and practical consequences. As Dewey understood it, the experimental method of inquiry employed in the natural sciences was not different in kind from the practice of moral inquiry; it was only more technically refined and more institutionalized than experimental methods in the ethical realm (Dewey, 1920; 1929).

This approach to moral experience was a radical departure from the more deductivistic and principle-driven style of ethical reasoning found in much of the Western ethical tradition. Moreover, Dewey's naturalism was strongly at odds with the leading non-naturalistic ethical theories and methods of the canon, such as Kantian transcendentalism, to name only the most influential alternative. But most importantly for our claims here, and as mentioned above, Dewey's naturalism had the important effect of making his approach to ethics compatible with the ontological commitments and especially the methods of the social and natural sciences. Dewey's insight on this count – his articulation of a unified logic of inquiry – opens up the possibility of more interdisciplinary models of human values, and does much to clear the philosophical ground for a conceptually integrated language of valuation to be spoken across the sciences and the humanities.

If Dewey's reconstructed liberalism and moral theory of the early and middle twentieth century pointed the way toward a new institutional framework for articulating public values and community goals (Lee, 1993), contemporary democratic theorists such as Benjamin Barber have variously carried on and extended key elements of Dewey's project. Like Dewey, Barber offers a robust politics of social engagement and democratic citizenship. In particular, Barber's 'strong democracy' – rejecting classical and contemporary 'thin' liberal accounts focused on private goods and metaphysical commitments to individualism and atomism – offers a bold participatory politics of transformation that owes much to Dewey's insights into the creation of public values through free and open discussion of community goals. In Barber's model, only socially engaged, democratic citizens, shaped and enabled through civic education and public debate and discussion, will be able to build a political community 'capable of transforming dependent, private individuals into free citizens and partial and private interests into public goods' (Barber, 1984, p. 132). Barber views community, public goods and citizenship as the three constituent elements of an authentic, 'strong' democratic public (ibid., p. 133–4).

In the same vein, though planted more in the theoretical soil of critical theory than Anglo-American liberalism, Jurgen Habermas has advanced a sympathetic moral and political project geared toward the justification of community norms (Habermas, 1993, 1996). Instead of arguing for a particular substantive account of any particular moral good or set of goods, Habermas offers a public procedure (what he terms 'practical discourse') for testing the normative validity of publicly articulated values.

Accordingly, Habermas's 'discourse ethics' emphasizes the articulation of discursive rules that will secure free, fair and open deliberative processes and promote reasoning about public interests and goods rather than private, individual preferences and interests. Habermas's work – which he describes as 'post-metaphysical,' emphasizes the presuppositions and conventions of communication in service of cooperative action. By noting the implicit acceptance by participants in public deliberation of norms of discourse – such as respect for other participants and their views – Habermas offers norms derived from commitment to cooperative action as a substitute for the unwavering principles of the environmental ethicists and the selfish desires of economists. Further, his explorations in 'ideal speech communities' may open up new areas for social science research, such as research on public deliberation within ecosystem and watershed management processes.

Despite their differences, with Dewey, Barber and Habermas we see the refashioning of moral inquiry into a public process of deliberation and normative argument among diverse citizens who share the goal of acting cooperatively in search of intelligent social action in response to perceived problems. This project has much to offer forward-thinking environmental ethicists who have moved beyond the extensionist program and have rejected the gravitational pull of monistic nonanthropocentrism in favor of a pluralistic and process orientation toward questions of environmental value. It also provides a framework supportive of more institutional treatments of environmental values as communal goods not fully captured by private-utility-maximizing models. Therefore, ethicists and economists searching for new normative ground for their environmental programs along political lines have a potential common foundation awaiting development.

4.   ENVIRONMENTAL ETHICS AS A PUBLIC PHILOSOPHY OF ADAPTIVE MANAGEMENT

In light of the previous discussion, we suggest that environmental ethicists embrace the deliberative model of ethics as politics and explore the implications of inquiry into environmental values as a democratic process of identifying and justifying community environmental goals through free and open public deliberation. Environmental ethics, in our view, must be thought of as a *public* philosophy, one that recognizes the irreducible plurality and yet communal nature of environmental values articulated in diverse normative vocabularies and experiential contexts. This means that environmental ethicists and environmental economists who seek to collapse such pluralism into a single theory of value, whether intrinsic value or consumers' willingness to pay, are failing to develop fully comprehensive and sufficiently democratic accounts of environmental goods. As a consequence, those choosing this path are incapable of offering much critical insight into the creation and defense of strategies and processes for resolving conflicts between competing environmental and social interests.

A truly public philosophy of the environment would recognize the descriptive and normative validity of ethical pluralism and would work to fashion a more practical and activist philosophical mission for environmental ethics. Such an agenda would emphasize the development of a contextual model of moral inquiry into environmental problems whereby citizens work together to resolve specific environmental disputes and set common goals for their communities. Here is one area where philosophy, if practiced at a local level at which real environmental problems are encountered, can actually make significant and lasting practical contributions to democratic processes of environmental valuation and policy formation. By helping stakeholders identify, clarify and evaluate environmental and social claims introduced into the flow of argument and debate in public environmental deliberation, environmental ethicists can play a major role in the development of the conditions necessary for social action on behalf of collectively endorsed environmental ends. Likewise, economists contribute to the same process by identifying ways to achieve proposed goals at least cost to economic goals.

In effect, what is being suggested here is that most discussion of environmental values has progressed, logically, from general questions of ontology and how to measure all types of environmental value (questions 1 and 2, above) toward questions of justification and process (questions 3 and 4). What may be more useful is to reverse this progression and begin by examining the processes by which particular environmental disputes are addressed and by asking what various theories of value can be offered as interpretations and clarifications of particular, on-the-ground debates about what to do in particular situations. If, that is, environmental ethicists and environmental economists could set aside their disagreements about the ultimate nature of environmental values and recognize that individuals – as participants in particular policy debates and deliberations – appeal to a multiplicity of values, members of the two fields might be effective in articulating, comparing and prioritizing the multiple values that are articulated by individuals and interest groups in actual public processes.

In order for this to happen, however, environmental ethics needs to adopt a more empirical approach to environmental values and goals; by an empirical approach, we mean something like Dewey's view of science and social action, and of social learning as a real possibility of democratically organized communities. On this count we believe that adaptive management, an emerging paradigm of environmental management developed by C.S. Holling and others in the late 1970s, provides the scientific and philosophical framework for this activist and empirical agenda (Holling, 1978; Walters, 1986; Lee, 1993; Gunderson et al., 1995). Adaptive management is, above all, *experimental* management, an approach that acknowledges the cognitive and political challenges of understanding and acting in the face of complex natural and social phenomena. Recognizing the dynamic and unpredictable character of ecological processes, adaptive managers expect surprises, and yet strive to design methods and manipulations of environmental systems that reduce this uncertainty through directed management practices. As a consequence, social institutions engaged in and affected by the management process must be structured in a manner that promotes a flexible, iterative process through which citizens can learn about the dynamics of the natural world as they voice and revise their values and goals in light of increasing information and evidence.

As we can see from even this cursory treatment of the adaptive management paradigm, many of Dewey's ideas are quite pertinent. The first, which has been discussed above, is his treatment of science and ethical inquiry as subject to the same pattern of inquiry. He simply denied there is a problem about the 'fact–value gulf' and embraced the idea that we resolve ethical dilemmas through experience, especially through community-based and community-sensitive, participatory experience. Because Dewey and the pragmatists engage values in real situations, with important stakes for communities, values are as open to revision in the face of new experiences as are uncertain beliefs. In real situations, values can be so compelling that they provide solid planks for undertaking experiments and reducing uncertainty by the judicious use of science within a management process. When engaged in active, adaptive management, we are encouraged to find refuge in consensus wherever possible and compromise otherwise; an epistemological community can be built upon shared social values. At other times, experience leads us to reconsider some of our values; at these times, values, like other beliefs, can be undermined by experience. For example, many US cities – especially our city of residence, Atlanta – have over the past few decades carried out an experiment in unlimited suburban growth. This experiment was animated by a certain value, the value of individual freedom and unlimited mobility, a value that is observed in the pervasive choice to travel in single-occupant vehicles. Time will tell whether residents in the future will consider this experiment a success; if not, they may come to question the values on which it was predicated.

Another Deweyan idea, 'social learning,' once refurbished and modernized, can serve us well as a guide to adaptive management. This idea has important implications for environmental policy process, and it also has implications for the way we think of stakeholders, the general public and professional policy-makers and bureaucratic managers. Dewey's concept of social learning provides a broad framework for understanding the goals of adaptive management within a diverse and democratic society. Here the purpose is not to seek to reduce environmental values to a simplified, single notion of economic or intrinsic good, but rather to design a process that allows citizens to introduce and, consequently, learn about the complex plurality of environmental and social values in a deliberative process.

This idea of social learning also requires an important shift in the role of environmental managers and experts involved in managing resources. Dewey perceived that the growth in complexity of modern industrial societies was such as to bewilder the layperson; so he conceived of communities as capable of strategically organizing themselves to incorporate directed, mission-oriented science at specific areas of uncertainty and disagreement (Dewey, 1927; Funtowicz and Ravetz, 1995). Dewey also saw that, under the best conditions, such an organization might lead to a cooperative interaction of the public and experts, unified by a shared goal of protecting an important environmental feature of their place, working together to learn about and discuss openly both the goals and also the methods of environmental management.

It is encouraging that a recent National Research Council report (1996) strongly endorses such an iterative, participatory and deliberative process in the management of risk, including choices regarding regulatory goals. The 1996 report – in direct and stark contrast to earlier approaches to risk management (National Research Council, 1983), which urged the isolation and serial treatment of scientific assessment and deliberation about values – advocates deliberation as essential to the characterization of risk. If the ideal of deliberation in search of cooperative action could be achieved in an open, iterative process of community-based adaptive management – through the use of citizens' advisory committees in conjunction with blue-ribbon scientific panels, for example – it may be possible for the community to cooperate to reduce uncertainty, to adjust environmental goals and to engage in management activities that both improve local conditions and at the same time contribute to the learning curve with regard to environmental values more generally.

The upshot is that we need an approach to environmental values and valuation that fits comfortably into the experimentalist framework of an adaptive management process. Such an approach must recognize the dynamic and transformative potential of environmental values as citizens enter into deliberation over community futures; it must also encourage the articulation of multiple, diverse values and proposed courses of action by stakeholders. This normative variation and the ensuing process of inquiry and experimentation are part of the selective process of adaptation, helping managers and citizens move toward more intelligent and sustainable environmental policies. The adaptive management paradigm can therefore be instrumental in helping to reconstruct environmental ethics as a public and pragmatic philosophy of the environment, one that traffics in the real-world problems, plans and policies of communities struggling to adjust to their changing ecophysical contexts.

5.   TOWARD A PLURALIST AND EXPERIMENTAL ANTHROPOCENTRISM

If we choose to follow the above line of argument in environmental ethics, we expand the field's framing of normative discourse beyond its conventional and narrowly defined anthropocentric and nonanthropocentric languages. The focus on the public process of value articulation and its connection to social action gives rise to a broader understanding of environmental values as communal goods requiring a politics of validation and justification, rather than as philosophical values requiring metaphysical founding. Here we have the emergence of a broad, democratic humanism: public environmental values are multiple and multi-vocal; they are expressed in a variety of normative discourses not exhausted by the limited grammars of utility maximization, intrinsic value, or any other single-criterion formulation. We should expect this to remain the case as long as human experience continues to grow and evolve as it reaches into and is conditioned by complex and dynamic ecological systems.

Our line of argument, further, directs us toward a form of anthropocentrism that is pluralist and experimental in attitude. It is pluralist in recognizing that participants in public deliberation derive values from nature in many ways and express these values in many ways. The adaptive approach to management is experimental, admitting we do not know how best to measure environmental values, and encourages experimentation with multiple methods for improving our understanding of what people value. One very useful exercise for a community is to try to choose 'integrative indicators,' indicators that will 'stand in' for multiple values. For example, the indicator 'percentage of ground area with pervious surfaces' can be easily measured and may prove representative of the values of advocates of green space, of biological diversity, of water quality, and of anti-sprawl. In some communities, perhaps, such an indicator can be agreed upon as a useful guide to policy, even if the various interest groups involved could never agree on the ultimate values that justify pursuing such a specific objective (Norton, 1991).

The proposed system of valuation, and the broader framework of adaptive management into which it is embedded, is, it must be acknowledged, anthropocentric in one sense, a sense which we will call 'methodological anthropocentrism.' By emphasizing as we do that valuation of public goods is part of a broader, deliberative and political process, we must insist that all values that are expressed in this discourse are human values, expressed and experienced by humans. Methodologically, then, we insist that all values be expressed as reasons that humans should act in certain ways and not others. They are understood, then, not as reified, human-independent values or as preferences formed exogenous to public decisions, but rather as ways that some humans do indeed value nature, and as possibly persuasive reasons to act or choose specific policies. This insistence, while limiting reasons based on values to human reasons, is nevertheless consistent with nonanthropocentrism in the broader sense that it recognizes, empirically, strong evidence in people's words and practices that they do indeed value nature intrinsically, that is, for reasons that have nothing to do with their own, selfish goals (Spash, 2000). References to intrinsic values in nature – and the desire to protect natural systems from further harm – are thus understood as one competing value espoused by some humans who express these values in conflict with other participants in the debate who have different and competing values. But they are not the presumptive moral 'trumps' or conversation-stoppers that many ethicists believe them to be. Rather, they are simply one way of speaking about nature that may or may not prove helpful in resolving specific environmental policy disputes (Minteer, 2001). The key point about participants is that they have decided – despite their recognition that other participants will seek to protect or enhance values they reject – to enter the process and to seek cooperative solutions to environmental problems, even if this requires compromise on efficiency measures or moral principles.

By focusing on *process*, then, one delays clashes over ontology, and poses the question of how to evaluate environmental changes in a more tractable, concrete form: what methods of valuation prove (have proven) helpful to real communities in responding to real environmental problems and disagreements about what to do about them? (Leach et al., 2001; Leach et al., under review) By trying to better understand value discourse and evaluation methods as endogenous to the adaptive management process, we hope to deflect attention away from ontological disagreements and a priori claims about the nature of all environmental value, and toward empirical studies of experiments in making evaluation procedures useful in actual management situations.

The primary message for environmental ethicists and environmental economists is that both camps need to move toward a more communal and pluralistic understanding of environmental values. This attitudinal and procedural shift requires, among other things, the relaxation of the demands of individualistic and monistic philosophical foundations and methods of analysis. If this change in perspective and commitments is accomplished, we believe that both fields will be able to play a more active and meaningful role in public environmental discourse, and the fields will also identify shared intellectual problems that will encourage interdisciplinary collaboration and increased communication between environmental ethicists and environmental economists.

To pull together the claims we have made throughout this chapter, then, and in preparation for the conclusion, we can offer the following set of suggestions for environmental economists and environmental ethicists who are willing to move beyond exclusivist, monistic theories (and ontologically driven accounts of environmental values in general) in favor of a more deliberative and process-oriented approach to evaluation of environmental change. While our remarks have been more historical than prospective, it should be clear that we think there is a rich future of collaboration between environmental ethics and environmental economics, provided a more pragmatic, deliberative and democratic approach is pursued in both fields.

First, we must stop thinking of methodological individualism as the only way to learn about human values and behavior. Even if we can usefully represent *some* values as having costs in competition with other consumer choices, it does not follow that calculation and aggregation of individual willingnesses to pay are the only useful ways of representing or studying environmental values. Therefore, instead of viewing environmental values as the outcome of the aggregation of individual preferences and utility functions, or as intrinsic to nature, we need to think of environmental value articulation as the product of social, deliberative and political processes – ones in which citizens advance and assess normative claims in an explicitly public context, a context in which real policy choices are open and real values are at stake. In this understanding, social commitments, norms and, especially, institutions are the foundational elements of environmental valuation, including, of course, institutions with strong economic dimensions. Through the give-and-take of public debate, environmental policies emerge as democratically validated social goals, supported by collectively assessed norms and values constructed through a fair process of deliberation, in which advantages and disadvantages – including, of course, costs and benefits – are considered and debated publicly. Methodological pluralism would support undertaking a variety of interdisciplinary comparisons of different evaluation techniques used in different situations, a trend that may already be well under way (Leach et al., 2001, Leach et al., under review; Norton and Steinemann, 2001). Programs such as the Environmental Protection Agency's Water and Watersheds program and joint programs of EPA and the National Science Foundation (including a joint workshop, Community Based Environmental Decision Making on 9 May 2000) have recently encouraged experimentation in new ways to learn about public values and to develop more effective processes that will empower communities to undertake actions to solve problems based on cooperative, community action. Researchers in Europe have already developed alternative techniques for understanding and interpreting environmental values through work with small groups (Burgess et al., 1988, 2000).

Second, we must reject the neoclassical economic notion of consumer sovereignty, especially in its most general form (Norton, 1994; Norton et al., 1998). Not only are environmental claims something more than the subjective desires of individual consumers; they are not properly conceived of as 'given,' unchanging entities that must be accepted as unquestioned articulations of public value. We must, as is explained by Funtowicz and Ravetz (1990, 1995), undertake mission-oriented science, both in the natural and social sciences. This includes science directed at questioning currently held values and goals. This change by no means challenges the authority of individuals to hold and express their desires and values in public debate. It only directs us to endorse a process by which such desires and values may be put to the critical test of public argument and scrutiny. It is clear that one of the potential outcomes of public deliberation is that citizens may revise their opinions, and even change their minds completely, when their beliefs are thoughtfully challenged by others (Gundersen, 1995). This dynamic, transformative aspect of environmental commitments, we believe, only underscores the necessity for more process-oriented methods of valuation.

Third, we must replace the fact–value distinction with a more relational, pragmatic model of moral and scientific inquiry in which the study of human values and the study of natural systems can jointly contribute to better decisions regarding the environment. This change will require rethinking decision models, such as the sequential risk analysis model (risk assessment/risk management) model, still popular at the Environmental Protection Agency, that sharply separates the gathering of facts about risk from social decisions about how to respond to it (National Research Council, 1983). Making decisions in a more iterative, deliberative framework in which articulated values shape scientific research, and in which values are revisited in the light of new scientific findings, will provide a more accurate and effective way to study and improve public decision-making (National Research Council, 1996; EPA, Science Advisory Board, 2000). This shift will require, in our view, that attention of researchers be shifted from the development of abstract, one-size-fits-all models of environmental decision-making to the tailoring of decision models to particular decision contexts in local situations in which there are some agreements and some disagreements. These consequences and disagreements can guide researchers to questions that are locally relevant, focusing attention on uncertainties that stand in the way of collective action. Such locally relevant research may not resemble the complex and abstract, general models of values and valuation preferred by economists and philosophers, but they may, if successful, point the way, from the bottom up, toward more general theories of environmental value and some consolidation of pluralistic expressions of values.

Fourth, we should accept and account for the empirical validity and normative force of value pluralism regarding the natural world (Minteer and Manning,

1999). Citizens express their environmental commitments in a variety of ways and in a range of normative languages, and the reduction of this diversity into a single type or vocabulary of value, as ethicists and economists often seek to do, simplifies the social and moral complexity of human experience. Most objectionable is the degree to which this approach disenfranchises public values that do not fit within settled, pre-defined categories, and how it seems to favor an isolated element of the moral situation (for example, intrinsic value, or preference satisfaction) at the expense of a more complete and inclusive accounting. Dewey, in fact, saw such reductionistic approaches to value as the improper singling out of particular aspects of a moral situation for special authority and emphasis, and regretted the implications of this practice for effective moral inquiry. Instead, he argued, as do we, that the *entire* experiential context be taken into account when a problematic situation requiring thoughtful decision-making and coordinated action arises. Therefore we must be attentive to all of the ways in which people express their environmental commitments in specific settings and situations requiring judgment.

Finally, and speaking directly to environmental economists, alternative frameworks that accommodate these methodological and substantive commitments need to be explored and developed. We believe that one promising direction lies with institutional or 'evolutionary' economic approaches, now gaining explicit attention in environmental circles (for example, Bromley, 1989; Jacobs, 1994; Hodgson, 1997; and Faucheux, 1997). Institutionalists, drawing from a tradition running back to Veblen and Galbraith, among others, depart from neoclassicists in ways particularly conducive to the environmental valuation agenda we have advocated here. Specifically, adherents of this school reject consumer sovereignty and the notion of exogenous, 'given' preferences for goods and services in favor of an understanding that emphasizes the dynamic nature of such interests and the constitutive power of cultural meanings and institutions for citizens' desires and attitudes. Moreover, an institutional economic approach endorses methodological and substantive pluralism concerning environmental values. Indeed, institutionalists (in the 'old' sense) focus on the actual, rather than hypothetical, economic behavior of individuals in specific cultural contexts, and open the door for a more empirical, and consequently more inclusive accounting of the varying socio-psychological underpinnings of economic values; research directed at problems such as this would involve a significant departure from neoclassical economic models. As a result of these commitments, institutionalists see individuals' preferences as objects of analysis rather than as presumptively accepted claims that must be satisfied (Jacobs, 1994). The socio-cultural focus of this approach also comports well with the deliberative methods of environmental value formation advocated here, and in that sense might provide a means for economists and process-oriented ethicists to join forces in environmental inquiry. Rich opportunities may open up for collaborations between economists and philosophers, as well as collaborations among these, together, with cognitive psychologists, to engage in interdisciplinary research on the development, formation and reformation of social values in deliberative situations (Gundersen, 1995).

6. CONCLUSION

Environmental ethics and environmental economics have both suffered from a tendency to begin their study of environmental values by committing, implicitly or explicitly, to a monistic ontological viewpoint, which reduces their flexibility in recognizing and describing observable patterns of human valuation of natural objects. This same inflexibility in describing observed values has – because the practitioners of both fields have for the most part committed themselves to inimical ontological understandings of the nature of environmental value – prevented economists and philosophers from identifying a set of shared intellectual problems. To break the resulting logjam in environmental discourse, we have suggested that it will be necessary and desirable to turn attention to the way environmental values and deliberation about them function in active political discourse, carried out in local situations, plagued by uncertainty, and riven by cross-currents of differing values and competing interests. By concentrating on actual decision processes, we can describe diverse values and identify disagreements that block consensus and collective actions. The attention would then shift to specific disagreements; and we countenance the possibility that increasing knowledge through pilot projects and limited experiments, and increasing deliberation, will uncover or create shared values, shared objectives and collective actions that can be undertaken to further reduce uncertainty and disagreement.

The social sciences and philosophy, collectively, have a responsibility to direct research at community-based environmental policy formation and to study the processes by which communities collectively articulate management goals and identify management indicators that are expressive of widely held social values (EPA, SAB, 2000). The topic of such studies should be, we believe, the identification of the conditions under which communities, faced with difficult problems and competing demands on limited resources, can engage in productive deliberation, and under what conditions social learning takes place in such processes.

REFERENCES

Arrow, Kenneth (1963), *Social Choice and Individual Values*, New York: John Wiley.
Arthur, W. Brian (1989), 'Competing Technologies, Increasing Returns, and Lock-In by Historical Events,' *The Economic Journal*, **99**, 116–32.

Barber, Benjamin (1984), *Strong Democracy*, Berkeley CA: University of California Press.
Barry, Brian (1978), 'Circumstances of Justice and Future Generations,' in R.I. Sikora and B. Barry (eds), *Obligations to Future Generations*,
Barry, Brian (1989), 'The Ethics of Resource Depletion,' in Brian Barry, *Democracy, Power, and Justice*, Oxford: Clarendon Press.
Blackstone, W.T. (ed.) (1974), *Philosophy and Environmental Crisis*, Athens, GA: University of Georgia Press.
Bromley, Daniel W. (1989) *Economic Interests and Institutions: The Conceptual Foundations of Public Policy*, Oxford: Blackwell.
Burgess, J., M. Limb and C.M. Harrison (1988), 'People, Parks And the Urban Green: A Study of Popular Meanings and Values for Open Spaces in the City,' *Urban Studies*, **25**, 455–73.
Burgess, J.,. J. Clark and C.M. Harrison (2000), 'Culture, Communication and the Information Problem in Contingent Valuation Surveys: A Case Study of a Wildlife Enhancement Scheme', *Environmental Planning C: Government and Policy*, **18**, 505–24.
Callicott, J. Baird (1989), *In Defense of the Land Ethic*, Albany, NY: State University of New York Press.
Callicott, J. Baird (1990), 'The Case Against Moral Pluralism,' *Environmental Ethics*, **12**, 99–124.
Clark, Colin (1974), 'The Economics of Over-Exploitation,' *Science*, **182**, 630–34.
Commons, John Rogers (1934), *Institutional Economics: Its Place in Political Economy*, New York: Macmillan.
Costanza, Robert, Ralph d'Arge, Rudolph de Groot, Stephen Farber, Monica Grasso, Bruce Hannon, Karin Limburg, Shahid Naeem, Robert V. O'Neill, Jose Paruelo, Robert G. Raskin, Paul Sutton, and Marjan van den Belt (1997), 'The Value of the World's Ecosystem Services and Natural Capital,' *Nature*, **387** (6630), 253–60.
Dailey, Gretchen (ed.) (1997), *Nature's Services: Societal Dependence on Natural Ecosystems*, Washington, DC: Island Press.
Daly, Herman and John Cobb (1989), *For the Common Good*, Boston, MA: Beacon Press.
Dewey, John (1920), *Reconstruction in Philosophy*, New York: Henry Holt & Co.
Dewey, John (1927), *The Public and its Problems*, New York: Henry Holt & Co.
Dewey, John (1929), *The Quest for Certainty*, New York: G.P. Putnam's Sons.
Dewey, John (2000), *Liberalism and Social Action*, New York: Prometheus Books. (Orig. New York: G.P. Putnam's Sons, 1935).
Environmental Protection Agency, Science Advisory Board (2000), *Toward Integrated Environmental Decision-Making*, EPA-SAB-EC-00.011 Washington, DC.
Faucheux, Sylvie (1997), 'Technological Change, Ecological Sustainability and Industrial Competitiveness,' in Andrew Dragun and Kristin Jacobson, (eds), *Sustainability and Global Environmental Policy*, Cheltenham, UK and Lyme, USA: Edward Elgar.
Foster, John (ed.) (1997), *Valuing Nature? Economics, Ethics and Envrionment* London: Routledge.
Funtowicz, S.O. and Jerome R. Ravetz (1990), *Uncertainty and Quality in Science for Policy*, Dordrecht: Kluwer.
Funtowicz, S.O. and Jerome R. Ravetz (1995), 'Science for the Post Normal Age,' in L. Westra and J. Lemons (eds), *Perspectives on Ecological Integrity*, Dordrecht: Kluwer, pp. 146–61.

Gundersen, Adolf (1995), *The Environmental Promise of Democratic Deliberation*, Madison, WI: University of Wisconsin Press.

Gunderson, L.H., C.S. Holling, and S.S. Light (1995), *Barriers and Bridges*, New York: Columbia University Press.

Habermas, Jurgen (1993), *Justification and Application: Remarks on Discourse Ethics*, Cambridge, MA: MIT Press.

Habermas, Jurgen (1996), *Between Facts and Norms: Contributions to a Discourse Theory of Law and Democracy*, Cambridge, MA: MIT Press.

Hardin, Garrett (1968), 'The Tragedy of the Commons,' *Science*, **162**, (3858), 1243–8.

Hodgson, Geoffrey (1997), 'Economics, Environmental Policy and the Transcendence of Utilitarianism,' in John Foster (ed.), *Valuing Nature*? Economics, Ethics and Environment, London: Routledge.

Holling, C.S. (1978), *Adaptive Environmental Assessment and Management*, London: John Wiley.

Jacobs, Michael (1994), 'The Limits to Neoclassicism: Towards an Institutional Environmental Economics,' in Michael Redclift and Ted Benton (eds), *Social Theory and the Global Environment*, London: Routledge, pp. 67–91.

Leach, W.D., N.W. Pelkey and P.A. Sabatier (2001), 'Making Watershed Partnerships Work: A Review of the Empirical Literature,' *Journal of Water Resources Planning and Management*, Nov./Dec. **127**(6), 378–85.

Leach, W.D., N.W. Pelkey and P.A. Sabatier (under review), 'Stakeholder Partnerships as an Emergent Form of Collaborative Policymaking: Evaluation Criteria Applied to Watershed Management in California and Washington,' *Journal of Policy Analysis and Management*.

Lee, K.N. (1993), *Compass and Gyroscope: Integrating Science and Politics for the Environment*, Covelo, CA: Island Press.

Leopold, Aldo (1949), *A Sand County Almanac*, Oxford: Oxford University Press.

Light, Andrew and Eric Katz (eds) (1996), *Environmental Pragmatism*, London: Routledge.

MacLean, Douglas and Peter Brown (eds) (1983), *Energy and the Future*, Totowa, NJ: Rowman and Littlefield.

Minteer, Ben (2001), 'Intrinsic Value for Pragmatists?' *Environmental Ethics*, **23**, 57–75.

Minteer, Ben A. and Robert E. Manning (1999), 'Pragmatism in Environmental Ethics: Democracy, Pluralism, and the Management of Nature,' *Environmental Ethics*, **21**, 191–207.

Minteer, Ben A. and Robert E. Manning (2000), 'Convergence in Environmental Values: An Empirical and Conceptual Defense,' *Ethics, Place and Environment*, **3**, 47–60.

National Research Council (1983), *Risk Assessment in the Federal Government*, Washington DC: National Academy Press.

National Research Council (1996), *Understanding Risk: Informing decisions in a democratic society*, Washington DC: National Academy Press.

Nelson, Richard R. and Sidney G. Winter (1985), *Evolutionary Theory of Economic Change*, Cambridge, MA: Harvard University Press.

North, Douglas C. (1990), *Institutions, Institutional Change, and Economic Performance*, Cambridge, UK: Cambridge University Press.

Norton, Bryan (1982), 'Environmental Ethics and Rights of Future Generations,' *Environmental Ethics*, **4** 319–37.

Norton, Bryan (1991), *Toward Unity Among Environmentalists*, New York: Oxford University Press.

Norton, Bryan (1992), 'Epistemology and Environmental Values,' *The Monist*, **75**, 208–26.
Norton, Bryan (1994), ' Economists' Preferences and the Preferences of Economists,' *Environmental Values*, **3**, 311–32.
Norton, Bryan (1995), 'Ecological Integrity and Social Values: At What Scale?', *Ecosystem Health*, **1**, 228–41.
Norton, Bryan (1996), 'Integration or Reduction: Two Approaches to Environmental Values, in Andrew Light and Eric Katz (eds), *Environmental Pragmatism*, London: Routledge.
Norton, Bryan (2002), 'Democracy and Environmentalism: Foundations and Justifications for Environmental Policy', in B.A. Minteer and B.P. Taylor (eds), *Democracy and the Claims of Nature: Critical Perspectives for a New Century*, Lanham, MD: Rowman and Littlefield.
Norton, Bryan and Anne Steinemann (2001), 'Environmental Values and Adaptive Management,' *Environmental Values*, **10**, 473–506.
Norton, Bryan and M.A. Toman (1997), 'Sustainability: Ecological and Economic Perspectives,' *Land Economics*, **73**, 553–68.
Norton, Bryan, Robert Costanza, and Richard Bishop (1998), 'The Evolution of Preferences: Why "Sovereign" Preferences May Not Lead to Sustainable Policies and What to Do About It,' *Ecological Economics*, **24**, 193–211.
O'Neill, John (1993), *Ecology, Policy and Politics: Human Well-Being and the Natural World*, London: Routledge.
Ostrom, Elinor (1991), 'Governing the Commons: The Evolution of Institutions for Collective Action (Political Economy of Institutions and Decisions),' Cambridge: Cambridge University Press.
Partridge, Ernest (ed.) (1981), *Responsibility to Future Generations*, Buffalo, NY: Prometheus Books.
Passmore, John (1974), *Man's Responsibility for Nature*, New York: Charles Scribner's Sons.
Rawls, John (1971), *A Theory of Justice*, Cambridge, MA: Harvard University Press.
Regan, Tom (1981), 'The Nature and Possibility of an Environmental Ethic,' *Environmental Ethics*, **3**, 19–34.
Regan, Tom (1983), *The Case for Animal Rights*, Berkeley, CA: University of California Press.
Rittel, Horst W.J. and Melvin M. Webber (1973), 'Dilemmas in the General Theory of Planning,' *Policy Sciences*, **4**, 155–69.
Rolston, III, Holmes (1975), 'Is there an Ecological Ethic?', *Ethics*, **85**, 1203–7.
Rolston, III, Holmes (1988), *Environmental Ethics*, Philadelphia: Temple University Press.
Routley, Richard (1973), 'Is there a Need for a New, an Environmental Ethic?' *Proceedings, 15th World Congress of Philosophy*, **1**, 205–10.
Routley, Richard and V. Routley (1979), 'Against the Inevitability of Human Chauvinism,' in Goodpaster K.E. and K.M. Sayre (eds), *Ethics and Problems of the 21st Century*, Notre Dame, ID: University of Notre Dame Press, pp. 36–59.
Sager, Tore (1997), 'Planning and the Liberal Paradox: A Democratic Dilemma in Social Choice,' *Journal of Planning Literature*, **12**(1), 16–29.
Sagoff, Mark (1988), *The Economy of the Earth*, Cambridge, UK: Cambridge University Press.
Sagoff, Mark (1998), 'Aggregation and Deliberation in Valuing Environmental Public Goods: A Look Beyond Contingent Pricing', *Ecological Economics*, **24**, 213–30.

Sen, Amartya (1970a), *Collective Choice and Social Welfare*, San Francisco, CA: Holden-Day.

Sen, Amartya (1970b), 'The Impossibility of a Paretian Liberal,' *Journal of Political Economy*, **78**, 152–7.

Sikora, R.I. and Brian Barry (eds) (1978), *Obligations to Future Generations*, Philadelphia: Temple University Press.

Singer, Peter (1975), *Animal Liberation: A New Ethics for Our Treatment of Animals*, New York: Avon Books.

Solow, Robert M. (1993), 'Sustainability: An Economist's Perspective', in *Economics of the Environment: Selected Readings*, R. Dorfman and N.S. Dorfman (eds), New York: W.W. Norton and Company.

Spash, Clive (2000), 'Multiple Value Expression in Contingent Valuation: Economics and Ethics,' *Environmental Science and Technology*, **34**, 1433–8.

Stone, Christopher (1974), *Should Trees Have Standing? Toward Legal Rights for Natural Objects*, Los Altos, CA: William Kaufmann.

Stone, Christopher (1987), *Earth and Other Ethics: The Case for Moral Pluralism*, New York: Harper and Row.

Taylor, Paul (1986), *Respect for Nature*, Princeton, NJ: Princeton University Press.

Veblen, T.B. (1919), *The Place of Science in Modern Civilization and Other Essays*, New York: Huebsch.

Wackernagel, Mathis and William Rees (1996), *Our Ecological Footprint: Reducing Human Impact on Earth*, Gabriola Island, BC, Canada: New Society Press.

Walters, C.J. (1986), *Adaptive Management of Renewable Resources*, New York: Macmillan.

White, Lynn (1967), 'The Historical Roots of Our Ecological Crisis,' *Science*, **155**, 361–76.

Williamson, Oliver E. (1987), *The Economic Institutions of Capitalism*, New York: Free Press.

Index

abatement 37, 88–91, 187, 188, 189, 190
Abdalla, C.W. 247
Abt Associates 135
acid rain trading program 328–40
acute illness 234, 235, 239, 243, 245, 249, 266
Adams, R.M. 280, 291, 301
adaptation 34–6, 42, 394–8
Adler, K.J. 133, 134
adverse selection 336
afforestation 280
Africa 9, 196
age 257–61
Agee, M.D. 234
aggregated goods 386
Aghion, P. 190
agricultural sector model (ASM) 301, 303
agriculture 102 *see also* carbon sequestration in
agricultural soils
agroecozone scales 290–1
air 123–9
air pollution:
   health effects of pollution 233, 236,
      243, 246, 248, 250, 253, 260,
      263–4, 268
   hedonic property value techniques
      117–18, 131, 136, 146, 152, 153
air quality *see* tradable permits for
air quality and climate change
Air Quality Investment Program (AQIP)
   346
air quality valuation model (AQVM)
   237, 239
Alberini, A. 233–71
Alcamo, J. 19
Anderson, J.W. 304
anthropocentrism 376–9, 382, 384, 385, 387
   pluralist and experimental 398–403

Antle, J.M. 278–306
applied general equilbrium 21, 22
Argentina 355
Armington, P.S. 79, 97
Aronsson, T. 172, 186
Arrow, K. 390
Arrow-Debreu general equilibrium 69
Arthur, W.B. 387
Asheim, G.B. 174, 177, 178, 182, 183, 185, 186, 189, 213
Asia 243
   Pacific 100
asthma 234, 244, 245
asymmetries 47, 48, 52
Atkeson, E. 334, 337
Atkinson 10
Atkinson, S.E. 195, 196, 198, 213, 253
auctions 359
Auerbach, A.J. 78
Australia 195, 284
Ausubel, J. 202
autonomous energy efficiency improve-
   ment (AEEI) 18, 24, 85
averaging schemes 357
averting behavior 252
Ayres, R. 166, 202, 203, 204, 208, 209

Babcock, B.A. 291, 296
Bailey, M.J. 122, 131
Ballard, C.L. 102
banking 317, 319, 354
Barber, B. 393, 394
Barbier, E.B. 171, 194
Barker, T. 15, 19
Barns, D. 19
Barrager, S.M. 130, 133
Barrett, L.B. 117, 124
Barrett, S. 15, 42, 47, 52
Barro, R.J. 174
Barry, B. 381, 382

414

Index

Criteria Document 127
ethics 401
health effects of pollution 237, 238,
    252, 256, 260, 261
hedonic property value techniques
    117, 124, 129–30, 133–6, 148
Remedial Investigation 149
Science Advisory Board:
Environmental Economics Committee
    133
tradable permits for air quality and
    climate change 317–18, 320–6,
    328–30, 334, 337–8, 347–51, 356
Water and Watersheds program 400
environmental quality 198
environmental regulation 98–9
environmental standards costs 99–100
environmetnal policies for developing
    countries 100–1
EPIC model 299
epistemological theory 374
Epple, D. 121
equity 27–9, 36–41
    intergenerational 174, 177, 210
    intragenerational 173–6, 198
ESCAPE 25
escape valve 354
ethics 373–403
    anthropocentrism, pluralist and
        experimental 398–403
    extensionist 379–85
    individualism, holism and
        extensionism 385–94
    as public philosophy of adaptive
        management 394–8
    Europe 284, 400
    climate change policy 18, 23, 32
    economics of sustainability 196, 197
    health effects of pollution 233, 237,
        243, 269
    ozone-depleting chemicals 16
    programs 325–6
    tradable permits for air quality and
        climate change 315, 356
    see also Eastern Europe; European
European Burden Sharing Agreement
    354
European Commission 14, 18, 325–6
European Union 316, 352
    climate change policy 1, 9, 11–12, 15,
        27, 29, 49, 53

computable general equilibrium
    models 67, 83, 93–7, 99, 101
evolution property value techniques
    119–23
expenditures aversion 247–9
experience 396
extensionism 385–94
external commitment 46
externalities 176–7
ExternE 237, 239
Eyckmans, J. 37

Faber, M. 201
family emission limit (FEL) 327
Fankhauser, S. 35
farm scales 286–8
Farmer, M.C. 209
Farrell, A. 347–8
Faucheux, S. 206, 208, 402
Feather, P. 295
Federal Highway Administration
    (FHWA) 131, 132
field scales 290–1
Fischer, C. 8
Fisher, A. 254
Fisher-Vaden, K.E.J. 19
fixed price ceiling 16
Fleming, R.A. 291
flexibility 358
Folmer, H. 47
foreign trade 79–81
forestation 100
former Soviet Union 23, 29, 32, 33
Fortin, E. 16
fossil fuel 279, 281
Foster, J. 379
Foster, V. 318–20
Framework Convention on Climate
    Change 20
France 87, 95, 206
free-riding 33, 41, 42, 46, 47, 50, 51
Freeman III, A.M. 120, 125, 263
Froger, G. 199
fuel consumption 278
FUND 25
Funtowicz, S.O. 397, 401

G-Cubed model 84, 97
Galbraith, J. 402

Index